THE MOON OF THE
MOUNTAIN
LIONS

THE THIRTEEN MOONS

The Moon of the Owls (JANUARY)

The Moon of the Bears (FEBRUARY)

The Moon of the Salamanders (MARCH)

The Moon of the Chickarees (APRIL)

The Moon of the Monarch Butterflies (MAY)

The Moon of the Fox Pups (JUNE)

The Moon of the Wild Pigs (JULY)

The Moon of the Mountain Lions (AUGUST)

The Moon of the Deer (SEPTEMBER)

The Moon of the Alligators (OCTOBER)

The Moon of the Gray Wolves (NOVEMBER)

The Moon of the Winter Bird (DECEMBER)

The Moon of the Moles (DECEMBER–JANUARY)

NEW EDITION   THE THIRTEEN MOONS

THE MOON OF THE
MOUNTAIN
LIONS

BY JEAN CRAIGHEAD GEORGE

ILLUSTRATED BY RON PARKER

HarperCollins*Publishers*

The illustrations in this book were
painted with designer's gouache
on watercolor board.

The Moon of the Mountain Lions
Text copyright © 1969, 1991 by Jean Craighead George
Illustrations copyright © 1991 by R.S. Parker

Typography by Al Cetta
1 2 3 4 5 6 7 8 9 10
NEW EDITION

Library of Congress Cataloging-in-Publication Data
George, Jean Craighead, date
    The moon of the mountain lions / by Jean Craighead George ;
illustrated by Ron Parker. — New ed.
        p.   cm. — (The Thirteen moons)
    Includes bibliographical references and index.
    Summary: Describes the experiences of a young mountain lion
during the month of August in his natural habitat on the side of Mount
Olympus, in Washington State.
    ISBN 0-06-022429-0. — ISBN 0-06-022438-X (lib. bdg.)
    1. Pumas—Washington (State)—Olympic Mountains—Juvenile
literature. [1. Pumas.] I. Parker, Ron, ill. II. Title.
III. Series: George, Jean Craighead, date. Thirteen moons.
QL795.P85G4   1991   90-39451
599.74′428—dc20   CIP
                                                               AC

Why is this series called The Thirteen Moons?

Each year there are either thirteen full moons or thirteen new moons. This series of books is named in their honor.

Our culture, which bases its calendar on sun-time, has no names for the thirteen moons. I have named the thirteen lunar months after thirteen North American animals. Primarily night prowlers, these animals, at a particular time of the year in a particular place, do wondrous things. The places are known to you, but the animal moon names are not because I made them up. So that you can place them on our sun calendar, I have identified them with the names of our months. When I ran out of these, I gave the thirteenth moon, the Moon of the Moles, the expandable name December-January.

Fortunately, the animals do not need calendars, for names or no names, sun-time or moon-time, they follow their own inner clocks.

—JEAN CRAIGHEAD GEORGE

T HE YOUNG MOUNTAIN LION
opened his mouth and rolled out his tongue in
a waking yawn. Lying in his summer den at
timberline, he turned his gaze upon his home
on the side of Mount Olympus in Washington.
Snowcapped peaks speared the darkness above
him. An alpine meadow splattered with flowers
lay below, and far down the mountain shaggy
forests hugged the slopes and glacial valleys.
Below them the northern rain forest reached to
the Pacific Ocean.

Stretching and cupping his whiskers forward,
the noble cat arose and quietly stepped into the

moonlight. He stood beneath the moon of August, the moon of change.

The hummingbirds, sippers of flower nectar, had already sensed the force of this moon. They were ready to migrate. The temperature had dropped only one or two degrees across North America and had actually risen that much on the Pacific Coast, yet the flower birds were ready to go. The sun was setting earlier and rising later. The days were growing shorter. Snow and darkness were coming to the mountains.

At the dawn of this day several male rufous hummingbirds, some of the tiniest birds in the world, had darted past the lion's den as they spun south on whirling wings. No bigger than daisy heads, they were off toward winter homes on the plateaus of Mexico three thousand miles away. Their females stayed behind to hurriedly feed the last brood of nestlings. They would see their bud-sized youngsters out of the nests and onto their wings, teach them how to sip the nectar of the last lilies and bellflowers, then all would follow the males to the sunny winter lands where flowers bloomed.

The swallows also felt the change of the August moon. Great flocks were gathering by the thousands and tens of thousands over lakes, marshes, and seacoasts. Almost always on the wing, these agile birds have tiny, feeble feet that they rarely use. Before the moon would wane they would climb high into the sky and, out of sight of man and beast, circle and rest on their wings. Then, on a cue from the sun, they would turn south and speed away. The next day the swallows would be gone, leaving the skies strangely empty, like beaches when winter comes.

Other animals were responding differently to the change. In the deserts, on the August-dry prairies, and in forests from Mexico up through Canada, the chipmunks, toads, and frogs were asleep. This was not the sleep of hibernation but of estivation, summer's torpor. In this quiet state these animals were avoiding the adversities of the month, dryness and heat.

One beast, however would combine the sleeps of summer and winter. In the rockslides, the Olympic marmots, the whistlers of high country, were getting ready for the longest sleep of all the mammals—the nine months from mid-August to mid-May. Some of the marmots were already taking naps that lasted a day or two. Fat and drowsy, they slept longer and longer with each snooze. As they did so, their hearts beat more slowly and their bodies cooled. Eventually they would not be able to awaken until spring. Those that were still running across the rockslides whistled to each other, like children calling their dogs.

The lion tasted the wind with his tongue and nose. It tasted of another change, the change of aging and ripening. The wind bore the scent of sweet huckleberries, ripe gooseberries, and twinberries. This change did not interest the mountain lion, for he was a meat eater, or carnivore. Having looked, smelled, and tasted, the young lion now listened. He rotated his ears. The elk and deer had changed their direction. They were no longer climbing among the peaks but were moving downward. He heard them snapping branches in the forest below.

Since spring they had been wandering upward toward the alpine meadows as the melting snow uncovered sweet grasses. Now the grasses were dying, the growing season of the high country was ending and like the birds, the deer and elk were on migration. Their migration, however, was not south but down the mountain, and this concerned the lion. The deer and elk were his staff of life. He had moved up the mountain with them in the spring, harvesting the weak and infirm as he went. At about five thousand feet above sea level, where the trees stopped and the rocks, ice, and alpine prairies took over, the young lion had denned for the summer. His shelter was a twisted thicket of alpine firs, the last trees to withstand the driving wind and stunting cold at the tops of the mountains. They mark the timberline beyond which no trees grow.

Tonight the elk and deer were two thousand feet below the lion in a lower and, therefore, different kind of forest. On mountains the forests change with the altitude, the tougher trees braving the rugged heights. The lion could smell the pungent cedars the herds were trampling lower down the mountain. He must follow.

Before he entered the forest, he stopped in the last alpine meadow and tipped his ears forward. An elk had injured his foot in a crevasse several days ago and was limping through the trees, *da, thump, thump, thump.* The lion swished his tail. This animal was wounded. In the scheme of things he would falter and eventually be harvested.

Slowly the lion crossed the meadow. Beneath his feet a different sort of change was taking place. Spring was beginning. Under the leaf stems of the tiny alpine willow trees, no taller than a thumb, new buds were forming. This was happening not only on the mountain but all across the northern United States and Canada. Next year's willows, elm, maple, beech, and apple leaf buds were forming. As they emerged, the cells that brought food and water to the old leaves shut down. When these were sealed off, the leaves would lose their chlorophyll, turn yellow, red, orange, or gold and fall to the ground.

The young lion stopped at the edge of the forest and listened. He had lost sight and sound of the limping elk, so he climbed a leaning cedar to search for him. Lean and muscular, the lion was magnificently beautiful. Tawny in color, he had black smudges under his eyes and along his nose. His back was as straight as a leveling rod, his paws immense. His tail was tipped with black and almost as long as he. It touched the ground and curled up at the end. He weighed more than two hundred pounds. He was a cougar, or mountain lion, of North America. Almost as large as African lions, cougars are the second largest species of cat in the New World. Only jaguars surpass them in length and weight.

A hundred years ago mountain lions were abundant in all the mountains of the United States and Canada. Now they are rare in the United States and found only in the lonely wilderness areas of the West, Southwest, and Florida. Washington's Olympic Peninsula, a land barely touched by humans, still has its appropriate number of mountain lions. Because of their presence the elk and deer do not become so numerous that they ravage trees, bushes, grasses, and the wildlife that depend on them for shelter and food. The lions keep the herds in balance with their environment.

From the tree, the young lion could see the Hoh River valley where he had been born and raised. Turning his head he glanced up the mountain. The snow-covered peaks of the Olympic Mountains shone like silver saw blades against the purple-black sky. In the moonlight the mountain glaciers looked like Rocky Mountain goats sleeping on the dark rocks. Some of the spots may even have been goats. The goats lived at timberline and above all year round.

The lion's sensitive ears could hear the largest glacier, Blue Glacier, moan as its tons of ice moved great boulders, slowly grinding them to dust. In the August heat, all sixty glaciers were melting. The melt spilled down the mountain, forming waterfalls, streams, and the many rivers that joined the sea.

The lion could not locate the lame elk. Silently he leaped to the ground and slipped into the forest.

Born three years ago under the August moon—lion cubs in the north arrive in spring and into the summer—the young lion had lived with his mother and two sisters in a high valley of the Hoh River. He rarely saw his father, who had remained with his mother only a short time before returning to his solitary life. He would seek out the young lion's mother again in two or three years, when the cubs were on their own. Meanwhile, like most cats, he would live alone.

After a three-month pregnancy the lioness had given birth to cubs who were about one foot long and covered with spotted fur. In ten days their eyes opened.

They were weaned in three months. By that time the young lion had shed the spots and ringed tail of his childhood. He weighed about forty pounds and ventured out of the rock den with his mother and sisters. Together they hunted around the den, catching grouse, rabbits, and occasionally a coyote. When they were almost fully grown, they hunted farther and farther afield until they knew all about the game in their kingdom of several square miles. Eventually they were able to hunt the prey of the adult mountain lion—deer and elk. Each dawn they returned to their den.

At home they rolled and played like house cats, batting stones and flowers around, jumping on each other. Like house cats they also made many sounds, expressing different feelings.

A year ago in July the young lion had left home. He climbed out of the valley, following the deer and elk up through tall forests, over rocks, and along cliffs. After several days he came to an alpine meadow high up on Mount Olympus where the herds grazed. No other lion ran him off

the rich find, so he stayed in a twisted alpine fir forest until the moon of change drove the herds down-mountain. He went with them down almost to sea level, where the stately northern rain forests grow. Here the herds and the young lion lived all winter in a forest kept forever green by the warm rains from the sea.

One night in spring a thrilling sound brought him to his feet. A female mountain lion was calling from the other side of the Hoh River. Her scream was the high-pitched cry that the young lion recognized to be a mother cat's danger call to her cubs. He sat down and stared at the far side of the river. His whiskers stood out straight and his tail swished in anticipation.

The thin cry of a lost cub came from the riverbed. The young lion did not move. A stick snapped across the river. A lioness and two cubs slipped out from among the alder trees at the river edge and ran toward the water. The cubs were both males. The mother meowed and the lost cub ran to meet them. This one was a

female—a lively cub of almost a year, who piqued the interest of the young lion. He watched her closely.

After the family was reunited, the mother led them to a log. The cubs sat down. The mother lay on her side and, reaching under the fallen tree with her strong paws, pulled out some game she had cached there. The cubs set upon it with snarls and growls. When their stomachs were round with food, the mother shoved the leftovers back under the log and, kicking leaves over it, led her tawny-colored youngsters into the eerie yellow-green forest. The young lion watched until they disappeared.

After that he was constantly on the alert for the family. Twice he heard the mother call and several times he saw the cubs. They were growing up. Their tumbles and rollicks became skilled pounces. Their thin cries developed into growls and roars. One night in June, he heard the lioness call from the northern end of her kingdom, and he saw the family no more. It was time for him to follow the elk and deer up the mountain.

Now, two months later, the moon of change was rising. The young lion was headed down-mountain again. As he went, like all cats, he climbed logs and rocks and cliffs to survey the land below. Having lost track of the limping elk, he strode to the top of a cliff to search for him. Rocks avalanched below him and once more he heard the *da, thump, thump, thump* of the limping buck. Dropping from the cliff like plunging water, he struck the earth and tracked the elk to the edge of a small lake, where he lost him. Around the lake grew bluebells, yarrow, glacier lilies, cinquefoil, and cow parsnips. They were all blooming at once. In the lowlands some of these are spring flowers, while others are fall flowers, but in the mountains the growing season is so short that everything must bloom and go to seed between June and September. Spring's bluebells come into flower with autumn's asters.

As the lion walked around the lake, he awakened a junco who was sleeping behind a curtain of moss beneath an embankment. The bird saw the lion's

shadow in the moonlight and called *tik-tik*, the danger signal of the junco. Her five youngsters, sleeping under roots and flowers nearby, awakened. They did not fly, for their mother's note warned them to tighten their feet on their perches and sit perfectly still.

The youngsters had been flying for only three days. Nevertheless, they knew where the seeds of the alpine flowers lay, and today they had learned to shell them. Tomorrow they would bathe and preen their feathers and the next day they would sun themselves, the last achievement of a baby bird before its adolescence. Then they would start down the mountain with the elk, the deer, and the lion. They would not spend much time with them, however. When the snows came they would migrate to the lowlands of British Columbia and even as far as Mexico. Everywhere they would be known affectionately as "snowbirds," as their white tail feathers flashed over cold gray fields and under bird feeders in backyards.

The mother junco watched a starlike avalanche

lily bounce above her head. When it became still, she waited and then softly called "all's well" to her family. The enemy was gone.

The young lion walked to the spillway where the lake poured over its embankment to become a stream. The stream rushed downhill forming waterfalls and pools. He listened, but the limping elk could not be heard over the sound of water. He continued down among mountain hemlocks, silver and Alaska firs, and gigantic red cedars. Pine drops and twinberries grew under these trees.

In silence the lion searched for the limping elk, who was aware of the hunter and was hiding in a dense clump of cedars not far from the lion. Sensing him, the lion climbed to a high ledge. The limping elk saw him outlined against the sky. Terrified, he dashed down-mountain to a stream at the foot of a waterfall. So soft was the floor of the forest that the lion did not hear him go.

A most remarkable bird heard the elk splash into the water. He was a dipper, or water ouzel, a small gray songbird. He peered out from behind a waterfall, where he was roosting in an air pocket, and shifted his weight from one foot to the other. He had flown there at dusk through a split in the falling water. Dippers are birds of rushing streams and falling cascades. Wild water is their home. Dry and well hidden, the wondrous bird preened his feathers until they lay so smoothly no water could seep in, then went back to sleep.

The dipper had hatched in a round nest of moss on the wall of the gorge above the cascade. He had remained there for three weeks—a long time for a songbird, which usually remains in the nest only ten to twelve days. But the longer the dipper stayed in the nest, the stronger he became. He needed to be strong because he had to fly from his nest across the raging cascade. Two weeks ago he had made the perilous flight.

Although he had landed safely and was exhausted, his parents would not let him rest. They led him right into the stream. Surprisingly, he floated on the water like a duck. His parents demonstrated how to use the swift currents to cross the raging torrent without being washed away. When he had succeeded, they led him to a quiet pool. They dove and swam underwater. The young bird hesitated, then dove. As silver bubbles passed his eyes, he instinctively pumped his wings and arrived on the bottom of the stream. There he grasped pebbles with the hooklike claws on his toes, and ran along the stream bottom. His parents gobbled the larvae of the black fly and so did the young dipper. Surfacing with them, he flew through the air and alit beside his parents on a ledge behind the cascade. There in an air pocket he rested, safe from hawk, bass, and weasel.

This night the young dipper was on his own, independent of his parents. Through the falling water he saw the young lion come to the stream. The bird was not afraid. He looked at the big cat, then stuck his beak in his feathers. Not even a mountain lion would dare to walk into the thunderous waterfall.

The lion saw the elk splash out of the stream. With a bound he followed.

Above the mountain lion, high up in the fir trees that lined the stream, slept the tiny birds of the treetops, the kinglets. They were waiting for September, when they would follow the hummingbirds south. Pine siskins, which would fly south as far as the snowbirds do, were asleep against the boles of tall trees. These small birds were of little interest to the lion. He was, however, interested in the sweet odor of the blue grouse sleeping at the edge of a cedar glen. These grouse of the Olympic Peninsula were tasty food. He crouched to catch one, but did not. The lame elk was crossing the stream again. The lion followed it downhill in deliberate pursuit.

Leaping the waterway, he ran quite a distance, then suddenly slowed down and stopped. A bull elk was pawing the ground and thrashing his huge antlers in a grassy glade. He was alone, preparing for the mating season. In September he would bugle like the monarch elk he was and call his harem to him. And he would fight all bulls who dared to come near.

The lion twisted his ears and sniffed. A large herd of elk was in a clearing above him. They were resting and browsing as they slowly worked their way down the Hoh Valley. The lion was about to stop and join their more leisurely ascent when he heard the limping elk. He was hobbling down the mountain in great fear. The lion pursued him down an elk trail and into the mysteriously beautiful northern rain forest. Here the huge Sitka spruce, western hemlock, and Douglas fir were two hundred and fifty feet tall. Their trunks were six to nine feet in diameter, and many of the trees were five hundred years old. Water-loving mosses, mushrooms, ferns, vines, and microbes grew in luxurious profusion. The lion stopped and listened. The moist vegetation hushed the forest.

He could not hear the elk. The elk was tired, and was standing only a few hundred feet away. Thirst assailed the lion, and he walked to a spring to drink. Tiny frogs, which had just emerged from their tadpole stage and come onto the land, felt his step. They leaped back into the water.

Waves from their dives knocked against the lion's nose. Unwittingly a large frog hopped onto his paw, then jumped ashore. It crawled up a fern and clung there by means of the suction pads on its feet. The lion turned his head to observe it. The frog plunged back into the spring.

The lion was about to drink when he saw beside his other paw another amphibian—a northwestern hop toad. She, too, had become an adult this month. The lion lifted his paw. The toad jumped, not into the spring like the frog, but toward the woods. After spending months in the spring the toad had changed from a water-loving pollywog into a land creature. The lion reached for her playfully. The toad leaped four feet and disappeared.

Sniffing the air, the lion picked up the scent of the lame elk, now moving away. He followed him along the stream that flowed from the spring.

A great splashing in the shallows caught his attention. A large coho salmon was fighting his way, half out of water, toward a gravel bar. It was the same gravel bar where he had hatched. Now, seven years later, he was coming back to it. He had swum from the deep ocean up the Hoh River, to the feeder stream, and finally to the gravel bar where he had started his life. Here he would spawn with one of the females who were also coming home to this bar. Together the salmon would spawn and die, the last deeds of these coho salmon and millions more like them.

The lion left the salmon and followed the scent of the lame elk.

The moon was low in the western sky. Dawn would soon follow. A killdeer awoke beside the stream and flew screaming into the darkness. The lion ignored her. His hunger was beginning to gnaw at him. He wanted the elk. He climbed to the top of a bluff and saw him directly below. Crouching to pounce, he took aim.

He did not leap. Across the river something moved. Among the skyscrapers of Sitka spruce, a shadow flitted in such harmony with the forest that only the night vision of a cat could tell who walked there. A surge of warmth rushed over him. He forgot his hunger. Down the top of the cliff on the other side of the river came the child lioness and her mother. Behind them strolled one brother.

He tensed. Coming toward the family on the same trail was an enormous black bear. His head was low, his shoulder blades pumping up and down. He marched with great strength and deliberation.

Before the young lion's eyes the mother lioness and bear met. Both were surprised. Both reacted. The lioness extended her razor-sharp claws, hissed, and leaped for the bear's neck. The bear reared to his hind feet, swung his powerful front paw, and tore open the back of the lioness. He locked his teeth in her shoulder and, as he did, lost his footing on the edge of the cliff. He fell, dragging the lioness with him to the river shore forty feet below. Although they pawed at trees and branches, they could not break their plunge. They crashed to the earth. A long silence followed.

Presently the bear rolled to his feet and limped away. The lioness did not get up.

With three bounds the young lion crossed the river to the lifeless cat. He caterwauled, a lonesome, bloodcurdling scream.

A leaf, as large as a dinner plate and yellow with the change of August, fell from the top of the cliff. The big maple leaf spiraled to the ground. The young lion looked up. Peering over the edge of the cliff was the child lioness. He called to her. Slowly she came down the trail on the rim of the cliff and stopped before him. He sniffed her ears and nose. They rubbed foreheads in greeting, then he led her into the rain forest.

The child lioness stayed close to the young lion's heels. Not far behind them, moving with hesitation, came the yearling brother. The young lion had a family. The orphans followed him as they had followed their mother, creating a new role for a solitary male mountain lion.

The three walked deeper into the forest. Where the trees made columned hallways, the child lioness took the lead. She led the young lion and her brother under the roots of fallen spruce, upholstered in soft club moss. She led them into a glade where lacy ferns grew everywhere—on trees, rocks, limbs, other ferns. She took them over a forest floor bright green with oxalis—a pretty wood sorrel that provides a carpet of three-leafed designs.

The child lioness led them to the foot of a moss-covered boulder. Leaping onto it, she turned and looked down at the young lion. He vaulted to her side. She crept under an enormous log covered with ferns and fragrant bedstraw. There she lay down. The brother climbed up the rock and stretched out beside her. They were home.

Lowering himself to his belly, shoulders and haunches jutting, head erect, the young lion sat sphinxlike on the rock and stared at the child lioness and her brother, not knowing quite what to do about them.

The young lion dozed in the quiet time just before dawn when the night animals are bedding down and the day animals are not yet up. He did not see the monkey flowers bob in the wind that stirs as the day breaks. He did not see the ferns absorb dew, or the wind pick up their spores and carry them away to drop and plant them. Nor did he hear the winter wren sing his morning song.

Exuberant little birds, the wrens are permanent residents of the northern rain forest. They do not migrate like the hummingbirds and swallows but stay in this environment all year. The wren sang only briefly, for it was August, and the singing and nesting seasons were over. He flew off to eat, paying no attention to the lions or the far-off drilling of a pileated woodpecker, a two-foot-high bird who was a match for the enormous trees of the rain forest.

A chickaree, a little red squirrel, scolded and announced the passing of a bobcat, a cat about a third the size of the young lion. A raven sneaked through the trees on her way to the coast to hunt mice. Then the sun came up and the lions briefly opened their eyes.

They purred to each other and went to sleep.

Dull swishing sounds in the forest marked the homecoming of a herd of black-tailed deer. As the sun came up, they bedded down for the day. Deer feed in the predawn and at twilight. They sleep in the bright daylight and during the dark of night.

All day the lions slept, occasionally waking and purring to each other. The sun shone—a rare event in this land where ten to twelve feet of rain falls in the course of a year.

At sundown the mountain lions got to their feet. The child lioness leaped from the boulder and ran down the family trail that led to the ocean. The young lion followed. Suddenly he crouched. There was a flash of movement, and a thud. The lion had felled a deer for his family. They dined, then proceeded leisurely toward the ocean.

When the moon had waxed from a sliver to ball and waned from ball to a sliver, the three lions reached the ocean. Curious about the sea and sky, they walked the beach until the sun came up and

drove them back to the shelter of the forest.

The young lion was weary of his kittens. He turned and walked away. Inland along a riverbed the first of the elk had gathered for the winter. He climbed a toppled tree six feet in diameter, waited and watched. Alone and content, he lounged in the feathery mosses and deer ferns.

The winter rainy season was upon the forest, the fog dense, and the plants dripping like chimes. He heard the child lioness call from close by. He waited. Presently she stole quietly out of the yellow-green forest and sat down on the far end of his log. He tucked his paws under his chest and stared at her. She tucked her paws under her chest and stared at him. They looked away, then back again. All night they stared and looked away.

In the darkness before dawn the lion yawned and went to hunt. The lioness arose and walked up the riverbank. Each looked back at the other. The courtship of the mountain lion had begun.

The moon of change had brought the young lion a mate.

Bibliography

Audubon, John James, and the Rev. John Bachman, D.C. *The Imperial Collection of Audubon Animals*. Maplewood, N.J.: Hammond, Inc., 1967.

Gray, Robert. *Cougar, the Natural Life of a North American Mountain Lion*. New York: Grosset, 1972.

Macdonald, David, ed. *The Encyclopedia of Mammals*. New York: Facts on File Inc., 1984.

McDearmon, Kay. *Cougar*. New York: Dodd Mead, 1977.

Palmer, Ralph S., *The Mammal Guide*. Garden City, N.Y.: Doubleday & Company, 1954.

Rumsey, Marian. *Lion on the Run*. New York: Morrow, 1973.

Wallace, Bill. *Shadow on the Snow*. New York: Holiday House, 1985.

Index

Evelyn Botti

Charlie Maxy – refrig. washers,
Dryers

Glen Carlson – Radio & TV

Elementary Algebra

Edited by Louis Leithold

Elementary Algebra

Thomas M. Green
Contra Costa College

Macmillan Publishing Co., Inc.
New York
Collier Macmillan Publishers
London

Macmillan Publishing Co., Inc.
866 Third Avenue, New York, New York 10022

Collier-Macmillan Canada, Ltd., Toronto

Library of Congress Cataloging in Publication Data

Green, Thomas M
  Elementary algebra.

  1. Algebra. I. Title.
QA152.2.G73   512.9'042   73–16600
ISBN 0–02–346400–3

Printing: 1 2 3 4 5 6 7 8   Year: 5 6 7 8 9 0

Preface

This text is written for adults who typically have not been students of mathematics but now, for one reason or another, desire to gain some familiarity with the method and content of algebra.

There are many good reasons to study algebra, not the least of which is to prepare for more advanced mathematical study. Often, however, the need to prepare for advanced mathematics courses is not a consideration. Indeed, the major concern of some individuals is to merely enter the mainstream of mathematical thinking through an introductory course in algebra. Accordingly, particular care has been exercised by the author and editors to present a text that will provide a smooth transition from arithmetic to algebra and subsequently to more advanced mathematics if desired.

The first six chapters are organized to provide the reader who has little or no previous knowledge of algebra with a development that bridges the gap from the concrete examples of arithmetic to the more abstract or generalized aspects of algebra. Presented in these chapters is the necessary background and structure for the real numbers. The methods for solving simple equations are also developed in these chapters. Together with Chapters 7 and 8 the first six chapters provide a good introduction to algebra for those readers who do not intend to continue to a more advanced course in mathematics.

Chapters 9 through 13 develop algebraic skills in manipulating polynomials and other algebraic expressions. Quadratic equations, more advanced graphing techniques, and inequalities are covered. These topics are important for those readers preparing for more advanced mathematical study. Depending on the background and purposes of the reader, he or she may wish to spend less time on the first six chapters and concentrate on the latter half of the book.

Each chapter is subdivided into sections. Hence, Section 3.2 is the second section of Chapter 3. Each section is followed by a set of exercises and each chapter is followed by a set of review exercises for that chapter. The answers to the odd-numbered exercises in each set are found at the back of the book.

Each section is usually developed around one or two topics. "Illustrations" are used throughout to amplify the formal statements of certain concepts which are numbered and named as definitions, axioms, theorems, or merely properties. For instance, Theorem 3.2.4 refers to the fourth formal statement of some concept in Section 3.2. The illustrations relate the concept to some specific fact or statement that the reader will likely be familiar with, often a statement from arithmetic.

Although some of the properties of algebra are presented as definitions, axioms, or theorems and the proofs of some of the theorems are provided, it is not intended that this presentation be a formal axiomatic development of a mathematical system. Rather, the generalization of arithmetic is stressed. When a proof of a theorem is presented, it is to illustrate the various logical consequences of properties or assumptions that have been previously presented.

"Examples" are presented within the sections that detail the manipulative steps that are important to the development of the computational and problem-solving skills. The functional use of a second color aids in this development. All of the substantive methods and algebraic process for problem solving at the beginning level are presented in the examples. The reader wishing only to review could easily scan the examples of the pertinent chapter and try the review exercises.

The author wishes to thank and express his gratitude to the editors and staff of Macmillan Publishing Co., Inc., and to the many others who have contributed in one way or another to the ultimate development of the manuscript, not excluding the author's family and friends whose contributions were considerable.

The author expressly acknowledges his indebtedness to Louis Leithold, who provided conducement, criticism, and refinement over the entire manuscript.

Finally, however, all liabilities in the manner of presentation must of necessity accrue to the author.

San Pablo, California   T. M. G.

Contents

Elementary Algebra

1

Introduction to Algebra

1.1 What Is Algebra?

The answer to the question "What is algebra?" will reveal itself as you progress through this book. To begin to answer the question we should ask another question, "What was arithmetic?" From your experience with arithmetic many of you probably will find that you know more about algebra than you realize.

Arithmetic is, most likely, the first acquaintance most people have with mathematics, and so it gives us a common starting point. It is here that one learns that arithmetic applies to almost everything, to apples and unicorns, to sheep and dollars, and to ideas of the mind. The type of things does not matter; numbers apply to sets or collections of things just because they are things. Of all things it is true that two and two make four. In contrast to arithmetic, algebra is more concerned with the study of processes and methods than with particular answers to particular problems.

Algebra is, in the traditional sense, a *generalization of arithmetic*. This statement is full of implications. The generalizing of certain properties of arithmetic is accomplished in a symbolic manner by using letters for numbers, other symbols for the operations, and still other symbols for equality and inequality relationships.

The numbers most familiar to everyone are the *whole numbers,* that is,

$$0, 1, 2, 3, \ldots$$

The three dots after the last number indicate a continuation of the sequence of numbers. These are the numbers we use for counting purposes and it is the process of counting that provides a basis from which most of the rules or properties of arithmetic are derived.

For example: in arithmetic the equalities

$$2 + 2 + 2 = 3 \times 2 \quad \text{and} \quad 4 + 4 + 4 = 3 \times 4$$

are special cases of the "general" rule,

$$n + n + n = 3 \times n$$

where the letter n represents any number. Any other letter could have been used. Thus, it is also true that

$$a + a + a = 3 \times a$$

Instead of the expression "$3 \times n$," the expression "$3n$" is the notation commonly used in algebra for the product of 3 and some number n, or in other words "3 times n." Thus, we write

$$n + n + n = 3n$$

A whole number times any number is called a *multiple* of that number. Hence, $3n$ is a multiple of the number n, and $7a$ is a multiple of the number a.

Illustration 1 If $a = 5$, then $7a = 7 \times 5$, that is, $7a = 35$. The number 35 is a multiple of 5.

In Illustration 1 we *evaluate* $7a$ by *substituting* the number 5 for the number a and then performing the operation of multiplication indicated by the expression $7a$. The substitution process is a very important process in mathematics.

Example 1 If y is 4, find the value of the following expressions: (a) $5y$; (b) $3y + 4y$.

Solution: We substitute the number 4 for y.
  (a) $5y = 5 \times 4$
          $= 20$
  (b) $3y + 4y = 3 \times 4 + 4 \times 4$
              $= 12 + 16$
              $= 28$

Generalizing statements and properties of arithmetic is a very important aspect of algebra. We symbolize properties of arithmetic by using letters to represent numbers.

Illustration 2 The following two statements are general assumptions that we make in arithmetic.
  (i) If zero is added to any given number, the sum is always that given number. We can symbolize this general property of arithmetic by the equality

$$a + 0 = a$$

   where a represents any number.
  (ii) If two numbers are added, the order of the numbers does not affect the sum. We can symbolize this general property of arithmetic by the

equality

$$x + y = y + x$$

where x and y represent any two numbers.

In Illustration 2 we have two equalities, each symbolizing a general property of arithmetic. Some equalities, like those in Illustration 2, are called *identities*. Identities can be *tested* by substituting arbitrary numbers for the letters. We must replace every occurrence of a given letter with the same number.

Illustration 3 The equality symbolizing the general rule in Illustration 2(ii) can be tested by substituting arbitrary numbers for x and y. Suppose we replace x by 2 and y by 7, then for the equality

$$x + y = y + x$$

we obtain,

$$2 + 7 = 7 + 2$$

Adding the numbers on the left side of the equality we obtain 9 and adding the numbers on the right side of the equality we obtain 9. Hence, we get

$$9 = 9$$

The equality is shown to be correct when x is 2 and y is 7.

Example 2 Test the general rule represented by the equality

$$a + a + a + a = 4a$$

by replacing a by 5.

Solution: Substituting 5 for a in the given equality we obtain

$$5 + 5 + 5 + 5 = 4 \times 5$$

Adding the numbers on the left side we obtain 20; multiplying the numbers on the right side we obtain 20. Hence, we get

$$20 = 20$$

The equality is shown to be correct when a is 5.

Example 3 Test the statement represented by the equality

$$3n + 5n = 8n$$

for a specific value of n.

Solution: Suppose we replace n by 4. Then the given equality becomes

$$3 \times 4 + 5 \times 4 = 8 \times 4$$
$$12 + 20 = 32$$
$$32 = 32$$

The equality is found to be valid when n is 4.

The use of symbols (letters) for numbers was introduced by François Vieta (1540–1603), a French lawyer and mathematician. This innovation was the one that gave real power and generality to the then infant science of algebra. For this reason Vieta is sometimes referred to as the "father of algebra."

The origin of the word algebra comes from the Arabic word "Al-Jabr" (a word employed by the Arabs, having to do with "solving equations") used in the title of a book on the subject by an Arabian mathematician, Musa-al-Khowarizmi (ca. 820 A.D.). This work found its way to Europe after the Dark Ages and its subject came to be known as "algebra." Algebra was then practically synonymous with the "science of solving *equations*." In its early development algebra was concerned with solving a problem, such as the following:

"Some number multiplied by 7 and then added to 19 is equal to that same number added to 91."

To solve this problem we obtain an *equation*.

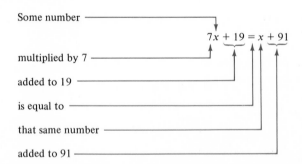

The expression $7x + 19$ is called the *left member* of the equation and the expression $x + 91$ is called the *right member* of the equation. Solving this equation is the process of finding the number represented by x so that the left and right members are equal.

Example 4 Write an equation that can be used to solve the following problem: some number multiplied by 5 and then added to 10 is equal to 24.

Solution: If x represents the unknown number, then we have the equation

$$5x + 10 = 24$$

In the process of solving equations we make use of the fact that most arithmetic operations can be "undone." Thus, for example if we have the equation

$$x + 5 = 8$$

we subtract the number five from both members of the equation and obtain

$$x + 5 - 5 = 8 - 5$$

or, equivalently,

$$x = 3$$

We have used the fact that subtraction is the *inverse* of addition. Subtracting a number is the *inverse* of adding that number. Adding a number is the *inverse* of subtracting that number. Multiplying by a number is the *inverse* of dividing by that number. Dividing by a number is the *inverse* of multiplying by that number if that number is not zero.

In Chapter 4 we study equations in greater detail. A few more examples will serve to illustrate how the concept of *inverse operations* is used in the process of solving equations.

Example 5 Solve the equation

$$x - 5 = 2$$

Solution: Because the inverse of "subtracting 5" is "adding 5," we add 5 to both members of the given equation and obtain

$$x - 5 + 5 = 2 + 5$$

or, equivalently,

$$x = 7$$

Example 6 Solve the equation

$$3x = 24$$

Solution: Because the inverse of "multiplying by 3" is "dividing by 3," we divide each member of the given equation by 3 and obtain

$$3x \div 3 = 24 \div 3$$

or, equivalently,

$$x = 8$$

An important characteristic of algebra is the logical-deductive nature of its development. Unlike most sciences, mathematics is primarily deductive rather than inductive. For instance, the experimental and natural sciences are inductive because we start from *specific* isolated facts and draw *general* results from many observations and experiments. However, in mathematics we start with a few general assumptions and from them deduce specific results.

Illustration 4 From the general assumption that the product of two numbers is zero only when at least one of the numbers is zero, we may deduce from the equation

$$3n = 0$$

the specific result

$$n = 0$$

Illustration 5 From the general assumption that the difference between two numbers is zero only when the numbers are equal, we may deduce from the equation

$$x - y = 0$$

the specific result

$$x = y$$

Furthermore, we may deduce from the equation

$$5 - x = 0$$

the specific result

$$x = 5$$

From some basic assumptions about whole numbers of arithmetic it is possible to prove by deduction many properties of numbers. One such property is the "summation property."

1.1.1 Summation Property   The sum of all the whole numbers from 1 to any given whole number is equal to one half of the product of the given whole number and the next consecutive whole number. Using symbols, where n is the given whole number, we write

$$1 + 2 + 3 + \cdots + n = \frac{1}{2} \times n \times (n + 1) \tag{1}$$

In equality (1) parentheses are used with $n + 1$ to indicate that $(n + 1)$ represents a single value. Thus, $\frac{1}{2} \times n \times (n + 1)$ represents the product of the three numbers $\frac{1}{2}$, n, and $(n + 1)$.

Example 7 Find the sum of all the whole numbers from 1 to 10.

Solution: From the Summation Property where n is 10 we have

$$1 + 2 + 3 + 4 + 5 + 6 + 7 + 8 + 9 + 10 = \frac{1}{2} \times 10 \times 11$$

$$= \frac{1}{2} \times 110$$

$$= 55$$

Example 8 Find the sum of all the whole numbers from 100 to 200.

Solution: First find the sum of all the whole numbers from 1 to 99 and then subtract this sum from the sum of all the whole numbers from 1 to 200.

The sum of all the whole numbers from 1 to 99 is $\frac{1}{2} \times 99 \times 100$.

$$\frac{1}{2} \times 99 \times 100 = \frac{1}{2} \times 9900$$

$$= 4950$$

The sum of all the whole numbers from 1 to 200 is $\frac{1}{2} \times 200 \times 201$.

$$\frac{1}{2} \times 200 \times 201 = \frac{1}{2} \times 40{,}200$$

$$= 20{,}100$$

We subtract and obtain

$$20{,}100 - 4950 = 15{,}150$$

Therefore, the sum of all the whole numbers from 100 to 200 is 15,150.

In answering our question "What is algebra?" we find equations and numbers as the objects that are studied. One set of numbers that we have already encountered is the set of whole numbers. Probably less familiar to you are certain other numbers known as the *integers,* which include the *negative integers*. For example, consider the temperature on a cold day. This measurement may be a number of degrees "below zero." If the scale on a thermometer is marked for temperatures above zero by 2, 4, 6, 8, and so on, some sort of designation is needed to mark the scale for temperatures below zero. Other examples are measurements of altitudes above and below sea level, profits and losses in financial matters, gains and losses in a game. The designations of "positive" and "negative" are used to denote numbers that in some sense are to be considered "opposites" of each other. Negative numbers are used for the purpose of measuring quantities oriented in a direction *opposite* to the positive direction.

Illustration 6 If "positive 10" denotes a credit of $10, then "negative 10" denotes a debit of $10. If "positive 5" denotes a distance of 5 miles east from some starting point then "negative 5" denotes a distance of 5 miles west from the starting point. If "positive 1" denotes a charge on a proton then "negative 1" denotes a charge on an electron.

The symbols used to denote the positive and negative designations are + and −.

> "positive 10" is denoted $^+10$
>
> "negative 10" is denoted $^-10$

If a number is written without a positive or a negative symbol, it is considered to be a positive number. Thus,

$$10 = {}^+10$$

All of the whole numbers greater than zero are considered to be positive. Corresponding to each positive number is a negative number. For instance, corresponding to $^+10$ is $^-10$; these corresponding numbers are called "opposites" of each other.

Illustration 7 $^+10$ is the opposite of $^-10$ and $^-10$ is the opposite of $^+10$.

When positive and negative numbers are depicted on a scale or line, one point on the line is designated as the "zero point"; this point is a reference point called the *origin* and corresponds to the number zero. Then all of the points on one side of the origin correspond to the positive numbers and all those points on the other side or opposite side of the origin correspond to the negative numbers. Zero is neither a positive nor a negative number. Figure 1.1.1 shows a scale that depicts land elevations above and below sea level; the elevation of a point at sea level corresponds to the number zero and such a point serves as the origin for the scale. Figure 1.1.2 shows a scale on a thermometer that uses positive and negative numbers to denote Fahrenheit temperatures above and below zero degrees.

The collection of whole numbers together with the opposites of the positive whole numbers form a set of numbers called the *integers*.

1.1.2 Definition   The collection of numbers 0, 1, 2, 3, ... together with $^-1, ^-2, ^-3, \ldots$ is the set of *integers*.

In our study of negative numbers we will primarily concern ourselves with learning how these numbers behave when subjected to the fundamental operations of addition and multiplication and the inverses of these operations, subtraction and division.

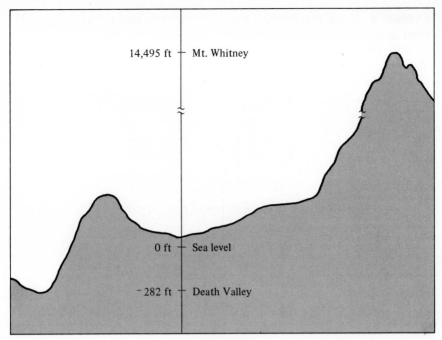

Figure 1.1.1

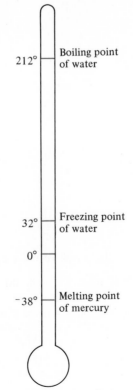

212° Boiling point of water

32° Freezing point of water

0°

⁻38° Melting point of mercury

Fahrenheit Temperature Scale

Figure 1.1.2

9

Example 9 If the temperature was 4° below zero and it warmed up 10°, what would be the temperature?

Solution: See the thermometer in Figure 1.1.3. Start at ⁻4° and count upward 10° and end at ⁺6°.

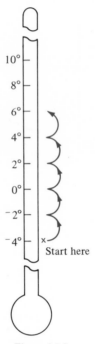

Figure 1.1.3

The process used in Example 9 corresponds to the operation of adding 10 to ⁻4.

$$^-4 + 10 = {}^+6$$

Exercises 1.1

In Exercises 1 and 2 find the value of each expression if $a = 2$.

1. (a) $3a$ (b) $a + a + a$ **2.** (a) $2a + 3a$ (b) $5a$

In Exercises 3 and 4 express each sum as a multiple.

3. (a) $6 + 6 + 6 + 6$ (b) $k + k + k + k$

4. (a) $a + a + a + a + a$ (b) $m + m$

5. Test the general rule for a specific value of n: $n + n + n + n + n = 5n$.

6. Express $a + a + a$ and $a + a + a + a$ as multiples. Predict the sum of $3a + 4a$ by noting that this is the same as $(a + a + a) + (a + a + a + a)$. Test your guess.

7. Write the given statement in symbolic form.
   (a) If any given number is multiplied by 1, the result is that same number.
   (b) Some number added to 20 is equal to 54.
   (c) Some number subtracted from 17 is equal to three times that number.

8. If the length of a line segment is y units, write an expression for the length of another line segment which is eight times as long.

9. Write an expression for the length of the line segment shown in Figure 1.1.4.

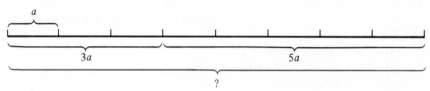

Figure 1.1.4

In Exercises 10 through 12 solve the given equations.

10. (a) $x + 5 = 12$ **(b)** $x + 10 = 10$ **(c)** $x - 5 = 9$

11. (a) $7x = 21$ **(b)** $8x = 32$ **(c)** $x \div 5 = 7$

12. (a) $2x + 1 = 7$ **(b)** $2x - 1 = 7$ **(c)** $3x - 3 = 0$

In Exercises 13 and 14, from the general assumption that the difference between two numbers is zero only when the numbers are equal, make some specific deductions.

13. (a) $x - 7 = 0$ **(b)** $m - n = 0$ **(c)** $10 - y = 0$

14. (a) $x - (5 + 2) = 0$
   (b) $10 - (x + 6) = 0$
   (c) $0 - (y - 4) = 0$

15. (a) Using the Summation Property find the sum of all the whole numbers from 1 to 100. (This problem, as the story goes, was solved by the great mathematician Gauss, in the matter of a minute, while still a schoolboy.)
   (b) Find the sum of the whole numbers from 1 to 1000.

16. It is thought that Gauss deductively arrived at his answer to the problem in Exercise 15(a) by the following reasoning:

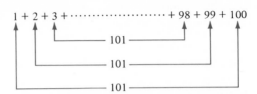

Each joined pair gives a sum of 101. And young Gauss probably reasoned there would be exactly 50 such pairs. Consequently he multiplied 101 by 50 and obtained $50 \times 101 = 5050$.

(a) Use this method of "deductive" reasoning to find the sum of all the *even* whole numbers from 1 to 100.

(b) Use this method to find the sum of all the whole numbers from 50 to 100.

17. If $^+15$ denotes the measure of a distance of a point that is 15 miles north of point P, then how would you denote the measure of a distance from P to Q if

(a) Q is 15 miles south of P?

(b) Q is 6 miles south of P?

(c) Q is 4 miles north of P?

(d) a person could go from point P to point Q by traveling 8 miles north and then traveling 12 miles south?

18. If 300 B.C. is denoted by $^-300$, how would you denote

(a) 300 A.D.?　　　(b) 32 B.C.?　　　　　　(c) the current year?

19. If the temperature at a given hour is 7° above zero (denoted $^+7$) and then the temperature drops 12° in the next 2 hours, how would you denote that temperature?

20. If in a given month a company shows $250 in losses and $5400 in profits, what numbers would you use to denote these amounts? What is the net profit or loss?

21. (a) What is the difference in elevation of the top of Mt. Whitney and the bottom of Death Valley? See Figure 1.1.1.

(b) What is the difference in the temperature reading of the freezing point of water and the melting point of mercury? See Figure 1.1.2.

22. Name the opposite of each of the following numbers.

(a) $^+10$　　　(b) $^-10$　　　　(c) 5　　　　　　(d) 0

Exercises 23 and 24 are given in order to provide some insight into the algebraic method of solving problems or equations.

23. Suppose you are given directions in a strange town to take you from one point A to another point B. Here are the directions:

From point *A* on the west side of Main Street, go 3 blocks north on Main Street and you will come to Elm Street. Turn left (west) on Elm and go 7 blocks to 7th Street. Turn left (south) on 7th Street and go 1 block and turn right (west). This puts you on Maple Lane. Proceed west on Maple Lane for $2\frac{1}{2}$ blocks to arrive at point *B* on the left (south) side of the street.

Now the problem is not just to follow these directions. Instead, with this information write directions for someone at point *B* to find you at point *A*. Of course, the directions will have to be reversed and this is the procedure used when solving equations. The important concept is that of inverse operations.

24. An elevator operator made the following moves starting at the ground floor: up 7 floors; up 2 floors; down 5 floors; up 1 floor; down 5 floors; up 6 floors; up 5 floors; down 8 floors. Where was the operator at the end of the last move mentioned? Write out the moves necessary for the operator to retrace every move made to end up at the ground floor again.

1.2 Sets

The theory of sets has provided mathematics with a convenient language for the expression of basic principles and relationships. It was with the theory of sets that Georg Cantor, in the 1880's, was able to give the first adequate mathematical analysis of "infinity."

There do exist objects of thought. Some of these objects are collections of other objects. Examples from everyday experience are collections such as the U.S. Track *Team,* the President's *Cabinet,* the *House* of Congress, a *herd* of elephants, a *flock* of birds, a singing *trio,* the *collection* of all numbers less than 50, the Jones' *family,* the *set* of odd numbers, and the *set* of whole numbers just to name a few.

A *set* is a specified *collection* of objects. Each object in a set is called a *member* or *element* of the set. We say that a collection is a *set* if the collection is *well defined,* that is, if given any object we can decide whether that object is or is not a member of the set in question. Hence, some of the collections of objects mentioned above are sets and some are not.

Illustration 1 A *trio* of the three greatest singers of the Twentieth Century is not a set because the determination of the elements of that collection cannot be decided. We do not know, for example, if Jack Jones is a member of the trio or not. There is no agreement on the criteria for greatness.

Illustration 2 The collection of whole numbers is a set, because if we are given any object, we can decide whether or not it is a whole number. (A whole number is an object although it is a mental object and not a physical object.)

Illustration 3 The President's Cabinet is not a set. However, if we are more specific about which President and which year the Cabinet is in office, that group can become a set.

The relationship between sets and the members of a set is so important that there is a special symbol to designate it. The symbol

$\in$ means "is an element of."

The symbol

$\notin$ means "is not an element of."

Illustration 4 $3 \in$ the set of whole numbers.

It is customary to designate sets by the capital letters of the alphabet. For example, we may let W represent the set of whole numbers. Then the sentence of Illustration 4 can be written as

$$3 \in W$$

which is read as

3 is an element of the set W.

We can write

$$2\frac{1}{2} \notin W$$

which is read as

$2\frac{1}{2}$ is not an element of the set W.

In this book the set designated by W is always understood to mean the set of whole numbers.

The elements of a set may be specified by listing them in braces.

Illustration 5 If $A = \{1, 2, 3, 4, 5\}$, then $2 \in A$, but $10 \notin A$.

Sometimes a set may have more elements than can be conveniently listed. Such a set is the set of whole numbers from 1 to 100. A list of the elements of this set can be given as follows:

$$\{1, 2, 3, \ldots, 100\}$$

The three dots are used to indicate the continuation of the sequence of numbers. Although the elements of a set are not necessarily in any special order, the use of dots to list the elements of a large collection of numbers facilitates the discussions of such sets.

Illustration 6 If $E = \{0, 2, 4, 6, \ldots, 100\}$, then E is the set of the first 51 *even* whole numbers. The number 100 is the so called last element.

When the elements of a set are not ordered in any particular way the reference to a "last" element is technically incorrect, but the convention is convenient and should not cause any confusion.

The sets in Illustrations 5 and 6 are *finite sets*, meaning that if we count the elements, the counting process will end and some whole number can be assigned to the "count" of the set. Some sets are *infinite*, meaning they are not finite, and if a count of the elements is attempted the process is unending. We can use the three dots to denote some infinite sets as shown in Illustrations 7 and 9.

Illustration 7 The set known as the *natural numbers* is designated as

$$N = \{1, 2, 3, \ldots\}$$

The set N is an infinite set containing all of the natural numbers. $10 \in N$, but $0 \notin N$ and $\frac{1}{2} \notin N$.

The set N in Illustration 7 is an infinite set with no "last" element. The three dots indicate a continuation of the sequence. In this book the set denoted by N is always understood to mean the set of natural numbers.

All of the natural numbers are whole numbers. We say that the set N is a "subset" of the set W.

1.2.1 Definition   Given two sets S and T,

(i) if every element of S is also an element of T, then S is a *subset* of T
and

(ii) if S is a *subset* of T, then every element of S is also an element of T.

The symbol

$\subseteq$ is read as "is a subset of."

Thus $S \subseteq T$ is read as "S is a subset of T." The symbol $\nsubseteq$ is read as "is not a subset of."

Illustration 8 (a) Because every element of $\{1, 2\}$ is also an element of $\{1, 2, 3, 4\}$, it follows from Definition 1.2.1(i) that $\{1, 2\}$ is a subset of $\{1, 2, 3, 4\}$ and we write

$$\{1, 2\} \subseteq \{1, 2, 3, 4\}$$

(b) Because $N \subseteq W$, it follows from Definition 1.2.1(ii) that every natural number is also a whole number.

An alternate way of stating Definition 1.2.1 by using the phrase "if and only if" is as follows:

Given two sets S and T,
S is a subset of T *if and only if* every element of S is also an element of T.

Note that the following statement is equivalent to part (i) of Definition 1.2.1: S is a subset of T if every element of S is also an element of T. Furthermore, the following statement is equivalent to part (ii) of Definition 1.2.1: S is a subset of T only if every element of S is also an element of T.

If S is a subset of T we say that T *contains* all of the elements of S.

Illustration 9 The set $\{0, 2, 4, 6, \ldots\}$ is called the set of *even* whole numbers. If $E = \{0, 2, 4, 6, \ldots\}$, then $E \subseteq W$. W contains all of the even whole numbers.

Two sets are "equal" if they contain exactly the same elements. That is, two sets are equal if each set is a subset of the other.

1.2.2 Definition Given two sets A and B, A *equals* B, written $A = B$ if and only if $A \subseteq B$ and $B \subseteq A$.

If set A is not equal to set B, we write $A \neq B$.

Illustration 10
(a) $\{1, 2, 3\} = \{1, 2, 3\}$
(b) $\{1, 1\} = \{1\}$ because $\{1, 1\} \subseteq \{1\}$ and $\{1\} \subseteq \{1, 1\}$
(c) $\{2, 6, 8\} = \{6, 2, 8\}$ (Note that the order of the elements does not change the fact that the sets are equal.)
(d) $\{1, 4\} = \{1, 1 + 3\}$
(e) $\{5, 10\} \neq \{0, 5, 10\}$
(f) $N \neq W$

One way to specify a set is to list the elements in braces as in the illustrations above. Another way is to describe the elements of the set by some rule that determines whether or not a given element belongs to that set. The notation on page 17 is used for this purpose and is called the *set-builder notation*. The letter x used in the set-builder notation is called a *variable*. A variable is a symbol (usually a lowercase letter of the alphabet) used to represent *any* element in a certain set. A specific element in that set is called a *value* of the variable.

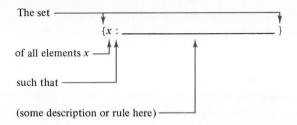

The set

{x : _____ }

of all elements x

such that

(some description or rule here)

Illustration 11 The set $\{1, 2, 3, \ldots, 100\}$ can be specified using the set-builder notation as

$$\{x : x \text{ is a natural number less than } 101\}$$

Illustration 12 The set of all the multiples of three is expressed symbolically as

$$\{x : x = 3n \text{ and } n \in W\}$$

This is read as "the set of all elements x, such that x equals three times n and n is an element of the set W." It follows that

$$\{x : x = 3n \text{ and } n \in W\} = \{0, 3, 6, 9, \ldots\}$$

Example 1 List the elements of $\{x : x \in N \text{ and } x \text{ is less than } 5\}$.

Solution: $\{1, 2, 3, 4\}$.

If we use the set-builder notation to specify sets, we may find several descriptions that define the same set.

Example 2 Specify the following set in two different ways by using the set-builder notation: $\{10, 20, 30, \ldots, 90\}$.

Solution:
(a) $\{x : x \text{ is a multiple of 10 between 1 and 100}\}$
(b) $\{y : y = 10n \text{ where } n \in \{1, 2, 3, \ldots, 9\}\}$

1.2.3 Definition   The *empty set* (or *null set*) is the set containing no elements. It is denoted by the symbol $\emptyset$.

Sometimes the empty set is denoted by $\{\ \}$; that is, $\emptyset = \{\ \}$.

Illustration 13 (a) The set $\{x : x \text{ is a whole number between 3 and 4}\}$ contains no elements because there is no whole number between 3 and 4. Hence, this set is the empty set, $\emptyset$.
(b) The set consisting of the largest whole number is the empty set, $\emptyset$.

The empty set can be associated with the concept of *nonexistence*. The antithesis of this concept is the concept of *all*. In set theory we consider a set, called the *universal set,* which is associated with this concept. For a given discussion a universal set is specified or it is understood and it contains every element in the discussion.

In many of the illustrations and examples of this section the universal set is W, the set of whole numbers. With this understanding the set $\{x : x$ is less than 5$\}$ is equal to the set $\{0, 1, 2, 3, 4\}$ and it is not necessary to include "and $x \in W$" in the description. If the universal set is N, the set of natural numbers, then $\{x : x$ is less than 5$\}$ is equal to the set $\{1, 2, 3, 4\}$.

Illustration 14 The collection of elements x, such that x is between 2 and 6, is not well-defined because the universal set has not been specified for this collection. Hence, this collection is not a set. If the universal set is known then we can refer to the collection as the set $\{x : x$ is between 2 and 6$\}$. If the universal set is W, then this set is equal to the set $\{3, 4, 5\}$.

Exercises 1.2

In Exercises 1 through 5 list all of the elements of the set described. You may use three dots if the set is an infinite set. $W = \{0, 1, 2, 3, \ldots\}$ and $N = \{1, 2, 3, \ldots\}$.

1. $\{x : x$ is less than 7 and $x \in N\}$

2. $\{x : x$ is greater than 100 and $x \in W\}$

3. $\{n : n \in W,$ but $n \notin N\}$

4. $\{y : y = 4n$ where $n \in W\}$

5. $\{x : x$ is not less than 4 and $x \in W\}$

In Exercises 6 through 9 use the set-builder notation to specify the set.

6. $\{0, 2, 4, 6, \ldots, 50\}$

7. $\{5, 10, 15, \ldots\}$

8. $\{6, 12, 18, \ldots, 60\}$

9. $\{0, 3, 5, 6, 9, 10, 12, 15, 18, \ldots\}$

10. Is the set consisting of the members of the United States Track team a well-defined set? Discuss.

11. Is the set $\{x : x$ is less than 5$\}$ a well-defined set? If so, list the elements, if not, why not?

12. **(a)** Is the set $\{1, 2, 3\}$ a subset of the set $\{1, 2, 3\}$?
    (b) If $A = \{f, a, s, t\}$ and $B = \{s, t, a, f\}$, does $A = B$?

13. (a) Discuss the meaning of $\{2\} \subseteq \{1, 2, 3\}$ and the meaning of $2 \in \{1, 2, 3\}$.

(b) If $A = \{37\}$, then is $3 \in A$?

(c) Discuss the differences between $\varnothing$, $\{0\}$, and $\{\varnothing\}$.

14. (a) If $A \subseteq B$ and $B \subseteq C$, is it true that $A \subseteq C$? Give an example.

(b) If $A \subseteq B$, is it true that $B \subseteq A$? Why?

15. List all the subsets of $\{1, 2, 3\}$ that contain

(a) one element;   **(b)** two elements;   **(c)** three elements.

16. Discuss the possibility of infinite sets other than sets of numbers.

17. (a) Suppose you have 10 sets and that each set has fewer than 9 elements. Do any two of these sets necessarily have the same number of elements? Discuss.

(b) Suppose you have a collection of m sets and that each set has fewer than $m - 1$ elements. Do any two of these sets necessarily have the same number of elements?

(c) Using the results of parts **(a)** and **(b)** show how you might prove that there are at least two trees in the world with the same number of leaves.

1.3 Operations on Sets

Two given sets may have some or all of their elements in common. For instance, if the set A is the set of even natural numbers and the set B is the set of whole multiples of three, then

$$A = \{2, 4, 6, 8, 10, 12, \ldots\}$$

and $$B = \{0, 3, 6, 9, 12, \ldots\}$$

The two sets A and B are not equal and neither one is a subset of the other; however, sets A and B have elements in common. The set of elements common to both set A and set B is the set C defined by listing the common elements.

$$C = \{6, 12, 18, \ldots\}$$

We call the set C the "intersection" of the sets A and B.

1.3.1 Definition   The *intersection* of sets A and B is the set which consists of only those elements which are in *both A and B*.

The symbol $\cap$ is used to designate the operation of intersection. Thus,

$A \cap B$ is read "the intersection of set A and set B."

Illustration 1   Let $A = \{2, 4, 6, 8, 10, 12, \ldots\}$
and $B = \{0, 3, 6, 9, 12, \ldots\}$

Then

$$A \cap B = \{6, 12, 18, \ldots\}$$

Furthermore, if $C = \{6, 12, 18, \ldots\}$, then

$$A \cap B = C$$

It follows that $x \in A \cap B$ if and only if $x \in A$ *and* $x \in B$; that is,

$$A \cap B = \{x : x \in A \text{ and } x \in B\}$$

If two sets have no elements in common, their intersection is the empty set.

Example 1   Let $A = \{1, 2, 3, 4, 5\}$, $B = \{4, 5, 6, 7, 8\}$, and $C = \{6, 7, 8, 9, 10\}$. List the elements of each of the following sets: (a) $A \cap B$; (b) $A \cap C$; (c) $B \cap C$.

Solution:
   (a) $A \cap B = \{4, 5\}$
   (b) $A \cap C = \emptyset$
   (c) $B \cap C = \{6, 7, 8\}$

Example 2   Let $A = \{1, 2, 3\}$, $B = \{2, 3, 4\}$, and $C = \{3, 4, 5\}$. List the elements of each of the following sets: (a) $(A \cap B) \cap C$; (b) $A \cap (B \cap C)$.

Solution:
   (a) $A \cap B = \{2, 3\}$. Therefore,

$$(A \cap B) \cap C = \{2, 3\} \cap \{3, 4, 5\}$$
$$= \{3\}$$

   (b) $B \cap C = \{3, 4\}$. Therefore,

$$A \cap (B \cap C) = \{1, 2, 3\} \cap \{3, 4\}$$
$$= \{3\}$$

1.3.2 Definition   If the intersection of two nonempty sets S and T is the empty set (that is, $S \cap T = \emptyset$), then the sets S and T are said to be *disjoint*.

Illustration 2   If $D = \{1, 3, 5, \ldots\}$ and $E = \{0, 2, 4, \ldots\}$, then $D \cap E = \emptyset$, and so D and E are disjoint sets. The set D is the set of *odd* whole numbers and the set E is the set of even whole numbers. No whole number is both odd and even; the sets are disjoint.

The set

$$C = \{0, 3, 5, 6, 9, 10, 12, 15, 18, 20, \ldots\}$$

can be defined by set-builder notation as follows:

$$C = \{x : x \text{ is either a multiple of 3 or a multiple of 5 or both}\} \quad (1)$$

If $A = \{x : x \text{ is a multiple of 3}\}$ and $B = \{x : x \text{ is a multiple of 5}\}$, then

$$A = \{0, 3, 6, 9, 12, 15, \ldots\}$$

and

$$B = \{0, 5, 10, 15, \ldots\}$$

and we call the set C defined by statement (1) the "union" of the sets A and B.

1.3.3 Definition   The *union* of sets A and B is the set which consists of all the elements which are *either* in A *or* in B (including any elements which may be in both).

The symbol $\cup$ is used to designate the operation of union. Thus,

$A \cup B$ is read "the *union* of set A and set B."

Illustration 3 Let $A = \{0, 3, 6, 9, 12, 15, \ldots\}$ and $B = \{0, 5, 10, 15, \ldots\}$. Then

$$A \cup B = \{0, 3, 5, 6, 9, 10, 12, 15, 18, 20, \ldots\}$$

Furthermore, if $C = \{0, 3, 5, 6, 9, 10, 12, 15, 18, 20, \ldots\}$, then

$$A \cup B = C$$

It follows that $x \in A \cup B$ if and only if $x \in A$ or $x \in B$; that is,

$A \cup B = \{x : x \in A \text{ or } x \in B\}$

Example 3 Let $A = \{1, 2, 3, 4, 5\}$, $B = \{4, 5, 6, 7, 8\}$ and $C = \{10, 15\}$. List the elements of each of the following sets: (a) $A \cup B$; (b) $A \cup C$; (c) $B \cup C$.

Solution:
 (a) $A \cup B = \{1, 2, 3, 4, 5, 6, 7, 8\}$
 (b) $A \cup C = \{1, 2, 3, 4, 5, 10, 15\}$
 (c) $B \cup C = \{4, 5, 6, 7, 8, 10, 15\}$

Example 4 Let $A = \{1, 2, 3\}$, $B = \{2, 3, 4\}$, and $C = \{3, 4, 5\}$. List the elements of each of the following sets: (a) $(A \cup B) \cup C$; (b) $A \cup (B \cup C)$; (c) $(A \cap B) \cup C$; (d) $A \cap (B \cup C)$.

Solution:

(a) $A \cup B = \{1, 2, 3, 4\}$. Therefore,

$$(A \cup B) \cup C = \{1, 2, 3, 4\} \cup \{3, 4, 5\}$$
$$= \{1, 2, 3, 4, 5\}$$

(b) $B \cup C = \{2, 3, 4, 5\}$. Therefore,

$$A \cup (B \cup C) = \{1, 2, 3\} \cup \{2, 3, 4, 5\}$$
$$= \{1, 2, 3, 4, 5\}$$

(c) $A \cap B = \{2, 3\}$. Therefore,

$$(A \cap B) \cup C = \{2, 3\} \cup \{3, 4, 5\}$$
$$= \{2, 3, 4, 5\}$$

(d) $B \cup C = \{2, 3, 4, 5\}$. Therefore,

$$A \cap (B \cup C) = \{1, 2, 3\} \cap \{2, 3, 4, 5\}$$
$$= \{2, 3\}$$

We now consider an operation on just one set called the operation of "complementation." If the universal set is the set of whole numbers, then the "complement" of the set of even whole numbers is the set of odd whole numbers.

1.3.4 Definition   The *complement* of set A is the set which consists of all the elements in the universal set which are *not* in A.

The symbol $'$ is used to designate the operation of complementation. Thus,

A' is read "the complement of set A."

Illustration 4 If the universal set is $\{1, 2, 3, \ldots, 10\}$ and $A = \{1, 3, 5, 7, 9\}$, then

$$A' = \{2, 4, 6, 8, 10\}$$

Illustration 5 If the universal set is the set of whole numbers, E is the set of even whole numbers, and D is the set of odd whole numbers, then

$$E' = D$$

Furthermore, $(E')' = D'$ and $D' = E$, therefore

$$(E')' = E$$

It follows that if $x \in U$, the universal set, then $x \in A'$ if and only if $x \notin A$; that is,

$$A' = \{x : x \notin A\}$$

Another symbol sometimes used for the complement of set A is $\overline{A}$.

Example 5 Let the universal set $U = \{0, 1, 2, 3, \ldots\}$, $E = \{0, 2, 4, 6, \ldots\}$, and $D = \{1, 3, 5, \ldots\}$. List the elements of (a) E', (b) D', (c) $E' \cap D'$, (d) $(E \cap D)'$, (e) $E' \cup D'$, and (f) $(E \cup D)'$.

Solution:
  (a) $E' = \{1, 3, 5, \ldots\} = D$
  (b) $D' = \{0, 2, 4, 6, \ldots\} = E$
  (c) $E' \cap D' = \emptyset$
  (d) $E \cap D = \emptyset$. Therefore, $(E \cap D)' = \{0, 1, 2, 3, \ldots\} = U$.
  (e) $E' \cup D' = \{0, 1, 2, 3, \ldots\} = U$
  (f) $E \cup D = U$. Therefore, $(E \cup D)' = \emptyset$.

Exercises 1.3

In Exercises 1 through 10 consider the universal set to be $U = \{1, 2, 3, 4, 5, 6\}$ with subsets $A = \{1, 3, 5\}$, $B = \{1, 2, 3, 4\}$, and $C = \{2, 4, 6\}$. List the elements of the given set.

1. $A \cup B$ **2.** $A \cap B$

3. $A \cup (B \cup C)$ **4.** $A \cap C$

5. $A \cap (B \cup C)$ **6.** A'

7. $A' \cup B'$ **8.** $C' \cup (B \cap A)$

9. $(B' \cup C')'$ **10.** $(A \cup B) \cap (A \cup C)$

In Exercises 11 through 23 let W be the universal set, E be the set of even whole numbers, and D be the set of odd whole numbers. Determine if the given set is equal to one of the sets W, E, D, or $\emptyset$.

11. $(D')'$ **12.** $E \cap \emptyset$

13. $E \cup D$ **14.** $E \cap D$

15. $E \cap W$ **16.** $E \cap E$

17. $E \cup \emptyset$ **18.** $E \cup W$

19. $\emptyset'$ **20.** W'

21. $E \cup E'$ **22.** $E \cup E$

23. $E \cap E'$

24. Let $U = \{1, 2, 3, \ldots, 10\}$. Select two sets A and B, such that $A \subseteq B$. Show that $B' \subseteq A'$.

25. If $A = \{1, 2, 3, 4, 5\}$ and $B = \{2, 4, 6, 8, 10\}$, then list the elements of each of the following sets.
    (a) $\{x : x \in A \text{ and } x \in B\}$ **(b)** $\{x : x \in A \text{ or } x \in B\}$

26. Give an example to show that $A \cap B \subseteq A$ and $A \cap B \subseteq B$.

27. Give an example to show that $A \subseteq A \cup B$ and $B \subseteq A \cup B$.

28. Use the sets A and B defined for Exercises 1 through 10 and show that $(A \cap B)' = A' \cup B'$.

29. Use the sets A and B defined for Exercises 1 through 10 and show that the number of elements in $A \cup B$ is not the same as the number of elements in set A plus the number of elements in set B.

In Exercises 30 through 33 let $A = \{x : x \in W \text{ and } x \text{ is a multiple of } 3\}$ and $B = \{x : x \in W \text{ and } x \text{ is a multiple of } 4\}$. List the elements of the given set.

30. $A \cup B$ **31.** $A \cap B$

32. A' **33.** B'

1.4 Sets of Numbers

A *numeral* is a name or symbol that is used to represent a number. For instance, the numerals used to represent the numbers in the set of natural numbers are

$$1, 2, 3, 4, 5, 6, 7, 8, 9, 10, 11, 12, \ldots$$

In particular the numeral "2" represents the natural number "two." In this book we refer to a number by the numeral representing it. For instance, we use the terminology: the number 2, the number 83, the number 256, and so on.

As well as being familiar with natural numbers, you are also familiar with numbers represented by numerals called *fractions*. For instance, the numerals

$$\frac{1}{2}, \frac{3}{5}, \frac{8}{5}, \frac{17}{3}, \text{ and } \frac{4}{1}$$

are fractions. The numbers represented by these fractions are called *rational numbers*. A rational number is defined formally in Section 5.2. Informally, we can think of a positive rational number as one that is the quotient of two natural numbers. For instance, the rational number $\frac{8}{5}$ is the quotient of 8 divided by 5. Because any natural number is the quotient of itself divided by 1, the set of natural numbers is a subset of the set of positive rational numbers. For example, $4 = \frac{4}{1}$, and so 4 is a positive rational number.

Illustration 1 The rational number $\frac{1}{2}$ can be represented by many different fractions. For instance,

$$\frac{1}{2}, \frac{2}{4}, \frac{3}{6}, \frac{4}{8}, \frac{5}{10}, \ldots$$

and so on, are all fractions representing the same rational number "one half."

In general, there are many fractions that can be used to represent a particular rational number.

Corresponding to each positive rational number is its opposite, a negative rational number. For instance, the opposite of $\frac{3}{4}$ is $\frac{-3}{4}$, the opposite of $\frac{7}{3}$ is $\frac{-7}{3}$, and so on. The set of opposites of the positive rational numbers is called the set of negative rational numbers.

The set of positive rational numbers together with the set of negative rational numbers as well as the set consisting of the single number zero forms the set of rational numbers. Hence, if

Q is the set of rational numbers
Q^+ is the set of positive rational numbers
Q^- is the set of negative rational numbers

and $\{0\}$ is the set consisting of the single number 0

then Q is the union of the three sets Q^+, Q^-, and $\{0\}$; that is

$$Q = Q^+ \cup Q^- \cup \{0\}$$

There are positive and negative numbers that are not rational numbers. Such a number is pi, represented by the numeral π. Another such number is the square root of 2, represented by the numeral $\sqrt{2}$. The numbers π and $\sqrt{2}$ are positive numbers that cannot be represented as the quotient of two natural numbers; hence, they are not rational numbers. They are called *irrational numbers*. Let I denote the set of irrational numbers. The sets I and Q are disjoint; that is,

$$I \cap Q = \varnothing$$

The union of the sets I and Q is called the set of *real numbers*. If R denotes the set of real numbers, then

$$R = Q \cup I$$

That is, the set of real numbers is the set of all positive numbers, all negative numbers, and 0.

We use the notation $a \in R$ to mean that a is a real number. Furthermore, if we write $a, b \in R$, we mean that a and b are real numbers.

The real numbers can be represented geometrically by points on a line. One point is chosen to represent zero; this point is a reference point called the *origin*. Each of the points on one side of the origin corresponds to a selected positive number and each of the points on the opposite side of the origin corresponds to a selected negative number. Each number is called the *coordinate* of its corresponding point on the line. Each point on the line is called the *graph* of its corresponding number. If the coordinates of all the points on the line are selected in a manner that preserves the natural order of magnitude of the numbers, then the line with its coordinate assignment is called a real number line. See Figure 1.4.1.

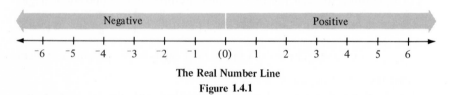

The Real Number Line
Figure 1.4.1

Example 1 Locate on a real number line the points corresponding to the numbers $-3, \dfrac{-1}{2}, 1, \dfrac{3}{2},$ and $\dfrac{5}{2}$.

Solution: See Figure 1.4.2.

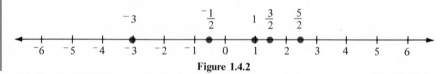

Figure 1.4.2

Example 2 Find the coordinates of the points A, B, C, and D shown in Figure 1.4.3.

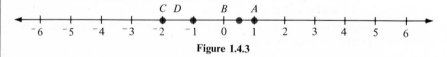

Figure 1.4.3

Solution: The coordinate of A is 1; the coordinate of B is 0; the coordinate of C is -2; and the coordinate of D is $\dfrac{-3}{2}$ (approx.).

If two natural numbers are added or multiplied, the result is another natural number. The property stating that the result of combining two numbers of a certain kind through some operation is a number of that same kind, is called a *closure law*.

Illustration 2   Given the natural numbers 3 and 5, $3 + 5$ is the natural number 8 and 3×5 is the natural number 15.

Because the sum of any two natural numbers is a natural number, the set of natural numbers is said to be "closed" with respect to the operation of addition. Furthermore, because the product of any two natural numbers is a natural number, the set of natural numbers is said to be closed with respect to the operation of multiplication.

Because $5 - 8$ and $8 \div 5$ do not represent natural numbers, the set of natural numbers is not closed with respect to the operations of subtraction and division.

We shall learn later that the set of integers is closed with respect to addition, multiplication, and subtraction, but this set is not closed with respect to division. For instance, $3 \div 2$ is not an integer. Furthermore, we shall learn that Q, the set of rational numbers, and R, the set of real numbers, are closed with respect to the four fundamental operations of arithmetic (addition, multiplication, subtraction, and division).

1.4.1 Property (The Closure Law for the Operations of Addition and Multiplication of Real Numbers)   If a, $b \in R$, then $(a + b) \in R$ and $(a \times b) \in R$.

Some subsets of the set of real numbers are closed with respect to the operations of addition and multiplication, such as the set of positive real numbers.

1.4.2 Property (Closure Law for the Operations of Addition and Multiplication of Positive Real Numbers)   If a and b are any positive real numbers, then $a + b$ and $a \times b$ are positive real numbers.

To gain a perspective of the relationship that some of the various subsets of the set of real numbers have to each other, study the diagram in Figure 1.4.4.

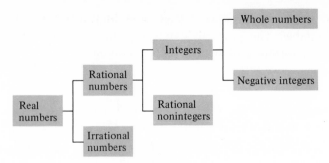

Figure 1.4.4

Exercises 1.4

In Exercises 1 through 5 find at least three other numerals for the given number.

1. $\dfrac{2}{3}$ **2.** $\dfrac{3}{4}$ **3.** 3   **4.** $\dfrac{9}{12}$

5. 0

6. Find the coordinates of the points A, B, C, D, and E in Figure 1.4.5.

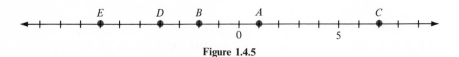

Figure 1.4.5

7. Find the coordinates of the points A, B, C, D, and E in Figure 1.4.6.

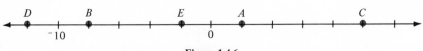

Figure 1.4.6

In Exercises 8 through 15 locate the approximate position of the given rational number on a number line. See Figure 1.4.2.

8. $\dfrac{1}{2}$ **9.** $\dfrac{3}{2}$ **10.** $^-3$ **11.** $\dfrac{^-1}{4}$

12. 0   **13.** $^-2$ **14.** $\sqrt{4}$ **15.** $\dfrac{^-5}{2}$

16. Given the sets N, W, Q, I, and R, write as many true statements as possible using the subset symbol, such as $N \subseteq W$.

17. Rewrite Property 1.4.2 changing the words "positive real numbers" to "whole numbers." Is the resulting statement a property of whole numbers? Discuss.

18. If the words "positive real numbers" are replaced by "even whole numbers" in Property 1.4.2, is the resulting statement true? Discuss and give an example.

19. Is the sum of any two odd whole numbers another odd whole number? Is the set of odd whole numbers *closed* with respect to addition? multiplication? Discuss and give examples.

20. Is the set of the whole multiples of 3 *closed* with respect to addition? multiplication? subtraction? division? Discuss and give examples.

21. Is the set $\{0, 1\}$ closed with respect to addition? multiplication? subtraction?

22. If the operation $\star$ is defined so that $a \star b =$ the average of a and b $\left(a \star b = \dfrac{a + b}{2}\right)$, then is the set of positive rational numbers Q^+ closed with respect to the operation $\star$? Discuss and give examples.

1.5 Equality and Inequality Relations

The most common relation used in algebra is equality. The symbol $=$ means "is equal to." Strictly speaking, $a = b$ if and only if a and b are numerals for the same number. If a and b represent different numbers, we write $a \neq b$.

Illustration 1
(a) $1 = \dfrac{1}{2} + \dfrac{1}{2}$. Both "1" and "$\dfrac{1}{2} + \dfrac{1}{2}$" are numerals for the number "one."
(b) $x = 2$. This equality is true if and only if x represents the number "two."
(c) $x + y = y + x$. This equality is always true if x and y are real numbers.
(d) $2 \neq 3$.
(e) $x + 1 \neq 2$. This statement is false if $x = 1$; otherwise this statement is true.

The Greeks were probably the first to recognize the potential value of statements such as "quantities equal to the same quantity are equal to each other." Such statements were considered "self-evident truths" and were called *axioms*. Today axioms are considered merely to be *assumptions* one makes about the operations and relations pertaining to a given set of numbers or elements. It is from these basic assumptions (axioms) that everything else logically follows. The consequences of the axioms are called *theorems* and are proved with logical deductive arguments. It is impossible to prove everything, but the axioms provide us with the necessary starting points. We now make some assumptions about the properties of equality.

1.5.1 Axiom (Reflexive Property of Equality)   Given any expression E, $E = E$.

Illustration 2   As examples of the Reflexive Property statements such as the following are assumed to be true without further justification: (a) $2 = 2$; (b) $x = x$; (c) $3y + 4 = 3y + 4$.

The Reflexive Property states that every number, or expression representing a number, is equal to itself.

1.5.2 Axiom (Substitution Property of Equality)   If E and F are expressions and if $E = F$, then either E or F may be substituted for the other in any algebraic expression or statement without altering the value or meaning of that expression or statement.

Illustration 3   Because $\dfrac{30}{3} = 10$ we may substitute 10 for $\dfrac{30}{3}$ in the statement

$$x - 2 = \frac{30}{3}$$

and we have

$$x - 2 = 10$$

The next two properties are logical consequences of Axioms 1.5.1 and 1.5.2 and can be "proved." We call these properties *theorems*. When proving a theorem, which is usually a statement of the form "If _____, then _____," one procedure is to assume the "if" part, called the *hypothesis,* and to try to establish the "then" part, called the *conclusion.*

1.5.3 Theorem (Symmetric Property of Equality)   Given any two expressions E and F, if $E = F$, then $F = E$.

Proof: Assume the hypothesis

$$E = F \tag{1}$$

By the Reflexive Property (Axiom 1.5.1) we know that

$$E = E \qquad (2)$$

Now we use the Substitution Property (Axiom 1.5.2) and in the left member of equality (2) we substitute the expression F for the expression E. We have then

$$F = E \qquad (3)$$

Because equality (3) is the conclusion of the theorem to be proved, the proof is completed.

The Symmetric Property states that the left and right members of an equality are interchangeable.

Illustration 4   If

$$3 = x + 2$$

then from the Symmetric Property we have

$$x + 2 = 3$$

The next theorem provides the justification for the often stated principle that quantities equal to the same quantity are equal to each other.

1.5.4 Theorem (Transitive Property of Equality)   Given three expressions, E, F, and G, if $E = F$ and $F = G$, then $E = G$.

Proof: Assume the hypothesis

$$E = F \qquad (4)$$

and

$$F = G \qquad (5)$$

Applying the Substitution Property and substituting G for F in equality (4), we have

$$E = G \qquad (6)$$

Illustration 5   If

$$2x = x + x \qquad \text{and} \qquad x + x = 10$$

then from the Transitive Property of Equality we have

$$2x = 10$$

Example 1   Name the property illustrated by the following statements.

(a) If $5 = x + 1$, then $x + 1 = 5$
(b) $x + y = x + y$
(c) If $x = y + 1$ and $y + 1 = 12$, then $x = 12$
(d) If $y = 3$, then $y + 7 = 3 + 7$
$$= 10$$

Solution:
(a) Symmetric Property (Theorem 1.5.3)
(b) Reflexive Property (Axiom 1.5.1)
(c) Transitive Property (Theorem 1.5.4)
(d) Substitution Property (Axiom 1.5.2)

In algebra we are also concerned with *order relations*. Statements employing these relations are sometimes called *inequalities*. First we discuss the "less than" relationship, denoted by the symbol $<$.

1.5.5 Definition   If $a, b \in R$, then *a is less than b,* denoted by $a < b$, if and only if there exists a positive number c such that $a + c = b$.

Illustration 6   Because $2 + 1 = 3$ it follows from Definition 1.5.5 that $2 < 3$ (read: two is less than three).

If a number line is positioned in a conventional way, horizontally with the positive direction to the right, then the number a is less than the number b $(a < b)$ if and only if the point on the number line corresponding to the number a is to the left of the point corresponding to the number b. See Figure 1.5.1.

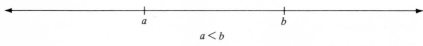

$a < b$

Figure 1.5.1

Illustration 7   Figure 1.5.2 shows a point corresponding to the number $^-3$ and a point corresponding to the number $^-1$. Because the point corresponding to $^-3$ is to the left of the point corresponding to $^-1$, we state that $^-3$ is less than $^-1$, that is $^-3 < ^-1$.

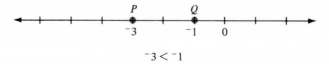

$^-3 < ^-1$

Figure 1.5.2

It follows that every negative number is less than any positive number.

If one number is neither less than nor equal to a second number, then it is said to be *greater than* the second number, and we use the symbol $>$ to denote this relation.

1.5.6 Definition   If $a, b \in R$, then *a is greater than b,* denoted by $a > b$, if and only if $b < a$.

Illustration 8 Because $2 < 3$ it follows from Definition 1.5.6 that $3 > 2$ (read: three is greater than two).

If a number line is positioned in a conventional way (see Figure 1.5.3), then the number a is greater than the number b ($a > b$) if and only if the point on the number line corresponding to the number a is to the right of the point corresponding to the number b.

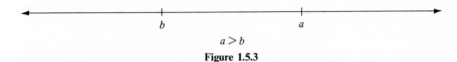

$a > b$

Figure 1.5.3

Illustration 9 If we have the inequality

$$5 > x$$

we can write the equivalent inequality

$$x < 5$$

Given any real number a, either

$$a \text{ is a negative number } (a < 0) \tag{7}$$

or

$$a \text{ is zero } (a = 0) \tag{8}$$

or

$$a \text{ is a positive number } (a > 0) \tag{9}$$

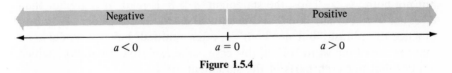

Figure 1.5.4

See Figure 1.5.4. Statements (7), (8), and (9) are a special case of the following axiom we call the Trichotomy Law.

1.5.7 Axiom (Trichotomy Law)   If $a, b \in R$, then exactly one of the following statements is true
   (i) $a < b$
   (ii) $a = b$
or
   (iii) $a > b$

Example 2 Replace the blank space with one of the following symbols $=$, $<$, or $>$ so that the resulting statement is true.

(a) $2 + 3$ _____ 2×3

(b) $^-6$ _____ $^-2$

(c) 0 _____ $^-10$

(d) $\dfrac{^-3}{2}$ _____ $\dfrac{1}{2}$

(e) $\pi + \sqrt{2}$ _____ $\sqrt{2} + \pi$

Solution:

(a) Because $2 + 3 = 5$ and $2 \times 3 = 6$ and $5 < 6$ we have $2 + 3 < 2 \times 3$.

(b) $^-6 < ^-2$

(c) $0 > ^-10$

(d) $\dfrac{^-3}{2} < \dfrac{1}{2}$

(e) $\pi + \sqrt{2} = \sqrt{2} + \pi$

Consider the negation of each of the three statements of the Trichotomy Law. We write

$$a \not< b \quad \text{(read: } a \text{ is not less than } b)$$
$$a \neq b \quad \text{(read: } a \text{ is not equal to } b)$$
$$a \not> b \quad \text{(read: } a \text{ is not greater than } b)$$

From the rules of logic and the Trichotomy Law it follows that if $a, b \in R$, then exactly two of the negation statements are true. For instance, if $a \neq b$, then either $a > b$ or $a < b$, but not both. And if $a \not< b$, then either $a > b$ or $a = b$, but not both. Similarly, if $a \not> b$, then $a < b$ or $a = b$, but not both.

The mathematical symbol for the relation "is greater than or equal to, but not both" is $\geq$. Thus, the statement $a \geq b$ is read "a is greater than or equal to b, but not both" and is equivalent to the statement $a \not< b$. In practice the phrase "but not both" is often omitted, but it is understood that the use of the word "or" in this case is the exclusive use of "or" which implies that not both parts of the statement are true.

Illustration 10 The statement $^-2 \geq ^-3$ is read as "negative two is greater than or equal to negative three." The statement $5 \geq 5$ is read as "five is greater than or equal to five," and this statement is also true because $5 \geq 5$ is equivalent to $5 \not< 5$, which is true.

The symbol for the relation "is less than or equal to" is $\leq$. Thus, the statement $a \leq b$ is read as "a is less than or equal to b" and is equivalent to the statement $a \not> b$.

Illustration 11 The statement $x \ngtr x + 1$ is read as "x is not greater than $x + 1$." This statement is true and is equivalent to the statement $x \le x + 1$, which is read as "x is less than or equal to $x + 1$."

Statements which include either the relation "is less than" or "is greater than" are called *inequalities*. A statement, such as $a \ne b$, which implies the use of the "less than" or "greater than" relationship, is also called an *inequality*. Each of the following statements (or their equivalents) is an inequality:

$$a < b$$
$$a > b$$
$$a \ne b \quad \text{(equivalent to } a > b \text{ or } a < b\text{)}$$
$$a \nless b \quad \text{(equivalent to } a \ge b\text{)}$$
$$a \ngtr b \quad \text{(equivalent to } a \le b\text{)}$$

The statement $a < x < b$ is read as "a is less than x and x is less than b." That is,

$$a < x < b \quad \text{means} \quad a < x \text{ and } x < b$$

Sometimes this statement is read as "x is between a and b." This statement is also an example of an inequality. Other inequalities of this type are the following:

$$a > x > b \quad \text{means} \quad a > x \text{ and } x > b$$
$$a \le x \le b \quad \text{means} \quad a \le x \text{ and } x \le b$$
$$a \ge x \ge b \quad \text{means} \quad a \ge x \text{ and } x \ge b$$

Example 3 List the elements of each of the following sets:
(a) $\{x : x < 5\}$
(b) $\{x : 2 \le x < 7\}$
(c) $\{x : 7 > x\} \cap \{x : x > 2\}$
(d) $\{x : 7 > x > 2\}$
The universal set is the set of whole numbers, W.

Solution:
(a) $\{x : x < 5\} = \{0, 1, 2, 3, 4\}$
(b) $\{x : 2 \le x < 7\} = \{2, 3, 4, 5, 6\}$
(c) $\{x : 7 > x\} = \{0, 1, 2, 3, 4, 5, 6\}$ and $\{x : x > 2\} = \{3, 4, 5, 6, \ldots\}$.
   Therefore,

$$\{x : 7 > x\} \cap \{x : x > 2\} = \{0, 1, 2, 3, 4, 5, 6\} \cap \{3, 4, 5, 6, \ldots\}$$
$$= \{3, 4, 5, 6\}$$

(d) $\{x : 7 > x > 2\} = \{3, 4, 5, 6\}$

If $a < b$, then the set of all the real numbers x such that $a \le x \le b$ is an example of what is called an *interval*. When making certain measurements in engineering or science, a "tolerance interval" is sometimes specified for a given measurement. For example, the measurement of a certain field is 120 feet $\pm$ 0.1 foot (read: 120 feet, plus or minus 0.1 foot). This means that if x feet is the length of the field, then

$$119.9 \leq x \leq 120.1$$

That is, x is at least 119.9, and at most 120.1.

Example 4 If x represents the "actual" measure in the following measurements, write an inequality involving x.

   (a) A measurement of 10 inches $\pm \dfrac{1}{2}$ inch.

   (b) A measurement of 0.015 inch measured to the nearest 0.001 inch.

Solution:

   (a) $9\dfrac{1}{2} \leq x \leq 10\dfrac{1}{2}$

   (b) $0.014 < x < 0.016$

Exercises 1.5

In Exercises 1 through 12 name the property illustrated by the given example.

1. If $10 = 2x$, then $2x = 10$.

2. $x + 2 = x + 2$

3. If $x = y + 1$ and $y + 1 = 17$, then $x = 17$.

4. If $y = 2x + 1$ and $y = 3x - 4$, then $2x + 1 = 3x - 4$.

5. If $x = 4$ and $x + 2 = 6$, then $4 + 2 = 6$.

6. If $x = 4$, then $x + 2 = 4 + 2 = 6$.

7. If $x = y$ and $y = z$, then $x = z$.

8. If $x = y$ and $x = z$, then $y = z$.

9. If $2 = 3x - 1$, then $3x - 1 = 2$.

10. If $2 = 3x - 1$ and $x = y + z$, then $3x - 1 = 2$.

11. If $2 = 3x - 1$ and $x + 2 = y$, then $x + 2 = x + 2$.

12. If $4x + 1 > 3$ and $y = 4x + 1$, then $y > 3$.

In Exercises 13 through 25 replace the blank space with one of the relation symbols $=$, $>$, or $<$, so that the resulting statement is true.

13. (a) $3 \times 3 + 4 \times 4$ _____ $3 \times 4 + 4 \times 3$

(b) $\dfrac{5}{9} + \dfrac{8}{7}$ _____ $\dfrac{8}{7} + \dfrac{5}{9}$

14. (a) 5×1 _____ $5 + 0$ (b) 8×0 _____ $^-5$

15. (a) $\dfrac{1}{2} + 1$ _____ $1 - \dfrac{1}{2} + \dfrac{3}{4}$ (b) $\dfrac{1}{4}$ _____ $\dfrac{1}{3}$

16. (a) 2 _____ $^-10$ (b) $\dfrac{1}{2} + \dfrac{4}{19}$ _____ $\dfrac{1}{2} - \dfrac{4}{19}$

17. (a) $1 + 2 + 3 + 2 + 1$ _____ 3×3

(b) $\dfrac{3}{25}$ _____ $\dfrac{2}{17}$

18. (a) $\dfrac{1}{2} \times \dfrac{1}{2}$ _____ $\dfrac{1}{2}$ (b) 0 _____ $^-9$

19. (a) 0.101 _____ 0.095 (b) $\dfrac{4 + 9}{2}$ _____ $\sqrt{4 \times 9}$

20. (a) $2 \times 2 \times 2$ _____ 3×3 (b) $2 + 2$ _____ 2×2

21. (a) $^-100$ _____ $^-200$ (b) $^-10$ _____ $^+1$

22. (a) x _____ x (b) x _____ $x + 1$

23. (a) x _____ $x - 1$ (b) x _____ $x + 2$

24. (a) $x - 1$ _____ $x - 2$ (b) $x + 1$ _____ $x + 2$

25. If $x > y$, then $x + 2$ _____ $y + 2$

In Exercises 26 through 30 list the elements of the set. If the set is infinite use three dots. The universal set is the set of whole numbers, W.

26. $\{x : x \leq 3\}$ 27. $\{x : x > 100\}$

28. $\{x : 9 > x\} \cap \{x : x > 4\}$ 29. $\{x : 9 > x > 4\}$

30. $\{x : 1 < x \leq 6\}$

In Exercises 31 through 35 write in words the meaning of each statement.

31. $a \not> 3$ 32. $x \not> y$ and $x \not< y$ 33. $2 < 3 < 4$

34. $4 \not\geq 5$ 35. $10 \geq x \geq 7$

In Exercises 36 through 40, if x is the "actual" measure to be found, write an inequality involving x.

36. A measurement of 10 inches $\pm \dfrac{1}{4}$ inch.

37. A measurement of 0.059 inch $\pm$0.0005 inch.

38. A measurement of 137 inches measured to the nearest 2 inches.

39. A measurement of 120 feet measured to the nearest foot.

40. A measurement of 120 feet measured to the nearest 10 feet.

41. If $a < b$ and $b < c$ $(a < b < c)$, then what is the relationship of a and c? Represent possible positions of a, b, and c on the number line.

42. If you add two positive numbers, the sum is greater than either addend. Give a counterexample to show that a similar statement is not true if you multiply two positive numbers.

43. If x units is the width of a rectangle and x is between 5 and 6, and if the length is two more units than the width, what are maximum and minimum values of the number of units in the length?
  (a) That is, if $5 < x < 6$, then _____ $< x + 2 <$ _____.
  (b) In general, if $a < x < b$, then _____ $< x + 2 <$ _____.
  (c) In general if $a < x < b$, then _____ $< x + c <$ _____, for any positive number, c.

44. Prove the following theorem:

$$\text{If } E = F \text{ and } G = F, \text{ then } E = G.$$

1.6 Review Exercises

1. Express each of the following as a multiple.
  (a) $m + m + m + m$ (b) $b + b$

2. List the first three or four multiples of 3.

3. If y is 6 find the value of each of the following.
  (a) $4y$ (b) $3y + y$

4. Find the sum of all the whole numbers from 1 to 60.

5. Find the sum of all the whole numbers from 30 to 60.

6. Write the equation that corresponds to the statement:

  "Some number multiplied by 5 and added to 40 is equal to 15 times that number."

7. Solve each equation.
  (a) $x - 5 = 9$ (b) $x \div 4 = 4$

8. Solve each equation.
  (a) $5x = 60$ (b) $x + 2 = 13$

9. (a) The opposite of 4 is _____.
  (b) The opposite of $^{-}9$ is _____.

10. List all of the elements in each of the following sets.
    (a) $\{x : x$ is an even whole number and $x \leq 10\}$
    (b) $\{x : x \not> 5$ and $x \in W\}$

11. Use the set-builder notation to specify each of the following sets.
    (a) $\{0, 5, 10, 15, \ldots\}$ (b) $\{102, 104, 106, \ldots, 198\}$

12. (a) If $A \subseteq B$ and $B \subseteq A$, then A_____B.
    (b) If $A \subseteq B$ and $B \subseteq C$, then A_____C.

In Exercises 13 through 17 let the universal set be $\{1, 2, 3, \ldots, 10\}$. Let $A = \{1, 2, 3, 4, 5\}$ and $B = \{2, 4, 6, 8, 10\}$ and list the elements in each of the given sets.

13. $A \cap B$ 14. A'

15. $A' \cap B'$ 16. $(A \cup B)'$

17. $A \cap A'$

18. Classify each of the following statements as true or false.
    (a) $Q \subseteq R$ (b) $Q \cap I = \varnothing$
    (c) $I \cup Q = R$ (d) $W \subseteq Q$

19. Is the set of whole numbers closed with respect to division? Give an example to support your answer.

20. Find the coordinates of the points A, B, C, and D shown in Figure 1.6.1.

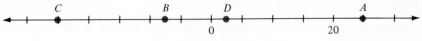

Figure 1.6.1

In Exercises 21 and 22 replace the blank space with $<$, $>$, or $=$, whichever is appropriate.

21. (a) $^-5$ _____ $^-1$ (b) x _____ $x + 1$

22. (a) $1 + 2 + 3 + \cdots + 10$ _____ $\dfrac{10 \times 11}{2}$

    (b) $\dfrac{1}{2}$ _____ $^-8$

23. Name the property (Reflexive, Symmetric, Transitive, or Substitution Property of Equality) illustrated by each of the following statements.
    (a) $x + 1 = x + 1$
    (b) If $x = y$ and $y = z$, then $x = z$.
    (c) If $x = y + 1$, then $y + 1 = x$.

2

The Fundamental Operations

2.1 The Operations of Addition and Multiplication

The operation of addition is indicated by the symbol + (read: plus). The addition of two numbers a and b is denoted by $a + b$, and the result of this addition is called the *sum* of a and b. Each of the numbers a and b is called an *addend*.

Illustration 1   The sum of 2 and 3 is denoted by

$$2 + 3$$

and this sum equals 5. Hence, we write

$$2 + 3 = 5$$

The numbers 2 and 3 are addends.

Addition is called a *binary operation* because addition is performed on two numbers. The order of the numbers involved in addition can be changed without affecting the sum. We call this property of addition the commutative law of addition.

2.1.1 Axiom (The Commutative Law of Addition)   If $a, b \in R$, then

$$a + b = b + a$$

Illustration 2
(a) $2 + 3 = 3 + 2$
(b) $x + 1 = 1 + x$
(c) The equation $1 + x = 7$ is equivalent to $x + 1 = 7$ because $1 + x = x + 1$.

Another property of addition of real numbers of particular interest at this time is the following one.

2.1.2 Axiom   If $a \in R$, then

$$a + 0 = a$$

Zero is called the *identity element for addition.*

Illustration 3
   (a) $3 + 0 = 3$
   (b) $0 + x = x$
   (c) $0 + (5 + n) = 5 + n$

Multiplication of whole numbers is the process of adding a given number of equal addends. It is essentially repeated addition. For real numbers we will need a "broader" interpretation for multiplication. We use either the symbol $\times$ or $\cdot$ (read: times) to denote the operation of multiplication. The multiplication of two numbers a and b is denoted by $a \times b$ or $a \cdot b$, and the result is called the *product* of a and b. Each of the numbers a and b is called a *factor* of the product. Often, in a multiplication process, the operation symbol is omitted, and we write

$$ab$$

to denote the product of a and b. Parentheses may also be used to denote the product of a and b in the following ways:

$$(a)(b)$$
$$a(b)$$
$$\text{and} \quad (a)b$$

The symbol $\times$ is not used much in algebra to denote multiplication since it can be confused with the letter x.

Illustration 4
   (a) 3 is a factor of 12, since $12 = 3 \cdot 4$
   (b) 3 is a factor of $3x$, since $3x = 3 \cdot x$
   (c) x is a factor of $3x$, since $3x = 3 \cdot x$

Example 1   Find all of the whole number factors of 12.

Solution: $1, 2, 3, 4, 6,$ and 12 are factors of 12 because 12 can be represented as a product in each of the following ways: $1 \cdot 12,\ 2 \cdot 6,$ and $3 \cdot 4$.

Example 2   Find all of the whole number factors of $3x$, where x is a whole number.

Solution: Because $1 \cdot 3 \cdot x = 3x$ the whole number factors of $3x$ are 1, 3, x, and $3x$.

In any given product, if we consider one particular factor, we say that the product of the remaining factors is the *coefficient* of the factor being considered.

Illustration 5

(a) 3 is the coefficient of x in the product $3x$ because $3 \cdot x = 3x$.

(b) $4x$ is the coefficient of 3 in the product $12x$ because $4x \cdot 3 = 12x$.

(c) 15 is the coefficient of xy in the product $15xy$.

(d) 1 is the coefficient of x in the product $1 \cdot x = x$.

The expression a^3 is a notation used in algebra to denote the product of three factors of a. That is,

$$a^3 = a \cdot a \cdot a$$

where a represents any number. A specific example of this notation is

$$4^3 = 4 \cdot 4 \cdot 4 = 64$$

An expression such as a^3 is called a *power*. The number 3 in the expression is called an *exponent*, and the number a is called the *base* of the power.

More generally, if n is a natural number, then

$$a^n = a \cdot a \cdot a \cdot \,\cdots\, \cdot a \quad (n \text{ factors of } a)$$

and a^n is read as "the nth power of a."

Illustration 6

$$4^3 \text{ is read "the third power of 4"}$$
$$a^3 \text{ is read "the third power of } a\text{"}$$
$$n^2 \text{ is read "the second power of } n\text{"}$$

Futhermore

$$4^3 = 4 \cdot 4 \cdot 4 = 64$$
$$a^3 = a \cdot a \cdot a$$
$$n^2 = n \cdot n$$

It is common practice to read the second power of a number, such as n^2, as "n squared" and the third power of a number, such as n^3, as "n cubed."

Illustration 7 The value of 2 cubed is 8 because $2^3 = 2 \cdot 2 \cdot 2 = 8$. The number 8 is the third power of 2.

Example 3 (a) Express $5x^3$ as a product without using exponents. (b) Express $3mmnnnn$ in more concise form using exponents.

Solution:

(a) $5x^3 = 5xxx$ (b) $3mmnnnn = 3m^2n^4$

Example 4 Find the value of the expression $3a^2$ if $a = 2$.

Solution: $\quad 3a^2 = 3(2)^2$
$$= 3(2)(2)$$
$$= 3(4)$$
$$= 12$$

   Multiplication, like addition, is a binary operation for which the order of the numbers involved in the multiplication can be changed without affecting the product. We call this property of multiplication the commutative law of multiplication.

2.1.3 Axiom (The Commutative Law of Multiplication)   If $a, b \in R$, then

$$ab = ba$$

Illustration 8   (a) $2 \cdot 3 = 3 \cdot 2$; (b) $4a = a(4)$; (c) $4(a + b) = (a + b)4$.

Illustration 9   The product $3 \cdot 4$ is a multiple of 4; that is,

$$3 \cdot 4 = 4 + 4 + 4 = 12$$

Also $4 \cdot 3$ is a multiple of 3; that is,

$$4 \cdot 3 = 3 + 3 + 3 + 3 = 12$$

Hence,

$$4 + 4 + 4 = 3 + 3 + 3 + 3$$

That is,

$$3 \cdot 4 = 4 \cdot 3$$

This is an illustration of the Commutative Law of Multiplication.

   Of particular interest at this time are the following two properties of multiplication.

2.1.4 Axiom   If $a \in R$, then

$$a \cdot 1 = a$$

The number 1 is called the *identity element for multiplication.*

Illustration 10   As special cases of Axiom 2.1.4 we note that

$$3 \cdot 1 = 3$$
$$1 \cdot x = x$$
$$1(a + 2) = a + 2$$
$$1 \cdot 1 = 1$$

2.1.5 Theorem **(Zero Factor Property)**   If $a \in R$, then

$$a \cdot 0 = 0$$

The proof of Theorem 2.1.5 is presented in Section 3.3.

Essentially Theorem 2.1.5 states that if any real number is multiplied by zero, the product is zero.

Illustration 11   As specific cases of Theorem 2.1.5 we note that

$$5 \cdot 0 = 0$$
$$0 \cdot x = 0$$
$$0(4 - x^2) = 0$$
$$(3 - 3)(3 + 3) = 0(3 + 3) = 0$$

As a special case of both Axiom 2.1.4 and Theorem 2.1.5 we note that

$$1 \cdot 0 = 0$$

Example 5   (a) Find a value of x for which $3x$ is 3. (b) Find a value of x for which $3x$ is 0. (c) Find a value of x for which $0x$ is 0.

Solution: (a) Because $3 \cdot 1 = 3$ by Axiom 2.1.4, it follows that if $x = 1$, then $3x = 3$.

(b) Because $3 \cdot 0 = 0$ by Theorem 2.1.5, it follows that if $x = 0$, then $3x = 0$.

(c) Because $0x = 0$ for any x by Theorem 2.1.5, it follows that if $x = 7$ or any other number, then $0 \cdot 7 = 0$.

Exercises 2.1

In Exercises 1 through 5 use Properties 2.1.2, 2.1.4, and 2.1.5 to find the value of x.

1. (a) $7 + x = 7$ (b) $x + 0 = 12$

2. (a) $x + 7 = 7$ (b) $12 + 0 = x$

3. (a) $5x = 5$ (b) $5x = 0$

4. (a) $7x = 0$ **(b)** $x \cdot 1 = 6$

5. (a) $4(x - 1) = 0$ **(b)** $4(x + 1) = 4$

In Exercises 6 through 12 find the set of whole number factors of the given number (assume x and y are whole numbers).

6. 18   **7.** 20   **8.** 13   **9.** $5y$

10. $6y$ **11.** $3xy$ **12.** $2x^2$

13. Find the value of each of the following powers.
     (a) 2^2 **(b)** 2^3 **(c)** 2^4

14. Find the value of each of the following powers.
     (a) 3^2 **(b)** 3^3 **(c)** 4^3

15. Find the value of each of the following powers.
     (a) 10^2 **(b)** 10^3 **(c)** 10^4

16. In the product $3x^2$ the 3 is called the _____ of x^2.

17. In the expression n^3 the 3 is called an _____, n is called the _____ and n^3 is called a _____.

18. Name the coefficient of x in each of the following.
     (a) $3x$ **(b)** $15x$
     (c) $2xy$ **(d)** x
     (e) x^2

19. Express each product as a power, using an exponent.
     (a) $5 \cdot 5 \cdot 5$ **(b)** $(10)(10)$ **(c)** $aaaa$ **(d)** $(n)(n)(n)$

20. (a) Express $3x^2y^3$ as a product without using exponents.
     (b) Express $7aaabb$ in more concise form using exponents.

21. Find the value of each expression if $x = 2$.
     (a) x^2 **(b)** x^3 **(c)** $x^2 \cdot x^3$ **(d)** x^5

22. Find the value of each expression if $x = 3$ and $n = 4$.
     (a) x^n **(b)** n^x **(c)** $2nx$ **(d)** $2n^3$

23. The statement

$$aa + bb \geq ab + ab$$

is always true for any real numbers a and b.
     (a) Choose several pairs of real numbers and test the validity of this statement.
     (b) Using exponents and coefficients rewrite the statement in a more succinct form.

In Exercises 24 through 32 name a property that justifies the statement.

24. $5 + 8 = 8 + 5$ **25.** $2(3 \cdot 4) = (3 \cdot 4)2$

26. $35 + 0 = 35$ **27.** $2 + \sqrt{2}$ is a real number.

28. $9(7 \cdot 10) = 9(10 \cdot 7)$ **29.** $5(3 + 4) = (3 + 4)5$

30. $5(3 + 4) = 5(4 + 3)$ **31.** $7 \cdot 0 = 0$

32. $1 \cdot x = x$

33. Let the binary operation $\star$ be defined as follows, $a \star b = \dfrac{a + b}{2}$, that is, $a \star b$ equals the average of the two numbers a and b. Is $\star$ a commutative operation? (Does $a \star b = b \star a$ for all real numbers a and b?)

34. If the sum of the factors of a whole number equals two times the number, then that number is said to be a *perfect number*. The whole number 6 is a perfect number, since the factors of 6 are 1, 2, 3, and 6 and the sum of these numbers is,

$$1 + 2 + 3 + 6 = 12$$

which is two times 6.

(a) Verify that 496 is a perfect number. This is the third known perfect number; 6 is the first.

(b) The second perfect number is less than 50. Find the second perfect number. (Hint: there are no known odd perfect numbers, and it is an unsolved problem in mathematics as to whether there are, in fact, any odd perfect numbers.)

2.2 The Distributive Law

Consider the following procedure, which involves both addition and multiplication. You wish to find the product of two numbers, for instance, 7 and 23. You reason in the following way: the product is 7 twenties plus 7 threes. Thus,

$$\begin{aligned}
(7)(23) &= (7)(20 + 3) \\
&= (7)(20) + (7)(3) \\
&= 140 + 21 \\
&= 161
\end{aligned}$$

We express the property involved in this procedure as a general law of arithmetic, and it is called the Distributive Law of Multiplication over Addition. This property stated in words is as follows:

> The product of a given number and the sum of two numbers is the sum of the product of the given number with the first addend and the product of the given number with the second addend.

We now express this property algebraically.

2.2.1 Axiom (The Distributive Law)   If $a, b, c \in R$, then

$$a(b + c) = ab + ac$$

From Axiom 2.2.1 and the Commutative Law of Multiplication we have

$$(b + c)a = ba + ca$$

Illustration 1   Let $a = 3$, $b = 6$, and $c = 4$. Then from the equality

$$a(b + c) = ab + ac$$

we have

$$3(6 + 4) = 3(6) + 3(4)$$

The left member is equal to $3(10) = 30$. The right member is equal to $18 + 12 = 30$. This tests the Distributive Law for the numbers 3, 6, and 4.

Illustration 2   If 30 tickets are sold at 60¢ per ticket and then another 70 tickets are sold at 60¢ per ticket, the sum of the number of cents in the total cost of these tickets is given by

$$(60)(30) + (60)(70) = 1800 + 4200$$
$$= 6000$$

The number of cents in the total cost of these tickets is also obtained by multiplying 60 by the sum of 30 and 70 and we have

$$(60)(30 + 70) = (60)(100)$$
$$= 6000$$

Note that

$$(60)(30) + (60)(70) = (60)(30 + 70)$$

and this equality illustrates the Distributive Law.

Illustration 3   The number of square units in Figure 2.2.1 can be found in the following two ways:
   (a) $(4)(3) + (4)(5) = 12 + 20 = 32$
   (b) $4(3 + 5) = (4)(8) = 32$
   Note then that

$$(4)(3) + (4)(5) = 4(3 + 5)$$

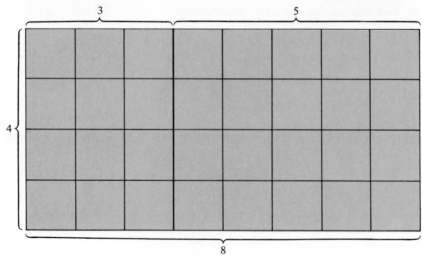

Figure 2.2.1

Example 1 Find the value of each expression.
  (a) 10(5 + 12)   (b) (10)(5) + (10)(12).

Solution:
  (a) 10(5 + 12) = 10(17) = 170
  (b) (10)(5) + (10)(12) = 50 + 120 = 170

Example 2 Replace the ☐ with the correct numeral or letter.
  (a) 15(10 + 3) = (15)(10) + (15)(☐)
  (b) 8(a + 3) = 8a + (☐)(3)
  (c) 9x + 9y = 9(☐ + y)

Solution:
  (a) 15(10 + 3) = (15)(10) + (15)(3)
  (b) 8(a + 3) = 8a + (8)(3)
  (c) 9x + 9y = 9(x + y)

Example 3 Find the value of 11(7 + 3) in two ways: (a) first adding and then multiplying and (b) first multiplying and then adding.

Solution:
  (a) 11(7 + 3) = 11(10) = 110
  (b) 11(7 + 3) = (11)(7) + (11)(3) = 77 + 33 = 110

Example 4 Compute by using the Distributive Law: $4\left(3\dfrac{3}{4}\right)$

Solution: $4\left(3\dfrac{3}{4}\right) = 4\left(3 + \dfrac{3}{4}\right)$

$$= (4)(3) + (4)\left(\dfrac{3}{4}\right)$$

$$= 12 + 3$$

$$= 15$$

Example 5 From the Distributive Law we have the following equality

$$n(n + 1) = n^2 + n$$

Apply this equality to find the product $x(x + 1)$.

Solution: Because $x(x + 1)$ is the same as $n(n + 1)$ if $n = x$, and

$$n(n + 1) = n^2 + n$$

we have

$$x(x + 1) = x^2 + x$$

Example 6 If A is the number of square units in the area of the rectangle shown in Figure 2.2.2, write an expression for A.

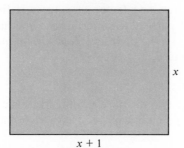

$x + 1$

Figure 2.2.2

Solution: The number A of square units in the area of a rectangle is found by multiplying the number of units in the length by the number of units in the width of the rectangle. Thus,

$$A = x(x + 1)$$
$$= x^2 + x$$

(Note the application of the Distributive Law.)

The Distributive Law of Multiplication over Subtraction is also valid. That is, if $a, b, c \in R$, then

$$a(b - c) = ab - ac$$

and

$$(b - c)a = ba - ca$$

Illustration 4 From the Distributive Law of Multiplication over Subtraction we have

$$7(x - 9) = 7 \cdot x - 7 \cdot 9$$
$$= 7x - 63$$

and

$$10x - 4x = (10 - 4)x$$
$$= 6x$$

Consider the sum $7x + 3x$. Note that both addends contain a factor of x. Therefore, by using the Distributive Law we have

$$7x + 3x = (7 + 3)x$$
$$= 10x$$

We refer to the expressions $7x$ and $3x$ as *terms*. Any expression which is expressed as a product of numbers or variables is a *term*. We refer to the process of adding (or subtracting) terms, such as, $7x$ and $3x$, as *combining terms*.

The coefficient of any one factor in a term is the product of all the remaining factors. Of particular importance is the *numerical coefficient* of a term. In the terms $3x$, $4x^2$, x^2, and $7abc$ the numerical coefficients are respectively 3, 4, 1, and 7.

2.2.2 Definition If two or more terms have exactly the same variable factors, excluding their numerical coefficients, then the terms are called *like terms*.

Illustration 5 $7x$ and $3x$ are like terms. $7x^2y$ and $\dfrac{1}{2}x^2y$ are like terms.

However, $7x^2$ and $7x$ are not like terms because they do not have exactly the same variable factors. The variable factors of $7x^2$ are x and x^2. The variable factor of $7x$ is only x.

Like terms can be added or subtracted (that is, combined) by adding or subtracting the numerical coefficients of each term and then multiplying by the common variable factors. The justification for this procedure comes from the Distributive Law.

Illustration 6

(a) $7x$ and $3x$ are like terms; therefore

$$7x + 3x = 10x$$

and

$$7x - 3x = 4x$$

(b) $5x^2y$ and $2x^2y$ are like terms; therefore

$$5x^2y + 2x^2y = 7x^2y$$

and

$$5x^2y - 2x^2y = 3x^2y$$

(c) x and x and x are like terms; therefore

$$x + x + x = 3x$$

and

$$x - x = 0$$

and

$$x + x - x = 2x - 1x = 1x = x$$

The distributive concept also applies to extended sums and combinations of sums and differences such as those in the next illustration.

Illustration 7

(a) $3(x + y + z) = 3x + 3y + 3z$
(b) $2(x - y + z) = 2x - 2y + 2z$
(c) $x + 2x + 3x + 4x = (1 + 2 + 3 + 4)x$

Example 7 Combine like terms in each of the following expressions:
(a) $3x + 4x + 2x$ (b) $3xy + 3xy + 3xy - 3xy$

Solution:

(a) $3x + 4x + 2x = (3 + 4 + 2)x$
$$= (9)x$$
$$= 9x$$

(b) $3xy + 3xy + 3xy - 3xy = (3 + 3 + 3 - 3)xy$
$$= (6)xy$$
$$= 6xy$$

The terms $7x$ and $3y$ are not like terms because different variables appear in each term. Hence, these terms cannot be combined. However, the terms $7x$ and $3y$ can be added or subtracted, but only as an indicated sum or difference. That is,

$$7x + 3y \qquad \text{and} \qquad 7x - 3y$$

represent the sum and difference of the terms $7x$ and $3y$ and no further simplification is possible.

Illustration 8

(a) $2x + 2x + 2 = 4x + 2$

(b) $3x + 5x + y + y = 8x + 2y$

(c) $2x + 2(x + 1) = 2x + 2x + 2$
$$= 4x + 2$$

Example 8 If P is the number of units in the perimeter of the rectangle shown in Figure 2.2.2, write an expression for P.

Solution: The number P of units in the perimeter of the rectangle is found by adding two times the number of units in the length and two times the number of units in the width. Thus,

$$P = 2x + 2(x + 1)$$
$$= 2x + 2x + 2$$
$$= 4x + 2$$

Exercises 2.2

In Exercises 1 through 4 compute the numerical value of each pair of expressions.

1. $10(5 + 15)$ $10(5) + 10(15)$

2. $4(3 + 17)$ $4(3) + 4(17)$

3. $9(51 + 19)$ $9(51) + 9(19)$

4. $6\left(2\frac{5}{6}\right)$ $6(2) + 6\left(\frac{5}{6}\right)$

In Exercises 5 through 9 replace the $\square$ with the correct number (use a numeral or a letter, whichever is appropriate).

5. $7(10 + 20) = 7(10) + 7(\square)$ 6. $6(27 + 3) = 6(27) + \square(3)$

7. $19(\square + 4) = 19(14) + 19(4)$ 8. $\square(5 + 2) = \square(5) + 4(2)$

9. $a(x + y) = a\square + a\square$

10. Draw a rectangle having a length of 15 units and a width of 4 units and compute the total number of square units in the area of the rectangle in two different ways. See Illustration 3.

11. Match those of the following products and sums that are equal by virtue of the Distributive Law.

Products	Sums
$2(x + y)$	$ax + az$
$a(x + z)$	$6 + 12$
$a(x + y)$	$ax + bx$
$3(2 + 4)$	$ax + ay$
$2(3 + 4)$	$6 + 8$
$x(a + b)$	$2x + 2y$

12. (a) If l and w represent the number of units in the length and width, respectively, of the rectangle shown in Figure 2.2.3, express the number of units in the perimeter in two ways: (i) as a product and (ii) as a sum.

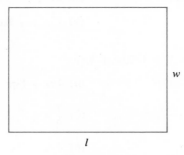

w

l

Figure 2.2.3

(b) Express the number of square units in the area of the rectangle shown in Figure 2.2.4 in two ways: (i) as a product and (ii) as a sum.

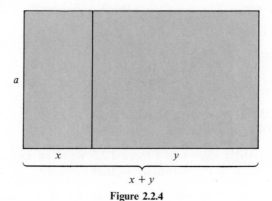

a

x y

$x + y$

Figure 2.2.4

13. Match the terms in the left column with a like term in the right column.

$3x$	$\frac{1}{2}xy^2$
$15xy$	x^2y^2
$4xyz$	$3yz$
$3x^2$	$15x^2y$
$7x^2y$	$100xyz$
$5xy^2$	$7x$
$23x^2y^2$	$23x^2$
yz	xy
$3wx$	$8xw$

In Exercises 14 through 26 combine like terms.

14. (a) $14xy + 9xy$ **(b)** $x + 2x + 3x$

15. (a) $4x^2 + 7x^2 - 2x^2$ **(b)** $21xy - 7xy + 3xy$

16. (a) $42xyz - 20xyz + 20xyz$ **(b)** $13x^2y + 8x^2y + 4x^2y - x^2y$

17. (a) $4x + 2 + 7x + 5$
     (b) $17xy + 3xy + 8xy + 2xy + 5xy$

18. (a) $29r^2 + 13r^2 - 17r^2$ **(b)** $4\pi r + 8\pi r - 2\pi r - \pi r$

19. (a) $\frac{1}{3}\pi r^2 + \pi r^2 - \frac{1}{2}\pi r^2$ **(b)** $\frac{1}{4}x + \frac{1}{2}x$

20. (a) $5y - y + 3y$ **(b)** $7xy - 2xy + 5xy - xy$

21. (a) $2ab - ab - ab$ **(b)** $7x - x - (2x + 3x)$

22. (a) $4xy + ab - (4xy + ab)$ **(b)** $3ab + ab + ab$

23. (a) $33R + 44R - 17R + 19T - 6T$
     (b) $4x^3 + 3x^3 + 2x - x$

24. (a) $7 + x + x - 7$ **(b)** $7 + x - x$

25. $3x + 6(x + 2)$

26. $2(x + 2) + 2(x + 1)$

27. If $1 + 2 + 3 + \cdots + n = \dfrac{n(n + 1)}{2}$, then

    $x + 2x + 3x + \cdots + nx = \underline{\hspace{1cm}}$.
    (Use the Distributive Law.)

28. For each triangle shown in Figure 2.2.5 write an expression for the number of units in the perimeter of that triangle.

29. If P is the number of units in the perimeter of the square shown in Figure 2.2.6, write an expression for P.

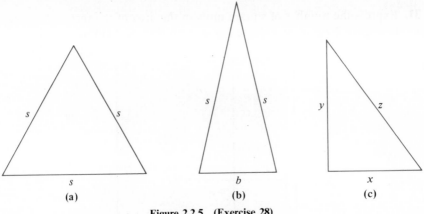

Figure 2.2.5 (Exercise 28)

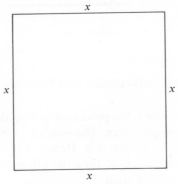

Figure 2.2.6 (Exercise 29)

30. Express the number of square units in the area of the rectangle shown in Figure 2.2.7 in two ways: (a) as a product and (b) as a sum.

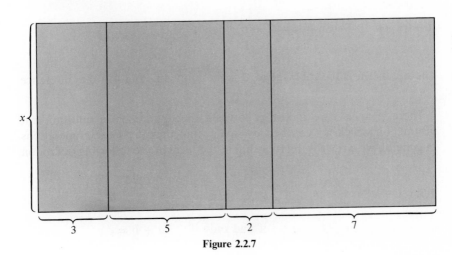

Figure 2.2.7

31. Express the number of square units in the area of the rectangle shown in Figure 2.2.8 in two ways: (a) as a product and (b) as a sum.

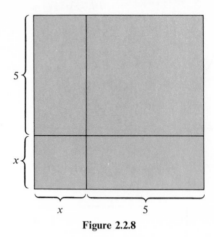

Figure 2.2.8

2.3 The Operations of Subtraction and Division

The operation of *subtraction* is the process of finding the other addend when one addend and the sum are given. The symbol — (read: subtract) is used to denote the operation of subtraction. Hence, if the sum of two numbers is c and one of the numbers is b, then the other number a is called the *difference* of c and b, and we write

$$c - b = a \quad \text{(read: } c \text{ subtract } b \text{ equals } a\text{)}$$

The number c is called the *minuend,* and the number b is called the *subtrahend.*

Illustration 1 Because $4 + 2 = 6$, then

$$6 - 2 = 4$$

The number 6 is the subtrahend, 2 is the minuend, and 4 is the difference.

There is a close relationship between the operations of addition and subtraction which is described by saying that they are *inverse* operations. In general, we write this relationship in the form of the following definition.

2.3.1 Definition If $a, b, c \in R$, then

$$c - b = a \quad \text{if and only if} \quad a + b = c$$

Illustration 2 (a) From Definition 2.3.1 and because

$$7 + 3 = 10 \quad \text{then} \quad 10 - 3 = 7$$

(b) From Definition 2.3.1 and if

$$x + 8 = 15 \quad \text{then} \quad 15 - 8 = x$$

(c) From Definition 2.3.1 and because

$$8 - 2 = 6 \quad \text{then} \quad 6 + 2 = 8$$

Example 1 Find the other addend if one addend is 5 and the sum is 14.

Solution: Let x represent the other addend. Then

$$5 + x = 14$$

Therefore, by Definition 2.3.1

$$x = 14 - 5$$
$$x = 9$$

From Definition 2.3.1 and the knowledge that 0 is the identity element for addition it follows that

$$a - a = 0 \quad \text{because} \quad 0 + a = a$$

and

$$a - 0 = a \quad \text{because} \quad a + 0 = a$$

We have, then, the following properties.

2.3.2 Theorem   If $a \in R$, then

$$a - a = 0$$

2.3.3 Theorem   If $a \in R$, then

$$a - 0 = a$$

Illustration 3 A special case of Theorem 2.3.2 is

$$5 - 5 = 0$$

and a special case of Theorem 2.3.3 is

$$5 - 0 = 5$$

Example 2 (a) Find a value of x for which $10 - x$ is 0. (b) Find a value of x for which $10 - x$ is 10.

Solution: (a) Because $10 - 10 = 0$ it follows from Theorem 2.3.2 that if $x = 10$, then $10 - x = 0$. (b) Because $10 - 0 = 10$ it follows from Theorem 2.3.3 that if $x = 0$, then $10 - x = 10$.

Example 3 Find a value of x for which $3(x - 1) = 0$.

Solution: Because $3 \cdot 0 = 0$ by Theorem 2.1.5 it follows that if $x - 1 = 0$, then $3(x - 1) = 0$. But because $1 - 1 = 0$ it follows from Theorem 2.3.2 that if $x = 1$, then $x - 1 = 0$.

The operation of *division* is the process of finding the other factor when one factor and the product of the two factors are given. The symbol $\div$ is used to denote division and we write $a \div b$ (read: a divided by b) to denote the division of a by b. The result of $a \div b$ is called the *quotient*. Hence, if the product of two numbers is a and one of the numbers is b $(b \neq 0)$, then the other number c is called the quotient of a and b, and we write

$$a \div b = c$$

The number a is called the *dividend,* and the number b is called the *divisor.*

Illustration 4 Because 8 is the quotient of 24 and 3 we write

$$24 \div 3 = 8$$

where 24 is the dividend and 3 is the divisor.

As was the case with addition and subtraction there is a close relationship between multiplication and division. Multiplication and division are *inverse* operations and the following definition expresses this relationship.

2.3.4 Definition   If $a, b, c \in R$ where $b \neq 0$, then

$$a \div b = c \qquad \text{if and only if} \qquad bc = a$$

Illustration 5 $24 \div 3 = 8$ because $3 \cdot 8 = 24$.

Example 4 If the product of two factors is 39 and one factor is 3, find the other factor.

Solution: Let s represent the other factor. Then

$$3s = 39$$

Therefore, by Definition 2.3.4, we have

$$s = 39 \div 3$$

and so

$$s = 13$$

Division can be indicated by a fraction. The quotient $a \div b$ may be represented by the fraction

$$\frac{a}{b}$$

where the number a is called the *numerator* of the fraction and the number b is called the *denominator* of the fraction. The notation a/b is also used to denote this fraction.

Using the fraction notation, Definition 2.3.4 can be written as

$$\frac{a}{b} = c \qquad \text{if and only if} \qquad bc = a$$

where $b \neq 0$.

If $b = 0$, then we cannot consider $a \div b$. The question is what is the value of $a \div 0$; that is, what number must be placed in the box $\square$ such that

$$\frac{a}{0} = \square$$

Remember, whatever number is placed in the box must, according to Definition 2.3.4, be such that

$$0 \cdot \square = a$$

But, by Theorem 2.1.5 we know that zero multiplied by any number gives a product of zero. Hence, regardless of what number is placed in the box, $0 \cdot \square$ cannot equal a if a is not zero. Therefore, if $a \neq 0$,

$$\frac{a}{0}$$

does not represent any number.

If a is 0, as well as b, then the question is what number must be placed in the box so that

$$\frac{0}{0} = \square$$

But Definition 2.3.4 states that

$$\frac{0}{0} = \square \qquad \text{if and only if} \qquad 0 \cdot \square = 0 \qquad\qquad (1)$$

According to Theorem 2.1.5 zero multiplied by any number gives a product of zero and so statement (1) is true if any number whatsoever is placed in the box. That is,

$$\frac{0}{0} = \boxed{1} \quad \text{or} \quad \frac{0}{0} = \boxed{0} \quad \text{or} \quad \frac{0}{0} = \boxed{10} \quad \text{or} \quad \frac{0}{0} = \boxed{153}$$

and so on, because $0 \cdot \boxed{1} = 0$, and $0 \cdot \boxed{0} = 0$, and $0 \cdot \boxed{10} = 0$, and $0 \cdot \boxed{153} = 0$. Hence, $\frac{0}{0}$ does not have a unique value.

In summary, then, if a is not equal to zero, $a \div 0$ does not represent any number and $0 \div 0$ is not a unique number. So, when considering the quotient $a \div b$, we do not allow the divisor, b, to have the value of zero. We say, then, that

division by zero is undefined.

Therefore,

$$\frac{a}{0} \quad \text{and} \quad \frac{0}{0}$$

are undefined; that is, they do not have a numerical value.

Example 5 Find the value of x for which each fraction is undefined.

(a) $\dfrac{3}{x}$

(b) $\dfrac{5}{x-1}$

Solution:

(a) $\dfrac{3}{x}$ is undefined if $x = 0$.

(b) $\dfrac{5}{x-1}$ is undefined if $x - 1 = 0$, but $x - 1 = 0$ if and only if $x = 1$.

From Definition 2.3.4 and the knowledge that 1 is the identity element for multiplication, if a is not zero, it follows that

$$a \div a = 1 \quad \text{because} \quad a \cdot 1 = a$$

and

$$a \div 1 = a \quad \text{because} \quad 1 \cdot a = a$$

We have, then, the following theorems.

2.3.5 Theorem If $a \in R$, and $a \neq 0$, then

$$\frac{a}{a} = 1$$

2.3.6 Theorem If $a \in R$, then

$$\frac{a}{1} = a$$

Illustration 6   Special cases of Theorem 2.3.5 are

$$\frac{5}{5} = 1 \quad \text{and} \quad \frac{x+y}{x+y} = 1 \quad \text{if} \quad x+y \neq 0$$

Illustration 7   Special cases of Theorem 2.3.6 are

$$\frac{5}{1} = 5 \quad . \quad \text{and} \quad \frac{x+y}{1} = x+y$$

Example 6

(a) Find a value of x for which $\frac{3}{x}$ is 1.

(b) Find a value of x for which $\frac{3}{3}$ is x.

(c) Find a value of x for which $\frac{3}{x}$ is 3.

(d) Find a value of x for which $\frac{x}{1}$ is 3.

Solution: From Theorem 2.3.5 we have

$$\frac{3}{3} = 1$$

and so

(a) if $x = 3$, $\frac{3}{x} = 1$

and

(b) if $x = 1$, $\frac{3}{3} = x$.

From Theorem 2.3.6 we have

$$\frac{3}{1} = 3$$

and so

(c) if $x = 1$, then $\frac{3}{x} = 3$

and

(d) if $x = 3$, then $\frac{x}{1} = 3$.

Example 7   Give a counterexample to show that division is not a commutative operation.

Solution: If division is a commutative operation, then the quotient $a \div b$ must equal the quotient $b \div a$. If $a = 6$ and $b = 3$, then

$$a \div b = 6 \div 3 = 2$$

and

$$b \div a = 3 \div 6 = \frac{1}{2}$$

Since $6 \div 3$ does not equal $3 \div 6$, division is not a commutative operation.

Dividing some number by two is equivalent to multiplying that number by one half. That is,

$$\frac{x}{2} = \frac{1}{2}x$$

This and other similar relationships between multiplication and division are developed in Chapter 5.

Exercises 2.3

In Exercises 1 through 6 use Theorems 2.3.2, 2.3.3, 2.3.5, and 2.3.6 to find the value of x.

1. (a) $7 - x = 0$ **(b)** $7 - x = 7$

2. (a) $x - 7 = 0$ **(b)** $12 - 12 = x$

3. (a) $x - 0 = 12$ **(b)** $12 - 0 = x$

4. (a) $\dfrac{x}{4} = 1$ **(b)** $\dfrac{x}{1} = 9$

5. (a) $\dfrac{x-1}{5} = 1$ **(b)** $\dfrac{x+2}{1} = 2$

6. (a) $\dfrac{5}{x} = 1$ **(b)** $\dfrac{5}{x} = 5$

In Exercises 7 through 12 use Definitions 2.3.1 and 2.3.4 to find the value of x.

7. (a) $7 + x = 12$ **(b)** $x + 3 = 9$

8. (a) $x - 5 = 10$ **(b)** $8 - x = 2$

9. (a) $x + 1 = 1$ **(b)** $x + a = b$

10. (a) $4x = 24$ **(b)** $7x = 42$

11. (a) $12x = 60$ **(b)** $\dfrac{x}{3} = 9$

12. (a) $\frac{x}{4} = 20$ **(b)** $\frac{12}{x} = 4$

In Exercises 13 through 21 find the value of x for which the given expression is undefined.

13. $\dfrac{5}{x}$ **14.** $\dfrac{10}{x}$ **15.** $\dfrac{9}{x-1}$

16. $\dfrac{9+x}{x-1}$ **17.** $\dfrac{x-1}{x-1}$ **18.** $\dfrac{5}{x-4}$

19. $\dfrac{2x}{x-5}$ **20.** $\dfrac{9}{3x}$ **21.** $\dfrac{25}{4(x-2)}$

In Exercises 22 through 29 with the given general equality a specific answer can be deduced. The important feature is the equality and not the particular letter used to represent the variable.

22. If $x + x = 2x$, then $y + y =$ _____

23. If $xx = x^2$, then $yy =$ _____

24. If $\frac{1}{2}x = \frac{x}{2}$, then $\frac{1}{2}ab =$ _____

25. If $\frac{1}{2}x = \frac{x}{2}$, then $\frac{1}{2}(a + b) =$ _____

26. If $x(x + 1) = x^2 + x$, then $n(n + 1) =$ _____

27. If $(a + b)^2 = a^2 + 2ab + b^2$, then $(x + y)^2 =$ _____

28. If $0 - (a - b) = 0 - a + b$, then $0 - (9 - 14) =$ _____

29. If $\dfrac{a + b}{c} = \dfrac{a}{c} + \dfrac{b}{c}$, then $\dfrac{x + 4}{4} =$ _____

30. Give a counterexample to show that division of even whole numbers is not a commutative operation.

2.4 Grouping Symbols and the Order of Operations

The use of parentheses, brackets, and other grouping symbols is very important in algebra. Parentheses are like punctuation marks; they are used to emphasize certain groupings of numbers. If parentheses or brackets are used to enclose an expression, then that expression is thought of as representing a single value. Thus,

$$(10 + 2) \cdot 5 \text{ represents the product of } (10 + 2) \text{ and } 5,$$

whereas

$10 + (2 \cdot 5)$ represents the sum of 10 and $(2 \cdot 5)$.

If we translate the phrase "ten plus two times five" into symbols we might get $(10 + 2) \cdot 5$ or we might get $10 + (2 \cdot 5)$; however, these two expressions have different values.

$$(10 + 2) \cdot 5 = 12 \cdot 5 = 60$$
$$10 + (2 \cdot 5) = 10 + 10 = 20$$

If an expression contains no parentheses, such as,

$$2 + 3 \cdot 4$$

then the convention is to perform the operation of multiplication before the operation of addition. Thus,

$$2 + 3 \cdot 4 = 2 + 12 = 14$$

If we wish to indicate that the sum is to be found first, then we use parentheses and we write

$$(2 + 3) \cdot 4 = 5 \cdot 4 = 20$$

By applying the Distributive Law we can write

$$(2 + 3) \cdot 4 = 2 \cdot 4 + 3 \cdot 4$$

where, by convention, the right member is evaluated by first performing the multiplication and then the addition. Thus, we have

$$(2 + 3) \cdot 4 = 2 \cdot 4 + 3 \cdot 4$$
$$= 8 + 12$$
$$= 20$$

Illustration 1 In the expression

$$2(4 + 18)$$

the addition is performed first and is followed by the multiplication. Thus,

$$2(4 + 18) = 2(22)$$
$$= 44$$

In the expression

$$5 + 3 \cdot 2$$

the multiplication is performed first and is followed by the addition. Thus,

$$5 + 3 \cdot 2 = 5 + 6$$
$$= 11$$

If powers are involved, the convention is to perform these operations before multiplications, unless parentheses or brackets are used to indicate otherwise.

Illustration 2 $2x^2$ means x is squared first, then multiplied by 2. On the other hand, $(2x)^2$ uses parentheses to change the conventional order. The operation of multiplication within the parentheses is performed first and the squaring is last.

Example 1 Evaluate:
   (a) $2 \cdot 3^2$ (b) $(2 \cdot 3)^2$ (c) $5 + 2 \cdot 3^2$

Solution:
  (a) $2 \cdot 3^2 = 2 \cdot 9 = 18$
  (b) $(2 \cdot 3)^2 = 6^2 = 36$
  (c) $5 + 2 \cdot 3^2 = 5 + 2 \cdot 9$
                  $= 5 + 18$
                  $= 23$

Suppose we have an expression containing more than one addition operation and more than one multiplication operation and no parentheses are used. Consider, for example,

$$2 + 3 \cdot 4 + 5 \cdot 3$$

In such a situation the multiplications are performed in order from left to right, followed by the additions in order from left to right. Thus,

$$2 + 3 \cdot 4 + 5 \cdot 3 = 2 + 12 + 15 = 14 + 15 = 29$$

The order of performing the operations of subtraction and division is the same as the order of performing the inverse operations of addition and multiplication, respectively.

Illustration 3 $2 + 12 \div 3 - 4 = 2 + 4 - 4$
                                  $= 6 - 4$
                                  $= 2$

We summarize the rules for order of operations by the following steps:

Step 1. If there are parentheses, perform the operations within the parentheses first.

Step 2. Perform all operations of raising to powers or taking roots as they occur in order from left to right.

Step 3. Perform all operations of multiplication and/or division in order from left to right.

Step 4. Perform all operations of addition and/or subtraction in order from left to right.

Example 2 Compute: $3 \cdot 4 + \dfrac{1}{2} - 9 \div \sqrt{9}$

Solution: $3 \cdot 4 + \dfrac{1}{2} - 9 \div \sqrt{9} = 3 \cdot 4 + \dfrac{1}{2} - 9 \div 3$

$$= 12 + \frac{1}{2} - 3$$

$$= 12\frac{1}{2} - 3$$

$$= 9\frac{1}{2}$$

In the following examples the color in each line shows where the operation is performed to yield the next line.

Example 3 Compute: $3 + 2 \cdot 4^2 + 2 \cdot 9 \div 3 - (4 - 2)6$

Solution:

$$
\begin{aligned}
& 3 \phantom{{}} + 2 \cdot 4^2 + 2 \cdot 9 \div 3 - (4 - 2)6 \\
&= 3 \phantom{{}} + 2 \cdot 4^2 + 2 \cdot 9 \div 3 - 2 \cdot 6 \\
&= 3 \phantom{{}} + 2 \cdot 16 + 2 \cdot 9 \div 3 - 2 \cdot 6 \\
&= 3 \phantom{{}} + 32 \phantom{{}} + 18 \phantom{{}} \div 3 - 12 \\
&= 3 \phantom{{}} + 32 \phantom{{}} + 6 \phantom{{}} - 12 \\
&= 35 + 6 \phantom{{}} - 12 \\
&= 41 - 12 \\
&= 29
\end{aligned}
$$

If parentheses are found inside brackets or other parentheses, then we begin by computing the expression within the innermost set of grouping symbols and follow the order of operations given by Step 2 through Step 4; then we go to Step 1 again and continue.

Example 4 Compute: $[2 + (4 - 2)] + 5(7 - 3)$

Solution:

$$
\begin{aligned}
& [2 + (4 - 2)] + 5(7 - 3) \\
&= [2 + 2] + 5(4) \\
&= 4 + 20 \\
&= 24
\end{aligned}
$$

Example 5 Compute: $25 + 3[5(4 - 2 \cdot 2 + 3^2) - 3 \cdot 5]^2$

Solution:

$$
\begin{aligned}
& 25 + 3[5(4 - 2 \cdot 2 + 3^2) - 3 \cdot 5]^2 \\
&= 25 + 3[5(4 - 4 + 9) - 3 \cdot 5]^2 \\
&= 25 + 3[5(9) - 3 \cdot 5]^2 \\
&= 25 + 3[45 - 15]^2 \\
&= 25 + 3[30]^2 \\
&= 25 + 3[900] \\
&= 25 + 2700 \\
&= 2725
\end{aligned}
$$

The order of some operations can be performed from right to left as well as from left to right. Addition and multiplication have this property, but subtraction and division do not.

Illustration 4 $2 + 3 + 4 = (2 + 3) + 4 = 5 + 4 = 9$

and

$$2 + 3 + 4 = 2 + (3 + 4) = 2 + 7 = 9$$

Furthermore,

$$2 \cdot 3 \cdot 4 = (2 \cdot 3) \cdot 4 = 6 \cdot 4 = 24$$

and

$$2 \cdot 3 \cdot 4 = 2 \cdot (3 \cdot 4) = 2 \cdot 12 = 24$$

The properties of addition and multiplication shown in Illustration 4 are called the Associative Law of Addition and the Associative Law of Multiplication.

2.4.1 Axiom (The Associative Law of Addition)   If $a, b, c \in R$, then

$$(a + b) + c = a + (b + c)$$

Example 6   Simplify the following expressions:
  (a) $(x + 3) + 4$ (b) $8 + x + 2$ (c) $x + y + x$

Solution:
  (a) $(x + 3) + 4 = x + (3 + 4)$
                $= x + 7$
  (b) By the conventional order of operations

$$8 + x + 2 = (8 + x) + 2$$

Applying the Commutative Law to the sum in parentheses we have

$$(8 + x) + 2 = (x + 8) + 2 \tag{1}$$

Applying the Associative Law in the right member of equality (1) we have

$$(x + 8) + 2 = x + (8 + 2)$$

Hence, starting from the beginning we have

$$\begin{aligned}
8 + x + 2 &= (8 + x) + 2 \\
&= (x + 8) + 2 \\
&= x + (8 + 2) \\
&= x + 10
\end{aligned}$$

(c) $x + y + x = (x + y) + x$
$= (y + x) + x$
$= y + (x + x)$
$= y + 2x$

The Associative Law of Addition permits a *regrouping* of terms in forming a sum. To contrast this with the Commutative Law, we note that the Commutative Law of Addition permits a *reordering* of the terms in forming a sum. Thus, a sum such as

$$1 + 2 + 3 + 4 + 5 + 6$$

can be written as

$$(1 + 3 + 5) + (2 + 4 + 6)$$

if it is desired to do so, and the justification for this rearrangement is the result of applying the Commutative and Associative Laws of Addition in the appropriate manner. Similar regroupings and reorderings can be made when the operation is multiplication, but not when the operation is either subtraction or division.

Consider now the product of 5 and the term $4x$. This means

$$4x + 4x + 4x + 4x + 4x \qquad \text{(5 addends)}$$

or in simpler form,

$$5(4x)$$

But, by the Distributive Law we know that

$$4x + 4x + 4x + 4x + 4x = (4 + 4 + 4 + 4 + 4)x$$
$$= 20x$$

and so we conclude that

$$5(4x) = 20x \qquad (2)$$

Equality (2) is an illustration of a more general law of arithmetic called the Associative Law of Multiplication.

2.4.2 Axiom (The Associative Law of Multiplication) If $a, b, c \in R$, then

$$(ab)c = a(bc)$$

Illustration 5 If we let $a = 5$ and $bc = 4x$ in Axiom 2.4.2, then we have

$$5(4x) = (5 \cdot 4)x$$

or, equivalently,

$$5(4x) = 20x$$

Example 7 Find the following products.

    (a) $5(3x)$ (b) $6(2x)$ (c) $(5 \cdot 2)x$

Solution:

    (a) $5(3x) = (5 \cdot 3)x$
                $= 15x$
    (b) $6(2x) = (6 \cdot 2)x$
                $= 12x$
    (c) $(5 \cdot 2)x = 10x$

Example 8 If A is the number of square units in the area of the large rectangle shown in Figure 2.4.1, write an expression for A in two ways: first (a) as the product of the measures of the length and width of the large rectangle, then (b) as the sum of the measures of the areas of the small rectangles.

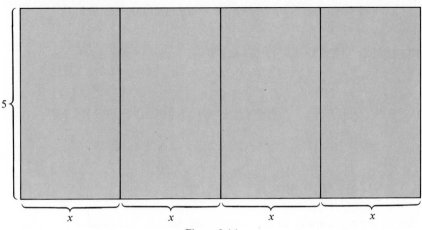

5

x x x x

Figure 2.4.1

Solution: (a) The measure of the length of the large rectangle is given by $x + x + x + x = 4x$, and the measure of its width is 5. Therefore,

$$A = 5(4x)$$
$$= 20x$$

(b) The large rectangle is subdivided into 4 smaller rectangles. The measure of the area of each small rectangle is given by $5x$. Therefore,

$$A = 5x + 5x + 5x + 5x$$
$$= 4(5x)$$
$$= 20x$$

In Example 8 if we compare the solutions of part (a) and part (b), we have incidentally shown by a geometrical method that

$$5(4x) = 4(5x)$$

which can also be shown algebraically by reordering and regrouping the factors according to the Commutative and Associative Laws of Multiplication.

Illustration 6 If C is the number of units in the circumference of a circle and d is the number of units in the diameter of the circle, then

$$C = \pi d$$

If r is the number of units in the radius of the circle, then $d = 2r$. Therefore

$C = \pi(d)$
$C = \pi(2r)$
$C = (\pi 2)r$ By the Associative Law of Multiplication
$C = (2\pi)r$ By the Commutative Law of Multiplication
$C = 2\pi r$

This last equation is probably the more familiar formula.

Illustration 7 $2 \cdot 3 \cdot 4 = (2 \cdot 3) \cdot 4$ or $2 \cdot 3 \cdot 4 = 2 \cdot (3 \cdot 4)$
$\qquad\qquad\qquad = 6 \cdot 4 \qquad\qquad\qquad\qquad\qquad = 2 \cdot 12$
$\qquad\qquad\qquad = 24 \qquad\qquad\qquad\qquad\qquad\quad = 24$

If we first apply the Commutative Law of Multiplication we have

$$2 \cdot 3 \cdot 4 = (2 \cdot 3) \cdot 4$$
$$= (3 \cdot 2) \cdot 4$$
$$= 3 \cdot (2 \cdot 4)$$
$$= 3 \cdot 8$$
$$= 24$$

Hence, by regrouping or reordering the factors 2, 3, and 4 the product $2 \cdot 3 \cdot 4$ can be computed as

$$6 \cdot 4 \quad \text{or} \quad 2 \cdot 12 \quad \text{or} \quad 3 \cdot 8$$

Any desired regrouping or reordering of factors in a product can be accomplished by the use of the Associative and Commutative Laws of Multiplication. Thus, a product such as,

$$2 \cdot 3 \cdot 2 \cdot 3 \cdot 3 \cdot 2$$

can be written as

$$(2 \cdot 2 \cdot 2) \cdot (3 \cdot 3 \cdot 3)$$

We justify this rearrangement by stating that it is the result of applying the Commutative and Associative Laws of Multiplication in the appropriate manner.

Some grouping is accomplished without parentheses by certain uses of the operation symbols. Thus, in the expression

$$\frac{x + y}{xy}$$

the division bar is treated like parentheses; that is, the operations $(x + y)$ and xy are performed first, followed by the division. Another way of writing this quotient is

$$(x + y) \div (xy)$$

Note that the parentheses around $x + y$ and xy are necessary. Thus, $(x + y) \div xy$ is not the same as $(x + y) \div (xy)$. To see this, let $x = 3$ and $y = 4$. Then

$$(x + y) \div xy = (3 + 4) \div 3 \cdot 4$$
$$= \frac{3 + 4}{3} \cdot 4 = \frac{7}{3} \cdot 4 = \frac{28}{3}$$

and

$$(x + y) \div (xy) = (3 + 4) \div (3 \cdot 4)$$
$$= 7 \div 12 = \frac{7}{12}$$

Exercises 2.4

1. In each part state which of the following laws is illustrated: the Associative Law of Addition, the Commutative Law of Addition, the Associative Law of Multiplication, the Commutative Law of Multiplication, or the Distributive Law of Multiplication over Addition.
   (a) $2(3 + 4) = 2(3) + 2(4)$ (b) $2(3 \cdot 4) = (2 \cdot 3)4$
   (c) $3(10) = 10(3)$ (d) $9(7 \cdot 10) = 9(10 \cdot 7)$
   (e) $4(6 + 2) = 4(2 + 6)$ (f) $(5 + 2) + 1 = 5 + (2 + 1)$
   (g) $\pi(2r) = (2\pi)r$

In Exercises 2 through 13 compute the value of each expression.

2. (a) $2 \cdot 3 \cdot 4$ (b) $\frac{1}{2} \cdot 3 \cdot 4$

3. (a) $3 \cdot 4 + 2$ (b) $3 + 4 \cdot 2$

4. (a) $(3 + 4)^2$ (b) $3^2 + 4^2$

5. (a) $3^3 \cdot 2 + 4$ (b) $3 \cdot 2^3 + 4$

6. (a) $(2 + 3) + 7$ (b) $2 + (3 + 7)$

7. (a) $2(3)^2$ (b) $(2 \cdot 3)^2$

8. (a) $18 - 8 \div 4 \cdot 6$ (b) $18 - 8 \div (4 \cdot 6)$

9. (a) $8 + 6 \div (3 \cdot 2)$ **(b)** $8 + 6 \div 3 \cdot 2$

10. (a) $2(7 - 3) + 4(5 - 2) - 3^2$ **(b)** $2(7 - (4 - 1)) + 3(5 - 2)^2$

11. (a) $4(4 - 1)(4 - 2)(4 - 3)$ **(b)** $1 - (1 - [1 - (1 - 1)])$

12. (a) $(4 \cdot 2 + 3 \cdot 2^2)^3$ **(b)** $3^2 + 4^2 \div 2 \cdot 4$

13. (a) $\dfrac{3^3 + 2^2}{2(3^2 + 6 \div 2)^2}$ **(b)** $\left[\dfrac{4(7 + 3) + \sqrt{25}}{3^2 + 2^2 - 4}\right] - \dfrac{10}{2}$

14. Discuss the difference between the following expressions:
(a) Three times x squared: $3x^2$.
(b) Three times x, the quantity squared: $(3x)^2$.
Suppose $x = 4$, then what do $3x^2$ and $(3x)^2$ equal?

In Exercises 15 through 18 simplify the given expressions.

15. (a) $(x + 3) + 7$ **(b)** $9 + (x + 5)$

16. (a) $6 + x + 4$ **(b)** $a + b + a$

17. (a) $(2 \cdot a) \cdot 5$ **(b)** $3 \cdot (a \cdot 4)$

18. (a) $\dfrac{1}{2} \cdot a \cdot 8$ **(b)** aba

19. John added the following column of numbers as shown:

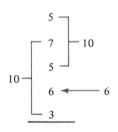

He considered the following sums: $5 + 5 = 10$, then $7 + 3 = 10$ and finally $10 + 10 + 6 = 26$. What properties of addition allow John to do this?

20. Regroup the numerals in each of the following in a way that produces a multiple of 10 to be added to some third number.
(a) $23 + (7 + 5)$ (b) $(49 + 5) + 35$ (c) $[8 + (3 + 4)] + 3$

21. How do you justify adding all the whole numbers from 1 to 10 by the scheme shown in Figure 2.4.2?

In Exercises 22 through 25 simplify the given expressions.

22. (a) $6(3x)$ **(b)** $5(2xy)$

23. (a) $5(2y) + 6(3y)$ **(b)** $3(7x^2) + 2(4x^2)$

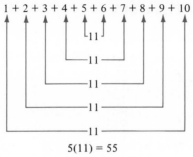

$$1 + 2 + 3 + 4 + 5 + 6 + 7 + 8 + 9 + 10$$

$$5(11) = 55$$

Figure 2.4.2   (Exercise 21)

24. (a) $20(5a) + 19(a) - 5(2a)$
   (b) $2(6m) + 4(5m) + 3(3n) - 2(2n)$
25. (a) $7(5x + 2y) + 3(2x + 8y)$
   (b) $10(2a + 5b) + 4(a - 5b)$

In Exercises 26, 27, and 28 let A be the number of square units in the area of the large rectangle. Then write an expression for A in two ways, first **(a)** as the product of the measures of the length and width of the large rectangle, then **(b)** as the sum of the measures of the areas of the small rectangles. (Refer to Example 8.)

26. The rectangle of Figure 2.4.3.

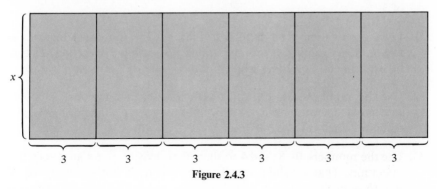

Figure 2.4.3

27. The rectangle of Figure 2.4.4.

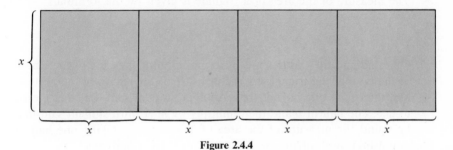

Figure 2.4.4

28. The rectangle of Figure 2.4.5.

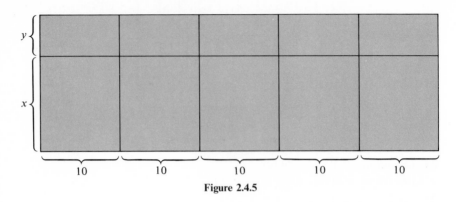

Figure 2.4.5

29. Let the operation ★ be defined by

$$a \star b = \frac{a + b}{2} \qquad \text{(the average of } a \text{ and } b)$$

Is ★ an associative operation? For instance, does $(2 \star 6) \star 14$ equal $2 \star (6 \star 14)$?

30. Noting that $6n = 3(2n)$ explain why all multiples of 6 are also multiples of 3.

31. Let the operation ↑ be defined so that $x \uparrow y =$ the larger one of the two numbers x and y. Is this operation an associative operation? Decide by experiment with some whole numbers. (If $x = y$, then $x \uparrow x = x$.)

32. Use the numbers 20, 10, and 5 to show that subtraction is not an associative operation. That is, show that $(a - b) - c$ does not generally equal $a - (b - c)$.

33. Use the numbers 16, 8, and 4 to show that division is not an associative operation. That is, show that $(a \div b) \div c$ does not generally equal $a \div (b \div c)$.

34. The measure of the area of a triangle is given by the formula,

$$A = \frac{1}{2}bh$$

One student said that this means to multiply the measure of the length of the base of the triangle by the measure of the length of the altitude and then take one half of that. Another student said that this means to take one half of b and then multiply by h. A third student said that he found the measure of the area of a triangle by taking one half of h and then multiplying by b. Now, who is right and why?

2.5 Review Exercises

1. Express each of the following products as a power.
   (a) $6 \cdot 6 \cdot 6 \cdot 6$ (b) $aaaaa$

2. Find the value of each of the following powers.
   (a) 2^4 (b) 5^3 (c) 3^4

3. Name the numerical coefficient of $9x^2$.

4. Write $aa + aa + aa$ by using a coefficient and an exponent.

5. List all of the whole number factors of $9x^2$ and assume that x is whole number.

6. Replace each ☐ with the correct value.
   (a) $5(10 + 7) = 5(10) + \boxed{}(7)$
   (b) $am + an = a(\boxed{} + \boxed{})$

7. Use the Distributive Law to evaluate the following expressions.
   (a) $x(x + 1) = $ _____   (b) $3y + 7y = $ _____

8. Write an expression for the number of units in (a) the area; and (b) the perimeter of the square shown in Figure 2.5.1.

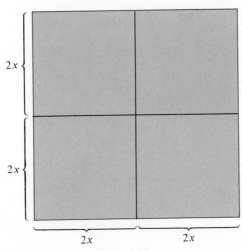

Figure 2.5.1

In Exercises 9 through 11 combine terms and simplify each of the given expressions.

9. (a) $14xy + 6xy$ (b) $x + 8 + x$

10. (a) $2x^2 + 4x^2$ (b) $2x^2 + 5x^2 + 7y + 2y$

11. (a) $3(2x) + 7(3x)$ (b) $8(2x + 5y) + 4x - 5(4y)$

12. Simplify each of the following expressions.

(a) $x - x$ (b) $x - 0$ (c) $\dfrac{x}{x}$ (d) $\dfrac{x}{1}$

13. Find the value of x for which each equation is true.

(a) $7x = 0$ (b) $3 - x = 0$

(c) $4(x - 2) = 4$ (d) $\dfrac{x - 1}{10} = 1$

14. For what value of x is the expression $\dfrac{2x}{x - 5}$ undefined?

15. Name an operation that is not commutative and give an example.

16. If x is 2, find the value of each of the following expressions.
    (a) $3x^4$ (b) $(3x)^4$

In Exercises 17 through 20 name a property that justifies each statement.

17. (a) $2 + (3 + 5) = (2 + 3) + 5$
    (b) $x \cdot 1 = x$

18. (a) $\dfrac{1}{2}(ab) = \left(\dfrac{1}{2}a\right)b$ (b) $x^2 \cdot 0 = 0$

19. (a) $x + 0 = x$ (b) $x(a + b) = xa + xb$

20. (a) If x is a real number, then $2x$ and x^2 are real numbers.
    (b) $x(a + b) = (a + b)x$

In Exercises 21 through 23 compute the value of each expression.

21. (a) $2 + 5 \cdot 3 - 1$.   (b) $2 \cdot 6 \div 2 \cdot 3$

22. (a) $3 \cdot 4^2 - 4$ (b) $8 - 6 \div 3 \cdot 2$

23. (a) $2 + 2[(1 + 2)^2 - 3]$ (b) $\dfrac{3(9 - 1)}{3 \cdot 3 - 1^3}$

3

The Set of Integers

3.1 The Concept of Opposite

If the operation of addition is performed using whole numbers, the result is a whole number. For instance,

$$9 + 16 = 25$$

That is, the sum of the whole numbers 9 and 16 is the whole number 25. More generally, if a and b are whole numbers, then the sum $a + b$ is a whole number. For this reason, we state that the set W is closed with respect to the operation of addition. Furthermore, because the product of two whole numbers is a whole number, the set W is closed with respect to the operation of multiplication.

A different situation occurs when we perform the operation of subtraction with whole numbers. First, consider the equation

$$x + 4 = 9$$

To solve this equation we subtract 4 from each member of the equation and we obtain

$$x + 4 - 4 = 9 - 4$$

or, equivalently,

$$x = 5$$

But, if we apply the same technique to solve the equation

$$x + 8 = 5 \qquad (1)$$

we subtract 8 from each member of the equation and obtain

$$x + 8 - 8 = 5 - 8$$

or, equivalently,

$$x = 5 - 8$$

Because $5 - 8$ is not a whole number, the set W is not closed with respect to subtraction.

We wish then to obtain a set of numbers which we call the set of "integers," with respect to which the operation of subtraction is closed and which contains the set W as a subset. In order to obtain this set of integers in a formal way we begin with the concept of the "opposite" of a number. Then in Section 3.2 we use this concept of "opposite" and define $5 - 8$ to be the opposite of $8 - 5$. Because $8 - 5 = 3$, we define $5 - 8$ to be the opposite of 3; thus we are able to solve an equation such as equation (1).

We use the symbol $\neg$ for the operation "the opposite of." For instance, the notation $\neg 3$ is read "the opposite of 3." The operation $\neg$ is defined by the following property, in which we make the assumption that the opposite of any integer is a unique integer.

3.1.1 Axiom For each integer k, there exists exactly one integer, the opposite of k, denoted by $\neg k$, such that

$$k + (\neg k) = 0$$

Illustration 1 $2 + (\neg 2) = 0$

Illustration 2 If $5 + x = 0$, then $x = \neg 5$ because Axiom 3.1.1 states that there is exactly one integer, the opposite of 5, such that $5 + (\neg 5) = 0$.

Because we require the set of integers to contain the set W as a subset, it follows that every natural number is an integer. Therefore, by Axiom 3.1.1 the opposite of every natural number is an integer. We define the set of the opposites of the natural numbers to be the set of *negative integers* and we denote this set by

$$\{^-1, ^-2, ^-3, \ldots\}$$

The set of the opposites of the negative integers is the set of natural numbers. Hereafter we refer to the set of natural numbers as the set of *positive integers,* which is denoted by

$$\{1, 2, 3, \ldots\}$$

or, equivalently,

$$\{^+1, ^+2, ^+3, \ldots\}$$

Illustration 3
$\neg(^+10) = ^-10$ (read: the opposite of positive ten equals negative ten)
$\neg(^-10) = ^+10$ (read: the opposite of negative ten equals positive ten)
$\neg(^-3) = 3$ (read: the opposite of negative three equals three)
$\neg 3 = ^-3$ (read: the opposite of three equals negative three)

Because zero is an integer it follows from Axiom 3.1.1 that zero plus the opposite of zero equals zero. That is,

$$0 + (\neg 0) = 0 \tag{2}$$

If $a \in R$, then $a + 0 = a$, and so if a is 0, we have

$$0 + 0 = 0 \qquad (3)$$

By comparing equalities (2) and (3), we must define the opposite of zero to be zero; that is, we define

$$\neg 0 = 0$$

Illustration 4 Because there is exactly one integer $\neg 5$ such that $\neg 5 + 5 = 0$, then if

$$x + 5 = 0$$

it follows that

$$x = \neg 5$$

Example 1
  (a) Find the value of x for which $x + 4 = 0$.
  (b) Find the value of x for which $\neg 9 + x = 0$.
  (c) Find the value of x for which $\neg 6 + 3x = 0$.

Solution:
  (a) If

$$x + 4 = 0$$

then because $\neg 4 + 4 = 0$ we have

$$x = \neg 4$$

  (b) If

$$\neg 9 + x = 0$$

then because $\neg 9 + 9 = 0$ we have

$$x = 9$$

  (c) If

$$\neg 6 + 3x = 0$$

then because $\neg 6 + 6 = 0$ we have

$$3x = 6$$

Therefore,

$$x = 2$$

3.1.2 Definition The opposite of any integer is called the *additive inverse* of that integer.

Illustration 5 $^-10$ is the additive inverse of $^+10$; $^+10$ is the additive inverse of $^-10$.

At first it may seem that the concept of "additive inverse" is the same as that of "opposite." When referring to "the opposite of a number," we are performing a unary operation (an operation on a single number) on that number to yield some number. The terminology "additive inverse" is descriptive; it describes one number relative to another number. Thus, when we state that the opposite of 10 is the additive inverse of 10, we perform "an operation on the number 10" to yield as a result "the additive inverse of 10."

We know from our discussion of subtraction that $5 - 5 = 0$ and from Axiom 3.1.1 we know that $5 + (\neg 5) = 0$. Hence, from these two equalities it follows that

$$5 - 5 = 5 + (\neg 5)$$

Because of this similarity to subtraction we now adopt the more conventional symbol to denote "the opposite of," which is the symbol, $-$. This symbol is also used for the binary operation of subtraction and when you find it between two numbers or expressions, it means subtraction. If you find the symbol $-$ in front of a number or expression it means the unary operation "the opposite of."

Illustration 6

$x - y$	means	"x subtract y"
$-x$	means	"the opposite of x"
$x + (-x)$	means	"x add the opposite of x"
$^-2$	means	"negative two"
-2	means	"the opposite of two"
$5 - 2$	means	"5 subtract 2"
$-x - y$	means	"the opposite of x subtract y"

[Note that $-2 = {}^-2$ (read: the opposite of two equals negative two)]

We now define one particular kind of subtraction involving integers. Definition 2.3.1 (the definition of subtraction) states that

$$c - a = b \qquad \text{if and only if} \qquad a + b = c \qquad (4)$$

If in statement (4), $c = 0$ and $b = -a$, we have

$$0 - a = -a \qquad \text{because} \qquad a + (-a) = 0 \qquad (5)$$

Thus, by statement (5) and Axiom 3.1.1 we have the following property.

3.1.3 Theorem   If a is any integer, then

$$0 - a = -a$$

Illustration 7

(a) $0 - 5 = -5$ (read: zero subtract five equals the opposite of five)

or, equivalently,

$0 - 5 = {}^-5$ (read: zero subtract five equals negative five)

because

$-5 = {}^-5$ (read: the opposite of five equals negative five)

(b) $0 - {}^-2 = -{}^-2$ (read: zero subtract negative two equals the opposite of negative two)

or, equivalently,

$0 - {}^-2 = 2$ (read: zero subtract negative two equals two)

because

$- {}^-2 = 2$ (read: the opposite of negative two equals two)

We denote the set of all the integers by the symbol J.

$$J = \{0, 1, {}^-1, 2, {}^-2, 3, {}^-3, \ldots\}$$

For the elements of the set J and the operations of addition and multiplication we assume certain laws. Most of these laws have been previously stated for real numbers. We restate them here for the set J, and we give an illustration of each law.

(I) Closure Law for Addition and Multiplication

If $a, b \in J$, then $(a + b) \in J$ and $ab \in J$.

Illustration 8   Because ${}^-3 \in J$ and $5 \in J$, then

$$({}^-3 + 5) \in J \qquad \text{and} \qquad ({}^-3)(5) \in J.$$

(II) Commutative Laws for Addition and Multiplication

If $a, b \in J$, then

$$a + b = b + a$$

and

$$ab = ba$$

Illustration 9   Because ${}^-4 \in J$ and ${}^-8 \in J$ then

$${}^-4 + {}^-8 = {}^-8 + {}^-4$$

and

$$({}^-4)({}^-8) = ({}^-8)({}^-4)$$

(III) Associative Laws for Addition and Multiplication

If $a, b, c \in J$, then

$$a + (b + c) = (a + b) + c$$

and

$$a(bc) = (ab)c$$

Illustration 10 Because $7 \in J$, $^-7 \in J$, and $12 \in J$, then

$$7 + (^-7 + 12) = (7 + {}^-7) + 12$$

and

$$7[(^-7)(12)] = [(7)(^-7)]12$$

(IV) Distributive Law of Multiplication over Addition

If $a, b, c \in J$, then

$$a(b + c) = ab + ac$$

Illustration 11 Because $1 \in J$ and $^-1 \in J$, then

$$^-1(1 + {}^-1) = (^-1)(1) + (^-1)(^-1)$$

(V) Identity Elements for Addition and Multiplication

If $a \in J$, then

$$a + 0 = a$$

and

$$a \cdot 1 = a$$

Illustration 12 Because $^-10 \in J$, then

$$^-10 + 0 = {}^-10$$

and

$$^-10 \cdot 1 = {}^-10$$

(VI) Additive Inverse Law

For each $a \in J$, there exists the opposite of a, $-a \in J$, such that

$$a + (-a) = 0$$

Illustration 13 Because $^-1973 \in J$, then $1973 \in J$ and

$$^-1973 + 1973 = 0$$

As a consequence of these laws we now wish to show that the opposite of the opposite of a given integer is the given integer. In particular,

$$-(^-10) = 10 \qquad (6)$$

Furthermore,

$$^-10 = -10 \qquad (7)$$

Substituting -10 for $^-10$ from equality (7) into equality (6) we get

$$-(-10) = 10$$

In general we have the following theorem, which can be justified by a similar argument.

3.1.4 Theorem   If $k \in J$, then

$$\boxed{-(-k) = k}$$

Illustration 14   (a) $-(-17) = 17$; (b) $-(-^-6) = {}^-6$

Illustration 15   If $-x = 3$, then

$$-(-x) = -3$$

or, equivalently,

$$x = {}^-3$$

Notice that $-k$ (the opposite of k) is not necessarily a negative number. The number $-k$ is a negative number only when k is a positive number, but $-k$ is a positive number when k is a negative number. For instance, if k is 5, then $-k$ is $^-5$, but if k is $^-3$, then $-k$ is $-(^-3) = 3$. See Figure 3.1.1.

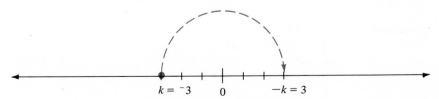

$k = {}^-3 \qquad 0 \qquad -k = 3$

(a)   If k is a negative number, then $-k$ is a positive number.

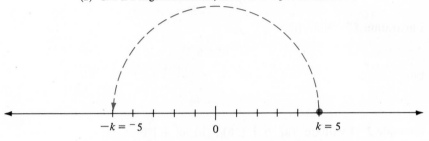

$-k = {}^-5 \qquad 0 \qquad k = 5$

(b)   If k is a positive number, then $-k$ is a negative number.

Figure 3.1.1

The concept of *magnitude* is closely allied to the concept of a number and its opposite. Both ⁺10 and ⁻10 have the same *magnitude*, namely 10. The magnitude 10 can be thought of as the number of units in the distance on the number line from the origin to either the point designated as ⁺10 or the point designated as ⁻10. See Figure 3.1.2.

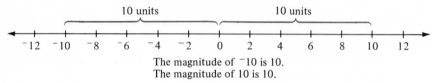

The magnitude of ⁻10 is 10.
The magnitude of 10 is 10.

Figure 3.1.2

We use the symbol

$$|x| \text{ to denote the } \textit{magnitude of } x$$

which is also called the *absolute value* of x. Hence, $|10| = 10$ and $|{}^-10| = 10$.

3.1.5 Definition If x denotes the *absolute value* of an integer x, then

$$|x| = x \text{ if } x \text{ is a positive integer or zero}$$

and

$$|x| = -x \text{ if } x \text{ is a negative integer.}$$

Illustration 16 $|10| = 10$
$|{}^-10| = -({}^-10) = 10$
$|{}^+2| = 2$
$|-2| = |{}^-2| = -({}^-2) = 2$
$|0| = 0$
$-|{}^-5| = -[-({}^-5)] = -5$

Illustration 17 Note that

$$^-6 < 6$$

but

$$|{}^-6| = |6|$$

Example 2 Evaluate: (a) $|6 + ({}^-6)|$; (b) $|6| + |{}^-6|$

Solution: (a) $|6 + ({}^-6)| = |0| = 0$ (b) $|6| + |{}^-6| = 6 + 6 = 12$

1. (a) $5 + {}^{-}5 = $ _____
   (b) $^{-}18 + 18 = $ _____

2. (a) $-(-13) = $ _____
   (b) $-(-(-21)) = $ _____

3. (a) $|^{-}100| = $ _____
   (b) $|^{-}1| + |1| = $ _____

4. (a) $0 - 8 = $ _____
   (b) $0 - 3 = $ _____

5. (a) $0 - {}^{-}8 = $ _____
   (b) $0 - (^{-}17) = $ _____

6. (a) $^{-}9 + 9 = $ _____
   (b) $2 + (-2) + [-(-2)] = $ _____

7. (a) $0 - k = $ _____
   (b) $(0 - k) + k = $ _____

In Exercises 8 through 15 complete each statement.

8. $-{}^{-}2 = $ _____

9. $-0 = $ _____

10. $-(-x) = $ _____

11. If x is a negative integer, then $-x$ is a_____

12. If x is a positive integer, then $-x$ is a_____

13. If x is a positive integer, then $|x| = $ _____

14. If $x < 0$, then $|x| = $ _____

15. If $x + y = 0$, then $x = $ _____

In Exercises 16 through 35 replace the blank space with the appropriate symbol $<$, $=$, or $>$.

16. $^{-}5$ _____ $^{-}1$
17. 0 _____ $^{-}1$

18. $^{-}100$ _____ 2
19. $^{-}10$ _____ $^{+}10$

20. $-{}^{-}2$ _____ $^{-}2$
21. $-{}^{+}2$ _____ $^{-}2$

22. -3 _____ $-(8 - 5)$
23. $-(-5)$ _____ -5

24. $|^{-}4|$ _____ $|2|$
25. $|8 + {}^{-}8|$ _____ 8

26. $|7| + |^{-}7|$ _____ 7
27. $|5 + {}^{-}5|$ _____ $|5| + |^{-}5|$

28. $|^{-}10|$ _____ $|10|$
29. $-|5|$ _____ $|^{-}5|$

30. If $x < 0$, then $|x|$ _____ x
31. If $x < 0$, then $|x|$ _____ $-x$

32. If $x \geq 0$, then $|x|$ _____ x
33. If $x > 0$, then $|x|$ _____ $-x$

34. If $x < y$, then $-x$ _____ $-y$
35. If $x = y$, then $-x$ _____ $-y$

In Exercises 36 through 46, match each of the statements in Column I with the appropriate Property listed in Column II. The lower case italic letters represent integers.

Column I (Statement)	Column II (Property)
36. $a + b = b + a$	(a) Associative Law for Multiplication
37. $a(bc) = (ab)c$	
38. $a(x + y) = ax + ay$	(b) Distributive Law
39. $a(b + c) = (b + c)a$	(c) Commutative Law for Multiplication
40. $a + (b + c) = (a + b) + c$	
41. $a + (b + c) = (b + c) + a$	(d) Identity Element for Multiplication
42. $a + (-a) = 0$	
43. $a + 0 = 0 + a$	(e) Associative Law for Addition
44. $a + 0 = a$	(f) Commutative Law for Addition
45. $a \cdot 1 = a$	
46. $a(b + c) = a(c + b)$	(g) Identity Element for Addition
	(h) Additive Inverse Law

3.2 Subtraction and Addition of Integers

Suppose you put 7 gallons of gasoline in a car's tank. Then you drive for several miles and burn up 4 gallons of gasoline. Intuitively, you recognize that a gain of 7 gallons followed by a loss of 4 gallons is equivalent to a net gain of 3 gallons. Mathematically this situation can be interpreted as either

$$7 + {}^-4 \qquad \text{(seven plus negative four)}$$

or

$$7 - 4 \qquad \text{(seven subtract four)}$$

Because the net result is 3 we have

$$7 + {}^-4 = 3$$

and

$$7 - 4 = 3$$

Therefore

$$7 + {}^-4 = 7 - 4$$

It is, in general, true that the addition of a negative integer is the same as the subtraction of its opposite, which is a positive integer. We justify this statement by the following argument.

Suppose we consider two arbitrary integers a and b. Let x denote the sum of a and the opposite of b. That is,

$$a + (-b) = x \tag{1}$$

To both members of equation (1) we add b and obtain

$$[a + (-b)] + b = x + b \tag{2}$$

Applying the Associative Law to the left member of equation (2) we obtain

$$a + [(-b) + b] = x + b$$

Because $(-b) + b = 0$, we have

$$a + 0 = x + b$$

from which it follows that

$$a = x + b \tag{3}$$

To solve equation (3) for x we use Definition 2.3.1, which states that $x + b = a$ if and only if $x = a - b$. Therefore,

$$a - b = x \tag{4}$$

Comparing equations (1) and (4), we conclude that

$$a + (-b) = a - b$$

We have therefore proved the following property of integers.

3.2.1 Theorem   If $a, b \in J$, then

$$a - b = a + (-b)$$

In Illustration 1 we apply Theorem 3.2.1 to find $a - b$ when a is a positive integer and b is a negative integer.

Illustration 1

(a) $10 - {}^{-}4 = 10 + (-{}^{-}4)$
$\qquad\quad = 10 + 4$
$\qquad\quad = 14$

(b) $8 - {}^{-}12 = 8 + (-{}^{-}12)$
$\qquad\quad\; = 8 + 12$
$\qquad\quad\; = 20$

In Illustration 2 we find $a + (-b)$ when a is a positive integer and $a > b$.

Illustration 2

(a) $10 + (-4) = 10 - 4$
$\qquad\qquad\;\; = 6$

(b) $9 + {}^-5 = 9 + (-5)$
$= 9 - 5$
$= 4$

(c) ${}^-8 + 10 = 10 + {}^-8$ (by the Commutative Law)
$= 10 + (-8)$
$= 10 - 8$
$= 2$

Example 1   Evaluate: (a) $12 + {}^-8$; (b) ${}^-9 + 9$; (c) $18 - {}^-6$.

Solution:

(a) $12 + {}^-8 = 12 + (-8)$
$= 12 - 8$
$= 4$

(b) ${}^-9 + 9 = 9 + {}^-9$
$= 9 + (-9)$
$= 9 - 9$
$= 0$

Note that we could also evaluate ${}^-9 + 9$ by applying the Additive Inverse Law.

(c) $18 - {}^-6 = 18 + (-{}^-6)$
$= 18 + 6$
$= 24$

The sum of the two integers ${}^-5$ and ${}^-8$ can be demonstrated by considering a loss of 5 followed by a loss of 8, which is equivalent to a loss of 13. That is,

$${}^-5 + {}^-8 = {}^-13$$

The set of negative integers is closed with respect to addition; that is, the sum of two negative integers is a negative integer. This fact is a particular consequence of the following property.

3.2.2 Theorem   If $a, b \in J$, then

$$-(a + b) = (-a) + (-b)$$

Proof: From the Additive Inverse Law we have

$$a + (-a) = 0 \quad and \quad b + (-b) = 0$$

and therefore, it follows that

$$[a + (-a)] + [b + (-b)] = 0 \tag{5}$$

By reordering and regrouping in the left member of equality (5) we obtain

$$(a + b) + [(-a) + (-b)] = 0$$

Because the sum $(a + b) + [(-a) + (-b)]$ is zero, it follows from the Additive Inverse Law that $(a + b)$ and $[(-a) + (-b)]$ are opposites of each other. Therefore, we state that

$$-(a + b) = (-a) + (-b)$$

which is what we wished to prove.

Illustration 3 Although Theorem 3.2.2 is true for all integers it is particularly useful for negative integers. Thus,

(a) $^{-}5 + {}^{-}8 \quad = (-5) + (-8)$
$\qquad\qquad\quad = -(5 + 8)$
$\qquad\qquad\quad = -13$

(b) $^{-}5 + {}^{-}1 \quad = -(5 + 1)$
$\qquad\qquad\quad = -6$

(c) $^{-}51 + {}^{-}64 = -(51 + 64)$
$\qquad\qquad\quad = -115$

In words, the rule for adding two negative integers is to add their opposites (which are positive) and then take the opposite of the sum (which makes the result a negative integer).

The operation of addition as applied to integers can be depicted on the number line by representing each integer by a "curved arrow" that spans a distance from "tail" to "head" equal to the absolute value of the integer. Positive integers are represented by arrows whose heads are directed towards the positive side of the number line and negative integers are represented by arrows directed in the opposite direction. The first addend in a sum is represented by an arrow whose tail is placed at the origin and the tail of each succeeding arrow, representing each succeeding addend, is placed at the point located by the head of the preceding arrow. The sum of the integers then is the coordinate of the point located by the head of the arrow representing the last addend. See Figure 3.2.1.

Thus far by using Theorems 3.2.1 and 3.2.2 we have been able to add and subtract certain combinations of integers. This has been possible because after applying Theorems 3.2.1 and 3.2.2 and the Additive Inverse Law we have had an operation that could be performed by using the nonnegative integers and the rules of ordinary arithmetic. We now develop two properties that enable us to subtract any two integers and consequently to add any two integers.

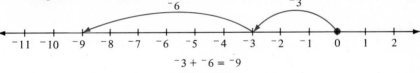

$$^{-}3 + {}^{-}6 = {}^{-}9$$

Figure 3.2.1

It is useful when working with differences to use the property called the Fundamental Principle of Differences: If given the difference $a - b$, then any number can be added to or subtracted from both the minuend a and the subtrahend b without changing the value of the difference.

Illustration 4 Consider the difference

$$10 - 7 = 3$$

Any number, for instance 5, can be added to both the minuend 10 and the subtrahend 7, and we have

$$(10 + 5) - (7 + 5) = 15 - 12$$
$$= 3$$

3.2.3 Theorem **(Fundamental Principle of Differences)** If $a, b, x \in J$, then

(i)
$$a - b = (a + x) - (b + x)$$

and

(ii)
$$a - b = (a - x) - (b - x)$$

We omit the proof of Theorem 3.2.3. We occasionally omit the proof of a theorem, but an ample number of illustrations and examples are provided to demonstrate the use of the theorem.

Illustration 5 Let $a = 24$, $b = 8$, and $x = 4$ in Property 3.2.3; then

(i)
$$24 - 8 = (24 + 4) - (8 + 4)$$
$$16 = 28 - 12$$
$$16 = 16$$

and

(ii)
$$24 - 8 = (24 - 4) - (8 - 4)$$
$$16 = 20 - 4$$
$$16 = 16$$

Example 2 Find the following differences using the Fundamental Principle of Differences: (a) $7 - 12$; (b) $10 - {}^-4$; (c) ${}^-7 - 8$.

Solution:
  (a) $7 - 12 = (7 - 7) - (12 - 7)$
$$= 0 - 5$$
$$= -5 \quad \text{(by Theorem 3.1.3)}$$

(b) $10 - {}^-4 = (10 + 4) - ({}^-4 + 4)$
$= 14 - 0$
$= 14$

(c) ${}^-7 - 8 = ({}^-7 + 7) - (8 + 7)$
$= 0 - 15$
$= -15$

Note in Example 2 parts (b) and (c) that a procedure to use when finding differences is as follows: if one of the numbers is negative, then add the opposite of that number to both the minuend and the subtrahend. This procedure then utilizes the Additive Inverse Law.

Illustration 6 If we wish to solve the equation

$$x + 8 = 5$$

we need to subtract 8 from both members and we obtain

$$x = 5 - 8$$

Applying the Fundamental Principle of Differences in the right member we have

$$x = (5 - 5) - (8 - 5)$$
$$= 0 - 3$$
$$= -3$$

Observe in Illustration 6 that the difference $5 - 8$ is the opposite of the difference $8 - 5$, namely, -3. Subtraction is not a commutative operation, so that $5 - 8 \neq 8 - 5$. However, $5 - 8$ does equal the opposite of $8 - 5$, that is,

$$5 - 8 = -(8 - 5) \tag{6}$$

Equation (6) is a particular case of the following property.

3.2.4 Theorem   If $a, b \in J$, then

$$a - b = -(b - a)$$

Proof: Using the Fundamental Principle of Differences we have

$$a - b = (a - a) - (b - a)$$

Because $a - a = 0$, we have

$$a - b = 0 - (b - a)$$

From Theorem 3.1.3 it follows that

$$a - b = -(b - a)$$

Example 3 Find the following differences: (a) $12 - 17$; (b) $^-5 - 2$; (c) $^-8 - 10$.

Solution: We apply Theorem 3.2.4.
  (a) $12 - 17 = -(17 - 12)$
                  $= -5$
  (b) $^-5 - 2 = -(2 - ^-5)$
                  $= -(2 + 5)$
                  $= -7$
  (c) $^-8 - 10 = -(10 - ^-8)$
                    $= -(10 + 8)$
                    $= -18$

We are now in a position to find the sum of any two integers. We consider the three possible cases.

Case 1. Both integers are either positive or zero. This is the situation in ordinary arithmetic. For instance,

$$^+7 + {}^+8 = {}^+15$$

Case 2. Both integers are negative. This is the situation based on Theorem 3.2.2. For instance,

$$^-6 + {}^-4 = {}^-10$$

Case 3. One of the integers is positive and the other is negative. In this case we use Property 3.2.1:

$$a + (-b) = a - b$$

Illustration 7 (a) Suppose we wish to add $^-5$ and $^+8$. We write

$$^-5 + {}^+8 = {}^+8 + {}^-5$$
$$= 8 + (-5)$$
$$= 8 - 5$$
$$= 3$$

(b) If we wish to add $^-7$ and $^+2$, we write

$$^-7 + {}^+2 = 2 + {}^-7$$
$$= 2 + (-7)$$
$$= 2 - 7$$
$$= -(7 - 2)$$
$$= -5$$

As shown in Illustration 7 when adding a positive integer and a negative integer, apply the Commutative Law, if necessary, and write the positive addend first. Then by applying Theorem 3.2.1, the addition problem becomes a subtraction problem to which we can apply Theorems 3.2.3 and 3.2.4.

Note in Case 3 that the sum of a positive integer and a negative integer can be obtained by finding the difference of the absolute values of the two integers, and affixing the sign of the integer that has the largest absolute value.

Example 4 Find the sum: (a) $^-8 + {}^-4$; (b) $^-8 + {}^+4$; (c) $^+8 + {}^-4$.

Solution:

(a) $^-8 + {}^-4 = -(8 + 4)$
$= -12$

(b) $^-8 + {}^+4 = {}^+4 + {}^-8$
$= 4 - 8$
$= -(8 - 4)$
$= -4$

(c) $^+8 + {}^-4 = 8 - 4$
$= 4$

The sums in Example 4 can be depicted on a number line. See Figure 3.2.2.

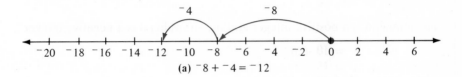

(a) $^-8 + {}^-4 = {}^-12$

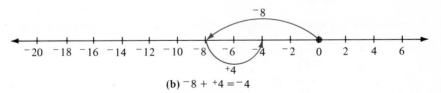

(b) $^-8 + {}^+4 = {}^-4$

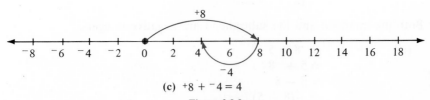

(c) $^+8 + {}^-4 = 4$

Figure 3.2.2

It is important to realize that if x is the coordinate of any point A (shown on the number line in Figure 3.2.3), then if a positive integer y is added to x, the sum of x and y is the coordinate of a point B, where B is to the right of A. If y is a negative integer and $x + y$ is the coordinate of the point B, then B is to the left of A. This is true regardless of whether x is a positive, zero, or negative integer.

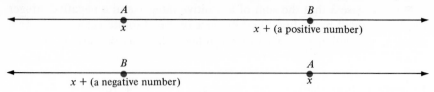

Figure 3.2.3

Because

$$a - b = a + (-b)$$

we can find the difference of two integers either by changing the problem to an addition problem or by using Theorems 3.2.3 and 3.2.4. Illustration 8 summarizes the various cases that can arise in a subtraction problem.

Illustration 8 Both the minuend and the subtrahend are positive integers.

(a) $^+8 - ^+5 = 3$
(b) $10 - 15 = -(15 - 10)$
            $= -5$

The minuend is a positive integer and the subtrahend is a negative integer.

(c) $10 - ^-6 \ = 10 + 6$
                  $= 16$
(d) $10 - ^-12 = 10 + 12$
                  $= 22$

The minuend is a negative integer and the subtrahend is a positive integer.

(e) $^-8 - 5 \ = ^-8 + ^-5$
                $= -13$
(f) $^-8 - 10 = ^-8 + ^-10$
                $= -18$

Both the minuend and the subtrahend are negative integers.

(g) $^-8 - ^-5 \ = ^-8 + 5$
                $= 5 + ^-8$
                $= 5 - 8$
                $= -(8 - 5)$
                $= -3$
(h) $^-10 - ^-13 = ^-10 + 13$
                  $= 3$

The operation of subtraction can always be performed in the set of integers. The set of integers is closed with respect to subtraction. Thus, the equation

$$x + a = b$$

where a and b are integers always has a solution, namely

$$x = b - a$$

Exercises 3.2

1. Find the following differences.
   (a) $3 - 0$ (b) $3 - 1$ (c) $3 - 2$
   (d) $3 - 3$ (e) $3 - 4$ (f) $3 - 5$
   (g) $3 - 6$

2. Find the following differences.
   (a) $3 - 3$ (b) $3 - 2$ (c) $3 - 1$
   (d) $3 - 0$ (e) $3 - {}^-1$ (f) $3 - {}^-2$
   (g) $3 - {}^-3$

3. Find the following differences.
   (a) ${}^-3 - {}^-3$ (b) ${}^-3 - {}^-2$ (c) ${}^-3 - {}^-1$
   (d) ${}^-3 - 0$ (e) ${}^-3 - 1$ (f) ${}^-3 - 2$
   (g) ${}^-3 - 3$

4. Find the following sums.
   (a) $2 + 2$ (b) $2 + 1$ (c) $2 + 0$
   (d) $2 + {}^-1$ (e) $2 + {}^-2$

5. Find the following sums.
   (a) ${}^-2 + 2$ (b) ${}^-2 + 1$ (c) ${}^-2 + 0$
   (d) ${}^-2 + {}^-1$ (e) ${}^-2 + {}^-2$

In Exercises 6 through 20 find the difference.

6. (a) $23 - 37$ (b) $37 - 23$

7. (a) $117 - 83$ (b) $83 - 117$

8. (a) ${}^-5 - 6$ (b) $6 - {}^-5$

9. (a) $5 - {}^-5$ (b) ${}^-5 - 5$

10. (a) ${}^-9 - {}^-12$ (b) ${}^-12 - {}^-9$

11. (a) ${}^-8 - {}^-8$ (b) $8 - 8$

12. (a) $15 - {}^-7$ (b) $7 - {}^-15$

13. (a) ${}^-13 - {}^-5$ (b) $5 - 13$

14. (a) ${}^-1 - 0$ (b) $0 - 1$

15. (a) ${}^-7 - {}^-10$ (b) $10 - 7$

16. (a) $9 - 12$ (b) ${}^-12 - {}^-9$

17. (a) $^-5 - 6$ (b) $^-6 - 5$

18. (a) $25 - 14$ (b) $^-14 - ^-25$

19. (a) $5 - ^-6$ (b) $6 - ^-5$

20. (a) $^-10 - 10$ (b) $10 - ^-10$

In Exercises 21 through 42 find the sum.

21. (a) $^-8 + ^-7$ (b) $^-8 + 7$

22. (a) $8 + ^-7$ (b) $8 + 7$

23. (a) $^-6 + ^-7$ (b) $^-6 + 7$

24. (a) $6 + ^-7$ (b) $6 + 7$

25. (a) $^-13 + ^-12$ (b) $^-13 + 12$

26. (a) $13 + ^-12$ (b) $12 + ^-13$

27. (a) $^-12 + 0$ (b) $0 + ^-12$

28. (a) $^-31 + ^-17$ (b) $^-31 + 17$

29. (a) $31 + ^-17$ (b) $^-17 + 31$

30. (a) $^-1 + ^-1$ (b) $^-1 + 1$

31. (a) $^-2 + 2$ (b) $2 + ^-2$

32. (a) $^-1 + ^-2 + ^-3$ (b) $^-1 + 2 + ^-3$

33. (a) $^-44 + 55$ (b) $44 + ^-55$

34. (a) $9 + (-4)$ (b) $(-9) + (-4)$

35. (a) $16 + (-16)$ (b) $(-5) + 3$

36. (a) $(-16) + (-17)$ (b) $(-9) + (16)$

37. (a) $(-451) + 239$ (b) $(-212) + (-107)$

38. (a) $(-66) + (34)$ (b) $(66) + (-34)$

39. (a) $(-72) + (72)$ (b) $0 + (-23)$

40. (a) $(-9) + (-6) + (-3)$ (b) $(-2) + (-2) + (-2)$

41. (a) $(^-8) + (-4) + (4)$ (b) $(-3) + (3) + (-3)$

42. (a) $[3 + (-8)] + 4$ (b) $3 + [(-8) + 4]$

In Exercises 43 through 48, replace the blank with either $=$, $<$, or $>$.

43. $^-8 + 6$_____$^-8 + ^-6$ 44. $^-3 + ^-2$_____$^-3 + 2$

45. $^-10 - 6$_____$^-10 - ^-6$ 46. $^-4 - ^-2$_____$^-4 - 2$

47. $x + 3$ $x + {}^-3$ **48.** $x - 3$ $x - {}^-3$

49. What must be added to ${}^-8$ to give a sum of 10?

50. What must be added to 7 to give a sum of ${}^-1$?

51. What must be added to ${}^-8$ to give a sum of ${}^-13$?

52. Test the general statement $a - b = (-b) - (-a)$ using several combinations of positive and negative values for the numbers a and b.

53. If $a - b = -(b - a)$ and $a - b = (-b) - (-a)$, then draw a conclusion about $-(b - a)$ and $(-b) - (-a)$.

54. Test the general statement $|a - b| = |b - a|$ using several combinations of positive and negative values for the numbers a and b.

55. Show that for any integer x that

$$x - (-x) = 2x$$

56. We know that $-(a + b) = (-a) + (-b)$. Obtain an expression for $-(a - b)$.

57. Prove: $-(a + b) = -a - b$.

3.3 Multiplication and Division of Integers

In Section 3.1 we assumed the Closure Law for Multiplication for the set of integers; that is, the product of two integers is an integer. In Section 2.1 we stated the Zero Factor Property without proof. We now prove the Zero Factor Property.

3.3.1 Theorem (Zero Factor Property)   If $a \in J$, then

$$a \cdot 0 = 0$$

Proof: Because 1 is the identity element for multiplication

$$a = a \cdot 1 \tag{1}$$

Substituting $1 + 0$ for 1 in the right member of equality (1) we have

$$a = a(1 + 0) \tag{2}$$

Applying the Distributive Law in the right member of equality (2) we have

$$a = a \cdot 1 + a \cdot 0 \tag{3}$$

Substituting a for $a \cdot 1$ in the right member of equality (3) we have

$$a = a + a \cdot 0 \tag{4}$$

Because 0 *is the unique identity element for addition such that* $a = a + 0$ *it follows from equality* (4) *that*

$$a \cdot 0 = 0$$

which is what we wished to prove.

We know that the product of two positive integers is a positive integer, because this is the case in ordinary arithmetic. Now we turn to the question of multiplying a negative integer by another integer, either positive or negative.

Consider the product $3x$ expressed as the sum of three equal addends of x. That is

$$3x = x + x + x \tag{5}$$

If equality (5) is to be true for any integer x, it must be true if x is a negative integer. For instance if $x = -4$, then equality (5) becomes

$$3(-4) = (-4) + (-4) + (-4)$$
$$= -12$$

It follows then that if equality (5) is to hold when $x = -4$, then the product of the positive integer 3 and the negative integer -4 is the negative integer -12. Because we assume the Commutative Law for Multiplication, we also have

$$(-4)(3) = 3(-4) = -12$$

In Illustration 1 we have an alternate proof that $(-4)(3) = -(4 \cdot 3)$, which can be generalized to prove that $(-a)(b) = -(ab)$.

Illustration 1 Because 0 is the Identity Element for Addition we have

$$(-4)(3) = (-4)(3) + 0 \tag{6}$$

Substituting $[(4)(3) + [-(4 \cdot 3)]]$ for 0 in equality (6) we have

$$(-4)(3) = (-4)(3) + [(4)(3) + [-(4 \cdot 3)]] \tag{7}$$

Applying the Associative Law for Addition to the right member of equality (7) we obtain

$$(-4)(3) = [(-4)(3) + (4)(3)] + [-(4 \cdot 3)] \tag{8}$$

Applying the Distributive Law to the expression $(-4)(3) + (4)(3)$ in equality (8) we obtain

$$(-4)(3) = [(-4) + (4)](3) + [-(4 \cdot 3)] \tag{9}$$

Because $(-4) + (4) = 0$ by the Additive Inverse Law, we substitute 0 for $(-4) + (4)$ in Equality (9) and we get

$$(-4)(3) = (0)(3) + [-(4 \cdot 3)] \tag{10}$$

Applying the Zero Factor Property in the right member of equality (10) we have

$$(-4)(3) = 0 + [-(4 \cdot 3)] \tag{11}$$

Because 0 is the Identity Element for Addition we obtain

$$(-4)(3) = -(4 \cdot 3) \tag{12}$$

3.3.2 Theorem   If $a, b \in J$, then

$$(-a)(b) = -(ab)$$

The proof of Theorem 3.3.2 is similar to the proof given in Illustration 1. See Exercise 17 of this section.

From Theorem 3.3.2 it follows that the product of a positive integer and a negative integer is a negative integer.

Example 1 Find the following products: (a) $(-8)(4)$; (b) $9(-3)$.

Solution:

(a) $(-8)(4) = -(8 \cdot 4)$
$\qquad\qquad = -32$

(b) $9(-3) = -(9 \cdot 3)$
$\qquad\qquad = -27$

[Note that $9(-3) = (-3)9 = -(3 \cdot 9) = -27$]

In Illustration 2 we prove, for a particular case, that the product of two negative integers is a positive integer.

Illustration 2 From Theorem 3.3.2 with $a = 3$ and $b = -4$ we have

$$(-3)(-4) = -[3(-4)] \tag{13}$$

Applying the Commutative Law in the right member of equality (13) we have

$$(-3)(-4) = -[(-4)3] \tag{14}$$

Applying Theorem 3.3.2 to the product $(-4)3$ in equality (14) we have

$$(-3)(-4) = -[-(4 \cdot 3)] \tag{15}$$
$$= 4 \cdot 3$$
$$= 3 \cdot 4$$

Hence,

$$(-3)(-4) = 12$$

3.3.3 Theorem   If $a, b \in J$, then

$$(-a)(-b) = ab$$

The proof of Theorem 3.3.3 is similar to the proof given in Illustration 2. See Exercise 19 of this Section.

Example 2   Find the following products: (a) $(-2)(-5)$; (b) $(-2)(5)(-3)$.

Solution:
   (a) $(-2)(-5) = 2 \cdot 5$
                 $= 10$
   (b) $(-2)(5)(-3) = [(-2)(5)](-3)$
                     $= (-10)(-3)$
                     $= 30$

Example 3   Find the following powers: (a) $(-1)^2$; (b) $(-1)^4$; (c) $(-1)^5$.

Solution:
   (a) $(-1)^2 = (-1)(-1) = 1$
   (b) $(-1)^4 = [(-1)(-1)][(-1)(-1)]$
               $= [1] \cdot [1]$
               $= 1$
   (c) $(-1)^5 = [(-1)(-1)][(-1)(-1)](-1)$
               $= [1] \cdot [1] \cdot (-1)$
               $= 1 \cdot (-1)$
               $= -1$

Note from Example 3 that a power involving an even number of negative factors results in a positive product and if an odd number of negative factors are involved, the product is a negative number.

Illustration 3   A correct interpretation of the expression -1^2 is "the opposite of one squared," and hence,

$$-1^2 = -(1)^2 = -1$$

If we want the square of -1, we write

$$(-1)^2 = 1$$

It is worth noting that

$$-1^2 \neq (-1)^2$$

The set of integers is not closed under the operation of division. However, if a, b, and c are any integers and $b \neq 0$, then $a \div b = c$ if and only if there exists an integer c, such that $a = bc$.

Illustration 4

(a) $\dfrac{12}{-3} = -4$ because $12 = (-3)(-4)$

(b) $\dfrac{-12}{3} = -4$ because $-12 = (3)(-4)$

(c) $\dfrac{-12}{-3} = 4$ because $-12 = (-3)(4)$

(d) $\dfrac{12}{-5}$ is not an integer because there does not exist an integer c such that $(-5)(c) = 12$. To provide an answer for this quotient we must extend the set of integers to a larger set, the set of rational numbers. This set is discussed in Chapter 5.

We can summarize into two statements the rules of signs for multiplying and dividing integers.

(I) The product and quotient of two integers are positive numbers if the integers are both positive or both negative.

(II) The product and quotient of two integers are negative numbers if one of the integers is positive and the other is negative.

Example 4 Simplify: $\dfrac{(-4)(-3)(-5)}{(-6)(-1)}$

Solution: $\dfrac{(-4)(-3)(-5)}{(-6)(-1)} = \dfrac{-60}{6}$

$= -10$

Exercises 3.3

1. Find the following products.
  (a) $2 \cdot (3)$ (b) $2 \cdot (2)$ (c) $2 \cdot (1)$
  (d) $2 \cdot (0)$ (e) $2 \cdot (-1)$ (f) $2 \cdot (-2)$
  (g) $2 \cdot (-3)$

2. Find the following products.
  (a) $(-2)(3)$ (b) $(-2)(2)$ (c) $(-2)(1)$
  (d) $(-2)(0)$ (e) $(-2)(-1)$ (f) $(-2)(-2)$
  (g) $(-2)(-3)$

In Exercises 3 through 20 find the product.

3. (a) $(-4) \cdot (+5)$ (b) $(-4)(-5)$

4. (a) $(+4)(-5)$.   (b) $(+4)(+5)$

5. (a) $(-10)(3)$ (b) $(-10)(-3)$

6. (a) $(-4)(-8)$ (b) $(-4)(8)$

7. (a) $(-5) \cdot 0$ (b) $0 \cdot (-7)$

8. (a) $(-1)(-1)(-1)$ (b) $(-1)(-1)(2)$

9. (a) $(-2)(-2)(-2)$ (b) $(-2)(2)(-2)$

10. (a) $(-1)(-2)(-3)(-4)$ (b) $(-1)(2)(3)(4)$

11. (a) $(-3)^3$ (b) $(-2)^4$

12. (a) $(-2)^5(-1)^2$ (b) $(-1)^5 \cdot (-1)^3$

13. (a) $(-2)(3 + 5)$ (b) $(-2)(3 - 5)$

14. (a) $4(-3 + 6)$ (b) $5(-3 + 8)$

15. (a) $(-4 + 1)^2$ (b) $(-2)^2 \cdot (^-6 + 4)^3$

16. Discuss the meanings of each of the following expressions.
    (a) $0 - 1^2$ (b) -1^2 (c) $(-1)^2$

17. Prove Theorem 3.3.2 by a procedure similar to that in Illustration 1 where -4 is replaced by $-a$ and 3 is replaced by b.

18. Prove: $-a = (-1) \cdot a$

19. Prove Theorem 3.3.3 by a procedure similar to that in Illustration 2 where -3 is replaced by $-a$ and -4 is replaced by $-b$.

20. Find each of the following powers.
    (a) $(-1)^{10}$ (b) $(-1)^{11}$

In Exercises 21 through 33 find the quotient if it exists in the set of integers.

21. (a) $\dfrac{6}{-6}$ (b) $\dfrac{6}{-3}$ (c) $\dfrac{6}{-2}$ (d) $\dfrac{6}{-1}$

22. (a) $\dfrac{-6}{6}$ (b) $\dfrac{-6}{3}$ (c) $\dfrac{-6}{2}$ (d) $\dfrac{-6}{1}$

23. (a) $\dfrac{-6}{-6}$ (b) $\dfrac{-6}{-3}$ (c) $\dfrac{-6}{-2}$ (d) $\dfrac{-6}{-1}$

24. (a) $\dfrac{0}{-3}$ (b) $\dfrac{-32}{8}$ (c) $\dfrac{32}{-8}$

25. (a) $\dfrac{-6}{12}$ (b) $\dfrac{-6}{0}$ (c) $\dfrac{-6}{4}$

26. (a) $\dfrac{-14}{-7}$ (b) $\dfrac{-14}{2}$ (c) $\dfrac{14}{-7}$

27. (a) $\dfrac{24}{-3}$ (b) $\dfrac{-24}{-3}$ (c) $\dfrac{-24}{3}$

28. (a) $\dfrac{27}{-3}$ (b) $\dfrac{-27}{-9}$ (c) $\dfrac{-27}{27}$

29. (a) $\dfrac{3 \cdot 4}{-6}$ (b) $\dfrac{-3 \cdot 4}{-6}$

30. (a) $\dfrac{(-4)(-5)}{(-2)(2)}$ (b) $\dfrac{9 \cdot (-4)}{(-3)(12)}$

31. (a) $\dfrac{(-2)(-10)(3)}{(-15)(-1)}$ (b) $\dfrac{(-5)(4)(-4)}{(-10)(-2)(-1)}$

32. (a) $\dfrac{(-1)^2}{(-1)}$ (b) $\left(\dfrac{+1}{-1}\right)^3$

33. (a) $\left(\dfrac{+8}{-2}\right)^2$ (b) $\left(\dfrac{+8}{-2}\right)^3$

In Exercises 34 through 41 replace the blank space with =, >, or <.

34. If $xy > 0$ and $x < 0$, then y_____0.

35. If $xy < 0$ and $x > 0$, then y_____0.

36. If $x < 0$ and $y < 0$, then xy_____0.

37. If $x < 0$ and $y > 0$, then xy_____0.

38. Regardless of whether $x < 0$ or $x > 0$, x^2_____0.

39. If $x > 0$, then $2x$_____x.

40. If $x < 0$, then $2x$_____x.

41. If $x = 0$, then $2x$_____x.

3.4 Computations Involving Integers

If several positive and negative integers are to be added, we make use of the Commutative and Associative Laws to group all of the positive integers together and all of the negative integers together. Refer to Illustration 1.

Illustration 1 To find the sum

$$(-4) + (^+3) + (^-1) + (8) + (^-9) + (12) + (-3)$$

we express each addend as either a positive or a negative integer. Then we group the positive integers together and the negative integers together and we have

$$[(3) + (8) + (12)] + [(^-4) + (^-1) + (^-9) + (^-3)] = (23) + (-17)$$
$$= 23 - 17$$
$$= 6$$

Example 1 Find the sum:

$$(4) + (^-3) + (-2) + (5) + (^-4) + (^-10) + (7) + (2) + (-1)$$

Solution:

$$(4) + (^-3) + (-2) + (5) + (^-4) + (^-10) + (7) + (2) + (-1)$$
$$= [(4) + (5) + (7) + (2)] + [(^-3) + (^-2) + (^-4) + (^-10) + (^-1)]$$
$$= (18) + (-20)$$
$$= 18 - 20$$
$$= ^-2$$

Sometimes the computation involves subtractions and additions of positive and negative integers. If there are very many of these operations, one procedure is to rewrite all of the subtractions as additions of opposites and employ the commutative and associative properties of addition as shown in Illustration 1 and Example 1. Note that

> *Subtracting a positive integer* gives the same result as *adding a negative integer having the same absolute value.*

and

> *subtracting a negative integer* gives the same result as *adding a positive integer having the same absolute value.*

Illustration 2 $5 - 8 = 5 + ^-8$ and $5 - ^-3 = 5 + ^+3$.

Every problem involving the subtraction of integers can be rewritten as a problem involving only the addition of integers.

Example 2 Compute:

$$(^-5) + (8) - (^-1) + (^-5) - (7) - (^-10) + (^-8)$$

Solution: Rewrite the problem changing all subtractions to additions.

$$(^-5) + (8) - (^-1) + (^-5) - (7) - (^-10) + (^-8)$$
$$= (^-5) + (8) + (^+1) + (^-5) + (^-7) + (^+10) + (^-8)$$
$$= [(8) + (^+1) + (^+10)] + [(^-5) + (^-5) + (^-7) + (^-8)]$$
$$= 19 + [-25]$$
$$= 19 - 25$$
$$= ^-6$$

Example 3 Combine like terms:
(a) $3x - 7x + 2x$
(b) $3a + 8a - 7a - 2a + a - 10a$
(c) $2x - (3x + 2x - 8x)$

Solution:

(a) $3x - 7x + 2x = 3x + (-7x) + 2x$
$$= (3x + 2x) + (-7x)$$
$$= 5x + (-7x)$$
$$= 5x - 7x$$
$$= -2x$$

(b) $3a + 8a - 7a - 2a + a - 10a$
$$= 3a + 8a + (-7a) + (-2a) + a + (-10a)$$
$$= [3a + 8a + a] + [(-7a) + (-2a) + (-10a)]$$
$$= [12a] + [-19a]$$
$$= -7a$$

(c) $2x - (3x + 2x - 8x) = 2x - [5x - 8x]$
$$= 2x - [-3x]$$
$$= 2x + [3x]$$
$$= 5x$$

Example 4 Simplify: $2a - 3b - (a + 2b)$

Solution: $2a - 3b - (a + 2b) = 2a - 3b + [-(a + 2b)]$
$$= 2a + (-3b) + (-a) + (-2b)$$
$$= a + (-5b)$$
$$= a - 5b$$

Example 5 Simplify: $-5(2x - 4y) + 3x$

Solution: $-5(2x - 4y) + 3x = (-5)(2x) - (-5)(4y) + 3x$
$$= -10x - (-20y) + 3x$$
$$= -10x + 20y + 3x$$
$$= (-10x + 3x) + 20y$$
$$= -7x + 20y$$

Note the use of the Distributive Law of Multiplication over Subtraction in the first step.

Raising an integer to a power is basically a multiplication problem. In Section 3.3 we found that raising a negative integer to an even power yields a positive result and raising a negative integer to an odd power yields a negative result. We also have the following results:

$$(x)(x) = x^2$$
$$(-x)(-x) = x^2$$
$$(x)(x)(x) = x^3$$
$$(-x)(-x)(-x) = -x^3$$

Example 6 Simplify: $(-2x)(-3x)(-x)$

Solution: We apply the Commutative and Associative Laws for Multiplication to regroup and reorder the factors in the given expression.

$$(-2x)(-3x)(-x) = [(-2)(-3)(-1)][(x)(x)(x)]$$
$$= [-6][x^3]$$
$$= -6x^3$$

Example 7 Evaluate $-x^3$ if $x = -2$.

Solution: $\quad -x^3 = -(x)^3$
$$= -(-2)^3$$
$$= -(-8)$$
$$= 8$$

Example 8 Evaluate $2x^2 - 3x$ if $x = -4$.

Solution: $\quad 2x^2 - 3x = 2(x)^2 - 3(x)$
$$= 2(-4)^2 - 3(-4)$$
$$= 2(16) - 3(-4)$$
$$= 32 - (-12)$$
$$= 32 + 12$$
$$= 44$$

Example 9 Evaluate $\dfrac{x^3 - x}{xy}$ if $x = -1$ and $y = 5$.

Solution: $\quad \dfrac{x^3 - x}{xy} = \dfrac{(-1)^3 - (-1)}{(-1)(5)}$

$$= \dfrac{-1 - (-1)}{-5}$$

$$= \dfrac{-1 + 1}{-5}$$

$$= \dfrac{0}{-5}$$

$$= 0$$

Exercises 3.4

In Exercises 1 through 5 find the sum.

1. $6 + (^-4) + 3 + (^-5)$

2. $(^-8) + 9 + (^-3) + 5$

3. $(-5) + (-6) + (-3) + 12$

4. $5 + (-2) + (-1) + 3 + 4 + (-5) + 11$

5. $(-4) + (^+4) + 10 + (-7) + (^+1) + (-2) + 100$

In Exercises 6 through 15 rewrite each subtraction operation as an addition operation and then add.

6. $8 - 5 + (-2)$

7. $4 + (-3) + (-8) - (6)$

8. $(-7) + (-8) - (-3)$

9. $4 - 3 - 2 - 1$

10. $(^-5) + (-8) - (-8) - (2)$

11. $(-2) - (10) - (-4)$

12. $(-2) - (-2) - 2 + (-2)$

13. $(-8) - (-12) + (-12) - (3) - (7)$

14. $-10 - (-4 - (-1))$

15. $(-9 - (-4)) - ((-3) - (-3))$

In Exercises 16 through 29 simplify the expression.

16. (a) $(-x) - (-y)$ (b) $-(m - n)$

17. (a) $(10 - 5) + (5 - 10)$ (b) $(x - y) + (y - x)$

18. (a) $x - (-x)$ (b) $-x - x$

19. (a) $a - (b - a)$ (b) $a - (a - b)$

20. (a) $2x - 5x$ (b) $8x - 18x$

21. (a) $-2x - 7x$ (b) $(-4m) - (-3m)$

22. (a) $5x + 2x - 9x$ (b) $3x - 9x + x - 2x + 4x$

23. (a) $2xy - 5xy + xy$ (b) $-5xy + 4xy - 2xy$

24. (a) $2y - (8y - 12y)$ (b) $x - 2x + (-3x)$

25. (a) $(2k - 3k) - 4k$ (b) $7x - 5x - (-5x - x)$

26. (a) $x + (-3a) - 4x - 2a$ (b) $x + 1 - 3x - 9$

27. (a) $9 - (x + 2) - (2x - 3)$ (b) $1 + 5x - (8x + x^2)$

28. (a) $-(x + 2) + (2x + 3)$ (b) $-4(x - 1) + 5x - 8$

29. (a) $3(2x + 5) - (x - 1)$ (b) $-2(3x - 1) - 2(x + 3)$

In Exercises 30 through 36 simplify each product or power.

30. (a) $(-x)(-x)$ (b) $(-2x)(-3x)$

31. (a) $(-x)(-x)(-x)$ **(b)** $(2x)(2x)(2x)$

32. (a) $(-a)(-a)(-a)(-a)$ **(b)** $(2a)(-4a)$

33. (a) $(-2x)(-3x)(-x)$ **(b)** $(-3y)(4y)(-2y)$

34. (a) $(-x)^2$ **(b)** $(-2x)^2$

35. (a) $(-x)^3$ **(b)** $(-20)(-5x)$

36. (a) $-(-4m)(-2m)$ **(b)** $(-2a)(-3b)(-c)$

In Exercises 37 through 42 evaluate each expression if $a = -2$ and $b = 3$.

37. (a) ab **(b)** $-(ab)$

38. (a) $3a - b$ **(b)** $a(a + b)$

39. (a) $5a^2$ **(b)** a^3b

40. (a) $(a + b)(a - b)$ **(b)** $a^2 - b^2$

41. (a) $\dfrac{a^3 - b}{b + 8}$ **(b)** $\dfrac{a^2 - 2ab + b^2}{(a - b)^2}$

42. (a) $2a^3$ **(b)** $(2a)^3$

43. Find the temperature in degrees Celsius that corresponds to $-40°$ Fahrenheit if $9C = 5(F - 32)$, where C is the number of degrees Celsius and F is the number of degrees Fahrenheit.

3.5 Review Exercises

1. Complete the following table.

Number	3	1	0	$^-2$	$^-17$	$-(^-5)$	$\sqrt{4}$	$0 - 7$	$^-6$
Additive Inverse of Number	$^-3$								

In Exercises 2 through 21 perform the computation.

2. $(^-7) + (-2) =$ **3.** $(^-5) + (9) =$

4. $5 - (-8) =$ **5.** $^-9 - 2 =$

6. $6 + (-3) - (-2) =$ **7.** $(-13) - (2) + 5 - (-10) =$

8. $\dfrac{(^-2)(18)}{-6} =$ **9.** $(^-2)^3 =$

10. $\dfrac{(-3)(10) + (^-12)}{-6} =$

11. $(^-2) \cdot (2) \cdot (^-3) \cdot (^-1) =$

12. $|5 - 13| =$

13. $|^-8| =$

14. $^-5[^-3 + (-5) - (^-1)] =$

15. $|17 - 5| =$

16. $-(-(^-3)) =$

17. $|-3| \cdot |5| =$

18. $(^-1)^3 \cdot (2)^2 =$

19. $5 - (3 - 10)$

20. $-16 - 16$

21. $^-5 - (3 - 8) + 4$

In Exercises 22 through 25 name the property that is illustrated.

22. $^-3 + 5 = 5 + {}^-3$

23. $^-3(^-2 \cdot 5) = (^-3 \cdot {}^-2) \cdot 5$

24. $^-3 + 3 = 0$

25. $25 - 30 = (25 - 25) - (30 - 25)$

26. The opposite of the quantity $2 - x$ is _____

27. If $x < 0$ and $xy > 0$, then y_____0.

28. What must be added to -6 to give a sum of 12?

29. If $9C = 5(F - 32)$, find C when $F = -4$.

In Exercises 30 through 36 find the value of the given expression if $a = 4$, $b = 3$, and $c = -2$.

30. (a) c^2

(b) $-c^2$

31. (a) $3c^2$

(b) $(3c)^2$

32. (a) $b^2 - a^2$

(b) $(b + a)(b - a)$

33. (a) $(b - a)^2$

(b) abc

34. (a) $a - (b + c)$

(b) $a - b - c$

35. (a) $a - (b - c)$

(b) $(a - b) + c$

36. (a) $a + (b - c)$

(b) $(a + b) - c$

In Exercises 37 through 40 combine like terms and simplify the expression.

37. (a) $8t - 14t$

(b) $-15xy - 9xy$

38. (a) $7a - 10a + 5a$

(b) $-3n^2 + 11n^2 - 4n^2$

39. (a) $a - (b - a)$

(b) $(x - a) - (y - a)$

40. (a) $-(u - v)$

(b) $2z - (3z + 4w) + 2w$

4

Equations

4.1 Kinds of Equations

An *equation* is a sentence using the relation of equality. The following are examples of equations.

$$3 = 3 \tag{1}$$
$$m + 1 = m + 1 \tag{2}$$
$$2x + 3 = 11 \tag{3}$$
$$x^2 + x - 6 = 0 \tag{4}$$

Upon examining these equations we note that (1) and (2) are always true. Equation (1) is an illustration of the Aristotelian maxim that A is A. Equation (2) also illustrates this truth, but it has the added feature of being true for *all* values which replace m. Equations (1) and (2) are known as *identities* because of their universal truth.

Equations (3) and (4) are true only under certain conditions, and they are called *conditional equations*. Equation (3) is true if x is 4 because when x is replaced by 4 we obtain the identity

$$2(4) + 3 = 11$$

Because the number 4 *satisfies* equation (3), 4 is a *solution* of equation (3). The number 4 is the only number that satisfies equation (3) because if x is replaced by any other number we obtain a false statement.

Equation (4) is satisfied by two values of x, namely 2 and -3 because

$$(2)^2 + (2) - 6 = 4 + 2 - 6$$
$$= 0$$

and

$$(-3)^2 + (-3) - 6 = 9 + (-3) - 6$$
$$= 0$$

Example 1 Decide if the given value of x satisfies the corresponding equation.
  (a) If x is 5, does $x + 7 = 12$?
  (b) If x is 2, does $3x + 1 = 5x - 4$?
  (c) If x is 10, does $x^2 - 10 = 7x + 20$?

110

Solution:

(a) If x is 5, then

$$x + 7 = 5 + 7$$
$$= 12$$

Therefore, 5 satisfies the given equation.

(b) If x is 2, then

$$3x + 1 = 3(2) + 1 \qquad \text{and} \qquad 5x - 4 = 5(2) - 4$$
$$= 6 + 1 \qquad\qquad\qquad\qquad\quad = 10 - 4$$
$$= 7 \qquad\qquad\qquad\qquad\qquad\quad = 6$$

Hence, 2 does not satisfy the given equation.

(c) If x is 10, then

$$x^2 - 10 = (10)^2 - 10 \qquad \text{and} \qquad 7x + 20 = 7(10) + 20$$
$$= 100 - 10 \qquad\qquad\qquad\qquad\quad = 70 + 20$$
$$= 90 \qquad\qquad\qquad\qquad\qquad\quad = 90$$

Therefore, 10 satisfies the given equation.

A given equation is neither a true nor a false statement until the variables are replaced by specific numbers. The set of numbers that contains the values used for replacement is called the *replacement set* for the equation. We can think of the replacement set as a "universal set" containing the elements under discussion. In most cases the replacement set for an equation is specified or understood to be a certain set of numbers. In this book, unless otherwise stated, the replacement set for an equation is the set of real numbers.

Some equations have only one solution while others may have many solutions or no solutions at all. The set of all solutions for a given equation is called the *solution set* of the equation. The solution set is, of course, a subset of the replacement set.

Illustration 1   The equation

$$2x = 5$$

is a conditional equation and the condition is that

$$x = \frac{5}{2}$$

If the replacement set is the set of whole numbers, then the equation has no solution. However, if the replacement set is the set of real numbers, then the solution is $\frac{5}{2}$ and so the solution set of the equation is $\left\{\frac{5}{2}\right\}$.

Illustration 2   Suppose we have the equation

$$x^2 = 4$$

whose replacement set is the set of real numbers. Because 2 and -2 are the only two real numbers whose square is 4, the solution set of this equation is $\{2, -2\}$. If the replacement set for this equation is the set of positive real numbers, then the solution set is $\{2\}$.

Illustration 3 The equation

$$x^2 = -4$$

has no solution in the set of real numbers because the square of any real number is not a negative number. If the replacement set is the set of real numbers, then the solution set of the equation is $\emptyset$.

Exercises 4.1

In Exercises 1 through 8 classify each of the given equations as either an identity or a conditional equation.

1. (a) $x + 7 - 7 = x$ **(b)** $x - 5 + 5 = x$

2. (a) $2x + 1 = 3$ **(b)** $2\left(\dfrac{1}{2}x\right) = x$

3. (a) $10 = 10$ **(b)** $2x \div 2 = x$

4. (a) $2x + 3 = 3x + 1$ **(b)** $x + 4 + 6 = 10 + x$

5. (a) $x^2 + 8x + 12 = 0$ **(b)** $x + y = y + x$

6. (a) $x + 3 = 5$ **(b)** $x + (y + z) = (x + y) + z$

7. (a) $x = 3$ **(b)** $y = 2 - y$

8. (a) $x = x$ **(b)** $x^2 = 9$

In Exercises 9 through 26 decide if the given value of x satisfies the corresponding equation.

9. If x is 7, does $x - 7 = 10$?

10. If x is 5, does $2x + 5 = 15$?

11. If x is -2, does $3x - 1 = -5$?

12. If x is 1, does $5x + 2 = x + 6$?

13. If x is 12, does $\dfrac{x + 1}{2} = 7$?

14. If x is 2, does $x^2 = 4$?

15. If x is -2, does $x^2 = 4$?

16. If x is -3, does $3(x - 1) = -15 - x$?

17. If x is 6, does $x^2 + 12 - 8x = 0$?

18. If x is $\frac{1}{2}$, does $2x + 1 = x$?

19. Does $3(x + 2) + 4(x - 1) = 2(x + 6)$, if x is 2?

20. Does $(x - 6)(x + 2) = 0$, if x is 6?

21. Does $(2x - 3)(6x + 1) = 0$, if x is $\frac{3}{2}$?

22. Does $5(2x - 3) + (x + 2)(x - 1) = x^2 + 4x$, if x is 3?

23. Does $\frac{1}{3} + \frac{1}{x} = \frac{1}{2}$, if x is 1?

24. Does $\frac{x}{3} = \frac{8}{x}$, if x is 5?

25. Does $\frac{x}{3} = \frac{8}{3}$, if x is 5?

26. Does $x^3 - 3x^2 + 3x - 1 = 0$, if x is 1?

27. If $x = 5$, then $x - 8 = -3$. If the replacement set for the equation $x - 8 = -3$ is the set of real numbers, what is the solution set for this equation?

28. If $x = -3$ or $x = 3$, then $x^2 = 9$. If the replacement set for the equation $x^2 = 9$ is the set of real numbers, what is the solution set for this equation?

29. If the replacement set for each of the following equations is the set of real numbers, find the solution set for each equation.
(a) $x^2 = 1$ (b) $x^2 = 0$ (c) $x^2 = -1$

30. If x is any real number, then $x + 1 > x$. Discuss, then, the truth value of the sentence $x + 1 = x$. What is the solution set of this equation?

4.2 The Principles of Inversion

In the next two sections we are concerned with "solving equations," and the method we use involves the "principles of inversion," which we introduce here.

Illustration 1

(a) $$(10 + 5) - 5 = 15 - 5$$

Hence,

$$(10 + 5) - 5 = 10 \tag{1}$$

(b) $$(7 - 11) + 11 = -4 + 11$$

Hence,

$$(7 - 11) + 11 = 7 \qquad (2)$$

(c) If we have an expression E to which we add 3, then we get $E + 3$. Now if we subtract 3 from the quantity $E + 3$ we get $(E + 3) - 3$, or simply $E + 3 - 3$, and this expression has the same value as the original expression E. Hence,

$$E + 3 - 3 = E \qquad (3)$$

Equations (1), (2), and (3) are particular cases of the "additive principle of inversion," which we now state.

4.2.1 Property (The Additive Principle of Inversion)

(i) If to an expression E we add the expression F, and then from this sum we subtract F, the result is the original expression E. Using symbols we write

$$(E + F) - F = E \qquad \text{and} \qquad (F + E) - F = E$$

or, equivalently,

$$E + F - F = E \qquad \text{and} \qquad F + E - F = E$$

(ii) If from an expression E we subtract the expression F, and then to this difference we add F, the result is the original expression E. Using symbols we write

$$(E - F) + F = E$$

or, equivalently,

$$E - F + F = E$$

Example 1 Use the Additive Principle of Inversion to evaluate each of the following expressions:

(a) $(3 - 8) + 8$
(c) $(3x + 5) - 9 + 9$

(b) $(7 - y) + y$
(d) $(8 + x) - 8$

Solution:

(a) $(3 - 8) + 8 = 3$
(b) $(7 - y) + y = 7$

(c) $(3x + 5) - 9 + 9 = (3x + 5) - 9 + 9$
$$= 3x + 5$$
(d) $(8 + x) - 8 = x$

Illustration 2

(a) $\qquad (10 \cdot 5) \div 5 = 50 \div 5$

Hence,
$$(10 \cdot 5) \div 5 = 10 \qquad\qquad (4)$$

(b) $\qquad (10 \div 5) \cdot 5 = 2 \cdot 5$

Hence,
$$(10 \div 5) \cdot 5 = 10 \qquad\qquad (5)$$

(c) If we multiply the expression E by 4, we get $E \cdot 4$. Now if we divide the quantity $E \cdot 4$ by 4 we get $(E \cdot 4) \div 4$, or simply $E \cdot 4 \div 4$, and this expression has the same value as the original expression E. Hence,
$$E \cdot 4 \div 4 = E \qquad\qquad (6)$$

Equations (4), (5), and (6) are particular cases of the "multiplicative principle of inversion," which we now state.

4.2.2 Property (The Multiplicative Principle of Inversion)

(i) If a given expression E is multiplied by the expression $F (F \neq 0)$, and then this product is divided by F, the result is the original expression E. Using symbols we write

$$(E \cdot F) \div F = E \qquad \text{and} \qquad (F \cdot E) \div F = E$$

or, equivalently,

$$\frac{E \cdot F}{F} = E \qquad \text{and} \qquad \frac{F \cdot E}{F} = E$$

(ii) If a given expression E is divided by an expression $F (F \neq 0)$, and then this quotient is multiplied by F, the result is the original expression E. Using symbols we write

$$(E \div F) \cdot F = E \qquad \text{and} \qquad F \cdot (E \div F) = E$$

or, equivalently,

$$\frac{E}{F} \cdot F = E \qquad \text{and} \qquad F \cdot \frac{E}{F} = E$$

Example 2 Use the Multiplicative Principle of Inversion to evaluate the following expressions:

(a) $(10x) \div 10$

(b) $(10x) \div x$

(c) $7 \cdot \dfrac{x}{7}$

(d) $\dfrac{4(x-3)}{4}$

(e) $\dfrac{2}{x+1}(x+1)$

(f) $\dfrac{x(x-1)}{x-1}$

Solution:

(a) $(10x) \div 10 = x$

(b) $(10x) \div x = 10$

(c) $7 \cdot \dfrac{x}{7} = x$

(d) $\dfrac{4(x-3)}{4} = x - 3$

(e) $\dfrac{2}{x+1}(x+1) = 2$

(f) $\dfrac{x(x-1)}{x-1} = x$

Example 3 Use the principles of inversion to evaluate each of the following expressions:

(a) $\dfrac{7x - 3 + 3}{7}$

(b) $\dfrac{5(x+4)}{5} - 4$

Solution:

(a) We first apply the Additive Principle of Inversion and then we apply the Multiplicative Principle of Inversion, and we have

$$\frac{7x - 3 + 3}{7} = \frac{7x}{7}$$

$$= x$$

(b) We first apply the Multiplicative Principle of Inversion and then we apply the Additive Principle of Inversion, and we have

$$\frac{5(x+4)}{5} - 4 = (x + 4) - 4$$

$$= x$$

Example 4 Someone says, "Take a number, add 5, double the result, subtract 10, divide by 2, add 4, and subtract your original number. Now your answer is 4." Show how this works.

Solution:

Take a number	:	x
Add 5	:	$x + 5$
Double the result	:	$2(x + 5) = 2x + 10$
Subtract 10	:	$(2x + 10) - 10$

Divide by 2 : $\dfrac{(2x + 10) - 10}{2}$

Add 4 : $\dfrac{(2x + 10) - 10}{2} + 4$

Subtract your original number : $\left[\dfrac{(2x + 10) - 10}{2} + 4\right] - x$

Now we must show that the expression on the last line equals 4. Thus,

$\left[\dfrac{(2x + 10) - 10}{2} + 4\right] - x = \left[\dfrac{2x}{2} + 4\right] - x$ By the Additive Principle of Inversion

$= [x + 4] - x$ By the Multiplicative Principle of Inversion

$= (4 + x) - x$ By the Commutative Law

$= 4$ By the Additive Principle of Inversion

Note that any number x may be chosen and the answer is always 4.

Exercises 4.2

In Exercises 1 through 30 use the Principles of Inversion to evaluate the given expression.

1. $14 + 3 - 3$
2. $7 \cdot 3 \div 3$
3. $8 - 6 + 6$

4. $0 \div 5 \cdot 5$
5. $3 + 7 - 3$
6. $7 + 7 - 7$

7. $5 + x - x$
8. $10 - 5x + 5x$
9. $2x + 1 + 8 - 8$

10. $7x \div 7$
11. $\dfrac{7x}{7}$
12. $\dfrac{x}{2} \cdot 2$

13. $\dfrac{5x}{2} \cdot 2$
14. $\dfrac{5x}{5}$
15. $\dfrac{9x - 1}{3} \cdot 3$

16. $(x - 1) \cdot 3 \div 3$
17. $3(x - 1) \div 3$
18. $\dfrac{3(x - 1)}{3}$

19. $\dfrac{3x + 1 - 1}{3}$
20. $\dfrac{2x - 5 + 5}{2}$

21. $\dfrac{8(x - 4)}{8} + 4$
22. $\dfrac{\frac{1}{2}(3x - 1)}{\frac{1}{2}} + 1$

23. $\dfrac{9(7x + 2)}{9} - 2$
24. $\dfrac{13(6x + 5)}{13} - 5$

25. $\left[\dfrac{17(3x+2)}{17} - 2\right] \div 3$

26. $\dfrac{5\left(x - \dfrac{1}{5}\right)}{5} + \dfrac{1}{5}$

27. $\left[\dfrac{10(3x-2)}{10} + 2\right] \div 3$

28. $14 - 20 + 20$

29. $2 - 5 + 5$

30. $0 - 10 + 10$

31. Someone says to you, "Take any number, add 10, double the result, subtract 20, divide by 2, add 5, and subtract your original number. Now, your answer is 5." Show how this works.

32. Someone says to you, "Take a number greater than 10, subtract 5, triple the result, add 15, subtract your original number, divide by 2, add 10, and subtract your original number plus 4. Now, your answer is 6." Show how this works.

33. As a variation of Exercises 31 and 32, and a good "parlor game," consider these instructions. Tell someone to write down the year of his birth without telling you what it is that he writes down. Next have him write down the year of any important event in his life. Now have him add these two numbers. To this have him also add his age as of this year. Also have him add the number of years since the important event as of this year. At this point you announce to him the sum of his four numbers, much to his amazement.

   The answer will always be two times this year's date. Show why this works.

34. Take a number, add 10, triple the result, subtract 30, double the result, divide by 6, and subtract your original number. What answer will you always get, regardless of the number with which you start? Why is this so?

4.3 Equivalent Equations

Determining the solution set of a conditional equation is called *solving* the equation. When solving an equation we use the concept of "equivalent equations."

4.3.1 Definition   Two equations are said to be *equivalent* if they have the same solution set.

Illustration 1
   (a) The equations

$$x - 8 = 5$$

and

$$x = 13$$

are equivalent equations because the solution set of each equation is {13}.
  (b) The equations

$$x + 7 = 11$$

and

$$x = 4$$

are equivalent equations because the solution set of each equation is {4}.
  (c) The equations

$$2x = 5$$

and

$$x = \frac{5}{2}$$

are equivalent equations because the solution set of each equation is $\left\{\frac{5}{2}\right\}$.

  (d) The equations

$$\frac{x}{3} = 9$$

and

$$x = 27$$

are equivalent equations because the solution set of each equation is {27}.

An equation equivalent to a given equation can be obtained by applying properties of the real numbers. Probably the most important such properties are the addition, subtraction, multiplication, and division principles of equality that are given in Theorems 4.3.2 through 4.3.5 which follow.

4.3.2 Theorem (Addition Principle of Equality)   If E, F, and G are algebraic expressions representing real numbers, and if

$$E = F$$

then

$$E + G = F + G$$

Proof: From the Reflexive Property of Equality (Axiom 1.5.1), we have

$$E + G = E + G \qquad (1)$$

By hypothesis, *E = F, and so we use the Substitution Property (Axiom 1.5.2)
and substitute F for E in the right member of equality (1). We have then*

$$E + G = F + G$$

and the theorem is proved.

Illustration 2   The first equation in Illustration 1(a) is

$$x - 8 = 5$$

From the Addition Principle of Equality (where *E* is *x* − 8, *F* is 5, and *G*
is 8), we can add 8 to each member of the equation, and we obtain

$$x - 8 + 8 = 5 + 8$$

The left member of this equation is *x* (from the Additive Principle of
Inversion) and the right member is 13; hence, we have

$$x = 13$$

which is the second equation in Illustration 1(a).

Example 1   Find the solution set of each of the following equations:
    (a) $x - 4 = -1$ (b) $x - 6 = {}^-10$

Solution:

(a)
$$x - 4 = -1$$
$$x - 4 + 4 = -1 + 4$$
$$x = 3$$

The solution set is {3}.
    (b)
$$x - 6 = {}^-10$$
$$x - 6 + 6 = {}^-10 + 6$$
$$x = {}^-4$$

The solution set is {⁻4}.

4.3.3 Theorem (Subtraction Principle of Equality)   If *E*, *F*, and *G* are
algebraic expressions representing real numbers, and if

$$E = F$$

then

$$E - G = F - G$$

Proof: From Theorem 4.3.2, because E = F, it follows that

$$E + (-G) = F + (-G)$$

However, $E + (-G) = E - G$ *and* $F + (-G) = F - G;$ *hence, we have*

$$E - G = F - G$$

and the theorem is proved.

Illustration 3 The second equation in Illustration 1(a) is

$$x = 13$$

From the Subtraction Principle of Equality we can subtract 8 from each member of this equation, and we have

$$x - 8 = 13 - 8$$

or, equivalently,

$$x - 8 = 5$$

which is the first equation in Illustration 1(a).

   In Illustration 2 we showed that if $x - 8 = 5$, then $x = 13$; and in Illustration 3 we showed that if $x = 13$, then $x - 8 = 5$. Therefore, the two equations of Illustration 1(a) are equivalent.

Example 2 Find the solution set of each of the following equations:
   (a) $x + 7 = 10$ (b) $8 + x = 2$

Solution:
   (a)
$$x + 7 = 10$$
$$x + 7 - 7 = 10 - 7$$
$$x = 3$$

The solution set is $\{3\}$.

   (b)
$$8 + x = 2$$
$$8 + x - 8 = 2 - 8$$
$$x = -6$$

The solution set is $\{-6\}$.

   A solution of an equation can be *checked* by substituting the solution for the variable in the given equation. In the following illustration we check the solutions found in Example 2.

Illustration 4
   (a) If $x = 3$, then

$$x + 7 = 3 + 7$$
$$= 10$$

Therefore, the solution of Example 2(a) checks.

(b) If $x = -6$, then
$$8 + x = 8 + (-6)$$
$$= 2$$

Therefore, the solution of Example 2(b) checks.

Example 3   Find the solution set of the equation
$$10 - x = 12$$

and check the solution.

Solution:
$$10 - x = 12$$
$$10 - x + x = 12 + x$$
$$10 = 12 + x$$
$$10 - 12 = 12 + x - 12$$
$$-2 = x$$
$$x = -2$$

The solution set is $\{-2\}$. If $x = -2$, then
$$10 - x = 10 - (-2)$$
$$= 10 + 2$$
$$= 12$$

Because 12 is the right member of the given equation, the solution checks.

4.3.4 Theorem (Multiplication Principle of Equality)   If E, F, and G are algebraic expressions representing real numbers, and if
$$E = F$$

then
$$E \cdot G = F \cdot G$$

Proof: From the Reflexive Property of Equality (Axiom 1.5.1), we have
$$E \cdot G = E \cdot G \qquad (2)$$
By hypothesis, $E = F$, and so we use the Substitution Property (Axiom 1.5.2) and substitute F for E in the right member of equality (2) and we have
$$E \cdot G = F \cdot G$$
and the theorem is proved.

Illustration 5   The first equation in Illustration 1(d) is
$$\frac{x}{3} = 9$$

From the Multiplication Principle of Equality, we multiply each member of this equation by 3, and we obtain

$$3 \cdot \frac{x}{3} = 3 \cdot 9$$

The left member of this equation is x (by the Multiplicative Principle of Inversion) and the right member is 27; hence, we have

$$x = 27$$

which is the second equation in Illustration 1(d).

Example 4 Find the solution set of each of the following equations and check.

(a) $\frac{x}{5} = 10$ 　　　　　　　　　　　(b) $\frac{x}{4} = -9$

Solution:

(a) 　　　　　　　　　　　$$\frac{x}{5} = 10$$

$$5 \cdot \frac{x}{5} = 5 \cdot 10$$

$$x = 50$$

The solution set is $\{50\}$. If $x = 50$, then

$$\frac{x}{5} = \frac{50}{5}$$

$$= 10$$

Because 10 is the right member of the given equation, the solution checks.

(b) 　　　　　　　　　　　$$\frac{x}{4} = -9$$

$$4 \cdot \frac{x}{4} = 4(-9)$$

$$x = -36$$

The solution set is $\{-36\}$. If $x = -36$, then

$$\frac{x}{4} = \frac{-36}{4}$$

$$= -9$$

Because -9 is the right member of the given equation, the solution checks.

4.3.5 Theorem (Division Principle of Equality)   If E, F, and G are algebraic expressions representing real numbers, and $G \neq 0$, and if

$$E = F$$

then

$$\frac{E}{G} = \frac{F}{G}$$

The proof of Theorem 4.3.5 is similar to the proof of Theorem 4.3.4 and is left as an exercise for the reader. See Exercise 31 at the end of this section.

Illustration 6. The second equation in Illustration 1(d) is

$$x = 27$$

From the Division Principle of Equality, we can divide each member of this equation by 3, and we have

$$\frac{x}{3} = \frac{27}{3}$$

or, equivalently,

$$\frac{x}{3} = 9$$

which is the first equation in Illustration 1(d).

In Illustration 5 we showed that if $\frac{x}{3} = 9$, then $x = 27$, and in Illustration 6 we showed that if $x = 27$, then $\frac{x}{3} = 9$. Hence, the two equations of Illustration 1(d) are equivalent.

Example 5   Find the solution set of each of the following equations and check.
   (a) $2x = -6$ (b) $5x = 12$

Solution:

   (a)
$$2x = -6$$
$$\frac{2x}{2} = \frac{-6}{2}$$
$$x = -3$$

The solution set is $\{-3\}$. If $x = -3$, then

$$2x = 2(-3)$$
$$= -6$$

Therefore, the solution checks because -6 is the right member of the given equation.

(b)
$$5x = 12$$
$$\frac{5x}{5} = \frac{12}{5}$$
$$x = \frac{12}{5}$$

The solution set is $\left\{\frac{12}{5}\right\}$. If $x = \frac{12}{5}$, then

$$5x = 5 \cdot \frac{12}{5}$$
$$= 12$$

Therefore, the solution checks because 12 is the right member of the given equation.

If $E = F$ is any equation, then from the Multiplication Principle of Equality, we can multiply both members of this equation by -1, and we have $-E = -F$. Thus, if E equals F, then the opposite of E equals the opposite of F.

Illustration 7 If $-x = 7$, then $-(-x) = -7$ or, equivalently,

$$x = -7$$

Example 6 Find the solution set of the equation

$$-x + 13 = 21$$

Solution:
$$-x + 13 = 21$$
$$-x + 13 - 13 = 21 - 13$$
$$-x = 8$$
$$x = -8$$

The solution set is $\{-8\}$.

Exercises 4.3

In Exercises 1 through 20, find the solution set of the given equation, and check.

1. $x + 6 = 9$

2. $4x = 20$

3. $x - 3 = 8$

4. $\frac{x}{4} = {}^-2$

5. $3x = {}^-18$

6. $x + 7 = 7$

7. $\frac{x}{3} = 3$

8. $x - 12 = -12$

9. $\frac{1}{2}x = 20$

10. $x + 2 = 0$ **11.** $x - \dfrac{2}{5} = 0$ **12.** $\dfrac{x}{2} = 28$

13. $6x = 15$ **14.** $10x = 0$ **15.** $x + 4 = 1$

16. $x - 1 = -1$ **17.** $\dfrac{x}{3} = \dfrac{2}{3}$ **18.** $x - 10 = 0$

19. $1 - x = 5$ **20.** $-x = {}^-9$

In Exercises 21 through 30 solve the given equation for x.

21. $-x + 4 = 6$ **22.** $-x + 8 = 20$

23. $-(x + 1) = -13$ **24.** ${}^-8 + (x + 1) = 0$

25. $x + {}^-7 = {}^-3$ **26.** $x + {}^-9 = 2$

27. $19 - x = -7$ **28.** $14 - x = {}^-17$

29. $23 - x = 18$ **30.** $-4x = -32$

31. Prove Theorem 4.3.5.

32. Prove: If $E = F$, then $-E = -F$.

33. Prove: If $E + G = F + G$, then $E = F$.

34. Prove: If $E \cdot G = F \cdot G$, then $E = F$.

35. Find a value for k in the equation $x + 3 = k$ so that this equation is equivalent to the equation $x - 1 = 10$.

4.4 Solving Equations

The following illustration gives a step-by-step procedure for solving a more complicated equation than we have so far considered.

Illustration 1   We wish to solve the equation

$$3x - 6 = 18$$
$$3x - 6 + 6 = 18 + 6 \quad \text{(We applied the Addition Principle of Equality.)}$$
$$3x = 24 \quad \text{(We applied the Additive Principle of Inversion in the left member.)}$$
$$\frac{3x}{3} = \frac{24}{3} \quad \text{(We applied the Division Principle of Equality.)}$$
$$x = 8 \quad \text{(We applied the Multiplicative Principle of Inversion in the left member.)}$$

The solution set is $\{8\}$.

When writing the subsequent equivalent equations used in solving an equation, we usually omit the equations that actually show the application of the Principles of Equality. We would omit the second and fourth equations of the step-by-step procedure in Illustration 1. Thus, we write

$$3x - 6 = 18$$
$$3x = 24$$
$$x = 8$$

We check the solution by substituting into the original equation. Doing this we have, if $x = 8$, then

$$3x - 6 = 3(8) - 6$$
$$= 24 - 6$$
$$= 18$$

Therefore, the solution checks because 18 is the right member of the original equation.

Solving an equation may be thought of as a series of operations performed on a beam balance. If we have the equation

$$3x - 6 = 18$$

we can think of the two members of this equation as being "balanced" on a beam. See Figure 4.4.1. By adding 6 to the numbers on both sides, this

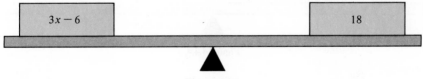

Figure 4.4.1

equation becomes

$$3x - 6 + 6 = 18 + 6$$

The balance is still maintained on the beam. See Figure 4.4.2. Now the quantity on the left is equivalent to $3x$ and the quantity on the right is

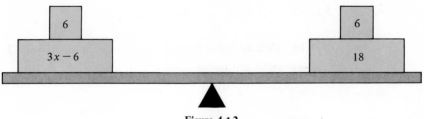

Figure 4.4.2

equivalent to 24. Thus, we have the equation

$$3x = 24$$

See Figure 4.4.3. Because $3x = x + x + x$ and $24 = 8 + 8 + 8$ we have

$$x + x + x = 8 + 8 + 8$$

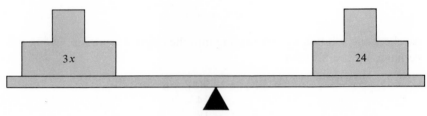

Figure 4.4.3

and so

$$x = 8$$

See Figure 4.4.4. We can obtain the same result by solving the equation

$$3x = 24$$

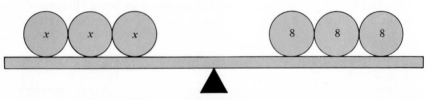

Figure 4.4.4

by using the Division Principle of Equality.

Example 1 Find the solution set of the equation

$$\frac{x}{5} - 5 = 13$$

and check.

Solution: $\frac{x}{5} - 5 = 13$

$\qquad\qquad \frac{x}{5} = 18$ (We added 5 to each member of the equation.)

$\qquad\qquad x = 90$ (We multiplied each member by 5.)

The solution set is {90}.

Check: if $x = 90$, then

$$\frac{x}{5} - 5 = \frac{90}{5} - 5$$
$$= 18 - 5$$
$$= 13$$

Therefore, the solution checks.

Example 2 Find the solution set of the equation
$$15 - 2x = 10$$

Solution:
$$15 - 2x = 10$$

$15 = 10 + 2x$ (We added $2x$ to each member.)

$5 = 2x$ (We subtracted 10 from each member.)

$\frac{5}{2} = x$ (We divided both members by 2.)

$x = \frac{5}{2}$ (We applied the Symmetric Property of Equality (Theorem 1.5.3).)

The solution set is $\left\{\frac{5}{2}\right\}$.

Example 3 Find the solution set of the equation
$$3x + 4x + 5 = 19$$

Solution:
$$3x + 4x + 5 = 19$$
$$7x + 5 = 19$$
$$7x = 14$$
$$x = 2$$

The solution set is $\{2\}$.

In the next illustration we give a step-by-step procedure for solving an equation in which the variable appears in both members of the equation. We wish to obtain an equivalent equation in which the terms involving the variable are on the same side of the equation.

Illustration 2 We wish to solve the equation

$3x + 2 = 4x - 1$

$3x + 2 - 3x = 4x - 1 - 3x$ (We subtracted $3x$ from each member.)

$2 + (3x - 3x) = (4x - 3x) - 1$ (We regrouped terms in each member.)

$2 = x - 1$ (We simplified each member.)

$2 + 1 = x - 1 + 1$ (We added 1 to each member.)

$3 = x$ (We applied the Additive Principle of Inversion in the right member.)

$x = 3$ (We applied the Symmetric Property of Equality.)

The solution set is $\{3\}$.

Example 4 Find the solution set of the equation

$$3(x + 2) + 4x = 2x - 4$$

Solution:
$$
\begin{aligned}
3(x + 2) + 4x &= 2x - 4 \\
3x + 6 + 4x &= 2x - 4 \\
7x + 6 &= 2x - 4 \\
5x + 6 &= -4 \\
5x &= -10 \\
x &= -2
\end{aligned}
$$

The solution set is $\{-2\}$.

Example 5 Find the solution set of the equation

$$\frac{5x - 3}{4} = x$$

Solution:

$$\frac{5x - 3}{4} = x$$

$$4\left(\frac{5x - 3}{4}\right) = 4x \qquad \text{(We multiplied each member by 4.)}$$

$$5x - 3 = 4x \qquad \text{(We applied the Multiplicative Principle of Inversion in the left member.)}$$

$$5x - 3 - 4x = 0 \qquad \text{(We subtracted } 4x \text{ from each member.)}$$

$$x - 3 = 0 \qquad \text{(We simplified the left member.)}$$

$$x = 3 \qquad \text{(We added 3 to each member.)}$$

The solution set is $\{3\}$.

Example 6 Find the solution set of the equation

$$4(x + 1) - x - 3 = 3x + 1$$

Solution:
$$
\begin{aligned}
4(x + 1) - x - 3 &= 3x + 1 \\
4x + 4 - x - 3 &= 3x + 1 \\
3x + 1 &= 3x + 1
\end{aligned}
$$

We note that this last equation is an identity. If we subtract $3x$ from each member, we get

$$1 = 1$$

which is also an identity. The significance of obtaining an identity is that the original equation is equivalent to an identity, and therefore, the solution set of the original equation is the universal set or the replacement set for the equation. The solution set is $\{x : x \in R\}$.

Not every statement of the form $E = F$, where E and F are algebraic expressions, is an equality. That is, there may be no replacement for the variable in the equation that makes the equation true. The solution set for such an equation is the empty set, $\varnothing$.

Illustration 3 If we have the equation

$$x = x + 1$$

and we subtract x from each member, we obtain

$$0 = 1$$

which is obviously a false statement. Hence, there is no value of x which satisfies the given equation. Thus, the solution set of the given equation is $\varnothing$.

Exercises 4.4

In Exercises 1 through 12 find the solution set of the given equation and check the solution.

1. $3x - 9 = 9$ 2. $4y - 2 = 18$ 3. $4x + 5 = -11$

4. $7x - 1 = 20$ 5. $3t = 0$ 6. $\dfrac{y}{2} - 3 = 15$

7. $\dfrac{2x}{5} = 3$ 8. $-13 = 7 - 3x$ 9. $2x + 5x = 35$

10. $\dfrac{4x}{3} = 1$ 11. $\dfrac{4x}{3} + 5 = 23$ 12. $\dfrac{1}{2}x + \dfrac{1}{2}x = 10$

In Exercises 13 through 28 find the solution set of the given equation.

13. (a) $12x - 3x = 27$ (b) $3y + y = -16$

14. (a) $4(y - 3) = 44$ (b) $5(x + 2) = -20$

15. (a) $5(2y - 3) = -15$ (b) $3(2x + 1) - 1 = 42$

16. (a) $5x = x + 8$ (b) $7x + 35 = 12x$

17. (a) $7x + 10 = 3x + 50$ (b) $t - 11 = 64 - 4t$

18. (a) $17 - 2x = 8$ (b) $8 - 3x = -4$

19. (a) $13 - 4x = -11$ (b) $25 - 7x = 4$

20. (a) $2 + 3y = 11 - 2y$ (b) $4x + 5 = 3x + 12$

21. (a) $3x + 1 = 2x + 1$ (b) $2x + 4 = 2x + 5$

22. (a) $7x - 4 = 5x - x + 35$ (b) $5y + 9 - 4y = 51 - 5y$

23. (a) $4x - 5 = x - 5 + 3x$ (b) $3(t - 5) = 2(t + 1)$

24. (a) $5(t + 2) + 7 = 5(2t - 3) - 8$
    (b) $15x + 3(x + 4) = 8x$

25. (a) $\dfrac{2x + 1}{3} = x$ (b) $\dfrac{3x - 1}{2} = x + 5$

26. (a) $\dfrac{5x + 2}{4} = 2x$ (b) $\dfrac{3x - 1}{2} - 5 = x$

27. (a) $6 - (x + 2) = -5$ (b) $\dfrac{6 - (4 - x)}{3} = x$

28. (a) $x + 2x + 3x + 4x = \dfrac{4(5)}{2}$

    (b) $x + 2x + 3x + 4x = \dfrac{5(4x)}{2}$

29. Find a value for k in the equation $2x - 3 = k$ so that this equation is equivalent to the equation $3 - x = 1$.

30. Find the solution set of the equation $3x = 2x + x$.

31. Find the solution set of the equation $3x = 2x$.

32. Find the solution set of the equation $3x = 3x - 3$.

4.5 Formulas and Literal Equations

The equation is a powerful tool for solving problems of many kinds. The problems we wish to solve can be classified into two types. The first type is the "ready-made" type. That is, some problems occur often enough that special equations, called *formulas*, are developed to solve these problems. The variables used in formulas usually represent the measure of some physical or geometrical quantity. Formulas are true because they express either a physical law that is determined by experiment or they are true by definition.

For instance, suppose we wish to find the Celsius temperature that corresponds to 86° Fahrenheit. This type of problem occurs often and there is a formula for solving it. If C is the number of degrees Celsius temperature and F is the number of degrees Fahrenheit temperature, then

$$C = \frac{5}{9}(F - 32)$$

Thus, if F = 86, then

$$C = \frac{5}{9}(86 - 32)$$

$$= \frac{5}{9}(54)$$

$$= 5(6)$$
$$= 30$$

Therefore, 30° Celsius corresponds to 86° Fahrenheit.

The second type of problem that we wish to solve is what we refer to as the "custom-made" type. That is, each problem has to be individually analyzed and an equation obtained to fit the conditions of the problem. We investigate many kinds of problems for which this is possible in the next section and in other chapters to follow.

In geometry we use formulas to find the volumes of solids and areas of plane regions. For instance, the formula for determining the area of the region enclosed by a rectangle is given by

$$A = lw$$

where l units is the length of the rectangle, w units is the width of the rectangle, and A square units is the area of the region enclosed by the rectangle. See Figure 4.5.1. The formula expresses A in terms of l and w.

Another familiar formula is the one for determining the area of the region enclosed by a circle. It is

$$A = \pi r^2$$

where r units is the radius of the circle and A square units is the area of the region enclosed by the circle. See Figure 4.5.2. In this formula the Greek

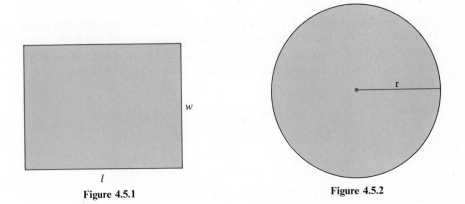

Figure 4.5.1   Figure 4.5.2

letter pi, π, represents a specific number approximately equal to 3.14. The number represented by π is called a *constant* in the formula.

Example 1 Which region has the greater area: the region enclosed by a rectangle with a length of 4 units and a width of 3 units, or the region enclosed by a circle with a radius of 2 units?

Solution: If A_1 square units is the area of the region enclosed by the rectangle, then A_1 is given by the formula

$$A_1 = lw$$

where $l = 4$ and $w = 3$. (Note: The 1 in the notation A_1 is called a subscript. The subscripted variable A_1 denotes a variable different from any of the variables A_2, A_3, etc.) Hence,

$$A_1 = (4)(3)$$
$$= 12$$

If A_2 is the area of the region enclosed by the circle, then A_2 is given by the formula

$$A_2 = \pi r^2$$

where $r = 2$. Therefore,

$$A_2 = \pi(2)^2$$
$$\doteq (3.14)(4) \quad \text{(read } \doteq \text{ as "approximately equal to")}$$
$$\doteq 12.56$$

Because A_2 is greater than A_1, the region enclosed by the circle has the greater area.

Example 2 The formula

$$s = 16t^2$$

represents the relationship of the time of travel to the distance traversed by a falling body. In the formula s feet is the distance of the body from the starting point t seconds after the body started to fall. Find the distance of a body from the starting point 4 seconds after it started to fall.

Solution: In the given formula, we replace t by 4 and we have

$$s = 16(4)^2$$
$$= 16(16)$$
$$= 256$$

Therefore, the distance a body falls in 4 seconds is 256 feet.

The equation

$$d = rt \qquad (1)$$

is a formula showing the relationship of the distance, d units; the rate of speed, r units of distance per unit of time; and the time, t units. We can solve equation (1) for either r or t. If we wish to solve for t, we divide both members of equation (1) by r $(r \neq 0)$, and obtain

$$\frac{d}{r} = t \qquad (2)$$

An equation, like equation (1), that has two or more variables or letters representing numbers, is sometimes called a *literal equation*. Most formulas are literal equations. The equation

$$ax + b = c$$

is also a literal equation.

Example 3 Solve the equation

$$ax + b = c$$

for x. Assume $a \neq 0$.

Solution:

$$ax + b = c$$
$$ax = c - b \quad \text{(We subtracted } b \text{ from each member.)}$$
$$x = \frac{c - b}{a} \quad \text{(We divided each member by } a.\text{)}$$

Example 4 Solve the following formula for C:

$$F = \frac{9}{5}C + 32$$

Solution:

$$F = \frac{9}{5}C + 32$$

$$F - 32 = \frac{9}{5}C \qquad \text{(We subtracted 32 from each member.)}$$

$$5(F - 32) = 5 \cdot \frac{9}{5}C \qquad \text{(We multiplied each member by 5.)}$$

$$5(F - 32) = 9C \qquad \text{(We applied the Multiplicative Principle of Inversion.)}$$

$$\frac{5(F - 32)}{9} = C \qquad \text{(We divided each member by 9.)}$$

Therefore,

$$C = \frac{5(F - 32)}{9}$$

As another example of a literal equation consider the formula for finding the volume of a *cylinder*. See Figure 4.5.3. If r = the number of units in the radius, h = the number of units in the height, and V = the number of cubic units in the volume of the cylinder, then

$$V = \pi r^2 h \qquad (3)$$

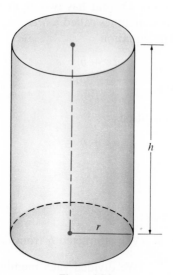

Figure 4.5.3

Example 5 Solve formula (3) for h.

Solution: If we divide each member of equation (3) by πr^2 we obtain

$$\frac{V}{\pi r^2} = h$$

or, equivalently,

$$h = \frac{V}{\pi r^2}$$

The measure, A, of the area of the region enclosed by a *trapezoid*, is given by the formula

$$A = \frac{1}{2}h(B + b) \qquad (4)$$

where B and b are the measures of the two bases and h is the measure of the altitude of the trapezoid shown in Figure 4.5.4.

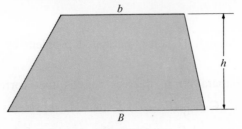

Figure 4.5.4

Example 6 Solve formula (4) for B.

Solution: $A = \dfrac{1}{2}h(B + b)$ (4)

Multiply both members of equation (4) by 2.

$$2A = h(B + b)$$ (5)

Divide both members of equation (5) by h.

$$\frac{2A}{h} = B + b$$ (6)

Subtract b from both members of equation (6).

$$\frac{2A}{h} - b = B$$

The equation in the next example requires the use of the Distributive Law for its solution.

Example 7 Solve the following equation for x if $a - c \neq 0$.

$$ax = b + cx$$ (7)

Solution: Subtract cx from both members of equation (7).

$$ax - cx = b$$ (8)

Use the Distributive Law and substitute $x(a - c)$ for $ax - cx$ in equation (8).

$$x(a - c) = b$$ (9)

Divide both members of equation (9) by $a - c$ (because $a - c \neq 0$)

$$x = \frac{b}{a - c}$$

In Exercises 1 through 11 solve the stated problem by using the given formula.

1. Find the temperature in degrees Celsius that corresponds to 100° Fahrenheit if $C = \dfrac{5}{9}(F - 32)$, where C represents the number of degrees Celsius and F represents the number of degrees Fahrenheit.

2. Find the distance, s feet, fallen by an object after 3 seconds if

$$s = 16t^2$$

where *t* seconds is the time of the fall.

3. Find the distance, s feet, fallen by an object after 4 seconds. See Exercise 2.

4. How far does an object fall during the 4th second of fall? See Exercises 2 and 3.

5. How fast is a particle moving if it travels at a constant velocity and covers 256 feet in 4 seconds? Use the formula

$$v = \frac{s}{t}$$

where *v* feet per second is the velocity, *s* feet is the distance, and *t* seconds is the time.

6. In a purely resistive electric circuit, if the applied voltage is E volts, the resistance is R ohms, and the current is I amperes,

$$E = RI$$

Find the applied voltage if a circuit has a resistance of 7 ohms and a current of 30 amperes.

7. Find the resistance of a circuit having an applied voltage of 12 volts and a current of 5 amperes. Refer to Exercise 6.

8. If the electric company charges C dollars for using an electrical appliance, then

$$C = \frac{wrt}{1000}$$

where *w* is the number of watts of power used by the appliance, *r* is the number of dollars charged for each kilowatt hour, and *t* is the number of hours that the appliance is used. Use the formula to find the cost of burning a 100 watt bulb for 24 hours if the rate is $3\dfrac{1}{2}$¢ per kilowatt hour ($0.035 per kilowatt hour, and so *r* = 0.035).

9. The sum of the whole numbers from 1 to n is given by the formula

$$S = \frac{n(n + 1)}{2}$$

Use this formula to find the sum of the counting numbers from 1 to 100.

10. If the measure of the volume of a pyramid is V, the measure of the area of the region enclosed by its base is B, and the measure of its height is h, then

$$V = \frac{1}{3} Bh$$

What is the volume of the pyramid shown in Figure 4.5.5?

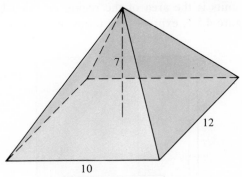

7

12

10

Figure 4.5.5

11. If the measure of the volume of a cone is V, the measure of the area of the region enclosed by its base is B, and the measure of its height is h, then

$$V = \frac{1}{3} Bh$$

If the base of a cone is a circle, then $B = \pi r^2$ where r is the number of units in the radius of the circle. Find the measure of the volume of a circular cone if $r = h = 6$. See Figure 4.5.6.

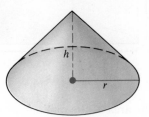

h

r

Figure 4.5.6

In Exercises 12 through 15 translate the given formula into algebraic symbols.

12. The measure A of the area of the region enclosed by a circle, is equal to the product of π and the square of the number r of units in the radius.

13. The number of square units in the area A of the region enclosed by a triangle, is equal to one half the number of units in its base b times the number of units in its altitude a.

14. The measure V of the volume of a cube is equal to the cube of the number e of units in the edge.

15. The number V of cubic units in the volume of a pyramid is equal to one third the number B of square units in the area of the region enclosed by its base multiplied by the number h of units in the altitude.

16. If A square units is the area of the region enclosed by the rectangle shown in Figure 4.5.7, express A in terms of x and y.

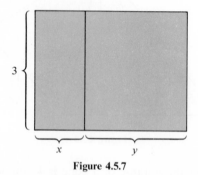

Figure 4.5.7

17. If A square units is the area of the region enclosed by the rectangle shown in Figure 4.5.8, express A in terms of a, b, x, and y.

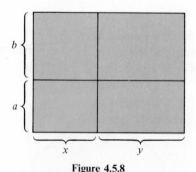

Figure 4.5.8

18. If A square units is the area of the region enclosed by the square shown in Figure 4.5.9, express A in terms of x and y.

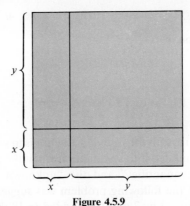

Figure 4.5.9

In Exercises 19 through 23 solve each equation for x or y, whichever appears.

19. (a) $5x = a$ **(b)** $x + 2 = m$

20. (a) $cy = 7$ **(b)** $2x + 1 = p$

21. (a) $b + x = a$ **(b)** $2(x + 4) = a$

22. (a) $\dfrac{x}{c} = 6$ **(b)** $a(x + 2) = b$

23. (a) $\dfrac{y}{r} = s$ **(b)** $A = \dfrac{hx}{2} \cdot (b + c)$

In Exercises 24 through 28 solve each equation for the indicated variable.

24. (a) $P = 2l + 2w$, for l **(b)** $x^2 + y^2 = r^2$, for y^2

25. (a) $A = lw$, for w **(b)** $C = 2\pi r$, for r

26. (a) $V = lwh$, for h **(b)** $V = \dfrac{1}{3}\pi r^2 h$, for h

27. (a) $C = \dfrac{5}{9}(F - 32)$, for F **(b)** $s = \dfrac{1}{2}gt^2$, for g

28. (a) $S = \dfrac{n + 1}{2}$, for n **(b)** $A = 2\pi rh$, for r

In Exercises 29 through 33, solve each equation for x. You may need to use the Distributive Law.

29. (a) $mx + nx = p$ **(b)** $mx = n + px$

30. (a) $mx + nx = m + n$ **(b)** $ax + b = mx + n$

31. (a) $ax - 2x = c$ **(b)** $ax - 2 = bx - 5$

32. (a) $3x - ax = a + b$ **(b)** $ax + bx = 10 - cx$

33. (a) $ax + 3 = 6x$ **(b)** $ax + mx + 10 = x$

34. Solve the equation $V = \dfrac{4}{3}\pi r^3$ for r^3.

4.6 Applications of Equations to Word Problems

One of the important reasons for studying algebra is to solve problems. Some problems can be formulated into an equation when the proper relationships between the "known quantities" and the "unknown quantities" are expressed. In Chapter 1 the following problem was suggested: find a number such that if it is multiplied by 7 and then added to 19 the result is the same as that number added to 91. To solve this problem we start by "defining the unknown."

Step 1. Let x represent the required number. Then

$$7x + 19 \quad \text{represents "19 added to seven times the number"}$$

and

$$x + 91 \quad \text{represents "91 added to the number"}$$

Step 2. The problem states that $7x + 19$ and $x + 91$ are equal, hence, we have the equation

$$7x + 19 = x + 91$$

Step 3. Solve the equation.

$$7x + 19 = x + 91$$
$$6x + 19 = 91$$
$$6x = 72$$
$$x = 12$$

The solution set of the equation is $\{12\}$.

Step 4. We check the solution to determine if it satisfies the conditions of the problem. Seven times 12 added to 19 is $84 + 19 = 103$, while 12 added to 91 is $12 + 91 = 103$. Therefore, 12 is the required number.

We used four basic steps to solve the preceding problem. We list these steps below to be used as a general guide that can be applied to help set up and solve word problems.

Step 1. Define the unknown(s).
Step 2. Write an equation involving the unknown(s).
Step 3. Solve the equation.
Step 4. Check the solution(s) of the equation to determine if the conditions of the problem are satisfied.

In order to write equations to solve word problems, we need to translate expressions found in the English language into algebraic expressions.

Example 1 Translate each of the following English expressions into algebraic expressions:
(a) Two times the sum of x and 5.
(b) Five more than the product of 2 and x.

Solution: (a) The phrase "the sum of x and 5" is written algebraically as $x + 5$. Thus, "two times the sum of x and 5" is written as

$$2(x + 5)$$

The parentheses are necessary to indicate the proper order of operations: first add x and 5, then multiply the sum by 2.

(b) The phrase "the product of 2 and x" is written algebraically as $2x$. Thus, "five more than the product of 2 and x" is written as

$$2x + 5$$

No parentheses are necessary here because the conventional order of operations is exactly what should occur.

Example 2 Translate each of the following expressions into algebraic symbols:
(a) The square of the sum of x and 3.
(b) The sum of the squares of x and 3.
(c) The other number if one number is x and the sum of the two numbers is 20.

Solution: (a) The phrase "the sum of x and 3" is written as $x + 3$. "The square of the sum of x and 3" is written as

$$(x + 3)^2$$

The parentheses are needed to assure the proper order of operations: first add x and 3, then square the sum.

(b) "The sum of the squares of x and 3" indicates the sum of two addends: the square of x, which is x^2, and the square of 3, which is 3^2. Hence, we write

$$x^2 + 3^2$$

No parentheses are necessary in this expression because the conventional order of operations is exactly what should occur.

(c) The other number is $20 - x$.

Example 3 The number of units in the length of a rectangle is three times the number of units in the width. The perimeter has a measurement of 40 units. Find the length and width. See Figure 4.6.1.

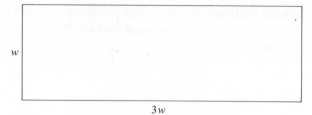

w

$3w$

Figure 4.6.1

Solution: Let w = the number of units in the width.

Then $3w$ = the number of units in the length.

The perimeter is the sum of the measures of the four sides. Hence, the required equation is

$$w + w + 3w + 3w = 40$$

We solve this equation for w and $3w$.

$$2w + 6w = 40$$
$$8w = 40$$
$$w = 5$$
$$3w = 15$$

Hence, the width is 5 units and the length is 15 units.

Example 4 Carl gained 8 pounds. If 8 pounds is one twentieth of his present weight, find his present weight.

Solution: Let x = the number of pounds in Carl's present weight. Then $\frac{1}{20}x$ = one twentieth of the number of pounds in Carl's present weight.

Hence, the required equation is

$$\frac{1}{20}x = 8$$

Multiplying both members by 20, we get

$$x = 160$$

Thus, Carl's present weight is 160 pounds.

Example 5 One number is four times another number. The sum of these numbers is 36. Find the numbers.

First Solution: Let x = the smaller number.

Then $4x$ = the larger number.

Hence, we have the equation

$$x + 4x = 36$$
$$5x = 36$$
$$x = \frac{36}{5}$$

Then

$$4x = 4\left(\frac{36}{5}\right)$$
$$= \frac{144}{5}$$

Thus, the two numbers are $\frac{36}{5}$ and $\frac{144}{5}$.

It is easy to verify that one number is four times the other number. However, we must also check to see if the sum of the two numbers is 36.

$$\frac{36}{5} + \frac{144}{5} = \frac{36 + 144}{5}$$
$$= \frac{180}{5}$$
$$= 36$$

Second Solution: Let $x =$ the larger number.

Then $36 - x =$ the smaller number.

Now because the larger number is four times the smaller number, we have the equation

$$x = 4(36 - x)$$

We solve the equation for x.

$$x = 4(36) - 4x$$
$$x = 144 - 4x$$
$$5x = 144$$
$$x = \frac{144}{5}$$

Then

$$36 - x = 36 - \frac{144}{5}$$
$$= \frac{180}{5} - \frac{144}{5}$$
$$= \frac{36}{5}$$

Thus, the two numbers are $\frac{144}{5}$ and $\frac{36}{5}$.

Example 6 Art is three times as old as Bill is now. Six years from now Bill will be half as old as Art is then. What is the present age of each person?

Solution: Let x years = Bill's present age. Then
$$3x \text{ years} = \text{Art's present age}$$
$$(x + 6) \text{ years} = \text{Bill's age six years from now}$$

and $(3x + 6)$ years = Art's age six years from now

Hence, we have the equation

$$x + 6 = \frac{1}{2}(3x + 6)$$

We solve the equation by first multiplying each member by 2.

$$2(x + 6) = 1(3x + 6)$$
$$2x + 12 = 3x + 6$$
$$12 = x + 6$$
$$6 = x$$

Then

$$3x = 18$$

Thus, Bill's present age is 6 years and Art's present age is 18 years.

Exercises 4.6

In Exercises 1 through 4 translate the given expression into algebraic symbols.

1. **(a)** x increased by 5   **(b)** 9 less than $4x$
   (c) x more than twice y **(d)** x decreased by $a + b$

2. **(a)** The product of 3 and the sum of a and b.
   (b) The sum of x and y divided by their product.
   (c) Twice x increased by the quantity five times y.
   (d) The quotient of y cubed and x squared.

3. **(a)** The sum of the squares of x and y.
   (b) The sum of x squared and y squared.
   (c) The sum of the squares of x and y is not equal to the square of the sum of x and y.
   (d) The difference between the squares of x and y is equal to the product of the sum and difference of x and y.

4. **(a)** The number of nickels required to equal the value of three dimes.
   (b) The number of nickels required to equal the value of n dimes.
   (c) The number of dollars in the cost of n cases of soda pop if one case costs three dollars. $C = n(\$3)$

(d) The number of dollars you have left if you had fourteen dollars and spent x dollars. $C = 14 - x$

5. (a) A line of length x units is divided into five equal parts. What is the number of units in each part?

(b) If you earn m dollars a day for x days and $m + n$ dollars a day for y days, how many dollars do you earn?

(c) If the sum of two numbers is 53 and one number is x, what is an expression for the other number?

(d) If a 20 foot board is cut into two parts and one part is x feet long, how long is the other part?

6. (a) Mary's mother is twice as old as Mary. If Mary's age is x years, how old is her mother?

(b) Mary's mother is twice as old as Mary. If Mary's age is x years, how old was her mother two years ago?

(d) In a class election a total of 66 votes are cast for two candidates. How many votes does the winner receive if the loser receives 29 votes?

(d) Refer to part (c). How many votes does the winner receive if the loser receives x votes?

In Exercises 7 through 12 write an equation for each problem and solve it.

7. (a) Five times a certain number equals 35. Find the number.

(b) A number decreased by 12 equals 15. Find the number.

8. (a) Four less than a number is 63. Find the number.

(b) Twice a number increased by 3 equals 21. Find the number.

9. (a) Five less than twice a certain number equals that number. Find the number.

(b) A number added to three times itself equals 60. Find the number.

10. (a) Twice a certain number equals itself. Find the number.

(b) Three times the number of years in Mark's age equals 24. Find Mark's age.

11. (a) Beth's age 12 years from now equals twice her present age. Find Beth's age now.

(b) One number is three times another number. The sum of the two numbers is -20. Find the numbers.

12. (a) The sum of eight times a number and 12 equals 60. Find the number.

(b) Eight times the sum of a number and 12 equals 60. Find the number.

13. The number of units in the length of a certain rectangle is twice the number of units in the width and the perimeter is 36 units. Find the length and width.

14. The number of units in the length of a certain rectangle is two more than the number of units in the width and the perimeter is 24 units. Find the length and width.

15. If 10 times a certain number is increased by 4, the result is 12 more than 9 times the number. Find the number.

 $12 = \frac{x}{15}$

16. Carl gained twelve pounds during the summer. If twelve pounds is one-fifteenth of his present weight, find his present weight.

17. Tom has 10 copper blocks. If he puts 3 blocks on one side of a beam balance with a 500 gram weight, he finds that these balance the other 7 blocks. How much does each block weigh? See Figure 4.6.2.

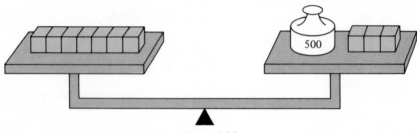

Figure 4.6.2

18. The sum of three numbers is 321. The first number is one less than the second while the third is one more than the second. What are the numbers?

19. The sum of two numbers is 40. Three times the smaller number is equal to twice the larger number. Find the numbers.

20. A mother is four times as old as her daughter. Five years ago the sum of their ages was 25. How old is each today?

21. A pen costs one dollar more than a pencil. The set cost $3.88. How much does each cost?

22. Every student in an English class of 34 students has read either book A or book B, and some students have read both books. If 21 students have read book A and 18 students have read book B, how many students have read both books?

4.7 Review Exercises

1. Classify each of the following equations as either a conditional equation or an identity.
   (a) $2x + 1 = x + 1 + x$ (b) $2x + 1 = x + 2$

2. Does $x^2 - 2x + 2x - 1 = 5$ if x is -2?

3. If x is -5, does $x^2 = 25$?

4. Use the Principles of Inversion to evaluate the given expression.

(a) $\dfrac{2(10) + 35 - 35}{2}$

(b) $\dfrac{5(2x - 1)}{5} + 1$

(c) $\dfrac{4(3x + 2)}{4} - 3x$

In Exercises 5 through 9 find the solution set of each equation.

5. (a) $x - 10 = 10$ (b) $2x + 5 = 1$

6. (a) $11 = 4x - 9$ (b) $2x + 7x = 12$

7. (a) $2x + 5 = 5x - 4$ (b) $3(2x + 5) = x + 15$

8. (a) $\dfrac{2x + 7}{4} = 2$ (b) $13 - 5x = -17$

9. (a) $\dfrac{-6y + 12}{10} = 4 - y$ (b) $2(5 - 8y) - y = -(y - 10)$

10. Find the temperature in degrees Fahrenheit that corresponds to $^-50°$ Celsius if

$$F = \frac{9C}{5} + 32$$

where F is the number of degrees Fahrenheit and C is the number of degrees Celsius.

11. If A square units is the total surface area of a cylinder, then

$$A = 2\pi r^2 + 2\pi rh$$

where r is the number of units in the radius of the circular base of the cylinder and h is the measure of the height of the cylinder. See Figure 4.7.1. Solve the formula for h.

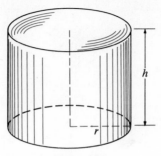

Figure 4.7.1

In Exercises 12 through 14 solve each equation for either x or y, whichever appears.

12. (a) $a - bx = c$ (b) $a(x + 1) = b + a$

13. (a) $\dfrac{ax}{b} - 1 = c$ (b) $mx + nx = 10$

14. (a) $18a = 3a - 5y$ (b) $mv = \dfrac{x}{v}$

15. A line of length 40 units is separated into two parts. If the shorter piece is x units long, what expression represents the number of units in the length of the other piece?

16. The sum of two numbers is 42. The larger number is 2 less than three times the smaller number. Find the numbers.

17. The number of units in the length of a rectangle is 5 more than the number of units in the width. If the perimeter is 20 units, find the length and width.

18. A customer purchases an item which is "On Sale" for $15. As she pays for the item the clerk tells her that the item was reduced for sale by one third of the original price. What was the original price of the item?

19. In a school of 1800 students everyone took either a course in algebra or a course in arithmetic or both. If 1400 students took a course in arithmetic and 1024 students took a course in algebra, how many students took both courses?

20. A man is 27 years older than his colleague. Together they have 45 years total professional experience. If each man entered the profession at age 24 years, what are their present ages?

5

The Rational Numbers

5.1 The Prime Numbers

The set of "prime numbers" is an important subset of the set of natural numbers. Before we give a definition of a "prime number" we consider the concept of "divisibility."

If 13 is divided by 3, there is a remainder equal to 1. If 12 is divided by 3, the remainder is 0. Hence, we say that 12 is "divisible" by 3 and that 3 *divides* 12. In general, if the remainder is zero when a whole number is divided by a natural number, then the whole number is "divisible" by the natural number and the natural number *divides* the whole number. Furthermore, the whole number is a multiple of the natural number.

Illustration 1   The whole number 12 is divisible by 3 because 12 is a multiple of 3. That is,

$$12 = 4 \cdot 3$$

The number 3 divides 12.

5.1.1 Definition   A whole number b is *divisible* by a natural number a if and only if

$$b = ka$$

where k is a whole number. The number a is called a *divisor* (or a *factor*) of b.

Illustration 2   The natural number 3 is a divisor (or a factor) of the whole number 12 because 12 is divisible by 3.

Example 1   List all of the factors of 12.

Solution: Because $12 = 1 \cdot 12$, $12 = 2 \cdot 6$, and $12 = 3 \cdot 4$, the set of factors of 12 is $\{1, 2, 3, 4, 6, 12\}$.

Example 2 List all of the factors of 5.

Solution: The set of factors of 5 is $\{1,5\}$.

Because the set of factors of 5 consists of only two numbers, 1 and 5, the number 5 is called a "prime number." In general, a "prime number" is a natural number, other than 1, whose only factors are 1 and itself.

5.1.2 Definition   A *prime number* is a natural number that has two and only two distinct factors.

Illustration 3 (a) The natural number 7 is a prime number because 1 and 7 are the only two factors of 7.

(b) The natural number 12 is not a prime number because 12 has six factors. See Example 1.

(c) The natural number 1 is not a prime number because 1 does not have two distinct factors. The only factor of 1 is 1.

The smallest prime number is 2 and Euclid, a Greek mathematician, ca. 300 B.C., proved that there is no largest prime number. There is a table of prime numbers in the appendix. The set of prime numbers less than 50 is

$$\{2, 3, 5, 7, 11, 13, 17, 19, 23, 29, 31, 37, 41, 43, 47\}$$

A natural number greater than 1 that is not a prime number is called a "composite number." The natural number 12 is a composite number.

5.1.3 Definition   A *composite number* is a natural number that has more than two distinct factors.

Illustration 4 The set of composite numbers less than 20 is $\{4, 6, 8, 9, 10, 12, 14, 15, 16, 18\}$.

Example 3 List all of the factors of each of the following composite numbers.
  (a) 4   (b) 6   (c) 8   (d) 9

Solution:
  (a) $\{1, 2, 4\}$ (b) $\{1, 2, 3, 6\}$
  (c) $\{1, 2, 4, 8\}$ (d) $\{1, 3, 9\}$

A property of whole numbers called the Fundamental Theorem of Arithmetic emphasizes the importance of the prime numbers.

5.1.4 Property (The Fundamental Theorem of Arithmetic)   Every composite number can be expressed uniquely as a product of prime numbers, and this expression is called the *prime factored form* of the composite number.

Illustration 5   Because $42 = 2 \cdot 3 \cdot 7$, the numbers 2, 3, and 7 are the prime factors of 42, and the product $2 \cdot 3 \cdot 7$ is called the prime factored form of 42. Note that the expression $2 \cdot 3 \cdot 7$ is not considered to be different from the expression $7 \cdot 3 \cdot 2$.

Example 4   Express 220 as a product of its prime factors.

Solution:
$$
\begin{aligned}
220 &= 10 \cdot 22 \\
&= (2 \cdot 5) \cdot (2 \cdot 11) \\
&= (2 \cdot 2) \cdot (5 \cdot 11) \\
&= 2^2 \cdot 5 \cdot 11
\end{aligned}
$$

Example 5   Express 408 in its prime factored form.

Solution:
$$
\begin{aligned}
408 &= 2 \cdot 204 \\
&= 2 \cdot (2 \cdot 102) \\
&= 2 \cdot 2 \cdot (2 \cdot 51) \\
&= 2 \cdot 2 \cdot 2 \cdot (3 \cdot 17) \\
&= 2^3 \cdot 3 \cdot 17
\end{aligned}
$$

There are many unanswered questions concerning prime numbers. For example, can every even composite number be expressed as the sum of two prime numbers. This question has not been answered. The plausibility of its being true was conjectured by C. Goldback in 1742. For example,

$$
\begin{aligned}
12 &= 5 + 7 \\
8 &= 5 + 3 \\
30 &= 7 + 23
\end{aligned}
$$

However, no one has proved that Goldback's conjecture is true for all even composite numbers, and no one has been able to find an even composite number for which Goldback's conjecture is not true.

Table 5.1.1 shows which of the natural numbers less than 30 are composite numbers and which are prime numbers. The columns in the table show a given natural number at the top and its other factors beneath it. Those natural numbers with only a 1 beneath them are the prime numbers. Table 5.1.1 can be extended to natural numbers greater than or equal to 30; the result is based on a process called the Sieve of Eratosthenes, a Greek mathematician, ca. 200 B.C.

The number 4 is a factor of both 8 and 12. We say that 4 is a *common factor* of the numbers 8 and 12. The set of common factors of the numbers

Table 5.1.1

1	2	3	4	5	6	7	8	9	10	11	12	13	14	15	16	17	18	19	20	21	22	23	24	25	26	27	28	29
	1		2		3		4		5		6		7		8		9		10		11		12		13		14	
		1			2			3			4			5			6			7			8			9		
			1				2				3				4				5				6				7	
				1					2					3					4					5				
					1						2						3						4					
						1							2							3							4	
							1								2								3					
								1									2									3		
									1										2									
										1											2							
											1												2					
												1													2			
													1														2	
														1														
															1													
																1												
																	1											
																		1										
																			1									
																				1								
																					1							
																						1						
																							1					
																								1				
																									1			
																										1		
																											1	
																												1

8 and 12 is the intersection of the set of factors of 8 and the set of factors of 12.

Illustration 6 Let $S = \{x : x \text{ is a factor of } 8\}$ and $T = \{x : x \text{ is a factor of } 12\}$. From Table 5.1.1 we find that $S = \{1, 2, 4, 8\}$ and $T = \{1, 2, 3, 4, 6, 12\}$. The set of common factors of the numbers 8 and 12 is

$$S \cap T = \{1, 2, 4\}$$

We now define the concept of "greatest common divisor" of a pair of natural numbers. This concept is useful when reducing fractions to "lowest terms," which is discussed in Section 5.3.

5.1.5 Definition   The *greatest common divisor* (GCD) of a set of natural numbers is the greatest natural number that is a divisor (or a factor) of each of the given numbers.

The greatest common divisor is sometimes called the *highest common factor*.

Example 6 Find the greatest common divisor of 18 and 24.

Solution: Let $S = \{x : x \text{ is a divisor of } 18\}$
and $T = \{x : x \text{ is a divisor of } 24\}$

From Table 5.1.1 we find that,

$$S = \{1, 2, 3, 6, 9, 18\}$$

and $$T = \{1, 2, 3, 4, 6, 8, 12, 24\}$$

Therefore, the set of *common* divisors of 18 and 24 is

$$S \cap T = \{1, 2, 3, 6\}$$

The greatest of the elements of $S \cap T$ is 6. Therefore, the greatest common divisor of 18 and 24 is 6.

Example 7 Find the greatest common divisor of 6 and 35.

Solution: Let $S = \{x : x \text{ is a divisor of } 6\}$
$= \{1, 2, 3, 6\}$
Let $T = \{x : x \text{ is a divisor of } 35\}$
$= \{1, 5, 7, 35\}$

The set of common divisors of 6 and 35 is

$$S \cap T = \{1\}$$

Hence, the greatest common divisor of 6 and 35 is 1.

The concept of "least common multiple," given in the following definition, is useful when adding rational numbers, which is discussed in Section 5.5.

5.1.6 Definition   The *least common multiple* (LCM) of a set of natural numbers is the smallest natural number that contains each of the given numbers as a divisor.

Example 8 Find the least common multiple of 6 and 8.

Solution: Let $S = \{x : x \text{ is a natural multiple of 6}\}$
$= \{6, 12, 18, 24, 30, 36, 42, 48, \ldots\}$
Let $T = \{x : x \text{ is a natural multiple of 8}\}$
$= \{8, 16, 24, 32, 40, 48, 54, \ldots\}$

Therefore, the set of common multiples of 6 and 8 is

$$S \cap T = \{24, 48, \ldots\}$$

The smallest of the elements of $S \cap T$ is 24. Therefore, the least common multiple of 6 and 8 is 24.

Example 9 Find the GCD and LCM of the numbers 72 and 60.

Solution: We express each number as a product of prime factors.

$$72 = 2 \cdot 2 \cdot 2 \cdot 3 \cdot 3$$
$$60 = 2 \cdot 2 \cdot 3 \cdot 5$$

By "tagging" each factor with a subscript to distinguish the equal factors we can form the set, P_{72}, of prime factors of 72 and the set, P_{60}, of prime factors of 60. We have

$$P_{72} = \{2_1, 2_2, 2_3, 3_1, 3_2\}$$
$$P_{60} = \{2_1, 2_2, 3_1, 5_1\}$$

Hence, the set of prime factors of the GCD is

$$P_{72} \cap P_{60} = \{2_1, 2_2, 3_1\}$$

Therefore the GCD is $2 \cdot 2 \cdot 3 = 12$.
    The set of prime factors of the LCM is

$$P_{72} \cup P_{60} = \{2_1, 2_2, 2_3, 3_1, 3_2, 5_1\}$$

Therefore, the LCM is $2 \cdot 2 \cdot 2 \cdot 3 \cdot 3 \cdot 5 = 360$.

Example 10 Find the GCD and LCM of the numbers 420, 600, and 900.

Solution: We express each number as a product of prime factors.

$$420 = 10 \cdot 42 \qquad\qquad 600 = 100 \cdot 6 \qquad\qquad 900 = 100 \cdot 9$$
$$= 2 \cdot 5 \cdot 6 \cdot 7 \qquad\qquad = 10 \cdot 10 \cdot 2 \cdot 3 \qquad\qquad = 10 \cdot 10 \cdot 3 \cdot 3$$
$$= 2 \cdot 5 \cdot 2 \cdot 3 \cdot 7 \qquad\qquad = 2 \cdot 5 \cdot 2 \cdot 5 \cdot 2 \cdot 3 \qquad\qquad = 2 \cdot 5 \cdot 2 \cdot 5 \cdot 3 \cdot 3$$
$$= 2^2 \cdot 3 \cdot 5 \cdot 7 \qquad\qquad = 2^3 \cdot 3 \cdot 5^2 \qquad\qquad = 2^2 \cdot 3^2 \cdot 5^2$$

If P_{420} is the set of prime factors of 420, then

$$P_{420} = \{2_1, 2_2, 3_1, 5_1, 7_1\}$$

If P_{600} is the set of prime factors of 600, then

$$P_{600} = \{2_1, 2_2, 2_3, 3_1, 5_1, 5_2\}$$

If P_{900} is the set of prime factors of 900, then

$$P_{900} = \{2_1, 2_2, 3_1, 3_2, 5_1, 5_2\}$$

The set of prime factors of the GCD is

$$P_{420} \cap P_{600} \cap P_{900} = \{2_1, 2_2, 3_1, 5_1\}$$

Therefore, the GCD is

$$2 \cdot 2 \cdot 3 \cdot 5 = 60$$

The set of prime factors of the LCM is

$$P_{420} \cup P_{600} \cup P_{900} = \{2_1, 2_2, 2_3, 3_1, 3_2, 5_1, 5_2, 7_1\}$$

Therefore, the LCM is

$$2 \cdot 2 \cdot 2 \cdot 3 \cdot 3 \cdot 5 \cdot 5 \cdot 7 = 12{,}600$$

If the intersection of the sets of prime factors of the given numbers is empty, then the GCD of the set of numbers is 1.

Example 11 Find the GCD and LCM of the numbers 15, 20, and 21.

Solution: $15 = 3 \cdot 5$
$20 = 2 \cdot 2 \cdot 5$
$21 = 3 \cdot 7$

Thus,

$$P_{15} = \{3_1, 5_1\}$$
$$P_{20} = \{2_1, 2_2, 5_1\}$$
$$P_{21} = \{3_1, 7_1\}$$

Hence,

$$P_{15} \cap P_{20} \cap P_{21} = \varnothing$$

Therefore, the GCD is 1.

$$P_{15} \cup P_{20} \cup P_{21} = \{2_1, 2_2, 3_1, 5_1, 7_1\}$$

Therefore, the LCM is $2 \cdot 2 \cdot 3 \cdot 5 \cdot 7 = 420$.

In Exercises 1 through 16 express the number as a product of prime factors.

1. 9	**2.** 8	**3.** 16	**4.** 24
5. 36	**6.** 200	**7.** 405	**8.** 360
9. 105	**10.** 132	**11.** 196	**12.** 78
13. 91	**14.** 71	**15.** 51	**16.** 57

In Exercises 17 through 25 find the LCM and GCD of the set of numbers.

17. $\{12, 16\}$	**18.** $\{8, 10\}$	**19.** $\{12, 27\}$
20. $\{7, 11\}$	**21.** $\{21, 44\}$	**22.** $\{90, 210\}$
23. $\{18, 24, 36\}$	**24.** $\{12, 15, 18\}$	**25.** $\{8, 12, 36, 40\}$

26. If a is divisible by b and b is divisible by c, does it follow that a is divisible by c? Choose some numbers, and test your answer.

27. Why is the number 1 not a prime number?

28. We know that prime numbers have just two factors. What kind of numbers have just 3 factors?

29. Some composite numbers have an even number of factors, and some have an odd number of factors. What kind of composite numbers have an odd number of factors?

30. If $P = \{x : x$ is a prime number$\}$ and $E = \{x : x$ is an even whole number$\}$, find $P \cap E$.

31. Is $P \subseteq W$? Is P an infinite set? See Exercise 30.

32. Goldbach's conjecture states that every even composite number can be expressed as the sum of two prime numbers. Verify this for all of the even composite numbers up to and including 30.

33. Consecutive odd numbers which are also prime numbers, such as 3 and 5, or 5 and 7, or 11 and 13 are known as "twin primes." Find three more pairs of twin primes.

34. Suppose the operation of finding the greatest common divisor is denoted by $\uparrow$; that is, $a \uparrow b =$ the GCD of a and b.
(a) Is the operation $\uparrow$ a closed operation in the set of natural numbers?
(b) Is the operation $\uparrow$ a commutative operation?
(c) Is the operation $\uparrow$ an associative operation?

35. Define $a \downarrow b =$ the LCM of a and b. Answer the same questions as in Exercise 34 for the operation $\downarrow$.

36. Using the definitions of $\downarrow$ and $\uparrow$ given in Exercises 34 and 35, test to see if $6 \downarrow (8 \uparrow 10)$ equals $(6 \downarrow 8) \uparrow (6 \downarrow 10)$. Choose three more numbers a, b, and c and test to see if $a \downarrow (b \uparrow c)$ equals $(a \downarrow b) \uparrow (a \downarrow c)$. Does it appear that the operation $\downarrow$ is distributive with respect to the operation $\uparrow$?

37. Find the GCD and LCM of 10 and 36. Does $10 \cdot 36$ equal (GCD of 10 and 36) $\cdot$ (LCM of 10 and 36)? Using other pairs of numbers perform this same experiment. Does this appear to be a valid property; that is, given two natural numbers a and b, does ab equal $(a \uparrow b) \cdot (a \downarrow b)$? See Exercises 34 and 35.

38. If the prime factors of a number n are a, b, and c $(n = abc)$, then what are the prime factors of n^2? Write n^2 as a product of prime factors.

39. If n^2 is even (that is, 2 is a factor of n^2) then does it follow that n is even?

40. Find the GCD and LCM of n and n^2.

5.2 Rational Numbers and Fractions

The "rational numbers" are necessary to determine one of the factors of a product when the other factor and the product are known. For instance, what number multiplied by 4 gives the product 3? This question can be answered by solving the equation

$$4x = 3 \tag{1}$$

The solution is not an integer; it is a "rational number." Solving equation (1) we divide 3 by 4. The quotient, $3 \div 4$, is a rational number.

In general, a rational number is the quotient of two integers a and b $(b \neq 0)$, which is written $a \div b$. Another symbol that is used to denote a rational number is a "fraction."

5.2.1 Definition   A *fraction* is a numeral in the form

$$\frac{a}{b}$$

where $a, b \in R$ and $b \neq 0$. The number a is called the *numerator* of the fraction and the number b is called the *denominator* of the fraction.

If both a and b are integers $(b \neq 0)$, then the fraction $\frac{a}{b}$ is a numeral (symbol) for a rational number.

Illustration 1   The numeral $\frac{3}{4}$ is a fraction in which 3 is the numerator and

4 is the denominator. This fraction represents the rational number that is the quotient of 3 divided by 4; that is

$$\frac{3}{4} = 3 \div 4$$

Illustration 2 The numeral $\frac{6}{8}$ is a fraction in which 6 is the numerator and 8 is the denominator. This fraction represents the solution of the equation

$$8x = 6 \qquad\qquad\qquad (2)$$

and it is the number that multiplied by 8 gives a product of 6.

5.2.2 Definition   A *rational number* is a number which is the solution of an equation of the form

$$bx = a$$

where a and b are integers and $b \neq 0$. This rational number is represented by the fraction $\frac{a}{b}$.

The solution of equation (1) is the rational number $\frac{3}{4}$ and the solution of equation (2) is the rational number $\frac{6}{8}$. Note that equations (1) and (2) are equivalent equations because if both members of equation (2) are divided by 2 we obtain equation (1). Hence, the rational number which is the solution of equation (1) is the same as the rational number which is the solution of equation (2). Therefore, the fractions $\frac{3}{4}$ and $\frac{6}{8}$ represent the same rational number. Actually, there are many other fractions which also represent this rational number. Some of them are

$$\frac{9}{12}, \quad \frac{15}{20}, \quad \frac{30}{40}, \quad \frac{-3}{-4}, \quad \frac{-6}{-8}, \quad \frac{300}{400}, \quad \frac{75}{100}, \quad \text{and} \quad \frac{3x}{4x} (x \neq 0)$$

All of these fractions are "equivalent."

5.2.3 Definition   The fraction $\frac{a}{b}$ is *equivalent* to the fraction $\frac{x}{y}$ if and only if

$$ay = bx$$

Illustration 3 (a) The fraction $\frac{3}{4}$ is equivalent to the fraction $\frac{6}{8}$ because

$$3 \cdot 8 = 4 \cdot 6$$

(b) The fraction $\frac{3}{4}$ is equivalent to the fraction $\frac{-3}{-4}$ because

$$3(-4) = 4(-3)$$

(c) The fraction $\frac{3}{4}$ is equivalent to $\frac{3x}{4x}$ $(x \neq 0)$ because

$$3(4x) = 4(3x)$$

Example 1   Are $\frac{39}{91}$ and $\frac{3}{7}$ equivalent fractions?

Solution: By Definition 5.2.3, $\frac{39}{91}$ is equivalent to $\frac{3}{7}$ if and only if $39 \cdot 7 = 91 \cdot 3$.

$$39 \cdot 7 = 273 \quad \text{and} \quad 91 \cdot 3 = 273$$

Therefore, $39 \cdot 7 = 91 \cdot 3$. Hence, $\frac{39}{91}$ and $\frac{3}{7}$ are equivalent fractions.

Every integer is a rational number because every integer can be represented as the quotient of itself and 1; for instance, 5 can be represented by $\frac{5}{1}$ (the quotient of 5 and 1), 0 can be represented by $\frac{0}{1}$, and -14 can be represented by $\frac{-14}{1}$. In a similar way we can show that every integer is a rational number and it can be represented by a fraction in which the numerator is the given integer and the denominator is 1. Because every integer is a rational number, the set of integers is a subset of the set of rational numbers. We denote the set of rational numbers by Q, and so we write

$$J \subseteq Q$$

To indicate a listing of the set of rational numbers we display a table of the fractions representing the rational numbers. Table 5.2.1 shows how a display of fractions representing the positive rational numbers is constructed.

The listing of the rational numbers by the method shown in Table 5.2.1 does not omit any positive rational number. In particular, the rational number represented by $\frac{17}{64}$ is listed in the 64th column and the 17th row. Note that because of equivalent fractions, each rational number is listed many

Table 5.2.1 The Positive Rational Numbers

	Natural Numbers	*The Halves*	*The Thirds*	*The Fourths*	*The Fifths*	*The Sixths*	*etc.*
Numerator 1	$\dfrac{1}{1}$	$\dfrac{1}{2}$	$\dfrac{1}{3}$	$\dfrac{1}{4}$	$\dfrac{1}{5}$	$\dfrac{1}{6}$	...
Numerator 2	$\dfrac{2}{1}$	$\dfrac{2}{2}$	$\dfrac{2}{3}$	$\dfrac{2}{4}$	$\dfrac{2}{5}$	$\dfrac{2}{6}$	...
Numerator 3	$\dfrac{3}{1}$	$\dfrac{3}{2}$	$\dfrac{3}{3}$	$\dfrac{3}{4}$	$\dfrac{3}{5}$	$\dfrac{3}{6}$	...
Numerator 4	$\dfrac{4}{1}$	$\dfrac{4}{2}$	$\dfrac{4}{3}$	$\dfrac{4}{4}$	$\dfrac{4}{5}$	$\dfrac{4}{6}$	...
Numerator 5	$\dfrac{5}{1}$	$\dfrac{5}{2}$	$\dfrac{5}{3}$	$\dfrac{5}{4}$	$\dfrac{5}{5}$	$\dfrac{5}{6}$	...
etc.	$\vdots$	$\vdots$	$\vdots$	$\vdots$	$\vdots$	$\vdots$	

times in Table 5.2.1. For instance, the fractions $\dfrac{1}{1}, \dfrac{2}{2}, \dfrac{3}{3}, \dfrac{4}{4}$, and so on are all representations for the same rational number.

The rational numbers listed in Table 5.2.1 in the top row belong to a subset of the set of rational numbers called the set of the "reciprocals" of the natural numbers. Every nonzero real number has a reciprocal.

5.2.4 Definition   If b is a real number, other than zero, then the quotient

$$\frac{1}{b}$$

is called the *reciprocal* of b.

If $b \neq 0$, then $\dfrac{1}{b}$ is the solution of the equation

$$bx = 1$$

The reciprocal of b then is the number which when multiplied by b gives a product of 1; that is,

$$b \cdot \frac{1}{b} = 1 \quad \text{and} \quad \frac{1}{b} \cdot b = 1$$

5.2.5 Axiom   For each nonzero real number b there exists exactly one reciprocal real number $\dfrac{1}{b}$, such that

$$b \cdot \frac{1}{b} = 1$$

Illustration 4   (a) The reciprocal of 6 is $\dfrac{1}{6}$, and

$$6 \cdot \frac{1}{6} = 1 \qquad \text{and} \qquad \frac{1}{6} \cdot 6 = 1$$

(b) The reciprocal of -4 is $\dfrac{1}{-4}$, and

$$(-4) \cdot \frac{1}{-4} = 1 \qquad \text{and} \qquad \frac{1}{-4} \cdot (-4) = 1$$

Illustration 5   From Definition 5.2.4 the reciprocal of $\dfrac{1}{6}$ is

$$\dfrac{1}{\dfrac{1}{6}}$$

However, because of Axiom 5.2.5, there exists exactly one real number that is the reciprocal of $\dfrac{1}{6}$ and that number when multiplied by $\dfrac{1}{6}$ gives a product of 1. We know from Illustration 4(a) that $\dfrac{1}{6} \cdot 6 = 1$, therefore, 6 is the reciprocal of $\dfrac{1}{6}$. Hence, it follows that

$$\dfrac{1}{\dfrac{1}{6}} = 6$$

That is, the reciprocal of $\dfrac{1}{6}$ is 6 and the reciprocal of 6 is $\dfrac{1}{6}$; 6 and $\dfrac{1}{6}$ are reciprocals of each other.

In general, the reciprocal of $\dfrac{1}{b}$ ($b \neq 0$) is b. The concept of the reciprocal of a number is similar to that of the opposite of a number. For example, the opposite of the oppposite of 4 is 4; that is,

$$-(-6) = 6$$

and the reciprocal of the reciprocal of 6 is 6; that is,

$$\dfrac{1}{\dfrac{1}{6}} = 6$$

As another example consider Axiom 5.2.5 and Axiom 3.1.1. Axiom 3.1.1 states that for each integer k there exists exactly one integer, the opposite of k, such that the sum of k and the opposite of k is equal to zero, which is the additive identity element. Axiom 3.1.1 is later called the Additive Inverse Law. Axiom 5.2.5 states that for each real number b ($b \neq 0$) there exists exactly one real number, the reciprocal of b, such that the product of b and the reciprocal of b is equal to 1, which is the multiplicative identity element. Axiom 3.1.1 refers to integers; however we will assume, subsequently, that the Additive Inverse Law is also true for real numbers. Axioms 3.1.1 and 5.2.5 then are similarly stated; when Axiom 3.1.1 refers to "opposite," Axiom 5.2.5 refers to "reciprocal"; when Axiom 3.1.1 refers to "sum," Axiom 5.2.5 refers to "product"; and when Axiom 3.1.1 refers to "additive identity element," Axiom 5.2.5 refers to "multiplicative identity element." If we examine the properties of Chapter 3 that refer to "opposites," "differences," "sums," and "additive identity elements," we will find in many cases that a similar property exists in this chapter where the references will be to "reciprocals," "quotients," "products," and "multiplicative identity elements." The following definition is in accord with this analogy.

5.2.6 Definition   The reciprocal of any given nonzero real number is called the *multiplicative inverse* of that real number.

Illustration 6   The multiplicative inverse of -2 is $\dfrac{-1}{2}$; the multiplicative inverse of $\dfrac{-1}{2}$ is -2.

The set of rational numbers is closed with respect to the four fundamental operations of addition, subtraction, multiplication, and division. The rules for the operations with positive and negative rational numbers are the same as they are for integers; that is, a positive rational number multiplied by a negative rational number is a negative rational number, and so on. The reason for this is that we assume all of the laws that were stated for the integers are laws for the set of real numbers as well as its subset of rational numbers. That is, for the set of rational numbers, Q, we assume the following:

(I) Closure Law for Addition and Multiplication
(II) Commutative Laws for Addition and Multiplication
(III) Associative Laws for Addition and Multiplication
(IV) Distributive Law of Multiplication over Addition
(V) Identity Elements for Addition and Multiplication
(VI) Additive Inverse Law

To this list of laws we now include the following law:

(VII) Multiplicative Inverse Law   For each nonzero $b \in Q$, there exists the reciprocal of b, $\dfrac{1}{b} \in Q$, such that

$$b \cdot \frac{1}{b} = 1$$

The set Q with the equality relation and the operations of $+$ and $\cdot$ and the above laws forms a mathematical system called a *field*. The laws I through VII are called *field properties* or *field axioms*. The rational number system is a field.

Exercises 5.2

1. What number multiplied by 2 gives a product of 3?
2. What number multiplied by 2 gives a product of -3?
3. Solve the equation $2x = 3$.
4. Solve the equation $2x = -3$.

In Exercises 5 through 13 use Definition 5.2.3 to determine whether or not the given fractions are equivalent.

5. (a) $\dfrac{9}{8}, \dfrac{8}{9}$ (b) $\dfrac{2}{3}, \dfrac{8}{12}$

6. (a) $\dfrac{3}{25}, \dfrac{2}{17}$ (b) $\dfrac{1}{2}, \dfrac{-2}{-4}$

7. (a) $\dfrac{-8}{12}, \dfrac{-6}{9}$ (b) $\dfrac{-9}{16}, \dfrac{-3}{4}$

8. (a) $\dfrac{10}{13}, \dfrac{7}{9}$ (b) $\dfrac{15}{20}, \dfrac{30}{40}$

9. (a) $\dfrac{2}{\frac{1}{4}}, \dfrac{4}{\frac{1}{2}}$ (b) $\dfrac{-30}{6}, \dfrac{5}{-1}$

10. $\dfrac{2}{x}, \dfrac{x}{1}$ 11. $\dfrac{3}{3}, \dfrac{1}{1}$

12. $\dfrac{2x}{3x}, \dfrac{2}{3}$ 13. $\dfrac{4x}{6x}, \dfrac{6y}{9y}$

14. Represent the integer 4 by a fraction.
15. Represent the rational number 10 by a fraction.

−1, −2, −3 **16. (a)** Give an example of an integer that is not a whole number.
  (b) Give an example of a rational number that is not an integer.

17. List four other fractions equivalent to $\frac{2}{3}$.

18. Prove that the fraction $\frac{a}{b}$ is equivalent to the fraction $\frac{-a}{-b}$.

Cite
definition **19.** Prove that the fraction $\frac{-a}{b}$ is equivalent to the fraction $\frac{a}{-b}$.

20. Prove that if $b \neq 0$, the fraction $\frac{0}{b}$ is equivalent to the fraction $\frac{0}{1}$.

21. Prove that if $b \neq 0$, then $b \cdot \frac{a}{b} = a$. (Hint: $\frac{a}{b}$ is the solution of the equation $bx = a$. See Definition 5.2.2.)

22. If Bill has $5 and Dennis has $3 more than Bill, how many times greater is the amount of money Dennis has than the amount Bill has? (The answer is a rational number. Express it as a fraction.)

23. In a class of 40 students, 25 students were boys. What fractional part of the class is made up of boys? of girls?

In Exercises 24 through 31 find the reciprocal of the given number.

24. 4   **25.** 100   **26.** $\frac{1}{2}$ **27.** $\frac{-1}{3}$

28. q **29.** $\frac{1}{q}$ **30.** -1 **31.** $\frac{1}{\frac{1}{2}}$ $\frac{1}{2}$

In Exercises 32 through 36 name the multiplicative inverse of the first factor and find the product.

$\frac{2}{1}, 1$ **32.** $\frac{1}{2} \cdot 2$ **33.** $-3 \cdot \frac{-1}{3}$ **34.** $x \cdot \frac{1}{x}$

35. $2y \cdot \frac{1}{2y}$ **36.** $(m + n) \cdot \frac{1}{m + n}$

37. (a) What is the reciprocal of the reciprocal of x? $\frac{1}{\frac{1}{x}} = x$

  (b) What is the reciprocal of the reciprocal of $\frac{1}{x}$?

38. Name the field axiom for the system of rational numbers that is different from those in the list for the system of integers.

39. What two rational numbers are their own reciprocals?

40. Suppose $F = \{-1, 0, 1\}$ and you have the equality relation and the operations of multiplication and addition. Is this system a field? That is, do you have

(a) Closure?   (b) Commutativity?
(c) Associativity?   (d) Distributivity?
(e) Identity elements?   (f) Inverse elements?

41. Consider the set $B = J \cup \left\{ \dfrac{1}{1}, \dfrac{-1}{1}, \dfrac{1}{2}, \dfrac{-1}{2}, \dfrac{1}{3}, \dfrac{-1}{3}, \dfrac{1}{4}, \dfrac{-1}{4}, \ldots \right\}$ where J is the set of integers.

(a) Does there exist an additive inverse in B for each number in B?
(b) Does there exist a multiplicative inverse in B for each nonzero number in B?
(c) Does B have an additive identity element? A multiplicative identity element?

5.3 Some Properties of Fractions

Ten times $\dfrac{1}{2}$ is equal to 10 divided by 2. Twelve times $\dfrac{1}{3}$ is equal to 12 divided by 3. In general, any number times $\dfrac{1}{k}$ $(k \neq 0)$ is equal to that number divided by k, the reciprocal of $\dfrac{1}{k}$.

Consider the equality

$$10 = 5 \cdot 2$$

and multiply each member by $\dfrac{1}{2}$ to obtain

$$10 \cdot \frac{1}{2} = (5 \cdot 2) \cdot \frac{1}{2} \qquad (1)$$

Applying the Associative Law of Multiplication in the right member of equality (1) and then applying the Multiplicative Inverse Law, we get

$$10 \cdot \frac{1}{2} = 5 \cdot \left(2 \cdot \frac{1}{2} \right)$$
$$= 5 \cdot 1$$
$$= 5$$

Furthermore,

$$10 \div 2 = 5$$

and so it follows that

$$10 \div 2 = 10 \cdot \frac{1}{2} \qquad (2)$$

Equation (2) states that the quotient of 10 divided by 2 is equal to the product of 10 multiplied by the reciprocal of 2. The following theorem is a generalization of equation (2).

5.3.1 Theorem   If $a, b \in R$ and $b \neq 0$, then

$$a \div b = a \cdot \frac{1}{b}$$

or, equivalently,

$$\frac{a}{b} = a \cdot \frac{1}{b}$$

Illustration 1 (a) $3 \div 10 = 3 \cdot \frac{1}{10}$; (b) $(-3) \cdot \frac{1}{4} = \frac{-3}{4}$; (c) $2y \cdot \frac{1}{x} = \frac{2y}{x}$;

(d) $x^2 \div 4 = x^2 \cdot \frac{1}{4}$; (e) $2 \div \frac{1}{3} = 2 \cdot 3$.

Illustration 2 The measure of the area of the region enclosed by a triangle is $\frac{1}{2}bh$, where b is the measure of the base of the triangle and h is the measure of the height of the triangle. From Theorem 5.3.1 we have

$$\frac{1}{2}bh = \frac{bh}{2}$$

Illustration 3 The term $\frac{1}{2}x$ is equal to $\frac{x}{2}$. Hence,

$$\frac{x}{2} + \frac{x}{2} + \frac{x}{2} = \frac{1}{2}x + \frac{1}{2}x + \frac{1}{2}x$$

$$= \left(\frac{1}{2} + \frac{1}{2} + \frac{1}{2}\right)x$$

$$= \left(3 \cdot \frac{1}{2}\right)x$$

$$= \frac{3}{2}x$$

As a consequence of Theorem 5.3.1, the fraction $\frac{a}{b}$ is the reciprocal of the fraction $\frac{b}{a}$ provided that $a \neq 0$ and $b \neq 0$. For example, from Theorem 5.3.1 it follows that

$$\frac{2}{3} = 2 \cdot \frac{1}{3} \qquad \text{and} \qquad \frac{3}{2} = 3 \cdot \frac{1}{2}$$

Therefore, the product of $\frac{2}{3}$ and $\frac{3}{2}$ is written as

$$\frac{2}{3} \cdot \frac{3}{2} = \left(2 \cdot \frac{1}{3}\right) \cdot \left(3 \cdot \frac{1}{2}\right) \tag{3}$$

Applying the Associative and Commutative Laws of Multiplication in the right member of equality (3) we obtain

$$\frac{2}{3} \cdot \frac{3}{2} = \left(2 \cdot \frac{1}{2}\right) \cdot \left(3 \cdot \frac{1}{3}\right) \tag{4}$$

Because of the Multiplicative Inverse Law the right member of equality (4) equals $1 \cdot 1$ and so

$$\frac{2}{3} \cdot \frac{3}{2} = 1$$

Because of the Multiplicative Inverse Law and the fact that $\frac{2}{3} \cdot \frac{3}{2} = 1$ we conclude that $\frac{2}{3}$ and $\frac{3}{2}$ are reciprocals of each other. A similar argument can be given to prove the following theorem.

5.3.2 Theorem   If $a, b \in R$, $a \neq 0$ and $b \neq 0$, then the reciprocal of $\frac{a}{b}$ is $\frac{b}{a}$.

Illustration 4 The reciprocal of $\frac{7}{10}$ is $\frac{10}{7}$ and $\frac{7}{10} \cdot \frac{10}{7} = 1$. The reciprocal of $\frac{x+y}{xy}$ is $\frac{xy}{x+y}$ provided that $x + y \neq 0$ and $xy \neq 0$. Furthermore, $\frac{x+y}{xy} \cdot \frac{xy}{x+y} = 1$.

In the fraction $\frac{a}{b}$, a and b can be any real numbers with the one exception that $b \neq 0$. Hence, we can have fractions in which the numerator and the denominator are fractions. Such fractions are called *complex fractions*. For instance, the fraction

$$\frac{\frac{2}{3}}{\frac{5}{6}}$$

is a complex fraction in which the numerator is $\frac{2}{3}$ and the denominator is $\frac{5}{6}$. If both the numerator and denominator of a fraction are integers, then the fraction is called a *simple fraction*. The fractions $\frac{2}{3}$ and $\frac{5}{6}$ are simple fractions.

The following theorem is useful both in simplifying fractions and in computations with fractions.

5.3.3 Theorem   If both the numerator and denominator of a fraction are (i) multiplied or (ii) divided by a number k ($k \neq 0$), then an equivalent fraction is obtained. Using symbols, we write

(i)
$$\frac{a}{b} = \frac{ak}{bk} \qquad (5)$$

and

(ii)
$$\frac{a}{b} = \frac{\dfrac{a}{k}}{\dfrac{b}{k}}$$

if $b \neq 0$.

Proof of (i):   By the Reflexive Property of Equality (Axiom 1.5.1)

$$abk = abk \qquad (6)$$

Applying the Associative and Commutative Laws of Multiplication in each member of equality (6), we have

$$a(bk) = b(ak)$$

Therefore, from Definition 5.2.3 it follows that the two fractions

$$\frac{a}{b} \quad and \quad \frac{ak}{bk}$$

are equivalent, and so equality (5) is valid.

Proof of (ii):   *If* $k \neq 0$, *then by Theorem 5.3.3(i)*

$$\frac{a}{b} = \frac{a \cdot \dfrac{1}{k}}{b \cdot \dfrac{1}{k}}$$

Hence, by applying Theorem 5.3.1, we have

$$\frac{a}{b} = \frac{\dfrac{a}{k}}{\dfrac{b}{k}}$$

Illustration 5   (a) If the numerator and denominator of the fraction $\dfrac{2}{5}$ are each multiplied by 3, we have

$$\frac{2}{5} = \frac{2 \cdot 3}{5 \cdot 3}$$

$$= \frac{6}{15}$$

(b) If the numerator and denominator of the fraction $\dfrac{4}{6}$ are each divided by 2, we have

$$\frac{4}{6} = \frac{\dfrac{4}{2}}{\dfrac{6}{2}}$$

$$= \frac{2}{3}$$

(c) If the numerator and denominator of the fraction $\dfrac{15}{\frac{1}{2}}$ are each multi-plied by 2, we have

$$\frac{15}{\dfrac{1}{2}} = \frac{15 \cdot 2}{\dfrac{1}{2} \cdot 2}$$

$$= \frac{30}{1}$$

$$= 30$$

(d) If the numerator and denominator of the fraction $\dfrac{3x}{5x}$ are each divided by x $(x \neq 0)$, we have

$$\frac{3x}{5x} = \frac{\dfrac{3x}{x}}{\dfrac{5x}{x}}$$

$$= \frac{(3x) \cdot \dfrac{1}{x}}{(5x) \cdot \dfrac{1}{x}}$$

$$= \frac{3\left(x \cdot \dfrac{1}{x}\right)}{5\left(x \cdot \dfrac{1}{x}\right)}$$

$$= \frac{3 \cdot 1}{5 \cdot 1}$$

$$= \frac{3}{5}$$

Note that $\dfrac{3x}{5x} = \dfrac{3}{5}$ is a direct consequence of Theorem 5.3.3(i); however, if we divide both $3x$ and $5x$ by x, then we apply Theorem 5.3.1 as shown in (d) above.

Theorem 5.3.3 is called The Fundamental Principle of Fractions. Because the fraction $\dfrac{a}{b}$ represents the quotient $a \div b$ we could also refer to Theorem 5.3.3 as the Fundamental Principle of Quotients and then compare it to Theorem 3.2.3, the Fundamental Principle of Differences. The two properties are analogous.

Theorem 5.3.3 is used to *reduce* fractions to what is called "lowest terms."

5.3.4 Definition   A simple fraction which does not represent the number zero is said to be in *lowest terms* if the greatest common divisor of the absolute value of the numerator and the absolute value of the denominator is 1.

To *reduce* a simple fraction to lowest terms, we divide the numerator and denominator by the GCD of the absolute values of the numerator and denominator.

Illustration 6   To reduce the fraction $\dfrac{24}{-18}$ to lowest terms we divide both

24 and -18 by the GCD of 24 and 18, which is 6. We have then

$$\frac{24}{-18} = \frac{\dfrac{24}{6}}{\dfrac{-18}{6}}$$

$$= \frac{4}{-3}$$

There is an unlimited number of fractions equivalent to a given fraction. From a set of equivalent fractions we define one of them to be the "simplest form" of all the fractions in the set.

5.3.5 Definition The simple fraction $\dfrac{a}{b}$ is the *simplest form* of all fractions equivalent to $\dfrac{a}{b}$ if $b > 0$ and the GCD of $|a|$ and b is 1. However, if $\dfrac{a}{b}$ is equivalent to an integer, then the integer is the *simplest form* of all fractions equivalent to $\dfrac{a}{b}$.

If we are given a fraction which is not the simplest form of all fractions equivalent to it, we state that the given fraction *simplifies* to that which is the simplest form.

Illustration 7 Given the set of equivalent fractions

$$\left\{ \frac{1}{2}, \frac{2}{4}, \frac{3}{6}, \frac{4}{8}, \ldots, \frac{-1}{-2}, \frac{-2}{-4}, \frac{-3}{-6}, \frac{-4}{-8}, \ldots \right\}$$

The fraction $\dfrac{1}{2}$ is the simplest form of any of the fractions in this set. Furthermore, the fraction $\dfrac{2}{4}$ (or any of the other fractions in the set) simplifies to $\dfrac{1}{2}$.

Illustration 8 The fraction $\dfrac{4}{-3}$ is equivalent to the fraction $\dfrac{-4}{3}$ because $4 \cdot 3 = (-3)(-4)$. Hence, $\dfrac{4}{-3}$ simplifies to $\dfrac{-4}{3}$ because Definition 5.3.5 requires the denominator to be a positive number when a fraction is in the simplest form.

Example 1 Simplify each of the following fractions:

(a) $\dfrac{8}{12}$ (b) $\dfrac{-2}{-3}$ (c) $\dfrac{0}{5}$ (d) $\dfrac{2}{1}$

Solution:

(a) The GCD of 8 and 12 is 4. Hence, we divide the numerator and denominator of $\dfrac{8}{12}$ by 4 and we have

$$\frac{8}{12} = \frac{8 \div 4}{12 \div 4}$$

$$= \frac{2}{3}$$

(b) By applying Theorem 5.3.3(i), we have

$$\frac{-2}{-3} = \frac{(-2)(-1)}{(-3)(-1)}$$

$$= \frac{2}{3}$$

(c) $\dfrac{0}{5}$ simplifies to 0.

(d) $\dfrac{2}{1}$ simplifies to 2.

5.3.6 Theorem   If $b \neq 0$, then

$$b \cdot \frac{a}{b} = a$$

Proof: From Theorem 5.3.1 we have

$$b \cdot \frac{a}{b} = b \cdot \left(a \cdot \frac{1}{b}\right) \tag{7}$$

Regrouping and reordering the factors in the right member of equality (7) we have

$$b \cdot \frac{a}{b} = a \cdot \left(b \cdot \frac{1}{b}\right) \tag{8}$$

Applying the Multiplicative Inverse Law and the Multiplicative Identity Law in the right member of equality (8), we have the desired result

$$b \cdot \frac{a}{b} = a$$

Example 2 Find each of the following products:

(a) $\dfrac{-3}{5} \cdot 5$ (b) $10 \cdot \dfrac{x}{10}$ (c) $2y \cdot \dfrac{x}{y} \, (y \neq 0)$

Solution:

(a) $\dfrac{-3}{5} \cdot 5 = 5 \cdot \dfrac{-3}{5}$

      $= -3$

(b) $10 \cdot \dfrac{x}{10} = x$

(c) $2y \cdot \dfrac{x}{y} = 2 \left(y \cdot \dfrac{x}{y} \right)$

      $= 2(x)$

      $= 2x$

5.3.7 Theorem   The fraction $\dfrac{-a}{b}$ is equivalent to $-\dfrac{a}{b}$.

Proof: *From Theorem 5.3.6 it follows that*

$$b \left(\dfrac{-a}{b} \right) = -a \tag{9}$$

Furthermore, because

$$b \cdot \dfrac{a}{b} = a$$

we have

$$b \left(-\dfrac{a}{b} \right) = -a \tag{10}$$

Because the right members of equalities (9) and (10) are equal, we have

$$b \left(\dfrac{-a}{b} \right) = b \left(-\dfrac{a}{b} \right) \tag{11}$$

and dividing each member of equality (11) by b, we have

$$\dfrac{-a}{b} = -\dfrac{a}{b}$$

which is what we wished to prove.

Example 3 Simplify each of the following fractions:

(a) $-\dfrac{8}{6}$ (b) $-\dfrac{1}{x}$ (c) $-\dfrac{-12}{-3}$ (d) $\dfrac{x}{-2}$

Solution:

(a) $-\dfrac{8}{6} = \dfrac{-8}{6}$

$ = \dfrac{-8 \div 2}{6 \div 2}$

$ = \dfrac{-4}{3}$

(b) $-\dfrac{1}{x} = \dfrac{-1}{x}$

(c) $-\dfrac{-12}{-3} = -\dfrac{-12 \div (-3)}{-3 \div (-3)}$

$ = -\left(\dfrac{4}{1}\right)$

$ = -4$

(d) $\dfrac{x}{-2} = \dfrac{x \cdot (-1)}{-2 \cdot (-1)}$

$ = \dfrac{-x}{2}$

Example 4 Find x so that

$$\frac{x}{20} = \frac{3}{4}$$

Solution: By the definition of equivalent fractions (5.2.3), $\dfrac{x}{20}$ is equivalent to $\dfrac{3}{4}$ if and only if

$$4x = 3 \cdot 20$$

or, equivalently,

$$4x = 60$$

and so

$$x = 15$$

In Exercises 1 through 7 simplify each fraction.

1. (a) $\dfrac{3}{6}$ (b) $\dfrac{5}{10}$ (c) $\dfrac{\frac{1}{2}}{1}$ (d) $\dfrac{16}{48}$

2. (a) $-\dfrac{1}{2}$ (b) $-\dfrac{-1}{-2}$ (c) $\dfrac{1}{-2}$ (d) $\dfrac{2}{4}$

3. (a) $\dfrac{-6}{-9}$ (b) $-\dfrac{6}{-9}$ (c) $-\dfrac{-6}{9}$ (d) $\dfrac{6}{9}$

4. (a) $-\dfrac{12}{4}$ (b) $\dfrac{-12}{4}$ (c) $\dfrac{12}{-4}$ (d) $-\dfrac{-12}{-4}$

5. (a) $\dfrac{6}{1}$ (b) $\dfrac{0}{4}$ (c) $\dfrac{6}{-1}$ (d) $\dfrac{0}{10}$

6. (a) $\dfrac{12}{\frac{1}{3}}$ (b) $\dfrac{3x}{10x}$ (c) $-\dfrac{3}{x}$ (d) $\dfrac{3}{-x}$

7. (a) $\dfrac{7}{\frac{1}{4}}$ (b) $\dfrac{-x}{-2}$ (c) $\dfrac{4x}{6}$ (d) $\dfrac{9y}{12y}$

In Exercises 8 and 9 express the reciprocal of each fraction in simplest form.

8. (a) $\dfrac{-4}{3}$ (b) $\dfrac{5}{4}$ (c) $\dfrac{x}{2}$

9. (a) $3\dfrac{1}{2}$ (b) $-\dfrac{x}{y}$ (c) $\dfrac{a+b}{a-b}$

In Exercises 10 through 18 find the product.

10. $\dfrac{3}{7} \cdot 7$ 11. $-\left(5 \cdot \dfrac{2}{5}\right)$ 12. $\dfrac{1}{2y} \cdot 2y$

13. $\dfrac{1}{8} \cdot 8$ 14. $x \cdot \dfrac{3}{x}$ 15. $(m+n) \cdot \dfrac{1}{m+n}$

16. $\dfrac{-5}{3} \cdot 3$ 17. $x \cdot \dfrac{1}{x}$ 18. $\dfrac{x}{-2} \cdot (-2x)$

19. Let $b = 3$ and $h = 24$, then find the value of each of the following expressions:

(a) $\dfrac{1}{2}bh$ (b) $\dfrac{bh}{2}$ (c) $\dfrac{1}{3}b^2h$ (d) $\dfrac{b^2h}{3}$

In Exercises 20 through 29 solve the given equation for x.

20. $\dfrac{5}{16} = \dfrac{x}{64}$

21. $-\dfrac{3}{2} = \dfrac{x}{10}$

22. $\dfrac{1}{x} = \dfrac{1}{3}$ $x = 3$

23. $\dfrac{0}{5} = \dfrac{x}{10}$

24. $\dfrac{-4}{7} = \dfrac{x}{-7}$

25. $\dfrac{5}{x} = -\dfrac{10}{4}$

26. $\dfrac{1}{2x} = \dfrac{1}{6}$

27. $\dfrac{1}{x+1} = \dfrac{1}{3}$

28. $\dfrac{1}{\frac{1}{x}} = 5$

29. $\dfrac{1}{\frac{1}{x}} = \dfrac{1}{5}$

30. Prove that $\dfrac{a}{b}$ is equivalent to $\dfrac{ax}{bx}$ where $x \neq 0$.

31. Prove that $-\dfrac{a}{b}$ is equivalent to $-\dfrac{a}{-b}$.

32. Prove that $-\dfrac{-a}{b}$ is equivalent to $-\dfrac{a}{-b}$.

5.4 Multiplication and Division of Rational Numbers

One half of one half is equivalent to one fourth. This can be interpreted as

$$\frac{1}{2} \cdot \frac{1}{2} = \frac{1}{4}$$

or, equivalently,

$$\frac{1}{2} \cdot \frac{1}{2} = \frac{1}{2 \cdot 2}$$

In general we would like to be able to state that the product of the reciprocals of two real numbers is equal to the reciprocal of the product of the two real numbers. In symbols we would have

$$\frac{1}{a} \cdot \frac{1}{b} = \frac{1}{a \cdot b}$$

Consider, for instance, the product $\dfrac{1}{2} \cdot \dfrac{1}{3}$. We know that

$$\frac{2}{2} \cdot \frac{3}{3} = 1 \quad \text{and} \quad \frac{2 \cdot 3}{2 \cdot 3} = 1$$

and therefore we have

$$\frac{2}{2} \cdot \frac{3}{3} = \frac{2 \cdot 3}{2 \cdot 3}$$ (1)

The left member of equality (1) can be written as $\left(2 \cdot \frac{1}{2}\right) \cdot \left(3 \cdot \frac{1}{3}\right)$ and the right member of equality (1) can be written as $(2 \cdot 3) \cdot \left(\frac{1}{2 \cdot 3}\right)$. Thus, we have

$$\left(2 \cdot \frac{1}{2}\right) \cdot \left(3 \cdot \frac{1}{3}\right) = (2 \cdot 3) \cdot \left(\frac{1}{2 \cdot 3}\right)$$

or, equivalently,

$$(2 \cdot 3) \cdot \left(\frac{1}{2} \cdot \frac{1}{3}\right) = (2 \cdot 3) \cdot \left(\frac{1}{2 \cdot 3}\right)$$

and hence, it follows that

$$\frac{1}{2} \cdot \frac{1}{3} = \frac{1}{2 \cdot 3}$$ (2)

A similar argument can be given to prove the following theorem.

5.4.1 Theorem   If $a, b \in R$, $a \neq 0$ and $b \neq 0$, then

$$\frac{1}{a} \cdot \frac{1}{b} = \frac{1}{a \cdot b}$$

Illustration 1

(a) $\dfrac{1}{2} \cdot \dfrac{1}{3} = \dfrac{1}{2 \cdot 3}$

$\qquad = \dfrac{1}{6}$

(b) $\dfrac{1}{4} \cdot \dfrac{1}{4} = \dfrac{1}{4 \cdot 4}$

$\qquad = \dfrac{1}{16}$

(c) $\dfrac{1}{-3} \cdot \dfrac{1}{5} = \dfrac{1}{-3 \cdot 5}$

$\qquad = \dfrac{1}{-15}$

$\qquad = \dfrac{-1}{15}$

(d) $\dfrac{-1}{3} \cdot \dfrac{1}{5} = (-1)\left(\dfrac{1}{3} \cdot \dfrac{1}{5}\right)$

$\qquad = (-1)\left(\dfrac{1}{15}\right)$

$\qquad = \dfrac{-1}{15}$

(e) $\dfrac{1}{2x} \cdot \dfrac{1}{y} = \dfrac{1}{(2x)y}$

$\qquad = \dfrac{1}{2xy}$

Now consider the product of any two rational numbers. For instance, the product $\frac{2}{3} \cdot \frac{4}{5}$ equals $\frac{2 \cdot 4}{3 \cdot 5}$. We show below that $\frac{2 \cdot 4}{3 \cdot 5}$ is the logical result of multiplying $\frac{2}{3}$ by $\frac{4}{5}$ by applying properties that have been previously stated. In particular note the application of Theorems 5.3.6 and 5.4.1

$$\frac{2}{3} \cdot \frac{4}{3} = \left(2 \cdot \frac{1}{3}\right) \cdot \left(4 \cdot \frac{1}{5}\right)$$

$$= (2 \cdot 4) \cdot \left(\frac{1}{3} \cdot \frac{1}{5}\right)$$

$$= (2 \cdot 4) \cdot \left(\frac{1}{3 \cdot 5}\right)$$

$$= \frac{2 \cdot 4}{3 \cdot 5}$$

or, equivalently,

$$\frac{2}{3} \cdot \frac{4}{5} = \frac{2 \cdot 4}{3 \cdot 5} \tag{3}$$

This discussion suggests the following theorem.

5.4.2 Theorem   If $a, b, c, d \in R$, $b \neq 0$ and $d \neq 0$, then

$$\frac{a}{b} \cdot \frac{c}{d} = \frac{a \cdot c}{b \cdot d}$$

The proof of Theorem 5.4.2 is a generalization of the procedure used to obtain equality (3), and is omitted here.

Example 1   Find each of the following products:

(a) $\dfrac{3}{7} \cdot \dfrac{2}{5}$ (b) $\dfrac{-4}{9} \cdot \dfrac{8}{3}$ (c) $\dfrac{2x}{5} \cdot \dfrac{x}{3}$

Solution:

(a) $\dfrac{3}{7} \cdot \dfrac{2}{5} = \dfrac{3 \cdot 2}{7 \cdot 5}$

$\qquad = \dfrac{6}{35}$

(b) $\dfrac{-4}{9} \cdot \dfrac{8}{3} = \dfrac{(-4) \cdot 8}{9 \cdot 3}$

$\qquad = \dfrac{-32}{27}$

(c) $\dfrac{2x}{5} \cdot \dfrac{x}{3} = \dfrac{(2x) \cdot x}{5 \cdot 3}$

$\qquad = \dfrac{2(x \cdot x)}{15}$

$\qquad = \dfrac{2x^2}{15}$

Illustration 2 We apply Theorem 5.4.2 to obtain the product of $\dfrac{9}{25} \cdot \dfrac{5}{6}$, and we have

$$\frac{9}{25} \cdot \frac{5}{6} = \frac{45}{150}$$

We now reduce the product to lowest terms, by dividing the numerator and denominator by the GCD of 45 and 150. We have

$$\frac{45}{150} = \frac{3(15)}{10(15)}$$

$$= \frac{3}{10}$$

If the given numerators and denominators are written in prime factored form before applying Theorem 5.4.2, we have

$$\frac{9}{25} \cdot \frac{5}{6} = \frac{3^2}{5^2} \cdot \frac{5}{2 \cdot 3}$$

$$= \frac{3^2 \cdot 5}{2 \cdot 3 \cdot 5^2}$$

$$= \frac{3(3 \cdot 5)}{(2 \cdot 5)(3 \cdot 5)}$$

$$= \frac{3}{2 \cdot 5}$$

$$= \frac{3}{10}$$

Example 2 Find each of the following products in lowest terms:

(a) $\dfrac{12}{25} \cdot \dfrac{15}{4}$ (b) $\dfrac{-8}{45} \cdot \dfrac{-27}{20}$ (c) $\dfrac{2x}{21y} \cdot \dfrac{14yz}{x}$ (d) $\dfrac{8a^2b}{5c^3} \cdot \dfrac{55c^3}{28a^2b^2}$

Solution:

(a) $\dfrac{12}{25} \cdot \dfrac{15}{4} = \dfrac{2^2 \cdot 3}{5^2} \cdot \dfrac{3 \cdot 5}{2^2}$

$$= \frac{2^2 \cdot 3^2 \cdot 5}{5^2 \cdot 2^2}$$

$$= \frac{3^2(2^2 \cdot 5)}{5(2^2 \cdot 5)}$$

$$= \frac{3^2}{5}$$

$$= \frac{9}{5}$$

(b) $\dfrac{-8}{45} \cdot \dfrac{-27}{20} = \dfrac{(-1) \cdot 2^3}{3^2 \cdot 5} \cdot \dfrac{(-1) \cdot 3^3}{2^2 \cdot 5}$

$= \dfrac{(-1)(-1) \cdot 2^3 \cdot 3^3}{2^2 \cdot 3^2 \cdot 5^2}$

$= \dfrac{2 \cdot 3(2^2 \cdot 3^2)}{5^2(2^2 \cdot 3^2)}$

$= \dfrac{2 \cdot 3}{5^2}$

$= \dfrac{6}{25}$

(c) $\dfrac{2x}{21y} \cdot \dfrac{14yz}{x} = \dfrac{2x}{3 \cdot 7y} \cdot \dfrac{2 \cdot 7yz}{x}$

$= \dfrac{2^2 \cdot 7xyz}{3 \cdot 7xy}$

$= \dfrac{2^2 z(7xy)}{3(7xy)}$

$= \dfrac{2^2 z}{3}$

$= \dfrac{4z}{3}$

(d) $\dfrac{8a^2b}{5c^3} \cdot \dfrac{55c^3}{28a^2b^2} = \dfrac{2^3a^2b}{5c^3} \cdot \dfrac{5 \cdot 11c^3}{2^2 \cdot 7a^2b^2}$

$= \dfrac{2^3 \cdot 5 \cdot 11a^2bc^3}{2^2 \cdot 5 \cdot 7a^2b^2c^3}$

$= \dfrac{2 \cdot 11(2^2 \cdot 5a^2bc^3)}{7b(2^2 \cdot 5a^2bc^3)}$

$= \dfrac{2 \cdot 11}{7b}$

$= \dfrac{22}{7b}$

We can apply Theorem 5.4.2 and the Associative Law of Multiplication to find the product of three or more numbers represented by fractions. For instance, if $b \neq 0$, $d \neq 0$, and $f \neq 0$, then

$$\frac{a}{b} \cdot \frac{c}{d} \cdot \frac{e}{f} = \frac{ace}{bdf}$$

Example 3 Find each of the following products in lowest terms:

(a) $\dfrac{3}{4} \cdot \dfrac{-8}{9} \cdot \dfrac{5}{4}$

(b) $\dfrac{2ac}{3b} \cdot \dfrac{3bc^2}{4a^2} \cdot \dfrac{-6a}{7c}$

Solution:

(a) $\dfrac{3}{4} \cdot \dfrac{-8}{9} \cdot \dfrac{5}{4} = \dfrac{3}{2^2} \cdot \dfrac{(-1)2^3}{3^2} \cdot \dfrac{5}{2^2}$

$= \dfrac{(-1) \cdot 3 \cdot 2^3 \cdot 5}{2^4 \cdot 3^2}$

$= \dfrac{(-1) \cdot 5(2^3 \cdot 3)}{2 \cdot 3(2^3 \cdot 3)}$

$= \dfrac{(-1) \cdot 5}{2 \cdot 3}$

$= \dfrac{-5}{6}$

(b) $\dfrac{2ac}{3b} \cdot \dfrac{3bc^2}{4a^2} \cdot \dfrac{-6a}{7c} = \dfrac{2ac}{3b} \cdot \dfrac{3bc^2}{2^2a^2} \cdot \dfrac{(-1) \cdot 2 \cdot 3a}{7c}$

$= \dfrac{(-1) \cdot 2^2 \cdot 3^2 a^2 bc^3}{2^2 \cdot 3 \cdot 7a^2 bc}$

$= \dfrac{(-1) \cdot 3c^2(2^2 \cdot 3a^2 bc)}{7(2^2 \cdot 3a^2 bc)}$

$= \dfrac{(-1) \cdot 3c^2}{7}$

$= \dfrac{-3c^2}{7}$

Illustration 3 (a) The expression $\left(\dfrac{2}{3}\right)^4$ means "the fourth power of $\dfrac{2}{3}$";
hence,

$$\left(\dfrac{2}{3}\right)^4 = \dfrac{2}{3} \cdot \dfrac{2}{3} \cdot \dfrac{2}{3} \cdot \dfrac{2}{3}$$

$$= \dfrac{2 \cdot 2 \cdot 2 \cdot 2}{3 \cdot 3 \cdot 3 \cdot 3}$$

$$= \dfrac{2^4}{3^4}$$

(b) The expression $\left(\dfrac{a}{b}\right)^5$ means "the fifth power of $\dfrac{a}{b}$"; hence,

$$\left(\dfrac{a}{b}\right)^5 = \dfrac{a}{b} \cdot \dfrac{a}{b} \cdot \dfrac{a}{b} \cdot \dfrac{a}{b} \cdot \dfrac{a}{b}$$

$$= \dfrac{a \cdot a \cdot a \cdot a \cdot a}{b \cdot b \cdot b \cdot b \cdot b}$$

$$= \dfrac{a^5}{b^5}$$

In Illustration 3 we have special cases of the following theorem.

5.4.3 Theorem   If $a, b \in R$, $b \neq 0$, and n is any positive integer, then

$$\left(\frac{a}{b}\right)^n = \frac{a^n}{b^n}$$

The proof of Theorem 5.4.3 is omitted.

Example 4 Find the following products:

(a) $\left(\frac{1}{2}\right)^3$

(b) $\left(\frac{-3}{4}\right)^2$

(c) $\left(\frac{x}{3}\right)^4$

(d) $\left(\frac{2}{x}\right)^2 \cdot \left(\frac{-y}{3}\right)^3$

Solution:

(a) $\left(\frac{1}{2}\right)^3 = \frac{1^3}{2^3}$

$= \frac{1}{8}$

(b) $\left(\frac{-3}{4}\right)^2 = \frac{(-3)^2}{4^2}$

$= \frac{9}{16}$

(c) $\left(\frac{x}{3}\right)^4 = \frac{x^4}{3^4}$

$= \frac{x^4}{81}$

(d) $\left(\frac{2}{x}\right)^2 \cdot \left(\frac{-y}{3}\right)^3 = \frac{2^2}{x^2} \cdot \frac{(-y)^3}{3^3}$

$= \frac{4}{x^2} \cdot \frac{-y^3}{27}$

$= \frac{-4y^3}{27x^2}$

5.4.4 Theorem   If $\frac{a}{b}$ and $\frac{c}{d}$ are rational numbers and $\frac{c}{d} \neq 0$, then

$$\frac{a}{b} \div \frac{c}{d} = \frac{a}{b} \cdot \frac{d}{c} \qquad (4)$$

Proof: *Theorem 5.3.1 states that if* $x, y \in R$ *and* $y \neq 0$, *then*

$$x \div y = x \cdot \frac{1}{y} \qquad (5)$$

Equation (5) states that the quotient of x divided by y is the product of x multiplied by the reciprocal of y. If x and y are rational numbers represented by the fractions

$$\frac{a}{b} \quad and \quad \frac{c}{d}$$

respectively, then the reciprocal of y is represented by the reciprocal of $\frac{c}{d}$, which is $\frac{d}{c}$. Then equation (5) becomes

$$\frac{a}{b} \div \frac{c}{d} = \frac{a}{b} \cdot \frac{d}{c}$$

In words, equality (4) states that to divide two rational numbers represented by fractions, we multiply the dividend by the reciprocal of the divisor.

Illustration 4

(a) $\dfrac{2}{3} \div \dfrac{5}{7} = \dfrac{2}{3} \cdot \dfrac{7}{5}$

$\qquad = \dfrac{2 \cdot 7}{3 \cdot 5}$

$\qquad = \dfrac{14}{15}$

(b) $\dfrac{3}{4} \div \dfrac{9}{16} = \dfrac{3}{4} \cdot \dfrac{16}{9}$

$\qquad = \dfrac{3}{2^2} \cdot \dfrac{2^4}{3^2}$

$\qquad = \dfrac{2^4 \cdot 3}{2^2 \cdot 3^2}$

$\qquad = \dfrac{2^2(2^2 \cdot 3)}{3(2^2 \cdot 3)}$

$\qquad = \dfrac{4}{3}$

(c) $4 \div \dfrac{1}{2} = 4 \cdot 2$

$\qquad = 8$

(d) $\dfrac{3}{5} \div (-4) = \dfrac{3}{5} \cdot \dfrac{-1}{4}$

$\qquad = \dfrac{(-1) \cdot 3}{5 \cdot 4}$

$\qquad = \dfrac{-3}{20}$

Example 5 Find the following quotients; none of the denominators is zero:

(a) $\dfrac{1}{x} \div \dfrac{1}{y}$

(b) $\dfrac{\dfrac{a}{x}}{\dfrac{b}{y}}$

(c) $6x \div \dfrac{2x^2}{3}$

Solution:

(a) $\dfrac{1}{x} \div \dfrac{1}{y} = \dfrac{1}{x} \cdot y$

$\qquad = \dfrac{y}{x}$

(b) $\dfrac{\dfrac{a}{x}}{\dfrac{b}{y}} = \dfrac{a}{x} \div \dfrac{b}{y}$

$\qquad = \dfrac{a}{x} \cdot \dfrac{y}{b}$

$\qquad = \dfrac{ay}{bx}$

(c) $6x \div \dfrac{2x^2}{3} = 6x \cdot \dfrac{3}{2x^2}$

$$= \dfrac{3(6x)}{2x^2}$$

$$= \dfrac{2 \cdot 3^2 x}{2x^2}$$

$$= \dfrac{3^2(2x)}{x(2x)}$$

$$= \dfrac{9}{x}$$

Example 6 Solve the equation

$$\dfrac{2}{3}x = \dfrac{3}{4}$$

Solution: Dividing each member of the given equation by $\dfrac{2}{3}$, we obtain

$$x = \dfrac{3}{4} \div \dfrac{2}{3}$$

$$= \dfrac{3}{4} \cdot \dfrac{3}{2}$$

$$= \dfrac{9}{8}$$

The solution set is $\left\{ \dfrac{9}{8} \right\}$.

Exercises 5.4

In Exercises 1 through 10 find each product. Express the result in simplest form.

1. (a) $\dfrac{1}{2} \cdot \dfrac{1}{3}$ (b) $\dfrac{1}{3} \cdot \dfrac{1}{2}$

2. (a) $\dfrac{1}{2} \cdot \dfrac{1}{4}$ (b) $\dfrac{-1}{2} \cdot \dfrac{-1}{4}$

3. (a) $-\dfrac{x}{3} \cdot \dfrac{x}{4}$ (b) $\dfrac{-x}{3} \cdot \dfrac{-x^2}{4}$

4. (a) $\dfrac{x}{3} \cdot \dfrac{y}{5}$ (b) $\dfrac{x}{3} \cdot \dfrac{-y}{5}$

5. (a) $\dfrac{1}{x} \cdot \dfrac{1}{y}$ **(b)** $\dfrac{1}{a} \cdot \dfrac{1}{b} \cdot \dfrac{1}{c}$

6. (a) $\dfrac{2}{3} \cdot \dfrac{3x}{4}$ **(b)** $\dfrac{-2}{3} \cdot \dfrac{3y}{4}$

7. (a) $\dfrac{4}{9x} \cdot \dfrac{3x}{8}$ **(b)** $\dfrac{7x^2}{10} \cdot \dfrac{5}{2x}$

8. (a) $\dfrac{x}{2} \cdot \dfrac{x}{2}$ **(b)** $\dfrac{x}{2} \cdot \dfrac{x}{3} \cdot \dfrac{x}{4}$

9. (a) $3y^3 \cdot \dfrac{4}{5y}$ **(b)** $6 \cdot \dfrac{-3}{8} \cdot \dfrac{1}{12}$

10. (a) $\dfrac{6r}{9t} \cdot \dfrac{20}{24} \cdot \dfrac{12t}{18r^2}$ **(b)** $\dfrac{5a^2}{2b} \cdot \dfrac{-3b}{10c^2} \cdot \dfrac{-4c}{3a}$

In Exercises 11 through 26 find each quotient and express the result in simplest form.

11. (a) $-4 \div 3$ **(b)** $4\pi \div 3\pi$

12. (a) $y \div 4$ **(b)** $y \div (-4)$

13. (a) $16 \div 2a$ **(b)** $16 \div \left(\dfrac{1}{-2}\right)$

14. (a) $\dfrac{1}{2} \div 5$ **(b)** $\dfrac{-1}{3} \div (-3)$

15. (a) $\dfrac{2}{3} \div 4m$ **(b)** $\dfrac{-1}{6} \div 2k$

16. (a) $5x \div \dfrac{x}{2}$ **(b)** $7y \div \left(\dfrac{-y}{3}\right)$

17. (a) $30 \div \dfrac{1}{4}$ **(b)** $10 \div \left(\dfrac{-3}{4}\right)$

18. (a) $\dfrac{2}{5} \div \dfrac{1}{3}$ **(b)** $\dfrac{3}{7} \div \dfrac{2}{3}$

19. (a) $\dfrac{5}{6a} \div \dfrac{3a^2}{4}$ **(b)** $\dfrac{-5}{4x} \div \dfrac{5}{2x}$

20. (a) $\dfrac{1}{2x} \div \dfrac{1}{4x^2}$ **(b)** $\dfrac{-9a}{4x} \div \dfrac{2a}{5x}$

21. (a) $\dfrac{y^3}{80} \div \dfrac{y}{10}$ **(b)** $\dfrac{-1}{3m} \div \dfrac{1}{15m^2}$

22. (a) $\dfrac{4x^2}{2} \div \dfrac{x}{6y}$ **(b)** $\dfrac{-1}{x} \div \dfrac{-1}{y}$

23. (a) $\dfrac{18}{\frac{3}{2}}$ (b) $\dfrac{14}{\frac{-7}{3}}$

24. (a) $\dfrac{0}{\frac{3}{10}}$ (b) $\dfrac{\frac{0}{4}}{\frac{1}{5}}$

25. (a) $\dfrac{x}{\frac{1}{10}}$ (b) $\dfrac{y}{\frac{5}{12}}$

26. (a) $\dfrac{\frac{x}{3}}{\frac{5x}{8}}$ (b) $\dfrac{\frac{-2}{3y}}{\frac{y}{4}}$

In Exercises 27 through 30 find the indicated power.

27. (a) $\left(\dfrac{1}{2}\right)^3$ (b) $-\left(\dfrac{3}{4}\right)^2$ — $\dfrac{9}{16}$ *error*   28. (a) $\left(\dfrac{-3}{5}\right)^2$ (b) $\left(\dfrac{-2}{3}\right)^3$

29. (a) $\left(\dfrac{-3}{2}\right)^4$ (b) $\left(\dfrac{1}{3}\right)^5$ 30. (a) $\left(\dfrac{x}{2}\right)^3$ (b) $-\left(\dfrac{x}{y}\right)^3$

In Exercises 31 through 34 write the expression in simplest form.

31. $\dfrac{4^3}{6^3}$ 32. $\dfrac{6^4}{8^4}$

33. $\left(\dfrac{2}{5}\right)^3 \cdot \left(\dfrac{5}{2}\right)^2$ 34. $\left(\dfrac{x}{2}\right)^3 \cdot \left(\dfrac{-2}{3}\right)^3$

In Exercises 35 through 40, solve the equation using the division transformation.

35. $\dfrac{1}{2}x = \dfrac{2}{3}$ $1 \cdot x = \dfrac{2}{3} \cdot 2$ 36. $3x = \dfrac{1}{2}$ 37. $\dfrac{3}{4}x = 2$

38. $-\dfrac{1}{8}x = \dfrac{1}{7}$ 39. $\dfrac{1}{5}x = \dfrac{-1}{10}$ 40. $\dfrac{3}{5}x = \dfrac{5}{12}$

41. (a) The set of whole numbers is closed with respect to what two operations?

    (b) The set of whole numbers is not closed with respect to what two operations?

42. With respect to what operation is the set of integers closed, but the set of whole numbers is not closed?

43. With respect to what operation is the set of rational numbers closed, but the set of integers is not closed?

44. If neither x nor y is zero, what is the reciprocal of $x \div y$?

45. Show that

    (a) $a \div b = \dfrac{1}{b} \div \dfrac{1}{a}$

and that

(b) $\dfrac{1}{b} \div \dfrac{1}{a} = \dfrac{1}{b \div a}$

and therefore it follows from (a) and (b) that

(c) $a \div b = \dfrac{1}{b \div a}$

46. Write the Fundamental Principle of Fractions (Theorem 5.3.3) and the Fundamental Principle of Differences (Theorem 3.2.2) in their symbolic form. Replace the division operation symbol in Theorem 5.3.3 with the subtraction operation symbol, and replace the concept of taking the reciprocal of number with the concept of taking the opposite of a number. Also replace the multiplication operation symbol with the addition operation symbol. How does the resulting statement compare to the Fundamental Principle of Differences?

5.5 Addition and Subtraction of Rational Numbers

We wish to determine how to find the sum of two rational numbers represented by fractions. First consider the rational numbers 2 and 3 whose sum is 5. Because $2 = \dfrac{4}{2}$, $3 = \dfrac{6}{2}$, and $5 = \dfrac{10}{2}$, the equality

$$2 + 3 = 5$$

is equivalent to

$$\frac{4}{2} + \frac{6}{2} = \frac{10}{2} \tag{1}$$

Consider now the sum of the two rational numbers $\dfrac{3}{10}$ and $\dfrac{5}{10}$. By Theorem 5.3.1 we have

$$\frac{3}{10} + \frac{5}{10} = \left(3 \cdot \frac{1}{10}\right) + \left(5 \cdot \frac{1}{10}\right)$$

Applying the Distributive Law to the right member of this equality, we have

$$\frac{3}{10} + \frac{5}{10} = (3 + 5) \cdot \frac{1}{10}$$

and applying Theorem 5.3.1 to the right member, we get

$$\frac{3}{10} + \frac{5}{10} = \frac{3 + 5}{10}$$

or, equivalently,

$$\frac{3}{10} + \frac{5}{10} = \frac{8}{10} \tag{2}$$

Equalities (1) and (2) are special cases of the following theorem.

5.5.1 Theorem   If $\dfrac{a}{c}$ and $\dfrac{b}{c}$ are fractions representing rational numbers, then

$$\frac{a}{c} + \frac{b}{c} = \frac{a+b}{c}$$

Proof:

$$\frac{a}{c} + \frac{b}{c} = \left(a \cdot \frac{1}{c}\right) + \left(b \cdot \frac{1}{c}\right) \qquad \textit{By Theorem 5.3.1}$$

$$= (a+b) \cdot \frac{1}{c} \qquad \textit{By the Distributive Law}$$

$$= \frac{a+b}{c} \qquad \textit{By Theorem 5.3.1}$$

Example 1   Find each of the following sums:

(a) $\dfrac{2}{7} + \dfrac{3}{7}$ (b) $\dfrac{5}{3} + \dfrac{-4}{3}$ (c) $\dfrac{x}{3} + \dfrac{y}{3} + \dfrac{z}{3}$ (d) $4 + \dfrac{1}{3}$

Solution: We apply Theorem 5.5.1.

(a) $\dfrac{2}{7} + \dfrac{3}{7} = \dfrac{2+3}{7} = \dfrac{5}{7}$

(b) $\dfrac{7}{3} + \dfrac{-4}{3} = \dfrac{7+(-4)}{3} = \dfrac{3}{3} = 1$

(c) $\dfrac{x}{3} + \dfrac{y}{3} + \dfrac{z}{3} = \dfrac{x+y+z}{3}$

(d) $4 + \dfrac{1}{3} = \dfrac{12}{3} + \dfrac{1}{3} = \dfrac{12+1}{3} = \dfrac{13}{3}$

Subtraction of rational numbers is defined as it is for integers, that is, the difference of $\dfrac{a}{c}$ and $\dfrac{b}{c}$ is equal to the sum of $\dfrac{a}{c}$ and the opposite of $\dfrac{b}{c}$. Thus,

$$\frac{a}{c} - \frac{b}{c} = \frac{a}{c} + \left(-\frac{b}{c}\right)$$

Hence,

$$\frac{a}{c} - \frac{b}{c} = \frac{a}{c} + \frac{-b}{c}$$

or, equivalently,

$$\frac{a}{c} - \frac{b}{c} = \frac{a + (-b)}{c}$$

or, equivalently,

$$\frac{a}{c} - \frac{b}{c} = \frac{a - b}{c} \tag{3}$$

Example 2 Perform each of the following subtractions:

(a) $\dfrac{6}{5} - \dfrac{2}{5}$
(b) $\dfrac{2x}{9} - \dfrac{5x}{9}$

Solution: We apply equality (3).

(a) $\dfrac{6}{5} - \dfrac{2}{5} = \dfrac{6-2}{5} = \dfrac{4}{5}$

(b) $\dfrac{2x}{9} - \dfrac{5x}{9} = \dfrac{2x - 5x}{9} = \dfrac{-3x}{9} = \dfrac{-x}{3}$

There are many equivalent fractions that can be used to represent a given rational number. To add two rational numbers represented by fractions with unequal denominators, we select from the equivalent fractions a pair that have a *common denominator,* and add them according to Theorem 5.5.1.

Illustration 1 We wish to add $\dfrac{1}{3}$ and $\dfrac{3}{4}$. Fractions equivalent to $\dfrac{1}{3}$ are in the set $\left\{\dfrac{1}{3}, \dfrac{2}{6}, \dfrac{3}{9}, \dfrac{4}{12}, \dfrac{5}{15}, \ldots\right\}$. Fractions equivalent to $\dfrac{3}{4}$ are in the set $\left\{\dfrac{3}{4}, \dfrac{6}{8}, \dfrac{9}{12}, \dfrac{12}{16}, \ldots\right\}$. From these two sets we select

$$\frac{4}{12} = \frac{1}{3} \quad \text{and} \quad \frac{9}{12} = \frac{3}{4}$$

Hence,

$$\frac{1}{3} + \frac{3}{4} = \frac{4}{12} + \frac{9}{12}$$

$$= \frac{4 + 9}{12}$$

$$= \frac{13}{12}$$

The process of finding a *common denominator* of two fractions is the same procedure as finding a *common multiple* of the denominators. It is usually desirable to find the *least common multiple* (LCM) of the denominators. This number is called the *least common denominator* (LCD) of the fractions.

Example 3 Find the LCD of $\frac{7}{18}$ and $\frac{15}{24}$.

Solution: The LCD of $\frac{7}{18}$ and $\frac{15}{24}$ is the LCM of 18 and 24. (If the LCM is not easily found by inspection, then we use the method of Section 5.1.)

$$18 = 2_1 \cdot 3_1 \cdot 3_2$$
$$24 = 2_1 \cdot 2_2 \cdot 2_3 \cdot 3_1$$

Therefore, we form the sets P_{18} and P_{24} of the prime factors of 18 and 24, respectively.

$$P_{18} = \{2_1, 3_1, 3_2\}$$

and

$$P_{24} = \{2_1, 2_2, 2_3, 3_1\}$$

Therefore, the set of prime factors of the LCM is

$$P_{18} \cup P_{24} = \{2_1, 2_2, 2_3, 3_1, 3_2\}$$

Hence, the LCM of 18 and 24 is

$$2 \cdot 2 \cdot 2 \cdot 3 \cdot 3 = 72$$

Hence the LCD of $\frac{7}{18}$ and $\frac{15}{24}$ is 72.

Example 4 Find the sum: $\frac{7}{18} + \frac{15}{24}$

Solution: The LCD of the two fractions is 72. See Example 3. Now we must write each addend as an equivalent fraction having 72 as the common denominator. Because $72 \div 18 = 4$, we multiply the numerator and denominator of $\frac{7}{18}$ by 4, and we have

$$\frac{7}{18} = \frac{7 \cdot 4}{18 \cdot 4}$$
$$= \frac{28}{72}$$

To express $\frac{15}{24}$ as an equivalent fraction with a denominator of 72 we first divide 72 by 24 and obtain 3. Hence,

$$\frac{15}{24} = \frac{15 \cdot 3}{24 \cdot 3}$$
$$= \frac{45}{72}$$

We now perform the addition.

$$\frac{7}{18} + \frac{15}{24} = \frac{28}{72} + \frac{45}{72}$$

$$= \frac{28 + 45}{72}$$

$$= \frac{73}{72}$$

Example 5 Find each of the following sums:

(a) $\frac{1}{2} + \frac{1}{5}$ (b) $\frac{3}{5} + \frac{-4}{3}$ (c) $\frac{x}{2} + \frac{y}{3} + \frac{z}{4}$

Solution:

(a) The LCD of the given fractions is 10. We have then

$$\frac{1}{2} + \frac{1}{5} = \frac{1 \cdot 5}{2 \cdot 5} + \frac{1 \cdot 2}{5 \cdot 2}$$

$$= \frac{5}{10} + \frac{2}{10}$$

$$= \frac{7}{10}$$

(b) The LCD of the given fractions is 15. We have then

$$\frac{3}{5} + \frac{-4}{3} = \frac{3 \cdot 3}{5 \cdot 3} + \frac{(-4)(5)}{3 \cdot 5}$$

$$= \frac{9}{15} + \frac{-20}{15}$$

$$= \frac{9 + (-20)}{15}$$

$$= \frac{-11}{15}$$

(c) The LCD of the given fractions is 12. We have then

$$\frac{x}{2} + \frac{y}{3} + \frac{z}{4} = \frac{x \cdot 6}{2 \cdot 6} + \frac{y \cdot 4}{3 \cdot 4} + \frac{z \cdot 3}{4 \cdot 3}$$

$$= \frac{6x}{12} + \frac{4y}{12} + \frac{3z}{12}$$

$$= \frac{6x + 4y + 3z}{12}$$

Example 6 Find the difference: $\frac{5}{8} - \frac{3}{4}$

Solution: The LCD of the given fractions is 8. We have then

$$\frac{5}{8} - \frac{3}{4} = \frac{5}{8} - \frac{3 \cdot 2}{4 \cdot 2}$$

$$= \frac{5}{8} - \frac{6}{8}$$

$$= \frac{5 - 6}{8}$$

$$= \frac{-1}{8}$$

Example 7 Simplify the expression $10\left(\dfrac{9}{10} - \dfrac{3}{5}\right)$

Solution: The LCD of the fractions $\dfrac{9}{10}$ and $\dfrac{3}{5}$ is 10. We have then

$$10\left(\frac{9}{10} - \frac{3}{5}\right) = 10\left(\frac{9}{10} - \frac{3 \cdot 2}{5 \cdot 2}\right)$$

$$= 10\left(\frac{9}{10} - \frac{6}{10}\right)$$

$$= 10\left(\frac{3}{10}\right)$$

$$= 3$$

To investigate addition involving fractions more closely consider the following examples developed alongside each other.

Arithmetic Example 8	Algebra Example 9
$\dfrac{1}{2} + \dfrac{1}{3}$	$\dfrac{1}{x} + \dfrac{1}{y}$
Solution:	*Solution:*
$\dfrac{1}{2} + \dfrac{1}{3} = \dfrac{1 \cdot 3}{2 \cdot 3} + \dfrac{1 \cdot 2}{3 \cdot 2}$	$\dfrac{1}{x} + \dfrac{1}{y} = \dfrac{1 \cdot y}{x \cdot y} + \dfrac{1 \cdot x}{y \cdot x}$
$= \dfrac{3}{6} + \dfrac{2}{6}$	$= \dfrac{y}{xy} + \dfrac{x}{xy}$
$= \dfrac{3 + 2}{6}$	$= \dfrac{y + x}{xy}$
$= \dfrac{5}{6}$	$= \dfrac{x + y}{xy}$

Example 10 Add the fractions $\dfrac{a}{b}$ and $\dfrac{x}{y}$.

Solution: The LCD of the given fractions is by. We have then

$$\frac{a}{b} + \frac{x}{y} = \frac{a \cdot y}{b \cdot y} + \frac{x \cdot b}{y \cdot b}$$

$$= \frac{ay}{by} + \frac{bx}{by}$$

$$= \frac{ay + bx}{by}$$

Example 11 Find the sum: $\dfrac{x}{x-y} + \dfrac{y}{x-y}$

Solution: The LCD of the given fractions is $x - y$. We have then

$$\frac{x}{x-y} + \frac{y}{x-y} = \frac{x+y}{x-y}$$

To solve an equation involving fractions we multiply each member of the equation by the LCD of the given fractions in order to obtain an equivalent equation that does not contain fractions.

Example 12 Solve the equation: $\dfrac{3}{5}x + \dfrac{1}{2} = \dfrac{7}{10}$

Solution: The LCD of the fractions $\dfrac{3}{5}, \dfrac{1}{2},$ and $\dfrac{7}{10}$ is 10. Therefore, we multiply both members of the equation by 10.

$$\frac{3}{5}x + \frac{1}{2} = \frac{7}{10}$$

$$10\left(\frac{3}{5}x + \frac{1}{2}\right) = \left(\frac{7}{10}\right)10$$

Applying the Distributive Law in the left member we have

$$10\left(\frac{3}{5}x\right) + 10\left(\frac{1}{2}\right) = 7$$

or, equivalently,

$$6x + 5 = 7$$

$$6x = 2$$

$$x = \frac{2}{6}$$

$$x = \frac{1}{3}$$

The following example illustrates how a complex fraction can be simplified by multiplying both the numerator and denominator by the LCD of the simple fractions.

Example 13 Simplify the complex fraction $\dfrac{\dfrac{1}{9} - \dfrac{3}{5}}{\dfrac{2}{15} + \dfrac{5}{9}}$.

Solution: The LCD of $\dfrac{1}{9}, \dfrac{3}{5}, \dfrac{2}{15}$ and $\dfrac{5}{9}$ is 45. Hence, we multiply the numerator and denominator of the complex fraction by 45. We have then

$$\frac{\dfrac{1}{9} - \dfrac{3}{5}}{\dfrac{2}{15} + \dfrac{5}{9}} = \frac{\left(\dfrac{1}{9} - \dfrac{3}{5}\right) \cdot 45}{\left(\dfrac{2}{15} + \dfrac{5}{9}\right) \cdot 45}$$

$$= \frac{5 - 27}{6 + 25}$$

$$= \frac{-22}{31}$$

Exercises 5.5

In Exercises 1 through 23 add or subtract as indicated and express the answer in simplest form.

1. (a) $\dfrac{2}{3} + \dfrac{2}{3}$ **(b)** $\dfrac{5}{6} + \dfrac{1}{6}$

2. (a) $\dfrac{1}{5} + \dfrac{3}{5}$ **(b)** $\dfrac{3}{8} + \dfrac{7}{8}$

3. (a) $\dfrac{5x}{9} + \dfrac{-4x}{9}$ **(b)** $\dfrac{7a}{12} + \dfrac{-11a}{12}$

4. (a) $\dfrac{-1}{4} + \dfrac{3}{4}$ **(b)** $\dfrac{-5}{10} + \dfrac{5}{10}$

5. (a) $\dfrac{-7}{16} + \dfrac{-15}{16}$ **(b)** $\dfrac{-3}{7} + \dfrac{3}{7}$

6. (a) $\dfrac{5}{2x} - \dfrac{3}{2x}$ **(b)** $\dfrac{5}{6y} - \dfrac{1}{6y}$

7. (a) $\dfrac{3}{20} - \dfrac{3}{20}$ **(b)** $\dfrac{9}{x - 6} - \dfrac{-3}{x - 6}$

8. (a) $\dfrac{2x}{3} + \dfrac{3x}{4}$ **(b)** $\dfrac{y}{2} + \dfrac{2y}{3}$

9. (a) $\dfrac{5}{12} + \dfrac{5}{6}$ (b) $\dfrac{3}{8} + \dfrac{3}{4}$

10. (a) $\dfrac{3}{4} + \dfrac{5}{6}$ (b) $\dfrac{3x}{20} + \dfrac{3x}{10}$

11. (a) $\dfrac{5y}{6} + \dfrac{3y}{8}$ (b) $3\left(\dfrac{3}{10} + \dfrac{-1}{8}\right)$

12. (a) $\left(\dfrac{-2}{7} + \dfrac{1}{3}\right)\left(\dfrac{1}{2}\right)$ (b) $\dfrac{-8xy}{9} + \dfrac{-5xy}{6}$

13. (a) $\left(\dfrac{2}{3}\right)\left(\dfrac{-1}{4} - \dfrac{-1}{5}\right)$ (b) $\dfrac{x}{2} - \dfrac{x}{3}$

14. (a) $\dfrac{x}{4} + \dfrac{x}{8}$ (b) $\left(\dfrac{x}{12} + \dfrac{y}{18}\right) \cdot 36$

15. (a) $\left(\dfrac{2x}{3} + \dfrac{x}{9}\right)\left(\dfrac{3}{7} - \dfrac{5}{7}\right)$ (b) $\dfrac{3x}{5} - \dfrac{x}{10}$

16. (a) $\dfrac{1}{3} + \dfrac{1}{4} + \dfrac{1}{5}$ (b) $\left(\dfrac{2}{3} + \dfrac{3}{4} - \dfrac{1}{2}\right)\left(1 + \dfrac{7}{8}\right)$

17. (a) $\dfrac{6}{5} - \dfrac{3}{10} + \dfrac{2}{15}$ (b) $\dfrac{1}{3} - \dfrac{1}{4} + \dfrac{1}{5}$

18. (a) $\dfrac{x}{3} + \dfrac{y}{3} + \dfrac{z}{4}$ (b) $\dfrac{2x}{5} + \dfrac{x}{10} - \dfrac{y}{10}$

19. (a) $\dfrac{3}{8} + \dfrac{1}{-4}$ (b) $\dfrac{x}{4} - \dfrac{x}{-3}$

20. (a) $\dfrac{x}{x} + \dfrac{2}{x}$ (b) $\dfrac{a}{a+b} + \dfrac{b}{a+b}$

21. (a) $\dfrac{a}{a-b} - \dfrac{b}{a-b}$ (b) $\dfrac{1}{x} + \dfrac{1}{y}$

22. (a) $\dfrac{a}{b} + \dfrac{a}{c}$ (b) $\dfrac{2x}{xy} + \dfrac{3}{xy}$

23. (a) $\dfrac{a}{b} + \dfrac{c}{d}$ (b) $\dfrac{a}{b} - \dfrac{c}{d}$

In Exercises 24 through 29 solve the given equation.

24. $\dfrac{2}{3}x + \dfrac{1}{2} = \dfrac{1}{4}$ 25. $\dfrac{3}{4}x - \dfrac{2}{5} = \dfrac{-3}{20}$

26. $\dfrac{1}{2}x - \dfrac{1}{5} = \dfrac{5}{2}$ 27. $\dfrac{4}{5}x + \dfrac{2}{3} = \dfrac{-4}{15}$

28. $\dfrac{1}{2}x + \dfrac{1}{5} = \dfrac{1}{3}x - \dfrac{1}{10}$

29. $\dfrac{5}{2}x - \dfrac{1}{3} = \dfrac{1}{4}x + \dfrac{5}{12}$

In Exercises 30 through 34 simplify the complex fraction.

30. $\dfrac{\dfrac{3}{4} + \dfrac{1}{2}}{\dfrac{3}{8} - \dfrac{7}{8}}$

31. $\dfrac{\dfrac{1}{2} + \dfrac{1}{3}}{\dfrac{2}{3} + \dfrac{1}{4}}$

32. $\dfrac{\dfrac{1}{x} + \dfrac{1}{y}}{\dfrac{1}{x} - \dfrac{1}{y}}$

33. $\dfrac{5}{6} + \dfrac{\dfrac{3}{4} - \dfrac{1}{3}}{\dfrac{5}{12} + \dfrac{1}{2}}$

34. $\left(\dfrac{\dfrac{9}{16} - \dfrac{3}{2}}{\dfrac{7}{8} - \dfrac{7}{4}}\right)^2$

35. Prove: $\dfrac{1}{a} + \dfrac{1}{b} = \dfrac{a + b}{ab}$

36. The formula for a parallel wiring circuit that has two branches is

$$\frac{1}{R} = \frac{1}{R_1} + \frac{1}{R_2}$$

where R_1 and R_2 are, respectively, the number of ohms of resistance of the two branches and R ohms is the total resistance in the circuit. Find the total resistance in the circuit if $R_1 = 3$ and $R_2 = 4$.

37. For a camera lens, a telescope, or a curved mirror, if

f = number of units in the focal length
D_o = number of units in the object distance
D_i = number of units in the image distance

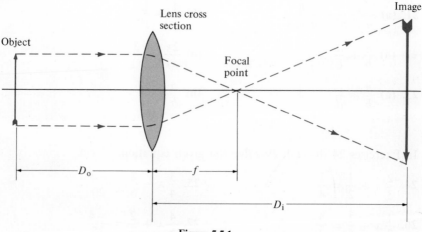

Figure 5.5.1

then

$$\frac{1}{f} = \frac{1}{D_o} + \frac{1}{D_i}$$

This formula is similar to the one used for the total resistance in an electric circuit. Figure 5.5.1 illustrates a real image formed through a lens. Find the focal length of a lens if the object distance is 40 centimeters and the image distance is 60 centimeters.

5.6 Ratio, Proportion, and Percent

A large number of problems of wide application can be solved by using the concepts of "ratio" and "proportion."

A "ratio" is a comparison of two numbers or quantities expressed by the division operation.

5.6.1 Definition   For any real numbers a and b, $b \neq 0$, the *ratio* of a to b is "a divided by b," denoted by $\frac{a}{b}$ or $a : b$ (read: the ratio of a to b).

Thus, the ratio of 6 to 3 is $\frac{6}{3}$. Because

$$\frac{6}{3} = \frac{2}{1}$$

the ratio of 6 to 3 is equivalent to the ratio of 2 to 1. Because

$$\frac{6}{9} = \frac{2}{3}$$

the ratio of 6 to 9 is equivalent to the ratio of 2 to 3.

We can compare measurements by considering the ratio of the corresponding measures when the measurements are expressed in the same units.

Illustration 1   To compare 1 quart to 1 pint we first note that 1 quart is equivalent to 2 pints. Thus, the comparison of 1 quart to 1 pint is equivalent to the comparison of 2 pints to 1 pint. The ratio of the corresponding measures is $2 : 1$ or, equivalently, $\frac{2}{1}$.

Illustration 2   To compare 3 inches to 2 feet we first note that 2 feet is equivalent to 24 inches. Thus, the comparison of 3 inches to 2 feet is equivalent to the comparison of 3 inches to 24 inches. The ratio of the corresponding measures is $3 : 24$ or, equivalently, $\frac{3}{24}$. Because $\frac{3}{24}$ is equivalent to $\frac{1}{8}$, we conclude that the ratio of the corresponding measures is $1 : 8$.

Example 1 Compare the areas of two squares if the length of the side of the second square is twice the length of the side of the first square.

Solution: Let s be the measure of the side of the first square, then $2s$ is the number of units in the length of the side of the second square. The ratio of the measures of the sides is $\dfrac{s}{2s} = \dfrac{1}{2}$ or 1 to 2. However, if A_1 is the number of square units in the area of the first square and A_2 is the number of square units in the area of the second square, the ratio of A_1 to A_2 is

$$\frac{A_1}{A_2} = \frac{s^2}{(2s)^2}$$

$$= \frac{s^2}{4s^2}$$

$$= \frac{1}{4}$$

Illustration 3 The ratio of the measure of the circumference of any circle to the measure of the diameter of that circle is the constant value, π. That is, if C is the number of units in the circumference of a circle and d is the number of units in the diameter of that circle, then

$$\frac{C}{d} = \pi$$

5.6.2 Definition   A *proportion* is an equation whose members are ratios.

Illustration 4 The equation

$$\frac{6}{3} = \frac{2}{1}$$

is a proportion.

A proportion can also be stated using the symbol : . Using the symbol : , the proportion of Illustration 4 is denoted by

$$6 : 3 = 2 : 1$$

which is read as either

"6 is to 3 as 2 is to 1"

or

"the ratio of 6 to 3 is equal to the ratio of 2 to 1."

Four numbers are "in proportion" when the ratio of the first two numbers equals the ratio of the second pair of numbers. The four numbers 6, 3, 2, and 1, considered in that order, are in proportion because

$$\frac{6}{3} = \frac{2}{1}$$

5.6.3 Definition   If the numbers a, b, c, and d are in proportion such that

$$a : b = c : d$$

then the numbers a and d are called the *extremes* of the proportion while b and c are called the *means* of the proportion.

Illustration 5   In the proportion $6 : 3 = 2 : 1$, 6 and 1 are called the extremes and 3 and 2 are called the means.

A relationship between the means and extremes of a proportion is given by the following theorem.

5.6.4 Theorem   If $a : b = c : d$, then $ad = bc$; that is, the product of the means equals the product of the extremes.

Proof: Given

$$\frac{a}{b} = \frac{c}{d}$$

we can multiply both members by b and obtain

$$a = \frac{bc}{d}$$

Next we multiply both members by d and obtain

$$ad = bc$$

Illustration 6   If x is to 3 as 2 is to 1, then we have

$$\frac{x}{3} = \frac{2}{1}$$

The product of the extremes if (x) (1) and the product of the means is $(3)(2)$. Therefore,

$$(x)(1) = (3)(2)$$

Hence,

$$x = 6$$

Example 2 Solve the proportion

$$\frac{6}{9} = \frac{15}{x}$$

Solution: Because the product of the means equals the product of the extremes, we have

$$6x = (9)(15)$$

and so

$$x = \frac{(9)(15)}{6}$$

$$= \frac{45}{2}$$

Example 3 If a recipe that serves 4 people calls for $1\frac{1}{2}$ cups of sugar, how many cups of sugar are needed to serve 6 people?

Solution: Let x be the number of cups of sugar needed to serve 6 people, then 4 is to $\frac{3}{2}$ as 6 is to x or, equivalently.

$$\frac{4}{\frac{3}{2}} = \frac{6}{x}$$

Because the product of the means equals the product of the extremes, we have

$$4x = 6 \cdot \frac{3}{2}$$

$$4x = 9$$

$$x = \frac{9}{4}$$

$$= 2\frac{1}{4}$$

Therefore, $2\frac{1}{4}$ cups of sugar are needed.

Percent means *hundredths* or *parts per hundred*. We use the symbol % to mean "percent." Therefore,

$$25 \text{ percent} = 25\%$$

Twenty-five percent is the ratio of 25 to 100. Hence,

$$25\% = \frac{25}{100}$$

$$= \frac{1}{4}$$

Illustration 7

(a) $33\frac{1}{3}\% = \dfrac{33\frac{1}{3}}{100}$

$$= \frac{\left(33\frac{1}{3}\right)(3)}{(100)(3)}$$

$$= \frac{100}{300}$$

$$= \frac{1}{3}$$

(b) $5\frac{1}{2}\% = \dfrac{5\frac{1}{2}}{100}$

$$= \frac{\left(5\frac{1}{2}\right)(2)}{(100)(2)}$$

$$= \frac{11}{200}$$

Illustration 8 25% of 40 is 10, because twenty-five hundredths of 40 is

$$\frac{25}{100} \cdot 40 = 10$$

or, equivalently,

$$\frac{25}{100} = \frac{10}{40}$$

In Illustration 8, 25% is the *rate* (percent ratio), 40 is the *base,* and 10 is the *percentage.* In general if p is the percentage, r is the rate, and b is the base, a formula for the relationship of these numbers is

$$r = \frac{p}{b} \tag{1}$$

Formula (1) is a proportion which states that the percent ratio equals the ratio of the percentage to the base. From Illustration 8, where $p = 10$ and

$b = 40$, we have

$$r = \frac{10}{40}$$

Because r is a percent ratio, r equals n parts per hundred. Hence, we have the proportion

$$\frac{n}{100} = \frac{10}{40}$$

and solving for n we find

$$n = 25$$

Thus, r equals 25 parts per hundred or, equivalently, 25%.

Any two of the three numbers p, r, and b can be given and the third may be determined from formula (1). Thus, there are three basic types of problems that one can encounter (see Examples 4, 5, and 6).

Example 4   90 is *what percent* of 240?

Solution: $p = 90$, $b = 240$, $r =$ the rate $\left(\text{percent ratio, } \dfrac{n}{100} \right)$. Because r equals n parts per hundred, we have the proportion

$$n \text{ is to } 100 \text{ as } 90 \text{ is to } 240$$

or, equivalently, from formula (1)

$$\frac{n}{100} = \frac{90}{240}$$

Solving this equation for n we obtain

$$n = 100 \left(\frac{90}{240} \right)$$

$$= 37\frac{1}{2}$$

Hence,

$$r = \frac{37\frac{1}{2}}{100}$$

$$= 37\frac{1}{2}\%$$

Example 5   40 is $33\frac{1}{3}\%$ of *what number?*

Solution: $p = 40$, $r = 33\frac{1}{3}\%$, $b =$ the base. The proportion is

$$33\frac{1}{3} \text{ is to } 100 \text{ as } 40 \text{ is to } b$$

or, equivalently, from formula (1)

$$\frac{33\frac{1}{3}}{100} = \frac{40}{b} \qquad\qquad (2)$$

Substituting $\frac{1}{3}$ for the left member of equation (2), we get

$$\frac{1}{3} = \frac{40}{b}$$

Because the product of the means equals the product of the extremes, we have

$$(1)(b) = (3)(40)$$
$$b = 120$$

Hence, 40 is $33\frac{1}{3}\%$ of 120.

Example 6 *What number is* $\frac{1}{2}\%$ *of 400?*

Solution: $b = 400$, $r = \frac{1}{2}\%$, $p =$ the percentage.

$$\frac{\frac{1}{2}}{100} = \frac{p}{400}$$
$$100(p) = \left(\frac{1}{2}\right)(400)$$
$$100p = 200$$
$$p = 2$$

Hence, 2 is $\frac{1}{2}\%$ of 400.

Example 7 A solution of salt in water is analyzed by comparing the weight of the salt to the weight of the solution. A 20% solution of salt in water means that the solution contains 20 parts of salt per 100 parts of solution. How many grams of salt are there in 80 grams of such a solution?

Solution: Let $p = $ the number of grams of salt in the solution. Then we have the proportion

$$\frac{20}{100} = \frac{p}{80}$$

$$100p = (20)(80)$$

$$p = \frac{(20)(80)}{100}$$

$$= 16$$

Hence, there are 16 grams of salt in 80 grams of a 20% solution of salt in water.

Example 8 The total cost of a stereo sound system is $386.30. This cost includes a 5% sales tax in addition to the selling price. What is the selling price?

Solution: Let $x = $ the number of dollars in the selling price. Then 105% of x equals the number of dollars in the total cost of the stereo system. Thus, we have the proportion

$$\frac{105}{100} = \frac{386.30}{x}$$

$$105(x) = (100)(386.30)$$

$$x = \frac{(100)(386.30)}{105}$$

$$= 368.00$$

Hence, the selling price of the stereo sound system is $368.00.

Exercises 5.6

In Exercises 1 and 2 compare the given quantities by expressing them as ratios.

1. (a) 12 to 15   **(b)** 36 to 24

2. (a) 1.5 to 0.5   **(b)** $\frac{5}{4}$ to $\frac{3}{4}$

3. (a) Compare $2\frac{1}{2}$ feet to 1 yard.

(b) Compare 12 ounces to $1\frac{1}{2}$ pounds.

(c) Compare 4 quarts to 1 gallon.

4. The man–land ratio (population density) is the ratio of the population count to the number 1, which represents one square unit of land area where the population is counted.

(a) Find the man–land ratio for California if its population is 20 million and its area is 158,600 square miles.

(b) Find the man–land ratio for the world. The population is three billion, and the land area is 135 million square kilometers.

(c) If the world population doubles, what is the man–land ratio?

5. Adverse "smog" conditions have been defined to be 0.15 parts of oxidant per million parts of air, or higher, when maintained for 1 hour or longer. What ratio corresponds to this comparison?

6. On a blueprint the scale claimed "1 inch is equivalent to 10 feet." Compare these measurements.

7. The area of a circle is A square units and $A = \pi r^2$, where r is the measure of the radius. If the length of the radius of a circle is doubled how do the respective areas compare?

8. Compare the areas of two squares if one had a side of length 4 inches and the other has a side of length 12 inches. What is the ratio of the measures of their sides?

In Exercises 9 through 14 find x in each of the proportions.

9. (a) $\dfrac{3}{4} = \dfrac{x}{28}$ (b) $\dfrac{12}{7} = \dfrac{x}{4}$

10. (a) $\dfrac{9}{3} = \dfrac{30}{x}$ (b) $\dfrac{5}{7} = \dfrac{9}{x}$

11. (a) $\dfrac{x}{9} = \dfrac{7}{70}$ (b) $\dfrac{x}{2} = \dfrac{2}{5}$

12. (a) $\dfrac{14}{x} = \dfrac{28}{2}$ (b) $\dfrac{50}{x} = \dfrac{75}{1}$

13. (a) $\dfrac{3}{x+1} = \dfrac{4}{7}$ (b) $\dfrac{3}{2x} = \dfrac{5}{x+1}$

14. (a) $\dfrac{9}{2x+1} = \dfrac{6}{4}$ (b) $\dfrac{x+5}{3} = \dfrac{2x}{1}$

15. If $7\frac{1}{2}$ gallons of water occupy 1 cubic foot of space, how much space is occupied by 1 gallon of water? (Write a proportion.)

16. A block of iron $6 \times 4 \times 48$ inches is drawn into a long rod with a $\frac{1}{4} \times \frac{1}{4}$ inch cross section. What is the ratio of the measures of the two volumes? What are the measures of the surface areas?

17. If $5z = 8t$, then find $\dfrac{t}{z}$.

18. Show that $x : x^2 = x^3 \cdot x^4$.

19. Prove that x is to 1 as 1 is to the reciprocal of x.

20. The "Golden Ratio" is defined to be the ratio of the measure of the width to the measure of the length of a certain rectangle such that the measure of the width of the rectangle is to the measure of the length as the measure of the length is to the sum of the measures of the length and width. See Figure 5.6.1. This rectangle was used in much of Greek art and architecture. Write the proportion stated above, and let l be the measure of the length and w be the measure of the width of the rectangle.

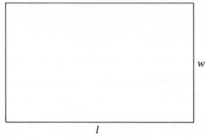

l

Figure 5.6.1

21. In the proportion $a \div b = c \div d$ we know that the product of the means equals the product of the extremes, that is,

$$ad = bc$$

Suppose that in the difference equation, $a - b = c - d$, the numbers a and d are called the "exteriors" and the numbers b and c are called the "interiors." Prove that the sum of the interiors equals the sum of the exteriors.

In Exercises 22 through 24 write a proportion and solve.

22. (a) 60% of _____ is 120.
(b) 50 is what percent of 75?

23. (a) 300 is 25% of _____.
(b) _____ is 20% of 78.

24. (a) $33\dfrac{1}{3}$% of 45 is _____.

(b) 600 is _____% of 400?

25. A town's population increased from 92,500 to 105,000. What percent increase does this represent?

26. Your weight on the moon is about $\frac{1}{6}$ of what it is here on earth, that is, about $16\frac{2}{3}\%$ of your earth weight. Suppose you weigh 140 pounds. How much would you weigh on the moon?

27. The total cost of an article is $15.34. This includes a 4% tax in addition to the selling price. What is the selling price?

28. A retail store paid $25.00 for an item of merchandise to offer for sale. The retailer marks the price up 20% of the amount he paid to realize a profit. Later the store had a "Sale" and this particular item was marked down 20% of the pre-sale price. What is the selling price during the "sale"? (The answer is not $25.00.)

29. (a) How many grams of salt are there in 80 grams of 15% solution of salt in water? See Example 7.
    (b) How many grams of water are there in the solution.

30. How much water must evaporate in Exercise 29 to give a 75% solution of salt in water?

31. How many grams of water and how many grams of sugar would you have to use to get 80 grams of a 5% solution?

32. Some psychologists define "intelligence quotient" as the ratio of a person's mental age to his chronological age expressed as a percent:

$$I = \frac{M}{C} \cdot 100$$

If a student has a mental age of 15 and an IQ of 135 (percent), what is his chronological age?

33. A number of horses on a certain ranch are shown in the following partition by sex and by color.

	Mare	Stallion
Black	15	5
Sorrel	10	40
Palomino	20	15
White	10	25

(a) Of all the horses, what percent are mares?
(b) Considering only the stallions, what percent are found in each color class?
(c) Of all the horses, what percent are sorrel?
(d) Considering only the palominos, what percent are stallions?

34. Suppose there are 20 women in a class that includes 40 men. What percent of the class do the women constitute?

5.7 Review Exercises

1. Express each number in prime factored form.
  (a) 210   (b) 240

2. Find the LCM and GCD of each set of numbers.
  (a) {48, 60}   (b) {1260, 2700}

3. Complete the following table.

Number	Simplest Form of the Number	Multiplicative Inverse of the Number
3		
-1		
0		
$\dfrac{4}{8}$		
$\dfrac{-17}{5}$		
$\dfrac{1}{3}$		
$-\dfrac{1}{5}$		

4. Name the property illustrated by each of the following equalities:

  (a) $6 \cdot \dfrac{1}{6} = 1$
  (b) $\dfrac{x}{3} = x \cdot \dfrac{1}{3}$
  (c) $\dfrac{1}{x} \cdot \dfrac{x}{y} = \dfrac{x}{y} \cdot \dfrac{1}{x}$

In Exercises 5 through 10 perform each of the indicated operations.

5. (a) $\dfrac{-x}{6} \div \dfrac{3x}{2}$
  (b) $8xy^2 \div \dfrac{x}{y}$

6. (a) $\dfrac{2}{xy} \cdot \dfrac{3x}{4}$
  (b) $\dfrac{9ab^2}{4} \cdot \dfrac{8b}{3a^2}$

7. (a) $\left(\dfrac{-x}{2}\right)^2$
  (b) $-\left(\dfrac{-1}{y^2}\right)$

8. (a) $\dfrac{x}{2} + \dfrac{x}{2}$ **(b)** $\dfrac{x}{3} + \dfrac{3x}{2} + \dfrac{4x}{9}$

9. (a) $\dfrac{x}{3} - \dfrac{x}{2}$ **(b)** $\dfrac{m}{m-n} - \dfrac{n}{m-n}$

10. (a) $\dfrac{4x}{xy} + \dfrac{3}{y} - \dfrac{2y}{x}$ **(b)** $\dfrac{2}{3}\left(\dfrac{5k}{6} + \dfrac{k}{2}\right)$

11. Simplify each of the following complex fractions.

    (a) $\dfrac{\dfrac{-t}{12}}{\dfrac{t^2}{9}}$ **(b)** $\dfrac{\dfrac{x}{3} + \dfrac{5x}{2}}{\dfrac{x}{4} - \dfrac{2x}{3}}$

12. Solve each of the following equations.

    (a) $\dfrac{1}{2}x + \dfrac{5}{6} = \dfrac{1}{3}$ **(b)** $20 - \dfrac{1}{3}x = \dfrac{5}{4}$

13. (a) Compare $2\dfrac{1}{2}$ feet to 5 inches using a ratio.

    (b) Compare $\dfrac{1}{4}$ inches to 100 feet using a ratio.

14. Solve each of the following proportions.

    (a) $2 : 7 = 5 : x$ **(b)** $\dfrac{6}{9} = \dfrac{8}{x}$

15. One square has a side of 4 inches and another has a side of 8 inches. What is the ratio of the measures of the
(a) perimeters of the two squares?
(b) areas of the two squares?

16. 24 is what percent of 60?

17. A secretary signs an invoice for office supplies. The total charge on the invoice is $37.80 and this includes a tax on the items ordered equal to 5% of the retail price of the items. Find the retail price of the items for the secretary.

18. Blood types are classified according to whether or not the blood contains the A antigen (Type A), the B antigen (Type B), both the A and B antigens (Type AB), or neither the A nor the B antigen (Type O). In a sample of 400 American Indians it was found that 56 Indians had blood containing the A antigen; 196 Indians had blood containing the B antigen; 164 Indians had blood that contained neither the A nor the B antigen. This classification of blood types is shown in the following diagram where

$A = \{$the people whose blood contains the A antigen$\}$
$B = \{$the people whose blood contains the B antigen$\}$

	A	A'
B	TYPE AB $A \cap B$	TYPE B $A' \cap B$
B'	TYPE A $A \cap B'$	TYPE O $A' \cap B'$

(a) How many Indians are found in each blood type?
(b) Of all the Indians, what percent is found in each blood type?
(c) Of all the Indians, what percent had blood free of the B antigen?
(d) Of all the Indians, what percent had either Type A or Type B blood?

6

The Real Numbers

6.1 Decimal Fractions

An important numeral used to represent some rational numbers is a "decimal fraction." A *decimal fraction* is a fraction whose denominator is a power of ten. That is, the denominator of a decimal fraction is an element of the set

$$\{10^1, 10^2, 10^3, 10^4, \ldots, 10^n, \ldots\}$$

where n is a positive integer.

Illustration 1   The following fractions are decimal fractions:

$$\frac{7}{10}, \quad \frac{3}{100}, \quad \frac{59}{100}, \quad \frac{427}{1000}, \quad \frac{81}{10,000}, \quad \frac{6243}{100,000}$$

A decimal fraction can be written in a more concise manner by using a decimal point. For instance,

$\dfrac{7}{10}$ is equivalent to 0.7

$\dfrac{3}{100}$ is equivalent to 0.03

$\dfrac{59}{100}$ is equivalent to 0.59

$\dfrac{427}{1000}$ is equivalent to 0.427

$\dfrac{81}{10,000}$ is equivalent to 0.0081

$\dfrac{6243}{100,000}$ is equivalent to 0.06243

The numeral 0.7 is called the *decimal form* of the decimal fraction $\dfrac{7}{10}$, the

numeral 0.03 is called the decimal form of the decimal fraction $\dfrac{3}{100}$, the

213

numeral 0.427 is called the decimal form of the decimal fraction $\frac{427}{1000}$, and

so on. A numeral in decimal form is called a *decimal*.

The following illustration shows how a numeral in decimal form can be expressed as an equivalent decimal fraction.

Illustration 2 $0.375 = 0.3 + 0.07 + 0.005$

$$= \frac{3}{10} + \frac{7}{100} + \frac{5}{1000}$$

$$= \frac{3 \cdot 100}{10 \cdot 100} + \frac{7 \cdot 10}{100 \cdot 10} + \frac{5}{1000}$$

$$= \frac{300}{1000} + \frac{70}{1000} + \frac{5}{1000}$$

$$= \frac{300 + 70 + 5}{1000}$$

$$= \frac{375}{1000}$$

The expression

$$\frac{3}{10} + \frac{7}{100} + \frac{5}{1000}$$

is called the *expanded form* of the decimal form 0.375.

To represent a rational number by a numeral in decimal form, we can use any fraction which represents the rational number and divide the numerator by the denominator. The next illustration shows the procedure.

Illustration 3 To represent $\frac{3}{8}$ by a numeral in decimal form we divide 3 by 8.

$$
\begin{array}{r}
0.375 \\
8\overline{)3.000} \\
\underline{2\,4} \\
60 \\
\underline{56} \\
40 \\
\underline{40} \\
0
\end{array}
$$

Thus, $\frac{3}{8}$ is equivalent to 0.375.

Not every rational number can be represented by a decimal fraction. Consider, for instance, the fraction $\frac{1}{3}$. Recall that

$\frac{1}{3}$ is not equivalent to $\frac{3}{10}$ because $1 \cdot 10 \neq 3 \cdot 3$

$\frac{1}{3}$ is not equivalent to $\frac{33}{100}$ because $1 \cdot 100 \neq 3 \cdot 33$

$\frac{1}{3}$ is not equivalent to $\frac{333}{1000}$ because $1 \cdot 1000 \neq 3 \cdot 333$

In fact, there is no value of n for which $\frac{1}{3}$ is equivalent to $\frac{a}{10^n}$ because $1 \cdot 10^n$ does not equal $3a$. For if $10^n = 3a$, then 3 would be a factor (divisor) of 10^n and consequently 3 would be a factor of 10. But 3 is not a factor of 10 $(10 = 2 \cdot 5)$. Hence, 3 cannot be a factor of 10^n. To say that there is no n for which $\frac{1}{3}$ is equivalent to $\frac{a}{10^n}$ is to say that $\frac{1}{3}$ cannot be expressed as a decimal fraction, no matter how great n is.

However, if we consider the sequence of decimal fractions

$$\frac{3}{10}, \frac{33}{100}, \frac{333}{1000}, \dots$$

we see that the values of these decimal fractions get progressively closer to the value of $\frac{1}{3}$. Refer to Figure 6.1.1.

$$\frac{3}{10} < \frac{33}{100} < \frac{333}{1000} < \dots < \frac{1}{3}$$

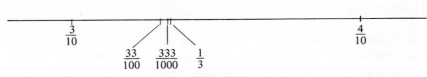

Figure 6.1.1

Illustration 4 If we attempt to represent $\frac{1}{3}$ by a numeral in decimal form we find that the process of dividing 1 by 3 is unending (or nonterminating).

$$
\begin{array}{r}
0.3333\dots \\
3\overline{)1.0000\dots} \\
\underline{9} \\
10 \\
\underline{9} \\
10 \\
\underline{9} \\
10 \\
\underline{9} \\
1
\end{array}
$$

Thus, $\frac{1}{3}$ is equivalent to the nonterminating decimal 0.3333 . . . .

The nonterminating decimal 0.3333 . . . is called a *repeating decimal* because the digit 3 is repeated.

Example 1 Represent $\frac{3}{11}$ by a decimal.

Solution: $\frac{3}{11} = 3 \div 11$

$$
\begin{array}{r}
0.27272\ldots \\
11)\overline{3.00000\ldots} \\
\underline{2\,2} \\
80 \\
\underline{77} \\
30 \\
\underline{22} \\
80 \\
\underline{77} \\
3
\end{array}
$$

Therefore, $\frac{3}{11} = 0.272727 \ldots .$

In Example 1 the digits 27 repeat in the decimal 0.272727 . . . , and so this decimal is a repeating decimal. We denote a repeating decimal by writing a bar over the group of digits that repeat. Thus, we have

$$\frac{1}{3} = 0.333 \ldots = 0.\overline{3}$$

$$\frac{3}{11} = 0.272727 \ldots = 0.\overline{27}$$

$$\frac{507}{9900} = 0.05121212 \ldots = 0.05\overline{12}$$

Every rational number can be represented by a decimal. In Illustration 3, Illustration 4, and Example 1, respectively, we showed that

$$\frac{3}{8} = 0.375$$

$$\frac{1}{3} = 0.\overline{3}$$

$$\frac{3}{11} = 0.\overline{27}$$

The decimal representation of a rational number is either terminating $\left(\text{as}\right.$ is the case with $\left.\frac{3}{8}\right)$ or nonterminating and repeating $\left(\text{as is the case with}\right.$ $\frac{1}{3}$ and $\left.\frac{3}{11}\right)$. There are real numbers that are represented by nonterminating, nonrepeating decimals, but these are not rational numbers (they are discussed in Section 6.2).

Example 2 Represent $\frac{3}{7}$ by a decimal.

Solution: $\frac{3}{7} = 3 \div 7$

$$
\begin{array}{r}
0.4285714\ldots \\
7\overline{)3.0000000\ldots} \\
2\,8 \\
\overline{20} \\
14 \\
\overline{60} \\
56 \\
\overline{40} \\
35 \\
\overline{50} \\
49 \\
\overline{10} \\
7 \\
\overline{30} \\
28 \\
\overline{2}
\end{array}
$$

Because the digit 2 is the same remainder that was obtained earlier (in the first subtraction), the digits in the quotient will repeat. Thus,

$$\frac{3}{7} = 0.\overline{428571}$$

We now describe a procedure for expressing a repeating decimal as an equivalent fraction. The method depends upon some advanced mathematics, so we do not prove it at this time. In any repeating decimal we designate the number in the group being repeated by a. The actual number of digits in the group is designated by r. Then a fraction that is equivalent to the repeating decimal is given by the formula

$$\frac{a}{10^r - 1}$$

Illustration 5 Given $0.\overline{5} = 0.555\ldots$. To express this repeating decimal by an equivalent fraction we see that the number in the group being repeated is 5; thus, $a = 5$. There is only one digit in the group that is being repeated, hence, $r = 1$. Therefore, we have

$$\frac{a}{10^r - 1} = \frac{5}{10^1 - 1}$$

$$= \frac{5}{9}$$

Hence,

$$0.\overline{5} = 0.555\ldots$$

$$= \frac{5}{9}$$

The result can be checked by dividing 5 by 9.

Example 3 Find a fraction equivalent to $0.\overline{123}$.

Solution: An equivalent fraction is $\dfrac{a}{10^r - 1}$ where $a = 123$ and $r = 3$. Hence, we have

$$\frac{a}{10^r - 1} = \frac{123}{10^3 - 1}$$

$$= \frac{123}{1000 - 1}$$

$$= \frac{123}{999}$$

However,

$$\frac{123}{999} = \frac{123 \div 3}{999 \div 3} = \frac{41}{333}$$

Therefore

$$0.\overline{123} = \frac{41}{333}$$

It is easy to compare the magnitudes of two rational numbers represented by decimal fractions. It is not always obvious which of two rational numbers represented by fractions, for instance, $\frac{4}{5}$ and $\frac{7}{9}$, is the larger. However,

$\frac{4}{5} = 0.8\overline{0}$ and $\frac{7}{9} = 0.\overline{7}$, and it is obvious that $0.8\overline{0}$ is greater than $0.\overline{7}$.

Example 4 Find a rational number between $0.8\overline{0}$ and $0.\overline{7}$.

Solution: There is an unlimited number of rational numbers between $0.8\overline{0}$ and $0.\overline{7}$,

$$0.8\overline{0} = 0.80000\ldots$$

and

$$0.\overline{7} = 0.77777\ldots$$

A rational number between $0.8\overline{0}$ and $0.\overline{7}$ is 0.78.
Others are 0.79 and 0.785. There are many possibilities.

$$0.8\overline{0}\ \ = 0.80000\ldots$$
$$0.79\ \ = 0.79000\ldots$$
$$0.785 = 0.785000\ldots$$
$$0.78\ \ = 0.780000\ldots$$
$$0.\overline{7}\ \ \ = 0.777777\ldots$$

Between every pair of distinct real numbers there is always another real number. In fact, between every pair of distinct rational numbers there is always another rational number. This is called the property of *density*.

6.1.1 Property (Density) If a and b are real numbers and $a < b$, there exists a real number r such that

$$a < r < b$$

Because of Property 6.1.1 the set of real numbers is said to be *dense*. Not all sets of numbers are dense. For instance, the set of integers is not dense because between any two integers there does not always exist another integer. Between 4 and 5 there does not exist another integer.

The set of rational numbers is dense. An obvious choice for finding a rational number that is between two others is the one exactly halfway between them. This number is the average of the two given rational numbers. The average of the two numbers a and b is $\dfrac{a+b}{2}$. Furthermore, if $a < b$, then

$$a < \frac{a+b}{2} < b$$

Example 5 Find the rational number halfway between $0.\overline{3}$ and $0.\overline{4}$.

Solution: The fraction $\dfrac{1}{3}$ is equivalent to $0.\overline{3}$ and the fraction $\dfrac{a}{10^r - 1}$ is equivalent to $0.\overline{4}$ where $a = 4$ and $r = 1$. Hence,

$$0.\overline{4} = \frac{4}{10^1 - 1}$$

$$= \frac{4}{10 - 1}$$

$$= \frac{4}{9}$$

✓ The average of $\frac{1}{3}$ and $\frac{4}{9}$ is given by

$$\frac{\frac{1}{3} + \frac{4}{9}}{2} = \frac{\left(\frac{1}{3} + \frac{4}{9}\right) \cdot 9}{(2) \cdot 9}$$

$$= \frac{3 + 4}{18}$$

$$= \frac{7}{18}$$

Therefore, $\frac{7}{18}$ is halfway between $\frac{1}{3}$ and $\frac{4}{9}$, furthermore, $\frac{7}{18} = 0.3\overline{8}$ (divide 7 by 18), and so $0.3\overline{8}$ is halfway between $0.\overline{3}$ and $0.\overline{4}$.

Example 6 Find the rational number halfway between $\frac{1}{3}$ and $\frac{7}{18}$.

Solution: The average of $\frac{1}{3}$ and $\frac{7}{18}$ is

$$\frac{\frac{1}{3} + \frac{7}{18}}{2} = \frac{\frac{6}{18} + \frac{7}{18}}{2}$$

$$= \frac{\frac{13}{18}}{2}$$

$$= \frac{13}{36}$$

Hence, $\frac{13}{36}$ is halfway between $\frac{1}{3}$ and $\frac{7}{18}$.

Using the method of Examples 5 and 6, we can find the rational number halfway between $\frac{1}{3}$ and $\frac{13}{36}$, and then repeat the process again and again for each new result we obtain. In this way we obtain an unlimited number of rational numbers between $\frac{1}{3}$ and $\frac{4}{9}$.

6.1.2 Property   If a and b are rational numbers, $a < b$, then there exists an unlimited number of rational numbers between a and b.

Because of Property 6.1.2 there is no "next" larger (or smaller) rational number greater than (or less than) a given rational number. For instance, there is no next larger rational number greater than $\frac{1}{3}$. Because $\frac{1}{3} = 0.\overline{3} = 0.333\ldots$, one might suspect that 0.340 is the next larger rational number greater than $\frac{1}{3}$. However, between $0.333\ldots$ and $0.34000\ldots$ there is the number 0.335, for example, and

$$0.333\ldots < 0.335 < 0.340$$

Thus, 0.340 is not the next larger rational number beyond $\frac{1}{3}$. A similar argument can be used for any suspected next larger rational number.

Exercises 6.1   *1-29 odd*

In Exercises 1 through 10 give an equivalent decimal representation for each rational number.

1. (a) $\frac{1}{2}$ (b) $\frac{2}{2}$ (c) $\frac{3}{2}$ (d) $\frac{4}{2}$ (e) $\frac{5}{2}$

2. (a) $\frac{1}{4}$ (b) $\frac{2}{4}$ (c) $\frac{3}{4}$ (d) $\frac{4}{4}$ (e) $\frac{5}{4}$

3. (a) $\frac{1}{3}$ (b) $\frac{2}{3}$ (c) $\frac{3}{3}$ (d) $\frac{4}{3}$ (e) $\frac{5}{3}$

4. (a) $\frac{1}{6}$ (b) $\frac{2}{6}$ (c) $\frac{3}{6}$ (d) $\frac{4}{6}$ (e) $\frac{5}{6}$

5. (a) $\frac{1}{5}$ (b) $\frac{2}{5}$ (c) $\frac{3}{5}$ (d) $\frac{4}{5}$ (e) $\frac{5}{5}$

6. (a) $\frac{1}{9}$ (b) $\frac{2}{9}$ (c) $\frac{3}{9}$ (d) $\frac{4}{9}$ (e) $\frac{5}{9}$

7. (a) $\frac{1}{10}$ (b) $\frac{2}{10}$ (c) $\frac{3}{10}$ (d) $\frac{4}{10}$ (e) $\frac{5}{10}$

8. (a) $\frac{6}{10}$ (b) $\frac{7}{10}$ (c) $\frac{8}{10}$ (d) $\frac{9}{10}$ (e) $\frac{10}{10}$

9. (a) $\frac{1}{10}$ (b) $\frac{1}{100}$ (c) $\frac{1}{1000}$ (d) $\frac{1}{10,000}$ (e) $\frac{1}{100,000}$

10. (a) $\dfrac{3}{10}$ **(b)** $\dfrac{3}{100}$ **(c)** $\dfrac{3}{1000}$ **(d)** $\dfrac{3}{10,000}$ **(e)** $\dfrac{3}{100,000}$

11. In (a) through (e) express the given power of $\dfrac{1}{10}$ as a fraction and also in decimal form.

    (a) $\dfrac{1}{10}$ **(b)** $\left(\dfrac{1}{10}\right)^2$ **(c)** $\left(\dfrac{1}{10}\right)^3$ **(d)** $\left(\dfrac{1}{10}\right)^4$ **(e)** $\left(\dfrac{1}{10}\right)^5$

In Exercises 12 through 15 express the given decimal in expanded form.

12. (a) 0.75   **(b)** 0.625   **13. (a)** 0.333444   **(b)** -0.875

14. (a) 2.045   **(b)** -21.375 **15. (a)** $-0.\overline{8}$ **(b)** $0.666\ldots$

In Exercises 16 through 18 express each expanded form in decimal form.

16. (a) $\dfrac{2}{10} + \dfrac{3}{100} + \dfrac{3}{1000}$

    (b) $\dfrac{5}{10} + \dfrac{5}{100} + \dfrac{5}{1000}$

17. (a) $\dfrac{5}{10} + \dfrac{0}{100} + \dfrac{5}{100} + \dfrac{0}{10000}$

    (b) $\dfrac{-4}{10} + \dfrac{-5}{10^2} + \dfrac{-4}{10^3} + \dfrac{-6}{10^4}$

18. (a) $\dfrac{-3}{10} + \dfrac{-5}{1000}$

    (b) $6\left(\dfrac{1}{10}\right) + 2\left(\dfrac{1}{10}\right)^2 + 5\left(\dfrac{1}{10}\right)^3$

In Exercises 19 through 29 express each decimal as a fraction in simplest form.

19. (a) 0.75   **(b)** 0.625   **20. (a)** 0.002   **(b)** 0.125

21. (a) -0.0005 **(b)** -3.4 **22. (a)** 0.405   **(b)** $0.\overline{6}$

23. (a) $0.\overline{7}$ **(b)** $-0.\overline{8}$ **24. (a)** $0.\overline{2}$ **(b)** $0.\overline{02}$

25. (a) $0.\overline{9}$ **(b)** $0.\overline{02}$ **26. (a)** $-0.\overline{16}$ **(b)** $0.8\overline{9}$

27. (a) $0.\overline{20}$ **(b)** $0.\overline{020}$ **28. (a)** $0.8\overline{3}$ **(b)** $0.1\overline{5}$

29. (a) $0.\overline{49}$ **(b)** $0.3\overline{60}$

30. Add $\dfrac{1}{3}$ and $\dfrac{2}{3}$ when they have been expressed in decimal form. What is the sum of $\dfrac{1}{3}$ and $\dfrac{2}{3}$?

31. Add the following:

(a) $3\left(\dfrac{1}{10}\right) + 4\left(\dfrac{1}{10}\right)^2 + 7\left(\dfrac{1}{10}\right)^3$

   $2\left(\dfrac{1}{10}\right) + 5\left(\dfrac{1}{10}\right)^2 + 2\left(\dfrac{1}{10}\right)^3$

(b) 0.347
    0.252
    _____

32. (a) Is $\dfrac{1}{10}$ the smallest positive rational number?

(b) Is $\dfrac{1}{100}$ the smallest positive rational number?

(c) Is there a smallest positive rational number?

33. Add the following:
(a) $0.3 + 0.03$
(b) $0.3 + 0.03 + 0.003$
(c) $0.3 + 0.03 + 0.003 + 0.0003$
(d) If the pattern established in (a) through (c) is continued indefinitely, what is the sum?

(e) $\dfrac{3}{10} + \dfrac{3}{10^2} + \dfrac{3}{10^3} + \dfrac{3}{10^4} + \cdots$ (Guess!)

34. (a) Find a rational number between $0.\overline{5}$ and $0.\overline{6}$.
(b) Find a rational number exactly halfway between $0.\overline{5}$ and $0.\overline{6}$.
(c) Find a rational number exactly halfway between 0.9 and $0.\overline{9}$.

35. (a) Find a rational number exactly halfway between $\dfrac{1}{2}$ and $\dfrac{2}{3}$.

(b) Find a rational number exactly halfway between $\dfrac{1}{2}$ and the answer to part (a).

(c) Find a rational number exactly halfway between $\dfrac{1}{2}$ and the answer to part (b).

(d) How long can the processes started in (a), (b), and (c) be carried out?

(e) How many rational numbers are between $\dfrac{1}{2}$ and $\dfrac{2}{3}$?

36. (a) Label each point shown in Figure 6.1.2 with a coordinate which is a rational number, $\dfrac{a}{b}$.

Figure 6.1.2

(b) Give the decimal form of each answer in part (a).

6.2 Irrational Numbers

In Section 6.1 we learned that any rational number can be represented by a decimal that is either terminating or nonterminating and repeating. In general, if p and q are integers and $q \neq 0$, and if p is divided by q, then there are at most $(q-1)$ positive integer remainders. Furthermore, if the fraction

$$\frac{p}{q}$$

is represented by a decimal, then the decimal either terminates with at most $(q-1)$ digits or repeats in groups of at most $(q-1)$ digits. For instance,

$$\frac{3}{8} = 0.375$$

The decimal 0.375 terminates with 3 digits.

$$\frac{3}{11} = 0.\overline{27}$$

The decimal $0.\overline{27}$ repeats a group of 2 digits.

$$\frac{3}{7} = 0.\overline{428571}$$

The decimal $0.\overline{428571}$ repeats a group of 6 digits.

Conversely, if a decimal terminates or repeats a group of digits, then the decimal represents a rational number. We now consider nonrepeating nonterminating decimals. For instance, the decimal

$$0.101001000100001 \ldots$$

is nonrepeating and nonterminating. Note that we deliberately made it nonrepeating by having each group of digits 0 between the two digits 1 contain one more 0 than the preceding group. We claim that the decimal 0.101001000100001 . . . does not represent a rational number because it is a nonterminating nonrepeating decimal.

If a real number is not a rational number it is called an *irrational number.* Because 0.101001000100001 . . . is a positive real number that is not a rational number, it is an irrational number, and, furthermore, it is the coordinate of some point on the real number line. Let

$$x = 0.101001000100001 \ldots$$

Then x is between 0.1 and 0.2. Furthermore x is between 0.10 and 0.11, and so on. That is,

$$0.1 < x < 0.2$$
$$0.10 < x < 0.11$$
$$0.101 < x < 0.102$$

$$0.1010 < x < 0.1011$$
$$0.10100 < x < 0.10101$$
$$0.101001 < x < 0.101002$$
$$\vdots \qquad \vdots \qquad \vdots$$

and so on. The sequence of rational numbers 0.1, 0.10, 0.101, 0.1010, 0.10100, 0.101001, . . . , is yielding numbers that are increasing in value but are all less than x, and the sequence of rational numbers 0.2, 0.11, 0.102, 0.1011, 0.10101, 0.101002, . . . , is yielding numbers that are decreasing in value but are all greater than x. If the number of terms in these sequences were to increase without bound and if the succeeding terms in the sequences were to continue to yield values according to the pattern established, then the "limiting value" of each sequence would be x.

We assume there exists a point on the real number line with a coordinate equal to x. We state this in the next property.

6.2.1 Axiom (Axiom of Completeness)
For every real number a we assume there exists a point on the real number line with a coordinate equal to a, and for every point on the real number line we assume there exists a real number as its coordinate. That is, we assume a one-to-one correspondence between the points on the real number line and the set of real numbers.

Illustration 1 We can associate a point on the real number line with each positive rational number of the form

$$\frac{p}{q}$$

where p and q are positive integers, in the following way. For instance, let q be 4 and consider all rational numbers of the form

$$\frac{p}{4}$$

where p is any positive integer. We divide each segment of unit length on the number line into 4 equal parts. These points of subdivision represent the positive rational numbers with denominator 4, that is, the set

$\left\{ \dfrac{1}{4}, \dfrac{2}{4}, \dfrac{3}{4}, \dfrac{4}{4}, \dfrac{5}{4}, \dfrac{6}{4}, \dfrac{7}{4}, \ldots \right\}$. See Figure 6.2.1. If this process is repeated

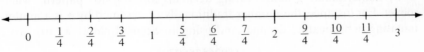

Figure 6.2.1

for any positive integer q then the points representing the positive rational numbers are obtained.

In Illustration 1 we have shown how a positive rational number is associated with a point on the real number line. In a similar way zero and the negative rational numbers are associated with other points on the real number line.

It is not as easy to show the correspondence between the irrational numbers and the remaining points on the real number line. However, for certain irrational numbers we can find the point corresponding to it. In Illustration 2 we find the point corresponding to the irrational number denoted by $\sqrt{2}$. In Section 6.3 $\sqrt{2}$ is defined to be the positive number when squared gives a product of 2. It has been proved that $\sqrt{2}$ is not a rational number. Hence, $\sqrt{2}$ is an irrational number.

Illustration 2 The ancient Greeks discovered that $\sqrt{2}$ is the measure of the diagonal of a square with sides of one unit of length. In Figure 6.2.2 a square is shown with its base on the real number line between the points whose coordinates are 0 and 1. An arc of a circle having center at the origin and radius $\sqrt{2}$ is then drawn and the point of intersection of this arc with the real number line is the point associated with $\sqrt{2}$.

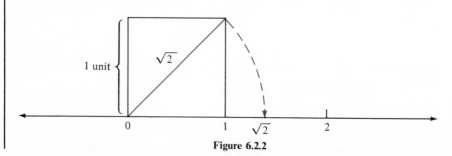

Figure 6.2.2

We cannot find all points associated with irrational numbers in the manner described in Illustration 2. However, the assumption made in the Axiom of Completeness is that every real number (and this includes irrational numbers) can be associated with a unique point of the real number line, and every point on the real number line can be associated with a real number. The real number line is a geometric representation of the set of real numbers.

Because the decimal form of the irrational number 0.101001000100001 . . . is composed of digits forming a specific "pattern" it can be described although it can not be represented by a numeral giving its exact value. There are many nonterminating nonrepeating decimals forming no "pattern" whatsoever. For instance, the number traditionally represented by π is a nonterminating nonrepeating decimal and using 16 decimal places we can write

$$\pi = 3.1415926535897932 \ldots$$

The number π has been computed to more than 100,000 decimal places and there is no observed pattern. Of course, computing the decimal form of π to 100,000 decimal places and finding no pattern is not sufficient evidence to conclude that no such pattern exists if more than 100,000 decimal places are computed. However, it has been shown by other more advanced methods that the number π is not a rational number.

The numeral π represents the "exact" value of a particular irrational number. The decimal form of an irrational number cannot completely represent the exact value of an irrational number. Another numeral is needed. For instance, the numeral $\sqrt{2}$ represents the exact value of a particular irrational number. In Table A.2 in the appendix you will find as the decimal form for $\sqrt{2}$ the numeral 1.4142. However, this is only an approximation to four decimal places.

The real number system satisfies all of the field axioms and the density property, and the completeness axiom.

Real numbers can be added, subtracted, multiplied, and divided and the results are real numbers. In particular, irrational numbers as well as rational numbers can be added, subtracted, multiplied, and divided. However, the set of irrational numbers does not satisfy the field axioms. For instance, the closure law for multiplication is not satisfied. In particular, $\sqrt{2} \cdot \sqrt{2} = 2$.

The sum of an irrational number and a rational number is an irrational number. For instance,

$$\sqrt{2} + 5, \quad \pi + 1, \quad \pi - 5$$

are irrational numbers. This fact is demonstrated in Illustration 3.

Illustration 3 Suppose a is an irrational number and b is a rational number. Consider the sum of a and b, $a + b = c$. If we do not know what kind of number c is, then we have two choices, either c is a rational number or c is an irrational number. If we assume c is a rational number, then $c - b$ is a rational number because b is also a rational number and the set of rational numbers is closed under subtraction. But $a = c - b$ (since $a + b = c$) and a is given as an irrational number and so we have a contradiction. Hence, the assumption that c is a rational number is incorrect, and therefore there is only one other choice, c must be an irrational number. Thus, the sum of a rational number and an irrational number is an irrational number.

In summary the set of real numbers is the union of the set of rational numbers and the set of irrational. Let R be the set of real numbers, Q the set of rational numbers, Q' the set of irrational numbers, J the set of integers, and W the set of whole numbers. Then

W is a subset of J; that is, $W \subset J$
J is a subset of Q; that is, $J \subset Q$
Q is a subset of R; that is, $Q \subset R$

Furthermore,

$$Q \cup Q' = R \quad \text{and} \quad Q \cap Q' = \emptyset$$

Exercises 6.2

In Exercises 1 through 10 classify the number as being either a rational number or an irrational number.

1. (a) $\sqrt{2}$ (b) $0.333\ldots$

2. (a) 1.01011 (b) $2.1010110111011110\ldots$

3. (a) 36 (b) $\dfrac{4}{9}$

4. (a) $40.\overline{2}$ (b) $\dfrac{1}{4}$

5. (a) $0.454554555455554\ldots$ (b) $0.123451234512345\ldots$

6. (a) $0.12345678910111121314\ldots$ (b) $0.\overline{869}$

7. (a) $\dfrac{\sqrt{2}}{2}$ (b) $\sqrt{2} + 1$

8. (a) 3π (b) $\pi + 1$

9. (a) $0.5 + 0.\overline{5}$ (b) $0.5 + 0.01001000100001\ldots$

10. (a) $(5 + \sqrt{2}) + (5 - \sqrt{2})$
    (b) $(0.505005000500005\ldots) + (0.050550555055550\ldots)$

11. Construct a sequence of rational numbers such that each number in the sequence is greater than the preceding one but less than $x = 0.424224222422224\ldots$, and another sequence of rational numbers such that each number in the sequence is less than the preceding one but greater than x. (Show 6 or 7 terms of each sequence to establish a pattern.) Write an inequality for each entry in the sequences, such as

$$0.4 < x < 0.5$$

12. Follow the instructions of Exercise 11 for the irrational number in Exercise 6(a).

13. What property does the system of real numbers have that the system of rational numbers does not? That is, what distinguishes the real number system from the rational number system?

14. If $\pi = 3.14159\ldots$, then (a) $1 + \pi = ?$ (b) $1 - \pi = ?$ (c) $(1 + \pi) + (1 - \pi) = ?$

15. Answer each of the following questions and give examples illustrating your answer:

    (a) Is the product of two irrational numbers always an irrational number?

    (b) Is the product of two rational numbers always a rational number?

    (c) Is the product of an irrational number and a rational number always an irrational number?

6.3 Square Roots

Some rational numbers are *perfect squares*. They are the square of another rational number. For instance, the numbers $4, 25,$ and $\dfrac{9}{16}$ are perfect squares because

$$2^2 = 4$$
$$(-2)^2 = 4$$
$$5^2 = 25$$
$$(-5)^2 = 25$$
$$\left(\frac{3}{4}\right)^2 = \frac{9}{16}$$
$$\left(-\frac{3}{4}\right)^2 = \frac{9}{16}$$

Consider now the problem of finding a number b whose square is a given number a; that is

$$b^2 = a$$

Suppose we have the equation

$$x^2 = 4$$

There are two solutions of this equation. A solution of this equation is 2 because $2^2 = 4$. Another solution is -2 because $(-2)^2 = 4$.

The numbers 2 and -2 are called "square roots" of the number 4.

6.3.1 Definition   If a and b are real numbers and

$$b^2 = a$$

then b is called a *square root* of a.

Illustration 1 (a) 2 is a square root of 4 because $2^2 = 4$; furthermore, -2 is also a square root of 4 because $(-2)^2 = 4$.

    (b) Both 5 and -5 are square roots of 25 because $5^2 = 25$ and $(-5)^2 = 25$.

(c) $\frac{3}{4}$ is a square root of $\frac{9}{16}$ because $\left(\frac{3}{4}\right)^2 = \frac{9}{16}$; $-\frac{3}{4}$ is also a square root of $\frac{9}{16}$ because $\left(-\frac{3}{4}\right)^2 = \frac{9}{16}$.

(d) Because $1^2 = 1$ and $(-1)^2 = 1$, both 1 and -1 are square roots of 1.

(e) 0 is a square root of 0 because $0^2 = 0$. Actually 0 is the only square root of 0 because 0 is the only number whose square is 0.

In Illustration 1 we see that the positive numbers 4, 25, $\frac{9}{16}$, and 1 each have two square roots. In fact, every positive number has two square roots, a positive number and its opposite, a negative number. To distinguish between these two square roots, we introduce the concept of "principal square root."

6.3.2 Definition If $a > 0$, then the *principal square root of a,* denoted by $\sqrt{a}$, is the positive square root of a.

Illustration 2 (a) $\sqrt{4} = 2$ (read "the principal square root of 4 is 2"). Note that -2 is a square root of 4 but it is not the principal square root of 4.

(b) $\sqrt{\frac{9}{16}} = \frac{3}{4}$ (read "the principal square root of $\frac{9}{16}$ is $\frac{3}{4}$").

The notation $\sqrt{a}$ is called a *radical,* the symbol $\sqrt{}$ is called a *radical sign,* and the number a is called the *radicand.*

The number zero has only one square root and we write $\sqrt{0} = 0$ (read "the square root of 0 is 0").

It was an important discovery made by the ancient Greeks that not every positive number has a principal square root equal to a rational number. The principal square root of a positive number r is a rational number if and only if r is the square of a rational number. However, there are positive numbers that are not squares of rational numbers. In particular it can be proved that the principal square root of 2 is not a rational number because there is no rational number whose square is 2. The principal square root of 2 is an irrational number. Other examples of irrational numbers are

$$\sqrt{3}, \quad \sqrt{5}, \quad \sqrt{6}, \quad \sqrt{7}, \quad \sqrt{8}, \quad \sqrt{10}, \quad \sqrt{\frac{1}{2}}, \quad \sqrt{\frac{1}{3}}, \quad \sqrt{\frac{1}{5}}, \quad \sqrt{\frac{2}{3}}, \quad \sqrt{\frac{5}{7}}$$

However,

$$\sqrt{1}, \quad \sqrt{4}, \quad \sqrt{9}, \quad \sqrt{16}, \quad \sqrt{25}, \quad \sqrt{\frac{1}{4}}, \quad \sqrt{\frac{9}{16}}, \quad \text{and} \quad \sqrt{0.01}$$

to name a few, are rational numbers.

If a positive integer x is not the square of an integer, then the principal square root of x is an irrational number. Hence, numbers such as $\sqrt{6}$, $\sqrt{20}$, $\sqrt{50}$, and $\sqrt{17}$ are examples of irrational numbers.

Table A.2 in the Appendix gives decimal approximations for some irrational numbers. In particular, from the table, we have

$$\sqrt{2} \doteq 1.4142$$

The symbol $\doteq$ is read "approximately equals."

Now consider the equation

$$x^2 = -4 \tag{1}$$

To have a solution of this equation requires that -4 be the square of some real number. But every positive number, when squared, yields a positive number, and every negative number, when squared, yields a positive number. Hence, the solution of equation (1) can be neither a positive nor a negative number, and it certainly is not zero. That is to say, there is no real number whose square is -4. More generally, if $a < 0$, there is no real square root of a because the square of any real number is a nonnegative number. Hence, $\sqrt{a}$ is not defined as a real number if $a < 0$.

If we wish to denote the negative square root of a positive number we use the minus sign with the radical. For instance, $-\sqrt{4}$ denotes the negative square root of 4, and so

$$-\sqrt{4} = -2$$

From Definitions 6.3.1 and 6.3.2 it follows that

$$(\sqrt{a})^2 = a$$

Consider now the radical $\sqrt{a^2}$ if $a \geq 0$. For instance,

$$\sqrt{3^2} = \sqrt{9} = 3$$
$$\sqrt{5^2} = \sqrt{25} = 5$$
$$\sqrt{0^2} = \sqrt{0} = 0$$
$$\sqrt{\left(\frac{3}{4}\right)^2} = \sqrt{\frac{9}{16}} = \frac{3}{4}$$

In general,

$$\sqrt{a^2} = a \quad \text{if} \quad a \geq 0 \tag{2}$$

But suppose $a < 0$. For instance, what is the value of $\sqrt{(-3)^2}$? Because $(-3)^2 = 9$, it follows that

$$\sqrt{(-3)^2} = \sqrt{9}$$

But $\sqrt{9} = 3$. Therefore,

$$\sqrt{(-3)^2} = 3$$

Hence, $\sqrt{(-3)^2} \neq -3$. However, because $|-3| = 3$, we can write

$$\sqrt{(-3)^2} = |-3| \; absolute \; value$$

$a \cdot$

More generally,

$$\sqrt{a^2} = |a| \qquad \text{if } a < 0 \tag{3}$$

However, because $|a| = a$ if $a \geq 0$, statement (2) can be written as

$$\sqrt{a^2} = |a| \qquad \text{if } a \geq 0 \tag{4}$$

Combining statements (3) and (4) we have

$$\boxed{\sqrt{a^2} = |a|} \qquad \text{if } a \text{ is any real number.}$$

Example 1 Express each of the following radicals in simpler form without the radical sign:

(a) $(\sqrt{5})^2$ (b) $\sqrt{7^2}$ (c) $\sqrt{(-8)^2}$ (d) $\sqrt{x^2}$ (e) $-\sqrt{(7x)^2}$

Solution:

(a) $(\sqrt{5})^2 = 5$
(b) $\sqrt{7^2} = |7| = 7$
(c) $\sqrt{(-8)^2} = |-8| = 8$
(d) $\sqrt{x^2} = |x|$
(e) $-\sqrt{(7x)^2} = -|7x|$

Example 2 Express $\sqrt{2^6}$ in a simpler form without the radical sign.

Solution: $\sqrt{2^6} = \sqrt{(2^3)^2}$
               $= 2^3$

Exercises 6.3

In Exercises 1 through 6 find the real square roots of the number if they exist.

1. 64 $8, -8$ 2. 100   3. 1 $1, -1$ 4. 0

5. -1 *impossible*   6. -16 *impossible*

In Exercises 7 through 10 find the principal square root of the number.

7. 36   8. $\dfrac{16}{25}$ 9. $\dfrac{1}{4} = \dfrac{1}{2}$ 10. 9 3

In Exercises 11 through 22 simplify the radical expression.

11. $(\sqrt{5})^2$ 12. $(\sqrt{9})^2$ 13. $\sqrt{49}$ 14. $-\sqrt{49}$

15. $-\sqrt{4}$ 16. $\sqrt{\dfrac{25}{36}}$ 17. $\sqrt{(-4)^2}$ 18. $-\sqrt{5^2}$

19. $\sqrt{3^4}$ 20. $\sqrt{2^8}$ 21. $\sqrt{(xy)^2}$ 22. $\sqrt{m^2}$

23. State the conditions for which $(\sqrt{x})^2 = \sqrt{x^2}$. That is, state whether x must be a positive number, zero, or a negative number.

24. If $\sqrt{x^2} = -x$, then x must be _____.

25. Solve the equation $\sqrt{x} = 5$.

6.4 Simplifying Radical Expressions

Numbers expressed in radical form, that is, numbers expressed in the form $\sqrt{a}$, are irrational numbers if $a > 0$ and if a is not the square of a rational number. These numbers represent only a subset of the set of irrational numbers. There are other expressions for irrational numbers, such as cube roots, fourth roots, π, and expressions involving the fundamental operations with irrational numbers. The system of real numbers satisfies all of the field properties. Irrational, as well as rational, numbers can be added, subtracted, multiplied, and divided.

Suppose we wish to add or subtract the two irrational numbers $\sqrt{3}$ and $\sqrt{2}$. These operations can be indicated by writing

$$\sqrt{3} + \sqrt{2} \qquad \text{or} \qquad \sqrt{3} - \sqrt{2}$$

Or if we wish to indicate the sum of π and 1, we write

$$\pi + 1$$

If we wish to multiply or divide numbers expressed in radical form, there are some alternative forms in which the product or quotient can be expressed. For instance, by definition the product of $\sqrt{5}$ and $\sqrt{5}$ is expressed either by $\sqrt{5} \cdot \sqrt{5}$ or 5. That is, $\sqrt{5} \cdot \sqrt{5} = 5$.

Illustration 1 (a) $\sqrt{4 \cdot 9} = \sqrt{36} = 6$
(b) $\sqrt{4} \cdot \sqrt{9} = 2 \cdot 3 = 6$

In Illustration 1, note that

$$\sqrt{4 \cdot 9} = \sqrt{4} \cdot \sqrt{9}$$

This equality is a special case of the following theorem.

6.4.1 Theorem   If a and b are nonnegative real numbers, then

$$\sqrt{a} \cdot \sqrt{b} = \sqrt{a \cdot b} \qquad\qquad (1)$$

Proof: Consider the second power of the left member of equation (1).

$$(\sqrt{a} \cdot \sqrt{b})^2 = (\sqrt{a})^2 (\sqrt{b})^2$$

But $(\sqrt{a})^2 = a$ *and* $(\sqrt{b})^2 = b$ *and so*

$$(\sqrt{a} \cdot \sqrt{b})^2 = a \cdot b$$

From Definition 6.2.1 it follows that

$$\sqrt{a} \cdot \sqrt{b} \text{ is a square root of } a \cdot b$$

Because $\sqrt{a} \geq 0$ *and* $\sqrt{b} \geq 0$, *then* $\sqrt{a} \cdot \sqrt{b} \geq 0$. *Therefore,* $\sqrt{a} \cdot \sqrt{b}$ *is the principal square root of* $a \cdot b$. *Thus,*

$$\sqrt{a} \cdot \sqrt{b} = \sqrt{a \cdot b}$$

Illustration 2 (a) $\sqrt{2} \cdot \sqrt{8} = \sqrt{2 \cdot 8} = \sqrt{16} = 4$
  (b) $\sqrt{2} \cdot \sqrt{5} = \sqrt{2 \cdot 5} = \sqrt{10}$

By using the symmetric property of equality, equation (1) becomes

$$\sqrt{a \cdot b} = \sqrt{a} \cdot \sqrt{b} \qquad \text{if } a \geq 0 \text{ and } b \geq 0 \qquad (2)$$

In the next illustration we show how statement (2) can be used to *simplify* a radical expression whose radicand contains a factor that is a perfect square.

Illustration 3 To *simplify* the radical $\sqrt{20}$, we first write 20 as a product of prime numbers. Because

$$20 = 2^2 \cdot 5$$

we have

$$\begin{aligned} \sqrt{20} &= \sqrt{2^2 \cdot 5} \\ &= \sqrt{2^2} \cdot \sqrt{5} \\ &= 2 \cdot \sqrt{5} \end{aligned}$$

Example 1 *Simplify* each of the following radicals:
  (a) $\sqrt{8}$ (b) $\sqrt{75}$ (c) $\sqrt{x^3}$ where $x \geq 0$ (d) $\sqrt{x^4}$

Solution:
  (a) $\sqrt{8} = \sqrt{2^3} = \sqrt{2^2 \cdot 2} = \sqrt{2^2} \cdot \sqrt{2} = 2\sqrt{2}$
  (b) $\sqrt{75} = \sqrt{3 \cdot 5^2} = \sqrt{5^2} \cdot \sqrt{3} = 5\sqrt{3}$
  (c) $\sqrt{x^3} = \sqrt{x^2 \cdot x} = \sqrt{x^2} \cdot \sqrt{x} = x\sqrt{x}$
  (d) $\sqrt{x^4} = \sqrt{(x^2)^2} = |x^2| = x^2$

By Definitions 6.3.1 and 6.3.2 we have

$$\sqrt{\left(\frac{3}{4}\right)^2} = \frac{3}{4}$$

or, equivalently,

$$\sqrt{\frac{9}{16}} = \frac{3}{4}$$

Notice that

$$\frac{\sqrt{9}}{\sqrt{16}} = \frac{3}{4}$$

Hence,

$$\sqrt{\frac{9}{16}} = \frac{\sqrt{9}}{\sqrt{16}}$$

This equality is a special case of the following theorem.

6.4.2 Theorem   If $a \geq 0$ and $b > 0$, then

$$\frac{\sqrt{a}}{\sqrt{b}} = \sqrt{\frac{a}{b}} \qquad\qquad (3)$$

The proof of Theorem 6.4.2 is similar to the proof of Theorem 6.4.1 and is omitted.

Illustration 4   From Theorem 6.4.2 we have

(a) $\dfrac{\sqrt{28}}{\sqrt{7}} = \sqrt{\dfrac{28}{7}} = \sqrt{4} = 2$

(b) $\dfrac{\sqrt{30}}{\sqrt{6}} = \sqrt{\dfrac{30}{6}} = \sqrt{5}$

By using the Symmetric Property of Equality with equation (3) we have

$$\sqrt{\frac{a}{b}} = \frac{\sqrt{a}}{\sqrt{b}} \qquad \text{if } a \geq 0 \text{ and } b > 0 \qquad (4)$$

Equality (4) can be used to replace a radical having a fraction in the radicand by an equivalent expression for which the radicand contains no fraction. The procedure is called *rationalizing the denominator,* and it consists of first building the fraction to an equivalent one in which the denominator is a perfect square. The next illustration shows the computation involved.

Illustration 5   To rationalize the denominator of the radical $\sqrt{\dfrac{3}{5}}$ we wish to build the fraction in the radicand to one in which the denominator is a perfect square. We therefore multiply the numerator and denominator by 5 and then apply equality (4).

$$\sqrt{\frac{3}{5}} = \sqrt{\frac{3 \cdot 5}{5 \cdot 5}}$$

$$= \frac{\sqrt{3 \cdot 5}}{\sqrt{5^2}}$$

$$= \frac{\sqrt{15}}{5}$$

Example 2 Rationalize the denominator of each of the following radicals:

(a) $\sqrt{\dfrac{1}{2}}$ (b) $\sqrt{\dfrac{3}{8}}$ (c) $\sqrt{\dfrac{1}{x^3}}$ where $x > 0$

Solution:

(a) $\sqrt{\dfrac{1}{2}} = \sqrt{\dfrac{1 \cdot 2}{2 \cdot 2}} = \dfrac{\sqrt{2}}{\sqrt{2^2}} = \dfrac{\sqrt{2}}{2}$

(b) $\sqrt{\dfrac{3}{8}} = \sqrt{\dfrac{3 \cdot 2}{8 \cdot 2}} = \dfrac{\sqrt{3 \cdot 2}}{\sqrt{16}} = \dfrac{\sqrt{6}}{\sqrt{4^2}} = \dfrac{\sqrt{6}}{4}$

(c) $\sqrt{\dfrac{1}{x^3}} = \sqrt{\dfrac{1 \cdot x}{x^3 \cdot x}} = \dfrac{\sqrt{x}}{\sqrt{x^4}} = \dfrac{\sqrt{x}}{\sqrt{(x^2)^2}} = \dfrac{\sqrt{x}}{x^2}$

Example 3 Rationalize the denominator in each of the following fractions:

(a) $\dfrac{2}{\sqrt{3}}$ (b) $\dfrac{5}{\sqrt{5}}$ (c) $\dfrac{7}{\sqrt{x}}$ where $x > 0$

Solution:

(a) $\dfrac{2}{\sqrt{3}} = \dfrac{2 \cdot \sqrt{3}}{\sqrt{3} \cdot \sqrt{3}} = \dfrac{2\sqrt{3}}{3}$

(b) $\dfrac{5}{\sqrt{5}} = \dfrac{5 \cdot \sqrt{5}}{\sqrt{5} \cdot \sqrt{5}} = \dfrac{5\sqrt{5}}{5} = \sqrt{5}$

(c) $\dfrac{7}{\sqrt{x}} = \dfrac{7 \cdot \sqrt{x}}{\sqrt{x} \cdot \sqrt{x}} = \dfrac{7\sqrt{x}}{x}$

By applying the preceding definitions and theorems we can express algebraic expressions involving square-root radicals in various equivalent forms. Usually, however, we wish the form to be the "simplest radical form."

6.4.3 Definition   An algebraic expression containing square-root radicals is said to be in *simplest radical form* if the following conditions are satisfied:

(i) The radicand, when expressed as a product of prime factors, does not contain a factor having an exponent greater than or equal to 2.
(ii) The radicand is not represented by a fraction.
(iii) There is no denominator containing a radical.

Example 4 Write each of the following expressions in simplest radical form.

(a) $\sqrt{18x^2y^5}$ where $x \geq 0$ and $y \geq 0$

(b) $\sqrt{\dfrac{4}{3}\pi r^3}$ where $r \geq 0$

(c) $\dfrac{1}{\sqrt{\pi r^2}}$ where $r > 0$

Solution:

(a) $\sqrt{18x^2y^5} = \sqrt{2 \cdot 3^2 \cdot x^2 \cdot y^4 \cdot y}$

$\qquad\qquad\ = \sqrt{(3^2 \cdot x^2 \cdot y^4)(2y)}$

$\qquad\qquad\ = \sqrt{(3xy^2)^2} \cdot \sqrt{2y}$

$\qquad\qquad\ = 3xy^2 \sqrt{2y}$

(b) $\sqrt{\dfrac{4}{3}\pi r^3} = \sqrt{\dfrac{4\pi r^3}{3}}$

$\qquad\qquad\ = \sqrt{\dfrac{4\pi r^3 \cdot 3}{3 \cdot 3}}$

$\qquad\qquad\ = \dfrac{\sqrt{(4r^2)(3\pi r)}}{\sqrt{3^2}}$

$\qquad\qquad\ = \dfrac{\sqrt{4r^2} \sqrt{3\pi r}}{3}$

$\qquad\qquad\ = \dfrac{2r \sqrt{3\pi r}}{3}$

(c) $\dfrac{1}{\sqrt{\pi r^2}} = \dfrac{1 \cdot \sqrt{\pi}}{\sqrt{\pi r^2} \cdot \sqrt{\pi}}$

$\qquad\qquad\ = \dfrac{\sqrt{\pi}}{\sqrt{\pi^2 r^2}}$

$\qquad\qquad\ = \dfrac{\sqrt{\pi}}{\pi r}$

Illustration 6   The expression

$$\sqrt{x^2 + y^2}$$

is in simplest radical form. Do not make the mistake of confusing this expression with $x + y$. For instance, let x be 3 and y be 4. Then

$$\sqrt{x^2 + y^2} = \sqrt{3^2 + 4^2}$$

$$= \sqrt{9 + 16}$$

$$= \sqrt{25}$$

$$= 5$$

However,

$$x + y = 3 + 4$$

$$= 7$$

The next two examples show how simplifying a radical can be of help in obtaining a decimal approximation of certain irrational numbers.

Example 5 Find a decimal approximation of $\sqrt{200}$ accurate to two decimal places.

Solution:
$$\begin{aligned} \sqrt{200} &= \sqrt{100 \cdot 2} \\ &= \sqrt{100} \cdot \sqrt{2} \\ &= 10\sqrt{2} \end{aligned}$$

From Table A.2 in the appendix we find $\sqrt{2} \doteq 1.4142$. Hence,

$$\sqrt{200} \doteq 10(1.4142)$$

Therefore,

$$\sqrt{200} \doteq 14.142$$

Example 6 Find a decimal approximation of $\sqrt{\dfrac{1}{3}}$ accurate to two decimal places.

Solution:
$$\sqrt{\frac{1}{3}} = \frac{\sqrt{1 \cdot 3}}{\sqrt{3 \cdot 3}}$$

$$= \frac{\sqrt{3}}{\sqrt{3^2}}$$

$$= \frac{\sqrt{3}}{3}$$

From Table A.2 in the appendix we find $\sqrt{3} \doteq 1.732$. Therefore,

$$\sqrt{\frac{1}{3}} \doteq \frac{1.732}{3}$$

Hence

$$\sqrt{\frac{1}{3}} \doteq 0.577$$

Note in Examples 5 and 6 above that 14.142 and 0.577 are terminating decimals and therefore represent rational numbers. These rational numbers are only approximately equal to the irrational numbers whose exact values are represented by $\sqrt{200}$ and $\sqrt{\dfrac{1}{3}}$, respectively.

In Exercises 1 through 31 simplify the radical expression.

1. $\sqrt{3} \cdot \sqrt{12}$ **2.** $\sqrt{x} \cdot \sqrt{x^3}$

3. $\dfrac{\sqrt{12}}{\sqrt{3}}$ **4.** $\dfrac{\sqrt{x^3}}{\sqrt{x}}$

5. $\sqrt{50}$ **6.** $\sqrt{12}$

7. $\sqrt{900}$ **8.** $\sqrt{2} \cdot \sqrt{7}$

9. $\sqrt{45}$ **10.** $\sqrt{32}$

11. $\sqrt{9x^5}$ where $x \geq 0$

12. $\sqrt{16x^3y^6}$ where $x \geq 0$ and $y \geq 0$

13. $\sqrt{8x^3y^3}$ where $x \geq 0$ and $y \geq 0$

14. $\sqrt{98x^4}$ **15.** $\dfrac{1}{\sqrt{3}}$

16. $\dfrac{6}{\sqrt{3}}$ **17.** $\sqrt{\dfrac{2}{3}}$

18. $\dfrac{\sqrt{3}}{\sqrt{8}}$ **19.** $\dfrac{1}{\sqrt{x}}$ where $x > 0$

20. $\dfrac{\sqrt{x}}{\sqrt{x^3}}$ where $x > 0$ **21.** $\sqrt{\dfrac{1}{2\pi r}}$ where $r > 0$

22. $\sqrt{\dfrac{1}{2}\pi r^2}$ where $r \geq 0$ **23.** $\sqrt{\dfrac{4x^3}{y^2}}$ where $x \geq 0$ and $y > 0$

24. $\dfrac{6x}{\sqrt{3x}}$ where $x > 0$ **25.** $\sqrt{0.75}$ $\left(\text{Hint: } 0.75 = \dfrac{3}{4}\right)$

26. $\sqrt{4.5}$ **27.** $\sqrt{3x + x}$ where $x \geq 0$

28. $\sqrt{6^2 + 8^2}$ **29.** $\sqrt{3^3 - 2}$

30. $\sqrt{2^2 + 2^2 + 1^2}$ **31.** $\sqrt{(3x)^2 + (4x)^2}$

32. Show that $\dfrac{1}{\sqrt{2}} = \dfrac{\sqrt{2}}{2}$.

In Exercises 33 through 36 find a decimal approximation of the radical accurate to two decimal places.

33. $\sqrt{50}$ **34.** $\sqrt{300}$ **35.** $\sqrt{\dfrac{4}{5}}$ **36.** $\sqrt{\dfrac{1}{2}}$

37. The length of the diagonal of a square is given by the formula

$$d = s\sqrt{2}$$

where d units is the length of the diagonal and s units is the length of the side of a square. See Figure 6.4.1.

(a) Find the length of the diagonal if the side of a square is 4 inches.

(b) Find the length of the diagonal if the side of a square is 2 inches.

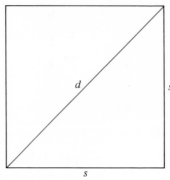

s

Figure 6.4.1

38. **(a)** If the perimeter of a square is 24 inches, find the length of the diagonal. See Exercise 37.

(b) If the length of the diagonal of a square is 18 units, find the perimeter of the square.

39. The length of the diagonal of a rectangle is given by the formula

$$d = \sqrt{l^2 + w^2}$$

where d is the measure of the diagonal, l is the measure of the length, and w is the measure of the width. See Figure 6.4.2. Find the length of the diagonal if the length is 4 units and the width is 3 units.

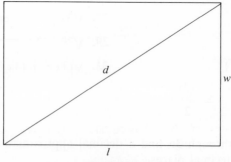

Figure 6.4.2

40. Can you fit a 36 inch yard stick onto the bottom of a suitcase that has

the dimensions of length equal to 32 inches and width equal to 24 inches? (Hint: See Exercise 39.)

41. The length of the diagonal of a box is given by the formula

$$d = \sqrt{l^2 + w^2 + h^2}$$

where d, l, w, and h are the measures of the diagonal, length, width and height respectively. See Figure 6.4.3.

(a) Use this formula to find the length of the diagonal of the box 2 feet long, 2 feet wide, and 1 foot high.

(b) Would a yard stick fit in the box described in part (a)?

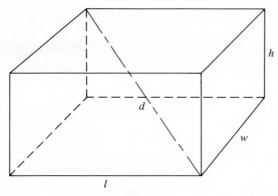

Figure 6.4.3

6.5 Review Exercises

1. Represent each of the following rational numbers by a numeral in decimal form.

(a) $\dfrac{5}{11}$ **(b)** $\dfrac{5}{12}$ **(c)** $\dfrac{5}{8}$

2. Represent each of the following rational numbers by a fraction in simplest form.

(a) 0.125 **(b)** $0.\overline{30}$ **(c)** $0.8\overline{9}$

3. Find the rational number halfway between $\dfrac{3}{4}$ and $0.\overline{8}$.

In Exercises 4 through 6 classify each of the numbers as either a rational number or an irrational number.

4. (a) 1.50555

   (b) $0.\overline{75}$

   (c) $1 + \pi$

5. (a) $\dfrac{\dfrac{1}{2}}{3}$

   (b) 0.303003000300003 ...
   (c) 0.0101001010010100 ... *block pattern, rational*

6. (a) $\sqrt{\dfrac{4}{9}}$

   (b) $\sqrt{2} + 3$
   (c) $(1 + \pi) + (1 - \pi)$ *= 2, rational*

7. Find the real square roots of each of the following numbers if the roots exist.
   (a) 0.36   (b) 0   (c) -4

8. Find the principal square root of each of the following numbers.
   (a) 36   (b) $\dfrac{9}{16}$ (c) $0.\overline{4}$

In Exercises 9 through 15 simplify each of the given radical expressions.

9. (a) $(\sqrt{2})^2$ (b) $\sqrt{3^4}$

10. (a) $\sqrt{(-3)^2}$ (b) $\sqrt{r^2}$

11. (a) $\sqrt{6} \cdot \sqrt{24}$ (b) $\dfrac{\sqrt{18}}{\sqrt{2}}$

12. (a) $\sqrt{7500}$ *$50\sqrt{3}$*   (b) $\sqrt{98}$ *$7\sqrt{2}$*

13. (a) $\sqrt{\dfrac{2}{5}}$ (b) $\sqrt{\dfrac{4}{3}}$

14. (a) $\dfrac{\sqrt{3}}{\sqrt{5}}$ (b) $\dfrac{6}{\sqrt{2}}$

15. (a) $\sqrt{12x^4}$ (b) $\sqrt{16x^6y^3}$ where $x \geq 0$ and $y \geq 0$

16. Find the value of y if $y = \sqrt{r^2 - x^2}$ and (a) $r = 15$ and $x = 12$;
    (b) $r = 10x^2$.   *$y = \sqrt{100x^4 - y^2}$*

17. The period of a pendulum (time for one cycle of a pendulum) is given by

$$t = 2\pi \sqrt{\dfrac{l}{g}}$$

where t seconds is the period, $\pi \doteq 3.14$, l feet is the length of the pendulum, and g feet per second squared is the measurement of the acceleration due to gravity. Find the period of a pendulum if its length is 18 feet and $g = 32$.

18. Enter the word "yes" in the table below if the system has the property described in the left-hand column, otherwise enter the word "no."

Property	System			
	Whole Numbers W	Integers J	Rational Numbers Q	Real Numbers R
Closure (+)	yes	yes	yes	yes
Closure (−)	no	yes	yes	yes
Closure (×)	yes	yes	yes	yes
Closure (÷)	No	No	yes	yes
Commutative (+)	yes	yes	yes	yes
Commutative (×)	yes	yes	yes	yes
Associative (+)	yes	yes	yes	yes
Associative (×)	yes	yes	yes	yes
Distributive (×)	yes	yes	yes	yes
Identity (+) 0	yes	yes	yes	yes
Identity (×) 1	yes	yes	yes	yes
Inverse (+)	No	yes	yes	yes
Inverse (×)	No	No	yes	yes
Density	No	No	yes	yes
Completeness	No	No	No	yes

Integers are rational numbers

multiplicative inverse, reciprocal

→ every point on xc line has a no. coordinate

for any number you pick, there's a number in between

7

Graphs of Equations

7.1 Graph of a Linear Equation

Suppose we are given that one number is one half of another number. There are many pairs of numbers that satisfy this condition: 1 and 2, 3 and 6, -5 and -10, $\frac{5}{2}$ and 5, and so on. If we let x and y represent the two numbers, we have the relationship defined by the equation

$$y = \frac{1}{2}x \tag{1}$$

Equation (1) has an unlimited number of solutions and each solution is a pair of values, one for x and one for y. We refer to these pairs of numbers as *ordered pairs*. An ordered pair is denoted by enclosing the members of the pairs in parentheses separated by a comma. For instance, the ordered pair $(1, 2)$ is not the same as the ordered pair $(2, 1)$; the order makes a difference. Each of the elements of an ordered pair is called a *component*, *first* and *second*.

If we designate the solutions of equation (1) as ordered pairs, the x value first and the y value second, then $(2, 1)$, $(6, 3)$, $(-10, -5)$, $\left(5, \frac{5}{2}\right)$, and so on, are elements of the solution set of equation (1). Using the set-builder notation the entire solution set is written as

$$\left\{(x, y) : y = \frac{1}{2}x\right\}$$

A set of ordered pairs can be represented pictorially by a graph on a rectangular coordinate system. This system is constructed by drawing two perpendicular lines intersecting at a point called the *origin*. On each of the lines we choose a convenient unit of measure. This unit is generally the same on each line. Each line then is a number line and is called an *axis* of the system. See Figure 7.1.1. The horizontal line is usually referred to as the *x-axis* and is a number line with positive direction to the right. The vertical line is usually referred to as the *y-axis* and is a number line with positive direction upward. From a property of geometry, two intersecting lines determine a *plane*. The plane determined by the x and y axes is called the *xy-plane*.

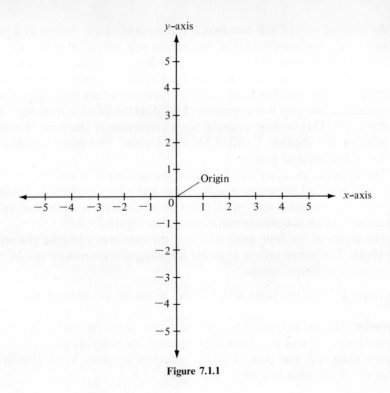

Figure 7.1.1

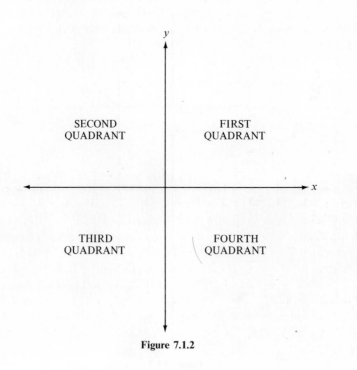

Figure 7.1.2

An ordered pair of real numbers is represented in this system as a point in the plane. The components of the ordered pair are called the *coordinates* of the particular point determined by the ordered pair. The first component of the ordered pair is the measure of the directed distance from the *y*-axis to the point. This number is called the *x-coordinate* of the point. The second component of the pair is the measure of the directed distance from the *x*-axis to the point. This number is called the *y-coordinate* of the point. Locating a point in this manner is called *plotting* a point. The point is called the *graph* of the ordered pair.

The *x*-coordinate of a point *P* is called the *abscissa* of *P*, and the *y*-coordinate of *P* is called the *ordinate* of *P*. The *x*- and *y*-axes are called *coordinate axes*. The coordinate axes divide the *xy*-plane into four regions called *quadrants,* which are numbered as shown in Figure 7.1.2.

The union of the four quadrants and the two axes comprise the entire *xy*-plane. The entire system is called a *rectangular coordinate system or a Cartesian coordinate system.*

Example 1   Plot the point which is the graph of the ordered pair $(2, 3)$.

Solution: Draw a vertical line through the point on the *x*-axis whose *x*-coordinate is 2 and a horizontal line through the point on the *y*-axis whose *y*-coordinate is 3. The point whose coordinates are given by $(2, 3)$ is at the intersection of these two lines. See Figure 7.1.3.

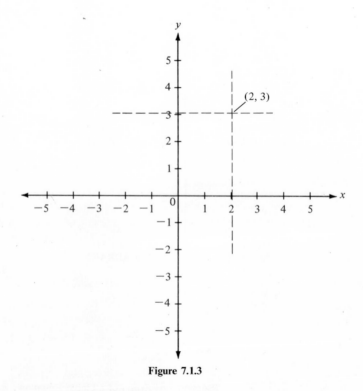

Figure 7.1.3

In Example 1 there is only one point in the plane whose coordinates are given by $(2, 3)$. More generally, for each pair of coordinates (x, y) there corresponds only one point in the plane. Conversely, given any point in the plane there is only one pair of coordinates corresponding to this point. Thus, a one-to-one correspondence has been established between the set of all ordered pairs of real numbers, and the set of points in the xy-plane.

Example 2 In Figure 7.1.4 give the coordinates of the points labeled A, B, C, D, E, and F.

Solution: A: $(3, 2)$; B: $(-2, 1)$; C: $(-3, -3)$; D: $(4, -3)$; E: $(-4, 0)$; F: $(0, -3)$.

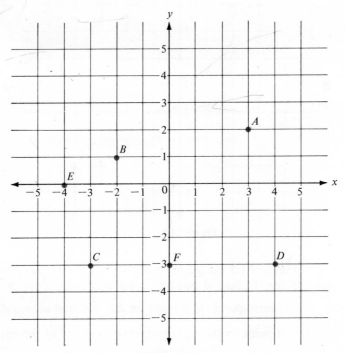

Figure 7.1.4

Example 3 Plot the set of points whose coordinates are such that the ordinate is always one half of the abscissa and the abscissa is an element of the set

$$\{-5, -4, -3, -2, -1, 0, 1, 2, 3, 4, 5\}$$

Solution: Because the ordinate (the y-coordinate) is one half of the abscissa (the x-coordinate) we have the equation $y = \frac{1}{2}x$. We plot points with co-ordinates given by $(x, y) = \left(x, \frac{1}{2}x\right)$. Therefore, because $x \in \{-5, -4, -3, -2, -1, 0, 1, 2, 3, 4, 5\}$ we plot the ordered pairs $\left(-5, -\frac{5}{2}\right), (-4, -2)$,

$\left(-3, -\dfrac{3}{2}\right)$, $(-2, -1)$, $\left(-1, -\dfrac{1}{2}\right)$, $(0, 0)$, $\left(1, \dfrac{1}{2}\right)$, $(2, 1)$, $\left(3, \dfrac{3}{2}\right)$, $(4, 2)$, and $\left(5, \dfrac{5}{2}\right)$. See Figure 7.1.5.

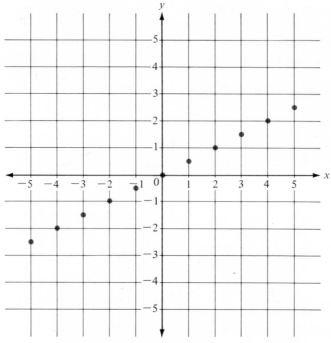

Figure 7.1.5

Note that in Figure 7.1.5 the graph shows eleven points that appear to lie on a straight line. In fact, it can be shown that every solution of the equation $y = \dfrac{1}{2}x$ corresponds to a point on the line, and conversely, the coordinates of each point on the line represents a solution of the equation. Therefore, the line of Figure 7.1.5 is the graph of the equation $y = \dfrac{1}{2}x$.

The equation representing the relationship exhibited by the ordinates and the abscissas of a set of points on a "straight line" is called a *linear equation*. Hence, $y = \dfrac{1}{2}x$ is a linear equation.

A linear equation is an equation that can be either of the form

$$y = mx + b \tag{2}$$

or of the form

$$Ax + By = C \tag{3}$$

where x and y are variables and m, b, A, B, and C are constants. Any equation equivalent to either equation (2) or (3) is a linear equation.

In linear equations the terms involving x and y are called "first degree terms" because the variables x and y are raised to the first power. The equation $y = x^2$ is not a linear equation. The term involving x is a second degree term; x^2 is a second degree term. Linear equations equivalent to equations (2) and (3) are also called *first degree equations*.

Illustration 1   Each of the following equations is a linear equation:

(a) $y = \dfrac{1}{2} x$

(b) $3x + 2y = 6$

(c) $y = 2$

Example 4   Draw a sketch of the graph of the linear equation

$$y = x + 3$$

Solution: Because the equation is linear, we know that the graph of the equation is a straight line. Because two points determine a line, we need to know the coordinates of at least two points. If we let $x = 0$, then from the equation we find that

$$\begin{aligned} y &= 0 + 3 \\ &= 3 \end{aligned}$$

Hence, one point on the line is given by $(0, 3)$. If we now let $x = 1$, then we find that

$$\begin{aligned} y &= 1 + 3 \\ &= 4 \end{aligned}$$

Hence, another point on the line is given by $(1, 4)$. (Although two points are sufficient to determine a line we plot more than two points to show that they do indeed lie on a "straight line." The coordinates of these points are found by arbitrarily selecting values for x and computing the corresponding values for y. The data are summarized in Table 7.1.1.

Table 7.1.1

x	$x + 3$	y
0	$0 + 3$	3
1	$1 + 3$	4
2	$2 + 3$	5
-1	$-1 + 3$	2
-2	$-2 + 3$	1
-3	$-3 + 3$	0
-4	$-4 + 3$	-1

We plot the points whose coordinates are $(0, 3)$, $(1, 4)$, $(2, 5)$, $(-1, 2)$, $(-2, 1)$, $(-3, 0)$, and $(-4, -1)$. See Figure 7.1.6.

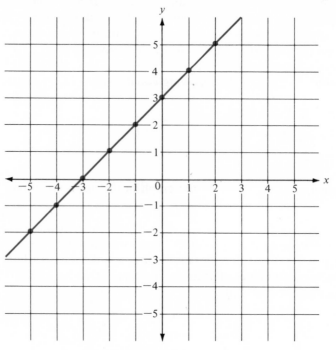

Figure 7.1.6

Example 5 Draw a sketch of the graph of the equation

$$3x + 2y = 6$$

Solution: The given equation is of the form of equation (3) and so it is a linear equation. Solving for y, we have

$$2y = 6 - 3x$$

$$y = \frac{6 - 3x}{2}$$

$$= 3 - \frac{3}{2}x$$

$$= -\frac{3}{2}x + 3 \qquad (4)$$

Equation (4) is equivalent to the given equation and it is of the form of equation (2), one of the general forms of a linear equation. We arbitrarily choose two values for x and make the table shown in Table 7.1.2. The

Table 7.1.2

x	$\dfrac{-3}{2}x + 3$	y
0	$\dfrac{-3}{2}(0) + 3$	3
2	$\dfrac{-3}{2}(2) + 3$	0

ordered pairs given by the table are the coordinates of the points plotted in Figure 7.1.7 and a straight line is drawn.

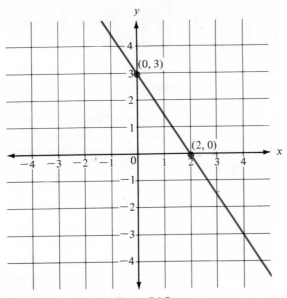

Figure 7.1.7

A third point could be plotted for the equation in Example 5 as a check to see if all three points are in the same line, that is, *collinear*. If the three points are not collinear, then one or more of them are plotted in error and they do not belong to the graph of the given equation.

Example 6 Draw a sketch of the graph of the set $\{(x, y) : y = 2\}$.

Solution: This set is the set of all ordered pairs (x, y) for which the y-coordinate is 2. Examples of some of the ordered pairs are $(0, 2)$, $(1, 2)$, $(3, 2)$, $(-1, 2)$, and $(2, 2)$. The graph is shown in Figure 7.1.8 and it is a horizontal line intersecting the y-axis at the point whose coordinates are given by $(0, 2)$.

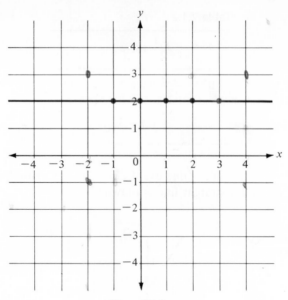

Figure 7.1.8

We see from Example 6 that a linear equation may be defined by an equation of the form $y = c$, where c is any constant. The graph of such an equation is a line parallel to the x-axis. The graph of the set $\{(x, y) : y = 0\}$ is the x-axis. The graph of the set $\{(x, y) : x = 0\}$ is the y-axis.

Exercises 7.1

Plot the points with coordinates given by the ordered pairs in Exercises 1 through 4. In each case name the quadrant in which the point lies. Label the points on the graph as A, B, C, D, and E in the order that they are given.

1. $(2, 3)$, $(3, 2)$, $(5, 5)$, $(4, 1)$, $(1, 4)$

2. $(-2, -3)$, $(-3, -2)$, $(-1, -1)$, $(-5, -2)$, $(-2, -5)$

3. $(2, -3)$, $(3, -2)$, $(1, -5)$, $(5, -1)$, $(2, -2)$

4. $(-3, 2)$, $(-2, 3)$, $(-5, 1)$, $(-1, 5)$, $(-2, 2)$

In Exercises 5 through 8 plot the set of points and join consecutive pairs of points with straight line segments in the order in which the points are given.

5. $\{(4, 3), (-2, 3), (-2, -1), (4, -1), (4, 3)\}$

6. $\{(3, 0), (-3, 7), (-8, -5), (3, 0)\}$

7. $\{(5, 0), (4, 3), (3, 4), (0, 5), (-3, 4), (-4, 3), (-5, 0), (-4, -3), (-3, -4),$
   $(0, -5), (3, -4), (4, -3), (5, 0)\}$

8. $\{(4, 1), (-4, 1), (3, -3), (0, 3), (-3, -3), (4, 1)\}$

9. Give the coordinates of each of the following points to be found in Figure 7.1.9: A, B, C, D, E, F, G.

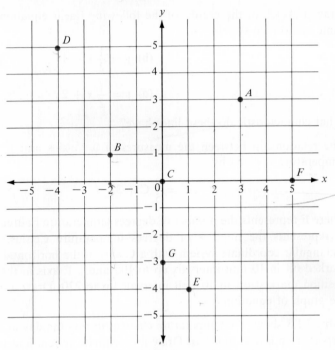

Figure 7.1.9

10. Plot the set of points whose coordinates are such that the ordinate is twice the abscissa, and the abscissa is an element of the set $\{-5, -4, -3, -2, -1, 0, 1, 2, 3, 4, 5\}$.

11. Plot the set of points whose coordinates are such that the ordinate is one less than twice the abscissa, and the abscissa is an element of the set $\{-5, -4, -3, -2, -1, 0, 1, 2, 3, 4, 5\}$. *X is restricted, so no lines*

12. Plot the set of points whose abscissa is always 0.

In Exercises 13 through 19 draw a sketch of the graph of the given set.

13. $\{(x, y) : y = x\}$

14. $\{(x, y) : y = 3\}$

15. $\{(x, y) : x = -2\}$ *y = 0*

16. $\{(x, y) : x - y = 0\}$

17. $\{(x, y) : x + y = 0\}$

18. $\left\{(x, y) : y = \frac{1}{2}x + 3\right\}$

19. $\{(x, y) : 2x + 5y = 10\}$

20. Draw a sketch of the graphs of the following linear equations on the same coordinate system:

(a) $y = 2x$ (b) $y = 2x + 1$
(c) $y = 2x + 2$ (d) $y = 2x + 3$

What characteristic do these lines have?

21. Draw a sketch of the graphs of the following linear equations on the same coordinate system.

(a) $y = \dfrac{1}{2} x$ (b) $y = \dfrac{1}{2} x - 1$

(c) $y = \dfrac{1}{2} x + 1$ (d) $y = \dfrac{1}{2} x + 2$

What characteristic do these lines have?

22. The relationship between the measures of a Celsius and Fahrenheit temperature is given by

$$F = \frac{9}{5} C + 32 \tag{5}$$

where F represents the number of degrees temperature Fahrenheit and C represents the number of degrees temperature Celsius. Make a rectangular coordinate system with a C axis in the horizontal position marked off in 10 unit intervals up to 100 and a F axis in the vertical position marked off in 10 unit intervals up to 220. Draw a sketch of the graph of equation (5).

23. Table 7.1.3 shows the temperature changes during the day at a certain airport from 6 A.M. to 6 P.M. Draw a coordinate system and plot each temperature reading. (Let the horizontal axis indicate the time units). Join the points with straight line segments.

Table 7.1.3

Hour	6	7	8	9	10	11	12	1	2	3	4	5	6
Temperature	$-5°$	$-2°$	$0°$	$0°$	$3°$	$10°$	$25°$	$28°$	$23°$	$25°$	$25°$	$15°$	$5°$

(a) Using the graph estimate the temperature at 11:30 A.M.; at 5:30 P.M. (This is a process called *interpolation*.)
(b) Using the graph project the trend and estimate the temperature at 7:00 P.M. (This is a process called *extrapolation*.)
(c) Between what hours is the temperature rising (as shown on the graph)?
(d) Between what two consecutive hours does the temperature increase most rapidly?
(e) Estimate how long the temperature is above 10°.

254 / [Chapter 7] Graphs of Equations

24. (a) On the same coordinate system draw sketches of the graphs of the equations $x + y = 5$ and $x - y = 7$. What are the coordinates of the point of intersection of the two lines?

(b) If $A = \{(x, y) : x + y = 5\}$ and $B = \{(x, y) : x - y = 7\}$, find $A \cap B$.

25. The area of an irregularly shaped region can be found if it is placed on a rectangular coordinate system and the coordinates of the points of the corners of the region can be determined. Suppose a triangle is placed so that its corner points have coordinates given by $(2, 3)$, $(0, 9)$, and $(-2, -3)$. Write the abscissas in a row and under them the corresponding ordinates. Start with any corner and take the succeeding corners in a counterclockwise direction around the region, writing the coordinates in two rows in this order. Indicate that you have made one complete closed path around the perimeter of the region by repeating the coordinates of the corner with which you started at the ends of the rows. See Figure 7.1.10. Multiply the numbers joined by diagonal solid lines and find the sum of the products. Multiply the numbers joined by diagonal dotted lines and find the sum of the products. Subtract the second sum from the first sum. Multiply by $\frac{1}{2}$ and the product is the number of square units of area in the region.

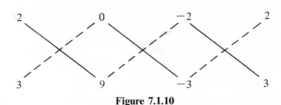

Figure 7.1.10

$$A = \frac{1}{2}\left([(2)(9) + (0)(-3) + (-2)(3)] - [(3)(0) + (9)(-2) + (-3)(2)]\right)$$

$$= \frac{1}{2}\left([18 + 0 + (-6)] - [0 + (-18) + (-6)]\right)$$

$$= \frac{1}{2}(18 + 0 - 6 - 0 + 18 + 6)$$

$$= \frac{1}{2}(36)$$

$$= 18$$

Therefore, the triangle has an area of 18 square units. Use this method to find the area of a four-cornered region whose coordinates are $(4, 0)$, $(1, 6)$, $(-3, 4)$, $(-2, -2)$, in that order as the region is traversed in a counterclockwise direction.

7.2 Slope of a Straight Line

Figure 7.2.1 shows in the first quadrant sketches of the graphs of the linear equations

$$y = \frac{1}{2}x \tag{1}$$

$$y = x \tag{2}$$

and

$$y = 2x \tag{3}$$

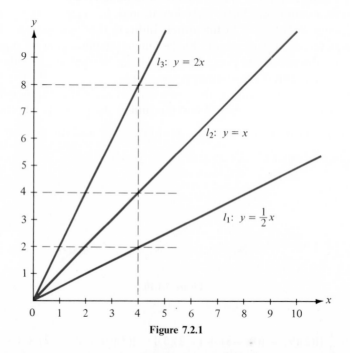

Figure 7.2.1

As the value of x increases (from left to right), we see that the graph of equation (3) "rises faster" than the graphs of equations (2) and (1), and the graph of equation (2) "rises faster" than the graph of equation (1). Notice that if x is 4, the value of y from equation (3) is 8, which is greater than the values of y from equations (2) and (1), which are 4 and 2, respectively. For $x = 5$ the value of y from equation (3) is 10, the value of y from equation (2) is 5, and the value of y from equation (1) is $\frac{5}{2}$. Thus, for a 1 unit change in x we find a 2 unit change in y defined by equation (3), a 1 unit change in y defined by equation (2), and only a $\frac{1}{2}$ unit change in y defined by equation (1).

This comparison of the changes in y for a change in x is the concept known as the "slope" of a line. For a linear equation the concept of slope is given in the following definition.

7.2.1 Definition　　Let (x_1, y_1) and (x_2, y_2), where $x_1 \neq x_2$, give the coordinates of two points on a line. Then the *slope* of the line containing these points is the number m given by the formula

$$m = \frac{y_2 - y_1}{x_2 - x_1} \qquad\qquad (4)$$

Illustration 1　 The points given by $(4, 8)$ and $(5, 10)$ are on the graph of the equation $y = 2x$ in Figure 7.2.1. In formula (4) let $(4, 8) = (x_1, y_1)$ and $(5, 10) = (x_2, y_2)$, then the slope of this line is given by

$$m = \frac{y_2 - y_1}{x_2 - x_1}$$
$$= \frac{10 - 8}{5 - 4}$$
$$= \frac{2}{1}$$
$$= 2$$

If we let $(5, 10) = (x_1, y_1)$ and $(4, 8) = (x_2, y_2)$, we see that we obtain the same value for m.

$$m = \frac{y_2 - y_1}{x_2 - x_1}$$
$$= \frac{8 - 10}{4 - 5}$$
$$= \frac{-2}{-1}$$
$$= 2$$

If we choose other points on this line, the value of m is still the same. For example, let $(x_1, y_1) = (0, 0)$ and $(x_2, y_2) = (3, 6)$; then

$$m = \frac{y_2 - y_1}{x_2 - x_1}$$
$$= \frac{6 - 0}{3 - 0}$$
$$= 2$$

See Figure 7.2.2.

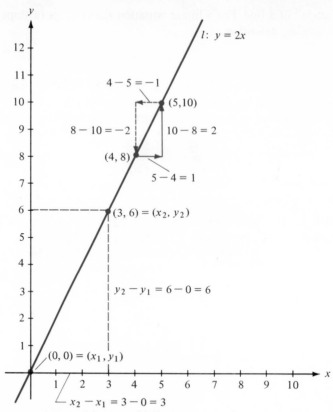

$l: y = 2x$

$4 - 5 = -1$

$(5,10)$

$8 - 10 = -2$

$10 - 8 = 2$

$(4, 8)$

$5 - 4 = 1$

$(3, 6) = (x_2, y_2)$

$y_2 - y_1 = 6 - 0 = 6$

$(0, 0) = (x_1, y_1)$

$x_2 - x_1 = 3 - 0 = 3$

Figure 7.2.2

Illustration 2 We find the slope of the line defined by the equation

$$y = x$$

Using formula (4) with $(4, 4)$ and $(5, 5)$ as the coordinates of two points on the graph of this equation, we have

$$m = \frac{5 - 4}{5 - 4}$$

$$= \frac{1}{1}$$

$$= 1$$

Therefore, the slope of the line defined by $y = x$ is 1. To find the slope of the line corresponding to the linear equation, $y = \frac{1}{2}x$ we choose two points in the line. Two such points are given by $(4, 2)$ and $\left(5, \frac{5}{2}\right)$. Using formula (4) we have

$$m = \dfrac{\dfrac{5}{2} - 2}{5 - 4}$$

$$= \dfrac{\dfrac{1}{2}}{1}$$

$$= \dfrac{1}{2}$$

Therefore, the slope of the line defined by $y = \dfrac{1}{2}x$ is $\dfrac{1}{2}$. See Figure 7.2.1.

Illustration 3 A line parallel to the y-axis does not have a slope. See Figure 7.2.3. The line of Figure 7.2.3 has no slope because the difference $x_2 - x_1$ for any pair of coordinates is always 0; and 0 in the denominator of the fraction of formula (4) gives an undefined expression.

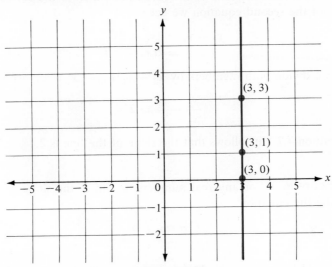

Figure 7.2.3

Example 1 Find the slope of the line containing the points whose coordinates are given by $(-1, 5)$ and $(4, -3)$.

Solution: Let $(x_1, y_1) = (-1, 5)$ and $(x_2, y_2) = (4, -3)$, then

$$m = \dfrac{y_2 - y_1}{x_2 - x_1}$$

$$= \dfrac{-3 - 5}{4 - (-1)}$$

$$= \dfrac{-8}{5}$$

The slope is $-\dfrac{8}{5}$.

By comparing the slopes of the graphs of the linear equations (1), (2), and (3), which are respectively $\frac{1}{2}$, 1, and 2. (See Illustrations 1 and 2), we see that in each case the slope and the coefficient of x are the same. Such a situation is always the case for linear equations of this form. Consider the equation

$$y = 2x$$

and let (x_1, y_1) and (x_2, y_2) be the coordinates of two points on the graph of this equation. Then

$$y_1 = 2x_1$$

and

$$y_2 = 2x_2$$

If we subtract each member of the first equation from the corresponding member of the second equation we get

$$y_2 - y_1 = 2x_2 - 2x_1$$
$$= 2(x_2 - x_1)$$

Now if we divide both members by $x_2 - x_1$ $(x_2 - x_1 \neq 0)$, we obtain

$$\frac{y_2 - y_1}{x_2 - x_1} = 2$$

By Definition 7.2.1 it follows that the slope of the line is 2.

7.2.2 Theorem   For any real numbers m and b, the slope of the line defined by the equation

$$y = mx + b \tag{5}$$

is m.

Illustration 4   To find the slope of the line defined by the equation

$$y = 3x + 2$$

we find the coordinates of two points in the line and and compute m from formula (4).

If $x = 0$, then $y = 2$ and if $x = 1$, then $y = 5$. Therefore $(0, 2)$ and $(1, 5)$ give the coordinates of two points on the line. And so,

$$m = \frac{5 - 2}{1 - 0}$$

$$= \frac{3}{1}$$

$$= 3$$

Thus, the slope is 3, as is predicted by Theorem 7.2.2.

If in equation (5) we let $x = 0$, then $y = b$. Hence, the ordered pair $(0, b)$ is a solution of the equation $y = mx + b$ and it gives a point on the graph of the equation. This point is on the y-axis because the abscissa is 0. The number b is called the *y-intercept* of the line.

Because the slope and the y-intercept are easily determined from the equation

$$y = \overset{\cdot}{m}x + b$$

this form of the linear equation is called the *slope-intercept form* of an equation of a line.

Example 2 Find the slope and y-intercept of the line whose equation is

$$y = \frac{1}{2}x - 1$$

Solution: Comparing the equation $y = \frac{1}{2}x - 1$ with equation (5), we conclude that

$$m = \frac{1}{2} \quad \text{and} \quad b = -1$$

Thus, the slope of the line is $\frac{1}{2}$ and the y-intercept is -1.

Example 3 Find the slope and y-intercept of the line whose equation is

$$3x + 2y - 6 = 0$$

Solution: Solve the equation for y.

$$2y = -3x + 6$$
$$y = \frac{-3x}{2} + \frac{6}{2}$$
$$= \frac{-3}{2}x + 3$$

Comparing this equation with equation (5), we conclude that $m = \frac{-3}{2}$ and $b = 3$. Thus, the slope of the line is $\frac{-3}{2}$ and the y-intercept is 3.

Example 4 Write an equation of the line whose slope is 5 and which intersects the y-axis at the point given by $(0, -1)$.

Solution: Because $m = 5$ and $b = -1$, we use the slope-intercept form of an equation of a line and obtain

$$y = 5x - 1$$

Example 5 Write an equation of the line shown in Figure 7.2.4.

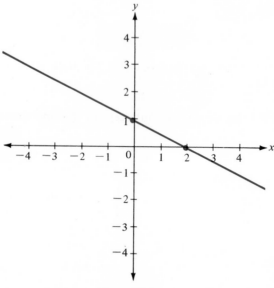

Figure 7.2.4

Solution: The line contains the points whose coordinates are given by $(0, 1)$ and $(2, 0)$. Hence,

$$m = \frac{0 - 1}{2 - 0}$$

$$= -\frac{1}{2}$$

and

$$b = 1$$

Therefore, applying the slope-intercept form of an equation of the line we get

$$y = -\frac{1}{2}x + 1$$

In geometry it is assumed that two distinct points are contained in one unique line, and we state that two points determine a line. In the next example we find an equation of a line when the coordinates of two points contained in the line are known.

Example 6   Write an equation of the line containing the points whose coordinates are given by $(5, 3)$ and $(1, 0)$.

Solution: The line contains the points given by $(5, 3)$ and $(1, 0)$. Hence, using formula (4) we have

$$m = \frac{3 - 0}{5 - 1}$$

$$= \frac{3}{4}$$

Substituting this value of m in equation (5) we get

$$y = \frac{3}{4}x + b$$

Because the point given by $(1, 0)$ is on the line, we substitute these coordinates into the equation and we get

$$0 = \frac{3}{4}(1) + b$$

and so

$$\frac{-3}{4} = b$$

Finally, substituting $\frac{3}{4}$ for m and $\frac{-3}{4}$ for b in equation (5) we get the required equation of the line

$$y = \frac{3}{4}x - \frac{3}{4}$$

Example 7   Write an equation of the line containing the point with coordinates given by $(4, 3)$ and having a slope of 2.

Solution: Because $m = 2$, we can write

$$y = 2x + b \tag{6}$$

as an equation of the line. The value of b is to be determined. The coordinates of the point must satisfy the equation. Hence we can substitute 4 for x and 3 for y in equation (6) and we obtain

$$3 = 2(4) + b$$

Solving this equation for b, we have

$$3 = 8 + b$$
$$-5 = b$$

Therefore, an equation of the required line is

$$y = 2x - 5$$

When three points lie on the same line, they are said to be *collinear*. To determine if three or more points are collinear we find the slopes of the lines containing any two of the points. If the slopes are equal, the points are collinear.

Example 8 Are the points whose coordinates are given by $(2, 6)$ $(5, 15)$ and $(3, 9)$ collinear?

Solution: One method for finding the slopes of the lines containing pairs of points is to arrange the coordinates according to increasing values of the abscissa, and compute the successive differences in the values of the abscissa and ordinates. This gives the necessary information for determining the slopes. That is, let $(x_1, y_1) = (2, 6)$, $(x_2, y_2) = (3, 9)$, and $(x_3, y_3) = (5, 15)$. Then

$$\frac{y_2 - y_1}{x_2 - x_1} = \frac{9 - 6}{3 - 2} = 3$$

and

$$\frac{y_3 - y_2}{x_3 - x_2} = \frac{15 - 9}{5 - 3} = 3$$

Therefore the slope of the line containing $(2, 6)$ and $(3, 9)$ is the same as the slope of the line containing $(3, 9)$ and $(5, 15)$. Furthermore, the point $(3, 9)$ is common to the lines. Because the lines have the same slope and contain a common point, the lines are the same. Therefore, we conclude that the points are collinear.

Another method of solution for Example 8 is to find an equation of the line containing two of the points, and then check the coordinates of the third point to see if they satisfy the equation to indicate whether or not the line contains the third point.

Two lines in a plane are said to be *parallel* if they do not intersect. If two lines have the same slope they are either parallel or they are the same line.

Illustration 5 The lines determined by the equations

$$y = 2x + 1$$

and

$$y = 2x - 2$$

each have a slope equal to 2. Because the y-intercept of the first line is 1 and the y-intercept of the second line is -2, the two lines are distinct. Hence, the two lines are parallel. See Figure 7.2.5. Because the two lines do not intersect, we can write

$$\{(x, y) : y = 2x + 1\} \cap \{(x, y) : y = 2x - 2\} = \emptyset$$

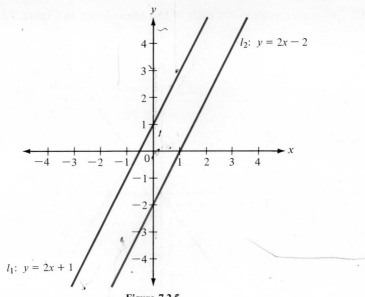

Figure 7.2.5

Exercises 7.2

In Exercises 1 through 4 find the slope of the line containing the points whose coordinates are given.

1. $(2, 0)$ and $(0, 3)$ **2.** $(3, -1)$ and $(-2, 5)$

3. $(4, 2)$ and $(-1, 2)$ **4.** $(-5, 1)$ and $(-5, 11)$

In Exercises 5 through 14 write the equation in the slope-intercept form and then determine the slope and the y-intercept of the line.

5. $y = 3x + 5$ **6.** $y = 5 - 3x$ **7.** $2x - y = 1$

8. $x + y = 0$ **9.** $x - y = 0$ **10.** $x + 3y - 7 = 0$

11. $2y = x + 3$ **12.** $2y - 6 = x$ **13.** $4(x + y) = -2$

14. $2x + 3(y - 1) = 10$

15. On the same coordinate system draw 3 lines, each having a slope of 2 and having y-intercepts of 0, 1, and 2. What geometric property do these lines appear to have? Repeat with a slope of $\frac{1}{2}$. What do you find?

16. Write an equation for each of the lines described in Exercise 15.

17. Write an equation for each of the lines shown in Figure 7.2.6.

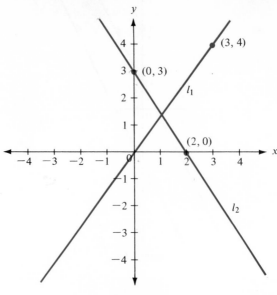

Figure 7.2.6

In Exercises 18 through 22 write an equation of the line containing the points whose coordinates are given.

18. $(0, 0)$, $(3, 4)$ **19.** $(3, 0)$, $(-3, -4)$ **20.** $(-6, 0)$, $(-2, 8)$

21. $(5, 8)$, $(-5, 2)$ **22.** $(-2, -3)$, $(4, -1)$

23. Write an equation of the line having a slope of 3 and containing the point whose coordinates are given by $(5, 1)$.

24. Write an equation of the line having a slope of $\frac{2}{3}$ and containing the point whose coordinates are given by $(-5, 2)$.

25. A temperature of $212°$ Fahrenheit corresponds to $100°$ Celsius and $32°$ Fahrenheit corresponds to $0°$ Celsius. Thus, we have two points whose coordinates are given by $(212, 100)$ and $(32, 0)$. Find an equation defining the relationship between these two temperature scales if you assume that this equation is linear.

26. Determine if the points whose coordinates are given by $(12, 1)$, $(8, 5)$, and $(7, 7)$ lie on the same line.

27. Determine if the points whose coordinates are given by $(0, 10)$, $(2, 7)$, and $(6, 1)$ lie on the same line.

28. At noon the supply of oxygen in a capsule measured 10 units. At 2:00

P.M. the supply of oxygen measured 7 units. If the supply of oxygen is s units t hours after noon and a constant rate of use is assumed, write an equation giving the relationship between t and s. Refer to a coordinate system where the t-axis is horizontal and $t = 0$ at noon. When will the supply of oxygen run out; that is, when does $s = 0$?

29. The measure of the distance between two points may be found by using the Pythagorean theorem in the form of

$$d = \sqrt{(x_2 - x_1)^2 + (y_2 - y_1)^2}$$

where d represents the measure of the distance and (x_1, y_1) and (x_2, y_2) give the coordinates of the two points. Find the distance between the points whose coordinates are given by $(-1, 2)$ and $(3, -1)$.

30. If (x_1, y_1) and (x_2, y_2) give the coordinates of the endpoints of a line segment, then the coordinates of the midpoint of this line segment are given by

$$\left(\frac{x_1 + x_2}{2}, \frac{y_1 + y_2}{2} \right)$$

Find the midpoint of the line segment whose endpoints have coordinates given by $(-1, 3)$ and $(7, 9)$.

31. In a laboratory experiment some crushed ice is warmed to the melting point, $0°C$, and melted. The water temperature is then increased to the boiling point and maintained as the water is converted into steam. The measure of the temperature T of the water in each of its states is found to depend upon the number of minutes of time t in such a way that the relationship is linear during the time interval of each state. Some of the data collected is shown in Table 7.2.1 and a sketch of the graph of the relationship between T and t is shown in Figure 7.2.7 (page 268).

Table 7.2.1

t	0	5	20	55	60	75
T	-20	0	0	100	100	100

(a) Find a linear equation giving the relationship between t and T for each of the following intervals: (i) $0 \leq t \leq 5$; (ii) $5 < t \leq 20$; (iii) $20 < t \leq 55$; (iv) $55 < t$.
(b) What is the slope of each line segment in the graph?
(c) In what interval does the temperature change most rapidly (greatest slope)? Most slowly (least slope)?
(d) At what time is the temperature of the water $40°C$?
(e) What is the temperature 45 minutes after the start of the experiment?

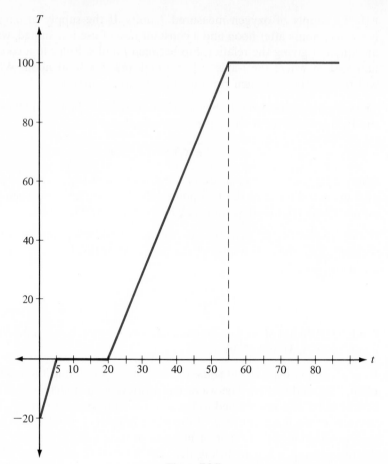

Figure 7.2.7

7.3 Systems of Linear Equations

Suppose we are given that the sum of two numbers is 5. If we let x and y represent the two numbers, we have the equation

$$x + y = 5 \tag{1}$$

This equation has two "unknowns" and an unlimited number of solutions that consist of a pair of values, one for x and one for y. Now suppose that another condition is imposed on the two numbers: the difference between the two numbers is 7. We now have a second equation

$$x - y = 7 \tag{2}$$

where x is the larger of the two numbers. Equations (1) and (2) together form a *system of equations*.

A *linear system* of equations is a set of linear equations. Hence, equations (1) and (2) form a linear system of two equations and two unknowns.

The solution set of a system of equations is the set of all solutions that simultaneously satisfy each of the equations in the system. Ordinarily, to solve a system of equations for a unique solution, we require as many equations as there are unknowns in the equations; however, there are exceptions to this requirement as the examples that follow indicate.

If we have a system of two linear equations and two unknowns and the system has a unique solution, then the solution consists of a pair of numbers. The graphical interpretation of the solution is that the numbers are the coordinates of the point of intersection of the lines that represent the two given equations.

Example 1 Draw a sketch of the graph of the linear equations (1) and (2), and find the coordinates of the point of intersection of the two lines that represent the equations.

Solution: If $A = \{(x, y) : x + y = 5\}$
  and $B = \{(x, y) : x - y = 7\}$

we wish to draw a sketch of the graph of the sets A and B and then find $A \cap B$. See Figure 7.3.1. From the figure we see that the x-coordinate of the point of intersection is 6 and the y-coordinate is -1. Thus, $A \cap B = \{(6, -1)\}$. Note that if we substitute 6 for x and -1 for y into the given equations, then the equations are satisfied. See Illustration 1.

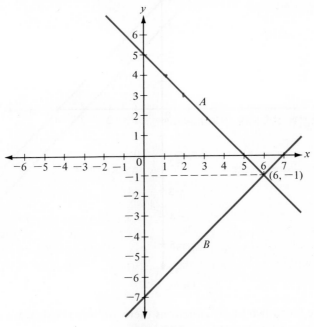

Figure 7.3.1

If there is a solution of a system of equations, then the equations are said to be *consistent*.

Illustration 1 The equations (1) and (2) are consistent because there is a solution, namely $x = 6$ and $y = -1$; these values of x and y satisfy both equations in the system.

$$
\begin{array}{cc}
x + y = 5 & x - y = 7 \\
6 + (-1) = 5 & 6 - (-1) = 7 \\
5 = 5 & 7 = 7
\end{array}
$$

Not every system of two equations and two unknowns has a unique solution. The system

$$x + y = 3 \tag{3}$$

$$x + y = 4 \tag{4}$$

has no solution that satisfies both equations simultaneously. No two numbers give a sum 3 and also a sum 4. Hence, equations (3) and (4) are inconsistent. The graph of the system of equations (3) and (4) consists of two parallel lines. See Figure 7.3.2.

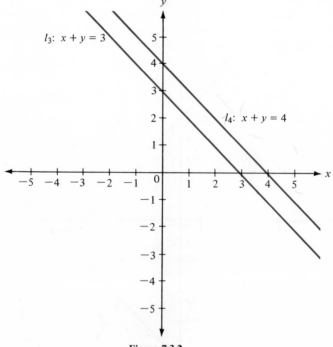

Figure 7.3.2

If we are given two linear equations there are three basic ways that their graphs can be related:

(i) The two lines intersect in a single point. See Example 1.

(ii) The two lines may not intersect; that is, they may be parallel. See Figure 7.3.2.

(iii) The two lines may in fact be one line; that is, the lines coincide. See Illustration 2.

If two lines have the same slope and different y-intercepts, they are parallel. If two lines have the same slope and equal y-intercepts, they coincide.

Illustration 2 Consider the system of equations

$$y = 4x - 3 \qquad\qquad (5)$$
$$2y = 8x - 6 \qquad\qquad (6)$$

The graphs of equations (5) and (6) are lines having the same slope. Because equation (5) is in the slope-intercept form, the coefficient of x is the slope of the line that represents the equation. Hence, the slope is 4. By dividing both members of equation (6) by 2, we see that the slope of the line that represents this equation is also 4. The y-intercept of each of the lines is -3. Thus, the two equations are equivalent and the graph of each equation is the same line. See Figure 7.3.3.

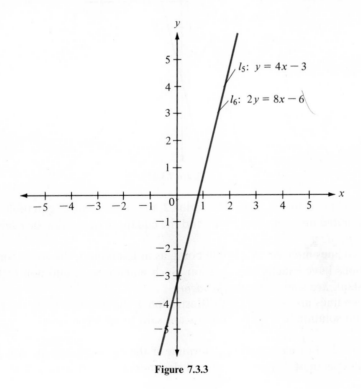

Figure 7.3.3

Illustration 3 The lines that are the graphs of the equations

$$y = 4x - 3$$

and

$$y = 4x + 3$$

have the same slope but different y-intercepts. These two lines are parallel lines. See Figure 7.3.4. If $A = \{(x, y) : y = 4x + 3\}$ and $B = \{(x, y) : y = 4x - 3\}$, then we write

$$A \cap B = \varnothing$$

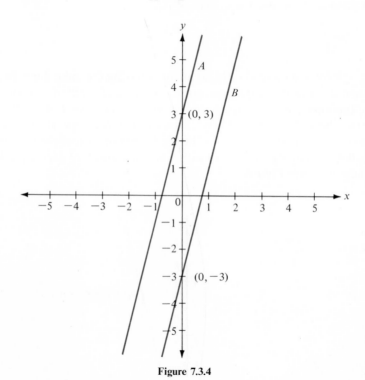

Figure 7.3.4

If two lines coincide, as in Illustration 2, the corresponding equations have an unlimited number of solutions and the equations are said to be *consistent* and *dependent*.

If two lines intersect in a single point, as in Example 1, the corresponding equations have exactly one solution. Such equations, in addition to being consistent, are said to be *independent*.

If two lines are parallel, as in Illustration 3, the corresponding equations have no solution and the equations are said to be *inconsistent*.

Example 2 For each system determine if the equations are (i) consistent and independent, (ii) consistent and dependent, or (iii) inconsistent.

(a) $3x + 2y = 6$ (b) $5x + 2y = 4$ (c) $y = -2x + 1$

    $3x + 2y = 12$ $10x + 4y = 8$ $y = \dfrac{1}{2}x + 1$

Solution: We write each equation in the slope-intercept form and consider the corresponding lines that represent the equations.

(a) $3x + 2y = 6$ $3x + 2y = 12$

    $2y = 6 - 3x$ $2y = 12 - 3x$

    $y = -\dfrac{3}{2}x + 3$ $y = -\dfrac{3}{2}x + 6$

Because the slope of each of the lines is $-\dfrac{3}{2}$ and the y-intercepts are not equal, the lines are parallel. Hence, the equations are inconsistent. There is no solution for the system.

(b) $5x + 2y = 4$ $10x + 4y = 8$

    $2y = 4 - 5x$ $4y = 8 - 10x$

    $y = -\dfrac{5}{2}x + 2$ $y = -\dfrac{10}{4}x + \dfrac{8}{4}$

                                  $y = -\dfrac{5}{2}x + 2$

We see that the two equations are equivalent. The corresponding lines coincide and therefore the equations are consistent and dependent. There is an unlimited number of solutions for the system.

(c) Because the slopes of the corresponding lines of this system are not equal, the lines intersect at a point; hence, the equations are consistent and independent. There is one solution for the system.

Exercises 7.3

In Exercises 1 through 10 draw a sketch of the graphs of the equations of the system. From these graphs find the solution of the system. Also, determine if the equations are (i) consistent and independent, (ii) consistent and dependent, or (iii) inconsistent.

1. $y = 2x + 1$ 2. $x + y = 6$
   $y = 1 - x$ $2x + 3y = 6$

3. $x - y = 5$ 4. $x + y = 2$
   $2x - 2y = 10$ $y = 4 - x$

5. $2y = x + 1$ 6. $y = 4$
   $7y = 3x + 14$ $x = 2$

7. $x = y$
    $y = -x$

8. $x + y = 4$
    $x = 3y$

9. $x + y = 4$
    $x - y = 4$

10. $y = x + 2$
    $x = y + 2$

In Exercises 11 through 14 examine the given graph of a system of equations. From these graphs find the solution of the system. Also, determine if the equations that are being represented by the graphs are (i) consistent and independent, (ii) consistent and dependent, or (iii) inconsistent.

11. See Figure 7.3.5.

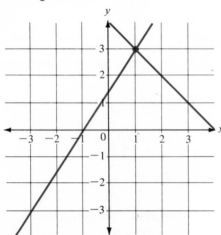

Figure 7.3.5

12. See Figure 7.3.6.

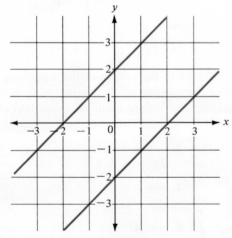

Figure 7.3.6

13. See Figure 7.3.7.

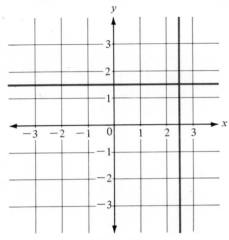

Figure 7.3.7

14. See Figure 7.3.8.

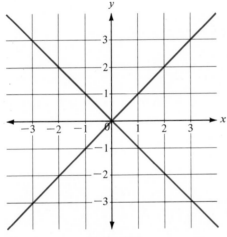

Figure 7.3.8

7.4 Solving Systems of Linear Equations

In Section 7.3 we found the solution of the system

$$x + y = 5 \tag{1}$$
$$x - y = 7 \tag{2}$$

from the graphs of these equations. This method of obtaining solutions of systems of equations is not reliable because, generally, the coordinates of a point of intersection can only be estimated. We now describe methods of obtaining precise solutions for a system of linear equations.

Example 1 Solve the system of equations (1) and (2).

Solution: If we add the left members of both equations and the right members of both equations, respectively, and equate the results, we eliminate the term involving y. Hence, we have

$$(x + y) + (x - y) = 5 + 7$$
$$2x = 12$$
$$x = 6$$

If we substitute 6 for x in equation (1), we obtain

$$6 + y = 5$$

and so,

$$y = -1$$

The solution then, is given by $x = 6$ and $y = -1$, or $(6, -1)$.

To check the solution of the system of equations in Example 1, we verify that the sum of x and y is 5 and the difference of x and y is 7. Thus, we have

$$x + y = 6 + (-1) = 5$$

and

$$x - y = 6 - (-1) = 7$$

In order to justify what we did in the solution of Example 1, we need the following theorem.

7.4.1 Theorem　If $E_1 = E_2$ and $E_3 = E_4$ are any two consistent equations, then

$$E_1 + E_3 = E_2 + E_4$$

Proof:

$E_1 = E_2$　　　　　　(1)　*Given.*
$E_1 + E_3 = E_2 + E_3$ (2)　*By adding E_3 to both members of equation (1) (Theorem 4.3.2).*
$E_3 = E_4$　　　　　　(3)　*Given.*
$E_1 + E_3 = E_2 + E_4$ (4)　*Substituting E_4 for E_3 in equation (2) on the right side (Axiom 1.5.2).*

With Theorem 7.4.1, the solution of Example 1 can be justified because we added the respective left and right members of the two equations of the given system.

Example 2   Solve the system

$$3x + 2y = 6$$
$$5x - 2y = 10$$

Solution: Given $3x + 2y = 6$ and $5x - 2y = 10$, we add the left and right members of these equations, respectively.

$$(3x + 2y) + (5x - 2y) = 6 + 10$$
$$8x = 16$$
$$x = 2$$

Now, we substitute 2 for x in either of the equations of the given system and solve for y. (We substitute in the first equation.)

$$3x + 2y = 6$$
$$3(2) + 2y = 6$$
$$6 + 2y = 6$$
$$2y = 0$$
$$y = 0$$

Therefore, the solution is given by $x = 2$ and $y = 0$.

7.4.2 Theorem   If $E_1 = E_2$ and $E_3 = E_4$ are consistent equations, then

$$E_1 - E_3 = E_2 - E_4$$

and

$$E_3 - E_1 = E_4 - E_2$$

The proof of Theorem 7.4.2 is similar to that of Theorem 7.4.1 and is left as an exercise for the reader. (See Exercise 21 at the end of Section 7.4.)

Example 3   Solve the given system and check the solution.

$$4x + 5y = 8$$
$$4x + 2y = 5$$

Solution: Given $4x + 5y = 8$ and $4x + 2y = 5$, we subtract the left member of the second equation from the left member of the first equation; this result is set equal to the corresponding difference of the right members of the two equations.

$$(4x + 5y) - (4x + 2y) = 8 - 5$$
$$3y = 3$$
$$y = 1$$

Now we substitute 1 for y in either of the equations of the given system and solve for x. We substitute in the second equation.

$$4x + 2y = 5$$
$$4x + 2(1) = 5$$
$$4x + 2 = 5$$
$$4x = 3$$
$$x = \frac{3}{4}$$

Therefore, the solution is given by $x = \frac{3}{4}$ and $y = 1$. We check by substituting $\frac{3}{4}$ for x and 1 for y in each equation.

$$4x + 5y = 4\left(\frac{3}{4}\right) + 5(1)$$
$$= 3 + 5$$
$$= 8$$
$$4x + 2y = 4\left(\frac{3}{4}\right) + 2(1)$$
$$= 3 + 2$$
$$= 5$$

Comparing the solutions of Examples 2 and 3 we see how Theorems 7.4.1 and 7.4.2 are used.

Suppose we have the equations

$$5x + y = 16 \tag{3}$$

and

$$2x + 3y = 22 \tag{4}$$

We cannot eliminate a variable by either adding or subtracting the respective members of the two equations. To solve the system we multiply both members of equation (3) by 3. Then the coefficients of y in the two equations are equal, and we proceed as in Examples 2 and 3. Study the next example.

Example 4 Solve the system of equations (3) and (4).

Solution: Multiplying equation (3) by 3, we have the equivalent equation

$$15x + 3y = 48 \tag{5}$$

The system of equations (5) and (4) is equivalent to the given system.

Now, comparing equation (4) with equation (5) we see that we can eliminate the terms involving y by subtracting the respective left and right members of these equations. Doing this we obtain

$$(2x + 3y) - (15x + 3y) = 22 - 48$$

By combining terms we get

$$-13x = -26$$

and so,

$$x = 2$$

Substituting 2 for x in equation (3), we obtain

$$5(2) + y = 16$$
$$10 + y = 16$$
$$y = 6$$

Therefore, the solution is given by $x = 2$ and $y = 6$.

In some cases it may be necessary to multiply both equations by appropriate factors.

Example 5 Solve the system

$$3x + 2y = 13 \tag{6}$$
$$2x + 5y = 27 \tag{7}$$

Solution: Multiplying both members of equation (6) by 2, we obtain

$$6x + 4y = 26 \tag{8}$$

Now multiplying both members of equation (7) by 3, we obtain

$$6x + 15y = 81 \tag{9}$$

The system of equations (8) and (9) is equivalent to the given system of equations.

We now subtract the corresponding members of equation (9) from those of equation (8).

$$(6x + 4y) - (6x + 15y) = 26 - 81$$

By combining terms we obtain

$$4y - 15y = -55$$
$$-11y = -55$$
$$y = 5$$

We substitute 5 for y in equation (6).

$$3x + 2y = 13$$
$$3x + 2(5) = 13$$
$$3x + 10 = 13$$
$$3x = 3$$
$$x = 1$$

Therefore, the solution is given by $x = 1$ and $y = 5$.

Some systems of equations are readily solved by the substitution process. See the next example.

Example 6 Solve the system

$$5x + 2y = 9 \qquad (10)$$
$$y = x - 3 \qquad (11)$$

Solution: We substitute the value of y given by equation (11) into equation (10), and we have

$$5x + 2(x - 3) = 9$$
$$5x + 2x - 6 = 9$$
$$7x - 6 = 9$$
$$7x = 15$$
$$x = \frac{15}{7}$$

We now substitute $\frac{15}{7}$ for x in equation (11).

$$y = x - 3$$
$$= \frac{15}{7} - 3$$
$$= \frac{15}{7} - \frac{21}{7}$$
$$= \frac{-6}{7}$$

Therefore, the solution is given by $x = \frac{15}{7}$ and $y = \frac{-6}{7}$.

The substitution process is also the basis for solving a system of equations where each equation has one member that consists of a single variable. Study Example 7.

Example 7 Solve the system

$$y = 2x + 1$$
$$y = 1 - x$$

Solution: Because the left member of each equation is the single variable y, we equate the right members, and we get

$$2x + 1 = 1 - x$$

Solving for x, we have

$$3x + 1 = 1$$
$$3x = 0$$
$$x = 0$$

We now substitute 0 for x in the first equation

$$y = 2(0) + 1$$
$$= 1$$

Therefore, the solution is given by $x = 0$ and $y = 1$.

Exercises 7.4

In Exercises 1 through 20 find a solution for the given system of equations.

1. $x + y = 12$
   $x - y = 4$

2. $t - r = 0$ *t=3*
   $t + r = 6$ *r=3*

3. $4x + 3y = 29$
   $2x - 3y = 1$

4. $x + y = 13$
   $x - y = 15$

5. $\frac{1}{2}x + y = 7$

   $\frac{1}{2}x - y = 5$

6. $4x + 5y = 16$
   $4x + y = 4$

7. $3(x + y) = 13$
   $x + 3y = 5$

8. $10x - y = 20$
   $15x + 2y = 30$

9. $x = 3y + 7$
   $x + y = 27$

10. $b = 3$
    $a + 3b = 11$

11. $4x + 2y = 8$
    $5x - 2y = 1$

12. $2a + 3b = 40$
    $5a + 2b = 35$

13. $5x + y = 6$
    $x + 3y = 18$

14. $4x - y = 30$
    $3x + 2y = 50$

15. Solve for x and y.   *dint*
    $x + y = a$
    $x - y = b$ *solve for*
      x+y sepr
      ately

16. $y = 3x - 2$
    $y = x + 1$

17. $2x + y = 8$
    $y = x + 2$

18. $x + 2y = 8$
    $2y = 3x$

19. $5x - y = 10$
    $5x - y = 15$

20. $x + 2y = 3$
    $5x + 10y = 15$
      0=0 dependent

21. Prove: Theorem 7.4.2.

22. In the statements of Theorems 7.4.1 and 7.4.2, the hypothesis requires that the equations are consistent. Discuss this requirement in the light of trying to apply the conclusion of these theorems to the inconsistent system given by

$$x - y = 3$$
$$x - y = 5$$

23. Solve the system of equations

$$x + y = 5$$
$$y + z = 10$$
$$x + z = 9$$

24. The variables E, I, R, and P represent the measures of the voltage,

current, resistance, and power in a direct current electrical circuit. Furthermore, $E = IR$ and $P = I^2 R$.

(a) Show that $P = E \cdot I$.

(b) If $E = 12$ and $R = 3$, find P.

25. If $A = \pi r^2$ and $d = 2r$, find a formula for A in terms of d.

7.5 Review Exercises

1. In what quadrant is the point whose coordinates are given by
   (a) $(-1, -1)$?   (b) $(1, -3)$?

2. Draw a sketch of the graph of the given set:
   (a) $\{(x, y) : 2x + 3y = 6\}$ (b) $\{(x, y) : 2x - 3y = 6\}$

3. What is the slope of the line containing the points whose coordinates are given by (a) $(3, -1)$ and $(-1, 5)$? (b) $(10, 0)$ and $(0, 10)$?

4. Find an equation of the line containing the point given by $(0, 5)$ and with (a) a slope equal to $\dfrac{1}{2}$; (b) a slope equal to -2.

5. The graphs of the given linear equations are straight lines. For each equation answer the following questions: (i) What is the slope of the line? (ii) What is the y-intercept of the line? (iii) What is the abscissa of the point of intersection of the line and the x-axis?
   (a) $y = 3x - 2$ (b) $x + y = 10$

6. Find an equation of the line containing the two points whose coordinates are given by (a) $(3, -1)$ and $(-1, 5)$; (b) $(10, 0)$ and $(0, 10)$.

7. If y dollars is the cost of the manufacture and distribution of x items and if

$$y = mx + b$$

then b dollars is called the *fixed cost* involved in the production. This is because if zero items are produced ($x = 0$), then the cost is b dollars ($y = b$). (The fixed cost pays for equipment, supplies, and the necessary overhead of production.) Find the fixed cost of the production if
   (a) the cost is \$10,400 to manufacture and distribute 100 items and the cost is \$14,400 to manufacture and distribute 200 items,
   (b) the cost is \$580 to manufacture and distribute 10 items and the cost is \$1000 to manufacture and distribute 52 items.

8. Draw a sketch of the graphs of A and B and find $A \cap B$ if
   (a) $A = \{(x, y) : x + y = 10\}$ and $B = \{(x, y) : x = 2y\}$
   (b) $A = \{(x, y) : x + y = -5\}$ and $B = \{(x, y) : y = x\}$

In Exercises 9 and 10 determine if each of the pairs of equations are (i) consistent and independent, (ii) consistent and dependent, or (iii) inconsistent.

9. (a) $y = x + 1$ *Graph each* **(b)** $y = x + 1$
    $y = x - 1$ *equation* $3y = 3x + 3$ *Graph*

10. (a) $y = x + 1$ } *same slope* **(b)** $y = x - 1$
     $y = x + 3$ $y = 1 - x$ *slopes different so intercept*

In Exercises 11 and 12 solve each system of equations.

11. (a) $2x + y = 10$ **(b)** $2x + 3y = 1$
       $2x - y = 2$ $4x - 2y = 26$

12. (a) $4x + 3y = 6$ **(b)** $2x - y = 5$
            $y = x - 5$ $y = -8 - x$

$x = 3$ $x = -1$
$y = -2$ $y = -7$

8

Test Mon.

Problem Solving

8.1 Problems Leading to Systems of Equations

The following problem leads naturally to a system of two equations and two unknowns.

Example 1 The sum of two numbers is 50 and their difference is 15. Find the two numbers.

Solution: Let x be the larger number and y be the smaller number. Then

$$x + y = 50$$

and

$$x - y = 15$$

To solve this system we add the corresponding left and right members of the two equations and we get

$$2x = 65$$

Therefore,

$$x = 32\frac{1}{2}$$

Now since $x + y = 50$, we have

$$32\frac{1}{2} + y = 50$$

or

$$y = 17\frac{1}{2}$$

Thus, $32\frac{1}{2}$ and $17\frac{1}{2}$ are the required numbers.

Check: Substitute the numbers $32\frac{1}{2}$ and $17\frac{1}{2}$ for x and y, respectively, in the original equations.

$$32\frac{1}{2} + 17\frac{1}{2} = 50$$

$$32\frac{1}{2} - 17\frac{1}{2} = 15$$

Both of the resulting statements are true.

In some instances a problem like that of Example 1 can be solved with one equation and one unknown. This sometimes, however, requires a little more effort to obtain the proper relationships. Thus, Example 1 can be solved by letting x represent the larger number and then $50 - x$ will represent the smaller number. (Note, if $x + y = 50$, then $y = 50 - x$.) Then the single equation will represent the information given about their difference, that is,

$$x - (50 - x) = 15$$

Example 2 A bottle and a cork cost $1.10 and the bottle costs one dollar more than the cork. How much does each cost?

Solution: Let $b =$ the number of cents in the cost of the bottle
and $c =$ the number of cents in the cost of the cork.
Then

$$b + c = 110 \qquad\qquad (1)$$

and

$$b = c + 100 \qquad\qquad (2)$$

This system can be solved by substituting the value for b from equation (2) in equation (1). Doing this, we obtain

$$(c + 100) + c = 110$$
$$2c + 100 = 110$$
$$2c = 10$$
$$c = 5$$

Because $b = c + 100$, we have

$$b = 5 + 100$$
$$= 105$$

Hence, the bottle costs $1.05 and the cork costs $0.05.

We can check these answers by noting that the total cost is $1.10 and that $1.05 is $1.00 more than $0.05.

Example 3 In a collection of coins the number of dimes is three less than twice the number of nickels. The total value of all the coins is $3.20. How many coins of each kind are there?

Solution: Let x = the number of nickels
and y = the number of dimes.

Then

$$y = 2x - 3 \qquad (3)$$

Now the value of x nickels is $5x$ cents, and the value of y dimes is $10y$ cents. Hence,

$$5x + 10y = 320 \qquad (4)$$

Solving these two equations, by substituting the value of y from equation (3) into (4) we obtain

$$5x + 10(2x - 3) = 320$$

Thus,

$$5x + 20x - 30 = 320$$
$$25x - 30 = 320$$
$$25x = 350$$
$$x = 14$$

Substituting this value of x into equation (3), we have

$$y = 2(14) - 3$$
$$= 28 - 3$$
$$= 25$$

Hence, the collection contains 14 nickels and 25 dimes. We can check this by noting first of all that 25 is 3 less than twice 14 and secondly, the value of 14 nickels is $0.70 and the value of 25 dimes is $2.50, a total of $3.20.

Example 4   Art is three times as old as Bill is now. Six years from now Bill will be half as old as Art is then. What is the present age of each person?

Solution: Let a years = Art's present age
and b years = Bill's present age.

Then

$$a = 3b \qquad (5)$$

Six years from now Art will be $(a + 6)$ years old and Bill will be $(b + 6)$ years old. At that time we have

$$b + 6 = \frac{1}{2}(a + 6) \qquad (6)$$

Solving these two equations by substituting the value of a from equation (5) into equation (6) we obtain

$$b + 6 = \frac{1}{2}(3b + 6)$$

Thus,

$$2(b + 6) = 3b + 6$$
$$2b + 12 = 3b + 6$$
$$12 = b + 6$$
$$6 = b$$

Substituting 6 for b into equation (5), we have

$$a = 3(6)$$
$$= 18$$

Hence, Art's present age is 18 years and Bill's present age is 6 years.

Exercises 8.1

Use a system of equations to solve each of the following problems.

1. The sum of two numbers is 76 and their difference is 48. Find the numbers.

2. The following problem is a variation of one of Euclid's (ca. 300 B.C.). Two peddlers were carrying loads of several measures each. One said to the other, "If I give you one of my measures, we shall have equal loads, but if you give me one of yours, I shall have twice as many measures as you." How many measures was each peddler carrying?

3. Separate 40 into two parts so that three times the smaller part equals twice the larger part.

4. The sum of two numbers is 53. The larger number is one more than three times the smaller. Find the two numbers.

5. John is three times as old as his son. In 10 years John will only be one year older than twice his son's age then. How old is each one now?

6. Beth is four fifths as old as Laura. Four years ago she was three fourths as old as Laura. How old is each one?

7. The numerator of a certain fraction is 3 less than the denominator. If each is increased by 2, the value of the resulting fraction is $\frac{2}{3}$. Find the original fraction.

8. The average of two numbers is 48. Their difference is 16. What are the two numbers?

9. If two pads and three pencils cost 70 cents and three pads and two pencils cost 95 cents, find the cost of each pad and each pencil.

10. If the perimeter of a certain rectangle is 60 feet and the measure of the length is three times that of the width, find the dimensions of the rectangle.

11. The son's share of an $18,000 inheritance was $5000 less than three times an uncle's share. Find the son's share.

12. An investment of $600 earned $35. Part of the $600 was invested at 5% and the rest at 6%. How much was invested at each rate?

13. At a school play students were charged 25 cents and others were charged 60 cents. If $61.50 was collected and 190 tickets sold one evening, how many nonstudents attended?

14. Two machines can process 1800 items in one hour. However, if the first machine operates for one-half hour and the second machine operates for two hours, 1500 items can be processed. How many items can each machine process in one hour?

15. A coin collection consists of 12 more nickels than three times the number of dimes. The total number of coins is 96. What is the total value of the collection?

16. The total value of a collection of dimes and nickels is $4.35. There are 12 more nickels than three times the number of dimes. How many of each kind of coin is there?

8.2 Mixture Problems

The following examples are typical of mixture problems.

Example 1 Mix a 5% acid solution (5% of the volume of the solution is acid and 95% of the volume of the solution is water) and a 15% acid solution to obtain 2 quarts of a 12% acid solution. How many quarts of each kind should be used?

Solution: Let x = the number of quarts of the 5% acid solution
and y = the number of quarts of the 15% acid solution.

Sometimes a diagram of the situation helps in formulating the equation. See Figure 8.2.1. The equation is based on the fact that the actual number of quarts of acid contained in the two solutions will be the same number of quarts of acid after they are mixed.

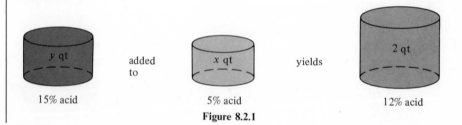

| y qt | added to | x qt | yields | 2 qt |
| 15% acid | | 5% acid | | 12% acid |

Figure 8.2.1

$0.05x =$ the number of quarts of acid in the 5% acid solution
$0.15y =$ the number of quarts of acid in the 15% acid solution
$0.12(2) =$ the number of quarts of acid in the mixture

Because the total number of quarts of acid contained in the original solutions equals the total number of quarts of acid in the final mixture, we have the equation

$$0.05x + 0.15y = 0.12(2) \qquad (1)$$

We also have the equation

$$x + y = 2 \qquad (2)$$

Hence, we can solve the system of equations (1) and (2). Multiply both members of equation (1) by 100 to eliminate the decimal notation.

$$5x + 15y = 12(2) \qquad (3)$$

Now multiply both members of equation (2) by 5 and obtain

$$5x + 5y = 5(2) \qquad (4)$$

Subtracting both members of equation (4) from the corresponding members of equation (3) we obtain

$$10y = 7(2)$$

Solving for y, we have

$$y = \frac{7(2)}{10}$$

$$= 1.4$$

Substituting this value for y into equation (2) we get

$$x + 1.4 = 2$$
$$x = 0.6$$

Hence, 1.4 quarts of the 15% acid solution should be mixed with 0.6 quarts of the 5% acid solution.

Example 1 can also be solved by using the percent of water in the solutions instead of the acid. See the next example.

Example 2   Solve Example 1 by considering the amount of water in the solutions instead of the acid.

Solution: Let $x =$ the number of quarts of the 95% water solution
and $y =$ the number of quarts of the 85% water solution.

Then

$0.95x =$ the number of quarts of water in the 95% solution
$0.85y =$ the number of quarts of water in the 85% solution
$0.88(2) =$ the number of quarts of water in the mixture

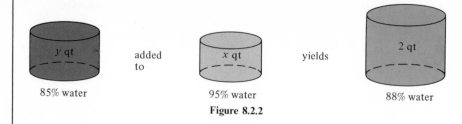
Figure 8.2.2

See Figure 8.2.2. The first equation is obtained by adding the number of quarts of water found in each container of the original solutions, and equating the sum to the number of quarts of water in the 2 quart mixture; that is,

$$0.95x + 0.85y = 0.88(2) \tag{5}$$

Multiplying both members of equation (5) by 100 gives us

$$95x + 85y = 176 \tag{6}$$

The other equation in the system is

$$x + y = 2 \tag{7}$$

Multiplying both members of equation (7) by 95 we obtain

$$95x + 95y = 190 \tag{8}$$

Subtracting the corresponding members of equation (6) from those of equation (8) gives

$$10y = 14$$
$$y = 1.4$$

Substituting this value of y into equation (7) gives

$$x + 1.4 = 2$$
$$x = 0.6$$

Hence, we find the same results as in Example 1.

Example 3 How much water must be evaporated from 100 gallons of a 20% salt solution to obtain a 25% salt solution.

Solution: Let x = the number of gallons of water to be evaporated.
$0.80(100)$ = the number of gallons of water present in the original mixture (20% salt).
$1.00(x)$ = the number of gallons of water evaporated.
$0.75(100 - x)$ = the number of gallons of water remaining.

See Figure 8.2.3. The number of gallons of water in the original solution is $[(0.80)(100)]$. Subtract $[1.00(x)]$, the number of gallons of water lost due

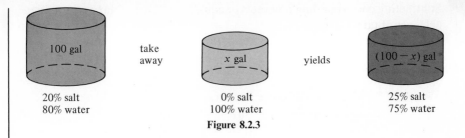

100 gal	take away	x gal	yields	(100 − x) gal
20% salt 80% water		0% salt 100% water		25% salt 75% water

Figure 8.2.3

to evaporation. The result equals the number of gallons of water remaining in the solution $[0.75(100 - x)]$. Hence, the required equation is

$$(0.80)(100) - 1.00(x) = 0.75(100 - x) \qquad (9)$$

Multiplying both members of equation (9) by 100, we obtain

$$8000 - 100x = 75(100 - x)$$
$$8000 - 100x = 7500 - 75x$$
$$-100x + 75x = 7500 - 8000$$
$$-25x = -500$$
$$x = \frac{-500}{-25}$$
$$= 20$$

Hence, 20 gallons of water must be evaporated.

Example 4 A grocer wishes to mix candy worth $1.50 per pound with some candy worth $1.00 per pound. He wants 500 pounds of this mixture to sell for $1.10 per pound. How many pounds of each kind of candy should he use?

Solution: Let $x =$ the number of pounds of candy worth $1.50 per pound and $y =$ the number of pounds of candy worth $1.00 per pound.

Then

$$1.50x = \text{the dollar value of the expensive candy used}$$
$$1.00y = \text{the dollar value of the less expensive candy used.}$$

We also note that there are 500 pounds of candy in the mixture selling at $1.10 per pound. Hence,

$$1.10(500) = \text{the dollar value of the entire mixture}$$

Thus, the equations are

$$x + y = 500 \qquad (10)$$

and

$$1.50x + 1.00y = 1.10(500) \qquad (11)$$

Subtracting corresponding members of equation (10) from those of equation (11), we obtain

$$0.50x = 1.10(500) - 500$$

and so

$$0.50x = 50$$

$$x = \frac{50}{0.50}$$

$$= 100$$

Substituting this value of x into equation (10) gives

$$100 + y = 500$$
$$y = 400$$

Hence, 100 pounds of expensive candy ($1.50 per pound) should be used and 400 pounds of the less expensive candy ($1.00 per pound) should be used.

Example 5 A 14 quart automobile radiator has in it a 20% antifreeze solution. It is desired to get a 30% antifreeze solution. How many quarts should be drained and replaced with pure (100%) antifreeze?

Solution: See Figure 8.2.4.
   Let $x =$ the number of quarts of solution to be drained and replaced.

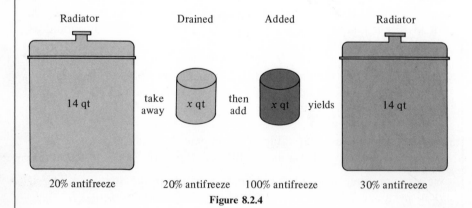

Radiator	Drained	Added	Radiator
14 qt	take away x qt	then add x qt yields	14 qt
20% antifreeze	20% antifreeze	100% antifreeze	30% antifreeze

Figure 8.2.4

Then

$$0.20(x) = \text{the number of quarts of antifreeze drained}$$
$$1.00(x) = \text{the number of quarts of antifreeze replaced.}$$

The number of quarts of antifreeze in the original solution is 0.20(14) and the number of quarts of antifreeze in the final solution is 0.30(14). Because the quarts of antifreeze in the radiator subtract the number of quarts of antifreeze drained plus the number of quarts of antifreeze replaced is equal to the number of quarts of antifreeze in the final solution we have the equation

$$0.20(14) - 0.20(x) + 1.00(x) = 0.30(14) \tag{12}$$

Solving equation (12) we have

$$2.8 - 0.20x + 1.00x = 4.2$$
$$2.8 + 0.80x = 4.2$$
$$0.80x = 1.4$$
$$x = \frac{1.4}{0.80}$$
$$= 1.75$$

Hence, 1.75 quarts should be drained and replaced with pure antifreeze.

Exercises 8.2

1. A grocer wishes to mix nuts worth 69¢ per pound with nuts worth 89¢ per pound to end up with 100 pounds of mixed nuts selling for 75¢ per pound. How many pounds of each should be mixed?

2. A grocer wishes to blend teas worth 88¢ per pound and $1.20 per pound to sell for $1.00 per pound. How many pounds of each kind should be used to end up with 50 pounds of blended tea? *work out in pennies*

3. How much pure gold (24 karat) must be added to 8 pounds of 10 karat gold to produce a jewelers specification of 14 karat gold?

4. A farmer has 1 ton of 10% nitrate fertilizer. He needs a total of 4 tons of fertilizer with 14% nitrate. If he buys 3 tons of fertilizer, what percent nitrate should it be?

5. An alloy 35% copper must be melted with another alloy 98% copper to create an alloy weighing $2\frac{1}{2}$ tons which is 60% copper. How much of each type alloy must be used?

6. How many gallons each of a 2% butterfat milk should be mixed with a 4% butterfat milk to produce 40 gallons of 2.5% butterfat milk?

7. How many 10¢ stamps and how many 13¢ stamps are in a packet of 24 stamps selling for $3.00?

8. How much water must be evaporated from a gallon of a 7% salt solution to obtain an 8% salt solution?

9. A high-octane and low-octane gasoline worth 60¢ per gallon and 54¢ per gallon, respectively, are to be used in filling a 9000 gallon tank and

each gallon of the mixture should sell for 58¢ per gallon. How many gallons of each should be used?

10. Oil at 180°F is piped into a vat at the same time an oil at 100°F from another pipe is entering the same vat. The resulting mixture filled one vat, and the resulting temperature was found to be 130°F. What part of the vat was filled with the oil originally at 180°F?

11. A 12 quart radiator, that has 2 quarts of antifreeze in it, is to be partially drained, and each quart of the solution removed is to be replaced with 100% antifreeze so that the resulting mixture will be 20% antifreeze. How much should be drained?

8.3 Work–Rate–Time Problems $W = rt$ (fraction by hours times time)

If part or all of a certain job can be accomplished in a given amount of time, then the measure of the average *rate* of work is the ratio of the fractional part of the job done to the number of units of time that it takes to do that part of the job. For instance, if it takes a man 8 hours to paint an apartment, then his average rate of work is $\frac{1}{8}$ of the apartment painted per hour. If a typist can type a 2000 word memo in 40 minutes, then the typist's average rate of work is $\frac{2000}{40}$ words typed per minute or, equivalently, 50 words typed per minute.

The measure of the total amount of work done is found by multiplying the measure of the rate of work by the number of units of time spent doing the work.

Illustration 1 If a house is completely painted in 8 hours, the average rate of work is $\frac{1}{8}$ of a house painted per hour. If a person works for 5 hours at this rate of work before stopping to rest, then the work done at that time is $\frac{5}{8}$ of a house painted: $5 \cdot \frac{1}{8} = \frac{5}{8}$.

Example 1 One painter can paint a standard apartment in 8 hours while it takes a second painter 6 hours to paint the same apartment. How long will it take the two painters working together to paint the apartment?

Solution: Let x = the number of hours it takes to paint the entire apartment when both painters are working.

The average rate of work for the first painter is $\frac{1}{8}$ of the apartment painted per hour. The average rate of work for the second painter is $\frac{1}{6}$ of the apartment painted per hour. Because both painters work for x hours, the work done by the first painter is $x \cdot \frac{1}{8}$ of the apartment and the work done by the second painter is $x \cdot \frac{1}{6}$ of the apartment. The fractional part of the apartment painted by the first painter plus the fractional part of the apartment painted by the second painter equals one (the whole apartment is painted). We have then

$$x \cdot \frac{1}{8} + x \cdot \frac{1}{6} = 1$$

or, equivalently,

$$\frac{x}{8} + \frac{x}{6} = 1$$

Multiplying each member of this equation by 24 (the LCD), we obtain

$$3x + 4x = 24$$

thus,

$$7x = 24$$
$$x = \frac{24}{7}$$
$$= 3\frac{3}{7}$$

Therefore, each painter works $3\frac{3}{7}$ hours.

Example 2   One inlet pipe can fill a tank in 3 hours. The drain pipe can empty the tank in 4 hours. If both pipes are open, how long will it take to fill the tank?

Solution: The average rate at which the tank is filled by the inlet pipe is $\frac{1}{3}$ tank filled per hour. The average rate at which the tank is emptied by the drain pipe is $\frac{1}{4}$ tank emptied per hour. Let t equal the number of hours needed to fill the tank. Then $\frac{1}{3}t$ and $\frac{-1}{4}t$ are the fractional parts of the tank filled by each pipe. Therefore,

$$\frac{1}{3}t - \frac{1}{4}t = 1$$

We solve the equation by multiplying each member by 12.

$$12\left(\frac{1}{3}t - \frac{1}{4}t\right) = 12 \cdot 1$$

$$12\left(\frac{1}{3}t\right) - 12\left(\frac{1}{4}t\right) = 12$$

$$4t - 3t = 12$$

$$t = 12$$

Hence, it takes 12 hours to fill the tank if both pipes are open.

Example 3   Three machines are put into use to produce 12,000 subassemblies. Machine A can produce 600 subassemblies per hour. Machine B can produce 300 subassemblies per hour, and machine C can produce 200 subassemblies per hour. How long will it take all three machines working together to produce the 12,000 subassemblies if machine A can only be used for a maximum of 4 hours?

Solution: The average rates of work for the three machines are given as 600, 300, and 200 subassemblies per hour. Let t hours be the time that machines B and C are used. Remember machine A is used only 4 hours. Then (600)(4), 300t, and 200t are the number of subassemblies produced by machines A, B, and C, respectively. Therefore,

$$12,000 = (600)(4) + 300t + 200t$$
$$12,000 = 2400 + 300t + 200t$$
$$9600 = 300t + 200t$$
$$9600 = 500t$$

$$\frac{9600}{500} = t$$

$$t = \frac{9600}{500}$$

$$= 19\frac{1}{5}$$

Hence, it takes $19\frac{1}{5}$ hours to produce the 12,000 subassemblies.

Example 4   Two boys working together can mow a lawn in $1\frac{1}{4}$ hours. If one boy can mow the whole lawn by himself in 2 hours, how long will it take the second boy working by himself?

Solution: Let x hours be the time it takes the second boy to mow the lawn by himself. Then his average rate of work is $\frac{1}{x}$ of the lawn mowed per hour.

The first boy's average rate of work is $\frac{1}{2}$ of the lawn mowed per hour, since it takes him 2 hours to do it by himself. They each work for $\frac{5}{4}$ hours. There-fore, the part of the lawn mowed by the first boy is $\frac{1}{2} \cdot \frac{5}{4}$ and the part of the lawn mowed by the second boy is $\frac{1}{x} \cdot \frac{5}{4}$. Therefore, the equation is

$$\frac{1}{2} \cdot \frac{5}{4} + \frac{1}{x} \cdot \frac{5}{4} = 1$$

or, equivalently,

$$\frac{5}{8} + \frac{5}{4x} = 1$$

Multiplying each member of this equation by $8x$, we obtain

$$5x + 10 = 8x$$
$$10 = 3x$$
$$\frac{10}{3} = x$$

Hence, it takes the second boy $3\frac{1}{3}$ hours to mow the lawn by himself.

Example 5 Dan can do a certain job in 5 hours. Ray can work at the same average rate of work as Dan. Both boys work for 1 hour before Ray has to leave. How long does it take Dan to finish the job?

Solution: Let x hours be the time required for Dan to finish the work. Dan's average rate of work is $\frac{1}{5}$ of the job per hour. Ray's average rate of work is $\frac{1}{5}$ of the job per hour. Dan works for $(1 + x)$ hours and Ray works for 1 hour. The equation is

$$\frac{1}{5}(1 + x) + \frac{1}{5}(1) = 1$$

Solving this equation we have

$$\frac{1}{5}(1) + \frac{1}{5}(x) + \frac{1}{5}(1) = 1$$
$$\frac{1}{5} + \frac{x}{5} + \frac{1}{5} = 1$$
$$\frac{x}{5} + \frac{2}{5} = 1$$
$$x + 2 = 5$$
$$x = 3$$

Therefore, Dan requires 3 more hours to finish the job.

1. What is the work done by a man working for 2 hours if he can do the whole job in (a) 5 hours; (b) 3 hours; (c) 2 hours; (d) x hours?

2. What is the work done by a woman working t hours if she can do the whole job in (a) 5 hours; (b) 3 hours; (c) 2 hours?

3. How many parts are produced by a machine producing parts for 5 hours, if the machine produces (a) 80 parts per hour; (b) 100 parts per hour; (c) x parts per hour?

4. Joel can mow a lawn in 2 hours. It takes Sam $1\frac{1}{2}$ hours to mow the same lawn. How long does it take them working together?

5. One pipe can fill a pool in 8 hours while a second pipe can fill the same pool in 10 hours. How long will it take to fill the pool if both pipes are open?

6. The drain of the pool in Exercise 5 can empty the pool in 6 hours. In each case find out how long it will take to fill the pool if the drain is open and just one of the pipes is filling the pool.

7. Refer to Exercises 5 and 6. Suppose both pipes are filling the pool and the drain is left open. How long will it take to fill the pool?

8. One printing press can run off 4000 papers per hour. Another press can run off 3000 papers per hour. How long will it take to run off 100,000 papers if both presses are being used?

9. Suppose the slower press of Exercise 8 works for 1 hour before the second press starts. Then how long will it take to print 100,000 papers?

10. If 10 identical machines can produce a required number of parts in 10 days, how long will it take 2 machines to produce the required number of parts?

11. If two men working together can do a job in 3 hours, and one of the men can do the job by himself in 5 hours, how long will it take the second man working by himself?

12. In an electronic computer center a card-sorter operator is asked to sort a given quantity of cards. He knows that an old sorter can do the job in 3 hours. If he also uses a newer machine the job is completed in 1 hour. How long will it take the new machine to do the same job alone?

13. Two girls can do a typing job in 6 hours. If one girl can type twice as fast as the other girl can type, how long does it take each girl to do the job alone?

14. Suppose the two girls of Exercise 13 are joined by a third girl who can

do the whole job in 10 hours by herself. How long does it take all three girls working together to do the typing job?

15. It takes Bob 3 hours to do a certain job while Mark can do it in 2 hours. Both boys work on the job, but for different amounts of time and finish $\frac{1}{4}$ of the total work. If Bob had worked as long as Mark did and if Mark had worked as long as Bob did, then $\frac{1}{3}$ of the total work would have been completed. How long does each person work? (Hint: Let $x =$ the number of hours Bob works and $y =$ the number of hours Mark works.)

16. Dan can do a certain job in 4 hours. After working for 1 hour he is joined by Ray who also can do the whole job by himself in 4 hours. How long does it take to complete the whole job?

17. Julio works twice as fast as Al. They are both on a job and Julio finishes $\frac{1}{2}$ of the job 3 hours before Al finishes his $\frac{1}{2}$ of the job. How long does each one work?

18. If a chicken and a half takes a day and a half to lay an egg and a half, how many eggs can 21 chickens lay in 7 days?

8.4 Distance–Rate–Time Problems

If an object moves with a constant rate of speed or if we consider only its overall average rate of speed, then the formula that expresses the relation of distance to rate of speed and time is given by the formula

$$d = rt \qquad (1)$$

where $d =$ the number of miles in the distance traveled
$\qquad r =$ the number of miles per hour in the rate of speed
and $\quad t =$ the number of hours in the time.

The average rate of speed is given in units of distance per unit of time. Solving formula (1) for r, we divide each member of the equation by t and obtain

$$r = \frac{d}{t} \qquad (2)$$

If we solve formula (1) for t by dividing both members by r, we obtain

$$t = \frac{d}{r} \qquad (3)$$

Illustration 1 If you are traveling in an automobile at 50 miles per hour and you continue at that rate of speed, you will travel 50 miles in 1 hour. If you travel 200 miles in 4 hours, then letting $d = 200$ and $t = 4$ in formula (1) we obtain

$$200 = r(4)$$

Dividing both members by 4, we have

$$r = \frac{200}{4} = 50$$

Hence, the average rate of speed is 50 miles per hour.

The measure of the average rate of speed is found by dividing the measure of the total distance traveled by the measure of the total time spent traveling that distance. Thus, even if the speed of an object varies, the average speed can be found.

Example 1 A boat takes $1\frac{1}{2}$ hours to go upstream 9 miles and then returns in 1 hour. Find the average rate of speed of the boat on the round trip. Find the average rate of speed of the boat going upstream. Find the average rate of speed of the boat returning.

Solution: Let $x =$ the number of miles per hour in the average rate of speed of the boat for the round trip.

The total distance traveled is 18 miles and the total time of travel is $2\frac{1}{2}$ hours. Using formula (2) with $d = 18$ and $t = 2\frac{1}{2} = \frac{5}{2}$, we have

$$x = \frac{18}{\dfrac{5}{2}} = 7.2$$

Hence, the average rate of speed on the round trip is 7.2 miles per hour.
Let $y =$ the number of miles per hour in the average rate of speed going upstream. The distance traveled upstream is 9 miles and the time traveled upstream is $1\frac{1}{2}$ hours. Using formula (2) with $d = 9$ and $t = 1\frac{1}{2} = \frac{3}{2}$, we have

$$y = \frac{9}{\dfrac{3}{2}} = 6$$

Hence, the average rate of speed of the boat going upstream is 6 miles per hour.

Let $z =$ the number of miles per hour in the average rate of speed returning downstream. The distance traveled downstream is 9 miles and the time traveled downstream is 1 hour. Using formula (2) with $d = 9$ and $t = 1$, we have

$$z = \frac{9}{1}$$

$$= 9$$

Hence, the average rate of speed returning downstream is 9 miles per hour.

Interesting problems result when two or more objects are moving at the same time. Consider the following examples.

Example 2 Two planes leave different airports at the same time and travel toward each other. One plane averages 200 miles per hour and the other plane averages 140 miles per hour. If the airports are 320 miles apart, how long after the start will they meet?

Solution: Let t hours $=$ the time after the start that it takes the planes to meet. Then

$\qquad 200t =$ the number of miles traveled by the faster plane

and

$\qquad 140t =$ the number of miles traveled by the slower plane

See Figure 8.4.1.

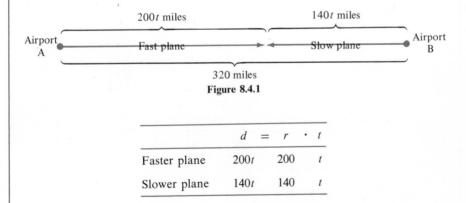

Figure 8.4.1

	d	$=$ r	$\cdot$ t
Faster plane	$200t$	200	t
Slower plane	$140t$	140	t

The number of miles traveled by the faster plane plus the number of miles traveled by the slower plane equals the number of miles in the distance between the airports. We have then, the equation

$$200t + 140t = 320$$

Solving this equation, we obtain

$$340t = 320$$

$$t = \frac{320}{340} = \frac{16}{17}$$

Therefore, the planes will meet in $\frac{16}{17}$ hours.

Example 3 A boat takes 2 hours to go to a bridge upstream against a current. On the return trip, with the current, it takes only $1\frac{1}{2}$ hours. If the rate of the current is 3 miles per hour, how fast is the boat in still water?

Solution Let x = the number of miles per hour in the rate of speed of the boat in still water. Then

$x - 3$ = the number of miles per hour in the rate of speed of the boat upstream

and

$x + 3$ = the number of miles per hour in the rate of speed of the boat downstream

See Figure 8.4.2.

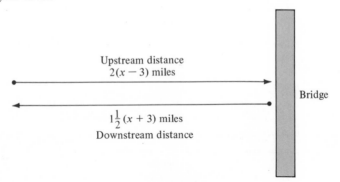

Upstream distance
$2(x - 3)$ miles

Bridge

$1\frac{1}{2}(x + 3)$ miles
Downstream distance

Figure 8.4.2

	d	=	r	·	t
Upstream	$2(x - 3)$		$x - 3$		2
Downstream	$1\frac{1}{2}(x + 3)$		$x + 3$		$1\frac{1}{2}$

Because the distance traveled upstream equals the distance traveled downstream, we have the equation

$$2(x - 3) = 1\frac{1}{2}(x + 3)$$

Solving this equation we have

$$2x - 6 = 1\frac{1}{2}x + 4\frac{1}{2}$$

$$2x = 1\frac{1}{2}x + 10\frac{1}{2}$$

$$\frac{1}{2}x = 10\frac{1}{2}$$

$$x = 21$$

Therefore, the average rate of speed of the boat in still water is 21 miles per hour.

Example 4 One bus leaves town at noon and averages 40 miles per hour. One hour later a car leaves the town on the same road and goes in the same direction and averages 50 miles per hour. At what time does the car overtake the bus?

Solution: Let $x = $ the number of hours the bus travels until overtaken by the car
and $y = $ the number of hours the car travels until it overtakes the bus.

We know that the number of miles in the distances traveled are represented by $40x$ and $50y$. See Figure 8.4.3. Because the distances are equal, one equation is

$$40x = 50y \qquad (4)$$

We also have the equation

$$x = y + 1 \qquad (5)$$

Substituting the value of x from equation (5) into equation (4) we have

$$40(y + 1) = 50y$$

Hence,

$$40y + 40 = 50y$$
$$40 = 10y$$
$$4 = y$$

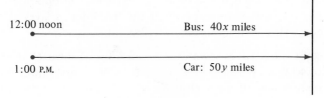

12:00 noon   Bus: $40x$ miles

1:00 P.M.   Car: $50y$ miles

Figure 8.4.3

Therefore, after 4 hours the car overtakes the bus. Because the car starts at 1 P.M., it overtakes the bus at 5 P.M.

Exercises 8.4

1. Find the average rate of speed of a particle that moves 88 feet in $\frac{1}{2}$ second. Express your answer in feet per second.

2. A miler runs a mile in 4 minutes. Find his average rate of speed expressed in miles per hour.

3. Find the average rate of speed of a particle dropped from a height of 400 feet as it falls to the ground. (Hint: The measure of the distance s a body falls is related to the measure of the time t by the formula $s = 16t^2$.)

4. An airplane that can fly 100 miles per hour without any wind makes a 100 mile trip against a 20 mile per hour wind and then returns with the wind. Find the average rate of speed of the airplane. (Note: The answer is not 100 miles per hour.)

5. In a novelty race a man runs $\frac{1}{2}$ mile in 3 minutes, swims 100 yards in 5 minutes, and drives a car 5 miles and 780 yards in 4 minutes. Find his average rate of speed expressed in miles per hour for the entire race.

6. A man is making a trip of 100 miles. He averages 30 miles per hour for the first 50 miles of his trip. What rate of speed will he have to average during the last 50 miles to have an overall average of 45 miles per hour?

7. The engine of a mile-long train enters a mile-long tunnel at noon. Two minutes later the caboose (at the rear of the train) emerges from the opposite end of the tunnel. Find the average rate of speed of the train.

8. Two cyclists, starting at the same time and 5 miles apart, travel toward each other. One cyclist averages 5 miles per hour and the other cyclist averages 10 miles per hour. How long does it take until they meet and how far does each travel?

9. Two cars start from the same point and travel in opposite directions. One car averages 35 miles per hour and the other car averages 45 miles per hour. How long until they are 288 miles apart?

10. A freight train leaves town P traveling toward town Q at an average rate of 40 miles per hour. Two hours later an express train leaves town P traveling toward town Q at an average rate of 60 miles per hour. How far from town P does the express train overtake the freight train?

11. Two boats, each capable of traveling 15 miles per hour in still water, start at the same time and travel towards each other at full speed. One boat is 6 miles upstream from the other boat and the current of the stream is 3 miles per hour. How long does it take before the boats pass each other?

12. Two planes leave Denver and travel in opposite directions. One plane averages 60 miles per hour faster than the other plane. At the end of 5 hours the planes are 1550 miles apart. What is the rate of speed of each plane?

13. Four scouts paddle a canoe 4 miles upstream in 2 hours and the return trip takes $\frac{1}{2}$ hour. What is the rate of speed of the canoe in still water and what is the rate of the current?

14. A courier travels by car, plane, and train for a total of 840 miles. By car the courier averages 30 miles per hour, by plane the courier averages 300 miles per hour, and by train the courier averages 75 miles per hour. The entire trip takes $5\frac{1}{2}$ hours. The number of hours spent traveling by plane is four times the number of hours spent traveling by car. How far did the courier travel at each rate of speed?

15. Two runners are training on a quarter mile oval track. The faster runner gives the slower runner a 1 minute head start and then starts after him. If the faster runner averages a quarter mile every 75 seconds and the slower runner averages a quarter mile every 90 seconds, how long will it take the faster runner to overtake the slower runner.

16. One car takes 3 hours longer to cover a 200 mile distance than another faster car, traveling at one and one-half times the average rate of speed of the slower car. Find the rate of speed of each car.

8.5 Using Ratios and Proportions to Solve Problems

Many elementary problems can be solved by using ratios and proportions. Consider the following examples.

Example 1   A solution is to be made from water and a certain concentrate. The ratio of the measure of the amount of water to the measure of the amount of concentrate is $5:3$. If 24 gallons of solution are needed, then how much water and how much concentrate should be used?

Solution: Let $x =$ the number of gallons of water
and $y =$ the number of gallons of concentrate.

Then we have the following equations:

$$\frac{x}{y} = \frac{5}{3} \tag{1}$$

and

$$x + y = 24 \tag{2}$$

Because in a proportion the product of the means equals the product of the extremes, we have from equation (1)

$$3x = 5y$$

Dividing both members of this equation by 3, we obtain

$$x = \frac{5y}{3}$$

Now, substituting $\frac{5y}{3}$ for x in equation (2), we obtain

$$\frac{5y}{3} + y = 24$$

$$\frac{5y}{3} + \frac{3y}{3} = 24$$

$$\frac{8y}{3} = 24$$

$$8y = 72$$

$$y = 9$$

Substituting 9 for y in equation (2) we get

$$x + 9 = 24$$
$$x = 15$$

Therefore, 15 gallons of water and 9 gallons of concentrate are needed.

In balancing a beam over a fulcrum, equal weights must be placed at equal distances from the fulcrum. Unequal weights can balance the beam if they are placed at unequal distances from the fulcrum. See Figure 8.5.1.

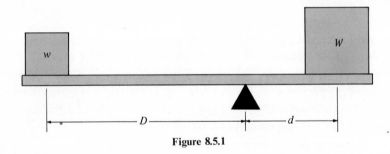

Figure 8.5.1

The exact relationship is stated as a proportion. That is, the ratio of the measures of the weights on the beam is equal to the reciprocal of the ratio of the measures of the distances of the weights from the fulcrum. If W pounds is placed on the beam d feet from the fulcrum and w pounds is placed D feet from the fulcrum on the opposite side and if the beam is in a state of equilibrium (the weights balance each other on the beam), then

$$\frac{W}{w} = \frac{1}{\frac{d}{D}}$$

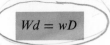

or, equivalently,

$$\frac{W}{w} = \frac{D}{d}$$

Hence, W is to w as D is to d. Because the product of the means equals the product of the extremes, we have

$$Wd = wD$$

Example 2 One boy weighs 14 pounds less than a second boy. They sit 5 feet and 7 feet from the fulcrum of a teetertotter and are in a balanced position. How much does each boy weigh?

Solution: Let $x =$ the number of pounds in the second boy's weight;
then $x - 14 =$ the number of pounds in the first boy's weight.
The heavier boy sits 5 feet from the fulcrum because this is the shorter distance.
The proportion is

$$\frac{x}{x - 14} = \frac{7}{5}$$

Solving for x, we find

$$5x = 7(x - 14)$$
$$5x = 7x - 98$$
$$5x + 98 = 7x$$
$$98 = 2x$$
$$49 = x$$

Thus, the heavier boy weighs 49 pounds and the other boy weighs $49 - 14$ pounds or 35 pounds.

A population sampling technique to estimate the total population of a given species in a given region involves a proportion. The technique is the "capture-mark-recapture" method. A group of specimens, such as, birds, fish, or animals, is captured from the population in the region of interest. These are marked or tagged in such a manner as not to harm the specimen and then returned to the region. After a sufficient amount of time has passed to allow thorough mixing, a new sample is captured, and among these will be a certain number of marked specimens. Then, from the various counts a proportion can be established and the total population can be estimated.

Example 3 In a small lake suppose that 120 fish are captured at random places, marked, and returned to the lake. Sometime later 80 fish are captured and among these we find 16 marked fish. Estimate the number of fish in the lake.

Solution: Let x = the total population of fish in the lake. Then the total number of marked fish is to the total population as the number of fish found marked in the recapture is to the total number of fish recaptured. That is,

$$120 : x = 16 : 80$$

or, equivalently,

$$\frac{120}{x} = \frac{16}{80}$$

Because the product of the means equals the product of the extremes, we have

$$16x = 120 \cdot 80$$

and so,

$$x = \frac{120 \cdot 80}{16}$$

$$= 600$$

Thus, we estimate that there are 600 fish in the lake.

Proportions also have an important use in geometry. A central concept in this connection is the notion of "similarity." Two geometric figures are similar if they have the same shape, but not necessarily the same size. The two triangles shown in Figure 8.5.2 are similar. The triangles in Figure 8.5.3 are not similar.

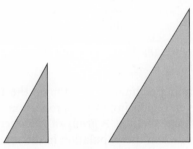

Figure 8.5.2

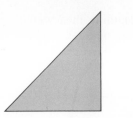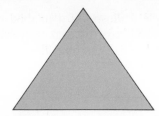

Figure 8.5.3

If two figures are similar, then they can be so arranged that pairs of corresponding sides are parallel, and furthermore, the measures of the lengths of these corresponding sides are proportional.

Example 4 A flag pole and a fence post cast shadows of 12 feet and 3 feet, respectively. The fence post is 5 feet tall. How tall is the flag pole? See Figure 8.5.4.

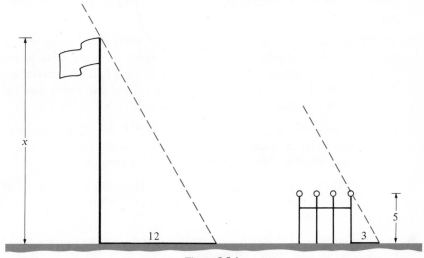

Figure 8.5.4

Solution: The triangles formed in Figure 8.5.4 are similar because corresponding sides are parallel. (Rays from the sun are assumed parallel.) Hence, if we let x = the number of units in the height of the flag pole, we have the proportion

$$\frac{x}{5} = \frac{12}{3}$$

Solving this equation we have

$$3x = 60$$
$$x = 20$$

Thus, the flagpole is 20 feet high.

Example 4 illustrates a method of obtaining measurements of objects indirectly. That is, by making certain measurements of objects that are accessible we can establish the measure of inaccessible objects.

Exercises 8.5

1. Two numbers are in the ratio $4:7$. Their sum is 70. Find the two numbers.

2. Fifty feet of copper wire weighs 3 pounds. How much does 225 feet of the wire weigh?

3. About 107 boys are born to every 100 girls that are born. In 1 million births how many girls can we expect to be born?

4. About 70% of our total body weight is due to the water content of our bodies. How many pounds of water are contained in a 180 pound person?

5. We know that the earth's diameter is about 8000 miles while that of the sun is about 866,000 miles, and the distance from the earth to the sun is about 93 million miles. If we use a 12 inch ball as a model for the sun, what diameter ball should we use for the earth and how far away should we place it from the 12 inch ball?

6. On the Celsius thermometer scale there are $5°C$ of change for every $9°F$ of change on the Fahrenheit scale. What would a change of $100°F$ on the Fahrenheit scale correspond to on the Celsius scale?

7. A board 40 feet long is cut into two pieces. The ratio of the length of the first piece to the length of the second is 2 to 3. What are the lengths of the two pieces?

8. If you enlarge a 5×7 inch photograph so that the shorter side measures 8 inches wide, how long will the enlargement be?

9. Eight hundred ninety-six offspring have brown-eyed parents who carry the recessive gene for blue eyes. According to Mendel's laws of heredity the probability ratio of offspring with brown eyes to those with blue eyes is 3 to 1 in this circumstance. How many of the 896 offspring would you expect to find with blue eyes?

10. The chemical formula for sugar (glucose) is $C_6H_{12}O_6$. The C, H, and O stand for the elements carbon, hydrogen, and oxygen. The numbers 6, 12, 6 indicate the numbers of atoms of each element to be found in a molecule of the compound (glucose in this case). In a pound (or any weight) of sugar these elements will be present in the same ratios. What is the ratio of the number of carbon atoms to the number of hydrogen atoms? To the number of oxygen atoms? If each oxygen atom

weighs 16 times as much as a hydrogen atom and each carbon atom weighs 12 times as much as a hydrogen atom, what part of the weight of a pound of this sugar is made up of oxygen?

11. According to Kepler's third law of planetary motion, the ratio of the cube of the measure of the distance of one planet from the sun to the cube of the measure of the distance of a second planet from the sun, is the same as the ratio of the square of the number of time units required for the first planet to complete one revolution around the sun to the square of the number of time units required for the second planet. If Saturn is half as far from the sun as Uranus, find the ratio of their respective number of time units required for one complete revolution.

Balanced beam problems:

12. If a 60 pound child balances a 120 pound adult by sitting 8 feet from the fulcrum of a seesaw, how far is the adult from the fulcrum?

13. One boy weighs 10 pounds more than his friend. They balance a teetertotter by sitting 6 and 8 feet from the fulcrum. How much does each boy weigh?

14. One boy weighs 80 pounds more than another boy. They balance on a teetertotter, but one is three times as far from the fulcrum as the other boy. How much does each boy weigh?

Population sampling problems:

15. In a waterfront warehouse, suppose that 30 rats were captured and marked and let free again. Later 42 rats were captured and among these were 12 marked rats. Estimate the number of rats in the warehouse.

16. On a large ranch, the rancher rounded up 360 cattle from different parts of the range, all of which were branded and returned to the range again. Some months later, 1440 cattle were rounded up and it was found that 288 were branded. How many more cattle can the rancher estimate he has to round up?

17. A large drum contained an unknown number of white ping pong balls. Fifty black balls were added to the drum and they were thoroughly mixed. Then 50 balls were randomly removed from the drum. This was done several times and the "average" number of black balls present at each sampling was $\frac{1}{2}$. Estimate how many balls were originally in the drum.

Geometry problems:

In Exercises 18 through 20 set up a proportion and find the value of x and/or y, assuming the triangles shown in each figure are similar.

18. See Figure 8.5.5.   **19.** See Figure 8.5.6.

Everybody should get

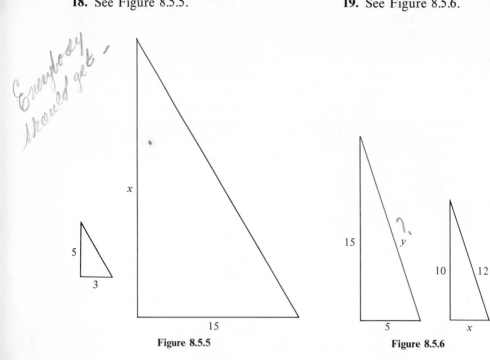

Figure 8.5.5   Figure 8.5.6

20. See Figure 8.5.7. (Hint: Use a system of equations.)

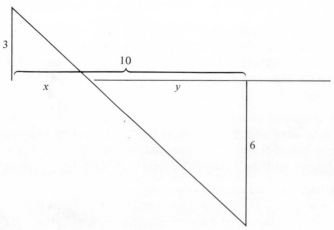

Figure 8.5.7

21. A building casts a shadow 150 feet long while a pole 5 feet long casts a shadow 20 feet long. How high is the building?

8.6 Review Exercises

1. The sum of two numbers is 40. The difference between the two numbers is 10. Find the numbers.

2. In a chess match a win of 1 game counts as 1 point, a draw counts as $\frac{1}{2}$ point and a loss as 0. After 14 games during a championship match the leader was 3 points ahead of his opponent. How many points did each player have?

3. The 1970 United States one-cent piece is made from an alloy of 95% copper and 5% zinc. How many pounds of pure zinc should be melted with 100 pounds of pure copper to produce this alloy?

4. A collection of quarters, dimes, and nickels has a face value of $6.30. There are five more nickels than dimes and eight more quarters than nickels. How many coins of each denomination are there?

5. One pipe can fill a tank in 6 hours. A second pipe can fill the same tank in $5\frac{1}{2}$ hours. If both pipes are open, how long will it take for them to fill an empty tank?

6. One truck can move 5 tons of gravel per hour to a given location. A second truck can move 7 tons of gravel per hour to that location. How long will it take both trucks to move 140 tons of gravel to the given location?

7. Bill can drive a certain race course in 5 hours. In a better car he can do it in 4 hours. If the better car averages 10 miles per hour faster than the other car, what is the average rate of speed of the better car?

8. A plane traveled a distance of 500 miles in 2 hours. But because of a rain storm during the last 30 minutes of the flight, the plane was slowed down by 40 miles per hour. How fast was the plane traveling in the storm?

9. A tower cast a shadow that is 90 feet long. At the same time a man 6 feet tall cast a shadow that is 5 feet long. Find the height of the tower.

10. The rangers working in a state park wanted to know the approximate size of the chipmunk population in the park. From several locations within the park they captured 180 chipmunks, marked them, and set them free again. The following week they captured 150 chipmunks and among these were 20 marked chipmunks. What is the approximate size of the chipmunk population?

9

Polynomials

9.1 What Is a Polynomial?

Certain kinds of algebraic expressions are known as *polynomials*. Before giving an explicit definition of a polynomial, we analyze several examples of a polynomial. Each of the following expressions is a polynomial:

(a) 5   (b) x (c) x^2 (d) $4y$ (e) $y + 3$ (f) $7x^2 + 3x + 1$
(g) $2x - 4$

From these examples we see that a polynomial may be a constant, a variable, a power of a variable, the product of a constant and a variable, the sum of a variable and a constant, and so forth. We refer to the expressions in (a), (b), (c), and (d) as terms. The expressions in (e), (f), and (g) are sums or differences of terms. We now define a special kind of polynomial called a *monomial*.

9.1.1 Definition   A *monomial* is a constant, a power of a variable, or a product, each of whose factors is a constant or a power of a variable.

Illustration 1   Each of the following expressions is a monomial:

$$5 \quad x \quad x^2 \quad 4y \quad 7x^2 \quad 4xy \quad 27ab^2c^3$$

Every monomial is a term. The numerical coefficient of each monomial involving variables is called simply the *coefficient* of the monomial.

Illustration 2   The coefficient of x^2 is 1 because $x^2 = 1 \cdot x^2$. The coefficient of $4y$ is 4. The coefficient of $27ab^2c^3$ is 27.

If the coefficient of a monomial is an integer, we refer to the monomial as a monomial with an integral coefficient. If the coefficient is a rational number, we refer to the monomial as a monomial with a rational coefficient. In a similar manner we refer to monomials with real coefficients.

Some monomials involve only one variable, while others may involve two or more variables. If a monomial involves only the variable x, we state that the monomial is a monomial *in x*.

Illustration 3 The expressions $4x$, x^2, and $7x^3$ are monomials in x with integer coefficients. The monomial $0.5y$ is a monomial in y with a rational coefficient.

The *degree* of a monomial in one variable is indicated by the power of the variable (that is, the number of times the variable is represented as a factor). The term x^2 is a second degree monomial and x^3 is a third degree monomial. First, second, and third degree terms are associated with geometric figures of one, two, and three dimensions. Plane figures, such as squares, are two dimensional; they have length and width. Line segments are one dimensional, and solids are three dimensional. See Figure 9.1.1.

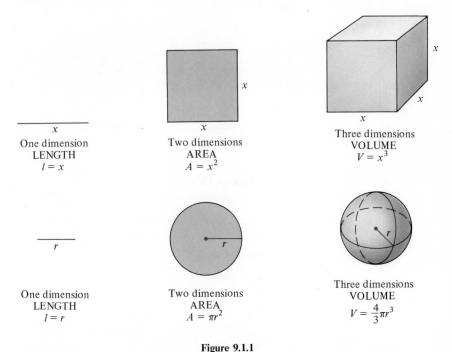

One dimension
LENGTH
$l = x$

Two dimensions
AREA
$A = x^2$

Three dimensions
VOLUME
$V = x^3$

One dimension
LENGTH
$l = r$

Two dimensions
AREA
$A = \pi r^2$

Three dimensions
VOLUME
$V = \frac{4}{3}\pi r^3$

Figure 9.1.1

Illustration 4 The degree of the monomial $4x^2$ is 2. We say that $4x^2$ is a second degree monomial in x with an integer coefficient. See Figure 9.1.2.

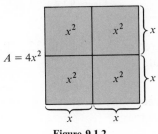

$A = 4x^2$

Figure 9.1.2

The degree of a monomial of more than one variable is the sum of the exponents of the variables. Remember it is understood that a variable, such as x, has an exponent equal to 1. That is,

$$x = x^1$$

The degree of a constant is zero, unless the constant is zero, in which case the degree is undefined.

Illustration 5   The terms xy and $3xy$ are second degree monomials because the sum of the exponents on the variable factors in each product x^1y^1 and $3x^1y^1$ is 2 $(1 + 1 = 2)$. See Figure 9.1.3.

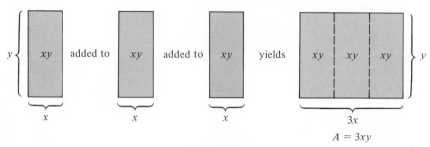

Figure 9.1.3

Illustration 6   The term x^2y is a third degree monomial because the variable x occurs as a factor twice and the variable y occurs as a factor once: $x^2y = x^2y^1$ and $2 + 1 = 3$. See Figure 9.1.4.

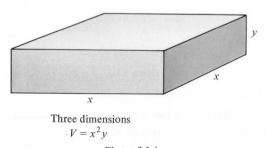

Three dimensions
$V = x^2y$

Figure 9.1.4

Illustration 7   The degree of the constant 25 is 0. There are no variable factors in this monomial.

Illustration 8   The degree of the constant 0 is not defined. This is the only monomial having no degree.

We are now ready to define a polynomial.

9.1.2 Definition　　A *polynomial* is a monomial or the sum of monomials.

Illustration 9　　The expressions $7x$, $3x^2 + 7x - 1$, and $2xy - 5$ are all polynomials. Even though $2xy - 5$ is a difference, we can express it as a sum because $2xy - 5 = 2xy + (-5)$.

9.1.3 Definition　　A polynomial consisting of the sum of exactly two monomials is called a *binomial*. A polynomial consisting of the sum of exactly three monomials is called a *trinomial*.

Illustration 10　　$2x + 11$ is a binomial. $x^2 + 3x - 5$ is a trinomial.

If the coefficients of each monomial in a polynomial and the constant term (if there is one) are all integers, then we refer to that polynomial as a polynomial with integer coefficients. Similarly if all the coefficients and constants are rational numbers, then we refer to that polynomial as a polynomial with rational coefficients. In like manner we also refer to polynomials with real coefficients.

Illustration 11　　$x^2 + 2x + 1$ is a polynomial with integer coefficients. It is also a polynominal with rational coefficients and one with real coefficients. $x^2 + \frac{1}{2}x + 1$ is a polynomial with rational coefficients. $7xy + \frac{1}{2}x - y + \sqrt{2}$ is a polynomial with real coefficients.

9.1.4 Definition　　A *polynomial in x* is a polynomial whose monomial terms are either monomials in x or constants.

Illustration 12　　$x^3 + 7x^2 - 2x + 5$ is a polynomial in x.

We can define polynomials in y or any other variable in the same way as we defined a polynomial in x.

Illustration 13　　$64t - 16t^2$ is a polynomial in t.

The *degree* of a polynomial is the highest degree of any of its monomial terms.

Illustration 14   The degree of the polynomial $x^3 + 7x^2 - 2x + 5$ is 3, because the degree of the monomial x^3 is higher than the degree of any of the other terms.

9.1.5 Definition   A polynomial of the form

$$ax + b$$

where $a \neq 0$, and a and b are real numbers, is called *a first degree polynomial in x*. The expression $ax + b$ is called the *standard form* of this kind of polynomial.

Illustration 15   The binomials $2x + 1$, $\frac{1}{2}x - 5$, and $\sqrt{2}x + 7$ are all first degree polynomials in x. The monomial $2x$ is also a first degree polynomial in x because it is of the form $ax + b$, where $a = 2$ and $b = 0$.

9.1.6 Definition   A polynomial of the form

$$ax^2 + bx + c$$

where $a \neq 0$, and a, b, and c are real numbers, is called a *second degree polynomial in x*, or a *quadratic polynomial in x*. The expression $ax^2 + bx + c$ is called the *standard form* of this kind of polynomial.

Illustration 16   The trinomial $2x^2 + \frac{1}{2}x - 1$ is a quadratic polynomial, where $a = 2$, $b = \frac{1}{2}$, and $c = -1$. The binomial $2x^2 - 1$ is a quadratic polynomial, where $a = 2$, $b = 0$, and $c = -1$. The monomial $2x^2$ is a quadratic polynomial, where $a = 2$, $b = 0$, and $c = 0$. Each of these polynomials is a second degree polynomial in x.

We can continue to define higher degree polynomials in a single variable in a pattern similar to that established for polynomials of the first and second degree. The set of all polynomials of this kind, to the nth degree in a single variable, do in fact form a very important set of quantities studied in great detail in higher mathematics. In this book we confine our study primarily to the first and second degree polynomials.

Exercises 9.1

The following expressions pertain to Exercises 1 through 8.

   (a) $x^2 + 4x$ (b) $x^3 + 7x + 1$ (c) t

(d) $\dfrac{1}{x}$ *not.* (e) 0 *poly* (f) $x^4 - \dfrac{1}{3}$

(g) $3x^2 + \sqrt{2}x + 9$ (h) $-x + 2$ (i) $\sqrt{x}$ *not poly why?*

(j) $-3xy$?

1. Identify the polynomials. **2.** Identify the monomials.

3. Identify the binomials. **4.** Identify the trinomials.

5. Identify the first degree polynomials in a single variable.

6. Identify the second degree polynomials in x.

7. For each polynomial, give its degree.

8. Identify the quadratic polynomials.

In Exercises 9 through 15 give the standard form of each polynomial and identify the constants a, b, and c of the standard form.

9. $3 + x$ **10.** $x + 2x^2 + 3$ **11.** $4x + 0$

12. $4 + 2x + x^2$ **13.** $64t - 16t^2$ **14.** $3 + 2x^2$

15. $\dfrac{1}{2} - \dfrac{2x}{3}$

16. Write a first degree polynomial in x with integer coefficients. ?

17. Write a second degree polynomial in y with real coefficients.

18. Write a third degree polynomial in t with rational coefficients.

19. Consider the set $D = \{0, 1, 2, 3, 4, 5, 6, 7, 8, 9\}$ and consider the set of all polynomials in x with coefficients from D. Some of these polynomials are the following:
(a) $2x^2 + 3x + 7$
(b) $x^3 + 3x^2 + 7x + 4$
(c) $x^3 + 8x + 6$
Let $x = 10$ in each of the above polynomials and find the value of each polynomial. Now for each polynomial write a sequence of only the coefficients. What do you find?

9.2 Addition and Subtraction of Polynomials

If we assume that the variable in any polynomial with real coefficients is also a real number, then we define the addition of polynomials to conform with the properties of addition of real numbers. That is, the Commutative, Associative, and Distributive laws apply.

Example 1   Add $7x$ and $3x$.

Solution: $7x + 3x = (7 + 3)x$
$\qquad\qquad\quad\ = 10x$

Example 2   Add $7x + 1$ and $3x - 4$.

Solution:

$$(7x + 1) + (3x - 4) = (7x + 3x) + (1 - 4)$$
$$= 10x - 3$$

The solution can also be written as follows:

$$\begin{array}{r} 7x + 1 \\ 3x - 4 \\ \hline 10x - 3 \end{array}$$

Example 3   Add $2x^2 - 3x + 1$ and $4x^2 - 5$.

Solution:

$$(2x^2 - 3x + 1) + (4x^2 - 5) = (2x^2 + 4x^2) + (-3x) + (1 - 5)$$
$$= 6x^2 - 3x - 4$$

The solution can also be written as follows:

$$\begin{array}{r} 2x^2 - 3x + 1 \\ 4x^2 \qquad\ - 5 \\ \hline 6x^2 - 3x - 4 \end{array}$$

Every polynomial has an additive inverse. That is, given a polynomial, we can find another polynomial such that the sum of the two polynomials is zero.

Example 4   Find the additive inverse of each of the following polynomials:
(a) $3x^2$ 　　　　　　　(b) $2x - 1$ 　　　　　　　(c) $x^2 - 6x + 9$

Solution:
(a) $3x^2$ and $-3x^2$ are additive inverses because $3x^2 + (-3x^2) = 0$.
(b) $2x - 1$ and $-(2x - 1) = -2x + 1$ are additive inverses because $(2x - 1) + (-2x + 1) = 0$.
(c) $x^2 - 6x + 9$ and $-(x^2 - 6x + 9) = -x^2 + 6x - 9$ are additive inverses because $(x^2 - 6x + 9) + (-x^2 + 6x - 9) = 0$.

To subtract one polynomial from another we add the additive inverse of the subtrahend. This follows from the definition of subtraction for real numbers: $a - b = a + (-b)$.

Example 5   Subtract $3x^2$ from $7x^2$.

Solution: $7x^2 - 3x^2 = 7x^2 + (-3x^2)$
$$= [7 + (-3)]x^2$$
$$= 4x^2$$

Example 6 Subtract $x^2 + 7x - 5$ from $x^3 + 8x^2 - 9$.

Solution:

$(x^3 + 8x^2 - 9) - (x^2 + 7x - 5) = (x^3 + 8x^2 - 9) + (-x^2 - 7x + 5)$
$$= x^3 + (8x^2 - x^2) + (-7x) + (-9 + 5)$$
$$= x^3 + 7x^2 - 7x - 4$$

The solution can also be written as follows:

$$
\begin{array}{r}
x^3 + 8x^2 \qquad\ - 9 \\
-\ \underline{\quad x^2 + 7x - 5} \\
\end{array}
$$

which becomes the following addition problem:

$$
\begin{array}{r}
x^3 + 8x^2 \qquad\ - 9 \\
+\ \underline{\quad -\ x^2 - 7x + 5} \\
x^3 + 7x^2 - 7x - 4 \\
\end{array}
$$

Exercises 9.2

In Exercises 1 through 10 add the given polynomials.

1. (a) $7x$
  $\underline{3x}$

  (b) $9y$
  $\underline{3y}$

  (c) $-3xy$
  $\underline{15xy}$

2. (a) $7x + 1$
  $\underline{3x + 5}$

  (b) $2x - 1$
  $\underline{13x + 4}$

  (c) $3x + 2y$
  $\underline{4x - 5y}$

3. (a) $2x^2 + 7x + 1$
  $\underline{4x^2 + 4x + 4}$

  (b) $7y^2 - 8y + \ 9$
  $\underline{6y^2 + 5y - 13}$

4. (a) $\dfrac{1}{2}x + \dfrac{1}{3}$
  $\underline{\dfrac{1}{2}x + \dfrac{1}{3}}$

  (b) $2x + \dfrac{1}{4}$
  $\underline{-2x - \dfrac{1}{4}}$

5. (a) $x^3 + 3x^2 + 2x - 7$
  $\underline{4x^3 \qquad\quad + 9x - 8}$

  (b) $-x^4 + 7x^3 + 2x^2 - 3x + 10$
  $\underline{5x^4 - 3x^3 + 9x^2 - 5x - 15}$

6. (a) $\ \ 2x + 7$
  $\ \ 3x - 8$
  $\underline{-4x + 2}$

  (b) $\ x^2 \qquad\quad - 1$
  $2x^2 + 4x$
  $\underline{\qquad\ - 2x + 1}$

7. (a) $(4x^2 + 5x - 1) + (7x^2 + 3x + 5)$
(b) $(2x + 5) + (-3x + 6) + (-4x - 8)$

8. (a) $(2x + 1) + (3x - 1)$
(b) $(x^2 + 1) + (x^2 - 1)$

9. (a) $(1 - x + x^2) + (4 - x^2 + 3x)$
(b) $16t^2 + (64t - 16t^2)$

10. $(x^5 + 5x^4 + 3x^3 - 7x^2 - x + 21) + (9x^4 - 3x^2 - 8 + 7x^3)$

In Exercises 11 through 20 subtract the second polynomial from the first.

11. (a) $7x$
$\quad\quad\ \underline{3x}$

(b) $9y$
$\quad\ \underline{3y}$

(c) $-3xy$
$\quad\quad\ \underline{15xy}$

12. (a) $7x + 1$
$\quad\quad\ \underline{3x + 5}$

(b) $2x - 1$
$\quad\ \underline{13x + 4}$

(c) $3x + 2y$
$\quad\quad\ \underline{4x - 5y}$

13. (a) $2x^2 + 7x + 1$
$\quad\quad\ \underline{4x^2 - 4x + 4}$

(b) $7y^2 - 8y + 9$
$\quad\ \underline{6y^2 + 5y - 13}$

14. (a) $\dfrac{1}{2}x + \dfrac{1}{3}$
$\quad\quad\ \underline{\dfrac{1}{2}x + \dfrac{1}{3}}$

(b) $2x + \dfrac{1}{4}$
$\quad\ \underline{-2x - \dfrac{1}{4}}$

15. (a) $x^3 + 3x^2 + 2x - 7$
$\quad\quad\ \underline{4x^3 \quad\quad\ + 9x - 8}$

(b) $-x^4 + 7x^3 + 2x^2 - 3x + 10$
$\quad\ \underline{5x^4 - 3x^3 + 9x^2 - 5x - 15}$

16. (a) $x^2 + 2x + 1$
$\quad\quad\ \underline{x^2 + 2x + 1}$

(b) $x^2 + 6x + 9$
$\quad\ \underline{-x^2 - 6x - 9}$

17. (a) $(4x^2 + 5x - 1) - (7x^2 + 3x + 5)$
(b) $(2x + 5) - (3x^2 + 7x - 8)$

18. (a) $(2x + 1) - (3x - 1)$
(b) $(x^2 + 1) - (x^2 - 1)$

19. (a) $(1 - x + x^2) - (4 - x^2 + 3x)$
(b) $16t^2 - (64t - 16t^2)$

20. $(x^5 + 5x^4 + 3x^3 - 7x^2 - x + 21) - (9x^4 - 3x^2 - 8 + 7x^3)$

21. Subtract $3x + 5$ from $7x + 8$.

22. Subtract 7 from $x^2 + x + 1$.

23. Subtract x from y.

24. From $x^2 + 4x + 44$ take $2x^2 - 1$.

25. From the sum of $x^2 - 9$ and $x^2 + 1$ take $x^2 - x - 1$.

26. Let P_x be the set of all polynomials in x with real coefficients.
  (a) Is P_x closed under addition?
  (b) Is there an identity element for addition in P_x?
  (c) Is there an additive inverse for every element in P_x?
  (d) Does P_x contain the set of real numbers as a subset?

27. Write 327 in expanded form as a polynomial as follows:

$$327 = 3(100) + 2(10) + 7$$
$$= 3 \cdot 10^2 + 2 \cdot 10 + 7$$

Now replace each 10 with an x and write the resulting polynomial. Keep this result. Now start with 561 and follow the same procedure. Now add 327 and 561 as whole numbers. Add 327 and 561 when both numbers are expressed in expanded form. Add the polynomials in x which you formed and compare all three answers. What do you find?

In Exercises 28 through 35 add the given polynomial expressions.

28. $3 \cdot 10^2 + 2 \cdot 10 + 7$
   $5 \cdot 10^2 + 6 \cdot 10 + 1$

29. $8 \cdot 10^3 + 0 \cdot 10^2 + 4 \cdot 10 + 1$
   $\qquad 9 \cdot 10^2 + 3 \cdot 10 + 0$

30. $4 \cdot 5^3 + 3 \cdot 5^2 + 1 \cdot 5 + 2$
   $0 \cdot 5^3 + 1 \cdot 5^2 + 3 \cdot 5 + 0$

31. $1 \cdot 2^4 + 0 \cdot 2^3 + 0 \cdot 2^2 + 1 \cdot 2 + 1$
   $\qquad 1 \cdot 2^3 + 1 \cdot 2^2 + 1 \cdot 2 + 0$

32. $7x^2 + 2x + 1$
   $3x^2 - 5x + 7$
   $\underline{x^2 - x - 3}$

33. $\qquad x^3 + 2x^2 - 7x + 5$
   $\qquad\qquad x^2 - 8x + 12$
   $\qquad 2x^3 - 5x^2 + 4x - 3$
   $\underline{-8x^3 + 0 + x - 9}$

34. $\qquad 2x^2 + 1$
   $\qquad 2x^2 - 1$
   $\qquad x + 1$
   $\qquad x - 1$
   $\underline{-4x^2 - 2x + 1}$

35. x
   $x + 1$
   $x + 2$
   $x + 3$
   $\underline{x + 4}$

9.3 Multiplication of Monomials

In Section 9.2, when we added and subtracted polynomials, we assumed the variable in the polynomial to be a real number. Continuing with this assumption, we discuss the multiplication of polynomials and we use the properties of real numbers.

The simplest case to consider is a monomial multiplied by a monomial.

Example 1 Find the product of the given monomials: (a) 3 and x; (b) x and x; (c) $3x$ and x^2; (d) $3x$ and $4x$; (e) x^3 and x^4.

Solution:
(a) $(3)(x) = 3x$
(b) $(x)(x) = x^2$
(c) $(3x)(x^2) = 3(x \cdot x^2)$
$\qquad\qquad = 3x^3$
(d) $(3x)(4x) = (3x)(x \cdot 4)$
$\qquad\qquad = (3x \cdot x)(4)$
$\qquad\qquad = (3x^2)(4)$
$\qquad\qquad = (4)(3x^2) = 12x^2$
(e) $(x^3)(x^4) = (x \cdot x \cdot x)(x \cdot x \cdot x \cdot x)$
$\qquad\qquad = x^7$

From Example 1, we observe the two facts which are stated as Properties 9.3.1 and 9.3.2.

9.3.1 Property For any two whole numbers m and n and for any real number x

$$x^m \cdot x^n = x^{m+n}$$

Illustration 1 $x^3 \cdot x^4 = (x \cdot x \cdot x)(x \cdot x \cdot x \cdot x)$
$\qquad\qquad\quad = x \cdot x \cdot x \cdot x \cdot x \cdot x \cdot x$
$\qquad\qquad\quad = x^7$

and

$$2^3 \cdot 2^4 = (2 \cdot 2 \cdot 2)(2 \cdot 2 \cdot 2 \cdot 2)$$
$$= 2^7$$

Note that x is used as a factor seven times, just as is 2.

9.3.2 Property If ax^m and bx^n are any two monomials in x and a and b are real numbers, their product is given by

$$(ax^m)(bx^n) = abx^{m+n}$$

Property 9.3.2 states that the coefficients of the monomials are multiplied and this product is the coefficient of the product of the monomials; furthermore, the degree of the product is the sum of the degrees of the factors.

Example 2 Find the product of $-3x^4$ and $4x^2$.

Solution: $(-3x^4)(4x^2) = -12 \cdot x^6$
$$= -12x^6$$

Example 3 Find: $(3x^4)^2$

Solution: $(3x^4)^2 = (3x^4)(3x^4)$
$$= 9x^8$$

Example 3 can be generalized to find any power of a monomial.

Illustration 2 To find the fourth power of $2x^3$ let us examine the meaning of the fourth power.

$$(2x^3)^4 = (2x^3)(2x^3)(2x^3)(2x^3)$$
$$= (2 \cdot 2 \cdot 2 \cdot 2)(x^3 \cdot x^3 \cdot x^3 \cdot x^3)$$
$$= 2^4 x^{3+3+3+3}$$
$$= 2^4 x^{4 \cdot 3}$$
$$= 2^4 x^{12}$$

Notice in Illustration 2 that the coefficient of the monomial is raised to the fourth power. Also notice that the degree of the result is the product of the degree of the monomial, which is 3, and the number 4. Illustration 2 is a special case of the following property.

9.3.3 Property If ax^m is a monomial in x and a is a real number, then the nth power of this monomial is given by

$$(ax^m)^n = a^n x^{mn}$$

Example 4 Find the third power of $4y^2$.

Solution: $(4y^2)^3 = 4^3 y^{2 \cdot 3}$
$$= 4^3 y^6$$

Properties 9.3.2 and 9.3.3 can be extended to include monomials in more than one variable.

Example 5 Find the product of $3x^2y$ and $2xy^3$.

Solution: $(3x^2y)(2xy^3) = (3 \cdot 2)(x^2 \cdot x)(y \cdot y^3)$
$$= 6x^3y^4$$

Example 6 Find the third power of the product of $3x^2$ and $4xy^2$.

Solution: $[(3x^2)(4xy^2)]^3 = [(3 \cdot 4)(x^2 \cdot x)(y^2)]^3$
$$= (12x^3y^2)^3$$
$$= 12^3 x^9 y^6$$

Special care must be taken when discussing powers of the opposite of a quantity and the opposite of a power of a quantity. If the opposite of a quantity is to be raised to a power then parentheses should be used. Thus,

$$(-x)^2 = x^2$$

and

$$(-x)^3 = -(x^3)$$

In the second case we can write $-x^3$ in the place of $-(x^3)$ because $-x^3$ equals $-(x^3)$.

In working with an expression such as $-(x^3)^2$, the power is the first operation performed on the quantity in parentheses, then the opposite of the result is found. Hence,

$$-(x^3)^2 = -(x^6) = -x^6$$

Illustration 3 If $x = -3$, then

$$
\begin{aligned}
(-x)^3 &= -x^3 \\
&= -(x)^3 \\
&= -(-3)^3 \\
&= -(-27) \\
&= 27
\end{aligned}
$$

However,

$$
\begin{aligned}
-x^2 &= -(-3)^2 \\
&= -(9) \\
&= -9
\end{aligned}
$$

but

$$
\begin{aligned}
[-x]^2 &= [-(-3)]^2 \\
&= (3)^2 \\
&= 9
\end{aligned}
$$

Example 7 Find the value of (a) -5^2 and (b) $(-5)^2$.

Solution: (a) $-5^2 = -(5^2) = -25$
 (b) $(-5)^2 = (-5)(-5) = 25$

Exercises 9.3

In Exercises 1 through 25 multiply the given factors.

1. (a) $(3x)(5x)$ (b) $(3x)(5y)$

2. (a) $(2x^2)(5x)$ (b) $(x^3)(x^5)$

3. (a) $(x^2)^3$ (b) $(x^3)^2$

4. (a) $(2x^3)^2$ (b) $(3x^2)(5x^3)$

5. (a) $(-x)(-x)(-x)$ (b) $(-x)(x^3)$

6. (a) $(-x)^2$ (b) $3^5 \cdot 3^3$

7. (a) $10^2 \cdot 10^2$ (b) $10^2 \cdot 10^4$

8. (a) $10^3 \cdot 10^3$ (b) $10^2 \cdot 10^2 \cdot 10^2$

9. (a) $10^{50} \cdot 10^{50}$ (b) $10^3 \cdot 10^6$

10. (a) $(10^3)^2$ (b) $(10^4)^3$

11. (a) $(10^{10})^{10}$ *Power to a power*
    (b) If $10^3 = 1000$, then express 1000^2 as a power of 10.

12. (a) $2^2 \cdot 2^3$ (b) $(-1)^5$

13. (a) $(-x)^5$ (b) $(-x)^6$

14. (a) $(-1)^{99}$ (b) $(-1)^{100}$

15. (a) $(-x)^{100}$ (b) $(-x^2)^3$

16. (a) $(-x^3)^2$ (b) $-(x^3)^4$

17. (a) $(3x^2y)(7x^3y)$ (b) $(10xyz)(5x^3)$

18. (a) $(3^2)^3$ (b) $(3^4)^3$

19. (a) $(3^3)^2(2^4)^3$ (b) $(3x^2)^4$

20. (a) $(3x^2)^4(2x^5)^2$ (b) $(3xy^2)(2xy)^3$

21. (a) $(-2x)^3(-3x^2)$ (b) $(-xy)^4(-x^2)^3$

22. (a) $(ab)^3$ (b) $(ab)^n$

23. (a) $x^a x^b$ (b) $x^n x^2$

24. (a) $(x^n)^2$ (b) $(x^n)^2 x^3$

25. (a) $x^{n+1} x^{n-1}$ (b) $x^{2n+3} x^{4-2n}$ *Cope with to here*

26. Let M_x be the set of all monomials in x with real coefficients.
    (a) Is M_x closed under multiplication? *yes*
    (b) Is M_x closed under addition? *No*
    (c) Is there an identity element for multiplication in M_x? *yes*
    (d) Is there a multiplicative inverse for every element in M_x? *yes*
    (e) Is there an additive inverse for every element in M_x? *yes*
    (f) Does M_x contain the set of real numbers as a subset? *No*

27. (a) Express the value of $2^3 + 2^3$ as a power of 2. (Hint: $2^3 + 2^3 = 2(2^3)$.)
    (b) Express the value of $3^2 + 3^2 + 3^2$ as a power of 3. (Hint: $3^2 + 3^2 + 3^2 = 3 \cdot 3^2$.)

(c) Express the value of

$$10^{10}+10^{10}+10^{10}+10^{10}+10^{10}+10^{10}+10^{10}+10^{10}+10^{10}+10^{10}$$

as a power of 10.

28. Suppose the sides of the square shown in Figure 9.3.1 have the dimensions indicated. **(a)** Express the number of units in the perimeter of the square as a monomial of degree 1. **(b)** Express the number of square units in the area of the square as a monomial of degree 2.

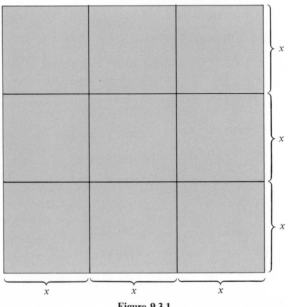

Figure 9.3.1

9.4 Multiplication of Polynomials

In Section 9.3 we discussed the product of a monomial multiplied by a monomial. We now consider the more general case of multiplying a monomial and a polynomial. To multiply polynomials we apply the Distributive Law: $a(b + c) = ab + ac$.

Example 1 Find the product of 3 and $x + 2$.

Solution: $3(x + 2) = (3 \cdot x) + (3 \cdot 2)$
$= 3x + 6$

Example 2 Find the product of x and $x + 2$.

Solution: $x(x + 2) = (x \cdot x) + (x \cdot 2)$
$= x^2 + 2x$

Example 3 Find the product of $-3y$ and $7x - 2y$.

Solution: $\begin{aligned} -3y(7x - 2y) &= (-3y \cdot 7x) - (-3y \cdot 2y) \\ &= -21xy - (-6y^2) \\ &= -21xy + 6y^2 \end{aligned}$

Example 4 Find the product of $2x^2$ and $5x^2 - 3x + 9$.

Solution:

$$\begin{aligned} 2x^2(5x^2 - 3x + 9) &= (2x^2 \cdot 5x^2) - (2x^2 \cdot 3x) + (2x^2 \cdot 9) \\ &= 10x^4 - 6x^3 + 18x^2 \end{aligned}$$

From Examples 1 through 4 observe that when multiplying a monomial and a polynomial we use the Distributive Law and multiply each term of the polynomial by the monomial. We then add these products (or indicate the addition) to form a new polynomial.

Consider the product of a binomial multiplied by a binomial. This computation also depends on the Distributive Law. Suppose we have the product

$$(x + 2)(x + 3)$$

To see the effect of the Distributive Law let the binomial $x + 2$ be temporarily replaced by the variable A. Hence, we have

$(x + 2)(x + 3) = A(x + 3)$ (This is now treated like the case of a monomial times a binomial.)

$\begin{aligned} &= A \cdot x + A \cdot 3 \\ &= xA + 3A \\ &= x(x + 2) + 3(x + 2) \end{aligned}$ (Replace A by $x + 2$ and multiply again.)

$\begin{aligned} &= (x^2 + 2x) + (3x + 6) \\ &= x^2 + 5x + 6 \end{aligned}$

The procedure may seem rather long, but it is presented to illustrate the use of the Distributive Law. If we leave out the explanation and do not replace $x + 2$ by A, we write

$$\begin{aligned} (x + 2)(x + 3) &= x(x + 3) + 2(x + 3) \\ &= x^2 + 3x + 2x + 6 \\ &= x^2 + 5x + 6 \end{aligned}$$

Note that each term of the first binomial is multiplied by each term of the second binomial and the products are added.

Example 5 Find the product of $2x + 5$ and $3x - 1$.

Solution: $\begin{aligned} (2x + 5)(3x - 1) &= 2x(3x - 1) + 5(3x - 1) \\ &= 6x^2 - 2x + 15x - 5 \\ &= 6x^2 + 13x - 5 \end{aligned}$

Example 6 Find the product of $x + 1$ and $x^2 + 2x + 1$.

Solution:

$$(x + 1)(x^2 + 2x + 1) = x(x^2 + 2x + 1) + 1(x^2 + 2x + 1)$$
$$= x^3 + 2x^2 + x + x^2 + 2x + 1$$
$$= x^3 + 3x^2 + 3x + 1$$

Example 7 Find the product of $3x$, $x + 2$, and $5x - 1$.

Solution: $3x(x + 2)(5x - 1) = 3x[(x + 2)(5x - 1)]$
$$= 3x[x(5x - 1) + 2(5x - 1)]$$
$$= 3x(5x^2 - x + 10x - 2)$$
$$= 3x(5x^2 + 9x - 2)$$
$$= 15x^3 + 27x^2 - 6x$$

Notice that the degree of the product in Examples 6 and 7 is three. In general, the degree of the product of two or more polynomials is the sum of the degrees of the individual factors. In Example 6, the two factors are of degrees one and two, and $1 + 2 = 3$. In Example 7 the three factors are all of the first degree and $1 + 1 + 1 = 3$.

If a first degree binomial is multiplied by itself, the product is a second degree trinomial (called a *perfect square trinomial*). A picture of a square with a side of measure $(a + b)$ is shown in Figure 9.4.1. The measure of

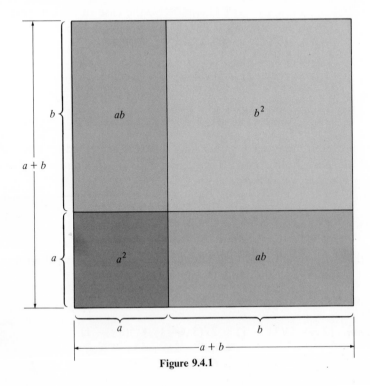

Figure 9.4.1

the area of the square in Figure 9.4.1 can be considered in two ways:

(i) the square of the binomial $(a + b)$, or

(ii) the whole area expressed as the sum of its parts.

Consider the square of the binomial $(a + b)$.

$$\begin{aligned}
(a + b)^2 &= (a + b)(a + b) \\
&= a(a + b) + b(a + b) \\
&= a^2 + ab + ba + b^2 \\
&= a^2 + ab + ab + b^2 \\
&= a^2 + 2ab + b^2
\end{aligned}$$

The measure of the area of the square in Figure 9.4.1 is also given by expressing the whole area as the sum of its parts.

$$\begin{aligned}
(a + b)^2 &= a^2 + ab + ab + b^2 \\
&= a^2 + 2ab + b^2
\end{aligned}$$

In either case we have

$$(a + b)^2 = a^2 + 2ab + b^2$$

The expression $a^2 + 2ab + b^2$ is called a *perfect square trinomial*.

Example 8   Find $(x + 1)^2$ and $(x + 1)^3$.

Solution: $\begin{aligned}[t]
(x + 1)^2 &= (x + 1)(x + 1) \\
&= x(x + 1) + 1(x + 1) \\
&= x^2 + x + x + 1 \\
&= x^2 + 2x + 1
\end{aligned}$

The expression $x^2 + 2x + 1$ is a perfect square trinomial. If we examine Example 6 and note that $(x + 1)^2 = x^2 + 2x + 1$, we discover that

$$(x + 1)(x^2 + 2x + 1)$$

is equivalent to

$$(x + 1)(x + 1)^2$$

which is equivalent to

$$(x + 1)^3$$

and hence, from Example 6 we have

$$(x + 1)^3 = x^3 + 3x^2 + 3x + 1$$

Exercises 9.4

In Exercises 1 through 17 find each product.

1. (a) $3(x + 7)$ (b) $-3(x - 4)$

2. (a) $x(2x - 5)$ (b) $(3x + 2)2x$

3. **(a)** $3x(x^2 + 1)$ **(b)** $-x^2(x^3 + x + 1)$

4. **(a)** $5x(x^4 + 2x^2 + 10)$
   (b) $2x^3(x^5 - x^4 + 2x^3 - x^2 + 7x - 12)$

5. **(a)** $-6x^2(2x^2 - 8x + 12)$ **(b)** $xy(x^2 - y^2)$

6. **(a)** $a(a - ab)$ **(b)** $ab(ab^2 + a^2b)$

7. **(a)** $(x - 1)(x - 2)$ **(b)** $(x + 1)(x - 2)$

8. **(a)** $(2x - 3)(x + 5)$ **(b)** $(2x - 3)(3x + 5)$

9. **(a)** $(x + 7)(x - 7)$ **(b)** $(x^2 + 1)(x^2 - 1)$

10. **(a)** $(x + 3)(x - 3)$ **(b)** $(x + y)(x - y)$

11. **(a)** $(a + b)(a - b)$ **(b)** $(x^2 + y^2)(x^2 - y^2)$

12. **(a)** $(-2x + 7)(3x - 1)$ **(b)** $3(x + 3)(x + 2)$

13. **(a)** $x(x + 1)(x + 2)$ **(b)** $4x(2x + 1)(2x - 1)$

14. **(a)** $(x + 1)(x^2 + x + 1)$ **(b)** $(x - 1)(x^2 + x + 1)$

15. **(a)** $(x + 1)(x^2 - x + 1)$ **(b)** $(x + 1)(x^2 + 5x + 6)$

16. **(a)** $(x + 1)^1$ **(b)** $(x + 1)^3$

17. **(a)** $(x + 1)^2$ **(b)** $(x + 1)^4$

18. **(a)** If $a(x + 4) = 3x + 12$, find a.
    (b) If $5(x + a) = 5x + 20$, find a.

19. **(a)** If $(a + 3)(x - 7) = x^2 - 4x - 21$, find a.
    (b) If $(x + 5)(x + a) = x^2 + 9x + 20$, find a.

20. Prove: $(a + b)^2 \neq a^2 + b^2$

21. Prove: $2k - 1 = k^2 - (k - 1)^2$

22. Prove: $3k(k - 1) = k^3 - (k - 1)^3 - 1$

23. Multiply $2x + 1$ by $3x + 2$. Now replace x with 10 so that $2x + 1$ becomes $2(10) + 1$, and $3x + 2$ becomes $3(10) + 2$. Multiply $2(10) + 1$ by $3(10) + 2$. Now multiply 21 by 32. Compare the coefficients of the polynomial products with the product of 21 and 32. What do you find?

24. Let P_x be the set of all polynomials in x with real coefficients.
    (a) Is P_x closed under multiplication?
    (b) Is P_x closed under addition?
    (c) Is there a multiplicative identity element in P_x?
    (d) Is there an additive identity element in P_x?
    (e) Does every element in P_x have an additive inverse?
    (f) Does every element in P_x have a multiplicative inverse?
    (g) Is the system P_x with the operations of addition and multiplication a field?

25. If the width of a rectangle is x units and the number of units in the length of the rectangle is 5 more than the number of units in the width, find a polynomial expression for the measure of the area of the rectangle. See Figure 9.4.2.

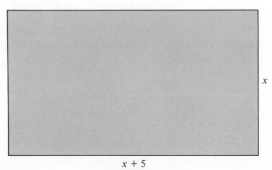

$x + 5$

Figure 9.4.2

26. Suppose the length of the rectangle in Exercise 25 is diminished by 3 units and the width is increased by 3 units. Find a polynomial expression for the measure of the area of this new rectangle.

27. Find the difference in the answers to Exercises 25 and 26. How does the area change when the rectangle of Exercise 25 is changed in Exercise 26?

28. Suppose the length of the side of the square in Figure 9.4.3 is $(x + 2)$ units. **(a)** Express the number of units in the perimeter of the square as a first degree binomial. **(b)** Express the number of square units in the area of the square as a quadratic trinomial.

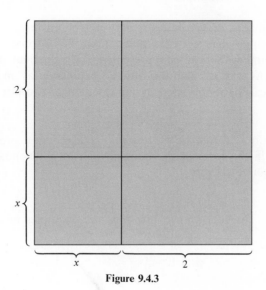

Figure 9.4.3

29. In Exercises 16 and 17 we find that

$$(x + 1)^1 = x + 1$$
$$(x + 1)^2 = x^2 + 2x + 1$$
$$(x + 1)^3 = x^3 + 3x^2 + 3x + 1$$
$$(x + 1)^4 = x^4 + 4x^3 + 6x^2 + 4x + 1$$

The coefficients of these polynomials can be arranged into a triangle known as "*Pascal's triangle*" (named after Blaise Pascal, a French mathematician and philosopher of the 17th century).

		1		1			The coefficients of the terms of $x + 1$
	1		2		1		The coefficients of the terms of $x^2 + 2x + 1$
1		3		3		1	The coefficients of the terms of $x^3 + 3x^2 + 3x + 1$
1	4		6		4		1	The coefficients of the terms of $x^4 + 4x^3 + 6x^2 + 4x + 1$

These coefficients form an interesting pattern and can be extended once that pattern is recognized. Note that except for the 1's forming the sides of the "triangle," each number is the sum of the two numbers above it to the right and left. Hence, the next line can be formed as follows:

```
 1   4   6   4   1
  \ / \ / \ / \ /
 1  5  10  10  5  1
```

Verify that the numbers 1, 5, 10, 10, 5, and 1 are the coefficients of the product $(x + 1)^5$.

9.5 Division of Polynomials

Just as the quotient of two integers may not be an integer, the quotient of two polynomials may not be a polynomial. We learned that a rational number is a number that can be represented by the quotient of two integers. In an analogous way we define a rational expression as an algebraic expression that can be represented by the quotient of two polynomials.

9.5.1 Definition   A *rational expression* is an algebraic expression that can be expressed in the form of the quotient of two polynomials, where the divisor does not equal zero.

Illustration 1   The following expressions are examples of some rational expressions:

$$7 = \frac{7}{1}$$

$$x^2 + 2x + 1 = \frac{x^2 + 2x + 1}{1}$$

$$\frac{1}{x}, \quad x \neq 0$$

$$\frac{x + 2}{x^2 + 2x + 1}, \quad x^2 + 2x + 1 \neq 0$$

$$\frac{x^3 - 1}{x^2 - 1}, \quad x^2 - 1 \neq 0$$

The reason for using the terminology "rational expression" is that the rules for adding, subtracting, multiplying, and dividing them are very much like those for performing the same operations with rational numbers.

The fundamental principle of quotients is, of course, the key to division. It is by this principle that we can divide both the dividend and the divisor by their common factors. Thus, if F, G, and E are algebraic expressions and G and E are not zero, then

$$\frac{F \cdot E}{G \cdot E} = \frac{F \cdot E \div E}{G \cdot E \div E} = \frac{F}{G}$$

In particular, if the algebraic expressions are polynomials, we have rational expressions that we can reduce to lowest terms.

Illustration 2

(a) $\dfrac{3x}{4x} = \dfrac{3}{4}, \quad x \neq 0$ (Both the numerator and denominator of the left member are divided by x.)

(b) $\dfrac{5(x + 2)}{8(x + 2)} = \dfrac{5}{8}, \quad x \neq -2$ (Both the numerator and denominator of the left member are divided by $x + 2$.)

(c) $\dfrac{x(x - 3)}{x - 3} = x, \quad x \neq 3$ (Both the numerator and denominator of the left member are divided by $x - 3$.)

(d) $\dfrac{(x + 2)(x + 3)}{x + 3} = x + 2, \quad x \neq -3$

(e) $\dfrac{3x^2(x + 1)(x - 1)}{2x^2(x - 1)} = \dfrac{3(x + 1)}{2}, \quad x \neq 0, \ x \neq 1$

(f) $\dfrac{(x - 3)(x^2 + 3x + 9)}{4(x^2 + 3x + 9)} = \dfrac{x - 3}{4}, \quad x^2 + 3x + 9 \neq 0$

Recall that division in the set R is possible when a, b, and c are in R, $b \neq 0$, and

$$\frac{a}{b} = c \quad \text{if and only if} \quad cb = a$$

The first case to consider is the case of a monomial divided by a monomial. For monomials in x having real numbers as coefficients we need the following property.

$$a^{-n} = \frac{1}{a} \qquad \textit{take reciprocal}$$

9.5.2 Property   If m and n are natural numbers and x is a real number, where $x \neq 0$, then

(i) $\dfrac{2^3}{2^2} \quad \dfrac{8}{4}$

$$\frac{x^m}{x^n} = x^{m-n} \quad \text{when } m > n$$

(ii) $2^2 \quad \dfrac{4}{8}$

$\dfrac{2^2}{2^3} = \dfrac{4}{8}$

$$\frac{x^m}{x^n} = \frac{1}{x^{n-m}} \quad \text{when } n > m$$

(iii) $\dfrac{1}{2^{3-2}}$

$$\frac{x^m}{x^n} = 1 \quad \text{when } m = n$$

In the illustrations and examples that follow, it is understood that the divisor is not zero.

Illustration 3 We can consider the quotient

$$\frac{x^5}{x^2}$$

in two ways.

First,

$$\frac{x^5}{x^2} = x^3 \quad \text{because} \quad (x^3)(x^2) = x^5$$

Second,

$$\frac{x^5}{x^2} = \frac{x \cdot x \cdot x \cdot x \cdot x}{x \cdot x}$$

$$= x \cdot x \cdot x$$

$$= x^3$$

because the dividend and divisor are divided by x^2. Thus, Property 9.5.2(i) is verified for this particular case; that is

$$\frac{x^5}{x^2} = x^{5-2} = x^3$$

Illustration 4 The quotient

$$\frac{x^2}{x^5} = \frac{1}{x^3}$$

because

$$\left(\frac{1}{x^3}\right)(x^5) = \frac{x^5}{x^3}$$

$$= x^{5-3}$$

$$= x^2$$

Also,

$$\frac{x^2}{x^5} = \frac{x \cdot x}{x \cdot x \cdot x \cdot x \cdot x}$$

$$= \frac{1}{x \cdot x \cdot x}$$

$$= \frac{1}{x^3}$$

Either way, Property 9.5.2(ii) is verified for this particular case; that is,

$$\frac{x^2}{x^5} = \frac{1}{x^{5-2}} = \frac{1}{x^3}$$

Illustration 5 By Property 9.5.2(iii)

$$\frac{x^5}{x^5} = 1$$

Example 1 Find the quotients $\dfrac{2^7}{2^3}$ and $\dfrac{2^3}{2^7}$.

Solution: $\dfrac{2^7}{2^3} = 2^{7-3} = 2^4$

$$\frac{2^3}{2^7} = \frac{1}{2^{7-3}} = \frac{1}{2^4}$$

We are now ready to divide a monomial in x by a monomial in x.

9.5.3 Property If ax^m and bx^n are monomials in x with real coefficients, such that $bx^n \neq 0$, the quotient of ax^m and bx^n is given by

$$\frac{ax^m}{bx^n} = \left(\frac{a}{b}\right)\left(\frac{x^m}{x^n}\right)$$

Example 2 Find the quotient of $15x^4$ divided by $3x$.

Solution: $\dfrac{15x^4}{3x} = \left(\dfrac{15}{3}\right)\left(\dfrac{x^4}{x}\right)$

$$= \frac{15}{3}x^{4-1}$$

$$= 5x^3$$

Example 3 Find the quotient of $3x$ divided by $15x^4$.

Solution:

$$\frac{3x}{15x^4} = \left(\frac{3}{15}\right)\left(\frac{x}{x^4}\right)$$

$$= \left(\frac{1}{5}\right)\left(\frac{1}{x^{4-1}}\right)$$

$$= \left(\frac{1}{5}\right)\left(\frac{1}{x^3}\right)$$

$$= \frac{1}{5x^3}$$

Example 4 Find the quotient of $-24x^5$ divided by the second power of $2x^3$.

Solution:

$$\frac{-24x^5}{(2x^3)^2} = \frac{-24x^5}{4x^6}$$

$$= \left(\frac{-24}{4}\right)\left(\frac{x^5}{x^6}\right)$$

$$= (-6)\left(\frac{1}{x}\right)$$

$$= \frac{-6}{x}$$

Example 5 Find $\left(\frac{8x^7}{4x^2}\right)^3$.

Solution:

$$\left(\frac{8x^7}{4x^2}\right)^3 = \left(\frac{8}{4}x^{7-2}\right)^3$$

$$= (2x^5)^3$$

$$= 2^3 x^{5\cdot3}$$

$$= 8x^{15}$$

The next property gives the power of a quotient of monomials.

9.5.4 Property   If ax^m and bx^n are monomials in x and a and b are real numbers such that $bx^n \neq 0$, then the rth power of the quotient of ax^m and bx^n is given by

$$\left(\frac{ax^m}{bx^n}\right)^r = \frac{(ax^m)^r}{(bx^n)^r}$$

In practice, the quotient is first simplified before raising to the power. Refer to the next example.

Example 6 Find $\left(\dfrac{-12x^2}{4x^5}\right)^6$.

Solution: $\left(\dfrac{-12x^2}{4x^5}\right)^6 = \left(\dfrac{-12}{4} \cdot \dfrac{x^2}{x^5}\right)^6$

$= \left(-3 \cdot \dfrac{1}{x^3}\right)^6$

$= \left(\dfrac{-3}{x^3}\right)^6$

$= \dfrac{(-3)^6}{(x^3)^6}$

$= \dfrac{3^6}{x^{18}}$

Properties 9.5.3 and 9.5.4 can be extended to include monomials in more than one variable.

Example 7 Divide $30x^2y^3$ by $6xy^5$.

Solution: $\dfrac{30x^2y^3}{6xy^5} = \left(\dfrac{30}{6}\right)\left(\dfrac{x^2}{x}\right)\left(\dfrac{y^3}{y^5}\right)$

$= (5)(x)\left(\dfrac{1}{y^2}\right)$

$= \dfrac{5x}{y^2}$

Example 8 Find $\left(\dfrac{42x^3y^4}{7x^3}\right)^3$.

Solution: $\left(\dfrac{42x^3y^4}{7x^3}\right)^3 = \left[\left(\dfrac{42}{7}\right)\left(\dfrac{x^3}{x^3}\right)(y^4)\right]^3$

$= [(6)(1)(y^4)]^3$

$= (6y^4)^3$

$= 6^3y^{12}$

The division of a polynomial of two or more terms by a monomial can be carried out by making use of the concept of a reciprocal. Recall that

$$\frac{a}{b} = a \cdot \frac{1}{b}$$

Thus, to divide $x^3 + 2x^4$ by $4x^2$, we write

$$\frac{x^3 + 2x^4}{4x^2} = (x^3 + 2x^4)\left(\frac{1}{4x^2}\right)$$

Using the Distributive Law, we have

$$(x^3 + 2x^4)\left(\frac{1}{4x^2}\right) = (x^3)\left(\frac{1}{4x^2}\right) + (2x^4)\left(\frac{1}{4x^2}\right)$$

$$= \frac{x^3}{4x^2} + \frac{2x^4}{4x^2}$$

$$= \left(\frac{1}{4}\right)\left(\frac{x^3}{x^2}\right) + \left(\frac{2}{4}\right)\left(\frac{x^4}{x^2}\right)$$

$$= \left(\frac{1}{4}\right)(x) + \left(\frac{1}{2}\right)(x^2)$$

$$= \frac{x}{4} + \frac{x^2}{2}$$

The preceding computation essentially involves dividing each term in the dividend by the divisor.

Example 9   Divide: $\dfrac{2x^3 + 8x^2 - 12x}{4x}$, $x \neq 0$.

Solution: $\dfrac{2x^3 + 8x^2 - 12x}{4x} = \dfrac{2x^3}{4x} + \dfrac{8x^2}{4x} - \dfrac{12x}{4x}$

$$= \frac{1}{2}x^2 + 2x - 3$$

Example 10   Divide $(x^2 + 2xy + y^2)$ by $2xy$.

Solution: $\dfrac{x^2 + 2xy + y^2}{2xy} = \dfrac{x^2}{2xy} + \dfrac{2xy}{2xy} + \dfrac{y^2}{2xy}$

$$= \left(\frac{1}{2} \cdot \frac{x^2}{x} \cdot \frac{1}{y}\right) + 1 + \left(\frac{1}{2} \cdot \frac{1}{x} \cdot \frac{y^2}{y}\right)$$

$$= \left(\frac{1}{2} \cdot x \cdot \frac{1}{y}\right) + 1 + \left(\frac{1}{2} \cdot \frac{1}{x} \cdot y\right)$$

$$= \frac{x}{2y} + 1 + \frac{y}{2x}$$

The case remaining to be considered is when the divisor is a polynomial of two or more terms and has a degree less than or equal to that of the dividend. To illustrate this division process we first identify certain aspects of polynomials that are critical to the discussion. Of all of the terms that are included in a polynomial, the monomial of highest degree is called the *leading monomial* (or leading term) of the polynomial. When writing polynomials it is customary to write the leading monomial first, followed by the other terms arranged in *descending order* of the degrees of each term in the polynomial.

Illustration 6 The terms of the polynomial

$$33x^4 - 7x^3 + 2x^2 + 6x - 12$$

are arranged in descending order of their degrees. The term $33x^4$ is the monomial of highest degree and is therefore the leading monomial.

To illustrate the division process we begin with an example from arithmetic. Suppose we wish to divide 252 by 12. First write these numbers in expanded form

$$252 = 200 + 50 + 2$$
$$12 = 10 + 2$$

We call 200 the leading monomial of $200 + 50 + 2$ and 10 is the leading monomial of $10 + 2$. Now we devise a process similar to that used for division of whole numbers. We write

$$10 + 2\overline{)200 + 50 + 2}$$

The division process is performed as follows:

Step 1. Divide the leading monomial of the dividend by the leading monomial of the divisor. Place this result (partial quotient) to the right of the division symbol on the line below the dividend. This partial quotient is one of the monomials in the full quotient.

$$10 + 2\overline{)200 + 50 + 2} \quad\Big|\quad 20$$

Step 2. Multiply this newly found monomial (20) by the divisor and write the result under the dividend so that terms of the same "degree" are in the same columns.

$$10 + 2\overline{)200 + 50 + 2} \quad\Big|\quad 20$$
$$\phantom{10 + 2\overline{)}}200 + 40$$

Step 3. Draw a line under this result and subtract from the dividend. We obtain a new polynomial called the difference.

$$10 + 2\overline{)200 + 50 + 2} \quad\Big|\quad 20$$
$$\phantom{10 + 2\overline{)}}\underline{200 + 40}$$
$$\phantom{10 + 2\overline{)200 + }}10 + 2$$

Step 4. If the degree of this difference is greater than or equal to the degree of the divisor, then repeat steps 1 through 4 and treat the difference as if it is the dividend. If the degree of this difference is less than the degree of the divisor, then this difference is the remainder and the division has been completed.

$$10 + 2\overline{)200 + 50 + 2} \quad\Big|\quad 20$$
$$\phantom{10 + 2\overline{)}}\underline{200 + 40}$$
$$\phantom{10 + 2\overline{)200 + }}\underline{10 + 2} \quad\Big|\quad 1$$
$$\phantom{10 + 2\overline{)200 + 50 + }}0$$

Step 5. If the remainder is zero add the monomials in the quotient. This is the full quotient.

$$
\begin{array}{r}
10 + 2 \overline{)\,200 + 50 + 2\,} \\
\underline{200 + 40} \quad\; 20 \\
10 + 2 \\
\underline{10 + 2} \quad\; 1 \\
0
\end{array}
\quad\Big\}\; 20 + 1
$$

Hence, the quotient in this example is $20 + 1 = 21$.

Now suppose we write

$$200 + 50 + 2$$

as

$$2 \cdot 10^2 + 5 \cdot 10 + 2$$

and let 10 be replaced by x. Then

$$200 + 50 + 2 \qquad \text{becomes} \qquad 2x^2 + 5x + 2$$

and

$$10 + 2 \qquad \text{becomes} \qquad x + 2$$

Furthermore, we now wish to divide $2x^2 + 5x + 2$ by $x + 2$. The process is identical to that outlined in steps 1 through 5 above. Refer to the next example.

Example 11 Divide $2x^2 + 5x + 2$ by $x + 2$, $x \neq -2$.

Solution: Performing steps 1 through 5 as described above, we obtain

$$
\begin{array}{r}
x + 2 \overline{)\,2x^2 + 5x + 2\,} \\
\underline{2x^2 + 4x} \quad\; 2x \\
x + 2 \\
\underline{x + 2} \quad\; 1 \\
0
\end{array}
\quad\Big\}\; 2x + 1
$$

To check the computation in division we multiply the quotient by the divisor. Thus, we check the computation in Example 11 by multiplying $2x + 1$ by $x + 2$.

$$
\begin{aligned}
(x + 2)(2x + 1) &= x(2x + 1) + 2(2x + 1) \\
&= 2x^2 + x + 4x + 2 \\
&= 2x^2 + 5x + 2
\end{aligned}
$$

If the remainder is not zero, write the remainder over the divisor to form a fraction and add this fraction to the quotient. In general,

$$\frac{\text{dividend}}{\text{divisor}} = \text{quotient} + \frac{\text{remainder}}{\text{divisor}}$$

Illustration 7 When 13 is divided by 4, the quotient is 3 and the remainder is 1. Thus,

$$\frac{13}{4} = 3 + \frac{1}{4}$$

Example 12 Divide $x^2 + 8x + 14$ by $x + 6$, $x \neq -6$.

Solution: We perform steps 1 through 5.

$$
\begin{array}{r}
x + 6 \overline{\smash{)}x^2 + 8x + 14} \\
\underline{x^2 + 6x} \qquad \boxed{x} \\
2x + 14 \\
\underline{2x + 12} \quad \boxed{2} \\
2
\end{array}
$$

$$\left. \right\} \; x + 2 + \frac{2}{x + 6}$$

Example 13 Divide: $\dfrac{x^2 - 3x + 5}{x + 9}$, $x \neq -9$

Solution:

$$
\begin{array}{r}
x + 9 \overline{\smash{)}x^2 - 3x + 5} \\
\underline{x^2 + 9x} \qquad\qquad \boxed{x} \\
-12x + 5 \\
\underline{-12x - 108} \quad \boxed{-12} \\
113
\end{array}
$$

$$\left. \right\} \; x - 12 + \frac{113}{x + 9}$$

Example 14 Divide: $\dfrac{x^3 - 27}{x - 3}$, $x \neq 3$

Solution: Note that $x^3 - 27 = x^3 + 0 \cdot x^2 + 0 \cdot x - 27$.

$$
\begin{array}{r}
x - 3 \overline{\smash{)}x^3 + 0 \cdot x^2 + 0 \cdot x - 27} \\
\underline{x^3 - 3x^2} \qquad\qquad\qquad \boxed{x^2} \\
3x^2 + 0 \cdot x - 27 \\
\underline{3x^2 - 9x} \qquad\qquad \boxed{3x} \\
9x - 27 \\
\underline{9x - 27} \qquad \boxed{9} \\
0
\end{array}
$$

$$\left. \right\} \; x^2 + 3x + 9$$

Example 14 shows that when dividing with polynomials, zero "place holders" are used as coefficients of the powers of the variable that do not appear in the polynomial.

Example 15. Divide: $\dfrac{x^3 - 8 + 3x + 5x^2}{x^2 - 3}$, $x^2 - 3 \neq 0$

Solution: Note that $x^3 - 8 + 3x + 5x^2 = x^3 + 5x^2 + 3x - 8$. Always arrange the terms of the polynomial in descending order.

$$
x^2 + 0x - 3 \overline{)\, x^3 + 5x^2 + 3x - 8}
$$

$$
\underline{x^3 + 0x^2 - 3x} \qquad \boxed{x}
$$

$$
5x^2 + 6x - 8
$$

$$
\underline{5x^2 + 0x - 15} \quad \boxed{5}
$$

$$
6x + 7
$$

$$
x + 5 + \frac{6x + 7}{x^2 - 3}
$$

Exercises 9.5

In Exercises 1 through 8 use the Fundamental Principle of Quotients to simplify the rational expressions. Assume the denominator does not equal zero. Give the values of x or y for which the denominator equals zero.

1. $\dfrac{3xy}{8xy}$

2. $\dfrac{5(x + 2)}{5(x + 3)}$

3. $\dfrac{5(x + 2)}{7(x + 2)}$

4. $\dfrac{(x + 1)(x + 2)}{x(x + 2)}$

5. $\dfrac{x(x + 1)}{x(x + 2)}$

6. $\dfrac{3(x + 1)(x + 2)}{x + 1}$

7. $\dfrac{(x + 1)(x^2 - 1)}{(x + 1)(x^2 + 1)}$

8. $\dfrac{4x(x + 1)(x^2 + 1)}{3x(x + 1)}$

In Exercises 9 through 48 perform the division. Assume the denominator is not zero.

9. (a) $\dfrac{10^7}{10^5}$ (b) $\dfrac{x^7}{x^5}$

10. (a) $\dfrac{10^{10}}{10^5}$ (b) $\dfrac{x^{10}}{x^5}$

11. (a) $\dfrac{2^{10}}{2^5}$ (b) $\dfrac{y^{10}}{y^5}$

12. (a) $\dfrac{y^3}{y^8}$ (b) $\dfrac{(xy)^3}{(xy)^8}$

13. (a) $\dfrac{3}{3^3}$ (b) $\dfrac{10}{10^3}$

14. (a) $\dfrac{10^7}{10^7}$ (b) $\dfrac{y^7}{y^7}$

15. (a) $\dfrac{-x^3}{x}$ (b) $\dfrac{-x^4}{x^6}$

16. (a) $\dfrac{12x^3}{4x^2}$ (b) $\dfrac{35x^2y}{7xy^4}$

17. (a) $\dfrac{48x^3y^6}{-96x^3y^5}$ (b) $\dfrac{84x^{10}y^7z}{26x^7y^{10}z^3}$

18. (a) $\dfrac{(2x^3)^2}{4x^4}$ (b) $\dfrac{(24x^3)^4}{6x}$

19. (a) $\left(\dfrac{42x^3}{7x^5}\right)^2$ (b) $\dfrac{2(x + 2)^3}{(x + 2)^2}$

20. $\dfrac{x^2 + 2x + 1}{x}$

21. $\dfrac{2x + 6}{2}$

22. $\dfrac{32x + 24}{8}$

23. $\dfrac{9x^2 + 12x - 21}{3}$

24. $\dfrac{10x^5 - 25x^3 + 100x}{5x}$

25. $\dfrac{a^2 + 2ab + b^2}{2ab}$

26. $\dfrac{-30a^2b^3 + 20ab^4 - 10ab}{10ab}$

27. $\dfrac{8x^2y^2 - 12xy^3 + 5xyz}{4x^3y^2}$

28. $\dfrac{x^a}{x^b}, \ a > b$

29. $\dfrac{x^a}{x^b}, \ a < b$

30. $\dfrac{x^n}{x^2}, \ n > 2$

31. $\dfrac{x^{2n}}{x^n}$

32. $\dfrac{x^{2n+3}}{x^{2n+1}}$

33. $\left(\dfrac{x^n}{x}\right)^2$

34. $\dfrac{x^2 + 4x + 4}{x + 2}$

35. $\dfrac{x^2 - 2x - 15}{x - 5}$

36. $\dfrac{x^2 - 8x + 15}{x - 5}$

37. $\dfrac{x^2}{x + 1}$

38. $\dfrac{x^2 - 1}{x + 1}$

39. $\dfrac{4x^2 + 4x + 1}{2x + 1}$

40. $\dfrac{x^2 + 1}{x + 1}$

41. $\dfrac{x^2 + 6x + 9}{x + 3}$

42. $\dfrac{x^2 - 6x + 9}{x - 3}$

43. $\dfrac{1 + 5x + 6x^2}{3x + 1}$

44. $\dfrac{4x^2 - 9}{2x + 3}$

45. $\dfrac{2x^2 + 4x + 3}{x + 1}$

46. $\dfrac{8 - x^3}{x - 2}$

47. $\dfrac{x^3 - 64}{x^2 + 4x + 16}$

48. $\dfrac{x^3 + 5x^2 + 3x - 9}{x^2 + 2x - 3}$

49. If $\dfrac{3x - 1}{2x + 7} = 1$, find x.

50. If a rectangle has an area of $(x^2 + 7x + 12)$ square units and the length is $(x + 4)$ units, find the measure of the width.

51. Divide $2x^2 + 7x + 3$ by $2x + 1$. Now replace x by 10 so that

$$2x^2 + 7x + 3 = 2 \cdot 10^2 + 7 \cdot 10 + 3$$

and

$$2x + 1 = 2 \cdot 10 + 1$$

Divide these "polynomial forms." Check by dividing 273 by 21.

52. Discuss what it means to take a square root of a polynomial and show that

$$\sqrt{x^2 + 2x + 1} = |x + 1|$$

53. The following problem is similar to Example 4 of Section 4.2 except that now you can use your knowledge of polynomials. Someone says to you, "Take a number greater than zero, add 1, square the result, subtract 1, divide this by your original number, multiply the result by 2 less than your original number, add 4, take the square root, triple the result, add 6, divide by 3, and finally subtract your original number. Now the answer is 2." Show how this works.

9.6 Review Exercises

1. (a) The coefficient of the monomial $4x^3$ is _____.
   (b) The degree of the polynomial $3x^2 + 2x - 1$ is _____.

2. (a) The degree of the monomial $4x^3$ is _____.
   (b) A polynomial with two terms is called a _____.

3. (a) Add: $\begin{array}{l} x^3 + 2x - 1 \\ 2x^3 + 4x + 6 \end{array}$ **(b)** Subtract: $\begin{array}{l} x^3 - 2x^2 + 7 \\ 2x^3 + 4x^2 - 3 \end{array}$

In Exercises 4 through 15 perform each of the indicated operations.

4. (a) $(2x^2 + 9x + 9) + (x^2 - 6x - 16)$
   (b) $(2x^2 + 9x + 9) - (x^2 - 6x - 16)$ *distributive law*

5. (a) $(x^3)(x^4)$ **(b)** $(x^3)^3$

6. (a) $(3x^5y)(4x^3y^2)$ **(b)** $(-2x^3)^6$

7. (a) $\dfrac{x^8}{x^5}$ **(b)** $\dfrac{x^4}{x^7}$

8. (a) $\dfrac{42ax^4}{12ax^3}$ **(b)** $\dfrac{-14x^2y^5}{7xy^3}$

9. (a) $4(2x - 5)$ **(b)** $2x(3x^2 - 4x + 1)$

10. (a) $(x + 1)(x + 5)$ **(b)** $(2x + 3)(x - 2)$

11. (a) $(x + 2)^2$ **(b)** $(x - y)^2$

12. (a) $(x - 1)(x^2 + x + 1)$ **(b)** $(x + 2)(x - 2)(x^2 + 4)$

13. (a) $\dfrac{ax^3 + bx^2 + cx}{x}$ **(b)** $\dfrac{4x^2 + 6x}{2x}$

14. (a) $\dfrac{x^2 + 5x + 5}{x + 2}$ **(b)** $\dfrac{2x^2 + 9x + 9}{2x + 3}$

15. (a) $\dfrac{x^3 + 1}{x + 1}$

(b) $\dfrac{8x^3 - 1}{4x^2 + 2x + 1}$

16. Write polynomial expressions for the measures of the perimeter and area of the rectangle shown in Figure 9.6.1.

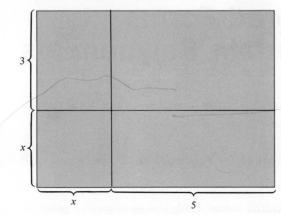

Figure 9.6.1

$A = (X + 5)(X + 3)$

$P = 4X + 16$

10

Factored Forms of Certain Polynomials

10.1 Common Factors in Polynomials

Because $10 = (5)(2)$ the numbers 5 and 2 are factors of 10. Furthermore, $(5)(2)$ is said to be a *factored form* of 10. It is also true that $(20)\left(\dfrac{1}{2}\right)$ and $(10)(1)$ are factored forms of 10. Unless otherwise indicated, in this chapter we are interested in those factored forms for which each factor is an integer, a variable, or a polynomial. Note that $(5)(2)$ is not only a factored form of 10, but also that each factor is a prime number, and recall that there is one unique prime factored form of any composite whole number.

Consider the polynomial $2x + 6$. Because

$$2x + 6 = 2(x + 3)$$

it follows that 2 and $x + 3$ are factors of $2x + 6$. Furthermore,

$$2x + 6 = 4\left(\frac{1}{2}x + \frac{3}{2}\right)$$

and so 4 and $\dfrac{1}{2}x + \dfrac{3}{2}$ can be considered as factors of $2x + 6$. However, it is customary to restrict the coefficients of the factors of a polynomial to be the same kind of number (an integer, a rational number, or a real number) as the coefficients of the given polynomial. Hence $2(x + 3)$ is considered to be the factored form of $2x + 6$. Most of our work in this book is with polynomials having integer coefficients. The process of expressing a given polynomial in completely factored form is called *factoring* the polynomial.

There are some basic kinds of factoring processes that we study. The first type consists of looking for a *common monomial factor* of all the terms of a polynomial. The basis for this process is the Distributive Law of Multiplication over Addition, that is,

$$a(x + y) = ax + ay$$

For the polynomial $ax + ay$ we observe that a is a common monomial factor of both terms. Hence we write

$$ax + ay = a(x + y)$$

Illustration 1 If we wish to factor the polynomial $2x + 10$, we examine each term for a common monomial factor. In this case, 2 is a factor of $2x$ and a factor of 10, and so 2 is a common factor. Hence,

$$2x + 10 = 2(x + 5)$$

where the factor $x + 5$ is obtained by dividing $2x + 10$ by 2.

If we wish to factor the polynomial $6x + 30$, we note that 2, 3, and 6 are common monomial factors. The greatest common monomial factor is 6 and so we write

$$6x + 30 = 6(x + 5)$$

The factor $x + 5$ has no common monomial factor except 1; hence, we say that $6(x + 5)$ is the *completely factored form* of $6x + 30$.

We adopt the following conventions when factoring polynomials with integer coefficients.

(i) Each factor is a polynomial with integer coefficients.
(ii) Each polynomial is expressed in *completely factored form,* that is,
  (a) the polynomial is a monomial, or
  (b) the polynomial is expressed in factored form and each polynomial factor other than a monomial does not have any other polynomial factors, or
  (c) the polynomial does not have any polynomial factors with integer coefficients and cannot be expressed in factored form.

Illustration 2
  (a) $3(2x + 10)$ is not the completely factored form of $6x + 30$, because the factor $2x + 10$ has the factors 2 and $x + 5$.
  (b) While $\frac{1}{x}(x^3 + x)$ is a factored form of $x^2 + 1$ it does not satisfy (i) of the above convention, because $\frac{1}{x}$ is not a polynomial.
  (c) The completely factored form of $x + 5$ is $x + 5$.
  (d) The completely factored form of the monomial $8x^2$ is $8x^2$ and we do not express $8x^2$ as $(2)(2)(2)(x)(x)$.

Example 1 Express $3x^2 + 6x$ in completely factored form.

Solution: $3x^2 + 6x = 3x(x + 2)$

Illustration 3 Suppose in Example 1, we first recognize that 3 is a common monomial factor. Then we write

$$3x^2 + 6x = 3(x^2 + 2x)$$

However, the factor $x^2 + 2x$ is not in completely factored form because x is a common monomial factor of the terms x^2 and $2x$. Therefore we continue the factoring process and obtain

$$3(x^2 + 2x) = (3)(x)(x + 2)$$

Example 2   Express $4x^3 + 12x^2 - 2x$ in completely factored form.

Solution: $4x^3 + 12x^2 - 2x = 2x(2x^2 + 6x - 1)$

To check a factoring process, determine if the given polynomial is the product of the factors.

Example 3   Express $-xy - 3y$ in completely factored form.

Solution: $-xy - 3y = y(-x - 3)$
or $-xy - 3y = -y(x + 3)$

Either of these answers is correct. However, if all of the coefficients of any polynomial factor consisting of two or more terms are negative, it is customary to express that factor in terms of its opposite. Hence, we write

$$-xy - 3y = -y(x + 3)$$

The factoring process is used to solve certain equations. Refer to Example 4.

Example 4   Solve for x: $ax + bx = c$

Solution: Express the left member of the equation in factored form.

$$ax + bx = c$$
$$x(a + b) = c$$

Dividing each member of this equation by the factor $a + b$, we have

$$x = \frac{c}{a + b}$$

In addition to common monomial factors we also look for *common binomial factors*.

Example 5   Express $x(x + 3) + 2(x + 3)$ in completely factored form.

Solution: If we temporarily let $A = x + 3$, we obtain

$$x(x + 3) + 2(x + 3) = (x)(A) + (2)(A)$$

Now A appears as a common monomial factor, and so

$$(x)(A) + (2)(A) = A(x + 2)$$

Replace A with $x + 3$ and obtain

$$A(x + 2) = (x + 3)(x + 2)$$

Therefore,

$$x(x + 3) + 2(x + 3) = (x + 3)(x + 2)$$

The use of the "dummy variable" A in the solution of Example 5 is not essential, but serves as an aid in seeing how the process is carried out.

The Distributive Law can be written in the following equivalent forms:

$$a(b + c) = ab + ac \qquad\qquad (1)$$
$$ab + ac = a(b + c) \qquad\qquad (2)$$
$$ba + ca = (b + c)a \qquad\qquad (3)$$

Because a, b, and c can be any real numbers, the Distributive Law can sometimes be used to perform operations on expressions involving radicals.

Equality (3) is used to simplify a sum of the form $ba + ca$ where a is a radical, as shown in the following illustration.

Illustration 4 $4\sqrt{3} + 7\sqrt{3} = (4 + 7)\sqrt{3} = 11\sqrt{3}$

Example 6 Simplify the following sum: $2\sqrt{x} + 3\sqrt{x} - 10\sqrt{x}$

Solution: Applying the distributive law, we have

$$2\sqrt{x} + 3\sqrt{x} - 10\sqrt{x} = (2 + 3 - 10)\sqrt{x} = -5\sqrt{x}$$

In Illustration 4 and Example 6, each term contains the same radical. Sometimes terms involving different radicals can be replaced by equivalent terms involving the same radical and then the Distributive Law can be applied. The next illustration shows such a situation.

Illustration 5 To add the two terms $3\sqrt{8} + \sqrt{50}$ we first express each radical in simplest radical form.

$$
\begin{aligned}
3\sqrt{8} + \sqrt{50} &= 3\sqrt{2^3} + \sqrt{2 \cdot 5^2} \\
&= 3\sqrt{2^2}\sqrt{2} + \sqrt{5^2}\sqrt{2} \\
&= 3 \cdot 2\sqrt{2} + 5\sqrt{2} \\
&= 6\sqrt{2} + 5\sqrt{2} \\
&= (6 + 5)\sqrt{2} \\
&= 11\sqrt{2}
\end{aligned}
$$

Example 7 Simplify the sum: $5\sqrt{x} - 3\sqrt{y} + 4\sqrt{y} - \sqrt{x}$

Solution:
$$5\sqrt{x} - 3\sqrt{y} + 4\sqrt{y} - \sqrt{x} = (5\sqrt{x} - \sqrt{x}) + (-3\sqrt{y} + 4\sqrt{y})$$
$$= (5 - 1)\sqrt{x} + (-3 + 4)\sqrt{y}$$
$$= 4\sqrt{x} + \sqrt{y}$$

Equality (1) can be used to find the product of expressions involving radicals as shown in the next two illustrations.

Illustration 6
$$\sqrt{5}(\sqrt{3} + \sqrt{7}) = \sqrt{5} \cdot \sqrt{3} + \sqrt{5} \cdot \sqrt{7}$$
$$= \sqrt{15} + \sqrt{35}$$

Illustration 7
$$(\sqrt{3} + 2)(\sqrt{3} + 4) = (\sqrt{3} + 2)\sqrt{3} + (\sqrt{3} + 2)4$$
$$= \sqrt{3}\sqrt{3} + 2\sqrt{3} + 4\sqrt{3} + 8$$
$$= 3 + (2 + 4)\sqrt{3} + 8$$
$$= 11 + 6\sqrt{3}$$

Example 8 Find the product $(\sqrt{3} + \sqrt{2})(\sqrt{3} - \sqrt{2})$

Solution:
$$(\sqrt{3} + \sqrt{2})(\sqrt{3} - \sqrt{2}) = (\sqrt{3} + \sqrt{2})\sqrt{3} + (\sqrt{3} + \sqrt{2})(-\sqrt{2})$$
$$= \sqrt{3}\sqrt{3} + \sqrt{2}\sqrt{3} - \sqrt{3}\sqrt{2} - \sqrt{2}\sqrt{2}$$
$$= 3 + \sqrt{6} - \sqrt{6} - 2$$
$$= 1$$

Exercises 10.1

In Exercises 1 through 10 write each expression in completely factored form by finding a common factor.

1. (a) $3x + 12$ (b) $45x + 60y$

2. (a) $ax^2 + bx - cx^2 + dx$ (b) $\pi A - \pi B$

3. (a) $xy^2 - x^2y$ (b) $3x^2 + 18x + 30$

4. (a) $10x^2y - 15xy^2 + 5xy$ (b) $x(x - 2) + 3(x - 2)$

5. (a) $a(x + y) + b(x + y)$ (b) $x^4 + 2x^3$

6. (a) $ax + bx - cx$ (b) $-3x - 6$

7. (a) $-x^2 - x$ (b) $\pi r^2 + 2\pi r$

8. (a) $64t - 16t^2$ (b) $x^3 - x^2 + x$

9. (a) $8x^3 - 24x^2 - 4x$ (b) $x(x - 1) - 4(x - 1)$

10. (a) $x^2 + 5x + 10x + 50$ (Hint: Group the first two terms and the last two terms. Find a common factor in each group, and then look for a common binomial factor.)

(b) $x(x + 1) + x + 1$

In Exercises 11 through 16 solve the equation for x.

11. $ax - bx = 10$

12. $x - \pi x = 3$

13. $ax + bx = a + b$

14. $ax + 5 = bx + 7$

15. $x\sqrt{2} - x\sqrt{3} = \sqrt{8} - \sqrt{12}$

16. $ax + bx + cx = m$

In Exercises 17 through 25 simplify each expression.

17. (a) $2\sqrt{5} + 3\sqrt{5}$

(b) $5\sqrt{3} + 6\sqrt{3}$

18. (a) $9\sqrt{2} - 4\sqrt{2}$

(b) $5\sqrt{x} + \sqrt{x} - 7\sqrt{x}$

19. (a) $x\sqrt{3} + 2x\sqrt{3}$

(b) $5\sqrt{y} + 4\sqrt{x} - 8\sqrt{y}$

20. (a) $\sqrt{50} + 3\sqrt{2}$

(b) $\sqrt{50} + \sqrt{18}$

21. (a) $\sqrt{75} - \sqrt{48}$

(b) $\sqrt{27} + 3\sqrt{12}$

22. (a) $\sqrt{3}(\sqrt{12} + \sqrt{27})$

(b) $2\sqrt{5}(\sqrt{5} + 2)$

23. (a) $\sqrt{6}(\sqrt{6} + \sqrt{3})$

(b) $\sqrt{2}(\sqrt{6} + \sqrt{8} + \sqrt{10})$

24. (a) $(\sqrt{7} + 2)(\sqrt{7} - 2)$

(b) $(\sqrt{3} + 5)^2$

25. (a) $(\sqrt{8} + \sqrt{3})(\sqrt{2} + \sqrt{3})$

(b) $(\sqrt{10} + \sqrt{7})(\sqrt{10} - \sqrt{7})$

26. Show that $(\sqrt{5} - 2)(\sqrt{5} + 2) = 1$ and, hence, $(\sqrt{5} - 2)$ is the reciprocal of $(\sqrt{5} + 2)$. That is,

$$\sqrt{5} - 2 = \frac{1}{\sqrt{5} + 2}$$

10.2 The Difference of Two Squares

In this section we consider the factored form of polynomials known as the *difference of two squares*. The polynomial $x^2 - 9$ is an example of the difference of two squares because

$$x^2 - 9 = x^2 - 3^2$$

The factored form of $x^2 - 9$ is $(x - 3)(x + 3)$; hence,

$$x^2 - 9 = (x - 3)(x + 3) \tag{1}$$

Equality (1) is verified by multiplying the factors in the right member.

Illustration 1 The product of the sum and difference of any two numbers is always equal to the difference of their squares. For instance, consider the two numbers 8 and 5. The sum of 8 and 5 is 13 and the difference of 8 and 5 is 3. The product of the sum and difference of 8 and 5 is $(13)(3) = 39$.

The square of 8 is 64 and the square of 5 is 25. The difference of the two squares is

$$64 - 25 = 39$$

In other words,

$$8^2 - 5^2 = (8 + 5)(8 - 5)$$

The difference $a - b$ is always a factor of the difference $a^n - b^n$. The factored forms below reveal this pattern.

$$x^2 - y^2 = (x - y)(x + y)$$
$$x^3 - y^3 = (x - y)(x^2 + xy + y^2)$$
$$x^4 - y^4 = (x - y)(x^3 + x^2y + xy^2 + y^3)$$
$$x^5 - y^5 = (x - y)(x^4 + x^3y + x^2y^2 + xy^3 + y^4)$$
$$\vdots \qquad \vdots$$

and so on. We can use these forms to factor the difference of two powers.

Example 1 Express $a^2 - 16$ in completely factored form.

Solution: $a^2 - 16$ is the difference of two squares, that is

$$a^2 - 16 = a^2 - 4^2$$

Hence,

$$a^2 - 16 = (a - 4)(a + 4)$$

Example 2 Express $x^3 - 4x$ in completely factored form.

Solution: x^3 and $4x$ have a common monomial factor of x. Thus,

$$x^3 - 4x = x(x^2 - 4)$$

This is not the completely factored form, because $x^2 - 4$ is the difference of two squares. Therefore, we write

$$x^3 - 4x = x(x - 2)(x + 2)$$

In Example 2 we use a process that we wish to emphasize. A common monomial factor is first found if there is one. After this is done, the other factor is investigated to determine if it can be further expressed in factored form.

Example 3 The area of a ring can be found by subtracting the area of the inner circle from the area of the outer circle. See Figure 10.2.1. The measure of the area of the ring is given by $\pi R^2 - \pi r^2$. Express this binomial in factored form.

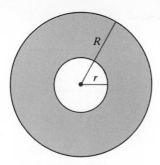

Figure 10.2.1

Solution:
$$\pi R^2 - \pi r^2 = \pi(R^2 - r^2)$$
$$= \pi(R - r)(R + r)$$

Example 4 Express $x^2(x + 1) - (x + 1)$ in completely factored form.

$$(x+1)[x^2-1]$$

Solution: We recognize the common binomial factor $(x + 1)$.

$$\begin{aligned}
x^2(x + 1) - (x + 1) &= x^2(x + 1) - (1)(x + 1)\\
&= (x + 1)(x^2 - 1)\\
&= (x + 1)(x + 1)(x - 1)\\
&= (x + 1)^2(x - 1)
\end{aligned}$$

Illustration 2 Given the product

$$(a - b)(a + b) = a^2 - b^2$$

it follows that

$$(\sqrt{3} - \sqrt{2})(\sqrt{3} + \sqrt{2}) = 3 - 2$$
$$= 1$$

Note that this product is a rational number.

Each of the two factors $(a - b)$ and $(a + b)$ in Illustration 2 is called the *conjugate* of the other factor. For instance, the factors $(\sqrt{3} - \sqrt{2})$ and $(\sqrt{3} + \sqrt{2})$ are the conjugates of each other. The concept of the conjugate is used to rationalize the denominator of a fraction when the denominator is a binomial containing a radical in either or both of the two terms.

Illustration 3 To rationalize the denominator of the fraction

$$\frac{3}{\sqrt{3} + 1}$$

we multiply both the numerator and denominator by the conjugate of the denominator and we have

$$\frac{3}{\sqrt{3}+1} = \frac{3(\sqrt{3}-1)}{(\sqrt{3}+1)(\sqrt{3}-1)}$$

$$= \frac{3\sqrt{3}-3}{3-1}$$

$$= \frac{3\sqrt{3}-3}{2}$$

Example 5 Rationalize the denominator of the fraction

$$\frac{\sqrt{5}-2\sqrt{3}}{3\sqrt{2}-\sqrt{5}}$$

Solution:

$$\frac{\sqrt{5}-2\sqrt{3}}{3\sqrt{2}-\sqrt{5}} = \frac{(\sqrt{5}-2\sqrt{3})(3\sqrt{2}+\sqrt{5})}{(3\sqrt{2}-\sqrt{5})(3\sqrt{2}+\sqrt{5})}$$

$$= \frac{(\sqrt{5}-2\sqrt{3})(3\sqrt{2})+(\sqrt{5}-2\sqrt{3})\sqrt{5}}{(3\sqrt{2})^2-(\sqrt{5})^2}$$

$$= \frac{3\sqrt{5}\sqrt{2}-6\sqrt{3}\sqrt{2}+\sqrt{5}\sqrt{5}-2\sqrt{3}\sqrt{5}}{9\cdot2-5}$$

$$= \frac{3\sqrt{10}-6\sqrt{6}+5-2\sqrt{15}}{18-5}$$

$$= \frac{3\sqrt{10}-6\sqrt{6}-2\sqrt{15}+5}{13}$$

Exercises 10.2

In Exercises 1 through 7 express the difference of two powers in completely factored form.

1. (a) x^2-1 (b) a^2-b^2

2. (a) $4x^2-9$ (b) y^2-25

3. (a) x^2y^2-1 (b) m^2-9

4. (a) A^2-16 (b) $(a+b)^2-4$

5. (a) x^3-1 (b) x^7-y^7

6. (a) $36-x^2$ (b) $64-25x^2$

7. x^4-1 (Hint: $x^4-1=(x^2)^2-1^2$. Let $A=x^2$ so that $(x^2)^2-1^2=A^2-1$. Now find the factored form of A^2-1 and replace A with x^2.)

8. If $x^4-1=(x-1)(x^3+x^2+x+1)$ and
   $x^4-1=(x-1)(x+1)(x^2+1)$

what conclusion can you make about the factored form of $x^3 + x^2 + x + 1$?

In Exercises 9 through 19 first find a common monomial factor, if there is one, and then write each polynomial in completely factored form.

9. $3x^2 - 75$ 10. $2x^3 - 8x$

11. $t^3 - t$ 12. $2x^3 - 16$

13. $10 - 10y^4$ 14. $x^3y - xy^3$

15. $x^8 - y^4$ 16. $2x^3 + 2x^2 + 2x$

17. $16x^2 - 36$ 18. $64t^2 - 16t^3$

19. $2x^2y^2 - 32$

20. We can find the product of 29 and 31 by multiplying $(30 - 1)$ and $(30 + 1)$. That is,

$$
\begin{aligned}
29 \cdot 31 &= (30 - 1)(30 + 1) \\
&= 30^2 - 1^2 \\
&= 900 - 1 \\
&= 899
\end{aligned}
$$

Use this method to find the following products: **(a)** $28 \cdot 32$; **(b)** $47 \cdot 53$; **(c)** $19 \cdot 21$; **(d)** $25 \cdot 35$.

In Exercises 21 through 26 the number of square units in the area of the colored region of each figure is given by the formula. Write each formula in completely factored form.

21. See Figure 10.2.2: $A = x^2 - y^2$.

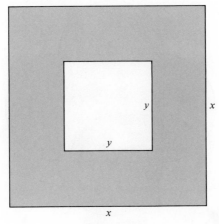

Figure 10.2.2

22. See Figure 10.2.3: $A = xy - 2y$.

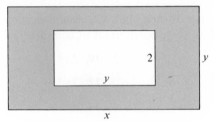

Figure 10.2.3

23. See Figure 10.2.4: $A = (2r)^2 + \dfrac{1}{2}\pi r^2$.

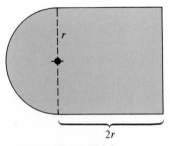

Figure 10.2.4

24. See Figure 10.2.5: $A = (2r)^2 + 4\left(\dfrac{1}{2}\pi r^2\right)$.

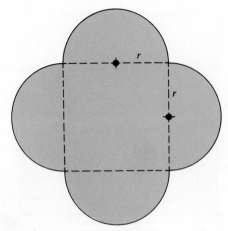

Figure 10.2.5

25. See Figure 10.2.6: $A = (x + 4)(y + 4) - xy$. (Hint: Multiply, combine terms, and then express in factored form.)

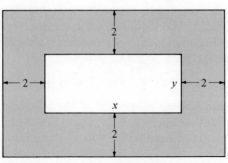

Figure 10.2.6

to here

26. See Figure 10.2.7: $A = \pi r^2 - 2r^2$.

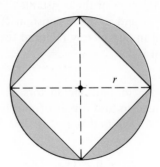

Figure 10.2.7

27. Find the number of square units in the area of the shaded region in Figure 10.2.2 if $x = 1.895649735$ and $y = 0.895649735$. [Hint: $x^2 - y^2 = (x + y)(x - y)$.]

In Exercises 28 through 33 rationalize the denominator of the fraction.

28. $\dfrac{1}{\sqrt{5} - 1}$ **29.** $\dfrac{\sqrt{3}}{\sqrt{3} + 2}$ **30.** $\dfrac{1}{\sqrt{5} + \sqrt{2}}$

31. $\dfrac{7}{5 + \sqrt{2}}$ **32.** $\dfrac{\sqrt{6} + 4}{\sqrt{6} - 4}$ **33.** $\dfrac{\sqrt{5} - 3}{2\sqrt{3} - \sqrt{2}}$

34. Show that if $n \geq 0$, $(\sqrt{n + 1} - \sqrt{n})(\sqrt{n + 1} + \sqrt{n}) = 1$.

35. Show that if $a \geq 1$, $(\sqrt{a} + \sqrt{a - 1})(\sqrt{a} - \sqrt{a - 1}) = 1$.

10.3 Factoring Trinomials in a Single Variable

The type of polynomial discussed in this section is a second degree trinomial in a single variable with integer coefficients. We are interested in expressing such polynomials in completely factored form. We consider two cases: trinomials whose leading monomial has a coefficient equal to 1 and trinomials whose leading monomial does not have a coefficient equal to 1.

Consider first the factors $x + 2$ and $x + 3$.

$$(x + 2)(x + 3) = x^2 + 5x + 6$$

The coefficient of the leading monomial of the trinomial $x^2 + 5x + 6$ is 1 and we may note that the coefficient 5 is equal to the sum of the constants 2 and 3 and that the coefficient 6 is equal to the product of 2 and 3. In general, consider the factors $(x + r_1)$ and $(x + r_2)$ where r_1 and r_2 are constants. Then we have

$$\begin{aligned}(x + r_1)(x + r_2) &= x(x + r_2) + r_1(x + r_2) \\ &= x^2 + xr_2 + r_1x + r_1r_2 \\ &= x^2 + x(r_2 + r_1) + r_1r_2\end{aligned}$$

Thus, we conclude that the sum of the constants r_1 and r_2 is the coefficient of x and the product of r_1 and r_2 is the constant coefficient. We use these facts to write a trinomial in completely factored form when the coefficient of the leading monomial is 1.

Illustration 1 If we wish to find the factors $(x + r_1)$ and $(x + r_2)$, of $x^2 + 5x + 6$, then we need to find a pair of numbers, r_1 and r_2, such that $r_1 + r_2 = 5$ and $r_1r_2 = 6$. We find that $2 + 3 = 5$ and $2 \cdot 3 = 6$. Thus, we write

$$x^2 + 5x + 6 = (x + 2)(x + 3)$$

This can be checked by multiplying $(x + 2)$ by $(x + 3)$.

Illustration 2 If we wish to express $x^2 - 5x + 6$ in completely factored form, then we need to find a pair of numbers, r_1 and r_2, such that $r_1 + r_2 = -5$ and $r_1 \cdot r_2 = 6$. These numbers are -2 and -3. Hence,

$$x^2 - 5x + 6 = (x - 2)(x - 3)$$

Example 1 Express $x^2 + 7x + 10$ in completely factored form.

Solution: Because $(5)(2) = 10$ and $5 + 2 = 7$, we write

$$x^2 + 7x + 10 = (x + 5)(x + 2)$$

Example 2 Express $x^3 + x^2 - 6x$ in completely factored form.

Solution: First we notice a common monomial factor of x. Thus,

$$x^3 + x^2 - 6x = x(x^2 + x - 6)$$

To express $x^2 + x - 6$ in factored form we need a pair of numbers whose sum is 1 and whose product is -6. These numbers are 3 and -2. Therefore,

$$x^3 + x^2 - 6x = x(x^2 + x - 6)$$
$$= x(x + 3)(x - 2)$$

Example 3 Express $2x^2 - 10x - 12$ in completely factored form.

Solution: The leading coefficient is not 1; however, there is a common monomial factor of 2.

$$2x^2 - 10x - 12 = 2(x^2 - 5x - 6)$$

To determine if $x^2 - 5x - 6$ can be expressed in factored form we need a pair of numbers whose sum is -5 and whose product is -6. The only possible pairs must be factors of -6 and these are -3 and 2, 3 and -2, -1 and 6, 1 and -6. The sum of the last pair of numbers is -5. Therefore,

$$2x^2 - 10x - 12 = 2(x^2 - 5x - 6)$$
$$= 2(x + 1)(x - 6)$$

Not all trinomials can be expressed in this manner as the product of two binomials. For example, $x^2 + x + 1$ cannot be expressed in a factored form such as $(x + r_1)(x + r_2)$ where r_1 and r_2 are integers, because we cannot find two integers, r_1 and r_2, whose sum is 1 and whose product is 1. The trinomial $x^2 + x + 1$ is said to be in completely factored form as it is.

Now we consider trinomials for which the coefficient of the leading monomial is not 1. Such a trinomial has the form $ax^2 + bx + c$, where $a \neq 0$ and $a \neq 1$. We first analyze the multiplication of two first degree binomials and introduce some terminology. Consider the product of the binomials $(2x + 3)$ and $(4x + 5)$.

$$(2x + 3)(4x + 5) = 2x(4x + 5) + 3(4x + 5)$$
$$= 8x^2 + 10x + 12x + 15$$
$$= 8x^2 + 22x + 15$$

We look at the four terms of the product $8x^2 + 10x + 12x + 15$. The term $8x^2$ is the product of $2x$ and $4x$ (the leading terms of the binomials) and 15 is the product of 3 and 5 (the constants of the binomials).

The terms $10x$ and $12x$ are combined to give the *middle term* of the trinomial

$22x$. The terms $2x$ and 5 are called the *outer terms* of the binomials and their product $10x$ is called the *outer product*. The terms 3 and $4x$ are called the *inner terms* of the binomials and their product $12x$ is called the *inner product*. These words describe relative positions only and depend upon the way the polynomials are written.

Outer product

Inner product

When we wish to factor a trinomial we look at the possible inner and outer terms to determine which combination, if any, will give the inner and outer products that can be combined to give the middle term of the trinomial. This determination can be accomplished by trial and error or in a more systematic manner. The next example illustrates the trial and error procedure.

Example 4   Express $3x^2 + 8x + 4$ in completely factored form.

Solution: The only possible leading terms of the binomial factors are x and $3x$; however, the constants of the binomial factors may be either 2 and 2, or 4 and 1. Thus, we write the possible binomial factors:

$$(x + 2)(3x + 2)$$
$$(x + 1)(3x + 4)$$

or

$$(x + 4)(3x + 1)$$

Of these factored forms the first form has an outer product of $2x$ and an inner product of $6x$. The combination of $2x$ and $6x$ gives $8x$, which is precisely the middle term of the trinomial $3x^2 + 8x + 4$. Therefore, we write

$$3x^2 + 8x + 4 = (x + 2)(3x + 2)$$

Suppose now that we wish to express $8x^2 + 22x + 15$ in completely factored form. If we approach this problem with the trial and error procedure, we find eight possible factored forms, only one of which can be correct. A more systematic procedure for factoring $8x^2 + 22x + 15$ is now outlined in the following steps:

Step 1. Find the product of the coefficient of the leading monomial and the constant of the trinomial $8x^2 + 22x + 15$. Thus,

$$(8)(15) = 120$$

Step 2. List all of the possible factored forms of this product.

$$\begin{array}{l} (1)(120) \\ (2)(60) \\ (3)(40) \\ (4)(30) \\ (5)(24) \\ (6)(20) \\ (8)(15) \\ (10)(12) \\ \text{- - - - -} \leftarrow \\ (12)(10) \end{array}$$

At this point we begin repeating factors that we already have.

Step 3. If the sign before the constant is +, then add each pair of factors found in step 2. If the sign before the constant is −, then find the difference of each pair of the factors found in step 2.

The sign before the constant, 15 in this case, is +. Thus, we add each pair of factors found in step 2.

$$\begin{array}{l} 1 + 120 = 121 \\ 2 + 60 = 62 \\ 3 + 40 = 43 \\ 4 + 30 = 34 \\ 5 + 24 = 29 \\ 6 + 20 = 26 \\ 8 + 15 = 23 \\ 10 + 12 = 22 \end{array}$$

These sums represent all the possible coefficients that the middle term of the polynomial can have if, in fact, the polynomial $8x^2 + \underline{}x + 15$ can be expressed in factored form. If the coefficient of x is a number other than those above, then the polynomial cannot be expressed in a factored form with integer coefficients.

Step 4. Look among the sums (or differences) found in step 3 for the coefficient of the middle term of the given polynomial (22 in this case). The numbers that gave this coefficient are the coefficients of the outer and inner products of the binomial factors that we seek (10 and 12 in this case).

Step 5. Choose one of these numbers to be the coefficient of the outer product and one to be the coefficient of the inner product, multiply each one by the variable (x in this case), and write the given polynomial with the middle term replaced by the sum (or difference) of the outer and inner products as found in step 4.

$$8x^2 + 10x + 12x + 15$$

Step 6. (a) Group the first two terms and the last two terms of the polynomial formed in step 5.

(b) Find the common monomial factor of the first two terms of this polynomial ($2x$ in this case).

(c) Find the common monomial factor of the last two terms of this same polynomial (3 in this case).

(d) Express these parts of the polynomial in factored form.

$$8x^2 + 10x + 12x + 15 = (8x^2 + 10x) + (12x + 15)$$
$$= 2x(4x + 5) + 3(4x + 5)$$

Step 7. Now there is a common binomial factor in the expression formed in step 6. Use this common binomial factor as one of the factors to express the polynomial in factored form.

$$8x^2 + 10x + 12x + 15 = (8x^2 + 10x) + (12x + 15)$$
$$= 2x(4x + 5) + 3(4x + 5)$$
$$= (2x + 3)(4x + 5)$$

Example 5 Express $6x^2 + 13x - 15$ in completely factored form.

Solution: Follow steps 1 through 7 outlined above.

1. $(6)(15) = 90$
2. Factors of 90 are 1 and 90, 2 and 45, 3 and 30, 5 and 18, 6 and 15, 9 and 10.
3. $90 - 1 = 89$ and $1 - 90 = -89$
   $45 - 2 = 43$ and $2 - 45 = -43$
   $30 - 3 = 27$ and $3 - 30 = -27$
   $18 - 5 = 13$ and $5 - 18 = -13$
   $15 - 6 = 9$ and $6 - 15 = -9$
   $10 - 9 = 1$ and $9 - 10 = -1$
4. We find the coefficient of the middle term of the given polynomial $13 = 18 - 5$. Therefore we write

$$13x = 18x - 5x$$

5. $6x^2 + 13x - 15 = 6x^2 + 18x - 5x - 15$
6. $ = 6x(x + 3) - 5(x + 3)$
7. $ = (x + 3)(6x - 5)$

Therefore,

$$6x^2 + 13x - 15 = (x + 3)(6x - 5)$$

In all cases, when attempting to express a polynomial in factored form, examine it first for a common monomial factor.

Example 6 Express $x^3 + 5x^2 - 36x$ in completely factored form.

Solution: First we notice that there is a common monomial factor of x. Then we write the trinomial as the product of two first degree binomials.

$$x^3 + 5x^2 - 36x = x(x^2 + 5x - 36)$$
$$= x(x + 9)(x - 4)$$

Example 7 Express $a^2 + 2ab + b^2$ in completely factored form.

Solution: We may think of $a^2 + 2ab + b^2$ as a second degree (quadratic) polynomial in a. Hence, we need a pair of numbers whose sum is $2b$ and whose product is b^2. These numbers are b and b. Thus

$$a^2 + 2ab + b^2 = (a + b)(a + b)$$
$$= (a + b)^2$$

As previously stated, a quadratic trinomial whose factored form is the square of a binomial (such as the one in Example 7) is called a *perfect square trinomial*. A perfect square trinomial always has the form

$$a^2 + 2ab + b^2$$

See Figure 9.4.1. The first and third terms are the squares of a and b, and the middle term is twice the product of the terms a and b.

Example 8 Determine if $x^2 + 6x + 9$ is a perfect square trinomial.

Solution: The first term is the square of x and the third term is the square of 3 and the middle term is 2 times $(3)(x)$. Therefore $x^2 + 6x + 9$ is a perfect square trinomial.

$$x^2 + 6x + 9 = (x + 3)^2$$

Example 9 What term must be added to $x^2 + 8x$ so that we obtain a perfect square trinomial?

Solution: The middle term is $8x$, which equals $(2)(4x)$. Hence, one half of the coefficient of x is 4 and the square of 4 is 16. Thus, 16 is the term we should add. We have then

$$x^2 + 8x + \underline{\ 16\ }$$

which is a perfect square trinomial.

We refer to the procedure used in the solution of Example 9 as *completing the square.*

Exercises 10.3

In Exercises 1 through 4 supply the missing signs ($+$ or $-$) so that each factored form is correct.

1. $x^2 + 6x + 9 = (x \quad 3)(x \quad 3)$

2. $x^2 - 10x - 24 = (x \quad 12)(x \quad 2)$

3. $x^2 + 10x + 24 = (x \quad 6)(x \quad 4)$

4. $x^2 + 10x - 24 = (x \quad 12)(x \quad 2)$

In Exercises 5 through 10 supply the missing factor.

5. $x^2 + 8x + 16 = (x + 4)(\qquad)$

6. $x^2 - 14x + 49 = (x - 7)(\qquad)$

7. $x^2 - 9x + 20 = (x - 5)(\qquad)$

8. $x^2 + 12x + 32 = (x + 4)(\qquad)$

9. $2x^2 + 13x + 15 = (x + 5)(\qquad)$

10. $4t^2 - 12t + 9 = (2t - 3)(\qquad)$

In Exercises 11 through 34 express the trinomial in completely factored form.

11. $x^2 - 12x + 36$ **12.** $y^2 + 8y + 16$

13. $x^2 + 7x + 12$ **14.** $x^2 + 10x + 24$

15. $x^2 - 10x - 24$ **16.** $x^2 + 9x + 8$

17. $x^2 + 10x - 24$ *wrong ans*   **18.** $x^2 + 11x + 24$

19. $x^2 + 36 + 13x$ **20.** $36 - 12x + x^2$

21. $x^2 + 2xy + y^2$ **22.** $x^2 - 2xy + y^2$

23. $x^2 - 2x - 8$ **24.** $7x^2 - 9x + 2$

25. $6x^2 + 19x + 15$ **26.** $2x^2 + 13x + 15$

27. $6x^2 + x - 15$ **28.** $-50 + 60t - 16t^2$

29. $10x^2 - 21x + 8$ **30.** $3x^2 + 5x - 12$

31. $2x^2 + 12x + 18$ **32.** $3x^2 + 33x - 72$

33. $10x^3 - 20x^2 + 10x$ **34.** $ax^2 + 2ax + a$

In Exercises 35 through 37 determine if each polynomial is a perfect square trinomial.

35. (a) $x^2 + 2x + 1$ **(b)** $x^2 + 4x + 4$

36. (a) $x^2 + 10x + 10$ **(b)** $x^2 - 10x + 25$

37. (a) $x^2 + 5x + 16$ **(b)** $x^2 - 2xy + y^2$

In Exercises 38 through 44, **(a)** find the missing term so that the given polynomial will be a perfect square trinomial; that is, complete the square; **(b)** express each trinomial as the square of a binomial.

38. $x^2 + 2x + \underline{\qquad}$ **39.** $x^2 - 2x + \underline{\qquad}$

$(x - 1)^2$

40. $x^2 + 8x +$ _____

41. $x^2 + 12x +$ _____

42. $x^2 - 10x +$ _____ ²⁵

43. $x^2 + 14x +$ _____

44. $x^2 + 3x +$ _____

45. The number of square units in the area of a rectangle is given by the trinomial $x^2 + 12x + 27$. The length and width of the rectangle are known to be integral numbers of units. If $x = 10$, what are the measures of the length and width?

46. Show that $(x - \sqrt{2})(x + \sqrt{2})$ is a factored form of $x^2 - 2$. Why is this not considered to be the completely factored form of $x^2 - 2$?

47. Show that $(x + 3 - \sqrt{6x})(x + 3 + \sqrt{6x})$ is a factored form of $x^2 + 9$. Why is this not considered to be the completely factored form of $x^2 + 9$?

10.4 Review Exercises

In Exercises 1 and 2 write each expression in completely factored form by finding a common factor.

1. (a) $4x^2 - 48$ **(b)** $6y^3 - 30y^2 + 18y$

2. (a) $x(x + 2) + 3(x + 2)$ **(b)** $x(x - 2) + x - 2$

3. Simplify each expression:
(a) $12\sqrt{3} - 7\sqrt{3}$ **(b)** $\sqrt{50} + \sqrt{72}$

4. Solve each equation for x:
(a) $mx - nx = 4$ **(b)** $ax + b = bx + a$

$x = \dfrac{4}{m-n}$

In Exercises 5 through 7 write each expression in completely factored form.

5. (a) $4x^2 - 1$ **(b)** $m^2 - n^2$

6. (a) $3x^3 - 27x$ **(b)** $n^4 - 16$

7. (a) $(x + 3)^2 - 4$ **(b)** $4x^2 - 64$

8. The formula for the measure of the volume of the solid shown in Figure 10.4.1 on page 368 is $V = \pi R^2 h - \pi r^2 h$. Write the formula in completely factored form.

9. Rationalize the denominator of each fraction:

(a) $\dfrac{1}{\sqrt{2} - 1}$ **(b)** $\dfrac{4}{\sqrt{5} + \sqrt{3}}$

In Exercises 10 through 12 write each expression in completely factored form.

10. (a) $x^2 + 10x + 24$ **(b)** $y^2 - y - 12$

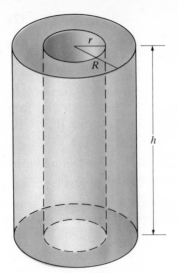

Figure 10.4.1 (Exercise 8)

11. (a) $4x^2 + 16x - 9$ **(b)** $y^2 - 13y + 36$

12. (a) $10x^3y - 15x^2y + 5xy$ **(b)** $8t^2 - 24t + 18$

13. Complete the square for each of the polynomials:

     (a) $x^2 + 10x +$ _____   **(b)** $x^2 - 20x +$ _____

11

Quadratic Equations

11.1 Introduction to Quadratic Equations

If a, b, and c are constants, $a \neq 0$, and x is a variable, then the expressions

$$ax + b \quad \text{and} \quad ax - b$$

are called "first degree expressions." If these expressions are set equal to some number c, then the resulting equations

$$ax + b = c \quad \text{and} \quad ax - b = c$$

are called "first degree equations." Solving the equation $ax + b = c$, we obtain

$$x = \frac{c - b}{a}$$

and solving the equation $ax - b = c$, we get

$$x = \frac{c + b}{a}$$

Illustration 1 $3x + 2$ is a first degree expression and $3x + 2 = 14$ is a first degree equation, with a solution

$$x = \frac{14 - 2}{3}$$

or, equivalently,

$$x = 4$$

If we take two first degree expressions and multiply them, we get a "second degree expression." Thus, if $a \neq 0$ and $c \neq 0$, then

$$(ax + b)(cx + d) \tag{1}$$

is a second degree expression.

Illustration 2 $(4x + 3)(x - 2)$ is a second degree expression which is like expression (1) where $a = 4$ and $c = 1$. If in (1) $a = 0$, then the expression

$ax + b$ becomes

$$(0)x + b = 0 + b = b$$

and, hence the product

$$(ax + b)(cx + d)$$

becomes

$$b(cx + d)$$

or

$$bcx + bd$$

another first degree expression. That is why the restriction that $a \neq 0$ and $c \neq 0$ is necessary in defining a second degree expression.

When we set expression (1) equal to some number e, then

$$(ax + b)(cx + d) = e$$

is called a "second degree equation." The solution of this equation involves some rather intricate transformations, most of which are familiar to you; however, we postpone finding the solution of this general case until Section 11.2. On the other hand, if we consider the special case of this equation when $e = 0$, then we discover a rather simple method of solution.

The solution of

$$(ax + b)(cx + d) = 0 \qquad (2)$$

depends on a property of zero called the Zero Product Property.

11.1.1 Theorem (Zero Product Property)   If E_1 and E_2 are two expressions and

$$E_1 \cdot E_2 = 0$$

then either $E_1 = 0$ or $E_2 = 0$.

Example 1   Solve

$$(2x - 3)(4x - 1) = 0$$

and check the solution.

Solution: Given $(2x - 3)(4x - 1) = 0$, then by the Zero Product Property (Theorem 11.1.1), we have

$$2x - 3 = 0$$

or

$$4x - 1 = 0$$

If
$$2x - 3 = 0$$
then
$$2x = 3$$
and so
$$x = \frac{3}{2}$$
If
$$4x - 1 = 0$$
then
$$4x = 1$$
and so
$$x = \frac{1}{4}$$

The solutions are $\frac{3}{2}$ and $\frac{1}{4}$.

The check is as follows: if $x = \frac{3}{2}$, then

$$(2x - 3)(4x - 1) = \left(2 \cdot \frac{3}{2} - 3\right)\left(4 \cdot \frac{3}{2} - 1\right)$$
$$= (3 - 3)(6 - 1)$$
$$= (0)(5)$$
$$= 0$$

If $x = \frac{1}{4}$, then

$$(2x - 3)(4x - 1) = \left(2 \cdot \frac{1}{4} - 3\right)\left(4 \cdot \frac{1}{4} - 1\right)$$
$$= \left(2 \cdot \frac{1}{4} - 3\right)(1 - 1)$$
$$= \left(\frac{1}{2} - 3\right)(0)$$
$$= 0$$

Because 0 is the desired result in both cases we say that both $\frac{3}{2}$ and $\frac{1}{4}$ are solutions.

There are, in general, two solutions for a second degree equation. The solutions of an equation are sometimes called the *roots* of the equation. The two roots of the second degree equation (2) are derived from the two factors in the left member of that equation. Because these factors are not necessarily distinct from one another, the number of distinct roots of equation (2) may be either 1 or 2. Example 2 demonstrates a second degree equation with one distinct solution.

Example 2 Solve the equation: $(2x - 8)^2 = 0$.

Solution: Because

$$(2x - 8)^2 = (2x - 8)(2x - 8)$$

we have the second degree equation

$$(2x - 8)(2x - 8) = 0$$

Therefore, because of the Zero Product Property

$$2x - 8 = 0 \quad \text{or} \quad 2x - 8 = 0$$

or, more simply,

$$2x - 8 = 0$$
$$2x = 8$$
$$x = 4$$

Thus, 4 is the only solution.

If the solution of a second degree equation consists of one distinct root, that solution is sometimes called a *double root*. The solution 4, of the second degree equation in Example 2, is a double root of that equation. With the understanding that some second degree equations have double roots, we state that every second degree equation has two roots.

Example 3 Solve the equation: $x^2 - 8x + 12 = 0$

Solution: Express the left member of the equation in factored form and use the Zero Product Property.

$$x^2 - 8x + 12 = 0$$
$$(x - 6)(x - 2) = 0$$

Therefore,

$$x - 6 = 0 \quad \text{or} \quad x - 2 = 0$$

and so

$$x = 6 \quad \text{or} \quad x = 2$$

Therefore, the solution set is $\{2, 6\}$.

The equation in Example 3 is a second degree equation, and this equation is also called a "quadratic equation."

In Section 9.1 we defined a quadratic polynomial in x (Definition 9.1.6). The standard form for such a polynomial is

$$ax^2 + bx + c$$

where $a \neq 0$ and a, b, and c are real numbers. If this polynomial is set equal to zero (or any real number), then we have a quadratic equation (or second degree equation).

11.1.2 Definition   If a, b, and c are real numbers and $a > 0$, then the equation

$$ax^2 + bx + c = 0$$

is a *quadratic equation in standard form.*

Illustration 3   The quadratic equation $-x^2 - 6x = 9$, or equivalently, $-x^2 - 6x - 9 = 0$, is expressed in standard form if we multiply each member by -1. Thus, we have

$$x^2 + 6x + 9 = 0$$

which is a quadratic equation in standard form, where $a = 1$, $b = 6$, and $c = 9$.

Example 4   Solve the equation: $16t - 64t^2 = 0$

Solution: Express the left member of the equation in factored form and use the Zero Product Property.

$$16t - 64t^2 = 0$$
$$16t(1 - 4t) = 0$$

Therefore,

$$16t = 0 \quad \text{or} \quad 1 - 4t = 0$$

and so

$$t = 0 \quad \text{or} \quad t = \frac{1}{4}$$

Hence, the solution set is $\left\{0, \dfrac{1}{4}\right\}$.

Example 5   Solve the equation: $x^2 = 9$

Solution:

$$x^2 = 9$$
$$x^2 - 9 = 0$$
$$(x - 3)(x + 3) = 0$$

Therefore,

$$x - 3 = 0 \quad \text{or} \quad x + 3 = 0$$

and so

$$x = 3 \quad \text{or} \quad x = -3$$

The solution set is $\{3, -3\}$.

Example 6   Solve the proportion: $2 : x = x : 8$

Solution: Because the product of the means equals the product of the extremes, we have

$$x^2 = 16$$

Solving this equation we have

$$x^2 - 16 = 0$$
$$(x - 4)(x + 4) = 0$$

Therefore,

$$x - 4 = 0 \quad \text{or} \quad x + 4 = 0$$

and so

$$x = 4 \quad \text{or} \quad x = -4$$

Hence, the solution set is $\{4, -4\}$.

Example 7   One number is three less than two times a second number. The product of the two numbers is 5. Find the two numbers.

Solution: Let x = the first number.
   Then $2x - 3$ = the second number.
The equation is

$$x(2x - 3) = 5$$

Solving this equation we have

$$2x^2 - 3x = 5$$
$$2x^2 - 3x - 5 = 0$$
$$(x + 1)(2x - 5) = 0$$

Therefore,

$$x + 1 = 0 \quad \text{or} \quad 2x - 5 = 0$$

and so

$$x = -1 \quad \text{or} \quad x = \frac{5}{2}$$

If $x = -1$, then

$$2x - 3 = -5$$

If $x = \frac{5}{2}$, then

$$2x - 3 = 2$$

Thus, there are two possible solutions. The two numbers are either -1 and -5 or $\frac{5}{2}$ and 2.

Exercises 11.1

In Exercises 1 through 10 solve the given equation.

1. $(4x - 8)(2x - 6) = 0$　　　　　**2.** $(2x - 5)(3x + 9) = 0$

3. $(5x - 25)(x - 5) = 0$　　　　　**4.** $y(2 - y) = 0$

5. $(4x - 12)\left(\frac{1}{2}x - 1\right) = 0$　　　　　**6.** $\left(\frac{2}{3}x - 4\right)\left(\frac{1}{2}x - 3\right) = 0$

7. $(x + 2)^2 = 0$　　　　　**8.** $(2x - 5)^2 = 0$

9. $(x - 4)(x + 3)(x + 2) = 0$　　　　　**10.** $(x^2 - 4)(x^2 - 9) = 0$

In Exercises 11 through 19 solve the quadratic equation by using the Zero Product Property.

11. $x^2 + 8x + 15 = 0$

12. $-x^2 + 4x = 0$　(Hint: Multiply both members by -1.)

13. $2x^2 - 7x + 6 = 0$　　　　　**14.** $x^2 - 4x = 0$

15. $x^2 - 4 = 0$　　　　　**16.** $x^2 + 4x = 0$

17. $x^2 + 8x + 12 = 0$　　　　　**18.** $x^2 + 13x + 42 = 0$

19. $6x^2 + 7x - 5 = 0$

20. Solve the equation $x^3 + 4x^2 - 12x = 0$

21. The square of a number increased by three times itself equals 40. Find the number.

22. The product of two consecutive integers is 240. Find the two integers.

23. Three natural numbers are selected at random. The first number is one more than twice the third number. The second number is one less than three times the third number. The product of the first and second numbers is 154. Find the three natural numbers.

24. The measure of the length of a rectangle is four more than the measure of the width. The area of the rectangle is 252 square units. Find the length and width of the rectangle.

25. Solve the proportion $4 : x = x : 25$

26. If a, b, and x are the measures of the lengths of the line segments shown in Figure 11.1.1, then a is to x as x is to b. Find x if $a = 6$ and $b = 24$.

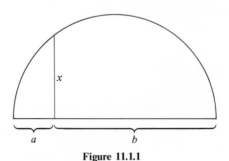

Figure 11.1.1

27. The sum of a number and its reciprocal is $\dfrac{13}{6}$. Find the number.

11.2 The Quadratic Formula

It is not always feasible to solve quadratic equations by the method used in Section 11.1. For instance, to solve the equation

$$x^2 - 2 = 0 \tag{1}$$

we need to consider the factored form of $x^2 - 2$. A factored form of this polynomial is

$$(x - \sqrt{2})(x + \sqrt{2})$$

and, hence, using the Zero Product Property we find that the roots of equation (1) are $\sqrt{2}$ and $-\sqrt{2}$.

The discussion above suggests the following theorem.

11.2.1 Theorem   If E and F are two expressions and

$$E^2 - F = 0$$

then

$$E = \sqrt{F} \quad \text{or} \quad E = -\sqrt{F}$$

Illustration 1 The equation

$$x^2 = 2$$

is equivalent to equation (1). From Theorem 11.2.1 we have

$$x = \sqrt{2} \qquad \text{or} \qquad x = -\sqrt{2}$$

The solution set of the given equation is $\{\sqrt{2}, -\sqrt{2}\}$.

For certain other quadratic polynomials, finding a convenient factored form is even less feasible than what we found for equation (1). Consider the following illustration.

Illustration 2 The length of a rectangle is 3 units more than the width. The area of the rectangle is 12 square units. Find the length and width of the rectangle.

Let x be the number of units in the width and $x + 3$ be the number of units in the length. See Figure 11.2.1. Then, we have the equation

$$x(x + 3) = 12$$
$$x^2 + 3x = 12$$
$$x^2 + 3x - 12 = 0 \qquad\qquad (2)$$

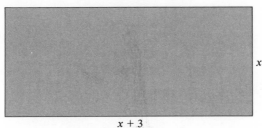

$$x + 3$$
Figure 11.2.1

Equation (2) is an example of a quadratic equation whose left member is not readily expressed as a product of two binomials. Therefore, it is not feasible to use the Zero Product Property to solve the equation. There is, however, a formula that enables us to solve equation (2). We now discuss this formula.

The *quadratic formula* is a general formula that is used to solve all quadratic equations of the form

$$ax^2 + bx + c = 0$$

where $a > 0$ and a, b, and c are real numbers. Before we develop the formula, we first outline the method used in deriving the formula. The method uses a procedure called *completing the square*. This procedure is outlined in the following steps using the equation

$$2x^2 + 3x - 1 = 0$$

which is a quadratic equation that is not readily solved by factoring.

Step 1. Express the equation in *standard form* and divide both members by the coefficient of the leading monomial.

$$2x^2 + 3x - 1 = 0$$

$$x^2 + \frac{3}{2}x - \frac{1}{2} = 0$$

Step 2. Add the additive inverse of the constant to both members.

$$x^2 + \frac{3}{2}x = \frac{1}{2}$$

Step 3. Add a constant to both members that gives us a perfect square trinomial. For this equation, the coefficient of x is $\frac{3}{2}$ and one half of this coefficient is

$$\frac{1}{2} \cdot \frac{3}{2} = \frac{3}{4}$$

Hence, we add $\left(\frac{3}{4}\right)^2$ to each member of the equation.

$$x^2 + \frac{3}{2}x + \left(\frac{3}{4}\right)^2 = \frac{1}{2} + \left(\frac{3}{4}\right)^2$$

$$x^2 + \frac{3}{2}x + \left(\frac{3}{4}\right)^2 = \frac{1}{2} + \frac{9}{16}$$

$$x^2 + \frac{3}{2}x + \left(\frac{3}{4}\right)^2 = \frac{17}{16}$$

Step 4. Express the polynomial in factored form.

$$\left(x + \frac{3}{4}\right)^2 = \frac{17}{16}$$

Step 5. Applying Theorem 11.2.1 to the equation in step 4, we obtain

$$x + \frac{3}{4} = \sqrt{\frac{17}{16}} \quad \text{or} \quad x + \frac{3}{4} = -\sqrt{\frac{17}{16}}$$

Step 6. Solve each equation for x.

$$x = \frac{-3}{4} + \sqrt{\frac{17}{16}} \qquad\qquad x = \frac{-3}{4} - \sqrt{\frac{17}{16}}$$

$$x = \frac{-3}{4} + \frac{\sqrt{17}}{4} \qquad\qquad x = \frac{-3}{4} - \frac{\sqrt{17}}{4}$$

$$x = \frac{-3 + \sqrt{17}}{4} \qquad\qquad x = \frac{-3 - \sqrt{17}}{4}$$

The two solutions can be written as follows:
$$x = \frac{-3 \pm \sqrt{17}}{4}$$

If the two roots of the equation $2x^2 + 3x - 1 = 0$ are denoted by r_1 and r_2, then
$$r_1 = \frac{-3 + \sqrt{17}}{4} \quad \text{and} \quad r_2 = \frac{-3 - \sqrt{17}}{4}$$

Example 1 Solve the equation $2x^2 + 6x + 3 = 0$ by completing the square.

Solution: We apply steps 1 through 6 given above.

$$2x^2 + 6x + 3 = 0$$

Step 1. $\qquad x^2 + 3x + \frac{3}{2} = 0$

Step 2. $\qquad x^2 + 3x = \frac{-3}{2}$

Step 3. $\qquad x^2 + 3x + \left(\frac{3}{2}\right)^2 = \frac{-3}{2} + \left(\frac{3}{2}\right)^2$

$\qquad\qquad x^2 + 3x + \left(\frac{3}{2}\right)^2 = \frac{-3}{2} + \frac{9}{4}$

$\qquad\qquad x^2 + 3x + \left(\frac{3}{2}\right)^2 = \frac{3}{4}$

Step 4. $\qquad \left(x + \frac{3}{2}\right)^2 = \frac{3}{4}$

Step 5. $\qquad x + \frac{3}{2} = \pm\sqrt{\frac{3}{4}}$

Step 6. $\qquad x = \frac{-3}{2} \pm \sqrt{\frac{3}{4}}$

$\qquad\qquad = \frac{-3}{2} \pm \frac{\sqrt{3}}{2}$

$\qquad\qquad = \frac{-3 \pm \sqrt{3}}{2}$

Hence, the solution set is $\left\{\dfrac{-3 + \sqrt{3}}{2}, \dfrac{-3 - \sqrt{3}}{2}\right\}$.

11.2.2 Theorem The roots of the quadratic equation
$$ax^2 + bx + c = 0$$

are $\qquad \dfrac{-b + \sqrt{b^2 - 4ac}}{2a} \quad \text{and} \quad \dfrac{-b - \sqrt{b^2 - 4ac}}{2a}$

Proof: *The given equation in standard form is*

$$ax^2 + bx + c = 0$$

Step 1. *Divide both members by* a.

$$x^2 + \frac{b}{a}x + \frac{c}{a} = 0$$

Step 2. *Add* $-\dfrac{c}{a}$ *to both members.*

$$x^2 + \frac{b}{a}x = -\frac{c}{a}$$

Step 3. *Complete the square of the left member by adding* $\left(\dfrac{b}{2a}\right)^2$ *to both members.*

$$x^2 + \frac{b}{a}x + \left(\frac{b}{2a}\right)^2 = -\frac{c}{a} + \left(\frac{b}{2a}\right)^2$$

Step 4. *Factor the left member and simplify the right member.*

$$\left(x + \frac{b}{2a}\right)^2 = -\frac{c}{a} + \frac{b^2}{4a^2}$$

$$= \frac{-4ac}{4a^2} + \frac{b^2}{4a^2}$$

$$= \frac{b^2 - 4ac}{4a^2}$$

Step 5. *Find the square root of both members by using the property that if* $E^2 = F$ *then* $E = \sqrt{F}$ *or* $E = -\sqrt{F}$ *(Theorem 11.2.1).*

$$x + \frac{b}{2a} = \pm\sqrt{\frac{b^2 - 4ac}{4a^2}}$$

Step 6. *Solve for* x.

$$x = \frac{-b}{2a} \pm \sqrt{\frac{b^2 - 4ac}{4a^2}}$$

$$x = \frac{-b}{2a} \pm \frac{\sqrt{b^2 - 4ac}}{2a} \quad \text{(Because } a > 0\text{)}$$

$$x = \frac{-b \pm \sqrt{b^2 - 4ac}}{2a}$$

We have proved that if $ax^2 + bx + x = 0$ *then*

$$x = \frac{-b \pm \sqrt{b^2 - 4ac}}{2a}$$

We need also to prove the converse: that is, if $x = \dfrac{-b \pm \sqrt{b^2 - 4ac}}{2a}$,

then $ax^2 + bx + c = 0$. This part of the proof is omitted. See Exercise 31 at the end of this section.

The equation

$$x = \frac{-b \pm \sqrt{b^2 - 4ac}}{2a}$$

is called the *quadratic formula*. It gives the roots of any quadratic equation.

Example 2   Use the quadratic formula to solve the equation

$$2x^2 + 3x - 1 = 0$$

Solution: Comparing

$$2x^2 + 3x - 1 = 0$$

with the general quadratic equation

$$ax^2 + bx + c = 0$$

we notice that $a = 2$, $b = 3$, and $c = -1$. Substituting these values into the quadratic formula, we obtain

$$
\begin{aligned}
x &= \frac{-b \pm \sqrt{b^2 - 4ac}}{2a} \\[2mm]
&= \frac{-(3) \pm \sqrt{(3)^2 - 4(2)(-1)}}{2(2)} \\[2mm]
&= \frac{-3 \pm \sqrt{9 + 8}}{4} \\[2mm]
&= \frac{-3 \pm \sqrt{17}}{4}
\end{aligned}
$$

The solution set is $\left\{ \dfrac{-3 + \sqrt{17}}{4}, \dfrac{-3 - \sqrt{17}}{4} \right\}$.

Before applying the quadratic formula it is important to write the equation in the form $ax^2 + bx + c = 0$. For example, if we wish to solve the equation $-2x^2 - x = 2x - 1$, we first write the equivalent equation

$$2x^2 + 3x - 1 = 0$$

This equation is solved in Example 2.

Example 3   Solve the equation $x^2 - 4x = 4(x - 3)$ by using the quadratic formula.

Solution: First write the equation in standard form.

$$x^2 - 4x = 4(x - 3)$$
$$x^2 - 4x = 4x - 12$$
$$x^2 - 8x + 12 = 0$$

Comparing $x^2 - 8x + 12 = 0$ with $ax^2 + bx + c = 0$ we see that $a = 1$, $b = -8$, and $c = 12$.

Substituting these values into the quadratic formula, we obtain

$$x = \frac{-b \pm \sqrt{b^2 - 4ac}}{2a}$$

$$= \frac{-(-8) \pm \sqrt{(-8)^2 - 4(1)(12)}}{2(1)}$$

$$= \frac{8 \pm \sqrt{64 - 48}}{2}$$

$$= \frac{8 \pm \sqrt{16}}{2}$$

$$= \frac{8 \pm 4}{2}$$

Hence,

$$x = \frac{12}{2} \quad \text{or} \quad x = \frac{4}{2}$$

Therefore, if r_1 and r_2 are the roots of the equation,

$$r_1 = 6 \quad \text{and} \quad r_2 = 2$$

The solution set is $\{6, 2\}$.

Example 4 Solve the equation $64t - 16t^2 = 0$ by using the quadratic formula.

Solution: The given equation is equivalent to

$$16t^2 - 64t = 0$$

Comparing this with the general quadratic equation

$$at^2 + bt + c = 0$$

we notice that $a = 16$, $b = -64$, and $c = 0$. Substituting these values into the quadratic formula, we obtain

$$t = \frac{-b \pm \sqrt{b^2 - 4ac}}{2a}$$

$$= \frac{64 \pm \sqrt{64^2 - 4(16)0}}{2(16)}$$

$$= \frac{64 \pm \sqrt{64^2}}{2(16)}$$

$$= \frac{64 \pm 64}{32}$$

Therefore, the two roots are

$$t_1 = 0 \quad \text{and} \quad t_2 = \frac{2(64)}{32} = 4$$

The solution set is $\{0, 4\}$.

The solutions of the equations in Examples 3 and 4 are rational numbers. Hence, these equations can be solved by factoring and using the Zero Product Property.

Example 5 Solve the quadratic equation $x^2 - 8x = -12$ by three methods: (a) by using the Zero Product Property; (b) by completing the square; (c) by using the quadratic formula.

Solution:

(a)
$$x^2 - 8x = -12$$
$$x^2 - 8x + 12 = 0$$
$$(x - 2)(x - 6) = 0$$

Therefore,

$$x - 2 = 0 \quad \text{or} \quad x - 6 = 0$$

Hence,

$$x = 2 \quad \text{or} \quad x = 6$$

The solution set is $\{2, 6\}$.

(b)
$$x^2 - 8x = -12$$
$$x^2 - 8x + 16 = -12 + 16$$
$$(x - 4)^2 = 4$$
$$x - 4 = \pm 2$$
$$x = 4 \pm 2$$

Therefore, if r_1 and r_2 are the roots of the equation, then

$$r_1 = 6 \quad \text{and} \quad r_2 = 2$$

The solution set is $\{2, 6\}$.

(c)
$$x^2 - 8x = -12$$
$$x^2 - 8x + 12 = 0$$

Comparing

$$x^2 - 8x + 12 = 0$$

with

$$ax^2 + bx + c = 0$$

we notice that $a = 1$, $b = -8$, and $c = 12$. Substituting these values into the quadratic formula, we obtain

$$x = \frac{-b \pm \sqrt{b^2 - 4ac}}{2a}$$

$$= \frac{-(-8) \pm \sqrt{(-8)^2 - 4(1)(12)}}{2(1)}$$

$$= \frac{8 \pm \sqrt{64 - 48}}{2}$$

$$= \frac{8 \pm \sqrt{16}}{2}$$

$$= \frac{8 \pm 4}{2}$$

$$= 4 \pm 2$$

Therefore, the two roots of the equation are

$$r_1 = 6 \quad \text{and} \quad r_2 = 2$$

The solution set is $\{2, 6\}$.

Not every quadratic equation has real numbers as solutions. For instance, there are no real numbers that satisfy the equation

$$x^2 = -9$$

because the square of every real number is a nonnegative real number.

In the quadratic formula

$$\frac{-b \pm \sqrt{b^2 - 4ac}}{2a}$$

where a, b and c are integers, the expression

$$b^2 - 4ac$$

is called the *discriminant* of the quadratic equation.

If the discriminant of a quadratic equation has a positive value, then the roots of the equation are real numbers. If the discriminant of a quadratic equation has a negative value, there are no real number roots of the equation.

If the discriminant of a quadratic equation is equal to zero, then the quadratic equation has a double root equal to $\frac{-b}{2a}$, and furthermore, if the discriminant is equal to the square of a rational number, then the two roots of the equation are rational numbers.

Illustration 3 For the equation $2x^2 + 3x - 1 = 0$ the discriminant is

$$b^2 - 4ac = 3^2 - 4(2)(-1)$$
$$= 9 + 8$$
$$= 17$$

Because $17 > 0$ we know that the roots of the equation are real numbers. Because 17 is not a perfect square we know that the roots of the equation are irrational numbers.

Exercises 11.2

In Exercises 1 through 6 solve the quadratic equation by completing the square.

1. $x^2 + 8x + 15 = 0$ **2.** $x^2 - 4x = 0$

3. $2x^2 + 6x + 3 = 0$ **4.** $x^2 + 8x - 2 = 0$

5. $x^2 - 10x = -20$ **6.** $3x^2 - 2x - 1 = 0$

In Exercises 7 through 20 solve the quadratic equation by using the quadratic formula.

7. $x^2 - 4x = 0$ **8.** $x^2 - x - 1 = 0$

9. $x^2 - 1 = 0$ **10.** $2x^2 + 2x - 1 = 0$

11. $2x^2 + 6x + 3 = 0$ **12.** $6x^2 + 7x = 5$

13. $2x - 1 = 3x^2 + x - 5$ **14.** $x^2 = -(x + 1)$

15. $5x^2 + 2x - 4 = 0$

16. $\dfrac{1}{2}x^2 + \dfrac{5}{2}x + 3 = 0$ (Hint: Multiply both members by 2.)

17. $2x^2 + 3x = 0$ **18.** $2x^2 - x + 3 = 0$

19. $(x + 2)^2 = (2x - 1)^2$ **20.** $(2x + 3)^2 = 2x + 3$

In Exercises 21 through 28 use the discriminant to determine whether the roots of the equation are real numbers or not. If the roots are real numbers, determine whether they are rational numbers or irrational numbers.

21. $x^2 + x + 1 = 0$ **22.** $x^2 + 3x - 3 = 0$

23. $2x^2 + 5x - 12 = 0$ **24.** $9x^2 + 15x + 4 = 0$

25. $x^2 - 2x = -1$ **26.** $3x^2 + 2x + 1 = 0$

27. $x^2 = 5x - 10$ **28.** $4x^2 + 4x + 1 = 0$

29. If r_1 and r_2 are the two roots of the quadratic equation

$$ax^2 + bx + c = 0$$

then show that $r_1 + r_2 = \dfrac{-b}{a}$.

30. The polynomial $x^2 + bx$ becomes a perfect square trinomial by adding _____ .

31. Show that if $x = \dfrac{-b \pm \sqrt{b^2 - 4ac}}{2a}$, then $ax^2 + bx + c = 0$.

32. Solve the problem of the rectangle stated at the beginning of this section and shown in Figure 11.2.1 on page 377.

11.3 Applications of the Quadratic Equation

Quadratic equations are obtained in the development of the solutions of many interesting problems. The examples that follow demonstrate a few of these applications.

Example 1 The length of a rectangle is twice as long as the width. If the width is increased by 3 units and the length is decreased by 1 unit the area of the rectangle is doubled. Find the length and width of the original rectangle. See Figure 11.3.1.

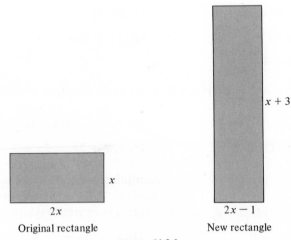

Figure 11.3.1

Solution: Let $x =$ the measure of the width of the original rectangle.
then $2x =$ the measure of the length of the original rectangle.
Hence $(2x)(x) = 2x^2 =$ the measure of the area of the original rectangle.

Now $x + 3$ = the measure of the width of the new rectangle,
and $2x - 1$ = the measure of the length of the new rectangle.
Hence
$(2x - 1)(x + 3)$ = the measure of the area of the new rectangle.
   An equation is obtained by equating the measure of the new area to twice the measure of the original area.

$$(2x - 1)(x + 3) = 2(2x^2)$$

Thus,

$$2x^2 + 5x - 3 = 4x^2$$
$$2x^2 - 5x + 3 = 0$$

We use the quadratic formula, where $a = 2$, $b = -5$, and $c = 3$.

$$x = \frac{-b \pm \sqrt{b^2 - 4ac}}{2a}$$

$$x = \frac{5 \pm \sqrt{5^2 - 4(2)(3)}}{2(2)}$$

$$= \frac{5 \pm \sqrt{25 - 24}}{4}$$

$$= \frac{5 \pm \sqrt{1}}{4}$$

$$= \frac{5 \pm 1}{4}$$

Therefore,

$$x = \frac{6}{4} = \frac{3}{2} \quad \text{or} \quad x = \frac{4}{4} = 1$$

   If $x = \frac{3}{2}$, then $2x = 3$. Hence, the width of the rectangle is $\frac{3}{2}$ units and the length is 3 units.
   If $x = 1$, then $2x = 2$. Hence, the width of the rectangle is 1 unit and the length is 2 units.
   Therefore, there are two possible original rectangles. One rectangle has dimensions $\frac{3}{2}$ units and 3 units, and the other rectangle has dimensions 1 unit and 2 units.

Example 2   A rectangular piece of sheet metal is three times as long as it is wide. From each of its four corners a square 5 inches on a side is cut out. The sides are then bent up to form an open box. If the volume of the box is 640 cubic inches, find the dimensions of the original rectangular piece of sheet metal. See Figure 11.3.2.

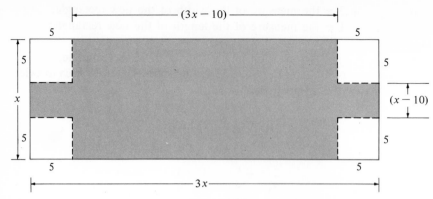

Figure 11.3.2

Solution: Let x inches = the width of the rectangle.

Then $3x$ inches = the length of the rectangle.

The volume of the box is given by the product of the three dimensions. See Figure 11.3.3. The product of the measures of the three dimensions of the box is equal to 640. Hence, we have the equation

$$5(x - 10)(3x - 10) = 640$$

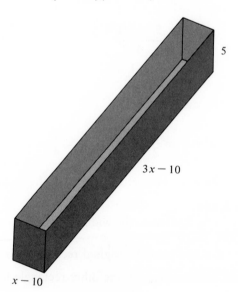

Figure 11.3.3

Dividing both members of this equation by 5, we obtain

$$(x - 10)(3x - 10) = 128$$
$$3x^2 - 40x + 100 = 128$$
$$3x^2 - 40x - 28 = 0$$
$$(3x + 2)(x - 14) = 0$$

Therefore,

$$3x + 2 = 0 \qquad \text{or} \qquad x - 14 = 0$$

and so

$$x = \frac{-2}{3} \qquad \text{or} \qquad x = 14$$

Because the measure of the width is a positive number, we reject the negative root. Therefore,

$$x = 14$$

and so

$$3x = 42$$

Hence, the dimensions of the original rectangular piece of sheet metal are 14 inches and 42 inches.

The following theorem is a theorem of geometry and is credited to Pythagoras, a Greek mathematician ca. 550 B.C., although there is evidence to indicate that the result of this theorem was known to the Babylonians even 1200 years earlier and possibly to the Egyptians even earlier.

This theorem has to do with the lengths of the sides of a *right triangle,* that is, a triangle with one right angle measuring 90°. See Figure 11.3.4.

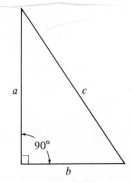

Figure 11.3.4

The longest side of a right triangle is called the *hypotenuse,* that is the side of measure c in the diagram. Pythagoras' Theorem states that "The area of the square on the hypotenuse is equal to the sum of the areas of the squares on the other two sides."

Algebraically, the Pythagorean Theorem is translated into the statement

$$a^2 + b^2 = c^2$$

where a, b, and c are, respectively, the measures of the altitude, the base, and the hypotenuse of the right triangle. See Figure 11.3.5.

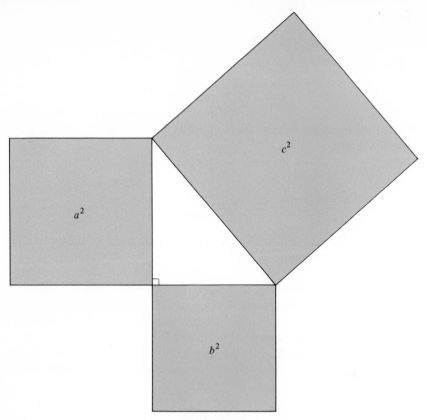

Figure 11.3.5

11.3.1 Theorem **(Pythagorean Theorem)**   If a, b, and c are positive real numbers representing the measures of the three sides of a right triangle, and if $c > a$ and $c > b$, then

$$a^2 + b^2 = c^2$$

The equation $a^2 + b^2 = c^2$ is called the *Pythagorean Formula*. This formula can be solved for any one of the numbers, a, b, or c. If two of the numbers are known, the third can be found.

Example 3 If $a = 4$ and $b = 3$, find c in the Pythagorean Formula.

Solution: $a^2 + b^2 = c^2$
$4^2 + 3^2 = c^2$
$16 + 9 = c^2$
$25 = c^2$
$0 = c^2 - 25$
$0 = (c - 5)(c + 5)$

Therefore,

$$c - 5 = 0 \qquad \text{or} \qquad c + 5 = 0$$

and so

$$c = 5 \qquad \text{or} \qquad c = -5$$

The negative root is not used as the measure of a line segment. Hence, the solution is 5.

Example 4 Find the length of the diagonal of a unit square. See Figure 11.3.6.

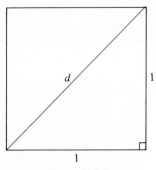

Figure 11.3.6

Solution: Let $d =$ the number of units in the length of the diagonal. The diagonal of the square is the hypotenuse of a right triangle formed from the line segments joining three corners of the square. Let $a = 1$, $b = 1$, and $c = d$, in the Pythagorean Formula. Then

$$a^2 + b^2 = c^2$$

becomes

$$1^2 + 1^2 = d^2$$

Thus,

$$1 + 1 = d^2$$
$$2 = d^2$$

Therefore, if $d^2 = 2$, then by Theorem 11.2.1

$$d = \sqrt{2} \qquad \text{or} \qquad d = -\sqrt{2}$$

Thus, disregarding the negative root, the length of the diagonal is $\sqrt{2}$ units.

The converse of the Pythagorean Theorem is also valid; that is, if $a^2 + b^2 = c^2$ and a, b, and c are positive numbers, then the triangle with sides having measures equal to a, b, and c is a right triangle. Furthermore, if the three numbers a, b, and c satisfy the Pythagorean Formula, then *ma*, *mb*, and *mc* also satisfy the Pythagorean Formula. This is true because if

$$a^2 + b^2 = c^2$$

then by multiplying both members by m^2, we have

$$m^2(a^2 + b^2) = m^2c^2$$

and hence,

$$m^2a^2 + m^2b^2 = m^2c^2$$

and so,

$$(ma)^2 + (mb)^2 = (mc)^2 \tag{1}$$

Illustration 1   We found in Example 3 that 3, 4, and 5 satisfy the Pythagorean Formula. Therefore, the numbers 6, 8, and 10 also satisfy the Pythagorean Formula because these numbers are multiples of 3, 4, and 5, respectively. Hence, if $a = 3$, $b = 4$, $c = 5$, and $m = 2$, formula (1) becomes

$$(2 \cdot 3)^2 + (2 \cdot 4)^2 = (2 \cdot 5)^2$$
$$6^2 + 8^2 = 10^2$$
$$36 + 64 = 100$$
$$100 = 100$$

which shows that 6, 8, and 10 satisfy the Pythagorean Formula.

Formula (1) gives useful information because it can save time in certain computations. For instance, we have already found in Example 4 that the length of the diagonal of a unit square is $\sqrt{2}$ units. Consequently, any square whose side is s units in length has a diagonal whose length is equal to $s \cdot \sqrt{2}$ units, a multiple of $\sqrt{2}$ units. See Figure 11.3.7.

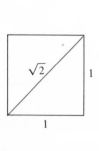
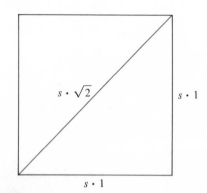

Figure 11.3.7

Example 5   The measure of the altitude of a right triangle is two times the measure of the base of the triangle. The measure of the hypotenuse is 15. Find the measures of the altitude and base.

Solution: Let $x =$ the measure of the base of the right triangle.

Then $2x =$ the measure of the altitude of the right triangle.

Using the Pythagorean Formula

$$a^2 + b^2 = c^2$$

where $a = 2x$, $b = x$, and $c = 15$, we have

$$(2x)^2 + x^2 = 15^2$$
$$4x^2 + x^2 = 225$$
$$5x^2 = 225$$
$$x^2 = 45$$

Hence,

$$x = \sqrt{45} \qquad \text{or} \qquad x = -\sqrt{45}$$

Disregarding the negative root, we have

$$x = \sqrt{45} \qquad \text{and} \qquad 2x = 2\sqrt{45}$$
$$x = 3\sqrt{5} \qquad\qquad\qquad 2x = 6\sqrt{5}$$
$$x \doteq 6.7 \qquad\qquad\qquad 2x \doteq 13.4$$

Therefore, the measure of the base of the triangle is approximately 6.7 and the measure of the altitude is approximately 13.4.

Example 6 The measure of one leg of a right triangle is 2 less than the measure of the hypotenuse, and the measure of the other leg of the right triangle is 4 less than the measure of the hypotenuse. Find the length of the hypotenuse.

Solution: Let $x =$ the measure of the hypotenuse.

Then $x - 2 =$ the measure of one leg,

and $x - 4 =$ the measure of the other leg.

Using the Pythagorean Formula

$$a^2 + b^2 = c^2$$

where $a = x - 2$, $b = x - 4$, and $c = x$, we have

$$(x - 2)^2 + (x - 4)^2 = x^2$$
$$x^2 - 4x + 4 + x^2 - 8x + 16 = x^2$$
$$x^2 - 12x + 20 = 0$$
$$(x - 2)(x - 10) = 0$$

Hence,

$$x - 2 = 0 \qquad \text{or} \qquad x - 10 = 0$$

Therefore,

$$x = 2 \qquad \text{or} \qquad x = 10$$

Because x is the measure of the hypotenuse we must reject the case $x = 2$, for then the measure of the shortest leg, $x - 4$, would be a negative number.

Therefore, the length of the hypotenuse is 10 units.

Problems involving falling bodies or projectiles shot through the air lead to second-degree equations. The formula

$$h = t(v_0 - 16t) \qquad (2)$$

gives the height, h feet, of an object projected with an upward initial velocity, v_0 feet per second, after a given time, t seconds.

Example 7 Determine how long it takes for a stone thrown straight upward with an initial velocity of 80 feet per second to return to the ground.

Solution: Because we wish to know the value of t when the stone returns to the ground, we set $h = 0$ (ground level), and $v_0 = 80$. Thus, substituting 0 for h and 80 for v_0 in formula (2), we obtain

$$0 = t(80 - 16t)$$

Applying the Zero Product Property we have

$$t = 0 \qquad \text{or} \qquad 80 - 16t = 0$$

Therefore,

$$t = 0 \qquad \text{or} \qquad t = 5$$

The solution $t = 0$ corresponds to the situation when the stone is at ground level before it is thrown. The solution $t = 5$ is the one we want. Hence, it takes 5 seconds for the stone to return to the ground.

Example 8 Determine how long it takes for a stone thrown straight up with an initial velocity of 64 feet per second to return to a point 10 feet above the ground.

Solution: We wish to find t when the stone returns to a point 10 feet above the ground. Therefore let $h = 10$ and $v_0 = 64$. Thus, formula (2) becomes

$$10 = t(64 - 16t)$$

We solve this equation for t.

$$10 = 64t - 16t^2$$
$$16t^2 - 64t + 10 = 0$$
$$2(8t^2 - 32t + 5) = 0$$

Thus, from the Zero Product Property, we have

$$8t^2 - 32t + 5 = 0$$

Using the quadratic formula where $a = 8$, $b = -32$, and $c = 5$, we have

$$t = \frac{-b \pm \sqrt{b^2 - 4ac}}{2a}$$

$$t = \frac{-(-32) \pm \sqrt{(-32)^2 - 4(8)(5)}}{2(8)}$$

$$= \frac{32 \pm \sqrt{1024 - 160}}{16}$$

$$= \frac{32 \pm \sqrt{864}}{16}$$

We find the approximate values of t. The square root of 864 is about 29.4 and so

$$t \doteq 3.84 \qquad \text{or} \qquad t \doteq 1.65$$

These values of t correspond to the two different times that the stone is at a height of 10 feet above the ground (once on the way up and once on the way down). We wish to know how long it takes the stone to reach the latter position. Hence, it takes approximately 3.84 seconds.

Exercises 11.3

1. The measure of the perimeter of a square equals the measure of the area of the square. Find the measure of the side of the square.

2. The larger rectangle in Figure 11.3.8 has measurements of 15 units by 30 units. The smaller rectangle has an area of 250 square units. The shaded border has the same width, x units, everywhere. Find the value of x.

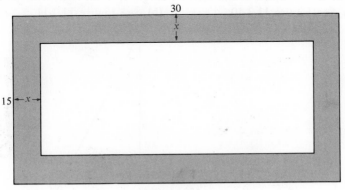

Figure 11.3.8

3. The measure of the width of a rectangular flower garden is one third

of the measure of its length. A pebble walkway 3 feet wide extends around the garden on all sides. The measure of the area of the region covered by the walkway equals the measure of the area of the region covered by the flower garden. Find the dimensions of the flower garden.

4. The measure of the area of the large circle in Figure 11.3.9 is twice the measure of the area of the small circle. The measure of the radius of the small circle is 2 less than the measure of the radius of the large circle. Find the measure of the radius of the large circle.

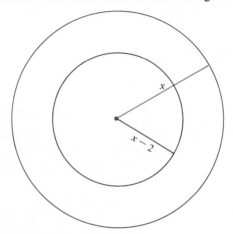

Figure 11.3.9

5. A rectangular piece of sheet metal is twice as long as it is wide. From each of its four corners a square piece 10 inches on a side is cut out. The remaining piece is then bent to form a box open at the top. If the volume of the box is 500 cubic inches, find the dimensions of the original rectangular piece of sheet metal.

6. Find the measure of the missing length in each right triangle.
   (a) See Figure 11.3.10.   (b) See Figure 11.3.11.

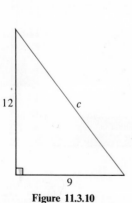

Figure 11.3.10

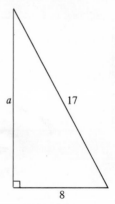

Figure 11.3.11

7. Find the measure of the missing length in each diagram.
   (a) See Figure 11.3.12.   (b) See Figure 11.3.13.

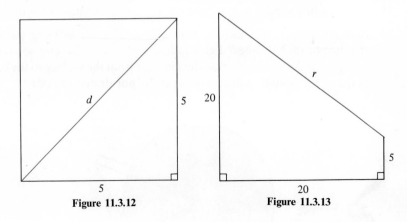

Figure 11.3.12   Figure 11.3.13

8. Find the area of the colored region shown in Figure 11.3.14.

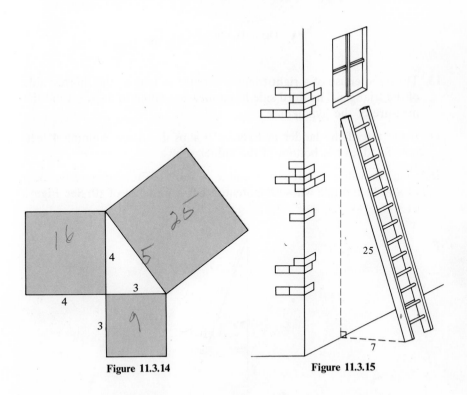

Figure 11.3.14   Figure 11.3.15

9. A ladder 25 feet long is placed so that its base is 7 feet from the building. How high on the building does the ladder reach? See Figure 11.3.15.

10. The length of the perimeter of a square is 40 inches. Find the length of the diagonal.

11. The area of a square is 36 square units. Find the length of the diagonal.

12. How far away is the horizon from a space capsule orbiting the earth at a height of 200 miles? Let d miles be this distance and solve for d in Figure 11.3.16. Assume that the distance from the surface to the center of the earth is 4000 miles. (The figure is not drawn to scale.)

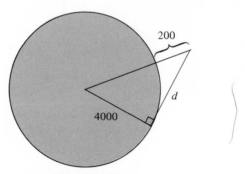

Figure 11.3.16

13. The hypotenuse of a right triangle is twice as long as the shortest side of the triangle. The third side has a measure equal to $5 \cdot \sqrt{3}$. Find the measure of the hypotenuse.

14. If the top of the ladder in Exercise 9 slips down the building 4 feet, how far does the bottom of the ladder slip?

15. Find the value of x if $x + 3$ and $x - 3$ are the measures of two legs of a right triangle whose hypotenuse has a measure of 10. See Figure 11.3.17.

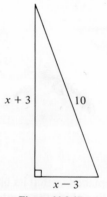

Figure 11.3.17

16. Two ventilating shafts each with a square cross section are to be replaced by one large shaft with a square cross section equal in area to the sum of the areas of the two smaller shafts. The length of the side of the smaller shafts are, respectively, 12 inches and 9 inches. Find the length of the side of the larger shaft. (Hint: Solve $12^2 + 9^2 = s^2$.)

17. The surface area of a cone, A square units, is given by $A = \pi rs$, where r is the measure of the radius of its base and s is the measure of the slant height and h is the measure of the height of the cone. Find the surface area if $r = 30$ and $h = 40$. See Figure 11.3.18.

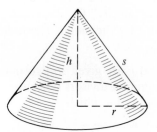

Figure 11.3.18

18. (a) How long will it take a projectile to return to the ground if it is shot straight up with an initial velocity of 960 feet per second? (Hint: Use formula (2) of this section.)

(b) Make a chart of the heights attained by the projectile of part (a) for each 10 second interval of flight, starting with $t = 0$.

t	0	10	20	$\dots$	
h					

19. Determine how long it takes a projectile that is shot straight up with an initial velocity of 128 feet per second to return to a point 32 feet above the ground. (Hint: Use formula (2) of this section.)

20. An object is dropped from a height of 4 feet. How long does it take to hit the ground? (Hint: Use the formula $h = 16t^2$.)

21. (a) The number 16 in the formulas $h = t(v_0 - 16t)$ and $h = 16t^2$ is one half the measure of the acceleration due to gravity g which is about 32 near the surface of the earth. On the moon the gravity is about $\frac{1}{6}$ of that on earth. If $h = \frac{1}{2}gt^2$, find out how long it takes an object to fall 4 feet on the moon.

(b) How long will it take an object to fall from the top of a 500 foot cliff to the bottom on earth? On the moon?

22. (a) If an object (rocket) is projected with a sufficiently fast upward velocity, it can escape the gravity of the planet and travel into space. The "escape velocity," v miles per second, is given by the formula $v^2 = 2gr$ where g is the measure of the acceleration due to gravity, and r is the measure of the radius of the planet. (Both g and r must be in compatible units. If r is in miles, g must be units of miles per second, and v is in miles per second.) Find the escape velocity for earth, if the acceleration due to gravity is 32 feet per second per second $\left(\dfrac{1}{165} \text{ mile per second per second}\right)$ and the radius is 4000 miles.

(b) Find the "escape velocity" for the moon. Refer to Exercise 21 to find the value of g for the moon. The radius of the moon is about 1080 miles.

23. If two numbers u and v are given so that one is even and one is odd and they have no common divisors other than one, with $v > u$, then the numbers a, b, and c, for which

$$a = v^2 - u^2$$
$$b = 2uv$$
and $$c = u^2 + v^2$$

form a *Pythagorean triple*. That is, $a^2 + b^2 = c^2$ and a, b, and c are the measures of the lengths of the sides of a right triangle. Let $u = 7$ and $v = 10$. Find a, b, and c and show that $a^2 + b^2 = c^2$.

11.4 The Graph of a Second-Degree Polynomial Equation

If y is the value of a second degree polynomial in x, then the value of y depends on the value of x.

Illustration 1 If $y = x^2 - 4x$, then the value of y is known when a value for x is given. If $x = 2$, then

$$y = (2)^2 - 4(2)$$
$$= 4 - 8$$
$$= -4$$

Illustration 2 If $y = x^2 - 4x$ and if we wish to know the value of x that gives a value of 0 for y, then we solve the equation

$$0 = x^2 - 4x$$
$$0 = x(x - 4)$$

Therefore, $\qquad x = 0 \qquad$ or $\qquad x - 4 = 0$

and so $\qquad x = 0 \qquad$ or $\qquad x = 4$

The solution set is $\{0, 4\}$. Hence, if $x = 0$ or $x = 4$, then $y = 0$.

The value of the variable x and the corresponding value of the polynomial in x, forms an ordered pair that can be represented by a point on a rectangular coordinate system. The graph of the set of all such ordered pairs of numbers that satisfy a given polynomial equation is a smooth curve.

The graph of the general quadratic equation

$$y = ax^2 + bx + c, \quad a \neq 0 \tag{1}$$

is a smooth curve called a *parabola*.

The simplest quadratic equation which is of the type given by equation (1) is

$$y = x^2 \tag{2}$$

Example 1 Draw a sketch of the graph of equation (2) if x is in the interval $\{x : -3 \leq x \leq 3\}$.

Solution: We compute the values of the polynomial for the integers and a few rational numbers in the interval $-3 \leq x \leq 3$. See Table 11.4.1. We plot the points given by the ordered pairs (x, y). Then we draw a smooth curve joining the points. See Figure 11.4.1. The curve is usually drawn freehand. The points are connected from the left side of the graph to the right side so that the x-coordinates of the points are increasing in value as they are joined in the sketch.

Table 11.4.1

x	-3	-2	-1	0	1	2	3	$\dfrac{1}{2}$	$\dfrac{1}{4}$	$\dfrac{3}{2}$
$y = x^2$	9	4	1	0	1	4	9	$\dfrac{1}{4}$	$\dfrac{1}{16}$	$\dfrac{9}{4}$

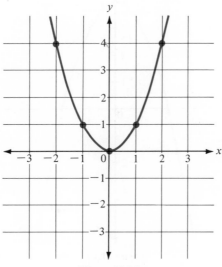

Figure 11.4.1

The parabola has many uses and applications. The surface of a concave lens in a reflecting telescope is parabolic. The reflectors in automobile headlamps, searchlights, and flashlights are parabolic. The path followed by a thrown object is parabolic. A stream of water ejected from a hose follows a parabolic path. The cables on some suspension bridges take a parabolic shape. The paths of some comets are parabolic.

Example 2 Draw a sketch of the graph of the parabola having the equation $y = -x^2 + 4$.

Solution: Make a table of coordinates of points in the parabola by arbitrarily choosing some values for x and computing the corresponding value of y. See Table 11.4.2. Plot the points and join them with a smooth curve. See Figure 11.4.2.

Table 11.4.2

x	$-x^2 + 4$	y
-3	$-(-3)^2 + 4$	-5
-2	$-(-2)^2 + 4$	0
-1	$-(-1)^2 + 4$	3
0	$-(0)^2 + 4$	4
1	$-1^2 + 4$	3
2	$-2^2 + 4$	0
3	$-3^2 + 4$	-5

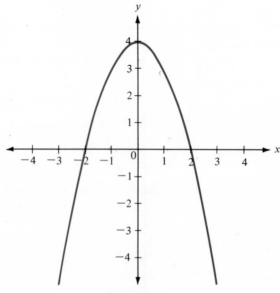

Figure 11.4.2

By examining the graphs of the parabolas in Figures 11.4.1 and 11.4.2 notice that they have the same shape, but they are in different positions. Also notice two features of this curve that are very apparent. First, the curve has either a high or a low point referred to as the *vertex point* of the parabola. The ordinate of this point is called a maximum or minimum value of the quadratic polynomial. Second, the curve has an axis of symmetry, which is the y-axis for these two curves. The part of the curve on the left side of the axis of symmetry is a "mirror image" of the part of the curve on the right side of the axis.

The position of the parabola is determined by the parameters of the quadratic equation $y = ax^2 + bx + c$. The parameter a determines whether the parabola will open upward or downward. If a is positive, the parabola opens upward and if a is negative, the parabola opens downward. In Example 1 $a = 1$ and the parabola shown in Figure 11.4.1 opens upward; in Example 2 $a = -1$ and the parabola shown in Figure 11.4.2 opens downward. The parameter a also determines the "shape" of the parabola in terms of its "flatness" or "sharpness." This is illustrated in Figure 11.4.3 for several values of a, $a > 0$, and in Figure 11.4.4 for several values of a, $a < 0$, for the quadratic equation $y = ax^2$.

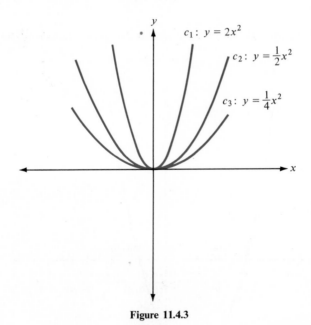

$c_1: y = 2x^2$

$c_2: y = \frac{1}{2}x^2$

$c_3: y = \frac{1}{4}x^2$

Figure 11.4.3

The values of the other parameters b and c have an effect on the positions of the vertex point and the axis of symmetry of the parabola. It can be shown, for instance, that the axis of symmetry represents the equation

$$x = \frac{-b}{2a}$$

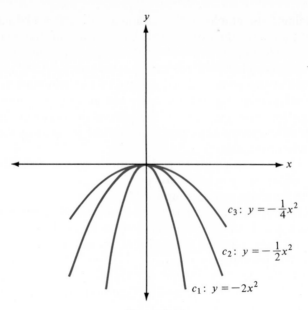

$c_3: y = -\frac{1}{4}x^2$

$c_2: y = -\frac{1}{2}x^2$

$c_1: y = -2x^2$

Figure 11.4.4

Example 3 Draw a sketch of the graph of the parabola having the equation

$$y = x^2 + 2x - 3 \qquad (3)$$

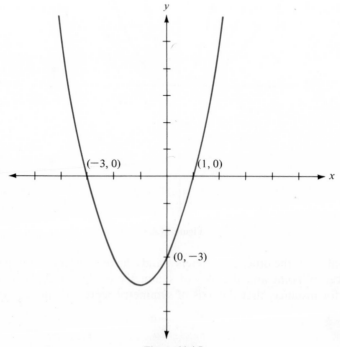

$(-3, 0)$ $(1, 0)$

$(0, -3)$

Figure 11.4.5

Solution: See Table 11.4.3 for the coordinates of some points on the parabola. Plot the points and join them with a smooth curve. See Figure 11.4.5.

Table 11.4.3

x	$x^2 + 2x - 3$	y
0	$0 + 0 - 3$	-3
1	$1 + 2 - 3$	0
-1	$1 - 2 - 3$	-4
2	$4 + 4 - 3$	5
-2	$4 - 4 - 3$	-3
3	$9 + 6 - 3$	12
-3	$9 - 6 - 3$	0
-4	$16 - 8 - 3$	5

The parabola shown in Figure 11.4.5 intersects the x-axis at two points. The ordinate of each of these points is zero and the abscissas are -3 and 1. The abscissas of the points of intersection of the parabola with the x-axis are called the zeros of the quadratic polynomial defined by equation (3).

11.4.1 Definition   A value of x, for which the value of a quadratic polynomial in x is zero, is called a *zero* of the quadratic polynomial.

Example 4 Find the zeros of the quadratic polynomial defined by equation (3). Give the points of intersection of the parabola and the x-axis.

Solution: We replace y by 0 in equation (3) and solve the resulting equation.

$$0 = x^2 + 2x - 3$$
$$0 = (x - 1)(x + 3)$$

Therefore,

$$x - 1 = 0 \quad \text{or} \quad x + 3 = 0$$

Hence, the solutions of the equation are

$$x_1 = 1 \quad \text{and} \quad x_2 = -3$$

and so the zeros of the quadratic polynomial defined by equation (3) are 1 and -3. The points where the parabola intersects the x-axis are given by $(1, 0)$ and $(-3, 0)$.

Knowing the zeros of a quadratic polynomial aids in drawing a sketch of the graph of the quadratic equation as well as helping to locate the vertex point of the parabola. The axis of symmetry of the parabola always contains the vertex point. The abscissa of the vertex point of the graph of the quadratic equation is therefore the same as the x-coordinate of the midpoint of the segment on the x-axis whose endpoints are the points where the parabola intersects the x-axis. In other words, the x-coordinate of the vertex point of the parabola is the average of the zeros of the quadratic polynomial.

The y-coordinate of the vertex point is either the maximum or the minimum value of the quadratic polynomial, depending on whether the parabola opens downward or upward, respectively. Study Example 5.

Example 5 Find the coordinates of the vertex point of the parabola that represents equation (3). What is the maximum or minimum value of the quadratic polynomial defined by this equation?

Solution: In Example 4 we found that the points where the parabola intersects the x-axis are given by $(1, 0)$ and $(-3, 0)$. The midpoint of the segment joining these points is given by

$$\left(\frac{1 + (-3)}{2}, \frac{0 + 0}{2}\right) = (-1, 0)$$

Hence, the x-coordinate of the vertex point is -1. To find the y-coordinate, substitute -1 for x in equation (3) and we have

$$
\begin{aligned}
y &= (-1)^2 + 2(-1) - 3 \\
&= 1 - 2 - 3 \\
&= -4
\end{aligned}
$$

Therefore, the vertex point is given by $(-1, -4)$. Because the leading coefficient of the quadratic equation (3) is positive, the parabola opens upward. Hence, the vertex point is a low point on the parabola and the ordinate of the vertex point is a minimum value of the quadratic polynomial. Denoting the minimum value of the quadratic polynomial by y_{min}, we have

$$y_{min} = -4$$

The coordinates of the vertex point of every parabola cannot be found by the method of Example 5. If when finding the zeros of the quadratic polynomial the roots of the quadratic equation are not real numbers, then the parabola does not intersect the x-axis. In such a situation the method for finding the x-coordinate of the vertex point is essentially unchanged, but we do not study operations with nonreal numbers in this book.

Example 6 Find the coordinates of the vertex point of the parabola having the equation

$$y = 2x^2 + 3x - 1$$

What is the maximum or minimum value of the quadratic polynomial defined by this equation?

Solution: First find the zeros of the quadratic polynomial by solving the equation

$$0 = 2x^2 + 3x - 1$$

Using the quadratic formula,

$$x = \frac{-b \pm \sqrt{b^2 - 4ac}}{2a}$$

where $a = 2$, $b = 3$, and $c = -1$, we have

$$x = \frac{-3 \pm \sqrt{3^2 - 4(2)(-1)}}{2(2)}$$

$$x = \frac{-3 \pm \sqrt{17}}{4}$$

Thus, the points where the parabola intersects the x-axis are given by

$$\left(\frac{-3 + \sqrt{17}}{4}, 0\right) \quad \text{and} \quad \left(\frac{-3 - \sqrt{17}}{4}, 0\right)$$

The midpoint of the segment joining these points on the x-axis is given by

$$\left(\frac{\dfrac{-3 - \sqrt{17}}{4} + \dfrac{-3 + \sqrt{17}}{4}}{2}, \frac{0 + 0}{2}\right) = \left(\frac{\dfrac{-3 - \sqrt{17} + (-3) + \sqrt{17}}{4}}{2}, 0\right)$$

$$= \left(\frac{-\dfrac{6}{4}}{2}, 0\right)$$

$$= \left(\frac{-3}{4}, 0\right)$$

The axis of symmetry of the parabola contains this point and hence, the abscissa of the vertex point is $\dfrac{-3}{4}$. To find the ordinate of the vertex point we substitute $\dfrac{-3}{4}$ for x in the given equation and we obtain

$$y = 2\left(\frac{-3}{4}\right)^2 + 3\left(\frac{-3}{4}\right) - 1$$

$$= 2 \cdot \frac{9}{16} + \frac{-9}{4} - 1$$

$$= \frac{9}{8} + \frac{-9}{4} - 1$$

$$= \frac{-17}{8}$$

Therefore, the vertex point is given by $\left(\dfrac{-3}{4}, \dfrac{-17}{8}\right)$. Because the leading coefficient of the quadratic expression is positive, the parabola opens upward and the vertex point is a low point. Hence, the ordinate of the vertex point is the minimum value of the quadratic polynomial. Furthermore,

$$y_{min} = \frac{-17}{8}$$

Example 7 Draw a sketch of the graph of the parabola of Example 6, by using the information found there.

Solution: See Figure 11.4.6.

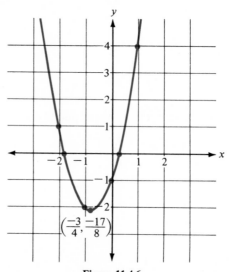

Figure 11.4.6

The next example shows how the knowledge of the maximum or minimum value of a quadratic polynomial can be applied to a practical problem.

Example 8 Find the area of the greatest rectangular region that can be enclosed with 75 feet of fencing. What is the length of the required rectangle?

Solution: Let $x = $ the number of feet in the length of the rectangle,
        and let $y = $ the number of feet in the width of the rectangle.
See Figure 11.4.7. The number of feet in the perimeter of the rectangle is 75 and, hence, one equation is

$$2x + 2y = 75 \qquad (4)$$

If A is the number of square feet in the area of the rectangle, then

$$A = xy \qquad (5)$$

If we solve equation (4) for y we obtain

$$y = \frac{75}{2} - x$$

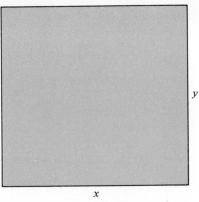

x

y

Figure 11.4.7

Substituting in equation (5) we get

$$A = x\left(\frac{75}{2} - x\right)$$

and so,

$$A = \frac{75}{2}x - x^2 \qquad (6)$$

Now A depends on x and equation (6) defines a quadratic polynomial. The maximum value of the quadratic polynomial is the ordinate of the vertex point of the parabola that is the graph of equation (6). The zeros of the quadratic polynomial are found by solving the equation

$$0 = \frac{75}{2}x - x^2$$

$$0 = x\left(\frac{75}{2} - x\right)$$

Therefore,

$$x = 0 \qquad \text{or} \qquad \frac{75}{2} - x = 0$$

and so the zeros of the quadratic polynomial are 0 and $\frac{75}{2}$. The x-coordinate of the vertex point is the average of these values, that is,

$$\frac{0 + \frac{75}{2}}{2} = \frac{75}{4}$$

Substituting $\dfrac{75}{4}$ for x in equation (6), we have

$$A_{\max} = \frac{75}{2} \cdot \left(\frac{75}{4}\right) - \left(\frac{75}{4}\right)^2$$

$$= \frac{75^2}{8} - \frac{75^2}{16}$$

$$= \frac{75^2}{16}$$

Therefore the area of the greatest rectangular region that can be enclosed with 75 feet of fencing is $\dfrac{75^2}{16}$ square feet, that is approximately 351.6 square feet. The length of the rectangle is $\dfrac{75}{4}$ feet.

Exercises 11.4

In Exercises 1 through 6 draw a sketch of the graph of the equation after plotting all the points with integer x-coordinates for all integer values of x in the interval $\{x : -3 \le x \le 3\}$. *restriction*

1. $y = -x^2$ **2.** $y = \dfrac{x^2}{3}$ **3.** $y = -\dfrac{x^2}{3}$

4. $y = 2x^2$ **5.** $y = -3x^2$ **6.** $y = \dfrac{1}{2}x^2 - 2$

For Exercises 7 and 8 draw a sketch of the three parabolas representing the three equations on one coordinate system.

7. $y = x^2$

$y = x^2 + 1$

$y = x^2 + 2$

8. $y = -\dfrac{1}{2}x^2 - 2$

$y = -\dfrac{1}{2}x^2 + 2$

$y = -\dfrac{1}{2}x^2 + 6$

In Exercises 9 through 14 draw a sketch of the graph of the equation.

9. $y = x^2 + 2x + 1$ **10.** $y = -x^2 + 2x + 1$

11. $y = 2x^2 + x$ **12.** $y = \dfrac{1}{2}x^2 + 2$

13. $y = -x^2 - x + 1$ **14.** $y = \dfrac{1}{2}x^2 + \dfrac{1}{3}x - 4$

In Exercises 15 through 24 find the zeros of the given quadratic polynomial if they exist, and find the maximum or minimum value of the quadratic polynomial by determining if the corresponding parabola opens upward or downward. Then draw a sketch of the graph of the set and label the vertex point of the parabola with its coordinates.

15. $\{(x, y) : y = x^2 - 1\}$

16. $\{(x, y) : y = -x^2 + 1\}$

17. $\{(x, y) : y = (x + 1)^2\}$

18. $\{(x, y) : y = (x - 1)^2\}$

19. $\{(x, y) : y = x^2 - 4x - 5\}$

20. $\left\{(x, y) : y = \dfrac{1}{2} x^2 + \dfrac{5}{2} x + 3\right\}$

21. $\{(x, y) : y = -2x^2 + 3x\}$

22. $\{(x, y) : y = 4x^2 - 3x - 1\}$

23. $\{(x, y) : y = -x^2\}$

24. $\{(x, y) : y = 9x^2 + 15x + 4\}$

25. In a manner similar to Example 1 of Section 11.4 draw a graph of the third degree polynomial equation, $y = x^3$ if x is in the interval $\{x : -2 \le x \le 2\}$. Plot points for choices of the x-coordinate at every $\dfrac{1}{2}$ unit.

26. Find the area of the greatest rectangular region that can be enclosed with 100 feet of fencing.

27. Find the area of the greatest rectangular region that can be enclosed with 100 feet of fencing if the fence is to be used on three sides only and the fourth side is positioned along a river bank.

28. The sum of two numbers is 15. Find the maximum value of their product.

29. If an object is shot upward with an initial velocity of 128 feet per second, and h feet is its height t seconds after it leaves the ground, then

$$h = t(128 - 16t)$$

Find the maximum height attained by the object. How long after the start will it take the object to reach the maximum height?

30. The sum of the whole numbers from 1 to n depends on n. The equation is

$$S = \frac{1}{2} n^2 + \frac{1}{2} n$$

where S is the sum. Draw a sketch of the graph of this equation and keep in mind the indicated replacement set for n. What is the minimum value of S?

11.5 Review Exercises

In Exercises 1 through 3 solve each equation by using the Zero Product Property.

1. (a) $(x - 3)(x + 7) = 0$ **(b)** $(2x + 6)(x - 5) = 0$

2. (a) $64t - 16t^2 = 0$ **(b)** $t(32 - 16t) = 0$

3. (a) $x^2 - 8x + 12 = 0$ **(b)** $2x^2 - 13x + 6 = 0$

4. (a) Twice the square of a number equals 16 more than 4 times that same number. Find the number.
  (b) Solve the proportion $4 : x = x : (x - 1)$.

5. (a) The Summation Property (Property 1.1.1) states that the sum of all the whole numbers from 1 to n is equal to $\frac{1}{2}n(n + 1)$. Suppose the sum of all the whole numbers from 1 to a certain number x is 253. Find x.
  (b) In some instances the speed of an automobile can be calculated by knowing the braking distance (skid marks) required to bring the automobile to a complete stop. The braking distance of D feet is given by the formula,

$$D = \frac{s^2}{30f}$$

  where s miles per hour is the speed at the time when the wheels begin skidding and f is the coefficient of friction between the road surface and the tires. Suppose it has been determined that a certain automobile on wet concrete has a coefficient of friction, $f = 0.45$. If the measured skid marks are 150 feet, find the speed of the automobile when the tires began skidding.

6. Solve each quadratic equation by completing the square.
  (a) $x^2 + 6x - 2 = 0$ **(b)** $2x^2 - 8x + 3 = 0$

In Exercises 7 and 8 solve each quadratic equation by using the quadratic formula.

7. (a) $x^2 - 4x + 1 = 0$ **(b)** $2x^2 + 5x - 12 = 0$

8. (a) $5(5 + x) = x^2$ **(b)** $4t - t^2 = 3$

9. Use the discriminant to determine whether the roots of each equation are real numbers or not. If the roots are real numbers determine whether they are rational numbers or irrational numbers.
  (a) $x^2 + 9x + 18 = 0$ **(b)** $3x^2 - 5x + 2 = 0$

10. (a) The measure of the area of a rectangle is 10. The measure of the length is 3 more than the measure of the width. Find the measures of the length and width of the rectangle.

(b) An open box with a volume equal to 320 cubic inches is to be made from a square piece of sheet metal. From each of its four corners a square piece 5 inches on a side is cut out. The remaining piece is then bent to form a box open at the top. Find the dimensions of the original square piece of sheet metal. See Figure 11.5.1.

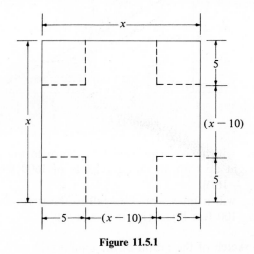

Figure 11.5.1

11. (a) The measures of the two legs of a right triangle are 1 and 8 less than the measure of the hypotenuse. Find the measure of the hypotenuse.

(b) The measure of the hypotenuse of a right triangle is 20. The other side is twice as long as the shortest side. Find the measures of the two sides.

12. (a) Find the values of x, y, and z as they are indicated in Figure 11.5.2.

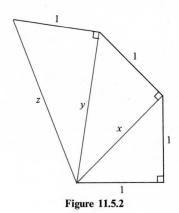

Figure 11.5.2

(b) Find the value of x as it is indicated in Figure 11.5.3.

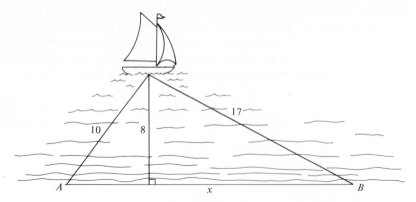

Figure 11.5.3

13. **(a)** How long will it take a projectile to return to the ground if it is shot straight up with an initial velocity of 1600 feet per second? $[h = t(v_0 - 16t)]$.
    (b) How long will it take a brick to fall to the street from the top of a builting 100 feet high? (Hint: $h = 16t^2$.)

14. **(a)** Draw a sketch of the graph of the equation $y = -\frac{1}{2}x^2$.

    (b) Draw a sketch of the graph of the set $\{(x, y) : y = 9 - x^2\}$.

15. Find the zeros of the given quadratic polynomial and find the maximum or minimum value of the quadratic polynomial by finding the coordinates of the vertex point of the corresponding parabola.
    (a) $y = x^2 + 3x - 10$ **(b)** $y = 9 - x^2$

12

Rational Expressions

12.1 Introduction to Rational Expressions

In Section 5.2 a rational number is defined as a number of the form

$$\frac{a}{b}$$

where a and b are integers and $b \neq 0$.

A *rational expression* is defined in Section 9.5 as an algebraic expression of the form

$$\frac{p_1}{p_2}$$

where p_1 and p_2 are polynomials and $p_2 \neq 0$.

Illustration 1   Examples of rational expressions are

(a) $\dfrac{1}{2}$ (b) 7 (c) $x^2 + 2x + 1$

(d) $\dfrac{x + 2}{x^2 + 2x + 1}$, $x^2 + 2x + 1 \neq 0$

(e) $\dfrac{x - 3}{x^2 + 7x + 12}$, $x^2 + 7x + 12 \neq 0$

Every real number is a rational expression and every polynomial is a rational expression. If the variables in a rational expression are replaced with real numbers so that the denominator is not zero, then the value of the rational expression is a real number. Thus, the properties of real numbers apply to rational expressions. In particular, all of the field axioms are valid for rational expressions when the expressions are defined.

Illustration 2   If x is replaced by 2 in the rational expression

$$\frac{x - 3}{x^2 + 7x + 12}$$

415

we have

$$\frac{x - 3}{x^2 + 7x + 12} = \frac{(2) - 3}{(2)^2 + 7(2) + 12}$$

$$= \frac{-1}{4 + 14 + 12}$$

$$= \frac{-1}{30}$$

For rational expressions the replacement of the variable by a real number is restricted to numbers that make the value of the expression meaningful. For example,

$$\frac{x}{x - 2}$$

is a rational expression which is undefined when x is replaced by 2 because then the denominator is 0. Hence, the rational expression

$$\frac{x}{x - 2}$$

is *undefined* if $x = 2$.

Example 1 Find the values of the variable for which the rational expression

$$\frac{x - 3}{x^2 + 7x + 12} \tag{1}$$

is undefined.

Solution: The rational expression is undefined for values of x for which the value of the denominator is zero. Letting the denominator equal zero and solving for x, we have

$$x^2 + 7x + 12 = 0 \tag{2}$$
$$(x + 3)(x + 4) = 0$$

Therefore, equation (2) is satisfied if

$$x + 3 = 0 \qquad \text{or} \qquad x + 4 = 0$$

or, equivalently, if

$$x = -3 \qquad \text{or} \qquad x = -4$$

Hence, rational expression (1) is undefined if $x = -3$ or $x = -4$.

Two rational expressions are said to be equal if they have the same value whenever they are defined. Consider, for instance, the two rational expressions

$$\frac{x}{x - 2} \tag{3}$$

and

$$\frac{x(x + 1)}{(x - 2)(x + 1)} \tag{4}$$

Rational expression (4) is obtained from rational expression (3) by multiplying the numerator and denominator by $(x + 1)$. The two rational expressions have the same value whenever they are defined and so they are equal. Note however that neither expression (3) nor expression (4) is defined when $x = 2$ and expression (4) is undefined when $x = -1$. Hence, we can write

$$\frac{x}{x - 2} = \frac{x(x + 1)}{(x - 2)(x + 1)} \qquad \text{if } x \neq 2 \text{ and } x \neq -1$$

12.1.1 Property   If $\dfrac{p_1}{p_2}$ and $\dfrac{p_3}{p_4}$ are rational expressions, $p_2 \neq 0$ and $p_4 \neq 0$, then

$$\frac{p_1}{p_2} = \frac{p_3}{p_4} \qquad \text{if and only if} \qquad p_1 \cdot p_4 = p_2 \cdot p_3$$

Illustration 3

$$\frac{x}{x - 2} = \frac{x(x + 1)}{(x - 2)(x + 1)} \qquad \text{if } x \neq 2 \text{ and } x \neq -1$$

because

$$x(x - 2)(x + 1) = (x - 2)x(x + 1)$$

The next property is an extension of the Fundamental Principle of Quotients and is used to "reduce" rational expressions to lower terms or to "build" them to higher terms.

12.1.2 Property   If $\dfrac{p_1}{p_2}$ is a rational expression, $p_2 \neq 0$, and q is a rational expression and $q \neq 0$, then

$$\frac{p_1}{p_2} = \frac{p_1 \cdot q}{p_2 \cdot q} \tag{5}$$

and

$$\frac{p_1}{p_2} = \frac{p_1 \div q}{p_2 \div q} \tag{6}$$

Illustration 4 If $p_1 = x$, $p_2 = x - 2$, and $q = 3$ in equation (5), then we have

$$\frac{x}{x - 2} = \frac{3x}{3(x - 2)}$$

If $p_1 = 3x$, $p_2 = 3x - 6$, and $q = 3$ in equation (6), then we have

$$\frac{3x}{3x - 6} = \frac{3x}{3(x - 2)}$$

$$= \frac{3x \div 3}{3(x - 2) \div 3}$$

$$= \frac{x}{x - 2}$$

Example 2 Reduce the following rational expression to lowest terms:

$$\frac{5x + 10}{5x^2 - 20} \quad \text{if } 5x^2 - 20 \neq 0$$

Solution: We write the factored form of both the numerator and denominator and then we divide the numerator and denominator by their greatest common factor.

Thus,

$$\frac{5x + 10}{5x^2 - 20} = \frac{5(x + 2)}{5(x^2 - 4)}$$

$$= \frac{[5(x + 2)] \cdot 1}{[5(x + 2)](x - 2)}$$

$$= \frac{1}{x - 2}$$

To *simplify* a rational expression means to reduce the expression to lowest terms, that is, so that the numerator and denominator have no common factors other than the number 1. In Example 2 the rational expression is simplified by dividing the numerator and denominator by their greatest common factor, $5(x + 2)$.

Each of the two expressions, $E - F$ and $F - E$, is the opposite of the other. In a rational expression if one of these forms is a factor of the numerator and the other is a factor of the denominator, then the rational expression is not in simplest form. Rational expressions of this type appear in Examples 3 and 4.

Example 3 Simplify the rational expression:

$$\frac{15 - 3y}{2y - 10}, \quad 2y - 10 \neq 0$$

Solution: $\dfrac{15 - 3y}{2y - 10} = \dfrac{3(5 - y)}{2(y - 5)}$

Observe that $5 - y$ is the opposite of $y - 5$ and so

$$5 - y = -(y - 5).$$

Substituting $-(y - 5)$ for $5 - y$ in the numerator we have

$$\frac{15 - 3y}{2y - 10} = \frac{3[-(y - 5)]}{2(y - 5)}$$

$$= \frac{3(-1)[y - 5]}{2[y - 5]}$$

$$= \frac{-3}{2}$$

Example 4 Simplify $\dfrac{4 - x^2}{x^2 - 4}$, $x^2 - 4 \neq 0$.

Solution: $\dfrac{4 - x^2}{x^2 - 4} = \dfrac{-(x^2 - 4)}{x^2 - 4}$

$$= -1$$

To build a rational expression to higher terms we can use the principle expressed in Property 12.1.2. See Examples 5 and 6.

Example 5 Build the following rational expression to one whose denominator is $(x - 3)(x + 2)$:

$$\frac{x + 1}{x - 3}, \quad x - 3 \neq 0$$

Solution: To obtain a denominator of $(x - 3)(x + 2)$ we multiply the numerator and denominator by $(x + 2)$. Thus, we have

$$\frac{x + 1}{x - 3} = \frac{(x + 1)[x + 2]}{(x - 3)[x + 2]}$$

Example 6 Build the following rational expression to one whose denominator is $4x^2 + x$:

$$\frac{2x + 3}{4x + 1}, \quad 4x + 1 \neq 0$$

Solution: We express the required denominator in factored form.

$$4x^2 + x = x(4x + 1)$$

Therefore, to obtain the denominator $4x^2 + x$ we multiply the numerator and denominator of the given rational expression by x. We have then

$$\frac{2x + 3}{4x + 1} = \frac{[x](2x + 3)}{[x](4x + 1)}$$

$$= \frac{2x^2 + 3x}{4x^2 + x}$$

Exercises 12.1

In Exercises 1 through 12 find the value (or values) of the variables for which the given rational expression is undefined.

need practice

1. $\dfrac{x + 4}{x - 4}$

2. $\dfrac{2x - 8}{3x - 12}$

3. $\dfrac{x^2 - 1}{x^2}$

4. $\dfrac{x + y}{x - y}$

5. $\dfrac{x^2 + 5x + 6}{x^2 - 9}$

6. $\dfrac{4x(x - 3)}{x^2 - 6x + 9}$

7. $\dfrac{5x + 25}{x^2 + 10x + 25}$

8. $\dfrac{y + 4}{y^2 + 2y - 3}$

9. $\dfrac{x^2 + 4x + 4}{x^2 + 8x + 12}$

10. $\dfrac{3 - x}{x^2 + 1}$

11. $\dfrac{1}{x^2 + 5x - 3}$

12. $\dfrac{x + 4}{x^3 - x}$

In Exercises 13 through 24 simplify the rational expression. Assume the expression is defined.

13. $\dfrac{4x^2}{12x}$

14. $\dfrac{6xy}{9x^2y}$

15. $\dfrac{x + 5}{x^2 - 25}$

16. $\dfrac{x^2 - 2x}{x^2 + 4x + 4}$

17. $\dfrac{5a + 15}{10a + 30}$

18. $\dfrac{x^2 + 8x + 15}{x + 5}$

19. $\dfrac{3x^5 - 12x}{3x^3 - 6x}$

20. $\dfrac{2x^2 + 14x + 24}{2x^2 + 12x + 18}$

21. $\dfrac{5 - x}{x^2 - 25}$

22. $\dfrac{3x^2 - 27}{9 - 3x}$

23. $\dfrac{-x - y}{x^2 - y^2}$ ✓

24. $\dfrac{-t^3}{t^4 - 2t^2}$

In Exercises 25 through 32 build the given rational expression to one having the given denominator.

25. $\dfrac{x + y}{x - y}$; $x^2 - y^2$

26. $\dfrac{2t}{4 - t}$; $64t - 16t^2$

27. $\dfrac{4y}{3xy}$; $12x^2y^2$

28. $\dfrac{1}{x - y}$; $y - x$

29. $\dfrac{3}{x + 5}$; $x^2 + 9x + 20$

30. $\dfrac{1 + y}{1 - y}$; $3 - 2y - y^2$

31. $\dfrac{2x + 1}{2x + 1}$; $x - 1$

32. $\dfrac{a + b}{a^2 + b^2}$; $a^2 + b^2$

33. Simplify the expression:

$$\frac{x_2{}^2 - x_1{}^2}{x_2 - x_1}$$

34. A freely falling body falls a distance s feet in t seconds, where

$$s = 16t^2$$

The same body will fall $s_f - s_0$ feet between the time t_0 seconds and t_f seconds, where

$$s_f = 16t_f^2 \qquad \text{and} \qquad s_0 = 16t_0^2$$

Thus,

$$s_f - s_0 = 16t_f^2 - 16t_0^2$$

If v_{av} feet per second is the average rate of speed of the body from the time t_0 seconds to the time t_f seconds, then

$$v_{av} = \frac{s_f - s_0}{t_f - t_0}$$

or, equivalently,

$$v_{av} = \frac{16t_f^2 - 16t_0^2}{t_f - t_0}$$

By simplifying the rational expression, show that

$$v_{av} = 16(t_f + t_0)$$

and find the average velocity of a falling body between 2 seconds and 3 seconds.

12.2 Multiplication and Division of Rational Expressions

We multiply and divide rational expressions in the same manner as rational numbers.

12.2.1 Definition   If $\dfrac{p_1}{p_2}$ and $\dfrac{p_3}{p_4}$ are two rational expressions, $p_2 \neq 0$ and $p_4 \neq 0$, then

$$\frac{p_1}{p_2} \cdot \frac{p_3}{p_4} = \frac{p_1 \cdot p_3}{p_2 \cdot p_4}$$

In order to simplify the product of two rational expressions first express each numerator and denominator in factored form and then apply Definition 12.2.1. The product is then reduced to lowest terms.

Example 1 Find the product:

$$\frac{7x - 14}{x^2 - 1} \cdot \frac{2x + 2}{5x - 10}$$

Solution:

$$\frac{7x - 14}{x^2 - 1} \cdot \frac{2x + 2}{5x - 10} = \frac{7(x - 2)}{(x + 1)(x - 1)} \cdot \frac{2(x + 1)}{5(x - 2)}$$

$$= \frac{(2)(7)(x - 2)(x + 1)}{5(x + 1)(x - 1)(x - 2)}$$

$$= \frac{(2)(7)[(x - 2)(x + 1)]}{5(x - 1)[(x - 2)(x + 1)]}$$

$$= \frac{14}{5(x - 1)}$$

Example 2 Multiply:

$$\frac{x^2 + x - 20}{2x - 6} \cdot \frac{9 - x^2}{x^2 - 2x - 8}$$

Solution:

$$\frac{x^2 + x - 20}{2x - 6} \cdot \frac{9 - x^2}{x^2 - 2x - 8} = \frac{(x + 5)(x - 4)}{2(x - 3)} \cdot \frac{(3 - x)(3 + x)}{(x + 2)(x - 4)}$$

$$= \frac{(x + 5)(x - 4)(3 - x)(3 + x)}{2(x - 3)(x + 2)(x - 4)}$$

The greatest common factor of the numerator and denominator is $(x - 3)(x - 4)$. Observe that $3 - x$ is the opposite of $x - 3$ and so,

$$3 - x = -(x - 3)$$

We substitute $-(x - 3)$ for $3 - x$ in the numerator and then divide the numerator and denominator by $(x - 3)(x - 4)$. Hence, we have

$$\frac{(x + 5)(x - 4)(3 - x)(3 + x)}{2(x - 3)(x + 2)(x - 4)} = \frac{(x + 5)(x + 3)[-(x - 3)(x - 4)]}{2(x + 2)[(x - 3)(x - 4)]}$$

$$= \frac{-(x + 5)(x + 3)}{2(x + 2)}$$

$$= \frac{-x^2 - 8x - 15}{2x + 4}$$

In Section 5.4 we stated that the quotient of two rational numbers is the product of the dividend and the reciprocal of the divisor. We now define the division of two rational expressions in a similar way.

12.2.2 Definition   If $\dfrac{p_1}{p_2}$ and $\dfrac{p_3}{p_4}$ are rational expressions, $p_2 \neq 0$, $p_3 \neq 0$, and $p_4 \neq 0$, then

$$\frac{p_1}{p_2} \div \frac{p_3}{p_4} = \frac{p_1}{p_2} \cdot \frac{p_4}{p_3}$$

Example 3   Divide $\dfrac{a^2 - b^2}{3a}$ by $\dfrac{2a - 2b}{6}$.

Solution:
$$\frac{a^2 - b^2}{3a} \div \frac{2a - 2b}{6} = \frac{a^2 - b^2}{3a} \cdot \frac{6}{2a - 2b}$$
$$= \frac{(a + b)(a - b)}{3a} \cdot \frac{6}{2(a - b)}$$
$$= \frac{6(a + b)(a - b)}{6a(a - b)}$$
$$= \frac{(a + b)[6(a - b)]}{a[6(a - b)]}$$
$$= \frac{a + b}{a}$$

Example 4   Divide the product of $\dfrac{x}{x + y}$ and $\dfrac{x^2 - y^2}{y}$ by $x - y$.

Solution:

$$\left(\frac{x}{x + y} \cdot \frac{x^2 - y^2}{y}\right) \div (x - y) = \left(\frac{x}{x + y} \cdot \frac{x^2 - y^2}{y}\right) \cdot \frac{1}{x - y}$$
$$= \frac{x}{x + y} \cdot \frac{(x + y)(x - y)}{y} \cdot \frac{1}{x - y}$$
$$= \frac{x(x + y)(x - y)}{(x + y)(y)(x - y)}$$
$$= \frac{x[(x + y)(x - y)]}{y[(x + y)(x - y)]}$$
$$= \frac{x}{y}$$

Example 5 Multiply the quotient $\dfrac{a^2 - 1}{a^2 - 4} \div \dfrac{3a - 3}{5a + 10}$ by $\dfrac{3a - 6}{5a}$.

Solution:

$$\left(\frac{a^2 - 1}{a^2 - 4} \div \frac{3a - 3}{5a + 10}\right) \cdot \frac{3a - 6}{5a} = \left(\frac{a^2 - 1}{a^2 - 4} \cdot \frac{5a + 10}{3a - 3}\right) \cdot \frac{3a - 6}{5a}$$

$$= \frac{(a + 1)(a - 1)}{(a + 2)(a - 2)} \cdot \frac{5(a + 2)}{3(a - 1)} \cdot \frac{3(a - 2)}{5a}$$

$$= \frac{(a + 1)(a - 1)(5)(a + 2)(3)(a - 2)}{(a + 2)(a - 2)(3)(a - 1)(5)(a)}$$

$$= \frac{(a + 1)[3 \cdot 5(a - 1)(a + 2)(a - 2)]}{a[3 \cdot 5(a - 1)(a + 2)(a - 2)]}$$

$$= \frac{a + 1}{a}$$

Exercises 12.2

In Exercises 1 through 20 perform the indicated operation and express the result in lowest terms.

1. $\dfrac{6y^3}{15} \cdot \dfrac{30x}{4y}$

2. $\dfrac{1 - x}{x} \cdot \dfrac{1 - x}{x}$

3. $\dfrac{6a - 3}{8a - 4} \cdot \dfrac{5a + 10}{10a - 15}$

4. $\dfrac{10y - y^2}{y^2 - 100} \cdot \dfrac{y^2 + 30y + 200}{10y + y^2}$

5. $\dfrac{x^2 - 2x + 1}{x^2 + x - 2} \cdot \dfrac{x^2 - x - 6}{x^2 - 9} \cdot \dfrac{x^2 - 2x + 1}{x^2 - x - 2}$ $\dfrac{(x - 1)^3}{(x + 3)(x - 2)(x + 1)}$

6. $\left(\dfrac{a - b}{a}\right)\left(\dfrac{a^3}{b^2 - a^2}\right)\left(\dfrac{a + b}{a}\right)$

7. $\left(\dfrac{x - 4}{x + 4}\right)^2 (x^2 + 8x + 16)$ $\dfrac{(x - 4)(x - 4)}{1}$

8. $\dfrac{4t + 12}{3t - 18} \cdot \dfrac{9t - 54}{2t + 6}$

9. $\dfrac{m^4 - n^4}{m - n} \cdot \dfrac{m + n}{m^2 + n^2}$

10. $\dfrac{u^2 - 4}{u^2 + 2u - 8} \cdot \dfrac{3u + 6}{u^2 + 4u + 4}$

11. $\dfrac{4x^2}{3y} \div \dfrac{x}{9y}$

12. $\dfrac{a + 4}{a^2 + 2a - 3} \div \dfrac{3a + 12}{a^2 + 3a}$

13. $\dfrac{y^2 - 4}{y^2 - 1} \div \dfrac{y + 2}{y - 1}$

14. $\dfrac{x^2 - 14x + 49}{x^2 - 2x - 35} \div \dfrac{x^2 - 5x - 14}{x^2 + 9x + 14}$ $\dfrac{x + 7}{x + 5}$

15. $\dfrac{z^2 - 25}{z^2 + 10z + 25} \div \dfrac{z^2 + 5z}{z^2 + 2z - 15}$

16. $\dfrac{x^2 + 7x + 12}{4x^2 - 1} \cdot \dfrac{x^2 - 25}{2x^2 + 13x + 15} \div \dfrac{x^2 - x - 20}{4x - 2}$

17. $\dfrac{4x + 12}{3x + 6} \div \dfrac{x - 1}{3x^2 - 12} \cdot \dfrac{x^2 + 4x + 3}{x^2 + 6x + 9}$

18. $\dfrac{9x^2 - 4}{3x + 3} \div (3x + 2)$

19. $\dfrac{10}{a^2 - b^2} \cdot \dfrac{b - a}{5}$

20. $\dfrac{1 - x^2}{x^4} \div \dfrac{x - 1}{x^2}$

21. The number of dots in the pattern in Figure 12.2.1 is calculated by multiplying the number of rows times one more than the number of dots in the last row divided by 2. If there are n rows, how many dots are in the last row? Write an expression for the total number of dots in the pattern with n rows. How many dots are in a pattern like this consisting of 100 rows?

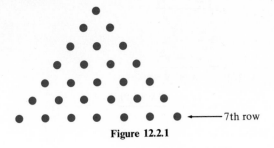

7th row

Figure 12.2.1

12.3 Addition and Subtraction of Rational Expressions

If two or more rational expressions have the same denominator, they can be added or subtracted just as rational numbers are added and subtracted.

12.3.1 Definition If $\dfrac{p_1}{p_2}$ and $\dfrac{p_3}{p_2}$ are rational expressions, $p_2 \neq 0,$ then

$$\frac{p_1}{p_2} + \frac{p_3}{p_2} = \frac{p_1 + p_3}{p_2}$$

and

$$\frac{p_1}{p_2} - \frac{p_3}{p_2} = \frac{p_1 - p_3}{p_2}$$

Example 1 Perform the indicated operations:

(a) $\dfrac{2x}{x+y} + \dfrac{2x}{x+y}$

(b) $\dfrac{x^2}{x+y} - \dfrac{y^2}{x+y}$

(c) $\dfrac{4x+2}{x^2+5x+6} + \dfrac{x+3}{x^2+5x+6} - \dfrac{4x+3}{x^2+5x+6}$

Solution:

(a) $\dfrac{2x}{x+y} + \dfrac{2y}{x+y} = \dfrac{2x+2y}{x+y}$

$$= \frac{2(x+y)}{x+y}$$

$$= 2$$

(b) $\dfrac{x^2}{x+y} - \dfrac{y^2}{x+y} = \dfrac{x^2-y^2}{x+y}$

$$= \frac{(x+y)(x-y)}{x+y}$$

$$= x - y$$

(c) $\dfrac{4x + 2}{x^2 + 5x + 6} + \dfrac{x + 3}{x^2 + 5x + 6} - \dfrac{4x + 3}{x^2 + 5x + 6}$

$$= \dfrac{(4x + 2) + (x + 3) - (4x + 3)}{x^2 + 5x + 6}$$

$$= \dfrac{x + 2}{x^2 + 5x + 6}$$

$$= \dfrac{x + 2}{(x + 2)(x + 3)}$$

$$= \dfrac{1}{x + 3}$$

To add or subtract rational expressions with different denominators, we must build the rational expressions to higher terms until they have a common denominator. We use Property 12.1.2 to do this.

The *least common multiple* (LCM) of two or more polynomials is found by the method of Section 5.1, where, instead of whole numbers, we have polynomials. The polynomials are first expressed in completely factored form.

Example 2 Find the LCM of x^2y and $2xy$.

Solution: Use the method of Section 5.1.

$$x^2y = (x)(x)(y)$$
$$2xy = (2)(x)(y)$$

By "tagging" each factor with a subscript to distinguish the equal factors we can form the set of factors of each monomial.

$$x^2y \longleftrightarrow \{x_1, x_2, y_1\}$$
$$2xy \longleftrightarrow \{2_1, x_1, y_1\}$$

The union of these sets is the set of factors of the required LCM.

$$\{x_1, x_2, y_1\} \cup \{2_1, x_1, y_1\} = \{2_1, x_1, x_2, y_1\}$$

Hence, the LCM of x^2y and $2xy$ is the product of the factors in the set $\{2_1, x_1, x_2, y_1\}$, that is,

$$(2)(x)(x)(y)$$

or, equivalently,

$$2x^2y$$

Example 3 Find the LCM of $2x + 4$ and $x^2 - 4$.

Solution: $2x + 4 = 2(x + 2)$
$x^2 - 4 = (x + 2)(x - 2)$

Hence, by subscripting the factors and forming the set of factors of each polynomial, we have

$$2x + 4 \longleftrightarrow \{2_1, (x + 2)_1\}$$
$$x^2 - 4 \longleftrightarrow \{(x + 2)_1, (x - 2)_1\}$$

The union of these sets is the set of factors of the required LCM.

$$\{2_1, (x + 2)_1\} \cup \{(x + 2)_1, (x - 2)_1\} = \{2_1, (x + 2)_1, (x - 2)_1\}$$

Hence, the LCM of $2x + 4$ and $x^2 - 4$ is the product of the factors in the set $\{2_1, (x + 2)_1, (x - 2)_1\}$, that is,

$$2(x + 2)(x - 2)$$

or, equivalently,

$$2x^2 - 8$$

The *least common denominator* (LCD) of two or more rational expressions is the LCM of the denominators of these rational expressions.

Example 4 Find the sum: $\dfrac{3}{x^2y} + \dfrac{1}{2xy}$

Solution: The LCD of the two rational expressions is the LCM of x^2y and $2xy$ which is $2x^2y$. See Example 2. Now we must build each rational expression to higher terms so that $2x^2y$ is the common denominator. Refer to Section 12.1.

Thus,

$$\frac{3}{x^2y} + \frac{1}{2xy} = \frac{3[2]}{x^2y[2]} + \frac{1[x]}{2xy[x]}$$
$$= \frac{6}{2x^2y} + \frac{x}{2x^2y}$$
$$= \frac{6 + x}{2x^2y}$$

Example 5 Find the sum: $\dfrac{1}{2x + 4} + \dfrac{2}{x^2 - 4}$

Solution: The LCD of the two rational expressions is the LCM of $2x + 4$ and $x^2 - 4$, which is $2(x + 2)(x - 2)$. See Example 3. Thus, we build each rational expression to higher terms so that the common denominator is $2(x + 2)(x - 2)$.

Therefore,

$$\frac{1}{2x + 4} + \frac{2}{x^2 - 4} = \frac{1}{2(x + 2)} + \frac{2}{(x + 2)(x - 2)}$$

$$= \frac{1[x - 2]}{2(x + 2)[x - 2]} + \frac{2[2]}{(x + 2)(x - 2)[2]}$$

$$= \frac{x - 2}{2(x + 2)(x - 2)} + \frac{4}{2(x + 2)(x - 2)}$$

$$= \frac{x - 2 + 4}{2(x + 2)(x - 2)}$$

$$= \frac{x + 2}{2(x + 2)(x - 2)}$$

$$= \frac{1[x + 2]}{2(x - 2)[x + 2]}$$

$$= \frac{1}{2(x - 2)}$$

Example 6 Subtract $\dfrac{x + y}{x - y}$ from $\dfrac{x - y}{x + y}$.

Solution: The LCD of the two rational expressions is $(x + y)(x - y)$. We build the rational expressions to higher terms with $(x + y)(x - y)$ as the common denominator.
Therefore,

$$\frac{x - y}{x + y} - \frac{x + y}{x - y} = \frac{(x - y)[x - y]}{(x + y)[x - y]} - \frac{(x + y)[x + y]}{(x - y)[x + y]}$$

$$= \frac{x^2 - 2xy + y^2}{(x + y)(x - y)} - \frac{x^2 + 2xy + y^2}{(x + y)(x - y)}$$

$$= \frac{x^2 - 2xy + y^2 - (x^2 + 2xy + y^2)}{(x + y)(x - y)}$$

$$= \frac{x^2 - 2xy + y^2 - x^2 - 2xy - y^2}{(x + y)(x - y)}$$

$$= \frac{-4xy}{(x + y)(x - y)}$$

Example 7 Simplify: $2a - b - \dfrac{a - b}{3}$.

Solution: We write the given expression as

$$\frac{2a}{1} - \frac{b}{1} - \frac{a - b}{3}$$

and determine that the LCD is 3. Thus,

$$2a - b - \frac{a-b}{3} = \frac{2a}{1} - \frac{b}{1} - \frac{a-b}{3}$$

$$= \frac{2a[3]}{1[3]} - \frac{b[3]}{1[3]} - \frac{a-b}{3}$$

$$= \frac{6a}{3} - \frac{3b}{3} - \frac{a-b}{3}$$

$$= \frac{6a - 3b - (a-b)}{3}$$

$$= \frac{6a - 3b - a + b}{3}$$

$$= \frac{5a - 2b}{3}$$

Example 8 Simplify: $\left(1 - \dfrac{x}{y}\right)\left(\dfrac{1}{x^2 - y^2}\right)$

Solution:

$$\left(1 - \frac{x}{y}\right)\left(\frac{1}{x^2 - y^2}\right) = \left(\frac{y}{y} - \frac{x}{y}\right)\left(\frac{1}{x^2 - y^2}\right)$$

$$= \frac{y - x}{y} \cdot \frac{1}{(x + y)(x - y)}$$

$$= \frac{y - x}{y(x + y)(x - y)}$$

$$= \frac{(-1)[x - y]}{y(x + y)[x - y]}$$

$$= \frac{-1}{y(x + y)}$$

Until now we have considered only rational expressions having a polynomial or a constant as the numerator and denominator. A rational expression for which this is not the case is called a *complex rational expression*.

Illustration 1 The expressions

$$\frac{\frac{3}{4}}{10}, \quad \frac{x}{\frac{1}{2}}, \quad \frac{\frac{x+2}{x^2-4}}{\frac{x}{x-2}}, \quad \text{and} \quad \frac{1 + \frac{1}{x}}{1 + \frac{1}{y}}$$

are complex rational expressions.

One method of simplifying a complex rational expression is to divide the numerator by the denominator. The next example illustrates this method.

Example 9 Simplify: $\dfrac{1 + \dfrac{1}{x}}{1 - \dfrac{1}{x}}$

Solution:

$$\frac{1 + \dfrac{1}{x}}{1 - \dfrac{1}{x}} = \left(1 + \frac{1}{x}\right) \div \left(1 - \frac{1}{x}\right)$$

$$= \left(\frac{x}{x} + \frac{1}{x}\right) \div \left(\frac{x}{x} - \frac{1}{x}\right)$$

$$= \left(\frac{x+1}{x}\right) \div \left(\frac{x-1}{x}\right)$$

$$= \frac{x+1}{x} \cdot \frac{x}{x-1}$$

$$= \frac{(x+1)x}{x(x-1)}$$

$$= \frac{(x+1)[x]}{(x-1)[x]}$$

$$= \frac{x+1}{x-1}$$

A second method for simplifying a complex rational expression is to multiply the numerator and denominator of the complex rational expression by the LCD of the other expressions in the complex expression.

Example 10 Simplify the rational expression of Example 9 by another method.

Solution: The LCD of the rational expressions in the numerator and denominator of the complex rational expression is x. Hence, we multiply the numerator and denominator by x.

$$\frac{1 + \dfrac{1}{x}}{1 - \dfrac{1}{x}} = \frac{x\left(1 + \dfrac{1}{x}\right)}{x\left(1 - \dfrac{1}{x}\right)}$$

$$= \frac{x+1}{x-1}$$

Example 11 Simplify:

$$\frac{\dfrac{x+2}{x^2-4}}{\dfrac{x}{x-2}}$$

Solution:

$$\frac{\dfrac{x+2}{x^2-4}}{\dfrac{x}{x-2}} = \frac{x+2}{x^2-4} \div \frac{x}{x-2}$$

$$= \frac{x+2}{x^2-4} \cdot \frac{x-2}{x}$$

$$= \frac{x+2}{(x+2)(x-2)} \cdot \frac{x-2}{x}$$

$$= \frac{(x+2)(x-2)}{(x+2)(x-2)(x)}$$

$$= \frac{1[(x+2)(x-2)]}{x[(x+2)(x-2)]}$$

$$= \frac{1}{x}$$

Example 12 Show that $\dfrac{1}{1-x^2} = \dfrac{\frac{1}{2}}{1-x} + \dfrac{\frac{1}{2}}{1+x}$

Solution: To show that the two members of the given equation are equal we show that the sum of the two rational expressions in the right member is equal to the rational expression in the left member.

$$\frac{\frac{1}{2}}{1-x} + \frac{\frac{1}{2}}{1+x} = \frac{\frac{1}{2}[2]}{(1-x)[2]} + \frac{\frac{1}{2}[2]}{(1+x)[2]}$$

$$= \frac{1}{2(1-x)} + \frac{1}{2(1+x)}$$

$$= \frac{1[1+x]}{2(1-x)[1+x]} + \frac{1[1-x]}{2(1+x)[1-x]}$$

$$= \frac{(1+x)+(1-x)}{2(1-x)(1+x)}$$

$$= \frac{2}{2(1-x)(1+x)}$$

$$= \frac{1}{(1-x)(1+x)}$$

$$= \frac{1}{1-x^2}$$

Exercises 12.3

In Exercises 1 through 30 perform the indicated operations.

1. $\dfrac{3}{x} + \dfrac{5}{x} - \dfrac{2}{x}$

2. $\dfrac{5}{4x} + \dfrac{3}{4x}$

3. $\dfrac{2a}{5x} + \dfrac{3a}{5x}$

4. $\dfrac{5}{x+y} + \dfrac{2}{x+y}$

5. $\dfrac{4x}{4x-y} - \dfrac{2x}{4x-y}$

6. $\dfrac{a}{a+b} + \dfrac{b}{a+b}$

7. $\dfrac{x+4y}{x+y} + \dfrac{x-2y}{x+y}$

8. $\dfrac{x^2}{x+4} - \dfrac{16}{x+4}$

9. $\dfrac{3x+9}{x^2+8x+12} - \dfrac{2x+3}{x^2+8x+12}$

10. $\dfrac{(x+1)^2}{4x^3-4x} - \dfrac{(x-1)^2}{4x^3-4x}$

11. $\dfrac{7}{2x^2} + \dfrac{3}{3x^3} - \dfrac{5}{6x}$

12. $\dfrac{1}{x} - \dfrac{1}{y}$

13. $\dfrac{x+3}{12} + \dfrac{x+2}{9}$

14. $\dfrac{2x-y}{x^2y} + \dfrac{x+y}{xy^2}$

15. $\dfrac{1}{a-b} - \dfrac{3}{a+b}$

16. $\dfrac{5}{t+4} - \dfrac{3}{3t+12}$

17. $\dfrac{16x}{x^2-4} + \dfrac{x-6}{x+2}$

18. $\dfrac{x^2+2x}{x^2+7x+10} - \dfrac{x-3}{x+2}$

19. $\dfrac{1}{x+1} + x - 1$

20. $\dfrac{m}{m-4} - \dfrac{3m}{4-m}$

21. $x + \dfrac{2x+4}{x-2}$

22. $1 - \dfrac{8}{x^2+4}$

23. $\left(x + \dfrac{2x+4}{x-2}\right)\left(1 - \dfrac{8}{x^2+4}\right)$

24. $\left(\dfrac{4y^2}{3} - 3\right) \div \left(1 + \dfrac{2y}{3}\right)$

25. $\dfrac{a+1}{a} \div \left(1 - \dfrac{1}{a^2}\right)$

26. $\dfrac{\frac{1}{x}}{\frac{1}{y}}$

27. $\dfrac{\frac{x}{y} + \frac{y}{x}}{\frac{x}{y} - \frac{y}{x}}$

28. $\dfrac{\frac{x}{x-y}}{\frac{x^2}{x^2-y^2}}$

29. $\dfrac{1 - \dfrac{x}{x-1}}{1 + \dfrac{1}{x-1}}$

30. $\dfrac{\dfrac{x^2 + x - 6}{3x^2 + 8x - 3}}{\dfrac{x^2 + 2x - 3}{2x^2 + 5x - 3}}$

31. Show that $\dfrac{1}{x^2 - a^2} = \dfrac{1}{2a}\left(\dfrac{1}{x - a} - \dfrac{1}{x + a}\right)$ when $x \neq \pm a$.

32. Show that $\dfrac{1}{n+1} = 1 - \dfrac{n}{n+1}$ when $n \neq -1$.

33. Study and verify the following equations. Predict the next equation. Write the nth equation in the list by using the variable n. (Hint: See Exercise 32.)

$$\dfrac{1}{1+1} = 1 - \dfrac{1}{1+1} \qquad (1)$$

$$\dfrac{1}{2+1} = 1 - \dfrac{2}{2+1} \qquad (2)$$

$$\dfrac{1}{3+1} = 1 - \dfrac{3}{3+1} \qquad (3)$$

$$\dfrac{1}{4+1} = 1 - \dfrac{4}{4+1} \qquad (4)$$

$$\cdot \qquad \cdot \qquad \cdot \qquad (5)$$
$$\cdot \qquad \cdot \qquad \cdot$$
$$\cdot \qquad \cdot \qquad \cdot \qquad \cdot$$
$$\cdot \qquad \cdot \qquad \cdot$$
$$\cdot \qquad \cdot \qquad \cdot \qquad (n)$$

34. Show that $\left(\dfrac{1}{x}\right)\left(\dfrac{1}{x+1}\right) = \dfrac{1}{x} - \dfrac{1}{x+1}$.

35. Show that $\left(\dfrac{1}{x}\right)\left(\dfrac{1}{ax+b}\right) = \dfrac{a}{b}\left(\dfrac{1}{ax} - \dfrac{1}{ax+b}\right)$.

36. An investigation of the following pattern

$$\dfrac{1}{2} = \dfrac{1}{2}$$

$$\dfrac{1}{3} + \dfrac{2}{3} = \dfrac{2}{2}$$

$$\dfrac{1}{4} + \dfrac{2}{4} + \dfrac{3}{4} = \dfrac{3}{2}$$

$$\dfrac{1}{5} + \dfrac{2}{5} + \dfrac{3}{5} + \dfrac{4}{5} = \dfrac{4}{2}$$

$$\vdots \qquad \vdots \quad \vdots$$

leads to the conjecture that

$$\frac{1}{n+1} + \frac{2}{n+1} + \frac{3}{n+1} + \cdots + \frac{n}{n+1} = \frac{n}{2}$$

Prove this formula by using the Summation Property of Chapter 1 (Property 1.1.1), that is,

$$1 + 2 + 3 + \cdots + n = \frac{1}{2}n(n+1)$$

12.4 Equations Containing Rational Expressions

If an equation contains rational expressions, we first multiply both members of the equation by the LCD of the rational expressions found in the equation.

Example 1 Solve the equation: $\frac{2}{3}x + \frac{1}{2} = \frac{7}{10}$

Solution: The LCD is 30. Thus we multiply both members of the given equation by 30.

$$30\left(\frac{2}{3}x + \frac{1}{2}\right) = 30\left(\frac{7}{10}\right)$$

$$20x + 15 = 21$$

$$20x = 6$$

$$x = \frac{6}{20}$$

$$x = \frac{3}{10}$$

Therefore, the solution set is $\left\{\frac{3}{10}\right\}$.

Example 2 Solve the equation: $\frac{1}{x} + \frac{1}{3} = \frac{1}{2}$

Solution: The LCD is $6x$. Thus, we multiply both members of the equation by $6x$.

$$6x\left(\frac{1}{x} + \frac{1}{3}\right) = 6x\left(\frac{1}{2}\right)$$

$$6 + 2x = 3x$$

$$6 = x$$

Therefore, the solution set is $\{6\}$.

Example 3 Solve the equation: $\dfrac{x}{x-1} = \dfrac{1}{x-1}$

Solution: The LCD is $x - 1$. We multiply both members of the given equation by $x - 1$.

$$(x-1)\left[\frac{x}{x-1}\right] = (x-1)\left[\frac{1}{x-1}\right]$$

$$x = 1$$

But, if $x = 1$, then $\dfrac{x}{x-1}$ and $\dfrac{1}{x-1}$ are undefined. Hence, 1 is not in the replacement set for x and so cannot be a solution of the given equation. The given equation has no solution. We state that the solution set is $\varnothing$.

Because of the situation that arises in Example 3, whenever we multiply both members of an equation by a polynomial containing a variable, the replacement set of the original equation should be explicitly defined.

Example 4 Solve the equation: $\dfrac{3}{2} - \dfrac{8}{x-1} = 5$

Solution: The replacement set for the equation is the set of all real numbers except 1. The LCD is $2(x - 1)$. We multiply both members of the given equation by $2(x - 1)$.

$$2(x-1)\left(\frac{3}{2} - \frac{8}{x-1}\right) = 2(x-1)(5)$$

$$3(x-1) - 2(8) = 10(x-1)$$

$$3x - 3 - 16 = 10x - 10$$

$$3x - 19 = 10x - 10$$

$$-7x = 9$$

$$x = \frac{-9}{7}$$

Because $\dfrac{-9}{7}$ belongs to the replacement set of the original equation, the solution set is $\left\{\dfrac{-9}{7}\right\}$.

Example 5 Solve the equation: $\dfrac{x}{x-1} + \dfrac{x}{x+1} = \dfrac{2x}{x^2-1}$

Solution: The replacement set of the given equation is the set of all real numbers except 1 and -1. The LCD is $(x + 1)(x - 1)$, and so we multiply both members of the given equation by $(x + 1)(x - 1)$.

$$(x + 1)(x - 1) \left[\frac{x}{x - 1} + \frac{x}{x + 1} \right] = (x + 1)(x - 1) \left[\frac{2x}{x^2 - 1} \right]$$

$$x(x + 1) + x(x - 1) = 2x$$

$$x^2 + x + x^2 - x = 2x$$

$$2x^2 - 2x = 0$$

$$2x(x - 1) = 0$$

By the Zero Product Property we have

$$x = 0 \qquad \text{or} \qquad x - 1 = 0$$

that is,

$$x = 0 \qquad \text{or} \qquad x = 1$$

Because 1 does not belong to the replacement set, we reject 1 as a solution. However, 0 belongs to the replacement set and so 0 is a solution. The solution set is $\{0\}$.

Example 6 Solve the equation: $\dfrac{5}{x} + \dfrac{x}{x - 2} = \dfrac{4}{3}$

Solution: The replacement set for the given equation is the set of all real numbers except 0 and 2. Multiplying both members of the given equation by the LCD, $3x(x - 2)$, we obtain

$$3x(x - 2) \left[\frac{5}{x} + \frac{x}{x - 2} \right] = 3x(x - 2) \left[\frac{4}{3} \right]$$

$$3(x - 2)(5) + 3x(x) = x(x - 2)(4)$$

$$15x - 30 + 3x^2 = 4x^2 - 8x$$

$$0 = x^2 - 23x + 30$$

Using the quadratic formula when $a = 1$, $b = -23$, and $c = 30$, we have

$$x = \frac{-b \pm \sqrt{b^2 - 4ac}}{2a}$$

$$= \frac{-(-23) \pm \sqrt{(-23)^2 - 4(1)(30)}}{2(1)}$$

$$= \frac{23 \pm \sqrt{529 - 120}}{2}$$

$$= \frac{23 \pm \sqrt{409}}{2}$$

Thus, the solutions are

$$x_1 = \frac{23 + \sqrt{409}}{2} \qquad \text{and} \qquad x_2 = \frac{23 - \sqrt{409}}{2}$$

Because $\sqrt{409} \doteq 20.2$, we obtain the approximate solutions

$$x_1 \doteq \frac{23 + 20.2}{2} \qquad \text{and} \qquad x_2 \doteq \frac{23 - 20.2}{2}$$

and so,

$$x_1 \doteq 21.6 \qquad \text{and} \qquad x_2 \doteq 1.4$$

Because these numbers belong to the replacement set, the solution set is $\{21.6, 1.4\}$.

Example 7 Solve the following formula for h.

$$A = \frac{1}{2} Bh - \frac{1}{2} bh$$

Solution: The factors of the right member are $\frac{1}{2} h$ and $(B - b)$. Thus,

$$A = \frac{1}{2} h(B - b)$$

$$2A = h(B - b)$$

$$\frac{2A}{B - b} = h \qquad \text{where } B - b \neq 0$$

Example 8 Solve the following equation for y.

$$x = \frac{y}{y + 2}$$

Solution: The replacement set of the variable y for the given equation is the set of all real numbers except -2. Multiplying both members of the given equation by $(y + 2)$, we have

$$(y + 2)[x] = (y + 2)\left[\frac{y}{y + 2}\right]$$

$$xy + 2x = y$$

$$2x = y - xy$$

$$2x = y(1 - x)$$

$$\frac{2x}{1 - x} = y \qquad \text{where } 1 - x \neq 0$$

The replacement set for the given equation is the set of ordered pairs $\left\{(x, y) : x = \dfrac{y}{y + 2}\right\}$ except that the value for y cannot be -2; and the value for x cannot be 1. This can be interpreted to mean that the graph of the given equation does not intersect the horizontal line having the equation $y = -2$ nor the vertical line having the equation $x = 1$.

Exercises 12.4

In Exercises 1 through 20 solve the equation.

1. $\dfrac{x}{3} + \dfrac{x}{4} = 14$

2. $\dfrac{1}{x} + \dfrac{1}{5} = \dfrac{1}{4}$

3. $\dfrac{m}{2} + \dfrac{2m}{3} = 7$

4. $\dfrac{2}{t} + \dfrac{3}{t} + \dfrac{4}{t} = 1$

5. $\dfrac{3}{x} - \dfrac{4}{3x} = \dfrac{5}{3}$

6. $\dfrac{100}{x} - 4 = \dfrac{200}{5x}$

7. $\dfrac{2y - 7}{2y + 3} = \dfrac{y + 1}{y - 1}$

8. $\dfrac{x - 3}{5} = 3x + 2$

9. $\dfrac{10}{x - 3} = \dfrac{9}{x - 5}$

10. $\dfrac{2}{t - 1} = \dfrac{3t}{1 - t}$

11. $3 - \dfrac{3x}{x - 2} = \dfrac{x}{x^2 - 4}$ $\times \dfrac{12 - 12}{7}$

12. $\dfrac{x + 5}{x + 10} = 0$

13. $\dfrac{x + 5}{x^2 - 25} = 0$ *0 Undefined*

14. $\dfrac{1}{x} + \dfrac{1}{x - 2} = \dfrac{4}{3}$

15. $\dfrac{2}{x} + \dfrac{x}{x - 2} = \dfrac{4}{3}$ $3 \times (x - 2) LCD$

16. $\dfrac{8}{x - 1} + \dfrac{x}{1 - x} = \dfrac{-2}{x^2 - 1}$

17. $\dfrac{y + 4}{y - 4} + \dfrac{y + 3}{y - 3} = 0$

18. $\dfrac{8}{x - 1} - \dfrac{3}{x^2 + x - 2} = 0$

19. $\dfrac{2}{a - 5} + \dfrac{1}{a + 5} = \dfrac{11}{a^2 - 25}$

20. $\dfrac{3x - 8}{x^2 - 8x + 16} - \dfrac{x}{x^2 - 8x + 16} = \dfrac{2}{x - 4}$ *Restrictions in denominator*

In Exercises 21 through 25 solve the equation for y. State the restrictions on the replacement values for x and y. *set equal to zero*

21. $\dfrac{1}{x} = \dfrac{1}{y}$

22. $2 = \dfrac{y}{x}$

23. $\dfrac{1}{y + 1} = \dfrac{1}{2x - 3}$

24. $\dfrac{x + 1}{3} = \dfrac{y - 1}{y + 1}$

25. $\dfrac{1}{x} + 3 = \dfrac{y}{y - 2}$ *Restriction of y?*

In Exercises 26 through 30 solve the equation for the variable indicated and state any restriction imposed on the remaining variables.

26. $d = rt$. Solve for t.

27. $\dfrac{1}{r} = \dfrac{1}{a} + \dfrac{1}{b}$. Solve for a.

28. $A = \dfrac{1}{2} h(B + b)$. Solve for h.

29. $E = \dfrac{1}{2} mv^2$. Solve for m.

30. $ax - b = cx - d$. Solve for x.

31. Examine the steps below and discover what mistake is made in this argument. Assume that

$$a = 2 \tag{1}$$

Multiplying both members of equation (1) by a, we have

$$a^2 = 2a \tag{2}$$

Subtracting 4 from both members of equation (2), we have

$$a^2 - 4 = 2a - 4 \tag{3}$$

Expressing both members of equation (3) in factored form, we have

$$(a + 2)(a - 2) = 2(a - 2) \tag{4}$$

Dividing both members of equation (4) by $(a - 2)$, we have

$$\frac{(a + 2)(a - 2)}{a - 2} = \frac{2(a - 2)}{a - 2} \tag{5}$$

Simplifying both members of equation (5), we have

$$a + 2 = 2 \tag{6}$$

Subtracting 2 from both members of equation (7), we have

$$a = 0 \tag{7}$$

Therefore, from equations (1) and (7) we conclude

$$2 = 0 \tag{8}$$

32. Every positive number a can be written in terms of x as

$$a = \frac{1 + x}{1 - x}$$

(a) Solve this equation for x.
(b) By replacing a by 10 in the equation find a value for x such that

$$10 = \frac{1 + x}{1 - x}$$

33. Show that the equation

$$\frac{x}{x - 3} = \frac{3}{x - 3} + c$$

where c is a constant, has no solution if $c \neq 1$ and has a solution if $c = 1$.

12.5 Applications Involving Rational Equations

Consider the formula

$$\frac{1}{R} = \frac{1}{R_1} + \frac{1}{R_2} \tag{1}$$

where R ohms is the total resistance in a parallel wiring circuit and R_1 ohms and R_2 ohms are the resistances in each branch of the circuit. Formula (1) is used in the following example.

Example 1 Find the resistance in one branch of a parallel wiring circuit if the resistance in the other branch is 3 ohms and the total resistance is 2 ohms.

Solution: We use formula (1) where $R = 2$ and $R_2 = 3$ and we let R_1 be the required number of ohms of resistance in the first branch of the circuit. Thus,

$$\frac{1}{2} = \frac{1}{R_1} + \frac{1}{3}$$

The LCD is $6R_1$. Multiplying both members of this equation by $6R_1$, we have

$$6R_1\left[\frac{1}{2}\right] = 6R_1\left[\frac{1}{R_1} + \frac{1}{3}\right]$$
$$3R_1 = 6 + 2R_1$$
$$R_1 = 6$$

Therefore, the required resistance is 6 ohms.

Example 2 If 80 is divided by a certain number and if 240 is divided by twice that certain number, the sum of the two quotients is 20. What is the number?

Solution: Let $x =$ the number. Then the two quotients are represented by

$$\frac{80}{x} \quad \text{and} \quad \frac{240}{2x}$$

We have then the equation

$$\frac{80}{x} + \frac{240}{2x} = 20$$

The LCD is $2x$ and multiplying both members of the equation by $2x$ gives

$$2x\left[\frac{80}{x} + \frac{240}{2x}\right] = 2x[20]$$
$$160 + 240 = 40x$$
$$400 = 40x$$
$$10 = x$$

Therefore the certain number is 10.

The next example involves a work–rate–time problem similar to those in Section 8.3.

Example 3 Two boys working together can mow a lawn in 1 hour and 12 minutes. The slower boy working alone takes 1 hour less than twice the number of hours required by the faster boy working alone. How long will it take each boy to mow the lawn if he works by himself?

Solution: Let x hours be the time required by the faster boy to mow the lawn by himself. Then $(2x - 1)$ hours in the time required by the slower boy to mow the lawn by himself. The average rate of work of the faster boy is $\frac{1}{x}$ lawns mowed per hour. The average rate of work of the slower boy is $\frac{1}{2x - 1}$ lawns mowed per hour.

The boys work together for 1 hour and 12 minutes $\left(\frac{6}{5} \text{ hours}\right)$. The fractional part of the total work (1 lawn mowed) done by each boy is found by multiplying his rate of work by the number of hours he works. Hence, the fractional part of the work done by the faster boy is $\left(\frac{1}{x}\right)\left(\frac{6}{5}\right)$ and the fractional part of the work done by the slower boy is $\left(\frac{1}{2x - 1}\right)\left(\frac{6}{5}\right)$.

Because the two boys complete the job

$$\left(\frac{1}{x}\right)\left(\frac{6}{5}\right) + \left(\frac{1}{2x - 1}\right)\left(\frac{6}{5}\right) = 1$$
$$\frac{6}{5x} + \frac{6}{5(2x - 1)} = 1 \qquad (2)$$

The LCD is $5x(2x - 1)$. Multiplying both members of equation (2) by $5x(2x - 1)$, we obtain

$$5x(2x - 1)\left[\frac{6}{5x} + \frac{6}{5(2x - 1)}\right] = 5x(2x - 1)[1]$$

$$6(2x - 1) + 6x = 5x(2x - 1)$$
$$12x - 6 + 6x = 10x^2 - 5x$$
$$-10x^2 + 23x - 6 = 0$$
$$10x^2 - 23x + 6 = 0$$
$$(x - 2)(10x - 3) = 0 \qquad\qquad (3)$$

Equation (3) is satisfied if either

$$x - 2 = 0 \qquad \text{or} \qquad 10x - 3 = 0$$

or, equivalently,

$$x = 2 \qquad \text{or} \qquad x = \frac{3}{10}$$

If $x = 2$, then $2x - 1 = 3$. If $x = \dfrac{3}{10}$, then $2x - 1 = -\dfrac{4}{10}$. Because $2x - 1$ can not be negative we reject the solution $x = \dfrac{3}{10}$. Therefore, it takes the faster boy 2 hours to mow the lawn by himself while the slower boy requires 3 hours.

Example 4   A plane leaves its base and travels to a given checkpoint 600 miles away. The plane then returns to the base. The entire flight takes 3 hours and the rate of speed of the plane on the return trip is 50 miles per hour less than the rate of speed going. What is the rate of speed of the plane going from its base to the checkpoint?

Solution: Let x miles per hour be the rate of speed of the plane going from the base to the checkpoint and $(x - 50)$ miles per hour be the rate of speed of the plane returning. Because

$$d = rt$$

it follows that

$$t = \frac{d}{r}$$

We use this formula to obtain the number of hours in the time going and the number of hours in the time returning. The results are summarized in Table 12.5.1.

Table 12.5.1

	d	$\div$	r	$=$	t
Going	600		x		$\dfrac{600}{x}$
Returning	600		$x - 50$		$\dfrac{600}{x - 50}$

Because the entire flight takes 3 hours, we have the equation

$$\frac{600}{x} + \frac{600}{x - 50} = 3$$

Multiplying both members of the equation by the LCD, $x(x - 50)$, we have

$$x(x - 50)\left[\frac{600}{x} + \frac{600}{x - 50}\right] = x(x - 50)[3]$$

$$(x - 50)(600) + 600x = 3x(x - 50)$$
$$600x - 30,000 + 600x = 3x^2 - 150x$$
$$0 = 3x^2 - 1350x + 30,000$$
$$0 = 3(x^2 - 450x + 10,000)$$

Therefore,

$$x^2 - 450x + 10,000 = 0$$

and so, applying the quadratic formula, we have

$$x = \frac{450 \pm \sqrt{(-450)^2 - 4(1)(10,000)}}{2(1)}$$

$$= \frac{450 \pm \sqrt{2500(81 - 16)}}{2}$$

$$= \frac{450 \pm \sqrt{2500 \cdot 65}}{2}$$

$$= \frac{450 \pm 50\sqrt{65}}{2}$$

$$= 225 \pm 25\sqrt{65}$$

Thus, if x_1 and x_2 denote the two roots, then

$$x_1 = 225 + 25\sqrt{65} \quad \text{and} \quad x_2 = 225 - 25\sqrt{65}$$

Because $\sqrt{65} \doteq 8.06$, we obtain the approximate solutions

$$x_1 \doteq 225 + 25(8.06) \quad \text{and} \quad x_2 = 225 - 25(8.06)$$

and so

$$x_1 \doteq 426.5 \quad \text{and} \quad x_2 \doteq 23.5$$

We must reject the root 23.5 because $23.5 - 50$ is a negative number. Therefore, the rate of speed going is approximately 426.5 miles per hour.

Exercises 12.5

1. Find the resistance in one branch of a parallel wiring circuit if the resistance in the other branch is $2\frac{1}{2}$ ohms and the total resistance is known

to be $1\frac{1}{2}$ ohms.

2. The resistance in one branch of a parallel wiring circuit is three times the resistance in the other branch. The total resistance is 1 ohm. Find the resistances in each branch.

3. If 60 is divided by a certain number and 108 is divided by three times that same number, the sum of the two quotients is 24. What is the number?

4. Find a fraction equivalent to $\frac{7}{10}$ and whose denominator exceeds its numerator by 21.

5. One boy by himself can assemble a machine 1 day less than the number of days it takes a second boy by himself. Working together it takes them 3 days to assemble the same machine. How long will it take the faster boy working alone?

6. One pipe can fill a tank at a rate twice as fast as the rate of a second pipe. If both pipes are open, it takes 5 hours to fill the tank. How long will it take each pipe alone to fill the tank?

7. Two cars begin a 500 mile race at the same time. The faster car averages 10 miles per hour faster than the slower car and finishes the race 1 hour ahead of the slower car. How long does it take the fast car to travel the 500 miles? *fast car $6\frac{2}{3}$ hr, slow $7\frac{2}{3}$ hr*

8. A boat has a rate of speed of 12 miles per hour in still water. This boat can travel 10 miles downstream in the same time it takes to travel 8 miles upstream. Find the rate of speed of the current.

9. The sum of two numbers is 10. The sum of their reciprocals is $\frac{1}{2}$. Find the two numbers.

10. An inlet pipe can fill an empty pool in 10 hours. A drain pipe can empty a full pool in 15 hours. If both pipes are open, how long will it take to fill an empty pool?

12.6 Review Exercises

In Exercises 1 and 2 simplify each rational expression and find the values of the variables for which the rational expression is undefined.

1. (a) $\dfrac{5}{10a + 15}$ (b) $\dfrac{x^2 - 9}{x^2 - 6x + 9}$

2. (a) $\dfrac{4x + 8}{x^2 - 4}$ (b) $\dfrac{x^2 + 8x + 12}{2x^2 + 13x + 6}$

In Exercises 3 through 7 perform each of the indicated operations and express the results in lowest terms.

3. (a) $\dfrac{4x^3}{36x} \cdot \dfrac{3xy}{y^2}$

   (b) $\dfrac{2a-6}{a^2-9} \cdot \dfrac{a+3}{2a^2+2a+8}$

4. (a) $\dfrac{x^2-64}{8-x} \div \dfrac{x^2+6x-16}{x+2}$

   (b) $\dfrac{x^2-13x+36}{x^2-36} \div \dfrac{x-4}{x^2-3x-54}$

5. (a) $\dfrac{x+3}{4x} + \dfrac{x-3}{4x}$

   (b) $\dfrac{2x}{x+5} + \dfrac{10}{x+5}$

6. (a) $\dfrac{x+6}{4x} + \dfrac{9}{4}$

   (b) $\dfrac{1}{4x-8} + \dfrac{-1}{4x+8}$

7. (a) $\dfrac{1}{x^2+3x-10} - \dfrac{1}{x^2-4}$

   (b) $\dfrac{4}{2y-4} - \dfrac{y+6}{y^2-4}$

8. Simplify the given complex rational expression:

   (a) $\dfrac{\dfrac{x}{y}+\dfrac{1}{x}}{\dfrac{3}{xy}}$

   (b) $\dfrac{v_1+v_2}{1+\dfrac{v_1v_2}{c^2}}$

In Exercises 9 through 11 solve each equation for x.

9. (a) $\dfrac{x}{3} + \dfrac{5x}{2} = 17$

   (b) $\dfrac{1}{3} + \dfrac{1}{x} = 1$

10. (a) $\dfrac{1}{x} + 4 = 12x$

   (b) $\dfrac{x}{x-5} = \dfrac{5}{x-5} + 2$

11. (a) $ax + 5 = bx - 3$

   (b) $\dfrac{1}{R} = \dfrac{1}{r} + \dfrac{1}{x}$

12. (a) One machine can process a given number of items twice as fast as another machine. When working together, the two machines process the entire shipment in 6 hours. How long does it take each machine to process the shipment by itself?

   (b) If 124 is divided by a certain number and if 124 is divided by 15 more than that certain number, the sum of the two quotients is 31. What is the number?

13

Inequalities

13.1 Order Relations

In this chapter we are concerned with relationships between numbers other than the equality relationship. These are the order relationships, "less than," "greater than," "less than or equal to," and "greater than or equal to."

In Section 1.5 we defined these relations. We restate the definition of "less than."

13.1.1 Definition   If $a, b \in R$, then a *is less than b,* denoted by $a < b$, if and only if there exists a positive number c such that $a + c = b$.

To state that "a is less than b" is equivalent to stating that "b is greater than a," denoted by $b > a$. Hence,

$$a < b \quad \text{is equivalent to} \quad b > a$$

Illustration 1   The statement $5 > 3$ is equivalent to $3 < 5$. If we have the statement $5 > x$ we can write the equivalent statement $x < 5$.

For any pair of real numbers a and b exactly one of the statements

$$a < b \tag{1}$$
$$a > b \tag{2}$$
$$a = b \tag{3}$$

is true. This property is known as the Trichotomy Law and was stated in Section 1.5.

We restate the Closure Law for the addition and multiplication of positive numbers that was originally stated in Section 1.4.

13.1.2 Axiom   If $a > 0$ and $b > 0$, then $a + b > 0$ and $ab > 0$.

Thus, we assume that the sum of two positive numbers is a positive number and the product of two positive numbers is a positive number.

All of the order relations share the "transitive property" which we now state for the "less than" relation.

13.1.3 Theorem (Transitive Property of Less Than)   If E, F, and G are expressions, and if $E < F$ and $F < G$, then $E < G$.

Illustration 2 If we are given that $x < 5$ and because we know that $5 < 9$, we can conclude from Theorem 13.1.3 that $x < 9$.

Proof of Theorem 13.1.3:   Because

$$E < F$$

it follows from Definition 13.1.1 of less than that there exists a number $N > 0$, such that

$$E + N = F \tag{4}$$

Also,

$$F < G$$

and so by Definition 13.1.1 there exists a number, $M > 0$, such that

$$F + M = G \tag{5}$$

Substituting the value of F from equation (4) into equation (5) we get

$$(E + N) + M = G$$

Applying the Associative Law to the left member of the above equation we obtain

$$E + (N + M) = G \tag{6}$$

Because $N + M$ is greater than zero if N and M are also greater than zero, it follows from equation (6) and the definition of less than that

$$E < G$$

which is what we wanted to prove.

Illustration 3 An example of Theorem 13.1.3, where $E = x + 3$, $F = y$, and $G = 8$, follows:

If $x + 3 < y$ and $y < 8$,   then $x + 3 < 8$

Statements that employ an order relation are called *inequalities*. Some inequalities that are often encountered are given in the next definition.

13.1.4 Definition

(i) The statement "x is at least y" or, equivalently, "x is not less than y" is written

$$x \geq y$$

if and only if

$$x > y \quad \text{or} \quad x = y$$

(ii) The statement "x is at most y" or, equivalently, "x is not greater than y" is written

$$x \leq y$$

if and only if

$$x < y \quad \text{or} \quad x = y$$

(iii) The statement "x is strictly between y and z" is written

$$y < x < z \quad \text{or} \quad y > x > z$$

depending on whether

$$y < z \quad \text{or} \quad y > z$$

(iv) The statement "x is at least y but at most z" is written

$$y \leq x \leq z$$

if and only if

$$y \leq x \quad \text{and} \quad x \leq z$$

Illustration 4 The statement "x is at least 7" is symbolized $x \geq 7$. This means that the value of x is 7 or a number greater than 7, that is, either $x = 7$ or $x > 7$.

Inequalities, like equations, can contain a variable or "unknown" and can be conditional statements. The solution set of an inequality is the set of all numbers that satisfy the given condition of the inequality.

Example 1 Decide if the following conditions satisfy the corresponding inequality and are therefore solutions of the inequalities.
(a) If $x = 3$, is the statement $x + 5 < 7$ true?
(b) If $x = 2$, is the statement $3x - 1 \geq 2x$ true?
(c) If $x = 9$, is the statement x is at most 10 true?

Solution:
(a) If $x = 3$, then $x + 5 = 3 + 5 = 8$ and $8 \not< 7$. Therefore, 3 is not a solution of $x + 5 < 7$.

(b) If $x = 2$, then $3x - 1 = 3(2) - 1 = 5$ and $2x = 2(2) = 4$. Thus, because $5 \geq 4$ we write

$$3x - 1 \geq 2x \quad \text{if} \quad x = 2$$

Therefore 2 is a solution of $3x - 1 \geq 2x$.

(c) The statement x is at most 10 is symbolized $x \leq 10$. Because $x = 9$ and $9 \leq 10$, the statement x is at most 10 is true.

Inequalities usually have more than just one solution in the solution set. Also, it is important to know what replacement set is being used, just as it is for equations. For example, the inequality

$$x \geq 4$$

has the solution set $\{4, 5, 6, \ldots\}$ if the replacement set is the set of integers. However, if the replacement set is the set of all real numbers, then the solution set is quite different, and is best shown by a graph. Since the set of real numbers is both *dense* and *complete* (see Sections 6.1 and 6.2) the graph of a "continuous" set of real numbers is depicted by a solid bar. Refer to the next examples.

Example 2
(a) Draw a sketch of the graph of the solution set of $x \geq 4$ if the replacement set is the set of real numbers.
(b) Draw a sketch of the graph of the solution set of $x \geq 4$ if the replacement set is the set of integers.

Solution:
(a) See Figure 13.1.1.

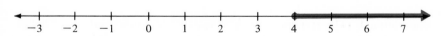

Figure 13.1.1

(b) See Figure 13.1.2.

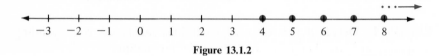

Figure 13.1.2

Example 3 Draw a sketch of the graph of the solution set of $x > 4$ if the replacement set is the set of real numbers.

Solution: See Figure 13.1.3. (Note: Since $x > 4$ we know that $x \neq 4$. To depict this on the graph, the point on the number line at 4 is not drawn as "solid," but is "open.")

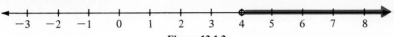
Figure 13.1.3

Example 4 On the number line draw a sketch of each of the following sets of real numbers.
  (a) $\{x : 3 \leq x \leq 6\}$
  (b) $\{x : 0 \leq x < 4\}$
  (c) $\{x : 8 > x > 5\}$
  (d) $\{x : x > 3\}$
  (e) $\{x : x \leq 2\} \cup \{x : 4 < x \leq 6\}$

Solution:
  (a) See Figure 13.1.4.

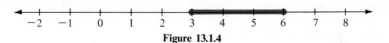
Figure 13.1.4

  (b) See Figure 13.1.5.

Figure 13.1.5

  (c) See Figure 13.1.6.

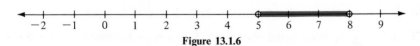
Figure 13.1.6

  (d) See Figure 13.1.7.

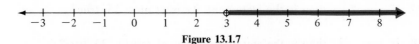
Figure 13.1.7

  (e) See Figure 13.1.8.

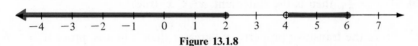
Figure 13.1.8

In Exercises 1 through 10 replace the blank space with the symbol $<$, $\leq$, $=$, $>$, or $\geq$, whichever applies.

1. If $x > y$ and $y > z$, then x _____ z.

2. If $x + 2 \leq 5$ and $5 \leq y$, then $x + 2$ _____ y.

3. If $x + 1 \geq x$ and $x \geq x - 1$, then $x + 1$ _____ $x - 1$.

4. If $x + 1$ is at least 7, then $x + 1$ _____ 7.

5. If $2x$ is at most 15, then $2x$ _____ 15.

6. If x is between 0 and 1, then 0 _____ x _____ 1.

7. If $x - 2$ is at most 12 but at least 10, then 10 _____ $x - 2$ _____ 12.

8. If $x > y$, then $x + 2$ _____ $y + 2$.

9. If $x > y$, then $x - 2$ _____ $y - 2$.

10. If $x < 0$, then $2x$ _____ x.

In Exercises 11 through 20 decide if the given condition satisfies the corresponding inequality and is therefore a solution of the inequality.

11. If $x = 2$, then is the statement $x + 5 > 8$ true?

12. If $x = 5$, then is the statement $2x - 1 < 9$ true?

13. If $x = -3$, then is the statement $x - 3 > 1$ true?

14. If $x = 1$, then is the statement $2x - 1 \geq x + 1$ true?

15. If $x = -5$, then is the statement $5 - x \leq -2x$ true?

16. If $x = \dfrac{1}{2}$, then is the statement x is at least 1 true?

17. If $x = 7\dfrac{1}{2}$, then is the statement $2x$ is at most 15 true?

18. If $x = -8$, then is the statement $2x$ is at most -20 true?

19. If $x = -1$, then is the statement $3x + 1$ is at least 0 true?

20. If $x = \dfrac{1}{2}$, then is the statement $x^2 < x$ true?

21. Prove the transitive property of "greater than"; that is, prove if $a > b$ and $b > c$, then $a > c$.

22. From the statement $a < x < b$, why is it permissible to conclude that $a < b$?

In Exercises 23 through 30 draw a sketch of the graph of the solution set of the given inequality if the replacement set is **(a)** the set of integers, **(b)** the set of real numbers.

23. $x < 3$ **24.** $x \geq -1$

25. $x > 0$ **26.** $x \leq 2$

27. x is at most 3   **28.** x is at least $\dfrac{1}{2}$

29. x is between 3 and 4   **30.** x is at least 3, but at most 4.

In Exercises 31 through 41 draw a sketch of the graph of the given set of real numbers on the number line.

31. $\{x : 2 < x \leq 5\}$ **32.** $\{x : 7 \geq x > 1\}$

33. $\{x : 10 > x > 5\}$ **34.** $\{x : 0 \leq x \leq 3\}$

35. $\{x : x < 3\}$ **36.** $\{x : x \leq 3\}$

37. $\{x : 2 < x < 5\} \cup \{x : 6 \leq x < 7\}$

38. $\{x : 2 \leq x < 5\} \cup \{x : 4 < x < 7\}$

39. $\{x : 2 \leq x < 5\} \cap \{x : 4 < x < 7\}$

40. $\{x : x > 3\} \cap \{x : x < 3\}$ **41.** $\{x : x \geq 3\}$

13.2 Solving Inequalities

If an inequality which is to be solved is complicated, it can, in many cases, be transformed into an equivalent inequality, which is less complicated and has the same solution set. The transformations are similar to the addition, subtraction, multiplication, and division transformations that are used for solving equations.

Theorems 13.2.1, 13.2.2, 13.2.3, and 13.2.4, are all stated in terms of the "less than" relationship; however, if the symbol $<$ is replaced by any of the symbols $>$, $\leq$, or $\geq$, the resulting statement of the theorem is also valid.

Unless stated otherwise, the replacement set of an inequality is the set of real numbers.

13.2.1 Theorem   If E and F are any algebraic expressions related by an inequality of the type

$$E < F,$$

then the inequality

$$E + G < F + G$$

is valid for all algebraic expressions G.

Illustration 1 If $x < 3$, then $x + 1 < 3 + 1$ or $x + 1 < 4$. And if $x > 3$, then $x + 1 > 3 + 1$.

The customary use of Theorem 13.2.1 is to simplify an inequality, such as

$$x - 2 < 5$$

By adding 2 to each member of the inequality, we have

$$x - 2 + 2 < 5 + 2$$

or, equivalently,

$$x < 7$$

Proof of Theorem 13.2.1: Since by hypothesis

$$E < F$$

it follows from the definition of less than that there is some number, $h > 0$, such that

$$E + h = F \tag{1}$$

Adding G to both members of equation (1) we get

$$(E + h) + G = F + G \tag{2}$$

Applying the Associative and Commutative Laws to the left member of equation (2), we obtain successively,

$$E + (h + G) = F + G$$
$$E + (G + h) = F + G$$

and applying the Associative law once again we obtain

$$(E + G) + h = F + G \tag{3}$$

By using the definition of less than, equation (3) gives

$$E + G < F + G$$

which is what we wished to prove.

Example 1 Find the solution set of the inequality

$$x - 7 < 3$$

and draw a sketch of the graph of the solution set.

Solution:

$$x - 7 < 3$$

Add 7 to both members of this inequality. This gives

$$x - 7 + 7 < 3 + 7$$

and so

$$x < 10$$

Thus, the solution set is $\{x : x < 10\}$. A sketch of the graph of the solution set is shown in Figure 13.2.1.

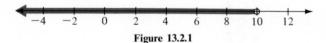

Figure 13.2.1

13.2.2 Theorem   If E and F are any algebraic expressions related by an inequality of the type

$$E < F$$

then the inequality

$$E - G < F - G$$

is valid for all algebraic expressions G.

Illustration 2   Since $0 < 2$, it follows that

$$0 - 3 < 2 - 3$$

or, equivalently,

$$-3 < -1$$

If $x + 5 < 8$, then

$$x + 5 - 5 < 8 - 5$$

or

$$x < 3$$

Proof of Theorem 13.2.2:   Because Theorem 13.2.1 is true for all algebraic expressions G, it is also true for the expression $-G$. Thus, if $E < F$, then

$$E + (-G) < F + (-G) \tag{4}$$

However,

$$E + (-G) = E - G$$

and

$$F + (-G) = F - G$$

so the inequality (4) becomes

$$E - G < F - G$$

which is what we wished to prove.

Example 2 Find the solution set of

$$x + 7 < 9$$

Draw a sketch of the graph of the solution set.

Solution: $x + 7 < 9$
$$x + 7 - 7 < 9 - 7$$
$$x < 2$$

Thus, the solution set is $\{x : x < 2\}$. See Figure 13.2.2.

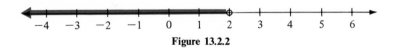

Figure 13.2.2

13.2.3 Theorem   If E and F are any algebraic expressions related by an inequality of the type

$$E < F$$

then
  (i) if $G > 0$, the inequality

$$E \cdot G < F \cdot G$$

is valid, and
  (ii) if $G < 0$, the inequality

$$E \cdot G > F \cdot G$$

is valid, and
  (iii) if $G = 0$, the equality

$$E \cdot G = F \cdot G$$

is valid.

Illustration 3 Consider the inequality

$$2 < 3 \tag{5}$$

If we multiply each member of inequality (5) by 2, we have

$$2 \cdot 2 < 3 \cdot 2$$

or

$$4 < 6$$

but if we multiply each member of inequality (5) by -2, we have

$$2(-2) > 3(-2)$$

and so
$$-4 > -6$$
The "sense" or "direction" of the symbol $<$ is changed to $>$ when each member of the given inequality is multiplied by the negative number -2.

Example 3 Solve and draw a sketch of the graph of the solution set of the inequality $\frac{1}{2}x + 2 < 6$.

Solution: Given
$$\frac{1}{2}x + 2 < 6$$

we obtain
$$\frac{1}{2}x < 4$$

By multiplying each member of this inequality by 2, we obtain
$$x < 8$$
Thus the solution set is $\{x : x < 8\}$. See Figure 13.2.3.

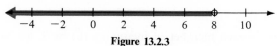

Figure 13.2.3

Example 4 Solve and draw a sketch of the graph of the solution set of the inequality $2 - \frac{1}{2}x \geq 0$.

Solution: Given
$$2 - \frac{1}{2}x \geq 0$$

we obtain
$$-\frac{1}{2}x \geq -2$$

By multiplying each member of this inequality by -2 we obtain
$$x \leq 4$$
(Note that the direction, or sense, of the symbol $\geq$ is changed to $\leq$ because we used a negative multiplier.) Thus, the solution set is $\{x : x \leq 4\}$. See Figure 13.2.4 on the next page.

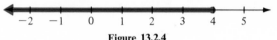

Figure 13.2.4

13.2.4 Theorem   If E and F are any algebraic expressions related by an inequality of the type

$$E < F$$

then

(i) if $G > 0$, the inequality

$$\frac{E}{G} < \frac{F}{G}$$

is valid, and
(ii) if $G < 0$, the inequality

$$\frac{E}{G} > \frac{F}{G}$$

is valid.

Illustration 4   Consider the inequality

$$-4 < 2 \tag{6}$$

then if we divide each member of inequality (6) by 2, we have

$$\frac{-4}{2} < \frac{2}{2}$$

or, equivalently,

$$-2 < 1$$

but if we divide each member of inequality (6) by -2, we have

$$\frac{-4}{-2} > \frac{2}{-2}$$

or, equivalently,

$$2 > -1$$

The sense or direction of the inequality symbol $<$ is changed to $>$.

Example 5   Find the solution set of the inequality $13x - 4 < 7x + 2$.

Solution: Given

$$13x - 4 < 7x + 2$$

By adding 4 to each member of the given inequality, we obtain

$$13x < 7x + 6 \qquad (7)$$

Now subtract $7x$ from each member of inequality (7). Hence, we have

$$6x < 6 \qquad (8)$$

Finally, divide each member of inequality (8) by 6, and we get

$$x < 1$$

Therefore, the solution set is $\{x : x < 1\}$.

In the above examples the given inequality is transformed into a simpler statement and the solution set is expressed in terms of this simpler statement. This solution set is the same as the solution set of the given inequality because the two inequalities are equivalent. Generally, the application of Theorems 13.2.1, 13.2.2, 13.2.3, and 13.2.4 will transform inequalities into other equivalent inequalities provided that the expression G referred to in each theorem contains no variables. However, in the application of Theorem 13.2.1 or 13.2.2 a variable may be used in the expression G if it is already present in the given inequality.

For instance, if we start with the inequality

$$x < 4 \qquad (9)$$

and transform it to

$$x + y < 4 + y \qquad (10)$$

then the inequality (10) has solutions that are ordered pairs of numbers, instead of just numbers as is the case of the solutions of the inequality (9). Thus, by adding the variable y to both members of inequality (9) we did not arrive at an equivalent inequality, because the replacements sets are quite different.

If $x > 0$ and we multiply each member of inequality (9) by x, we get

$$x^2 < 4x \qquad (11)$$

or, if $x < 0$, we get

$$x^2 > 4x \qquad (12)$$

Thus, if we multiply each member of inequality (9) by x, we get either inequality (11) or (12). Without additional information we cannot know which inequality, (11) or (12), is correct. On the other hand, if we add or subtract x from each member of inequality (9), the result will be equivalent to inequality (9).

As stated previously, Theorems 13.2.1 through 13.2.4 are valid for other inequality relationships, such as $>$, $\leq$, or $\geq$. See the next example.

Example 6 Solve and draw a sketch of the graph of the solution set of the inequality $10 \geq 3x + 4 \geq 7$.

Solution: Given

$$10 \geq 3x + 4 \geq 7$$

Subtracting 4 from each of the three members of the given inequality, we get

$$6 \geq 3x \geq 3 \qquad (13)$$

Now, dividing each member of inequality (13) by 3, we obtain

$$2 \geq x \geq 1$$

Thus, the solution set is $\{x : 2 \geq x \geq 1\}$. See Figure 13.2.5.

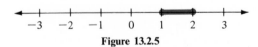

Figure 13.2.5

Example 7 Let the universal set, U, be the set of real numbers. Let $A = \left\{x : \dfrac{1}{2}x - 3 \leq 4\right\}$ and $B = \{x : 2x - 5 > 7\}$. Find and draw a sketch of the graph of the sets: (a) $A \cup B$; (b) $A \cap B$.

Solution: Because $\dfrac{1}{2}x - 3 \leq 4$ in set A we have

$$\frac{1}{2}x \leq 7$$

or, equivalently,

$$x \leq 14$$

Thus,

$$A = \left\{x : \frac{1}{2}x - 3 \leq 4\right\}$$
$$= \{x : x \leq 14\}$$

The graph of A is shown in Figure 13.2.6(a).

Because $2x - 5 > 7$ in set B we have

$$2x > 12$$

and so

$$x > 6$$

Thus,

$$B = \{x : 2x - 5 > 7\}$$
$$= \{x : x > 6\}$$

The graph of B is shown in Figure 13.2.6(b).

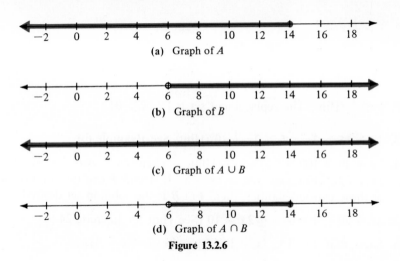

(a) Graph of A

(b) Graph of B

(c) Graph of A ∪ B

(d) Graph of A ∩ B

Figure 13.2.6

By examining the graphs of sets A and B, we can see that $A \cup B = U$ and that

$$A \cap B = \{x : 6 < x \leq 14\}$$

The graphs of these sets are shown in Figure 13.2.6(c) and (d).

Exercises 13.2

In Exercises 1 through 25 solve the given inequality and draw a sketch of the graph of the solution set. Assume the replacement set is the set of real numbers.

1. $x + 3 > 7$

2. $2x > 4$

3. $2x + 3 > 7$

4. $5x - 3 \geq 32$

5. $x - \dfrac{1}{2} < 1$

6. $8 - x > 1$

7. $\dfrac{1}{2}x - 1 \leq -5$

8. $8 - x > 0$

9. $x - 8 > 0$

10. $\dfrac{1}{3}x + \dfrac{1}{4} \leq \dfrac{1}{2}$

11. $2x + 1 < 3x - 5$

12. $x + 3 \leq 5x - 1$

13. $x + 1 < x + 3$

14. $x + 1 > x + 3$

15. $4x - 3 \leq x$

16. $1 < 2x < 4$

17. $3 \leq 2x - 1 \leq 5$

18. $17 \geq x + 5 \geq 10$

19. $3 \geq \dfrac{1}{2}x - 5 \geq 7$

20. $2x - 5 \leq \dfrac{20 - x}{2}$

21. $2\left(5 - \dfrac{1}{3}x\right) - 7 < x$

22. $3 < \dfrac{1}{x}$ (Hint: The replacement set is $\{x : x > 0\}$.)

23. $2x + 15 > 3x + 5 > 2x + 10$ (Hint: See Example 6.)

24. $2x + 20 \geq 100 \geq 2x - 5$ (Hint: Consider two inequalities, $2x + 20 \geq 100$ and $100 \geq 2x - 5$. If A and B are the solution sets of these two inequalities, then $A \cap B$ is the solution set desired.)

25. $2x - 20 \leq 100 - x \leq 2x - 10$ (See Hint for Exercise 24.)

26. Show that $\{x : 3 < 2x - 1 < 5\} = \{x : 2 < x < 3\}$.

In Exercises 27 through 31, **(a)** draw a sketch of the graph of $A \cup B$ and **(b)** draw a sketch of the graph of $A \cap B$. Assume the universal set is the set of real numbers.

27. $A = \{x : 3x + 2 < 20\}$ $B = \{x : 2x \geq 6\}$

28. $A = \left\{x : \dfrac{1}{2}x - 3 \geq 4\right\}$ $B = \{x : 2x - 5 > 7\}$

29. $A = \{x : 3 < x < 5\}$ $B = \{x : 4 \leq x \leq 6\}$

30. $A = \{x : 3 \leq 2x \leq 6\}$ $B = \{x : 3 \leq x \leq 6\}$

31. $A = \{x : 3 \leq 2x < 6\}$ $B = \{x : 4 < x + 1 < 9\}$

32. If $A = \{x : 3x + 2 \geq 4\}$ and the universal set, $U = \{x : x$ is a real number$\}$, then draw a sketch of the graph of A'.

33. If $A = \{x : 8 - x < 5 \leq 12 - x\}$ and the universal set, $U = \{x : x$ is a real number$\}$, then draw a sketch of the graph of A'.

34. Replace $<$ with $>$ and prove Theorem 13.2.1.

In Exercises 35 through 41 verify each statement for some particular numbers. (Use at least three numbers in each test.)

35. (a) If $a > 1$, is $\dfrac{1}{a} < 1$?   **(b)** If $0 < a < 1$, is $\dfrac{1}{a} < 1$?

36. (a) If $x > 0$, is $x^2 > x$?   **(b)** If $x > 0$, is $(1 + x)^2 > x$?

37. (a) If $x > 0$, is $\dfrac{x + 1}{x} > 1$?   **(b)** If $x > 0$, is $\dfrac{x}{x + 1} < 1$?

38. (a) If $0 < x < y$, is $\dfrac{1}{x} > \dfrac{1}{y}$?   **(b)** If $a < x < b$, is $\dfrac{1}{a} > \dfrac{1}{x} > \dfrac{1}{b}$?

39. (a) If $x > y > 0$, is $\dfrac{1}{x} < \dfrac{1}{y}$?   **(b)** If $a < b$, is $b - a > 0$?

(c) If $a > b$ and $x > y$, is $a + x > b + y$?

40. (a) If $n \geq 1$, is $2^n > n^2$?   **(b)** If $n \geq 3$, is $2^n > n^2$?

(c) If $n \geq 5$, is $2^n > n^2$?

41. (a) If $x > 0$, is $x + \dfrac{1}{x} \geq 2$?   **(b)** If $a \neq b$, is $a^2 + b^2 > 2ab$?

(c) If $a^2 > b^2$, and a and b are positive numbers, is $a > b$?

42. Prove that the arithmetic mean (the average) of two unequal numbers is between the two numbers. That is, prove that if $a < b$, then $a < \dfrac{a + b}{2} < b.$ $\left(\text{Hint: Add } a \text{ to each member of } a < b. \text{ Divide the}\right.$ resulting expressions by 2. This proves that $a < \dfrac{a + b}{2}.\Big)$

13.3 Applications of Inequalities to Problems

When expressing phrases or sentences involving the words "more" or "less" in algebraic notation, care must be taken to distinguish phrases from complete sentences. Study the following illustrations.

Illustration 1

(a) "7 more than x" is symbolized by "$x + 7$"
   "7 is more than x" is symbolized by "$7 > x$"
(b) "x is three more than y" is symbolized by "$x = y + 3$"
   "x is more than y" is symbolized by "$x > y$"
(c) "x is at least 3 more than y" is symbolized by "$x \geq y + 3$"
   "x is at most 3 more than y" is symbolized by "$x \leq y + 3$"

Here are a few examples typical of problems involving inequalities.

Example 1   A certain truck and its load weigh at least 8 tons. If the load weighs one more ton than the truck weighs, find the minimum weight of the load.

Solution: Let $x =$ the number of tons in the weight of the truck.
   Then $x + 1 =$ the number of tons in the weight of the load.
Hence,

$$\underbrace{x}_{} \quad + \quad \underbrace{x + 1}_{} \quad \underbrace{\geq}_{} \quad \underbrace{8}_{} \tag{1}$$

the measure of the weight of the truck	the measure of the weight of the load	is at least	the measure of the total weight

Solving inequality (1) we have

$$2x + 1 \geq 8$$
$$2x \geq 7$$
$$x \geq 3\frac{1}{2}$$

and so,

$$x + 1 \geq 4\frac{1}{2}$$

Therefore, the load weighs at least $4\frac{1}{2}$ tons; that is, $4\frac{1}{2}$ tons is the minimum weight of the load.

Example 2 When a certain number is doubled it is at least 5 more than its original value. When it is tripled it is at most 12 more than its original value. Find the set of possible values for the number.

Solution: Let x be the number. Then $2x$ is the double of the number. We now write two inequalities. The first inequality is

$$\underbrace{2x}_{\substack{\text{double of} \\ \text{the number}}} \quad \underbrace{\geq}_{\substack{\text{is at} \\ \text{least}}} \quad \underbrace{x + 5}_{\substack{\text{5 more than the} \\ \text{original value}}} \qquad (2)$$

By subtracting x from both members of inequality (2), we have

$$x \geq 5 \qquad (3)$$

That is, x is at least 5.

The second inequality is obtained by considering $3x$ as the triple of the number. Hence,

$$\underbrace{3x}_{\substack{\text{triple of} \\ \text{the number}}} \quad \underbrace{\leq}_{\substack{\text{is at} \\ \text{most}}} \quad \underbrace{x + 12}_{\substack{\text{12 more than the} \\ \text{original number}}} \qquad (4)$$

Subtracting x from both members of inequality (4) we get

$$2x \leq 12$$

Therefore,

$$x \leq 6 \qquad (5)$$

That is, x is at most 6.

Combining inequalities (3) and (5), we state that

$$5 \leq x \leq 6$$

The solution set is the interval $\{x : 5 \leq x \leq 6\}$.

Example 3 A certain alloy of nickel and silver is required to contain between 10 and 20 fewer grams of nickel than twice the number of grams of silver used. The total weight of the alloy is to be 100 grams. Find the permissible values of the number of grams of silver that can be used.

Solution: Let x = the number of grams of silver to be used.
Then $100 - x$ = the number of grams of nickel to be used.
Hence,

$$2x - 20 \quad < \quad 100 - x \quad < \quad 2x - 10 \tag{6}$$

the measure of 20 grams fewer than twice the number of grams of silver used	the measure of the $(100 - x)$ grams of nickel used is between the other measures	the measure of 10 grams fewer than twice the number of grams of silver used.

Inequality (6) is equivalent to the two inequalities

$$2x - 20 < 100 - x \tag{7}$$

and

$$100 - x < 2x - 10 \tag{8}$$

Solving inequality (7), we have

$$2x - 20 < 100 - x$$
$$3x - 20 < 100$$
$$3x < 120$$
$$x < 40 \tag{9}$$

Solving inequality (8), we have

$$100 - x < 2x - 10$$
$$100 < 3x - 10$$
$$110 < 3x$$
$$36\frac{2}{3} < x \tag{10}$$

Thus, from inequalities (9) and (10) we state that x is between $36\frac{2}{3}$ and 40, and we write

$$36\frac{2}{3} < x < 40$$

Therefore, the amount of silver to be used in the alloy must be more than $36\frac{2}{3}$ grams and less than 40 grams.

Exercises 13.3

1. One number is three more than another number and their sum is at most 75. Find the maximum values of the two numbers.

2. One number is three more than four times a second number. The sum of the two numbers is at least 28 and at most 33. Find the minimum values of these two numbers.

3. One number is ten less than twice a smaller number and the difference between them is at most 25. Find the maximum values of the two numbers.

4. One number is at most three more than four times a second number. The sum of the two numbers is 30. Find the minimum value of the second number.

5. A minimum of 270 cubic feet of air is required for each student in a new school building. To meet this requirement, what should be the minimum height of the ceiling of a class room whose floor measurements are 30 feet by 36 feet, seating 40 students?

6. An isosceles triangle is one having two sides of equal length. The measure of the base of a certain isosceles triangle is six less than the sum of the measures of the two equal sides. The perimeter is between 10 units and 30 units. Find the possible lengths of the three sides. See Figure 13.3.1.

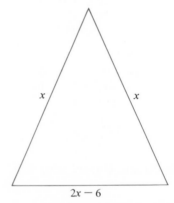

Figure 13.3.1

7. A certain company employs 100 people. There are at least twice as many men as women employees. What is the minimum number of male employees? (Note: The replacement set is the set of whole numbers.)

8. A certain company employs at least 100 people. There are twice as many men as women employees. What is the minimum number of male employees? (The answer is not the same as the answer of Exercise 7.)

9. A coin collection consists of pennies, nickels, and dimes. There are at least twice as many pennies as nickels and dimes combined. There are

at least twice as many nickels as dimes. All together there are at least 500 coins. Find the minimum number of each type of coin. (What replacement set should be considered?)

10. The average of two numbers is 5. The smaller number is at least $\frac{3}{4}$ of the larger. Find the interval of possible values for the larger number.

11. The denominator of a certain fraction is greater than the numerator. The numerator is three less than twice the denominator. If the numerator and denominator are positive integers, what is the maximum value of the denominator?

12. At least one third of the instruments in a certain symphony orchestra are violins. If there are no more than 76 instruments in the orchestra what is the minimum number of violins in the orchestra?

13. One number is between 20 and 24 and a second number is between 10 and 20.
    (a) Find an interval for the average of the two numbers.
    (b) Find an interval for the sum of the two numbers.
    (c) Find an interval for twice the first number increased by the second.

14. The average of two numbers is between 40 and 60 and one of the numbers is between 20 and 30. Find an interval for the other number.

15. You are traveling and come upon a crossroad with a broken sign post reading "Nearsville 46 miles" in one direction and "Farsville 62 miles" in possibly another direction. Find the minimum and maximum possible straight line distances between the two towns.

16. Fire lookout A is responsible for all the territory less than or equal to 24 miles from the lookout in any direction. Fire lookout B is responsible for all the territory up to and including a distance of 30 miles in any direction from the lookout. Lookout A is 40 miles as the crow flies from lookout B. What is the maximum width of the territory served by the two lookouts?

17. A certain mountainous region can always expect at most 5 inches of rainfall fewer than twice the number of inches of rainfall on the valley floor. If the combined total for both regions is never less than 40 inches, find the minimum amount of rainfall each region can expect.

18. In a certain solution of water and acid, it is required that the number of cubic centimeters of water be within 1 cubic centimeter of twice the number of cubic centimeters of acid. If the solution is to contain 100 cubic centimeters, find the maximum and minimum number of cubic centimeters of acid present.

19. If Mark were able to increase his cycling average rate of speed by 5 miles per hour, he would be able to cover in 3 hours a distance at least

as great as that which now takes him 4 hours. What is the maximum average rate of speed he achieves at present?

20. The sum of the lengths of the base and altitude of a right triangle is at least 12 units. The length of the altitude is 2 units more than the length of the base. Find the minimum length of the hypotenuse of the triangle if it is a whole number.

13.4 Review Exercises

1. Replace the blank with the symbol $<$, $>$, $=$, $\leq$, or $\geq$, whichever applies.
   (a) If $x < y$, then $10 - x$ _____ $10 - y$.
   (b) If $2x - 1$ is at most 25, then $2x - 1$ _____ 25.

2. (a) If $x = 1$, then is the statement $2x - 1 > x^2 - 1$ true?
   (b) If $x = 5$, then is the statement x is at least 7 true?

In Exercises 3 through 8 on the number line draw a sketch of the graph of the given set if the replacement set is (a) the set of integers, (b) the set of real numbers.

3. $\{x : 2 \leq x < 5\}$
4. $\{x : x < 3\} \cap \{x : x \geq 0\}$
5. $\{x : 4x - 5 \leq 7\}$
6. $\{x : 2 - 3x \geq 8\}$
7. $\{x : 5 < 2x - 1 < 10\}$
8. $\{x : x + 3 > 1 > x - 1\}$

9. If the universal set is the set of real numbers and if $A = \{x : x > 2x\}$ and $B = \{x : -2 \leq x \leq 2\}$, on the number line draw a sketch of the graph of
   (a) $A \cup B$
   (b) $A \cap B$

10. The measure of the length of a rectangle is at least two times the measure of the width of the rectangle. The measure of the perimeter of the rectangle is at most 12. Find the greatest possible measure of the width of the rectangle.

Appendix

Table A.1   The Prime Numbers Less Than 1000

2	3	5	7	11	13	17	19	23	29	31	37
41	43	47	53	59	61	67	71	73	79	83	89
97	101	103	107	109	113	127	131	137	139	149	151
157	163	167	173	179	181	191	193	197	199	211	223
227	229	233	239	241	251	257	263	269	271	277	281
283	293	307	311	313	317	331	337	347	349	353	359
367	373	379	383	389	397	401	409	419	421	431	433
439	443	449	457	461	463	467	479	487	491	499	503
509	521	523	541	547	557	563	569	571	577	587	593
599	601	607	613	617	619	631	641	643	647	653	659
661	673	677	683	691	701	709	719	727	733	739	743
751	757	761	769	773	787	797	809	811	821	823	827
829	839	853	857	859	863	877	881	883	887	907	911
919	929	937	941	947	953	967	971	977	983	991	997

Table A.2   Squares and Principal Square Roots

N	N^2	$\sqrt{N}$
.1	.01	.31622
.2	.04	.44721
.3	.09	.54772
.4	.16	.63245
.5	.25	.70710
.6	.36	.77459
.7	.49	.83666
.8	.64	.89442
.9	.81	.94868
1.0	1.00	1.00000
2.0	4.00	1.41421
3.0	9.00	1.73205
4.0	16.00	2.00000
5.0	25.00	2.23606
6.0	36.00	2.44949
7.0	49.00	2.64575
8.0	64.00	2.82842
9.0	81.00	3.00000
10.0	100.00	3.16227
11.0	121.00	3.31662
12.0	144.00	3.46410
13.0	169.00	3.60555
14.0	196.00	3.74165
15.0	225.00	3.87298
16.0	256.00	4.00000
17.0	289.00	4.12310
18.0	324.00	4.24264
19.0	361.00	4.35889
20.0	400.00	4.47213
21.0	441.00	4.58257
22.0	484.00	4.69041
23.0	529.00	4.79583
24.0	576.00	4.89897
25.0	625.00	5.00000
26.0	676.00	5.09901
27.0	729.00	5.19615
28.0	784.00	5.29150
29.0	841.00	5.38516
30.0	900.00	5.47722
31.0	961.00	5.56776
32.0	1024.00	5.65685
33.0	1089.00	5.74456
34.0	1156.00	5.83095
35.0	1225.00	5.91608
36.0	1296.00	6.00000
37.0	1369.00	6.08276
38.0	1444.00	6.16441

Table A.2 Squares and Principal Square Roots
(*Continued*)

N	N^2	$\sqrt{N}$
39.0	1521.00	6.24499
40.0	1600.00	6.32455
41.0	1681.00	6.40312
42.0	1764.00	6.48074
43.0	1849.00	6.55743
44.0	1936.00	6.63324
45.0	2025.00	6.70820
46.0	2116.00	6.78233
47.0	2209.00	6.85565
48.0	2304.00	6.92820
49.0	2401.00	7.00000
50.0	2500.00	7.07106
51.0	2601.00	7.14142
52.0	2704.00	7.21110
53.0	2809.00	7.28010
54.0	2916.00	7.34846
55.0	3025.00	7.41619
56.0	3136.00	7.48331
57.0	3249.00	7.54983
58.0	3364.00	7.61577
59.0	3481.00	7.68114
60.0	3600.00	7.74596
61.0	3721.00	7.81024
62.0	3844.00	7.87400
63.0	3969.00	7.93725
64.0	4096.00	8.00000
65.0	4225.00	8.06225
66.0	4356.00	8.12403
67.0	4489.00	8.18535
68.0	4624.00	8.24621
69.0	4761.00	8.30662
70.0	4900.00	8.36660
71.0	5041.00	8.42614
72.0	5184.00	8.48528
73.0	5329.00	8.54400
74.0	5476.00	8.60232
75.0	5625.00	8.66025
76.0	5776.00	8.71779
77.0	5929.00	8.77496
78.0	6084.00	8.83176
79.0	6241.00	8.88819
80.0	6400.00	8.94427
81.0	6561.00	9.00000
82.0	6724.00	9.05538
83.0	6889.00	9.11043
84.0	7056.00	9.16515

Table A.2 Squares and Principal Square Roots
(*Continued*)

N	N^2	$\sqrt{N}$
85.0	7225.00	9.21954
86.0	7396.00	9.27361
87.0	7569.00	9.32737
88.0	7744.00	9.38083
89.0	7921.00	9.43398
90.0	8100.00	9.48683
91.0	8281.00	9.53939
92.0	8464.00	9.59166
93.0	8649.00	9.64365
94.0	8836.00	9.69535
95.0	9025.00	9.74679
96.0	9216.00	9.79795
97.0	9409.00	9.84885
98.0	9604.00	9.89949
99.0	9801.00	9.94987
100.0	10000.00	10.00000

Answers to Odd-Numbered Exercises

Exercises 1.1 (Page 10)

1. (a) 6 **(b)** 6

3. (a) 4×6 **(b)** $4k$

5. $n + n + n + n + n = 5n$
$3 + 3 + 3 + 3 + 3 = 5 \times 3$
$15 = 15$

7. (a) $n \times 1 = n$ **(b)** $20 + x = 54$ **(c)** $17 - x = 3x$

9. $8a$

11. (a) $x = 3$ **(b)** $x = 4$ **(c)** $x = 35$

13. (a) $x = 7$ **(b)** $m = n$ **(c)** $y = 10$

15. (a) 5050 **(b)** 500500

17. (a) $^-15$ **(b)** $^-6$ **(c)** $^+4$ **(d)** $^-4$

19. $^-5$

21. (a) 14,777 feet **(b)** 250°F

23. From point B on the south side of the street proceed east on Maple Lane for $2\frac{1}{2}$ blocks, turn left (north) on 7th and go 1 block. Turn right (east) on Elm and go 7 blocks. Turn right (south) on Main Street and go 3 blocks and arrive at point A on the right (west) side of the street.

473

Exercises 1.2 (Page 18)

1. $\{1, 2, 3, 4, 5, 6\}$

3. $\{0\}$

5. $\{4, 5, 6, \ldots\}$

7. $\{x : x = 5n \text{ where } n \in N\}$

9. $\{x : x = 3n \text{ or } x = 5n \text{ where } n \in W\}$

11. The set $\{x : x \text{ is less than } 5\}$ is not a well-defined set because the universal set is not specified.

13. (a) $\{2\} \subseteq \{1, 2, 3\}$ means the set containing 2 is a subset of the set containing 1, 2, and 3; $2 \in \{1, 2, 3\}$ means 2 is an element of the set $\{1, 2, 3\}$. **(b)** No. **(c)** The empty set is denoted by $\varnothing$; the set containing the element 0 is denoted by $\{0\}$; the set containing the empty set is denoted by $\{\varnothing\}$.

15. (a) $\{1\}, \{2\}, \{3\}$ **(b)** $\{1, 2\}, \{1, 3\}, \{2, 3\}$ **(c)** $\{1, 2, 3\}$.

17. (a) Yes, because there are only 9 values (0, 1, 2, 3, 4, 5, 6, 7, and 8) for the number of elements in each of the 10 sets, hence, at least two of the sets will have to have the same number of elements. **(b)** Yes. **(c)** Assume that there are many more trees in the world than the number of leaves to be found on any one tree. Then we have m trees and each tree has fewer than $m - 1$ leaves. This is the situation of part **(b)** of this exercise.

Exercises 1.3 (Page 23)

1. $\{1, 2, 3, 4, 5\}$ **3.** $\{1, 2, 3, 4, 5, 6\}$

5. $\{1, 3\}$ **7.** $\{2, 4, 5, 6\}$

9. $\{2, 4\}$ **11.** D

13. W **15.** E

17. E **19.** W

21. W **23.** $\varnothing$

25. (a) $\{2, 4\}$ **(b)** $\{1, 2, 3, 4, 5, 6, 8, 10\}$

27. Let $A = \{1, 2, 3\}$ and $B = \{4, 5, 6\}$.

29. The number of elements in the set $A \cup B$ is 5, the number of elements in set A is 3, and the number of elements in set B is 4; $3 + 4$ does not equal 5.

31. $\{0, 12, 24, 36, \ldots\}$

33. $\{1, 2, 3, 5, 6, 7, 9, 10, 11, 13, 14, 15, 17, \ldots\}$

Exercises 1.4 (Page 28)

1. $\dfrac{4}{6}, \dfrac{8}{12}, \dfrac{20}{30}$

3. $\dfrac{6}{2}, \dfrac{12}{4}, \dfrac{30}{10}$

5. $\dfrac{0}{1}, \dfrac{0}{2}, \dfrac{0}{3}$

7. The coordinate of $A = 2$
the coordinate of $B = {}^-8$
the coordinate of $C = 10$
the coordinate of $D = {}^-12$
the coordinate of $E = {}^-2$

9., 11., 13., 15.

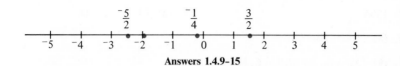

Answers 1.4.9–15

17. If a and b are any whole numbers, then $a + b$ and $a \times b$ are whole numbers. This statement is true for whole numbers.

19. No. The set of odd whole numbers is not closed with respect to addition, but is closed with respect to multiplication.

21. The set $\{0, 1\}$ is closed with respect to multiplication, but not with respect to either addition or subtraction.

Exercises 1.5 (Page 36)

1. The Symmetric Property of Equality

3. The Transitive Property of Equality

5. The Substitution Property of Equality

7. The Transitive Property of Equality

9. The Symmetric Property of Equality

11. The Reflexive Property of Equality

13. (a) $>$ (b) $=$

15. (a) $>$ (b) $<$

17. (a) $=$ (b) $>$

19. (a) $>$ (b) $>$

21. (a) $>$ (b) $<$

23. (a) $>$ (b) $<$

25. $>$

27. $\{101, 102, 103, \ldots\}$

29. $\{8, 7, 6, 5\}$

31. a is not greater than 3

33. 3 is between 2 and 4.

35. 10 is greater than or equal to x and x is greater than or equal to 7.

37. $0.0585 \le x \le 0.0595$

39. $119 < x < 121$

41. $a < c$

43. (a) $7 < x + 2 < 8$
    (b) $a + 2 < x + 2 < b + 2$
    (c) $a + c < x + c < b + c$

1.6 Review Exercises   (Page 38)

1. (a) $4m$ (b) $2b$

3. (a) 24   (b) 24

5. 1395

7. (a) 14   (b) 16

9. (a) $^-4$ (b) 9

11. (a) $\{x : x = 5n \text{ and } n \in W\}$
    (b) $\{x : x \text{ is an even whole number between 100 and 200}\}$

13. $\{2, 4\}$

15. $\{7, 9\}$

17. $\varnothing$

19. No; $5 \div 2$ is not a whole number.

21. (a) $<$ (b) $<$

23. (a) Reflexive Property
    (b) Transitive Property
    (c) Symmetric Property

Exercises 2.1   (Page 44)

1. (a) 0   (b) 12

3. (a) 1   (b) 0

5. (a) 1   (b) 0

7. $\{1, 2, 4, 5, 10, 20\}$

9. $\{1, 5, y, 5y\}$

11. $\{1, 3, x, y, 3x, 3y, xy, 3xy\}$

13. (a) 4   (b) 8   (c) 16

15. (a) 100   (b) 1000   (c) 10,000

17. exponent, base, power

19. (a) 5^3 (b) 10^2 (c) a^4 (d) n^3

21. (a) 4   (b) 8   (c) 32   (d) 32

23. (a) Let $a = 2$ and $b = 3$, then

$$aa + bb = 13$$

and

$$ab + ab = 12$$

and

$$13 \geq 12$$

(b) $a^2 + b^2 \geq 2ab$

25. The Commutative Law of Multiplication

27. The Closure Law for the Addition of Real Numbers

29. The Commutative Law of Multiplication

31. Zero Factor Property

33. Yes

Exercises 2.2 (Page 52)

1. 200; 200

3. 630; 630

5. 20

7. 14

9. x, y

11. $2(x + y) = 2x + 2y$
$a(x + z) = ax + az$
$a(x + y) = ax + ay$
$3(2 + 4) = 6 + 12$
$2(3 + 4) = 6 + 8$
$x(a + b) = ax + bx$

13. $3x, 7x$
$15xy, xy$
$4xyz, 100xyz$
$3x^2, 23x^2$
$7x^2y, 15x^2y$
$5xy^2, \dfrac{1}{2}xy^2$
$23x^2y^2, x^2y^2$
$yz, 3yz$
$3wx, 8xw$

15. (a) $9x^2$ **(b)** $17xy$

17. (a) $11x + 7$ **(b)** $35xy$

19. (a) $\dfrac{5}{6}\pi r^2$ **(b)** $\dfrac{3}{4}x$

21. (a) 0   **(b)** x

23. (a) $60R + 13T$ (b) $7x^3 + x$

25. $9x + 12$

27. $x \cdot \dfrac{n(n + 1)}{2}$

29. $P = 4x$

31. (a) $(x + 5)(x + 5)$ (b) $x^2 + 10x + 25$

Exercises 2.3   (Page 62)

1. (a) 7   (b) 0   **3.** (a) 12   (b) 12

5. (a) 6   (b) 0   **7.** (a) 5   (b) 6

9. (a) 0   (b) $b - a$ **11.** (a) 5   (b) 27

13. 0   **15.** 1

17. 1   **19.** 5

21. 2   **23.** y^2

25. $\dfrac{a + b}{2}$ **27.** $x^2 + 2xy + y^2$

29. $\dfrac{x}{4} + \dfrac{4}{4}$ or, equivalently, $\dfrac{x}{4} + 1$

Exercises 2.4   (Page 71)

1. (a) The Distributive Law of Multiplication over Addition
   (b) The Associative Law of Multiplication
   (c) The Commutative Law of Multiplication
   (d) The Commutative Law of Multiplication
   (e) The Commutative Law of Addition
   (f) The Associative Law of Addition
   (g) The Associative Law of Multiplication and the Commutative Law of Multiplication

3. (a) 14   (b) 11   **5.** (a) 58   (b) 28

7. (a) 18   (b) 36   **9.** (a) 9   (b) 12

11. (a) 24   (b) 1   **13.** (a) $\dfrac{31}{288}$ (b) 0

15. (a) $x + 10$ (b) $x + 14$

17. (a) $10a$ (b) $12a$

19. The Associative Law of Addition and the Commutative Law of Addition

21. The Associative Law of Addition and the Commutative Law of Addition

23. (a) $28y$ (b) $29x^2$

25. (a) $41x + 38y$ (b) $24a + 30b$

27. (a) $A = x(4x)$ (b) $A = x^2 + x^2 + x^2 + x^2$
        $= 4x^2$ $= 4x^2$

29. No, because $(2 \star 6) \star 14 = 9$ and $2 \star (6 \star 14) = 6$.

31. Yes

33. $(16 \div 8) \div 4 = 2 \div 4$ and $16 \div (8 \div 4) = 16 \div 2$
$$= \frac{1}{2} \qquad\qquad\qquad\qquad = 8$$

2.5 Review Exercises   (Page 75)

1. (a) 6^4 (b) a^5 **3.** 9

5. $\{1, 3, 9, x, x^2, 3x, 9x, 3x^2, 9x^2\}$

7. (a) $x^2 + x$ (b) $10y$ **9.** (a) $20xy$ (b) $2x + 8$

11. (a) $27x$ (b) $20x + 20y$

13. (a) 0   (b) 3   (c) 3   (d) 11

15. Division, $8 \div 4 \neq 4 \div 8$

17. (a) The Associative Law of Addition
     (b) Identity Element for Multiplication

19. (a) Identity Element for Addition
     (b) The Distributive Law of Multiplication over Addition

21. (a) 16   (b) 18

23. (a) 14   (b) 3

Exercises 3.1   (Page 85)

1. (a) 0   (b) 0   **3.** (a) 100   (b) 2

5. (a) 8   (b) 17   **7.** (a) $-k$ (b) 0

9. 0   **11.** positive integer

13. x **15.** $-y$

17. $>$ **19.** $<$

21. $=$ **23.** $>$

25. $<$ **27.** $<$

29. $<$ **31.** $=$

33. $>$ **35.** $=$

37. (a)   **39.** (c)

41. (f)   **43.** (f)

45. (d)

Exercises 3.2   (Page 95)

1. (a) 3   (b) 2   (c) 1   (d) 0   (e) $^-1$ (f) $^-2$ (g) $^-3$

3. (a) 0   (b) $^-1$ (c) $^-2$ (d) $^-3$ (e) $^-4$ (f) $^-5$ (g) $^-6$

5. (a) 0   (b) $^-1$ (c) $^-2$ (d) $^-3$ (e) $^-4$

7. (a) 34   (b) $^-34$ **9.** (a) 10   (b) $^-10$

11. (a) 0   (b) 0   **13.** (a) $^-8$ (b) $^-8$

15. (a) 3   (b) 3   **17.** (a) $^-11$ (b) $^-11$

19. (a) 11   (b) 11   **21.** (a) $^-15$ (b) $^-1$

23. (a) $^-13$ (b) 1   **25.** (a) $^-25$ (b) $^-1$

27. (a) $^-12$ (b) $^-12$ **29.** (a) 14   (b) 14

31. (a) 0   (b) 0   **33.** (a) 11   (b) $^-11$

35. (a) 0   (b) $^-2$ **37.** (a) $^-212$ (b) $^-319$

39. (a) 0   (b) $^-23$ **41.** (a) $^-8$ (b) $^-3$

43. $>$ **45.** $<$

47. $>$ **49.** 18

51. $^-5$ **53.** $-(b - a) = (-b) - (-a)$

55. By Theorem 3.2.1 we have

$$x - (-x) = x + [-(-x)]$$

and so,

$$x - (-x) = x + x$$
$$= 2x$$

57. By Theorem 3.2.2 we have $-(a + b) = (-a) + (-b)$. By Theorem 3.2.1 we have $(-a) + (-b) = (-a) - (b)$. Therefore, by the Transitive

Property it follows that

$$-(a + b) = (-a) - (b)$$

or, equivalently,

$$-(a + b) = -a - b$$

Exercises 3.3 (Page 101)

1. (a) 6 (b) 4 (c) 2 (d) 0 (e) ⁻2 (f) ⁻4 (g) ⁻6

3. (a) ⁻20 (b) 20 5. (a) ⁻30 (b) 30

7. (a) 0 (b) 0 9. (a) ⁻8 (b) 8

11. (a) ⁻27 (b) 16 13. (a) ⁻16 (b) 4

15. (a) 9 (b) ⁻32

17. Because 0 is the Identity Element for Addition we have

$$(-a)(b) = (-a)(b) + 0 \tag{1}$$

Substituting $[(a)(b) + -(ab)]$ for 0 in equality (1) we have

$$(-a)(b) = (-a)(b) + [(a)(b) + [-(ab)]] \tag{2}$$

Applying the Associative Law for Addition to the right member of equality (2), we obtain

$$(-a)(b) = [(-a)(b) + (a)(b)] + [-(ab)] \tag{3}$$

Applying the Distributive Law to the expression $(-a)(b) + (a)(b)$ in equality (3) we obtain

$$(-a)(b) = [(-a) + (a)](b) + [-(ab)] \tag{4}$$

Because $(-a) + (a) = 0$, we substitute 0 for $(-a) + (a)$ in equality (4) and we get

$$(-a)(b) = (0)(b) + [-(ab)] \tag{5}$$

Applying the Zero Factor Property in the right member of equality (5) we have

$$(-a)(b) = 0 + [-(ab)] \tag{6}$$

Because 0 is the Identity Element for Addition we obtain

$$(-a)(b) = -(ab) \tag{7}$$

19. From Theorem 3.3.2 we have

$$(-a)(-b) = -[a(-b)] \tag{1}$$

Applying the Commutative Law in the right member of equality (1) we have

$$(-a)(-b) = -[(-b)a] \tag{2}$$

Applying Theorem 3.3.2 to the product $(-b)a$ in equality (2) we have

$$(-a)(-b) = -[-(ba)]$$
$$= ba$$
$$= ab$$

Hence,

$$(-a)(-b) = ab$$

21. (a) $^-1$ (b) $^-2$ (c) $^-3$ (d) $^-6$

23. (a) 1   (b) 2   (c) 3   (d) 6

25. (a) Not an integer.   (b) Undefined quantity.   (c) Not an integer.

27. (a) $^-8$ (b) 8   (c) $^-8$

29. (a) $^-2$ (b) 2

31. (a) 4   (b) $^-4$

33. (a) 16   (b) $^-64$

35. $<$ 37. $<$ 39. $>$ 41. $=$

Exercises 3.4   (Page 106)

1. 0   3. $^-2$

5. 102   7. $^-13$

9. $^-2$ 11. $^-8$

13. $^-18$ 15. $^-5$

17. (a) 0   (b) 0   19. (a) $2a - b$ (b) b

21. (a) $-9x$ (b) $-m$ 23. (a) $-2xy$ (b) $-3xy$

25. (a) $5k$ (b) $8x$

27. (a) $10 - 3x$ (b) $-x^2 - 3x + 1$

29. (a) $5x + 16$ (b) $-8x - 4$

31. (a) $-x^3$ (b) $8x^3$ 33. (a) $-6x^3$ (b) $24y^3$

35. (a) $-x^3$ (b) $100x$ 37. (a) -6 (b) 6

39. (a) 20   (b) $^-24$ 41. (a) -1 (b) 1

43. $-40°$ Celsius

3.5 Review Exercises (Page 108)

1. $^-1, 0, 2, 17, ^-5, -\sqrt{4}, 7, ^-6$

3. 4   **5.** $^-11$

7. 0   **9.** $^-8$

11. $^-12$ **13.** 8

15. 12   **17.** 15

19. 12   **21.** 4

23. Associative Law of Multiplication

25. Fundamental Principle of Differences

27. $<$ **29.** $^-20$

31. (a) 12   **(b)** 36   **33. (a)** 1   **(b)** $^-24$

35. (a) $^-1$ **(b)** $^-1$ **37. (a)** $-6t$ **(b)** $-24xy$

39. (a) $2a - b$ **(b)** $x - y$

Exercises 4.1 (Page 112)

1. (a) Identity   **(b)** Identity

3. (a) Identity   **(b)** Identity

5. (a) Conditional equation   **(b)** Identity

7. (a) Conditional equation   **(b)** Conditional equation

9. No   **11.** No

13. No   **15.** Yes

17. Yes   **19.** Yes

21. Yes   **23.** No

25. No   **27.** $\{5\}$

29. (a) $\{1, -1\}$ **(b)** $\{0\}$ **(c)** $\varnothing$

Exercises 4.2 (Page 117)

1. 14   **3.** 8

5. 7   **7.** 5

9. $2x + 1$ **11.** x

13. $5x$

15. $9x - 1$

17. $x - 1$

19. x

21. x

23. $7x$

25. x

27. x

29. 2

31.

Instruction	Result
Take a number	: x
Add 10	: $x + 10$
Double the result	: $2x + 20$
Subtract 20	: $2x$
Divide by 2	: x
Add 5	: $x + 5$
Subtract original number	: 5

33. Let $x =$ this year's date

    $b =$ the year of the person's birth

    $e =$ the year of an important event in the life of this person

Then

$$x - b = \text{the person's age}$$

and

$$x - e = \text{the number of years since the important event}$$

Instruction	Result
Write the year of your birth	: b
Write the year of any important event	: e
Add these numbers	: $b + e$
Add your age as of this year	: $b + e + (x - b) = e + x$
Add the number of years since the important event	: $b + e + (x - b) + (x - e) = 2x$

Thus, $2x$ is two times this year's date.

Exercises 4.3 (Page 125)

1. $\{3\}$

3. $\{11\}$

5. $\{-6\}$

7. $\{9\}$

9. $\{40\}$

11. $\left\{\dfrac{2}{5}\right\}$

13. $\left\{\dfrac{5}{2}\right\}$ **15.** $\{^-3\}$

17. $\{2\}$ **19.** $\{^-4\}$

21. $\{^-2\}$ **23.** $\{12\}$

25. $\{4\}$ **27.** $\{26\}$

29. $\{5\}$

31. Proof: From the Reflexive Property of Equality (Axiom 1.5.1), we have

$$\frac{E}{G} = \frac{E}{G} \tag{1}$$

By hypothesis, $E = F$, and so we substitute F for E in the right member of equality (1) and we have

$$\frac{E}{G} = \frac{F}{G}$$

33. Proof: By hypothesis we have

$$E + G = F + G$$

From Theorem 4.3.3, the Subtraction Principle of Equality, we have

$$E + G - G = F + G - G$$

Hence, applying Property 4.2.1, the Additive Principle of Inversion, we have

$$E = F$$

35. $k = 14$

Exercises 4.4 (Page 131)

1. $\{6\}$ **3.** $\{^-4\}$

5. $\{0\}$ **7.** $\left\{\dfrac{15}{2}\right\}$

9. $\{5\}$ **11.** $\left\{\dfrac{27}{2}\right\}$

13. (a) $\{3\}$ (b) $\{^-4\}$ **15.** (a) $\{0\}$ (b) $\left\{\dfrac{20}{3}\right\}$

17. (a) $\{10\}$ (b) $\{15\}$ **19.** (a) $\{6\}$ (b) $\{3\}$

21. (a) $\{0\}$ (b) $\varnothing$ **23.** (a) R (b) $\{17\}$

25. (a) $\{1\}$ (b) $\{11\}$ **27.** (a) $\{9\}$ (b) $\{1\}$

29. $k = 1$ **31.** $\{0\}$

Exercises 4.5 (Page 138)

1. $37\frac{7}{9}° \text{ C}$ **3.** 256 feet

5. 64 feet per second   **7.** 2.4 ohms

9. 5050   **11.** 72π

13. $A = \frac{1}{2} ba$ **15.** $V = \frac{1}{3} Bh$

17. $A = (a + b)(x + y)$ or $A = ax + bx + ay + by$

19. (a) $x = \frac{a}{5}$ (b) $x = m - 2$

21. (a) $x = a - b$ (b) $x = \frac{a - 8}{2}$

23. (a) $y = rs$ (b) $x = \frac{2A}{h(b + c)}$

25. (a) $w = \frac{A}{l}$ (b) $r = \frac{C}{2\pi}$

27. (a) $F = \frac{9C + 160}{5}$ (b) $g = \frac{2s}{t^2}$

29. (a) $x = \frac{p}{m + n}$ (b) $x = \frac{n}{m + p}$

31. (a) $x = \frac{c}{a - 2}$ (b) $x = \frac{3}{b - a}$

33. (a) $x = \frac{3}{6 - a}$ (b) $x = \frac{-10}{a + m - 1}$

Exercises 4.6 (Page 146)

1. (a) $x + 5$ (b) $4x - 9$ (c) $2y + x$ (d) $x - (a + b)$

3. (a) $x^2 + y^2$ (b) $x^2 + y^2$ (c) $x^2 + y^2 \neq (x + y)^2$
     (d) $x^2 - y^2 = (x + y)(x - y)$

5. (a) $\frac{x}{5}$ (b) $xm + y(m + n)$ (c) $53 - x$ (d) $(20 - x)$ feet

7. (a) $5x = 35,\ x = 7$ (b) $x - 12 = 15,\ x = 27$

9. (a) $2x - 5 = x$, $x = 5$ **(b)** $x + 3x = 60$, $x = 15$

11. (a) $b + 12 = 2b$, $b = 12$ **(b)** $x + 3x = -20$, $x = {}^-5$, $3x = {}^-15$

13. 12 units and 6 units   **15.** 8

17. 125 grams   **19.** 16 and 24

21. Pen: $2.44, pencil: $1.44

4.7 Review Exercises   (Page 148)

1. (a) Identity   **(b)** Conditional equation

3. Yes   **5. (a)** $\{20\}$ **(b)** $\{{}^-2\}$

7. (a) $\{3\}$ **(b)** $\{0\}$ **9. (a)** $\{7\}$ **(b)** $\{0\}$

11. $h = \dfrac{A - 2\pi r^2}{2\pi r}$

13. (a) $x = \dfrac{b(c + 1)}{a}$ **(b)** $x = \dfrac{10}{m + n}$

15. $40 - x$ **17.** $7\dfrac{1}{2}$ units and $2\dfrac{1}{2}$ units

19. 624

Exercises 5.1   (Page 158)

1. $3 \cdot 3$ **3.** $2 \cdot 2 \cdot 2 \cdot 2$

5. $2 \cdot 2 \cdot 3 \cdot 3$ **7.** $3 \cdot 3 \cdot 3 \cdot 3 \cdot 5$

9. $3 \cdot 5 \cdot 7$ **11.** $2 \cdot 2 \cdot 7 \cdot 7$

13. $7 \cdot 13$ **15.** $3 \cdot 17$

17. GCD is 4, LCM is 48   **19.** GCD is 3, LCM is 108

21. GCD is 1, LCM is 924   **23.** GCD is 6, LCM is 72

25. GCD is 4, LCM is 360

27. The number 1 does not have two distinct factors.

29. Perfect squares   **31.** Yes, Yes

33. 17 and 19, 29 and 31, 59 and 61

35. (a) Yes   **(b)** Yes   **(c)** Yes

37. GCD is 2, LCM is 180; Yes; $ab = (a \uparrow b) \cdot (a \downarrow b)$

39. Yes

1. $\dfrac{3}{2}$

3. $x = \dfrac{3}{2}$

5. (a) $\dfrac{9}{8} \neq \dfrac{8}{9}$ (b) $\dfrac{2}{3} = \dfrac{8}{12}$

7. (a) $\dfrac{-8}{12} = \dfrac{-6}{9}$ (b) $\dfrac{-9}{16} \neq \dfrac{-3}{4}$

9. (a) $\dfrac{2}{\frac{1}{4}} = \dfrac{4}{\frac{1}{2}}$ (b) $\dfrac{-30}{6} = \dfrac{5}{-1}$

11. $\dfrac{3}{3} = \dfrac{1}{1}$

13. $\dfrac{4x}{6x} = \dfrac{6y}{9y}$

15. $\dfrac{10}{1}$

17. $\dfrac{2}{3} = \dfrac{4}{6} = \dfrac{8}{12} = \dfrac{6}{9} = \dfrac{20}{30}$

19. The fraction $\dfrac{-a}{b}$ is equivalent to the fraction $\dfrac{a}{-b}$ because $(-a)(-b)$ equals $(a)(b)$ by Definition 5.2.3.

21. By Definition 5.2.2 we know that $\dfrac{a}{b}$ is the solution of the equation $bx = a$. Therefore, substituting $\dfrac{a}{b}$ for x, we have

$$b \cdot \dfrac{a}{b} = a$$

23. $\dfrac{5}{8}$ of the class is made up of boys, $\dfrac{3}{8}$ of the class is made up of girls.

25. $\dfrac{1}{100}$

27. -3

29. q

31. $\dfrac{1}{2}$

33. $\dfrac{-1}{3}, 1$

35. $\dfrac{1}{2y}, 1$

37. (a) x; (b) $\dfrac{1}{x}$

39. 1 and $^-1$

41. (a) Yes (b) Yes (c) Yes, yes

1. (a) $\dfrac{1}{2}$ **(b)** $\dfrac{1}{2}$ **(c)** $\dfrac{1}{2}$ **(d)** $\dfrac{1}{3}$

3. (a) $\dfrac{2}{3}$ **(b)** $\dfrac{2}{3}$ **(c)** $\dfrac{2}{3}$ **(d)** $\dfrac{2}{3}$

5. (a) 6   **(b)** 0   **(c)** -6 **(d)** 0

7. (a) 28   **(b)** $\dfrac{x}{2}$ **(c)** $\dfrac{2x}{3}$ **(d)** $\dfrac{3}{4}$

9. (a) $\dfrac{2}{7}$ **(b)** $\dfrac{-y}{x}$ **(c)** $\dfrac{a-b}{a+b}$

11. -2 **13.** 1

15. 1   **17.** 1

19. (a) 36   **(b)** 36   **(c)** 72   **(d)** 72

21. $x = -15$ **23.** $x = 0$

25. $x = -2$ **27.** $x = 2$

29. $x = \dfrac{1}{5}$

31. By Definition 5.2.3 and because $a(-b) = b(-a)$, it follows that the fraction $\dfrac{a}{b}$ is equivalent to the fraction $\dfrac{-a}{-b}$. Thus,

$$\frac{a}{b} = \frac{-a}{-b}$$

and so,

$$-\frac{a}{b} = -\frac{-a}{-b}$$

1. (a) $\dfrac{1}{6}$ **(b)** $\dfrac{1}{6}$ **3. (a)** $\dfrac{-x^2}{12}$ **(b)** $\dfrac{x^3}{12}$

5. (a) $\dfrac{1}{xy}$ **(b)** $\dfrac{1}{abc}$ **7. (a)** $\dfrac{1}{6}$ **(b)** $\dfrac{7x}{4}$

9. (a) $\dfrac{12y^2}{5}$ **(b)** $\dfrac{-3}{16}$ **11. (a)** $\dfrac{-4}{3}$ **(b)** $\dfrac{4}{3}$

13. (a) $\dfrac{8}{a}$ **(b)** -32 **15. (a)** $\dfrac{1}{6m}$ **(b)** $\dfrac{-1}{12k}$

17. (a) 120   **(b)** $\dfrac{-40}{3}$ **19. (a)** $\dfrac{10}{9a^3}$ **(b)** $\dfrac{-1}{2}$

21. (a) $\dfrac{y^2}{8}$ **(b)** $-5m$ **23. (a)** 12   **(b)** -6

25. (a) $10x$ **(b)** $\dfrac{12y}{5}$ **27. (a)** $\dfrac{1}{8}$ **(b)** $\dfrac{9}{16}$

29. (a) $\dfrac{81}{16}$ **(b)** $\dfrac{1}{243}$ **31.** $\dfrac{8}{27}$

33. $\dfrac{2}{5}$ **35.** $x = \dfrac{4}{3}$

37. $x = \dfrac{8}{3}$ **39.** $x = \dfrac{-1}{2}$

41. (a) Addition, multiplication   **(b)** Subtraction, division

43. Division

45. (a) $a \div b = a \cdot \dfrac{1}{b} = \dfrac{1}{b} \cdot a = \dfrac{1}{b} \div \dfrac{1}{a}$

   (b) $\dfrac{1}{b} \div \dfrac{1}{a} = \dfrac{1}{b} \cdot \dfrac{a}{1} = \dfrac{a}{b} = \dfrac{1}{\frac{b}{a}} = \dfrac{1}{b \div a}$

   (c) From (a) and (b) and the Transitive Property of Equality it follows that

$$a \div b = \frac{1}{b \div a}$$

Exercises 5.5   (Page 196)

1. (a) $\dfrac{4}{3}$ **(b)** 1   **3. (a)** $\dfrac{x}{9}$ **(b)** $\dfrac{-a}{3}$

5. (a) $\dfrac{-11}{8}$ **(b)** 0   **7. (a)** 0   **(b)** $\dfrac{12}{x-6}$

9. (a) $\dfrac{5}{4}$ **(b)** $\dfrac{9}{8}$ **11. (a)** $\dfrac{29y}{24}$ **(b)** $\dfrac{21}{40}$

13. (a) $\dfrac{-1}{30}$ **(b)** $\dfrac{x}{6}$ **15. (a)** $\dfrac{-2x}{9}$ **(b)** $\dfrac{x}{2}$

17. (a) $\dfrac{31}{30}$ **(b)** $\dfrac{17}{60}$ **19. (a)** $\dfrac{1}{8}$ **(b)** $\dfrac{7x}{12}$

21. (a) 1   **(b)** $\dfrac{x + y}{xy}$ **23. (a)** $\dfrac{ad + bc}{bd}$ **(b)** $\dfrac{ad - bc}{bd}$

25. $x = \dfrac{1}{3}$ **27.** $x = \dfrac{-7}{6}$

29. $x = \dfrac{1}{3}$ **31.** $\dfrac{10}{11}$

33. $\dfrac{85}{66}$

35. By Theorem 5.3.3 (Fundamental Principle of Fractions) we have

$$\frac{1}{a} = \frac{b}{ab} \quad \text{and} \quad \frac{1}{b} = \frac{a}{ab}$$

Hence, we have

$$\frac{1}{a} + \frac{1}{b} = \frac{b}{ab} + \frac{a}{ab} \tag{1}$$

By Theorem 5.5.1 the right member of equality (1) is equal to $\dfrac{b + a}{ab}$

or, equivalently, $\dfrac{a + b}{ab}$. Therefore, we have

$$\frac{1}{a} + \frac{1}{b} = \frac{a + b}{ab}$$

37. 24 centimeters

Exercises 5.6   (Page 206)

1. (a) $\dfrac{4}{5}$ **(b)** $\dfrac{3}{2}$ **3. (a)** $\dfrac{5}{6}$ **(b)** $\dfrac{1}{2}$ **(c)** $\dfrac{1}{1}$

5. $\dfrac{3}{20,000,000}$ **7.** $\dfrac{1}{4}$

9. (a) 21   **(b)** $\dfrac{48}{7}$ **11. (a)** $\dfrac{9}{10}$ **(b)** $\dfrac{4}{5}$

13. (a) $\dfrac{17}{4}$ **(b)** $\dfrac{3}{7}$ **15.** $\dfrac{2}{15}$ cubic feet

17. $\dfrac{5}{8}$

19. Proof: We must prove

$$\frac{x}{1} = \frac{1}{\frac{1}{x}} \tag{1}$$

By Axiom 5.2.5 we have

$$x \cdot \frac{1}{x} = 1 \qquad (2)$$

Dividing each member of equality (2) by $\frac{1}{x}$ we obtain

$$x = \frac{1}{\frac{1}{x}} \qquad (3)$$

Substituting $\frac{x}{1}$ for x in the left member of equality (3) we obtain equality (1).

21. Proof: Given

$$a - b = c - d \qquad (1)$$

we obtain

$$a + d = b + c \qquad (2)$$

by adding $(b + d)$ to each member of equality (1). Thus, the sum of the "interiors" equals the sum of the "exteriors."

23. (a) 1200 **(b)** $\dfrac{78}{5}$ **25.** 13.5% (approx.)

27. $14.75 **29. (a)** 12 **(b)** 68

31. 76 grams of water and 4 grams of sugar

33. (a) 39.3% (approx.) **(b)** 5.88% Black (approx.), 47.1% Sorrel (approx.), 17.6% Palomino (approx.), 29.4% White (approx.) **(c)** 35.7% (approx.) **(d)** 42.9% (approx.)

5.7 Review Exercises (Page 210)

1. (a) $2 \cdot 3 \cdot 5 \cdot 7$ **(b)** $2^4 \cdot 3 \cdot 5$

3.

Number	Simplest form of the Number	Multiplicative Inverse of the Number	
3	3	$\dfrac{1}{3}$	
-1	-1	-1	
0	0	None	
$\dfrac{4}{8}$	$\dfrac{1}{2}$	2	*Table continues next page*

Number	Simplest form of the Number	Multiplicative Inverse of the Number
$\dfrac{-17}{5}$	$\dfrac{-17}{5}$	$\dfrac{-5}{17}$
$\dfrac{1}{3}$	$\dfrac{1}{3}$	3
$-\dfrac{1}{5}$	$\dfrac{-1}{5}$	-5

5. (a) $\dfrac{-1}{9}$ (b) $8y^3$ 7. (a) $\dfrac{x^2}{4}$ (b) $\dfrac{1}{y^2}$

9. (a) $\dfrac{-x}{6}$ (b) 1 11. (a) $\dfrac{-3}{4t}$ (b) $\dfrac{-34}{5}$

13. (a) $\dfrac{6}{1}$ (b) $\dfrac{1}{4800}$ 15. (a) $\dfrac{1}{2}$ (b) $\dfrac{1}{4}$

17. $36

Exercises 6.1 (Page 221)

1. (a) 0.5   (b) 1.0   (c) 1.5   (d) 2.0   (e) 2.5

3. (a) 0.333 ...   (b) 0.666 ...   (c) 1.0   (d) 1.333 ...   (e) 1.666 ...

5. (a) 0.2   (b) 0.4   (c) 0.6   (d) 0.8   (e) 1.0

7. (a) 0.1   (b) 0.2   (c) 0.3   (d) 0.4   (e) 0.5

9. (a) 0.1   (b) 0.01   (c) 0.001   (d) 0.0001   (e) 0.00001

11. (a) $\dfrac{1}{10} = 0.1$ (b) $\left(\dfrac{1}{10}\right)^2 = \dfrac{1}{100} = 0.01$ (c) $\dfrac{1}{1000} = 0.001$

(d) $\dfrac{1}{10000} = 0.0001$ (e) $\dfrac{1}{100000} = 0.00001$

13. (a) $3\left(\dfrac{1}{10}\right) + 3\left(\dfrac{1}{10}\right)^2 + 3\left(\dfrac{1}{10}\right)^3 + 4\left(\dfrac{1}{10}\right)^4 + 4\left(\dfrac{1}{10}\right)^5 + 4\left(\dfrac{1}{10}\right)^6$

(b) $-\left[8\left(\dfrac{1}{10}\right) + 7\left(\dfrac{1}{10}\right)^2 + 5\left(\dfrac{1}{10}\right)^3\right]$

15. (a) $-\left[8\left(\dfrac{1}{10}\right) + 8\left(\dfrac{1}{10}\right)^2 + 8\left(\dfrac{1}{10}\right)^3 + \cdots\right]$

(b) $6\left(\dfrac{1}{10}\right) + 6\left(\dfrac{1}{10}\right)^2 + 6\left(\dfrac{1}{10}\right)^3 + \cdots$

17. (a) 0.5050   **(b)** −0.4546

19. (a) $\dfrac{3}{4}$ **(b)** $\dfrac{5}{8}$ **21. (a)** $\dfrac{-1}{2000}$ **(b)** $\dfrac{-17}{5}$

23. (a) $\dfrac{7}{9}$ **(b)** $\dfrac{-8}{9}$ **25. (a)** 1   **(b)** $\dfrac{2}{90}$

27. (a) $\dfrac{20}{99}$ **(b)** $\dfrac{2}{99}$ **29. (a)** $\dfrac{1}{2}$ **(b)** $\dfrac{40}{111}$

31. (a) $5\left(\dfrac{1}{10}\right) + 9\left(\dfrac{1}{10}\right)^2 + 9\left(\dfrac{1}{10}\right)^3$ **(b)** 0.599

33. (a) 0.33   **(b)** 0.333   **(c)** 0.3333   **(d)** $\dfrac{1}{3}$ **(e)** $\dfrac{1}{3}$

35. (a) $\dfrac{7}{12}$ **(b)** $\dfrac{13}{24}$ **(c)** $\dfrac{25}{48}$ **(d)** Indefinitely   **(e)** An unlimited
number

Exercises 6.2 (Page 228)

1. (a) Irrational number   **(b)** Rational number

3. (a) Rational number   **(b)** Rational number

5. (a) Irrational number   **(b)** Rational number

7. (a) Irrational number   **(b)** Irrational number

9. (a) Rational number   **(b)** Irrational number

11. $0.4 < x < 0.5$
          $0.42 < x < 0.43$
        $0.424 < x < 0.425$
      $0.4242 < x < 0.4243$
    $0.42422 < x < 0.42423$
  $0.424224 < x < 0.424225$

13. Property 6.2.1 (Axiom of Completeness)

15. (a) No, $\sqrt{2} \cdot \sqrt{2} = 2$ **(b)** Yes, $\dfrac{1}{2} \cdot \dfrac{1}{3} = \dfrac{1}{6}$ **(c)** Yes, $2\sqrt{2}$ is irrational.

Exercises 6.3 (Page 232)

1. $\{8, -8\}$ **3.** $\{1, -1\}$

5. No real square roots exist.   **7.** 6

9. $\dfrac{1}{2}$

11. 5

13. 7

15. -2

17. 4

19. 3^2

21. $|xy|$

23. The value o̲ must be a positive number or zero, because $\sqrt{x}$ is undefined if ̲ ̲ ̲ ̲ ̲ ̲ ̲ ̲ ̲ negative number.

25. $x = 25$

Exercises 6.4 (̲ ̲ ̲ ̲ ̲ 239)

1. 6

3. 2

5. $5\sqrt{2}$

7. $2\sqrt{3}$

9. $3\sqrt{5}$

11. $3x^2\sqrt{x}$

13. $2xy\sqrt{2xy}$

15. $\dfrac{\sqrt{3}}{3}$

17. $\dfrac{\sqrt{6}}{3}$

19. $\dfrac{\sqrt{x}}{x}$

21. $\dfrac{\sqrt{2\pi r}}{2\pi r}$

23. $\dfrac{2x\sqrt{x}}{y}$

25. $\dfrac{\sqrt{3}}{2}$

27. $2\sqrt{x}$

29. 5

31. $5|x|$

33. 7.07

35. 0.89

37. (a) $4\sqrt{2}$ inches ̲ ̲ ̲ ̲ $2\sqrt{2}$ inches

39. 5 units

41. (a) 3 feet   (b) ̲ ̲ ̲ ̲ f it's very narrow.

6.5 Review Exercise̲ age 241)

1. (a) $0.\overline{45}$ (b) 0.4̲ ̲   (c) 0.625

3. $\dfrac{59}{72}$

5. (a) Rational numbe̲ ̲ ̲   (b) Irrational number   (c) Rational number

7. (a) $\{0.6, -0.6\}$ **(b)** 0   **(c)** No real square root exists.

9. (a) 2   **(b)** 3^2 **11. (a)** 12   **(b)** 3

13. (a) $\dfrac{\sqrt{10}}{5}$ **(b)** $\dfrac{2\sqrt{3}}{3}$ **15. (a)** $2x^2\sqrt{3}$ **(b)** $4x^3y\sqrt{y}$

17. 4.71 seconds

Exercises 7.1   (Page 252)

1.

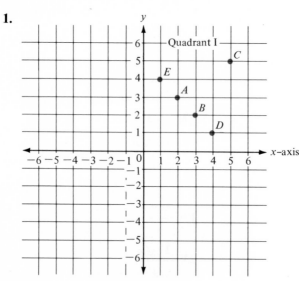

Answer 7.1.1

3.

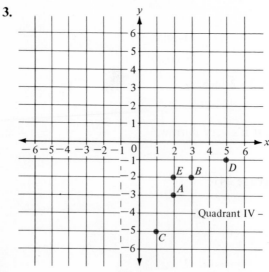

Answer 7.1.3

5.

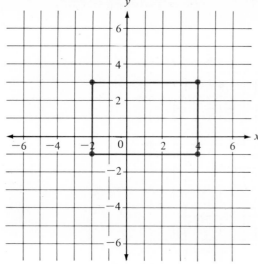

Answer 7.1.5

7.

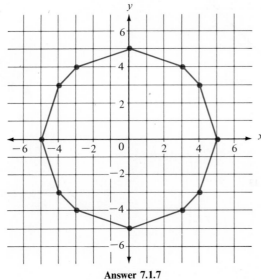

Answer 7.1.7

9. $A : (3, 3)$, $B : (-2, 1)$, $C : (0, 0)$, $D : (-4, 5)$, $E : (1, -4)$, $F : (5, 0)$, $G : (0, -3)$

11.

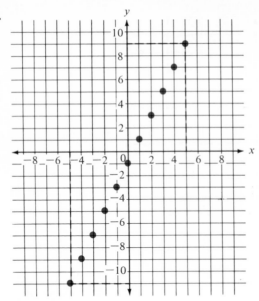

Answer 7.1.11

13.

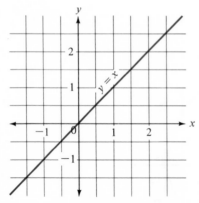

Answer 7.1.13

15.

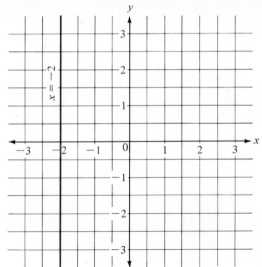

Answer 7.1.15

17.

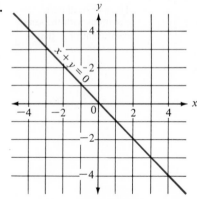

Answer 7.1.17

19.

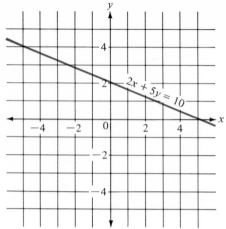

Answer 7.1.19

21.

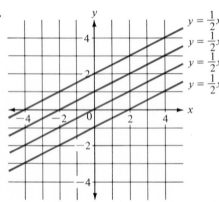

$y = \frac{1}{2}x + 2$ These lines are parallel.

$y = \frac{1}{2}x + 1$

$y = \frac{1}{2}x$ These lines all have equations with the same coefficient of x, that is, $\frac{1}{2}$.

$y = \frac{1}{2}x - 1$

Answer 7.1.21

23.

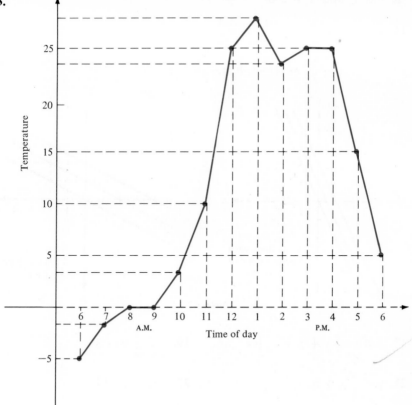

Answer 7.1.23

(a) $17\frac{1}{2}°$ (approx.) 11:30 A.M., 10° at 5:30 P.M.

(b) $-5°$ (approx.)

(c) 6 A.M. to 8 A.M., 9 A.M. to 1 P.M., 2 P.M. to 3 P.M.

(d) 11 A.M. to 12 noon

(e) From 11 A.M. to about 5:30 P.M., or $6\frac{1}{2}$ hours

25. 34 square units

Exercises 7.2   (Page 265)

1. $\dfrac{-3}{2}$ **3.** 0

5. $y = 3x + 5, m = 3, b = 5$

7. $y = 2x - 1, m = 2, b = -1$

9. $y = x$, $m = 1$, $b = 0$

11. $y = \dfrac{1}{2}x + \dfrac{3}{2}$, $m = \dfrac{1}{2}$, $b = \dfrac{3}{2}$

13. $y = -x - \dfrac{1}{2}$, $m = -1$, $b = \dfrac{-1}{2}$

15.

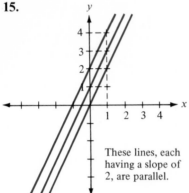

These lines, each having a slope of 2, are parallel.

These lines, each having a slope of $\dfrac{1}{2}$, are parallel.

Answer 7.2.15

17. $y = -\dfrac{3}{2}x + 3$, $y = \dfrac{4}{3}x$

19. $y = \dfrac{2}{3}x - 2$

21. $y = \dfrac{3}{5}x + 5$

23. $y = 3x - 14$

25. $C = \dfrac{5}{9}F - \dfrac{160}{9}$

27. The points are collinear.

29. 5 units

31. **(a)** (i) $T = 4t - 20$ (ii) $T = 0$ (iii) $T = \dfrac{20}{7}t - \dfrac{400}{7}$

  (iv) $T = 100$

  (b) (i) 4 (ii) 0 (iii) $\dfrac{20}{7}$ (iv) 0

  (c) Interval of most rapid change is given by $20 < t \leq 55$. Interval of slowest change is given by $5 < t \leq 20$ and $55 < t$.
  (d) 34 minutes **(e)** $71.4°$ C (approx.)

1.

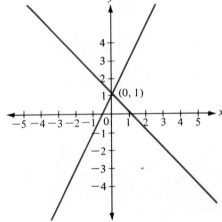

These equations are consistent and independent.

Answer 7.3.1

3.

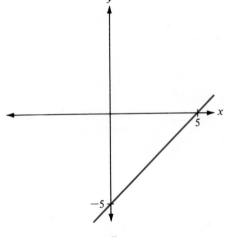

There is an unlimited number of solutions.
These equations are consistent and dependent.

Answer 7.3.3

5.

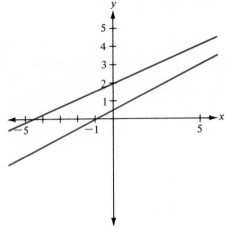

Lines are not parallel; they intersect at the point $(21, 11)$, but this is difficult to ascertain from the sketch.
These equations are consistent and independent.

Answer 7.3.5

7.

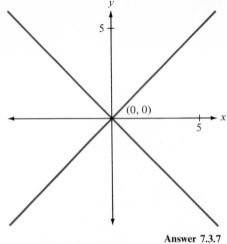

(0, 0)

These equations are consistent and independent.

Answer 7.3.7

9.

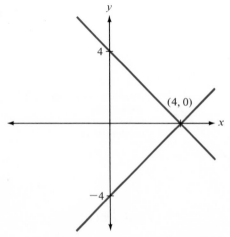

(4, 0)

These equations are consistent and independent.

Answer 7.3.9

11. $x = 1$, $y = 3$, the equations are consistent and independent.

13. $x = \dfrac{5}{2}$, $y = \dfrac{3}{2}$, the equations are consistent and independent.

Exercises 7.4 (Page 281)

1. $x = 8$, $y = 4$

3. $x = 5$, $y = 3$

5. $x = 12$, $y = 1$

7. $x = 4$, $y = \dfrac{1}{3}$

9. $x = 22$, $y = 5$ **11.** $x = 1$, $y = 2$

13. $x = 0$, $y = 6$ **15.** $x = \dfrac{a+b}{2}$, $y = \dfrac{a-b}{2}$

17. $x = 2$, $y = 4$ **19.** No solution

21. Proof:

$E_1 = E_2$	(1)	Given
$E_1 - E_3 = E_2 - E_3$	(2)	By subtracting E_3 from both members of equation (1) (Theorem 4.3.3).
$E_3 = E_4$	(3)	Given
$E_1 - E_3 = E_2 - E_4$	(4)	Substituting E_4 for E_3 in equation (2) on the right side (Axiom 1.5.2).

23. $x = 2$, $y = 3$, $z = 7$ **25.** $A = \dfrac{\pi d^2}{4}$

7.5 Review Exercises   (Page 282)

1. (a) III   **(b)** IV   **3. (a)** $\dfrac{-3}{2}$ **(b)** -1

5. (a) (i) 3   (ii) -2 (iii) $\dfrac{2}{3}$

     (b) (i) -1 (ii) 10   (iii) 10

7. (a) $6400   **(b)** $480

9. (a) Inconsistent   **(b)** Consistent and dependent

11. (a) $x = 3$, $y = 4$ **(b)** $x = 5$, $y = -3$

Exercises 8.1   (Page 287)

1. 14 and 62   **3.** 16 and 24

5. John is 33 years old, his son is 11 years old.

7. $\dfrac{4}{7}$ **9.** Pads: 29¢, pencils: 4¢

11. $12,250   **13.** 40

15. $5.85

1. 30 pounds at 89¢ per pound and 70 pounds at 69¢ per pound

3. 3.2 pounds

5. $\dfrac{125}{126}$ tons of the 98% copper alloy and $1\dfrac{32}{64}$ tons of the 35% copper alloy.

7. 20 13¢ stamps and 4 10¢ stamps

9. 6000 gallons at 60¢ per gallon and 3000 gallons at 54¢ per gallon

11. ~~4.8 quarts~~ .148 qt

Exercises 8.3 (Page 298)

1. (a) $\dfrac{2}{5}$ of the job   **(b)** $\dfrac{2}{3}$ of the job   **(c)** 1 whole job   **(d)** $\dfrac{2}{x}$ of the job

3. (a) 400 parts produced   **(b)** 500 parts produced   **(c)** $5x$ parts produced

5. $4\dfrac{4}{9}$ hours   **7.** $17\dfrac{1}{7}$ hours

9. $14\dfrac{6}{7}$ hours   **11.** $7\dfrac{1}{2}$ hours

13. 9 hours and 18 hours

15. Bob worked $\dfrac{3}{5}$ hours and Mark worked $\dfrac{1}{10}$ hours.

17. Julio works 3 hours and Al works 6 hours.

Exercises 8.4 (Page 304)

1. 176 feet per second   **3.** 80 feet per second

5. 30 miles per hour   **7.** 60 miles per hour

9. 3.6 hours   **11.** 20 minutes

13. 5 miles per hour is the rate of speed in still water and 3 miles per hour is the rate of speed of the current.

15. 5 minutes

Exercises 8.5 (Page 310)

1. $25\frac{5}{11}$ and $44\frac{6}{11}$

3. about 483,092

5. Diameter of about 0.11 inches, placed about 1289 inches away.

7. 16 feet and 24 feet

9. 224

11. $\frac{\sqrt{2}}{2}$ (approx. 1.41 to 2) Saturn requires 1.41 time units for one complete revolution to 2 time units for one complete revolution on Uranus around the sun.

13. 30 pounds and 40 pounds

15. 105

17. 4950

19. $x = 3\frac{1}{3}$, $y = 16\frac{1}{2}$

21. $37\frac{1}{2}$ feet

8.6 Review Exercises (Page 313)

1. 25 and 15

3. 5.26 pounds (approx.)

5. $3\frac{15}{17}$ hours

7. 50 miles per hour

9. 108 feet

Exercises 9.1 (Page 318)

1. (a), (b), (c), (e), (f), (g), (h), (j)

3. (a), (f), (h)

5. (c), (h)

7. (a) 2   (b) 3   (c) 1   (e) None   (f) 4   (g) 2   (h) 1
   (j) 2

9. $x + 3$, $a = 1$, $b = 3$

11. $4x$, $a = 4$, $b = 0$

13. $-16t^2 + 64t$, $a = -16$, $b = 64$, $c = 0$

15. $\frac{-2}{3}x + \frac{1}{2}$, $a = \frac{-2}{3}$, $b = \frac{1}{2}$

17. $y^2 + 2y + 1$ or something similar

19. (a) $2(10^2) + 3(10) + 7 = 237$ (coefficients: 2, 3, and 7)
(b) $1(10^3) + 3(10^2) + 7(10) + 4 = 1374$ (coefficients: 1, 3, 7, and 4)
(c) $1(10^3) + 8(10) + 6 = 1086$ (coefficients: 1, 8, and 6)

The numerals are formed using the coefficients. Numerals in positional notation base 10 are polynomials in 10.

Exercises 9.2 (Page 321)

1. (a) $10x$ (b) $12y$ (c) $12xy$

3. (a) $6x^2 + 11x + 5$ (b) $13y^2 - 3y - 4$

5. (a) $5x^3 + 3x^2 + 11x - 15$ (b) $4x^4 + 4x^3 + 11x^2 - 8x - 5$

7. (a) $11x^2 + 8x + 4$ (b) $-5x + 3$

9. (a) $2x + 5$ (b) $64t$

11. (a) $4x$ (b) $6y$ (c) $-18xy$

13. (a) $-2x^2 + 11x - 3$ (b) $y^2 - 13y + 22$

15. (a) $-3x^2 + 3x^2 - 7x + 1$ (b) $-6x^4 + 10x^3 - 7x^2 + 2x + 25$

17. (a) $-3x^2 + 2x - 6$ (b) $-3x^2 - 5x + 13$

19. (a) $2x^2 - 4x - 3$ (b) $32t^2 - 64t$

21. $4x + 3$ **23.** $y - x$

25. $x^2 + x - 7$

27.
$$\begin{array}{lll} 3x^2 + 2x + 7 & 327 & 3(10^2) + 2(10) + 7 \\ \underline{5x^2 + 6x + 1} & \underline{561} & \underline{5(10^2) + 6(10) + 1} \\ 8x^2 + 8x + 8 & 888 & 8(10^2) + 8(10) + 8 \end{array}$$

The coefficients of the polynomials are the same as the digits in the numerals.

29. $8(10^3) + 9(10^2) + 7(10) + 1$

31. $1(2^4) + 1(2^3) + 1(2^2) + 2(2) + 1$

33. $-5x^3 - 2x^2 - 10x + 5$

35. $5x + 10$

Exercises 9.3 (Page 326)

1. (a) $15x^2$ (b) $15xy$ **3.** (a) x^6 (b) x^6

5. (a) $-x^3$ (b) $-x^4$ **7.** (a) 10^4 (b) 10^6

9. (a) 10^{100} **(b)** 10^9 **11. (a)** 10^{100} **(b)** 10^6

13. (a) $-x^5$ **(b)** x^6 **15. (a)** x^{100} **(b)** $-x^6$

17. (a) $21x^5y^2$ **(b)** $50x^4yz$ **19. (a)** $3^6 2^{12}$ **(b)** $3^4 x^8$

21. (a) $24x^5$ **(b)** $-x^{10}y^4$ **23. (a)** x^{a+b} **(b)** x^{n+2}

25. (a) x^{2n} **(b)** x^7 **27. (a)** 2^4 **(b)** 3^3 **(c)** 10^{11}

Exercises 9.4 (Page 331)

1. (a) $3x + 21$ **(b)** $-3x + 12$

3. (a) $3x^3 + 3x$ **(b)** $-x^5 - x^3 - x^2$

5. (a) $-12x^4 + 48x^3 - 72x^2$ **(b)** $x^3y - xy^3$

7. (a) $x^2 - 3x + 2$ **(b)** $x^2 - x - 2$

9. (a) $x^2 - 49$ **(b)** $x^4 - 1$

11. (a) $a^2 - b^2$ **(b)** $x^4 - y^4$

13. (a) $x^3 + 3x^2 + 2x$ **(b)** $16x^3 - 4x$

15. (a) $x^3 + 1$ **(b)** $x^3 + 6x^2 + 11x + 6$

17. (a) $x^2 + 2xy + y^2$ **(b)** $x^4 + 4x^3y + 6x^2y^2 + 4xy^3 + y^4$

19. (a) $a = x$ **(b)** $a = 4$

21. Proof: $k^2 - (k - 1)^2 = k^2 - (k^2 - 2k + 1)$
$$= k^2 - k^2 + 2k - 1$$
$$= 2k - 1$$

23. $(2x + 1)(3x + 2) = 6x^2 + 7x + 2$
$(2 \cdot 10 + 1)(3 \cdot 10 + 2) = 6 \cdot 100 + 7 \cdot 10 + 2$
$21 \cdot 32 \qquad\qquad = 672$

The coefficients of $6x^2 + 7x + 2$ are the digits of 672.

25. $A = x^2 + 5x$

27. The area increases by 6 square units.

29. $(x + 1)^5 = x^5 + 5x^4 + 10x^3 + 10x^2 + 5x + 1$

Exercises 9.5 (Page 344)

1. $\dfrac{3}{8}$, $x = 0$, $y = 0$ **3.** $\dfrac{5}{7}$, $x = -2$

5. $\dfrac{x + 1}{x + 2}$, $x = 0$ or $x = -2$ **7.** $\dfrac{x^2 - 1}{x^2 + 1}$, $x = -1$

9. (a) 10^2 (b) x^2

11. (a) 2^5 (b) y^5

13. (a) $\dfrac{1}{3^2}$ (b) $\dfrac{1}{10^2}$

15. (a) $-x^2$ (b) $\dfrac{-1}{x^2}$

17. (a) $\dfrac{-y}{2}$ (b) $\dfrac{42x^3}{13y^3z^2}$

19. (a) $\dfrac{36}{x^4}$ (b) $2(x+2)$

21. $x + 3$

23. $3x^2 + 4x - 7$

25. $\dfrac{a}{2b} + 1 + \dfrac{b}{2a}$

27. $\dfrac{2}{x} - \dfrac{3y}{x^2} + \dfrac{5z}{4x^2y}$

29. $\dfrac{1}{x^{b-a}}$

31. x^n

33. x^{2n-2}

35. $x + 3$

37. $x - 1 + \dfrac{1}{x+1}$

39. $2x + 1$

41. $x + 3$

43. $2x + 1$

45. $2x + 2 + \dfrac{1}{x+1}$

47. $x - 4$

49. $x = 8$

51.
$$\frac{2x^2 + 7x + 3}{2x + 1} = x + 3$$
$$\frac{2(100) + 7(10) + 3}{2(10) + 1} = 10 + 3$$
$$\frac{273}{21} = 13$$
$$13 = 13$$

53.

Take a number greater than 0	: n
Add 1	: $n + 1$
Square the result	: $(n+1)^2 = n^2 + 2n + 1$
Subtract 1	: $n^2 + 2n$

Divide by the original number : $\dfrac{n^2 + 2n}{n} = n + 2$

Multiply by 2 less than the original number	: $(n+2)(n-2) = n^2 - 4$
Add 4	: n^2
Take the square root	: n
Triple the result	: $3n$
Add 6	: $3n + 6$

Divide by 3 : $\dfrac{3n + 6}{3} = n + 2$

Subtract the original number   : 2

The answer is 2

9.6 Review Exercises (Page 346)

1. (a) 4   **(b)** 2

3. (a) $3x^3 + 6x + 5$ **(b)** $-x^3 - 6x^2 + 10$

5. (a) x^7 **(b)** x^9

7. (a) x^3 **(b)** $\dfrac{1}{x^3}$

9. (a) $8x - 20$ **(b)** $6x^3 - 8x^2 + 2x$

11. (a) $x^2 + 4x + 4$ **(b)** $x^2 - 2xy + y^2$

13. (a) $ax^2 + bx + c$ **(b)** $2x + 3$

15. (a) $x^2 - x + 1$ **(b)** $2x - 1$

Exercises 10.1 (Page 352)

1. (a) $3(x + 4)$ **(b)** $15(3x + 4y)$

3. (a) $xy(y - x)$ **(b)** $3(x^2 + 6x + 10)$

5. (a) $(x + y)(a + b)$ **(b)** $x^3(x + 2)$

7. (a) $-x(x + 1)$ **(b)** $\pi r(r + 2)$

9. (a) $4x(2x^2 - 6x - 1)$ **(b)** $(x - 1)(x - 4)$

11. $x = \dfrac{10}{a + b}$ **13.** $x = 1$

15. $x = 2$ **17. (a)** $5\sqrt{5}$ **(b)** $11\sqrt{3}$

19. (a) $3x\sqrt{3}$ **(b)** $4\sqrt{x} - 3\sqrt{y}$

21. (a) $\sqrt{3}$ **(b)** $9\sqrt{3}$

23. (a) $6 + 3\sqrt{2}$ **(b)** $4 + 2\sqrt{3} + 2\sqrt{5}$

25. (a) $7 + 3\sqrt{6}$ **(b)** 3

Exercises 10.2 (Page 356)

1. (a) $(x - 1)(x + 1)$ **(b)** $(a - b)(a + b)$

3. (a) $(xy - 1)(xy + 1)$ **(b)** $(m - 3)(m + 3)$

5. (a) $(x - 1)(x^2 + x + 1)$
   (b) $(x - y)(x^6 + x^5y + x^4y^2 + x^3y^3 + x^2y^4 + xy^5 + y^6)$

7. $(x - 1)(x + 1)(x^2 + 1)$ **9.** $3(x - 5)(x + 5)$

11. $t(t - 1)(t + 1)$

13. $10(1 - y)(1 + y)(1 + y^2)$

15. $(x^2 - y)(x^2 + y)(x^4 + y^2)$

17. $4(2x - 3)(2x + 3)$

19. $2(xy - 4)(xy + 4)$

21. $A = (x - y)(x + y)$

23. $A = r^2 \left(4 + \dfrac{1}{2}\pi\right)$

25. $A = 4(x + y + 4)$

27. 2.791299470 (this is $x + y$)

29. $-3 + 2\sqrt{3}$

31. $\dfrac{35 - 7\sqrt{2}}{23}$

33. $\dfrac{2\sqrt{15} + \sqrt{10} - 6\sqrt{3} - 3\sqrt{2}}{10}$

35. $(\sqrt{a} + \sqrt{a - 1})(\sqrt{a} - \sqrt{a - 1}) = (\sqrt{a})^2 - (\sqrt{a - 1})^2$
$$= a - (a - 1)$$
$$= 1$$

Exercises 10.3 (Page 365)

1. $+, +$

3. $+, +$

5. $x + 4$

7. $x - 4$

9. $2x + 3$

11. $(x - 6)(x - 6)$

13. $(x + 3)(x + 4)$

15. $(x - 12)(x + 2)$

17. $(x + 10)(x - 2)$ ✓

19. $(x + 9)(x + 4)$

21. $(x + y)(x + y)$

23. $(x - 4)(x + 2)$

25. $(3x + 5)(2x + 3)$

27. $(3x + 5)(2x - 3)$

29. $(5x - 8)(2x - 1)$

31. $2(x + 3)(x + 3)$

33. $10x(x - 1)(x - 1)$

35. (a) Yes $(x + 1)^2$ **(b)** Yes $(x + 2)^2$

37. (a) No   **(b)** Yes $(x - y)^2$

39. (a) 1 **(b)** $(x - 1)^2$

41. (a) 36 **(b)** $(x + 6)^2$

43. (a) 49 **(b)** $(x + 7)^2$

45. 19 units long and 13 units wide

47. The product $(x + 3 - \sqrt{6x})(x + 3 + \sqrt{6x})$ is not considered to be a completely factored form of $x^2 + 9$ because $x + 3 + \sqrt{6x}$ and $x + 3 - \sqrt{6x}$ are not polynomials and the coefficients are not all integers. However,

$$(x + 3 + \sqrt{6x})(x + 3 - \sqrt{6x}) = x^2 + 9$$

10.4 Review Exercises (Page 367)

1. (a) $4(x^2 - 12)$ **(b)** $6y(y^2 - 5y + 3)$

3. (a) $5\sqrt{3}$ **(b)** $11\sqrt{2}$

5. (a) $(2x - 1)(2x + 1)$ **(b)** $(m - n)(m + n)$

7. (a) $(x + 1)(x + 5)$ **(b)** $4(x - 4)(x + 4)$

9. (a) $2 + 1$ **(b)** $2\sqrt{5} - 2\sqrt{3}$

11. (a) $(2x - 1)(2x + 9)$ **(b)** $(y - 9)(y - 4)$

13. (a) 25 **(b)** 100

Exercises 11.1 (Page 375)

1. $\{2, 3\}$

3. $\{5\}$

5. $\{3, 2\}$

7. $\{2\}$

9. $\{4, -3, -2\}$

11. $\{-3, -5\}$

13. $\left\{\dfrac{3}{2}, 2\right\}$

15. $\{2, -2\}$

17. $\{-6, -2\}$

19. $\left\{\dfrac{-5}{3}, \dfrac{1}{2}\right\}$

21. 5 or -8

23. 11, 14, and 5

25. $\{10, -10\}$

27. $\dfrac{2}{3}$ or $\dfrac{3}{2}$

Exercises 11.2 (Page 385)

1. $\{-3, -5\}$

3. $\left\{\dfrac{-3 + \sqrt{3}}{2}, \dfrac{-3 - \sqrt{3}}{2}\right\}$

5. $\{5 + \sqrt{5}, 5 - \sqrt{5}\}$

7. $\{0, 4\}$

9. $\{1, -1\}$

11. $\left\{\dfrac{-3 + \sqrt{3}}{2}, \dfrac{-3 - \sqrt{3}}{2}\right\}$

13. $\left\{\dfrac{4}{3}, -1\right\}$

15. $\left\{\dfrac{-1 + \sqrt{21}}{5}, \dfrac{-1 - \sqrt{21}}{5}\right\}$

17. $\left\{0, \dfrac{-3}{2}\right\}$

19. $\left\{3, \dfrac{-1}{3}\right\}$

21. There are no real number roots.

23. Two real number roots, both rational numbers.

25. One real number root, a rational number.

27. There are no real number roots.

29. $r_1 = \dfrac{-b + \sqrt{b^2 - 4ac}}{2a}$ and $r_2 = \dfrac{-b - \sqrt{b^2 - 4ac}}{2a}$ Hence,

$$r_1 + r_2 = \frac{-b + \sqrt{b^2 - 4ac}}{2a} + \frac{-b - \sqrt{b^2 - 4ac}}{2a}$$

$$= \frac{-b + \sqrt{b^2 - 4ac} - b - \sqrt{b^2 - 4ac}}{2a}$$

$$= \frac{-2b}{2a}$$

$$= \frac{-b}{a}$$

31. If $x = \dfrac{-b + \sqrt{b^2 - 4ac}}{2a}$, then

$$ax^2 + bx + c = a\left(\frac{-b + \sqrt{b^2 - 4ac}}{2a}\right)^2 + b\left(\frac{-b + \sqrt{b^2 - 4ac}}{2a}\right) + c$$

$$= a\left(\frac{b^2 - 2b\sqrt{b^2 - 4ac} + b^2 - 4ac}{4a^2}\right)$$

$$\quad + \frac{-b^2 + b\sqrt{b^2 - 4ac}}{2a} + c$$

$$= \frac{2b^2 - 2b\sqrt{b^2 - 4ac} - 4ac}{4a} + \frac{-b^2 + b\sqrt{b^2 - 4ac}}{2a} + c$$

$$= \frac{b^2 - b\sqrt{b^2 - 4ac} - 2ac}{2a} + \frac{-b^2 + b\sqrt{b^2 - 4ac}}{2a} + c$$

$$= \frac{b^2 - b\sqrt{b^2 - 4ac} - 2ac - b^2 + b\sqrt{b^2 - 4ac}}{2a} + c$$

$$= \frac{-2ac}{2a} + c$$

$$= -c + c$$

$$= 0$$

Exercises 11.3 (Page 395)

1. 4

3. 9.29 feet by 27.87 feet (approx.)

5. 22.07 inches by 44.14 inches (approx.)

7. (a) $5\sqrt{2}$ **(b)** 25   **9.** 24 feet

11. $6\sqrt{2}$ units   **13.** 10

15. $x = \sqrt{41}$ **17.** 1500π square units

19. 7.74 seconds (approx.)

21. (a) $\dfrac{\sqrt{6}}{2}$ seconds (approx. 1.22 seconds)

     (b) 5.6 seconds on earth (approx.), 13.7 seconds on the moon (approx.)

23. $a = 51, b = 140, c = 149$

$$51^2 + 140^2 = 149^2$$
$$2601 + 19600 = 22201$$
$$22201 = 22201$$

Exercises 11.4   (Page 410)

1.

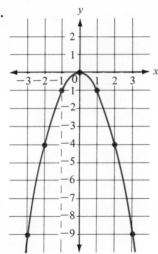

Answer 11.4.1

3.

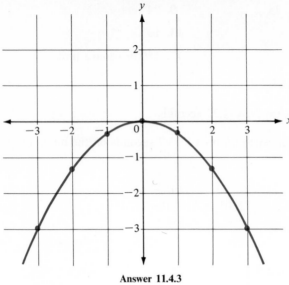

Answer 11.4.3

5.

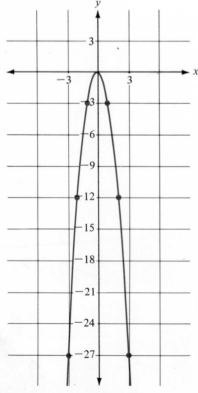

Answer 11.4.5

7.

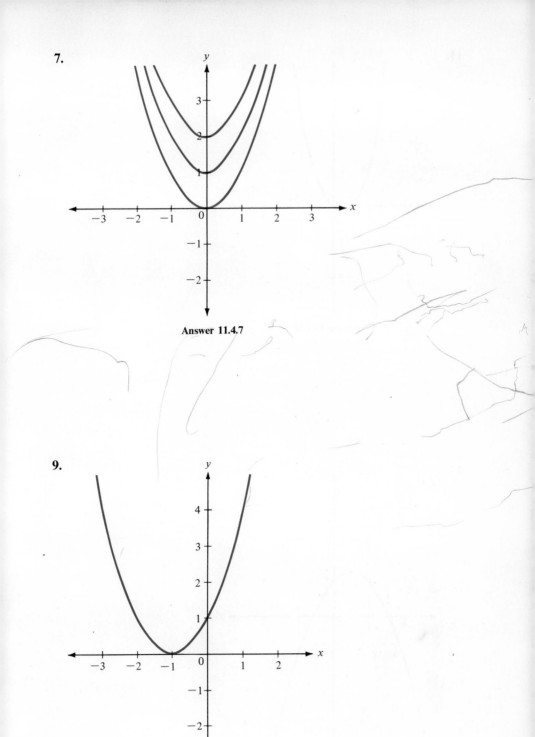

Answer 11.4.7

9.

Answer 11.4.9

11.

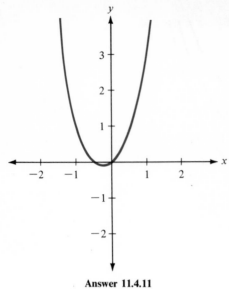

Answer 11.4.11

13.

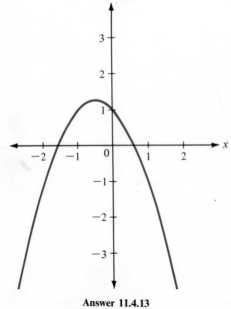

Answer 11.4.13

15. Zeros: $-1, 1$; $y_{min} = -1$

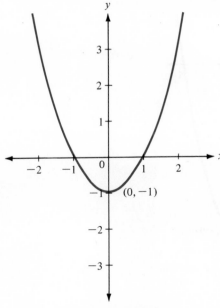

Answer 11.4.15

17. Zero: -1; $y_{min} = 0$.

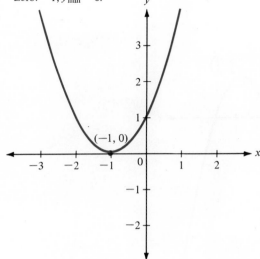

Answer 11.4.17

19. Zeros: $5, -1; y_{min} = -9.$

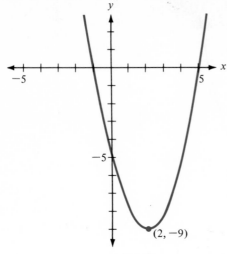

$(2, -9)$

Answer 11.4.19

21. Zeros: $0, \dfrac{3}{2}; y_{max} = \dfrac{9}{8}.$

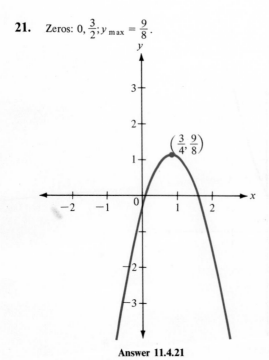

$\left(\dfrac{3}{4}, \dfrac{9}{8}\right)$

Answer 11.4.21

23. Zero: 0; $y_{max} = 0$

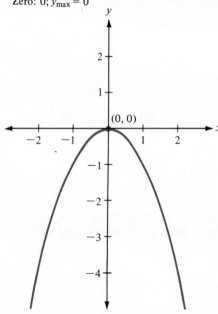

Answer 11.4.23

25.

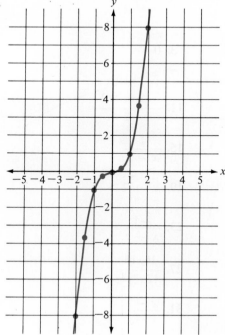

Answer 11.4.25

27. 1250 square feet

29. 256 feet maximum height, 4 seconds

11.5 Review Exercises (Page 412)

1. (a) $\{3, -7\}$ **(b)** $\{-3, 5\}$ **3. (a)** $\{6, 2\}$ **(b)** $\left\{\dfrac{1}{2}, 6\right\}$

5. (a) 22   **(b)** 45 miles per hour

7. (a) $\{2 + \sqrt{3}, 2 - \sqrt{3}\}$ **(b)** $\left\{\dfrac{3}{2}, -4\right\}$

9. (a) The roots are real numbers. Both roots are rational numbers.
   (b) The roots are real numbers. Both roots are rational numbers.

11. (a) 13   **(b)** $4\sqrt{5}$ and $8\sqrt{5}$

13. (a) 100 seconds   **(b)** 2.5 seconds

15. (a) Zeros : 2, -5; $y_{\min} = \dfrac{-49}{4}$

   (b) Zeros : 3, -3; $y_{\max} = 9$

Exercises 12.1 (Page 420)

1. 4

3. 0

5. 3, -3

7. -5

9. -6, -2

11. $\dfrac{-5 \pm \sqrt{37}}{2}$

13. $\dfrac{x}{3}$

15. $\dfrac{1}{x-5}$

17. $\dfrac{1}{2}$

19. $x^2 + 2$

21. $\dfrac{-1}{x+5}$

23. $\dfrac{-1}{x-y}$

25. $\dfrac{x^2 + 2xy + y^2}{x^2 - y^2}$

27. $\dfrac{16xy^2}{12x^2y^2}$

29. $\dfrac{3x + 12}{x^2 + 9x + 20}$

31. $\dfrac{x-1}{x-1}$

33. $x_2 + x_1$

Exercises 12.2 (Page 424)

1. $3xy^2$

3. $\dfrac{3(a+2)}{4(2a-3)}$

5. $\dfrac{(x-1)^3}{(x+3)(x-2)}$

7. $-a$

9. $(m+n)^2$

11. $12x$

13. $\dfrac{y-2}{y+1}$

15. $\dfrac{(z-3)(z-5)}{z(z+5)}$

17. $\dfrac{4(x-2)(x+1)}{x-1}$

19. $\dfrac{-2}{a+b}$

21. n dots in the last row; the total number of dots in n rows is $\dfrac{n(n+1)}{2}$;
5050 dots in 100 rows.

Exercises 12.3 (Page 433)

1. $\dfrac{6}{x}$

3. $\dfrac{a}{x}$

5. $\dfrac{2x}{4x-y}$

7. 2

9. $\dfrac{1}{x+2}$

11. $\dfrac{-5x^2+21x+6}{6x^3}$

13. $\dfrac{7x+17}{36}$

15. $\dfrac{-2a+4b}{a^2-b^2}$

17. $\dfrac{x+6}{x-2}$

19. $\dfrac{x^2}{x+1}$

21. $\dfrac{x^2+4}{x-2}$

23. $x+2$

25. $\dfrac{a}{a-1}$

27. $\dfrac{x^2+y^2}{x^2-y^2}$

29. $\dfrac{-1}{x}$

31. $\dfrac{1}{2a}\left(\dfrac{1}{x-a}-\dfrac{1}{x+a}\right)=\dfrac{1}{2a}\left(\dfrac{1[x+a]}{(x-a)[x+a]}-\dfrac{1[x-a]}{(x+a)[x-a]}\right)$

$$=\dfrac{1}{2a}\left(\dfrac{x+a-(x-a)}{(x+a)(x-a)}\right)$$

$$=\dfrac{1}{2a}\left(\dfrac{2a}{(x+a)(x-a)}\right)$$

$$=\dfrac{1[2a]}{(x^2-a^2)[2a]}$$

$$=\dfrac{1}{x^2-a^2}$$

33. Next equation : $\dfrac{1}{5+1}=1-\dfrac{5}{5+1}$

n^{th} equation: $\quad\dfrac{1}{n+1}=1-\dfrac{n}{n+1}$

35. $\dfrac{a}{b}\left(\dfrac{1}{ax}-\dfrac{1}{ax+b}\right)=\dfrac{a}{b}\left(\dfrac{1[ax+b]}{ax[ax+b]}-\dfrac{1[ax]}{(ax+b)[ax]}\right)$

$$=\dfrac{a}{b}\left(\dfrac{ax+b-ax}{ax(ax+b)}\right)$$

$$=\dfrac{a}{b}\left(\dfrac{b}{ax(ax+b)}\right)$$

$$=\dfrac{1[ab]}{x(ax+b)[ab]}$$

$$=\dfrac{1}{x(ax+b)}$$

$$=\left(\dfrac{1}{x}\right)\left(\dfrac{1}{ax+b}\right)$$

Exercises 12.4   (Page 439)

1. $\{24\}$

3. $\{6\}$

5. $\{1\}$

7. $\left\{\dfrac{2}{7}\right\}$

9. $\{23\}$

11. $\left\{\dfrac{12}{7}\right\}$

13. $\varnothing$

15. $\{7+\sqrt{37},\,7-\sqrt{37}\}$

17. $\{2\sqrt{3},\,-2\sqrt{3}\}$

19. $\{2\}$

21. $y=x,\ x\neq 0$ and $y\neq 0$

23. $y=2x-4,\ x\neq\dfrac{3}{2}$ and $y\neq -1$

25. $y = \dfrac{6x + 2}{1 + 2x}$, $x \neq 0$, $x \neq \dfrac{-1}{2}$, $y \neq 2$

27. $a = \dfrac{rb}{b - r}$, $r \neq 0$, $b \neq 0$, $r \neq b$

29. $m = \dfrac{2E}{v^2}$, $v \neq 0$

31. The mistake was made in step (5), dividing by $(a - 2)$, because this assumes that $a \neq 2$ (otherwise $a - 2 = 0$), and so this contradicts the statement in step (1) that $a = 2$.

33. If we multiply both members of the equation by $(x - 3)$ we obtain

$$x = 3 + c(x - 3)$$
$$x = 3 + cx - 3c$$
$$x - cx = 3 - 3c$$
$$x(1 - c) = 3(1 - c)$$

Assuming $(1 - c) \neq 0$, and hence, $c \neq 1$, we divide each member by $(1 - c)$ and we obtain

$$x = \frac{3(1 - c)}{(1 - c)}$$
$$= 3$$

However, 3 is not in the replacement set for x. Thus, the equation has no solution. Remember, we are assuming $c \neq 1$. If we assume $c = 1$, the given equation becomes

$$\frac{x}{x - 3} = \frac{3}{x - 3} + 1$$

Multiplying both members of this equation by $x - 3$ we obtain

$$x = 3 + x - 3$$
$$x = x$$

This last equation is an identity and is interpreted to mean that any number in the replacement set for x is a solution of the equation.

Exercises 12.5   (Page 444)

1. $3\dfrac{3}{4}$ ohms

3. 4

5. 5.54 days (approx.)

7. 4 hours

9. $(5 + \sqrt{5})$ and $(5 - \sqrt{5})$

12.6 Review Exercises (Page 445)

1. (a) $\dfrac{1}{2a + 3}, \dfrac{-3}{2}$ **(b)** $\dfrac{x + 3}{x - 3}, 3$

3. (a) $\dfrac{x^3}{3y}$ **(b)** $\dfrac{1}{a^2 + a + 4}$

5. (a) $\dfrac{1}{2}$ **(b)** 2

7. (a) $\dfrac{-3}{(x - 2)(x + 2)(x + 5)}$ **(b)** $\dfrac{1}{y + 2}$

9. (a) $x = 6$ **(b)** $x = \dfrac{3}{2}$

11. (a) $x = \dfrac{8}{b - a}$ **(b)** $x = \dfrac{Rr}{r - R}$

Exercises 13.1 (Page 452)

1. $>$ **3.** $\geq$ **5.** $\leq$

7. $\leq, \leq$ **9.** $>$ **11.** No

13. No   **15.** Yes   **17.** Yes

19. No

21. Proof: The statement $a > b$ and $b > c$ is equivalent to the statement $b < a$ and $c < b$ or, equivalently,

$$c < b \quad \text{and} \quad b < a \tag{1}$$

From statement (1) and the Transitive Property of Less Than (Theorem 13.1.3) we conclude

$$c < a$$

or, equivalently,

$$a > c$$

23. (a)

(b)

25. (a)

(b)

27. (a)

(b)

29. (a) ⊘

(b)

31.

33.

35.

37.

39.

41.

Exercises 13.2 (Page 461)

1. $\{x : x > 4\}$

3. $\{x : x > 2\}$

5. $\left\{x : x < \dfrac{3}{2}\right\}$

7. $\{x : x \le -8\}$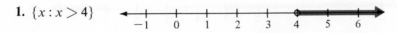

9. $\{x : x > 8\}$

11. $\{x : x > 6\}$

13. $\{x : x \in R\}$

15. $\{x : x \le 1\}$

17. $\{x : 2 \le x \le 3\}$

19. $\varnothing$

21. $\left\{x : x > \dfrac{9}{5}\right\}$

23. $\{x : 10 > x > 5\}$

25. $\left\{x : 40 \ge x \ge \dfrac{110}{3}\right\}$

27. (a)

(b)

29. (a)

(b)

31. (a)

(b) $\varnothing$

33.

35. (a) Yes (b) No

37. (a) Yes (b) Yes

39. (a) Yes (b) Yes (c) Yes

41. (a) Yes (b) Yes (c) Yes

1. 36 and 39

3. 35 and 60

5. 10 feet

7. 67

9. The minimum number of pennies under any conditions is 334. The minimum number of either the nickels or the dimes can be zero, if you increase the number of pennies.

11. 2

13. (a) If a = the average of the two numbers, then $15 < a < 22$.
(b) If s = the sum of the two numbers, then $30 < s < 44$.
(c) If x = twice the first number increased by the second number, then $50 < x < 68$.

15. 16 miles and 108 miles

17. The minimum number of inches of rainfall on the valley floor under any conditions is 15. The minimum number of inches of rainfall in the mountainous region can be zero under unusual conditions (where it rains on the valley floor, but not in the mountainous region). In that case the number of inches of rainfall on the valley floor increases to at least 40.

19. 15 miles per hour

13.4 Review Exercises (Page 468)

1. (a) $>$ (b) $\leq$

3. (a)

(b)

5. (a)

(b)

7. (a)

(b)

9. (a)

(b)

Index

A

B

C

Closure Law (*cont.*)
  for Addition
    of integers, 81
    of positive real numbers, 27, 447
    of rational numbers, 164
    of real numbers, 27
    of whole numbers, 77
  for Multiplication
    of integers, 81
    of positive real numbers, 27, 447
    of rational numbers, 164
    of real numbers, 27
    of whole numbers, 77
  for Subtraction, 77–78, 94–95
Coefficient
  of a factor, 42
  of a monomial, 314
  numerical, 50
Collinear points, 251, 264
Combining terms, 50
Common denominator, 191
Common factor of a set of whole
    numbers, 153–55
Common monomial factor, 348
Commutative Law
  of Addition, 40, 81, 164
  of Multiplication, 43, 81, 164
Complement of a set, 22–23
Completely factored form, 349
Completeness, Axiom of, 225
Completing the square, 365
Complex fraction, 169–70, 430–32
  simplifying, 196
  see also Rational expression,
    complex
Composite number, 152
Conclusion of a theorem, 30
Conditional equation, 110
Conjugate of a binomial, 355
Consistent equations, 270
Constant, 134
Coordinate, 26
  axes, 245
  x-, 245
  y-, 245
Coordinate system, 245

Coordinates
  of a point, 245
  rectangular, 245
Counterexample, 61–62
Counting numbers, *see* Natural
    numbers, 15
Cube
  of a binomial, 331, 334
  of a number, 42
  volume of, 315
Curve, parabolic, 401–408

D

Decimal expansion, 214
Decimal fraction, 213
Decimal notation, 213–14, 216
Decimals
  nonrepeating nonterminating, 224
  nonterminating, 216
  repeating, 216
  terminating, 217
Degree
  of an equation, 249, 369–70
  of a monomial, 315
  of a polynomial, 317–18
Denominator
  common, 191
  of a fraction, 59, 159
  least common (LCD), 191–92,
    428–30
  rationalizing the, 355–56
Denseness
  of rational numbers, 219–21
  of real numbers, 219
Density, Property of, 219
Dependent equations, 272
Difference
  definition of, 56
  of integers, 87
  of polynomials, 320–21
  of radical expressions, 233, 351–52
  of rational expressions, 334–35
  of rational numbers, 190–93
  symbol for, 56, 80

of two squares, 353

see also Subtraction

Differences, Fundamental Principle of, 90

Discriminant of a quadratic equation, 384–85

Disjoint sets, 20

Distance between two points, 267

Distributive Law, 46–52, 82, 164

Dividend, 58

Divisibility, concept of, 151

Division

definition of, 58

of integers, 100–101

operation of, 58–62

of polynomials, 334–44

of radical expressions, 234–35, 355–56

of rational expressions, 423–24

of rational numbers, 184–86

of real numbers, 58

of whole numbers, 151

by zero, 59–60

Division Principle of Equality, 124

Divisor, 58

greatest common (GCD), 155

of a whole number, 151

E

Element(s)

additive inverse, 79–80

identity, 41, 43

multiplicative inverse, 164–65

of a set, 13–14

Empty set, 17–18

Equal sets, 16

Equality

Addition Principle of, 119

axioms of, 30

Division Principle of, 124

Multiplication Principle of, 122

Reflexive Property of, 30

relation, 29

Substitution Property of, 30

Subtraction Principle of, 120

Symmetric Property of, 30

theorems of, 30–31

Transitive Property of, 31

Equation, 4, 110

checking the solution of an, 121

conditional, 110

containing rational expressions, 195, 435–38

first degree, 249, 369

formula, 132

identity, 110

left member of an, 4

of a line, 248–52, 261

linear, 248–52

slope-intercept form, 261

literal, 135

of a parabola, 401

quadratic, 372–85

replacement set for an, 111

right member of an, 4

second degree, 370

solution of an, 110

solution set of an, 111

solving an, 118, 126–31

Equations

consistent, 270

dependent, 272

equivalent, 118

inconsistent, 272

independent, 272

systems of, 268–73

linear, 269

solving, 275–81

Equivalent equations, 118

Euclid, 152

Even number, 16

Exponent, 42

laws of, 324–25, 336

Expression

algebraic, 2

first degree, 369

radical, 230–38

rational, 334–35, 415–44

second degree, 369

Extrapolation, 254

Extremes of a proportion, 201

Extremes of a proportion (*cont.*)
see also Proportion

F

Factor(s)
  coefficient of, 42
  common binomial, 350–51
  common monomial, 348
  conjugate of a binomial, 355
  prime, 153
  of a product, 41
  of a whole number, 41, 151
Factored form, completely, 349
  of the difference of two powers, 354
  of the difference of two squares, 353
  of polynomials, 348–65
  prime, 153
  of trinomials, 360–65
    general, 362–64
    perfect square, 365
Factoring
  difference of two powers, 359
  difference of two squares, 353–54
  solving equations by, 370–75
Factors of a whole number, 151–53
Field axioms, 164–65
Field properties, 164–65
Finite set, 15
First degree equation, 249, 369
First degree expression, 369
  see also Polynomial, standard form
  of
Formula, 132
  for the distance between two points, 267
  for the midpoint of a line segment, 267
  Pythagorean, 390
  quadratic, 381
  see also Geometric formulas
Fraction, 24
  complex, 169–70
  decimal, 213
  definition of, 159
  denominator of, 59, 159

numerator of, 59, 159
as a quotient, 59, 159
rational number represented by, 24, 160
reduced, 172
simple, 170
  lowest terms of, 172
  simplest form, 173
  simplifying, 170–74
Fractions
  equivalent, 160
  Fundamental Principle of, 172
Fundamental operations, 8, 40–44, 56–62
Fundamental Principle of Differences, 90
Fundamental Principle of Fractions, 172
Fundamental Principle of Quotients, 172
Fundamental Theorem of Arithmetic, 153

G

Gauss, 11–12
Geometric formulas
  area
    of a circle, 133
    of a rectangle, 49, 133
    of a square, 75
    of a trapezoid, 136–37
    of a triangle, 74
  circumference of a circle, 70
  perimeter
    of a rectangle, 52
    of a square, 54
    of a triangle, 54
  surface area
    of a cone, 399
    of a cylinder, 149
  volume
    of a box, 338
    of a cone, 139
    of a cube, 140, 315
    of a cylinder, 136

of a pyramid, 139
of a sphere, 315
Goldbach, C., 153
Golden ratio, 208
Graph
of an equation
as a line, 248–52
as a parabola, 400–408
of an inequality, 450–51
of a number, 26
of an ordered pair of numbers, 245
Graphical solution of a system of equations, 269–73
Greater than relationship, 32–35, 447
Greater than or equal to relationship, 34–35, 449
Greatest common divisor (GCD), 155
Grouping symbols, 63–65, 70–71

H

Higher terms of a fraction, 419–20
Highest common factor, *see* Greatest common divisor
Hypothesis of a theorem, 30

I

Identity, 3, 110
Identity element
for addition, 41, 82, 164
for multiplication, 43, 82, 164
If and only if, meaning of, 16
Inconsistent equations, 272
Independent equations, 272
Inequality, 32–36, 447–65
definition of, 35, 448–49
as an interval, 35–36
relationships, 32–35, 447–49
solution set of an, 449–51
solving an, 452–61
Infinite set, 15
Integer

additive inverse of an, 79–80
opposite of an, 7–9, 77–83
Integers, 7–9, 77–106
difference of, 87
negative, 7–9, 78
positive, 7–9, 78
product of, 97–100, 101
properties of, 81–83
quotient of, 100–101
set of, 8, 81
sum of, 89, 92–93
Intercept, y-, 261
Interpolation, 254
Intersection
of lines, 269
of sets, 19–20
Interval, 35–36
Inverse
additive, 79–80
multiplicative, 164–65
operations, 5, 8, 56, 58
Inversion
Additive Principle of, 114
Multiplicative Principle of, 115
Irrational numbers, 25, 224–28, 230–31
exact value of, 227, 238

L

Law(s)
Associative, 67, 68, 82, 164
Closure, 27, 77–78, 81, 164
Commutative, 40, 43, 81, 164
Distributive, 46–52, 82, 164
Identity, 41, 82, 164
Inverse, 78, 82, 164–65
Trichotomy, 33, 447
see also Property
Leading term of a polynomial, 340
Least common denominator (LCD), 191–92
of two or more rational expressions, 428–30
Least common multiple (LCM), 156
of two or more polynomials, 427–28
Left member of an equality, 4

Union of sets, 21–22
Universal set, 18

V

Variable(s), 16
  replacement set for, 111
  value of, 16
Vertex of a parabola, 403
Vieta, François, 4
Volume
  of a box, 338
  of a cone, 139
  of a cube, 140, 315
  of a cylinder, 136
  of a pyramid, 139
  of a sphere, 315
  see also Geometric formulas

W

Well-defined set, 13, 16
Whole numbers, 1, 14
  composite, 152
  even, 16
  factors of, 41, 151
  odd, 20–21
  prime, 152
Word problems
  concerning
    geometry, 133–34, 139–40,
      308–310, 386–89, 391–94
    numbers, 142–48
    physical quantities, 132–33,
      134–35, 198–99, 306–307,
      394–95, 441
  involving
    formulas, 132–42

fractional equations, 441–44
inequalities, 463–65
Pythagorean theorem, 389–94
quadratic equations, 386–95
ratio and proportion, 202–208,
  305–312
systems of equations, 284–88
types of
  distance–rate–time, 299–305,
    443–44
  mixture problems, 288–94
  percent, 204–206
  population sampling, 307–308
  similar figures, 308–310
  work–rate–time, 294–99, 442–43

X

x-axis, 244
x-coordinate, 245
xy-plane, 244

Y

y-axis, 244
y-coordinate, 245
y-intercept, 261

Z

Zero, 8
  division by, 59–60
  as an identity element for addition,
    41
  of a polynomial, 405
Zero Factor Property, 44, 97
Zero Product Property, 370